ISP Survival Guide

Strategies for Running a Competetive ISP

Geoff Huston

Wiley Computer Publishing

John Wiley & Sons, Inc.
New York ◆ Chichester ◆ Weinheim ◆ Brisbane ◆ Singapore ◆ Toronto

Publisher: Robert Ipsen
Editor: Carol Long
Assistant Editor: Pam Sobotka
Managing Editor: Angela Murphy
Text Design & Composition: D&G Limited, LLC

Library of Congress Cataloging-in-Publication Data:

Huston, Geoff.
    ISP survival guide : strategies for running a competitive ISP /
    Geoff Huston.
        p.   cm.
    Includes bibliographical references and index.
        ISBN 0-471-31499-4 (pbk. : alk. paper)
        1. Internet service providers.   I. Title.
    TK5105.875.I57H87   1998
    004.87'8--dc21   98-38660

Printed in the United States of America.
10 9 8 7 6

To the gentleman from Cyprus, who asked me some years ago in Prague, "Where is the book?" The answer, finally, is *here*.

contents

acknowledgments

First, I'd like to express my gratitude to Paul Ferguson, who collaborated with me for two chapters, "Quality of Service" and "Virtual Private Networks." Thanks indeed, Paul.

I'd like to express appreciation to my management at Telstra, who have allowed me the latitude to structure my work to accommodate the demands of this project. The views I express here do not always align with my employer, but the healthy debate that ensues is one which has led me to respect a workplace that encourages the interaction of ideas.

I am indebted to many folk over the years who have helped me gain a better understanding of this Internet business in all its detail. We have had some extraordinarily fine conversations in many fine locations over the years, and much of what we talked about has made its way into this book.

Half of the input to this book has come from a decade's worth of personal experience in operational management of an Internet Service Provider. To Peter Elford and David Woodgate, in particular, my thanks for many stimulating discussions. The other half of this book is the outcome of the teaching material generated for the Internet Society's Developing Countries Workshops. Each year, I have the privilege of teaching people from all over the globe how the Internet actually works, and in return, I have learned how it could happen for them. To my workshop friends, who have taught me about what the Internet means to them, thank you. To my fellow instructors, Barbara Fraser, Nur Zincir, Scott Bradner, and David Conrad, who have been an inspiration for much of the material in this book, thanks.

And, to the staff at Wiley and Pam Sobotka and Carol Long, my thanks for their assistance in converting my longwinded, rambling, and obtuse prose into something readable and consistent. What mistakes and omissions that remain are, of course, all mine!

A project of this size takes large quantities of time and effort. I'd like to say a heartfelt "thank you" to my loving wife, Michele, and my children, Alice, Sam, and Chris, for their patient forbearance throughout. Without their constant support, this book would never have been.

—*Geoff Huston*

introduction

I had written him a letter which I had, for want of better
  Knowledge, sent to where I met him down the Lachlan years ago;
He was shearing when I knew him, so I sent the letter to him,
  Just 'on spec', addressed as follows, "Clancy, of The Overflow."

And an answer came directed in a writing unexpected
  (And I think the same was written with a thumb-nail dipped in tar);
'Twas his shearing mate who wrote it, and verbatim I will quote it:
  "Clancy's gone to Queensland droving, and we don't know where he
  are."

From Clancy of the Overflow
— Banjo Paterson

The Internet brings with it a remarkable change to the way in which we communicate. From the postal system of a century ago, when this poem was written by Banjo Paterson, to the Internet of today has been quite a journey. And, the story is by no means finished. The pace of upheaval in the communications industry is now at a stage where the rate of surprises far exceeds the rate of many corporate entities to make sound decisions. No sign of any slackening of this pace is visible in the near future, so that further rapid change is a reasonable prediction.

At the root of much of this change is the Internet. The Internet forges one of the more powerful alliances we've seen—that of computing and communications. Rather than a communications network that operates within a single service mode, such as the telephone network or the radio network, the Internet uses the power of computing to allow a single communications system to be used for a wide variety of applications. The system simultaneously supports messaging, publication, voice and video, real-time collaboration, and a wide variety of other more specialized applications. The computing capability is sufficiently functional that the assumptions about the capability of the communications network are not particularly onerous: The Internet can tolerate varying packet size, varying delay, varying bandwidth, varying error rates, and even varying topology. This alliance of computing and communications has lead to an explosive change in the communications environment, in which the boundaries between the various communications service sectors are being blurred. Some have described this situation as *convergence*, and others use the more startling term of a *digital blizzard*. In a similar way, this alliance is leading to further changes in the computing environment, in which the traditional model of a computer as a data-processing device is giving way to personal digital assistants, Web-enabled televisions, network surveillance cameras, and other appliances that use communications capabilities to complement their internal processing capability.

No matter what term is used to describe the phenomenon, the undeniable fact is that it has now entered the mainstream of the communications industry and in doing so, it appears to have caught the established industry players unaware. The vanguard of this dramatic entrance to the communications industry has been the Internet Service Providers (ISPs). The ISP is the new face of the deregulated communications industry. Tens of thousands of these enterprises already exist all over the globe. Some ISPs are small enterprises, servicing a local neighborhood. Other ISPs are organized as a collective, operated as a community project in the developing world. Other ISPs are very large business enterprises, which change hands for sums in the hundreds of millions of dollars.

In this book, we look at the ISP in detail, looking not only at how the ISP itself operates, but also at the environment in which the ISP operates.

In looking at the ISP, the key question we are answering in this book is, "Why?" Many different vendor solutions are available in the market, and an ISP can construct a service environment in many different ways. Attempting to indicate precisely how a particular type of equipment should be configured is not very useful. Your situation may be different from that of the recipe in the book, and you may be using equipment that is configured in a completely different fashion. Your business structure will be tailored to your local environment and your particular business objectives, so that your business plan will be a very specific document, built to meet your requirements. Rather than provide a set of specific recipes for a small set of particular environments, this books addresses the underlying question of *why* situations arise and *what* can be achieved to address the issues. In this way, we can highlight the technology and business issues that are presented in each situation and outline the form of responses that will be of most benefit to the ISP. We trust that you find this form of approach useful to your needs.

How This Book Is Organized

This book is arranged in a way that first presents the background to the ISP environment, looking at how the ISP industry evolved from the original Internet research experiments. We then examine the technology components of an ISP, looking at the Internet protocol itself, routing issues, network management, carrier services, and network security. Following this look at the technology of an ISP, we follow on with a business and marketing perspective, looking at the enterprise side of the ISP operation. The communications market has been undergoing a number of fundamental changes of a policy nature, with the move to a deregulated market worldwide. We look at the Internet policy environment, examining the various driving factors that are shaping the regulatory environment of the ISP. In conclusion, we will indulge in a forecast for the ISP industry sector, looking at the future within this constantly changing and evolving landscape.

Chapter 1: A Look Back at the Internet

In this chapter, we look at how the Internet started in the late 1960s and how the effort evolved and gathered momentum in the following years. Not only is this invaluable briefing information for those Internet trivia evenings, this information is also helpful to understand how the Internet Culture has come into existence. This chapter looks at how the Internet emerged from a research experiment into an academic service network and from there into the multi-provider ISP environment.

Chapter 2: The Evolution of the Internet Service Provider

The ISP industry did not appear overnight. In each country an evolutionary path has developed from the early experiments with collaborative message-passing networks leading, ultimately, to the diverse ISP industry. While the time taken to move along this evolutionary path has varied from country to country, the major stepping points along this path are very similar. In this chapter, you learn what those points are and understand the business and technology factors that have created today's ISP environment. We then look at how these pressures may shape the immediate future of the Internet and the associated ISP environment.

Chapter 3: The Internet Architecture

In this chapter, we begin our examination of the technology base of the ISP. We first examine the IP protocol itself, looking at the composition of an IP packet header and then looking at the functionality of the Transmission Control Protocol (TCP) and the User Datagram Protocol (UDP). You then learn about the structure of IP address space and the relationship between the address space and the address deployment mechanisms used by ISPs. From addresses come names, and we then look at the Internet Domain Name System (DNS), its background, and current role. We then introduce the bodies that are involved in the defining of the technical documents that carry the status of Internet Standards and how these documents are created within the Internet Standards process.

Chapter 4: Internet Architectures

We continue with looking at the technology base of the ISP by examining the architecture of ISP networks. You learn about architectural principles, which are the framework of an effective network design. We then put these principles to work when we look at the design of ISP networks, looking first at the overall design of the network and then at the various design models of connecting clients to the ISP's network. The examination then shift to the design choices for the internal ISP network, looking at the various ways the ISP's internal network can be constructed. These principles are put to practice when we describe a number of common ISP profiles and how their network's are designed. To conclude the chapter, we look at emerging technologies that will influence ISP designs in the near future.

Chapter 5: Network Infrastructure

The two major technology components of an ISP network are the IP router and data carriage services. We take a detailed view of both of these areas in this chapter. You learn how a router works and how the router is used to support traffic filtering, routing protocols, and network management. You also learn the difference between routing and switching and the relative strengths and weaknesses of each approach. Routers are now specialized devices, and different routers are used in different roles within an ISP network. We then look at the parameters to use when purchasing a router for an ISP network. The second half of this chapter looks at available carriage service options. Following an examination of the carrier's hierarchy of digital services, the chapter looks at the strengths and weaknesses of various carriage technologies. You learn about modems, digital circuits, and SONET systems. The chapter also looks at various forms of switched carriage systems, including ISDN, X.25, Frame Relay, ATM, and SMDS. The chapter also looks at WDM futures. The chapter concludes with an examination of the parameters for an ISP to use when choosing carriage services for use in the network.

Chapter 6: Managing Routing

Managing the routing environment is a major task of every ISP. In this chapter, we clear away many of the myths and uncertainties regarding routing and take a commonsense view of how to manage the ISP's routing environment. You learn about interior routing protocols, how they work, and what they are attempting to achieve in their operation. We then examine the exterior routing protocol, BGP, the various ISP connection environments, and how BGP is used to support each one. We then put this information into a practical framework by examining how routing configurations can be used to support various components of the ISP's network, looking at supporting customer connections, the internal ISP network, and the various external ISP connections.

Chapter 7: Network Management

In this chapter, we move from design to the operational environment when we examine the role of network management. The chapter looks at practical management tools and their application in the ISP's network, including the use of the Simple Network Management Protocol (SNMP) as a management tool. The ISO Network Management Forum divides the task of network management into the functional areas of fault management, configuration management, performance management, accounting management, and security management. We examine the first four of these areas in this chapter; the issues relating to security warrant separate treatment, and are addressed in Chapter 9, which is dedicated to the topic.

Chapter 8: Quality of Service

Part of the role of network management is that of performance management. ISP's customers are now voicing a more sophisticated requirement—that of various forms of quality of service. In this chapter, we define the elements of Quality of Service (QoS) and how they can be applied to an ISP network. You learn about QoS mechanisms that can be applied at the circuit level, including the use of QoS mechanisms within Frame Relay and ATM networks. We then look at the various options available to deploy differentiated QoS within the IP environment, looking at various queue management disciplines that can yield differentiated service profiles. Customers are now voicing their service quality requirements within the framework of a Service Level Agreement (SLA), and we examine the role of the SLA within this area. QoS is a very challenging area for an ISP, and we conclude the chapter with some helpful guidelines and observations about deployment of QoS in an ISP network.

Chapter 9: Security

Security of an ISP network is a very important network attribute, as your customers will be trusting you to manage their data with all due care and attention to the confidentiality of the data. You learn about the nature of security incidents and the importance of formulating a security policy to assist you to respond to security incidents carefully and effectively. We then look at the ways to secure the ISP's network infrastructure and how to assist your customers in securing their networks from intrusion.

Chapter 10: Servicing Internet Markets

We move into the business operational areas of the ISP with this chapter. One of the major services retailed by the ISP is Internet access. We look at how this access service can be packaged to the business and personal markets and the various refinements to the basic Internet access product. You will also learn about various access technologies to service this market, including modems, Digital Subscriber Lines (DSL), and Hybrid Fiber Coax (HFC), and various roaming and mobility services. Services can extend beyond Internet access, and we examine the opportunities presented by fax services and GSM paging. You also learn about the emerging market of Internet-based voice services and their potential as an important business stream for the ISP.

Chapter 11: The ISP Service Profile

Besides Internet access, the ISP typically provides a set of additional services to its customers. The intention for the ISP is to augment access with value-added services that enable the customer to outsource various business functions to the ISP. In this chapter, we describe these services, how they are provided, and the value proposition provided to the customer. We examine electronic mail services, including POP servers, mail-relay agents, mailing lists, and secondary mail servers. We then look at domain name services, including name hosting, forwarders, and secondary name server functions. Web caching offers customers improved performance in the delivery of Web pages through local storage and delivery. We also look at the emerging market for Web hosting, looking at the various solutions available in this market area. Usenet is another major service activity, involving the support of specialized service platforms to support the Usenet traffic flows.

Chapter 12: Virtual Private Networks

Moving further into the area of providing higher valued services to the customer base that address business solutions, this chapter looks at the provision of Virtual Private Networks (VPNs). You learn what a VPN is and the motivations for customers to purchase VPN-based communications solutions. We then look at the various ways VPNs can be constructed and the strengths and weaknesses of each approach. The chapter concludes with an examination of the VPN service market, looking at the opportunities presented by this particular service activity.

Chapter 13: ISP Business Plans

This chapter looks at the business aspect of the ISP operation. Essential to the success of any business enterprise is a clear understanding of the objectives of the business, and the business plan is a method to outline clearly how the objective is to be achieved. The chapter takes a step-by-step approach through the components of the business plan, examining the aspects of market identification, cost determination, and the elements of a retail pricing structure. All this is combined in a sample business plan, illustrating the steps described in the chapter.

Chapter 14: Interacting with Other ISPs

The Internet is the combined outcome of tens of thousands of component networks. In this environment, no ISP can operate in complete isolation, and the enterprise has to reconcile the aspects of competition and cooperation. We examine the various roles of an ISP, from retail to wholesale, examining the issue of the difference between a peer or a client of an ISP. The chapter then examines the physical structures used by ISPs to interconnect, looking at exchange routers, exchange LANs, Network Access Points (NAPs), and distributed exchanges, evaluating their strengths and weaknesses. The major issue in the area of interconnection is not how to interconnect, but the financial and business aspects of interconnection. We explore various models of inter-provider financial settlement, looking at a number of potential models for a financial settlement structure for the inter-ISP domain. This area remains one of the more difficult areas to resolve in a stable fashion within the ISP industry, and we look at why financial settlement has proved to be so elusive in the Internet.

Chapter 15: Public Policy and the Internet

Part of the catalyst for the ISP industry has been the recent shift in public policy in many parts of the world that has deregulated the communications service industry. The Internet environment is not a mature environment from a policy perspective, and the current situation is highly fluid. Four major forces are attempting to shape public policy: the collaborative academic and research community, the public policy-makers, the established telephone network service providers, and the deregulated ISP industry. We examine the motivations of each of these sectors and look at the way they interact within various Internet policy and governance domains.

Chapter 16: Futures for the ISP Industry

Futures for the ISP industry lie on two planes: the technology plane and the business plane. The first part of this chapter looks at various technology futures for the ISP. We first look at whether the ISP industry can withstand the shift from modems towards higher speed access connections. The chapter then looks at the major technology futures within the Internet architecture itself, as they relate to the ISP environment. The second part of the examination of potential futures takes a business perspective. Much has happened in the past few years, not the least of which is the growth of ISPs from less than 10 to considerably more than 10,000. We look at the larger issues facing the ISP market, including whether the environment can sustain further growth in ISP numbers. We also examine the pressures leading to aggregation in the industry, in which mergers and acquisitions feature in the daily press, and examine the role of the regulator in this area.

Who Should Read This Book

This is not a book that tries to be all things to all readers. This book is directed at the Internet Service Provider area and explains the ISP in some detail. This book attempts to provide essential material for anyone who is thinking of starting an ISP and contains a number of useful strategies and approaches that should assist the new market entrant. The Internet is perceived as an area of significant opportunity, and the ISP is commonly believed to be one way of reaping the benefits of such opportunity. For some, this may well be the case. Others may not become instant millionaires. However, for everyone, not only is a large effort in store, but also a very brutal learning experience awaits those attempting to combine aspects of technology, business, and industry politics. This book is an effort intended to make the learning part a little less brutal and unforgiving, by documenting the essential aspects of the ISP operation, in advance of the lessons handed out through first-hand experience.

The book also is directed at those who operate an ISP business or work within the ISP industry. The material in the book should assist you in working through the major strategic opportunities for your business and help you to understand the various external pressures that the business faces now and in the near future. For the engineering manager, the material assists you in ensuring that your network is positioned to grow in line with business expectations. For the business manager, the book provides you with some strategies for the future course of your business.

This book also assists those who are purchasing services from an ISP, as it provides some essential details as to what services can be offered by the ISP and how they are provided. As the requirements become more sophisticated, they now include differentiated service levels, commitments to service level agreements, virtual private networks, and a diverse set of access arrangements. Defining a productive match between the requirements of the customer to the capabilities of the potential ISP provider does entail the customer being able to understand what can be offered by the ISP and how such services are provided.

If you don't fit into these categories, this book may still be useful for you. The communications industry is undergoing rapid change at present, and the major driver of these industry-wide changes is the Internet, heralded by the ISP sector. If you work within this industry, or if your work brings you near it, then this book will assist you in understanding the nature of the changes happening at present, from the Internet perspective.

An Initial Word

Any business enterprise has associated business risks. The ISP business is no exception. Some ISPs will fail, while others will grow beyond their wildest expectations. One of the key ingredients to business success is understanding the environment in which the ISP operates, allowing the business to correctly identify opportunities as they arise.

This book is intended to address this understanding of the environment of ISP operation and looks at the technology, business, and policy landscape of the Internet. The endeavor here is to assist the ISP operator to understand how to make the business a success, both for themselves, and for their clients.

PART ONE

THE EMERGENCE OF THE ISP

chapter one

A Look Back at the Internet

This chapter describes the developmental timeline of the Internet provider environment. This chapter contains a chronology of the Internet's development, focusing on the major events that shaped the Internet into a major communications sector and the unfolding process that has led to today's Internet Service Provider (ISP) industry.

In examining the ISP industry, the task of reviewing the ISP's chosen domain of operation, the Internet itself, is an appropriate first step. This is such a daunting task that I am tempted to assert that accurately describing today's Internet is not possible. So many aspects of its operation and character appear to lead inevitably towards a description of chaos, rather than order, and attempting to describe a chaotic environment is indeed a significant challenge. It is easier to go back to how it started, and from the simple origins, describe the path that has led to today's environment.

The technology, business, and social roles of many aspects of communications are very well understood in today's society. We unconsciously use the technologies of the print media through newspapers, magazines, and books. We place absolute reliance on the global postal and courier networks for the reliable and efficient delivery of documents. With equal ease, we use the public telephone network to communicate and transmit facsimiles of documents and use the radio and television networks as a source of entertainment, diversion, and information.

So, where does the Internet sit within this environment? Obvious to the millions of individuals who use the Internet daily is the concept that the applications that populate the Internet are a recent, but no less integral, component of the public communications environment. Also obvious to the millions of

Internet users is that this is a communications medium that will have significant longevity and influence within our society. The millions of computers sold every year into the consumer and corporate market will provide the fuel to feed this communications environment for many decades to come. However, placing the Internet into a particular service niche within the communications environment is difficult. The Internet's utility model encompasses many of the roles of the established communications paradigms, without reproducing their component technologies. More telling is that this is achieved by the Internet with considerable cost efficiencies over the traditional models. For example, information can be published and disseminated to an audience without ever being printed. Similarly, individually addressed messages can be delivered without use of a postal delivery system. Voice over the Internet is gaining momentum as a viable alternative to long-distance telephony.

The construction of the world's electronic communications networks commenced with the patenting of telegraphy in 1837. By 1880 a network of overland wires, undersea cables, and many thousands of telegraph operators was creating a world view that was simply unheard of previously. The telephone made its public debut in 1876 at the Philadelphia Exposition, creating a second wave of electronic communications expansion. The ensuing 100 years has seen this system play a critical role in reshaping our world, creating a mesh of multinational corporate enterprises and global marketplaces held together with the reach of telephony. Into this environment in the last two decades has burst the marriage of computing and communications technologies, reinvigorating the communications environment with a new set of imperatives. The current focus appears to be on messaging, content publication, and commerce, but the Internet utility model continues to evolve, including diverse media and communication models. The Internet has yet to discover where the boundaries lie and to establish what it cannot do. The world will change in response to the new opportunities offered by these technologies. Already, we are seeing the advent of the global small business, where small-business operators can take new and innovative products to a receptive global market, and in a more general sense, we are seeing the network itself replace the middle roles of distribution and retail. This realignment may see a more direct relationship between the producer and the consumer, eliminating much of the middleware that currently sits between these two basic roles. The Internet will be the vehicle for these likely changes, and it will play as pivotal a role in the coming years as that played by the telephone system in the past century.

How Did It All Start?

With the explosion of the Internet into social awareness in recent years, the history of the Internet is passing into the realms of folklore. The visible milestones of its development—the Advanced Research Projects Agency Network (ARPANET), the National Science Foundation Network (NSFNET), the Commercial Internet Exchange (CIX), and the Network Access Points (NAPs)—will no doubt remain as constant features in every version of the history, while the finer details will waiver just out of sharp focus, changing subtly with each retelling as first-hand memory of the events and the players fades. Let's look at these major milestones in the developmental path of the Internet. This will provide some understanding of the likely future directions of the Internet, as the future of the associated ISP industry will be evident in the path of events that has led to this point.

A more detailed history, authored by a number of the individuals involved in the events described here, can be found at www.isoc.org/internet/history/brief.html.

The Experimental Network

The Internet is undoubtedly the unintended outcome of the initial research objectives articulated by the Advanced Research Projects Agency (ARPA) of the United States Department of Defense (DoD) in the late 1960s, but the antecedents of this effort go back a few years earlier in the U.S. research community. The so-called *think-tank* of the cold war, the RAND Corporation, was an early vehicle for the concept of computer networking. There, Paul Baran, whom many consider to be the father of computer networking, presented his ideas on the subject in a seminal work published by RAND in the early 1960s, *On Distributed Communications* [Baran 1964]. Leonard Kleinrock was studying for his dissertation at the Massachusetts Institute of Technology (MIT) at the same time and published a paper in 1961 on information flow [Kleinrock 1961]. He subsequently published a book on the subject in 1964, *Communications Nets: Stochastic Message Flow and Delay* [Kleinrock 1964], that defined a formative model for the design and performance evaluation of computer networks.

T he entire set of Baran's classic RAND papers on packet-switching from the early 1960s is now available online at www.rand.org/ publications/RM/baran.list.html.

> . . . one day we will require more capacity for data transmission than needed for analogue voice transmission. . . . it would appear prudent to broaden our planning consideration to include new concepts for future data network directions. Otherwise, we may stumble into being boxed in with the uncomfortable restraints of communications links and switches originally designed for high quality analogue transmission. New digital computer techniques using redundancy make cheap unreliable links potentially usable. A new switched network compatible with these links appears appropriate to meet the upcoming demand for digital service. This network is best designed for data transmission and for survivability at the outset.

—"On Distributed Communications: I - Introduction to Distributed Communications Networks," RM-3420-PR, August 1964
    Acknowledgment is due to Noel Chiappa for this reference and to Dave Goldberg of Xerox PARC, who helped scan in the entire series.

Into this formative environment entered ARPA. Remember that ARPA does not undertake research itself, nor does it directly operate research facilities. ARPA's role is to define the research topic and then manage programs that fund various research groups to work within the defined area. In the mid-1960s ARPA formulated a research interest in computer networks. ARPA funded a study through Lawrence Roberts at MIT's Lincoln Laboratory in late 1965, largely as a result of Kleinrock's earlier work at MIT. The study report, *A Cooperative Network of Time-Sharing Computers*, proposed the establishment of an experimental three-computer network to investigate the concepts of computer networking. This proposal was successfully implemented one year later by Roberts and Thomas Merill, creating a two-host computer network consisting of a TX-2 at MIT and a Q-32 in California [Roberts 1966]. Phenomenal growth rates were a feature even at this stage, and this network grew by 50 percent with the addition of a third computer, located at ARPA. This experimental network generated significant interest in the computer research community, and an ad hoc Communication Group was established to examine how to connect a larger number of computers using telephone lines as the communications medium.

Within this group, that early incarnation of the router was developed, with the proposed architecture of a dedicated communications computer that would sit between the multiuser host system and the telephone lines. These proposed design elements were termed Interface Message Processors (IMPs), and the work of the ad hoc Communication Group then started to focus on the design use of IMPs as the foundation element of the network architecture, examining the IMP-to-host communications protocol, IMP-to-IMP communications protocol, error control, queuing control, and dynamic routing.

This story is not entirely based in the United States. The initial investigative work in the early 1960s was refined in the United Kingdom at the National Physical Laboratory (NPL), where a NPL Data Network design was proposed, which included local networks with interface computers that communicated with a number of high-capacity processing systems. The first packet-switching network was implemented in the United Kingdom in 1968 at the National Physical Laboratories, under the direction of Donald Davies and Roger Scantlebury. (As an item of trivia, the term *packet* was originally coined within the NPL effort.)

In late 1966, Lawrence Roberts went to DARPA (through its life, the name of the Advanced Research Projects Agency has added and dropped "Defense" from its name, swapping to *Defense Advanced Research Projects Agency* at various times, possibly to reflect the political climate of the United States administration of the day) to develop the computer network concept. He published his proposal for an ARPANET in 1967. At this stage, the relatively independent efforts at MIT, RAND, and the NPL recognized each other's efforts. Somewhat surprisingly, they had been all working in this area independently for some years.

In August 1968, ARPA invited prospective suppliers to propose a research network that used the Communication Group's generic architecture. In December 1968, ARPA awarded the contract for ARPANET to Bolt Beranek and Newman (BBN). On September 1, 1969, the first IMP was shipped to the University of California at Los Angeles (UCLA), which was used to connect with the IMPs subsequently shipped to the Stanford Research Institute (SRI), the University of California at Santa Barbara (UCSB), and the University of Utah. The initial work in developing network protocols was directed toward asymmetric client/server remote terminal access and data transfer support. This work was refined to include a symmetric host-host protocol, known as Network Control Protocol (NCP), completed under the direction of Steve Crocker in December 1970.

Interest in this project widened, and by 1971 the ARPANET connected 15 sites and 23 host computers. At this time, interest in computer network technologies and protocols within the U.S. research community was strongly stimulated. A time-slotted radio network, ALOHAnet, was developed by Norman Abrahamson at the University of Hawaii, which was connected into the ARPANET in 1972. The elements of this architecture were further refined by Bob Metcalfe in his 1973 doctoral thesis, which outlined the Ethernet architecture as the basis for a common broadcast local network environment. Further expansion of the ARPANET included satellite connections to the University College of London (England) and Royal Radar Establishment (Norway) in 1973, the first international connections of the ARPANET.

The subsequent refinement of the ARPANET networking model was one undertaken initially by Bob Kahn in 1972. He took the approach of examining the current architectural model, which was that of a collection of various host computers, connected through a homogeneous network. The refinement was to allow the network itself to be composed of a diverse collection of network elements, including local networks, wide area networks, and radio-based packet networks. The radical foresight embraced by this abstraction is, even today, difficult to fully appreciate. We have become so used to communication technology models that place a uniform communication model on top of a uniform transmission architecture, that it is close to impossible to even visualize this type of communications model. This model embraces an end-to-end coherent communications structure that makes no binding uniform requirements on the underlying transport elements. Although originally part of the packet radio program, it quickly became a research program in its own right, involving Vint Cerf, in the initial implementation effort.

The initial design of this protocol, first termed the *Kahn-Cerf protocol* after its major architects and later named TCP/IP (Transmission Control Protocol/ Internet Protocol), took place across 1973–74, with the paper, *A Protocol for Packet Network Interconnection*, published in May 1974 [Cerf-Kahn 1974]. This paper embraced the model of diverse communications elements with differing characteristics and made no assumptions regarding the imposition of *state* within the network. The functionality required for the network switches is a minimal set, focusing on best-effort forwarding actions. Every switch attempts to pass each data packet to a neighboring switch, which is topologically closer to the ultimate destination. The switch also is allowed to delay or discard the data packet if the switch is operating at an overload level. These packet switches do not have to maintain the state of any active connections, nor do they have to send a reverse notification back to the sender in the case of packet drop nor undertake any hop-by-hop reliable flow control. Each packet includes a globally significant destination identifier, and the local forwarding decision is based on the local knowledge of the location of that destination relative to the switch. The key protocol issues that required attention included the use of protocol algorithms to detect and retransmit lost packets from the source and allowing pipelining of data to increase network efficiency and associated end-to-end packet flow control. The protocol also had to allow for heterogeneous network characteristics, so that switches might be required to further fragment a packet to allow communication. In addition, the protocol required end-to-end checksums to allow for correct reassembly of the original datastream, and global addressing to allow stateless switching systems. The power of this remarkably simple model was evident in July 1975, with the first demonstration of ARPANET/Packet Radio Net/SATNET operation of Internet protocols with BBN-supplied gateways.

In 1975, the ARPANET administration was passed to the Department of Defense Communications Agency (DCA), indicating its evolving role from a research experiment to an operational facility. The applications at the time were the output of an enthusiastic group of graduate researchers and included *telnet* to support interactive remote access, *ftp* to support data transfer, and *SMTP* to support e-mail transfers.

Further expansion of the network took place in subsequent years. Related research networks were appearing at that time, including CSNET, a United States–based academic and research network focused on computer science departments. Critical in the promulgation of the Internet was an agreement that any ARPANET-connected CSNET hub could open up the use of the ARPANET to all students, employees, and faculty. The outcome was the creation of a generation of graduates who were exposed to the possibilities of a capable networking environment and the Internet in particular. Many of these individuals took this requirement with them to the workplace, fueling the subsequent commercial demand for the Internet. Coinciding with CSNET was BITNET, introduced in 1981 (although it must be noted that BITNET used IBM-based NJE protocols rather than IP). In 1983, the ARPANET was converted to run only TCP/IP, removing the remainder of the earlier NCP protocols from the network. In 1984, we heralded the next phase of the history of the Internet, where within the ARPANET the network was split between a Department of Defense Data Network operational network, MILNET (Military Network), and the ARPANET research and development platform. Scaling of the academic and research network as a utility prototype commenced.

The Internet as a Service Network

The early 1980s saw the widespread introduction of three significant technologies: the IBM Personal Computer (PC), the Ethernet Local Area Network (LAN), and the Unix operating system. All three technologies were to profoundly change the information technology world in their own way.

Prior to the introduction of PC technology, computers were large specialized systems that were located in protected environments with conditioned power, air, and access. The access network that reached out from such hosts was typically one of twisted-pair wires supporting the RS-232 serial line protocol to allow the dedicated connection of text-only terminals. The PC introduced the wave of cheap personal computers on desktops, replacing this model of large central host computers and its terminals with a model of a distributed data environment. The PCs were capable of exchanging data without the attendant need to use the central host system as the common data repository. The PCs could emulate the behavior of any text-only terminal, while also emulating the behavior of the host computer itself, albeit in a smaller scale and in a dedicated fashion. With this change in the landscape of computing came a change in the landscape of networking. Networking protocols were now the means by which these PCs were linked into the local environment. Networking protocols now had to provide the *glue* for this distributed environment, which was originally hard wired into the single mainframe host computer. Network protocols now had to support access to shared storage and distributed file systems, as well as supporting access to common resources, such as printers and mass archival storage, while also supporting the more traditional host-to-host models of remote terminal access, bulk data transfer, and electronic messaging.

Ethernet was to assist this change by introducing a matching change in the environment of the local area network. The original access networks were constructed using dedicated 2-pair copper wires, spanning out from the computer room or wiring hub to each workstation. The access system was designed to operate at very slow serial transmission speeds of 9600 baud or less. This speed was simply inadequate for the demands of a distributed environment of PCs. Ethernet changed all that in a very radical fashion. The early prototypes supported a common wiring plant operating at 3Mbps, and the production equipment was configured to operate at 10Mbps. Ethernet also changed the existing wiring topology, replacing the wiring hub closet and radial spans with a single cable that passed every workstation. This form of local networking spawned a diverse set of developments in networking. At this stage, the global high-energy physics and space aeronautics community undertook the deployment of two global networks based on the DECnet protocol suite.

T *he DECnet protocol suite was a proprietary network protocol technology developed by Digital Equipment Corporation (DEC). At the time, many vendors had developed proprietary network protocols to match the hardware and software environments of their range of computing products. DECnet served as a common protocol to interconnect the range of DEC minicomputer and mainframe computers. DEC computers were widely used in the academic and research environments in the late 1970s and the 1980s, and in the wake of deployment of these computer systems, DECnet was widely deployed to interconnect these systems.*

These DECnet networks—the High Energy Physics Network (HEPnet) in the physics community, and the Space Physics Aeronautical Network (SPAN) in the space aeronautics community—used local Ethernet networks for onsite connectivity and a mix of leased circuits and X.25 public switched data services for long-distance circuits. Also, at this period, the initial study work undertaken within Technical Committee 97, Information Processing, of the International Organization for Standardization, published its first set of Open Systems Interconnection (OSI) standards, with the CCITT Red Book series of 1984.

Unix was the third component of this technology trio. The computing environment to that time typically encompassed a software environment customized to the hardware platform. Clients were locked into vendor-specific information technology environments, which presented few options for portability and allowed vendors to operate in a market that did factor in vendor lock-in. Into this environment came Unix. For academic institutions, Unix was offered worldwide at nominal license fees and allowed the client to migrate between an increasingly large range of hardware platforms, while preserving a software environment. In addition, DARPA had contracted the University of California, Berkeley, to develop an implementation of TCP/IP for

Unix, and this implementation, with its source code, was freely available to the public. This was a critical step away from vendor-specific environments into a world of open technology where competition refocused into areas of price and quality.

F or much of the 1980s, the Internet was described as a research net-work investigating the significant issues surrounding efficient packet-based data networks. Most of the industry accepted that the OSI standardization effort would produce the deployment technologies for the next generation of public data networks, and while effort proceeded with the refinement of the OSI-based technologies, the Internet would solve some immediate requirements of the research community. At the same time, the research work within the Internet would yield some valuable outcomes in terms of understanding how such packet-switched networks operate and behave. The unfolding history did not adhere to such an orderly planned regime. The OSI effort, which a number of Internet technologists described as a triumph of vaporware over the requirement to produce functional technological specifications, has now largely dissipated within the overwhelming attention being focused on today's Internet.

In 1986, the next major transition of the evolving Internet commenced with the initial deployment of NSFNET, a networking project funded by the U.S. National Science Foundation (NSF). Interestingly enough, a decision was made that the network would support only TCP/IP in the first instance and would not support DECnet, then still in widespread use within the academic and research community. The initial effort within the NSF itself was led by Dennis Jennings, while the initial engineering of NSFNET was performed by the University of Illinois at Urbana-Champaign (UIUC), using Digital LSI-11/72 gateway systems, termed *fuzzballs* [Mills 1988]. The technical lead for this project passed to a Michigan university consortium, MERIT, in December 1987, with the collaboration of IBM and MCI for the provision of switching and transmission capabilities. This project was perhaps one of the most startling success stories in this history. The project had an original objective of linking the five supercomputer centers with an Internet backbone network. However, it quickly grew beyond that original objective and encompassed a broader objective of servicing the research communications needs of the national academic and research community.

Perhaps two aspects of the 1988 NSFNET program were truly long sighted and revolutionary. The first of these was to launch a project that had technical specifications, which could be confidently met by no existing services or equipment. The specification of 1.544Mbps transmission rates and high-speed gateways was certainly unique at that time, and provided a high-speed platform free of the operational issue of congestion overload for some years. The second quite novel aspect of the NSFNET program was the adoption of the organizational model of using the mid-level networks as the means of local distribution of the backbone long-haul core network. The mid-level networks not only were a focus for local effort in the development of Internet infrastructure, but these entities had to quickly include a funding base that was more embracing than absolute reliance on federal funding, and, as such, provided an early template for the emerging ISP market. Note that the prevailing model of network operation could be summarized by the catch cry of "one network, one operator," while the NSFNET deliberately started with an operation model of "one network, many providers." This structure has been a continual aspect of the Internet, and the current number of distinct entities that operates part of the Internet is now in excess of 30,000 ISPs worldwide.

The Multiprovider Internet

As the academic and research Internet gathered speed, so did the pressure to construct a more commercial orientation of networking. The U.S. federal agency networks and the NSFNET were no exception, operating under an Appropriate Use Policy (AUP), which effectively prevented their use for commercial purposes. Originally created as an experimental UUCP service node for USENIX, UUNET was one of the first commercial ISPs to meet this emerging market demand. The initial trial gathered momentum through 1987 and 1988, and by 1989, UUNET was positioning itself as one of the major ISPs within the commercial Internet marketplace, together with Performance Systems International (PSI).

The Internet history now starts to see rapid multiplication, as academic and research networks proliferated with the U.S. federal sector and abroad and as commercial ISP operators started to make their debut. The interaction between these networks quickly became the area of prime focus. Rather than following a single thread of development, the environment of interconnection became the major theme at this point. Indeed, this theme of interconnection, both as an aspect of network engineering, and as a commercial interaction between ISPs, has been an enduring aspect of the ISP domain.

To address the problem of interaction and interconnection within the United States, the emerging U.S. federal agency networks introduced the concept of interaction across an exchange point (or in this particular case, two distinct exchange points). The agency backbone networks—NSFNET, the NASA Science Internet (NSI), the Energy Sciences Network (ESnet), the military MILNET, and the DARPA wideband experimental network—interconnected with each other and participated in routing peer sessions at two points in the United States. These points were termed Federal Internet eXchanges (FIXes). They were FIX-W at NASA Ames Research Center in the San Francisco area and FIX-E at SURANET, College Park, Maryland, in the Washington, D.C., area. Each agency configured its routers to peer with other FIX routers to achieve the various policy objectives of the agency. Although this provided *open* points of exchange for the participants of the FIX, the transit between the two FIX points was provided by multiple paths that were individually subject to each agency's constraints.

Perhaps *open* is not the most appropriate word here. The entire U.S. FIX structure operated within U.S. federal government policy constraints, so that the use of the FIX as an exchange point for nonagency traffic was constrained by government policy, in the form of AUPs and agency requirements. This apparently clear delineation between research networks and commercial ISP networks was never particularly simple in practice, and the delineation became highly confused when the NSFNET operations were undertaken by Advanced Networking Systems (ANS), who in 1991 spawned a commercial offshoot to sell access to the same network that was providing the NSFNET platform. In addition, the NSFNET mid-level networks adopted an increasing commercial stance as they developed their roles as Internet service providers to a mix of academic, research, and commercial clients.

The Commercial Internet Exchange (CIX) emerged in this environment to provide a mechanism for the interconnection of the commercial ISP networks, in the same fashion as the FIXes provided a mechanism for the interconnection of the agency systems. This third exchange location added considerable complexity to the routing problems, and some NSFNET mid-level networks, although they were members of the CIX, did not implement a CIX connection because the routing required to support the multiple exterior connectivity was considered too unstable. Again, the issue of interconnection was a prime point of focus for the Internet.

The effort in 1993 concentrated on the complexity of network interaction. An AUP-free exchange point, MAE-EAST (some assert that the name MAE was an acronym for Metropolitan Area Exchange, and others see the elegance of the name simply as a nice play on words in reference to the renowned actress Mae West), was constructed adjacent to FIX-E, providing a neutral point of interconnection for national and international networks, allowing both research and commercial networks to serve their respective clients and providing a mechanism to exchange traffic. The exchange architecture proliferated over the following years, further spurned on by the NSF, who, following the expiration of the original NSFNET program in 1995, lent its support to a set of exchange points that were intended to facilitate the interconnection of research and commercial networks. These NAPs were joined by exchange points to form a very rich mesh of connectivity, both within the United States and elsewhere across the world.

The Internet Today

The Internet is now a network that, in January 1998 [Lottor 1998], serves some 30 million connected computers. (The number of Internet users is a much more challenging number to estimate, and current estimates for January 1998 range from 40 million to 70 million users. Much of the discrepancy in these numbers reflects some uncertainty in defining a user of the Internet, particularly in the corporate environment.) These systems are serviced by more than 30,000 Internet service providers across the world, predominately operating on a commercial basis as a service provider. The ISP business now includes the participation of the telephone service providers across the globe, as well as the active participation of medium- and small-business enterprises. Their services range from the mass-marketing of simple access products to service-intensive operations that provide specialized service levels to more localized Internet markets.

T he number of ISPs operating within the Internet at any point in time is a relatively imprecise number. In the same way as the number of hosts connected to the Internet shifted from a precise count to a statistical estimate as the Internet grew, the count of ISPs in the world is now at best an estimate. Part of the problem is definitional, in that many types of ISP operations exist, ranging from organizations that retail Internet access to the public to publicly funded programs servicing a defined community to operations that service a community of interest using a structure of shared costs to operate.

Its structure is one that can best be described as a self-organizing collection of semiautonomous components. No central authority or governing body exists, and any cohesive outcomes are as much a by-product of chaos and the application of complexity theory as they are of a more rational and organized process. This element of chaos is a major asset of the Internet, allowing it to respond to the continuing challenges of scale without the strictures of mandated structures and solution processes. The early vision of the ARPA program managers and the NSF members has largely been realized: The specific application of research funding has ultimately created a viable and highly valuable new industry, which in turn has been used to service the continuing communications needs of the research community using the cost efficiencies that are possible through the deployment of a large-scale public service offering.

The Internet is now predominately a commercially provided service with formal involvement of government-funded programs now waning. The market bears all the hallmarks of an immature market with great expectations yet to be realized. The *Financial Times* reported in March 1998 that of the 25 most valuable Internet companies, with a combined value of $37 billion, 20 of these companies are still operating at a deficit. Despite this, the mood of optimism pervades the Internet industry.

Exponential growth of the Internet continues, as indicated in Figure 1.1. Annual growth rates of the number of connected host systems range from 63 percent per year in Europe, 90 percent in North America, 111 percent in Africa, 136 percent in Asia, and an astounding 152 percent in Latin America. The number of users, the number of connected systems, the volume of traffic, and similar metrics of the size of the Internet continue to exhibit exponential growth. This growth probably will not continue in the long term, and at some stage, market saturation will be evident. But, at this point, new applications continue to fuel the Internet, ranging from the adaptation of existing activities into the Internet, such as electronic commerce and Internet telephony, to the emerging area of the Internet utility appliance, such as the Web camera. Although strong innovation continues in the base commodities of hardware and software environments, the Internet itself will continue to grow. Market saturation and a consequent leveling off of this growth will become evident when the utility model of the Internet becomes more rigid and when the associated client population of such utilities is serviced through Internet infrastructure. Predicting when this may occur is impossible.

Internet Hosts

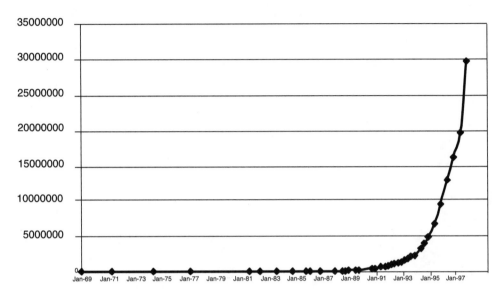

Figure 1.1 Internet host count.

This brief history has provided some background as to how the Internet has developed during the past three decades. This history repeated itself within many countries as the Internet developed within their respective national environments. In the next chapter, we examine how this repetition has happened and the common phases of development that occur in each country.

chapter two

The Evolution of the Internet Service Provider

This chapter describes the generic steps that led to the creation of the Internet Service Provider environment. Many components of this process need to align to allow this industry to take off. These components include access to local technical capabilities to support the industry, an initial level of local demand, a regulatory framework to allow these businesses to operate, and sufficient communications infrastructure services to support the industry. How these components come into alignment to create and sustain an Internet provider industry is described in this chapter.

The brief history of the Internet in the preceding chapter has concentrated on the mainstream development of the Internet within the United States, where much of the development of the character of today's Internet has taken place. However, a similar developmental effort has taken place in many countries around the world in the past two decades. Rather than attempt to describe these developments in detail, country by country, looking at the more generic phases of development, which are common to these individual histories, is more useful. This approach also describes how today's Internet Service Provider industry has evolved.

Within many regions of the world, the development of the Internet has a number of common landmarks that appear in similar sequence. Accordingly, the phases of evolution that have occurred in Egypt are quite similar to those experienced in Poland or in Sweden. Note that the evolutionary development of the Internet industry does entail an increasingly sophisticated carriage infrastructure within the country concerned, so that this evolution is meshed with the overall evolution of data carriage services as part of the national communications capability. The major differences that exist in this generic evolutionary path are those within the timescale in each developmental phase.

Although the early adopters took more than a decade to undertake the evolution from the original research experiments to a vibrant Internet Service industry, the later adopters managed to compress this evolutionary process into a small number of years.

What is perhaps most striking today is that, as an outcome of this evolution, in all parts of the developed world and in many parts of the developing world, the situation today is remarkably similar. The observation to be made is that where such evolutionary steps start to synchronize worldwide, fewer models exist to relate to in order to understand what the next phase may entail. Within such an environment, the ability to draw upon other experiences to create national policies, which ensures that the rational development of the Internet creates an efficient and effective communications infrastructure, is curtailed. The process of policy determination becomes itself very similar to the original research experiments that heralded the start of this entire process.

In this chapter, we will examine these phases of Internet evolution, looking at why they occur and the role each phase plays in the development of the ISP industry we see today.

This chapter is written as a history, using the past tense as if these events really happened. Events did not unfold precisely this way in any particular country. This history is a generalization of what already has happened in many countries and what is likely to happen in many other countries as the Internet starts to appear as a global ubiquitous technology. The intent of the chapter is to look at the major landmarks in the development of an ISP-dominated Internet environment.

The Bright Idea

The initial spark in many countries was carried by individuals who were strongly fascinated by what computer networking applications could achieve, and they started experimenting and investigating to bring the Internet into some initial reality. Listing each of the individuals who worked hard at this in so many countries is not possible, nor is this type of list the key aspect of the evolutionary process. The key question here is, "Why must the initial step start from an individual vision, rather than from the work of committees and panels?" The answer lies in the radical nature of the vision of computer networking when compared to existing communications networks. New concepts, new paradigms, and new technologies do not have carefully controllable outcomes, nor do they follow paths that can be predicted at the outset. A typical committee or large corporate approach strives for careful construction of controlled outcomes. This is not the path to attain acceptance of radically new concepts.

Observing where a challenge and vision is likely to be heard and shared is necessary and important. Here, the role of the national academic and research community is critical, as this community has taken on the role of high-risk innovation and experimentation. This sector, in its research guise, has agreed to be a guinea pig for such concepts, applying a rigorous process of experimentation to prove whether a concept is one that can ultimately be of benefit if deployed in the commercial world. The commercial world, on the other hand, entertains and develops ideas and concepts only when the outcomes are well understood in terms of their exploitative value, and when the risks involved in the development process are quantified. Therefore, the commercial world must balance the inherent conservatism of shareholders, financial institutions, and public policies with the task of innovation and fundamental change.

Individuals within the academic and research community must be receptive to novel concepts and innovative ideas. Of course, this community is itself a harsh testing environment, where both academic rigor and the realities of limited budgets act as intense filters on progress from concept to initial experimentation and finally to adoption.

The Research Experiment

Typically, the next evolutionary phase was one in which the initial concepts were realized within an experimental framework that allowed testing and refined the concept as a working prototype. Such experiments were by no means grand, but were often a powerful filter to determine whether an initial concept could be translated into a working system.

In the Internet context, this initial phase typically focused on message-passing computer networks. The experimental network that was generally adopted was that of a collection of small computer systems and modems, and a dial-based network. Each configured link in the network was opened with a modem call. Queued messages, which were directed to the computer at the remote end of the call, or were to be relayed through the remote end host computer in order to reach their ultimate destination, were passed across the dial connection, while queued messages were passed in the opposite direction. When the two queues were drained, or at the expiration of the configured call period, the call was torn down to be reestablished at the next scheduled call interval.

This concept is powerful and is borrowed from the paradigm of the postal system rather than traditional telephony. The network does not need fully meshed, direct connectivity in order to allow comprehensive end-to-end message delivery. Each host system acts not only as a message generation and termination point, but also as a message relay on behalf of other hosts, undertaking a dual role of both network client and network agent. The messages exchanged in this fashion were typically electronic mail items and data files. Subsequent refinement of the way in which the messages were generated and the refinement of the corresponding termination point message handlers allowed remote printing, distributed bulletin boards, and similar distributed communications functions. The major suite of tools to manage such a network was developed on Unix-based host systems, and the major protocol used in these systems was termed the Unix to Unix Copy Program (UUCP).

The innovation in this model had been addressing scaling of the network to cope with larger networks and larger traffic volumes. One of the major areas of development within these experimental message-passing networks was the refinement of the routing structure, allowing each relay host to determine the optimal next-hop queue for the message to reach its ultimate destination. From an initial model of static configuration in which a single fixed routing table is placed on each host, the refinement had been to make this structure adaptive. In this way, new hosts and new links could be added and could have this information automatically flooded through the message-passing network without the need for comprehensive reconfiguration. The data link message-passing protocol also had been refined, allowing for a checkpoint restart so that large messages could be successfully passed across a sequence of calls. One of the more impressive innovations was an early implementation of non-preemptive differentiated service levels. Here, the call was multiplexed into a number of parallel virtual channels, in which a greater share of the transmission time was given to the virtual channel that supported the carriage of high-priority messages, while still allowing the simultaneous transfer of lower priority messages in a lower priority channel. In this way, a high-priority message could overtake a message of lower priority within the message-passing network.

Outcomes of the Experiment

The major outcomes of this form of experimentation are as follows:

- ◆ It created a cadre of enthusiasts who could participate in developing a useful and very low cost computer network.
- ◆ It created a second population of individuals who used the network as a functional communications tool.

Such experiments often quickly extended outwards from the university computer science departments, where they typically originated, into other areas of the university campus and from there to schools, community groups, and ultimately into commercial messaging networks.

Such networks were extremely inexpensive to set up and operate. They operated as a collection of modem-based intermittent call circuits overlaid on top of the telephone network—the public switched telephone network (PSTN)—and were programmed to optimize the network's cost within the prevailing PSTN tariffs. The technology base these networks commonly drew upon was the PC and modem combination, and the scale of the network encompassed hundreds, sometimes thousands, of store-forward relay elements. The effective bandwidth of the network was measured in 10s of kilobits per second, although the intermittent call nature of the network tends to make this value average out to 10 or so kilobits per second as the average throughput quantity.

These distributed message-passing networks were generally constructed in a piecemeal fashion with a pooling of resources. One of the common attributes of such a system was the ethos of a grassroots approach, which was, by its very nature, strongly resistant to any external attempts to impose a central organization or control the scope of the activities of the network. But, using a bottom-up functional approach to building a communications system of this sort had much to recommend it. These network systems invariably enjoyed success in creating a very inexpensive and highly functional communications environment.

Stress Points in the Network

However, such systems have an inevitable problem—a success-disaster waiting to happen. A *success-disaster* is when the success of a service is so great that it overwhelms the capability of the service to meet the rampant growth demand, and the service then collapses under overload.

Strong pressures for the network to grow in size and scope existed. Host systems not only used the network, but also acted as relay hosts to other parts of the network, so there was no clear delineation between a consumer and a provider of the service. Consequently, the distinction between a client and a provider of network services blurred. Such systems typically had very basic, if any, tariffing for use of the service.

As the number of users increased, attracted by the low entry and usage costs, and as each user made more use of the network with the increasing population of people with which to communicate, the load on the network increased. This load was not uniformly imposed but tended to concentrate on the relay hosts that were at either end of the major message relay links supporting the central backbone of the message network. A typical example of load degradation was the Australian experience, in which the ACSnet messaging network had reached such load levels that it was experiencing a delivery delay of up to 14 days for some domestic end-to-end relay paths by 1988.

At such a stage, the viability of the experiment in computer networking was now evident, but new solutions were necessary to allow further growth. Such solutions were ones that also required significantly greater levels of financial investment and significantly greater levels of organizational capability to respond to the pressures of success.

The Grand Experiment: The National Academic and Research Network

Two common attributes of the ventures into cooperative message-passing networks are as follows:

- ◆ First, they were invariably highly successful in creating an inexpensive and highly functional communications environment that exhibited strong growth and strong interest in networking services.
- ◆ Second, absence of centralized management of expertise, deployment, operations, and financial resources created challenges when attempting to scale the functional core of the distribution network to meet ever-increasing demands.

The mesh of the store forward relay network did not load uniformly across all links. The operators of the relay systems at the core of the network quickly had all their available resources consumed. These operators were forced to either formalize their function and operation, or the network community had to devise an alternative network structure that could meet these increasing levels of demand.

Both approaches, introducing a managerial structure into the core of the messaging network, and the construction of an alternative network structure, had been used to address this problem. The UUCP network in the United States spawned the birth of the UUNet operation, which assumed a major role within a semiformalized core component of the network. The BITNET network was more directly a formalization of network structure to ensure that adequate resources could be brought to bear on the critical central components of the network.

However, there was an inevitable point at which a store forward messaging system would prove strongly resistant to further growth. The demand for additional functionality, reliability, carriage capacity, and end-to-end delivery speed was ever present. This demand, coupled with the increasing appreciation of the inherent value of computer networked applications, inevitably resulted in the next evolutionary step in the process. This step was to construct a dedicated carriage network that could support direct end-to-end application interaction across the network. In this evolutionary step, the intermittent call structure was replaced by dedicated transmission circuits. The messages of the store forward network were broken down into network protocol transmission units, or packets, and the relay function was passed into dedicated network routers that passed the data packets to the next hop with delay factors of milliseconds rather than hours or even days. The network structure was altered to manage higher volumes of traffic with improved service levels, and the proposal to construct a national academic and research Internet emerged.

At this stage, the Internet emerged as a grand experiment, undertaken as a community of interest network service.

The Emerging Internet

This initial venture into the deployment of a national Internet network has been typically a role undertaken by the national academic and research sector. Such projects also had many features in common: They generally were university-based networks, with some element of external program funding, operating on a noncommercial use basis, with a fixed term of operation mandated by the funding contract. At this point, the emphasis of the network also changed, reaching out from an experimentation with computer networking techniques into a grander experiment into content provision and service levels at a national level.

The initial effort to propose such a project into the national academic and research sector is never easy. Many competing demands are placed on research funding, and the effort to gather the necessary levels of support for such a large-scale project must be sufficiently flexible to allow it to meet a number of perceived requirements from various research sectors. Yet, the project should remain cohesive in design, so as to allow it to be constructed and operated as a useful and cost-effective communications resource.

The initial answer in many countries was invariably the multiprotocol national network. Multiprotocol networks attempt to emulate the protocol independence of the Local Area Network (LAN) by simultaneously supporting a number of different protocols within the larger wide area network.

T*hose who made early attempts to construct large wide area networks by simply bridging constituent LANs found it difficult to scale into the wide area, as large-scale bridged networks tend to be highly unstable.*

Many such national academic and research networks commenced as multiprotocol systems, with simultaneous support for TCP/IP, DECnet Phase IV, and X.25 as common elements. Some systems had experimental support for the OSI CLNS protocol, but this protocol never gained a critical mass of user acceptance. Such efforts were intended to ensure that a single network infrastructure could service the communications requirements of a large number of applications and service environments. A network cannot be positioned inflexibly with respect to supported services if it is to remain viable and relevant. Supporting an unused service option also is pointless, and the Darwinian principle of the survival of the fittest applies to these networks as well as the natural world. DECnet, X.25, and OSI CLNS have largely receded in popular adoption during the past decade, and service platforms based solely on TCP/IP have become viable in their own right.

The technology base of such networks moved towards an environment of campus-scale LANs, which served hundreds or thousands of individual PCs and workstations. The number of LANs serviced in this network typically numbered between 10 and 100, making a total client population of some 10,000 or so. The network moved away from host computers also acting as switching elements, and the architecture of such a network used dedicated router platforms to perform the multiprotocol packet-switching function. The circuit technology also changed from dial-up modems to permanent circuits. The nature of the circuits tended to vary in line with locally available data carriage services and ranged from X.25 switched data calls through various dedicated leased data circuits, various satellite-based communications services, and many forms of terrestrial radio. The bandwidth of the network rose typically by an order of magnitude, and the network typically commenced with circuits that operated at around 64Kbps, although the pressure to grow to larger capacity was evident from the start.

The national academic and research network had central management and funding structures, usually with a dedicated operations staff and some form of managerial committee. The mandate of the network was to provide a national academic and research service facility, with a strong emphasis on the provision of content with the active participation of the library sector. The network typically assumed the profile of an academic and research community of interest, with a defined appropriate use policy that precluded exploitation or the use of the network for commercial purposes.

The major aspect of these academic and research projects was the commonly adopted funding regime. The research infrastructure budgets never operated at a high national priority, and the agenda for the budgets always vastly exceeded the available funds. Consequently, funding agencies tend to pick a small number of projects to fund for a limited period and then move on to other projects. These agencies assume that providing a level of funding, which is likely to yield some form of outcome, to a small number of projects is better than providing inadequate funding to a broader set of projects. Therefore, these national network projects either had a fixed funding amount for a fixed period or a declining funding level, again for a fixed period. This lack of funding created significant internal pressure to evolve, as the network generally enjoyed a very high level of success in providing services to a community who were highly receptive to the possibilities. The consequence was very strong growth in the use of the network from the serviced community. Other communities on the periphery of the university sector, including government research agencies, public libraries, and similar institutions, also started to express a strong desire to join the network, adding to the pressure to grow.

The typical outcome of this phase was that the demand outstripped supply as the network outgrew its funding base.

Emergence of Internet Service Providers

The fixed funding regime of academic and research networks produced its inevitable pressures. To enlist support for the project, the network proposed a fully funded service to its academic and research client base, which was a free service to the end users. In a commercial environment, explosive growth is generally viewed as a highly desirable situation. Under a regime of fixed program budgets, the growth in demand that a free service generally creates can be disastrous. No effective control mechanism exists to prevent network over-subscription, which in turn results in degradation of service levels through congestion. To address this growth demand, strong pressure is placed on the network management to devise a broader funding base that allows client institutions to augment central funding with institutional funding. Also lurking in the background is the temptation to operate on more commercial lines as a communications service provider.

Overcoming the Obstacles

A number of factors often prevent a final step into the commercialization of the academic and research network. The role of publicly funded network programs is generally not to be positioned as a competitor to commercially operated services. Indeed, its role normally is stated as a precursor to such services, assisting in the creation of the levels of interest and expertise necessary to operate viable commercial services. Restricting the charter of the national network to a well-defined academic and research community is seen as a viable path to assisting in the formation of commercial services. In such an environment there is a consequent high risk that the commercial marketplace never achieves critical size to sustain a commercial operator. However, this risk is invariably minor. This approach of segmenting the network user community was followed in many countries in the late 1980s and early 1990s, leading to the emergence of two distinct network environments: the national academic and research service network and its community of users and information providers and a collection of commercial Internet Service Providers and their associated fee-for-service operation.

This evolutionary step could be assisted in a number of ways, and the model adopted by the National Science Foundation (NSF) in the United States is a good example. In the NSF service model, the NSF provided the funding for a national high-speed facility, which provided a service to the client base that was free of usage service charges. The clients of the service were themselves network operations that serviced a local regional client base, the mid-level networks. These mid-level networks were spawned with NSF seed funding but were positioned to evolve to a fully self-funding operation, serving academic and research institutions and using this client base as their funding base. Not surprisingly, many of these mid-level networks have evolved to be the core of the current commercial environment within the United States.

However, this path was not the most prevalent in national Internet development, due in no small part to an artifact of carrier circuit pricing. Circuit tariffs from carriers generally do not exhibit constant unit pricing, and higher capacity circuits are tariffed at lower unit costs. For example, a 64-Kbps circuit may be leased for $5,000 per month, but a 128-Kbps circuit may be leased for $7,000 per month, and a 2-Mbps circuit for $20,000 per month. In this example, the unit cost leverage of the 2-Mbps circuit is a factor of 8. In other words, capacity increases eightfold over increases in expenditure in this example.

The consequent outcome of such a pricing model for the academic and research network was that the temptation to resell network services to communities outside of the defined funded base was often overwhelming. Not only did the network possess a significant user population from its core user sector, but it was usually well populated with content and associated content services. With these assets, the academic and research network was already under strong external pressure to open access to other interested user sectors, which indicated a willingness to do so under fee-for-service structures. Admitting such fee-for-service users allowed the network to achieve additional carriage volumes, which in turn admitted financial economies of scale in the underlying circuit tariffs. In this way, the admission of fee-for-service users allowed the central funding component to achieve greater leverage through access to lower unit costs for transmission capacity.

Mission Impossible: Continued Network Growth

This hybrid model of a core academic and research network with a central funding component providing free service and an associated fee-based commercially oriented resale operation was a common phase at this point in the evolutionary path. The resale operation was typically constructed so as to enable structural cross-subsidization of the costs of providing service to the core academic and research constituency. This cross-subsidization, together with access to increasing economies of scale in transmission costs, enabled the network to undertake the seemingly impossible: to continue to grow at rates that were exponential, so that usage doubled in 8- to 12-month intervals, while exposing the academic and research institutional members of the network to no cost increase, or, at worst, linear cost increases.

This step was not without its consequent pressures for further change to the core network structure, as this move effectively spawned not only a larger directly served client base but also created an embryonic ISP industry sector. The typical model of the academic and research core service network was that of an ISP transit provider, linking into the campus networks of the academic and research institutions. These institutions then provided the infrastructure and service support to the individual client population. In broadening the client base, the academic and research network naturally sought commercial clients with similar service profiles. These clients included large corporations and government agencies in which there already existed a major area of interaction with the academic and research sector. The service model of IP transit connecting to a capable corporate infrastructure matched this core network service model. However, this was not an individual retail commercial service offering, in that a core transit network did not possess the resources or service processes to manage and deliver the components of an ISP retail operation. This retail niche that appeared as a market opportunity was quickly filled by the emergence of small businesses that purchased a wholesale ISP transit service from the academic and research network and then augmented this service with modems, metering, and billing systems, in order to launch a service into the direct retail market.

At this point the Internet Service Provider emerged as a distinct service operation.

The ISP Market Niche

The core network, at the stage when the ISPs emerged as a visible sector of the industry, was provisioned with high-speed routers and transmission systems, indirectly servicing some thousands or tens of thousands of clients within the academic and research institutions. The ISP industry augmented this core service model with a retail periphery, using modem banks for customer access and PC platforms to provide various value-added services, such as electronic mail, bulletin board services, and others. At this stage of early market entry, an individual ISP would commence operation within a single dial call area, leasing a single access circuit from the dial access server back to the core service network.

The low entry cost to enter the ISP market, and the general perception of high growth opportunities, which are a product of the strong retail market in PCs, created a very vibrant retail market. At this point, the market was occupied by a rapid proliferation of retail ISPs. The academic and research network was placed under new pressures in continuing to service this market. The initial opportunities to access lower unit transmission tariffs through increased carriage volume started to be offset by the change in focus of the network's operation. The business focus of the academic and research network started to shift to provide quality service to its retail ISP family, changing the emphasis of the core network into a commercial wholesale operation. This transition was not an easy one in any circumstances. The collegiate decision-making process, which is a hallmark of many academic and research communities, was ill-suited to the rapidly changing business environment that the core network was now servicing. Often, the influx of issues requiring business decisions exceeded the capacity of the decision-making process of the network's management. The consequent managerial crisis was inevitable.

The Competitive Internet Service Industry

This situation led to the next distinct phase of evolution, where the emerging ISP sector saw a viable path to operate an ISP transit network as well as a retail operation. This stage is one of the most prevalent in Internet markets today.

The economies of scale in communications tariffs that apply to the academic and research network apply equally to the ISP operation. In the drive to reduce communications costs, the ISP business direction is towards expanding its infrastructure as an independent network. This direction removes undue reliance on the academic and research network to continue to adapt to meet the evolving ISP business requirements. The outcome is the emergence of multiple Internet service networks, operated on a commercial basis, offering a variety of wholesale-like and direct retail access services.

These networks cannot operate with complete independence. The expectation of the client population is one of comprehensive reachability, and each ISP must ensure that it obtains connectivity to all other components of the overall Internet environment. The original model to sustain this connectivity requirement is the use of the academic and research network as the core connectivity exchange, in which this network undertakes the role of common transit provider to the collection of ISPs. However, this model quickly changes so that some ISPs undertake both retail services to end users and resell Internet access to other ISPs. As a result, the issues of creating a diversity of interconnection arrangements is limited more by the capabilities of the routing protocol and the ISP's technical resources than by any other factor.

The Commodity Market for Internet Access

At this stage, the Internet Service Provider business is engaged in its basic function of providing services to a client population. Basic access becomes a market commodity without obvious differentiation, and, as such, is the subject of prolonged price pressure.

Service providers shift to differentiating service based on factors other than price alone. The Internet market is carefully dissected, and business plans target various retail service sectors. Packaging of Internet access services at the point of sale of PC equipment appears in the retail sector, as do packaged service offerings that combine mail services, Web hosting, and other similar services that add value to the base commodity access service.

The original cash flow growth model of the early ISP business tends to succumb to investment pressure as larger ISPs, with the capability to call on greater investment resources, can use their leverage to buy market positions from which further growth can be undertaken. The investment market also sees the ISP industry as a very strong growth sector, and initial public floats of ISP businesses yield high returns as the market expresses its confidence that this is a robust growth industry. A visible proportion of ISP businesses position themselves for takeover or public offering as their primary objective within this robust investment market.

The original basis for the establishment of a centrally funded academic and research network has reached a natural conclusion. A funding program no longer needs to provide a specialist network to the academic and research sector, given that precisely the same set of services is now available on a commercial basis. Commercial services for the supply of Internet access exist in a robust competitive marketplace, and the will to continue to divert research funding directly into a service network quickly dissipates as a result. At the same point, the academic and research operation has now evolved into a fee-charging business enterprise in its own right, and the transition away from central funding to a charging regime in which member institutions are fee-paying clients is as natural as it is inevitable. However, in this environment the academic and research institutions are now clients in a competitive marketplace and can elect to purchase services from any provider. This further forces the academic and research network into a business outlook little different from its original client ISPs. For the academic and research sector, one final evolutionary step must be taken in this process: The network and its service structure are reshaped as a commercial ISP, either through the sale of the operation or the restructuring of the operation into a conventional business. The academic and research sector often regroups, not as a service provider, but as a purchasing block, using its collective volume of purchase to ensure that it optimizes its position within the competitive market. What was the academic and research network becomes a commercial ISP.

Between 1994 and 1998, this evolutionary step was played out in many countries around the world, and the Internet landscape is a vibrant environment, with tens of thousands of Internet service businesses operating in one of the most actively expanding markets of this century. The Internet market is one of the most aggressively open markets, with few onerous regulatory constraints on the operation of the enterprises that service this market. The environment is one in which access tariffs are driven down to reflect the commodity price of carriage, and a new value-added service market has emerged to service a new environment of Internet-based commerce and communication.

The Evolving Communications Industry

In many countries, this evolutionary path has been followed with a simultaneous evolution in the public regulatory environment for communications. The 1980s heralded a worldwide deregulation of the communications industry, in which the traditional monopoly position of the public telecommunications operator was diluted to allow commercial enterprises to operate within this market sector on a competitive basis. The rationale for this deregulation was to allow for increased investment in the national communications infrastructure through private investment channels, although the complementary observation is that deregulation of the industry allows public sector investment levels to decrease at the same time. This deregulation was anticipated to bring competitive business practices to bear on the efficiency of the operation of the incumbent provider, resulting in the rapid lowering of real communications prices in the retail market.

The focus of market deregulation may have been on the operation of the traditional PSTN service and its operator. The reality of deregulation is that its focus has been most clearly evident within the emergent ISP sector, and the outcome of deregulation is not as much a major shift in retail PSTN structure, but the emergence of a deregulated ISP industry. Instead, a very strong competitive ISP industry sector has arisen, in which the most competitive areas of the market today are currently being serviced with one ISP operation for every 40,000 in population and one ISP operation for every 6,000 Internet users. This service factor is very dense for an industry that needs scale of operation to realize cost efficiencies, and as investment pressures and pricing pressures play out within this market, the density of ISP operations is likely to decline.

Although the initial deployment of the Internet service is observed by the incumbent PSTN providers with scant level of interest, the size and rapid growth of the ISP market rapidly attracts the interest of the PSTN provider. Its initial role was that of leased circuit provider to the emerging Internet networks, then as leased circuit and PSTN access infrastructure providers to the retail ISP market. The original PSTN sector's strategic direction had encompassed electronic messaging and electronic commerce and trading, but its vision had encompassed this as occurring on public systems, which were intended to be evolutionary phases of the earlier public X.25-based network infrastructure. Its data services plot commonly assumed an evolution of the X.25 packet-switched network along the lines of the OSI service model, evolving into a large-scale centrally operated public data service with associated valued-added operations.

The similarities of this vision with the operation of the PSTN are, of course, not coincidental. Following a strong, but ultimately unsuccessful, push at the government purchasing sector in the late 1980s to position the OSI architecture as the only standard open networking model, the OSI model quickly waned, and has all but vanished in the Internet fervor of the mid 1990s. For the PSTN sector, this has caused a rapid reevaluation of the longer-term data service strategy. Now that the Internet market has appeared in a fully deregulated structure, the PSTN sector is required to quickly reposition itself into this market. In many markets, the PSTN provider entry has been accomplished by buying an ISP, as a way to quickly enter the Internet market. A number of PSTN providers also have embarked on ISP operations without an initial ISP purchase as a means of market entry.

The presence of a large incumbent communications provider into the ISP market has added a dimension to the factors that shape the future of the market. These PSTN sector moves are viewed with concern in the ISP domain, given the PSTN provider's ability to rely on its investment in carriage infrastructure to have significant influence over the market price. To date, the open Internet service market has certainly not collapsed under the influence of such investment pressure. The current position as the 1990s draw to a close is that the growth of the market remains at levels that stress the capability of any large player to match this demand with deployment of service. In the face of this growth, the market continues to allow both large and small ISP operators to coexist within an approximate level of stability. When such growth levels slow down, a new wave of competitive pressure may well cause poorly structured ISP operations to collapse within the resulting market shake-out.

Future Scenarios

While making predictions is always easy, it's much more of a challenge to get them right. Although hindsight makes much of this evolutionary progress appear inevitable, such certainty in outcomes was not present at the time. Looking at the future from the perspective of the late 1990s, we could see this market head in many directions.

We have been living with a network that has exhibited exponential growth for the past three decades. Believing that this growth must eventually taper off and that the market will exhibit some degree of service saturation seems natural. At that time, the growth model should shrink back to a level based on population and economic growth indicators. If this happens, we will see a restructuring of the ISP service market. As the growth tapers off, larger providers can bring their economies of scale to bear on market pricing across the entire market space. Inevitably, stronger ISPs will overtake the weak, and larger ISPs will further consolidate their position by acquiring smaller ventures that show strong promise. Some evidence of this trend already exists in the United States at the present.

The counter view is that predicting market saturation of a utility service when the utility model keeps expanding is impossible. The Internet today is often visualized as millions of people sitting behind personal computers, surfing the Web, reading and responding to e-mail, and filling Usenet newsgroup threads with the electronic chatter of the times. And, so it certainly is. But the Internet also is a protocol to allow computers to exchange data in a reliable and managed fashion. Computers in this sense are not just personal workstations with screens and keyboards. An entire separate universe exists, which consists of pagers, alarm systems, remote sensors, and similar utility devices that use computing and communications to undertake its specialized tasks. Does the Internet expand to encompass a model of embedded computing into specialized devices? If so, does the world of value-added services become a layer above a utility platform, which, like the existing electricity distribution grid, is neutral with respect to use? In such a world, does the ISP business model pass its value-added function into a capable appliance in which the functionality is embedded?

Perhaps one of the largest looming futures is the role of the Internet within the voice telephony world. In the same way that the telephone network largely supplanted the telegraph system during the middle of the twentieth century with a model of cheaper service and enhanced functionality (the answer came back as soon as the question was asked), the Internet will be able to carry large volumes of voice traffic and offer the same value proposition of cheaper service and enhanced functionality. Currently, a strong relationship exists between telephony service providers and carriage providers. The strength of this relationship is that the two functions are generally undertaken by the same business enterprise. Now that a viable alternate application for carriage is emerging, which also offers a service model that is competitive to telephony, will the strong binding between carriage and telephony service remain intact in the future? Will the incumbent operators in the carriage and telephony service environment adapt to encompass the Internet carriage and service model? If so, will it adapt in the same way that in many parts of the world the telephone service model of monopoly public PSTN operators effectively evolved from the original monopoly public telegraph network operators?

Such questions are relatively easy to pose. However, progress often mixes rational and ordered evolution with a dash of chaos, so that there is always some level of uncertainty about the outcomes, no matter how probable they may seem at the time.

For Now . . .

This chapter has taken us back to the origins of the Internet, unearthing its organizational roots, showing how the Internet service model has evolved, and describing the major factors that shape the Internet today.

Perhaps a sobering observation is that 30 years ago the Internet was a research topic shared by a handful of individuals. In the intervening period, the technology base has evolved to allow scaling of operation. The business model has created a fully deregulated competitive market for services. Finally, the deployment model is now surpassing special-interest communities and entering the phase of ubiquitous availability, and yet the system has remained largely coherent as a single communications environment. Compared to the century of evolution of the telephone network, this is truly an impressive achievement in a very brief span of time.

However, the certainties that a slower evolutionary process may bring are absent from the Internet environment, which is rapidly shifting and fueled by explosive growth. As such, the environment presents higher risks to those who chose to invest in this space, but also presents much higher levels of reward for success. The strategic task of the ISP today is to attempt to minimize the investment risk, through the application of business and technical expertise to the operation of the service enterprise, while attempting to maximize the financial outcomes from the investment.

PART TWO

ISP Technology and Engineering

chapter three

The Internet Protocol

The core business of every ISP is the Internet itself. This statement encompasses both the technology of the Internet protocol, as well as the way in which Internet protocol objects, the IP addresses and DNS names, are managed. The Internet environment also includes the way in which various bodies operate within the Internet sphere and how they influence each other in considering a common issue. Any successful business enterprise must come to grips with its operational environment, as a comprehensive understanding of the environment is an essential means of minimizing business risks. In the ISP business, each ISP must come to a thorough understanding of what the Internet is and how it operates. This chapter addresses this topic from the perspective of the architecture of the Internet.

Claiming that the Internet has some grand architecture is a highly provocative assertion. The Internet is viewed by some as a continuous sequence of alterations and refinements, without any particular consistency or overall theme. However, while some features have been reworked many times to adapt to the patterns of evolution and growth, the core components of the architecture have remained quite stable over the lifetime of the Internet. The fundamental aspects of the Internet protocol architecture have not changed at all in the past two decades. Considering that at the time of its design, the objective of connecting 100 hosts at speeds of 56Kbps was considered state of the art, the fact that this protocol architecture is now embedded in tens of millions of computers and supports transmission speeds of gigabits per second is a fitting testament to an outstandingly robust architecture. In this chapter, we review this architecture, looking at the protocol architecture and its various elements and then look at the organizational structure that oversees the continued evolution of the Internet architecture and its associated Internet standards.

First, we will look at the Internet Protocol itself, describing the capabilities of the protocol through examination of the formats used in the packet headers, examining the base IP protocol, the ICMP control protocol, and the end-to-end protocols, UDP and TCP.

We will then look at names and addresses within the Internet environment and conclude with an examination of the bodies who are active within the evolution of the Internet architecture.

The Internet Protocol

The overall architectural philosophy of the Internet Protocol can be best expressed by observing that it combines the use of smart hosts and a dumb switching network. This generic description includes the design concept of a distributed computer network that should not attempt to impose a restrictive or fixed data flow or host computer connectivity model upon the connected host systems. Instead, the distributed network protocol should do a simple and well-defined task and undertake this task as efficiently as possible. More complex host-to-host transactional models can be constructed above this simple network model by adding functionality to the end host systems, rather than by attempting to add further functionality into the network model.

These host systems can adapt their behavior to the perceived state of the network at each point in time, using intelligence derived from the state of the end-to-end traffic flow to derive the cu rrent network state. In this way, the host systems can continually modify their flow behavior to match the dynamic capabilities of the network. This model of adapting to prevailing conditions is like a road traffic system: When traffic on the road is light, individual cars travel faster; and as the road starts to fill with traffic individual cars reduce their speeds or suffer often fatal outcomes. This host-controlled adaptive model of the distributed network allows every host to behave cooperatively to optimize the carriage efficiency of the network, which yields an optimal fair share of this carriage resource to be allocated to each host. No network-based traffic control exists within the Internet, and instead the network is managed by the dynamic behavior of the host systems on the periphery of the network.

The opposite model is that of dumb hosts on a shared smart network. In this case, the hosts require the network to behave predictably under all circumstances, which in turn dictates a static partitioning of the network into fixed service elements. Here, each host can either connect to an available fixed service element or be denied service completely. This model is effectively that of the PSTN network, in which the fixed service element of the network can be approximately equated to a 64K end-to-end circuit established between telephone handsets.

The architectural approach of an adaptive interaction between the host and the network was first presented in a paper by J. H. Saltzer, D. P. Reed, and D. D. Clark, "End-to-End Arguments in Systems Design" [Saltzer 1984]. This philosophy, often termed the *end-to-end* architecture, was espoused by David Clark during his tenure on the Internet Architecture Board [Clark 1988]. The paper advocated that decisions regarding the interaction between the host and the network should, as far as is possible, be delegated to the host, rather than attempting to supplant or duplicate this host functionality with network functionality. Functions such as flow control, error detection, retransmission of lost packets, connection establishment, and termination should be host functions rather than network operations, and hosts should be able to insert control signals into the datastream and listen for corresponding signals from the remote host to ensure both integrity of communication and that optimal data flow rates are maintained.

This paper formed the origin of the Internet concept, where the intention was to create an end-to-end communications architecture that was capable of spanning a diverse sequence of individual networks [RFC 1958]. Given the appearance of a diversity of network media and the desire to communicate end-to-end across various combinations of these media, creating gateways between each of these single-hop networks was appropriate. These gateways (*routers*, as they were subsequently termed) would strip off the network-dependent encapsulation and then apply a forwarding decision to the packet based on the next layer's end-to-end encapsulation. This action would generate a network-to-network hop, so that the packet would be encapsulated once more for the next network transit. This generic function is indicated in Figure 3.1. The function of end-to-end sequence control and data transfer reliability was designed into the end-to-end control algorithm, as was flow control. The overall design criteria was to make an absolutely minimal set of assumptions regarding the capability of each component network in the end-to-end path. The basic assumption was that the network would undertake best-effort delivery of datagrams (or "packets"), without any delivery guarantee. This implies that there is no implicit indication from the network when a packet is discarded, or when it is successfully delivered, and any network component may elect to silently discard the packet as a response to local congestion. The gateway model was also simplified by the deliberate omission of state in the gateway design. With the omission of state there is no concept of a "call" and the use of locally significant address switching, as is found in state-based packet-switched systems. A stateless system uses only a global addressing level, where each packet contains the globally significant address of the packet's destination. Each gateway requires sufficient knowledge of the global address state in order to undertake a local forwarding decision. In addition, gateways perform neither flow control nor retransmission functions, as the stateless mode of operation infers that once a packet is forwarded no further action is required from the gateway in relation to the packet.

The Internet architecture uses four core protocols: IP, UDP, TCP, and ICMP. Their relationship is indicated in Figure 3.2. In terms of a fully functional protocol stack, a number of functional elements are missing here, namely the

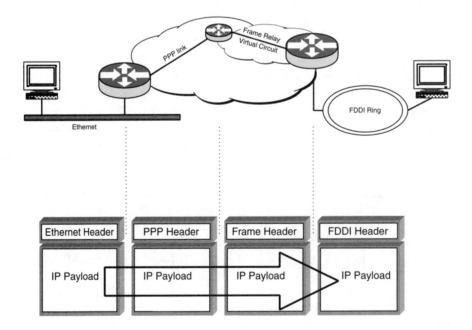

Figure 3.1   End-to-end packet delivery.

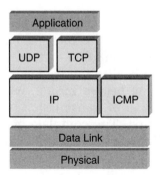

Figure 3.2   Internet layering.

lower data link layer protocols and the upper-layer application interface protocols. This omission was deliberate. The relationship of these component protocols into the general OSI Open Systems networking model is indicated in Figure 3.3.

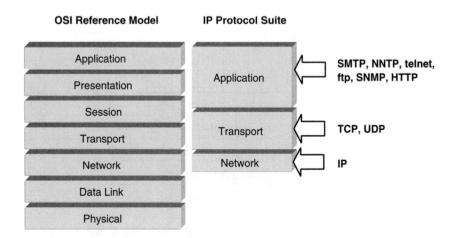

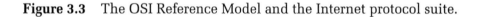

Figure 3.3   The OSI Reference Model and the Internet protocol suite.

IP

Every host and every switch on the Internet operates an instance of the Internet Protocol. IP is an encapsulation method that surrounds its payload, using a header structure prefixed to the payload, as indicated in Figure 3.4. Every IP packet has the same header format, with fields aligned on 32-bit word boundaries. The bit order of transmission is big-endian, with the most significant bit transmitted first. The complete header is aligned on a 32-bit word boundary, with padding used to ensure that the header length is aligned to a multiple of 32 bits.

IP is a datagram protocol, in which individual packets are passed through the IP network on a best-effort basis. No guarantee is made within the IP protocol that individual packets will arrive at the destination, nor is there any guarantee made that a sequence of packets will arrive in the same order as they were sent. A datagram includes a single level of addressing for the destination address, using an address that has global significance. In the delivery of a datagram, all routers along the path process each datagram individually, with local forwarding decisions based on this unique destination address. The router is not required to keep any history of how previous packets were processed nor to maintain a completely fixed view of the path of any given destination. In this way, IP makes minimal demands on the underlying network structure in terms of its functionality.

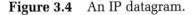

Figure 3.4 An IP datagram.

Version

The version field is used to define the semantics of the following fields in the IP header. The intent was to allow multiple protocol versions to coexist on a single network infrastructure, in which the subsequent header fields of the packet, and their semantic interpretation, were implicitly defined by the version number.

The IP protocol today uses a value of 4 in this version field. The IETF has been working on a successor protocol to IP version 4 (IPv4), intended predominately to address issues of growth in the current Internet exhausting the available fixed 32-bit address values. This effort has resulted in the standardization of IP version 6, although deployment of this version still appears to be some time away. Values of 1, 2, and 3 in this field were used by earlier versions of IP, and version 5 was used by the real-time experimental steam protocol ST-2.

IP Header Length

Because the IP header allows the use of a variable number of control options appended to the fixed header fields, the length of the total header is variable. This value describes, in units of 32-bit words, the total length of the IP header, including all IP options.

Type of Service

The Type of Service (TOS) field is an 8-bit field intended to enable this packet to specify the form of service it is requesting from the network. The original semantics for this field were specified in [RFC 791]. This field can be broken down into two components, a precedence value and a service type, as shown in Figure 3.5.

The precedence field is used to indicate the queuing function within routers. The IP specification defines eight values and their associated suggested use, as indicated in Figure 3.6. The intention within this specification is that router queues are sorted by precedence as the primary sort key and then by time of arrival or some other function as the secondary sort key. If this set of seven absolute priorities, which override the default priority, were to be implemented on all routers within a network, then there is a distinct risk of denial of service. A sustained high-volume stream of high-precedence packets would prevent the scheduling of packets of a lower priority. Such potential for denial of service and implied seizure of network resources by hosts places the network in a position of undue exposure.

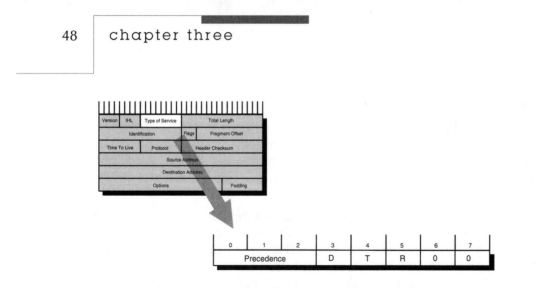

Figure 3.6 IP Type of Service precedence field.

Networks that have successfully used these fields with some form of priority queuing interpretation have used ingress filters, which clear the precedence on all incoming packets and then set precedence levels according to their predetermined policy as a network-based setting. When the packet leaves the network and is passed to the next network in the end-to-end transit path, no guarantee is made that the precedence field will be accepted and honored. This practice is rather at odds with the overall architecture of the IP

Figure 3.5 IP Type of Service selector.

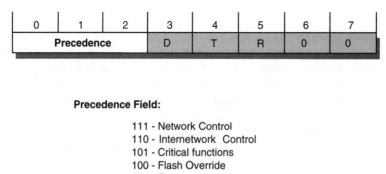

Precedence Field:

111 - Network Control
110 - Internetwork Control
101 - Critical functions
100 - Flash Override
011 - Flash
010 - Immediate
001 - Priority
000 - Routine

protocol, which attempts to use the header for information and assumes significance end-to-end. Currently, no clear outcome of the IETF investigation into differentiated service provision can be predicted. This investigation of whether the precedence field can take on an end-to-end semantic interpretation of relative precedence is predominately hosted within the Differentiated Services Working Group. An alternative interpretation of the precedence field is that it is used to invoke a differentiated behavior from an underlying switched transmission system. Where multiple virtual circuits exist, or where there is a selectable drop precedence function within the transmission system, this field could be used by the router to select a transmission level encapsulation that explicitly maps the IP precedence into a transmission behavior indicator. Such a potential use of the precedence field is yet to attain wide acceptance, and at present it is unclear whether the field can be used to invoke a transmission mechanism that yields some form of service differentiation.

The service type bits were intended to be used as indicators of path selection, requesting that the packet be routed along paths allowing minimal delay, maximized throughput, maximized transmission reliability, and minimized cost. Although these paths correspond to four distinct bits in the service field, only single-bit selection is meaningful, and the setting of multiple bits is an undefined service as indicated in Figure 3.7. Note that to implement support for such service selections, the relationship of this service field to the routing mechanics must be recognized. Multiple path selection capability implies multiple routing topologies, each optimized so that the topology minimizes (or maximizes) a topology metric that is associated with the service type. Attempts to define such multiple metrics were undertaken within the Open Shortest Path First (OSPF) routing protocol, but these metrics have not been used frequently.

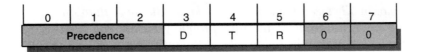

Path Selector Field:

Bit 3: 0 = Normal Delay   1 = Low Delay
    4: 0 = Normal Throughput   1 = High Throughput
    5: 0 = Normal Reliability   1 = High Reliability

Figure 3.7   IP Type of Service path selector field.

To date, little acceptance has been given to the common deployment of these values and their associated semantics of service differentiation. This task is the subject of developmental effort within the IETF, which recently has chartered the Differentiated Services Working Group [IETF 1998]. Although the use of such a field may appear to be a relatively simple issue, it has not proved to be so. The issues of control over the Type of Service selectors settings and of preserving the semantics of the field within a network path that encompasses a number of providers are still actively debated. This discussion raises both technical and business issues, which have not been adequately addressed to date. The default action of most routers is to ignore this field when switching a packet. Accordingly, this field, and the entire area of providing differentiated service, is effectively ignored over much of the Internet today.

If, as appears likely, this field continues to have no effective network-wide significance, then these 8 bits can be regarded as bits that are significant only within the context of an administratively bounded network. One way to interpret this field is as a per-ISP local bit set, which can be used to trigger various locally defined functions.

Total Packet Length

The packet length is a 16-bit quantity that specifies the total length of the packet, including both the header and the payload of the packet. The value is in units of octets, and the total field value of 16 bits allows the maximum IP packet size to be 65,535 octets.

Remember that when the protocol was designed in the mid-1970s, the state of the art was transmission speeds of 56Kbps. At this speed, a maximally sized packet would take a little more than nine seconds to enter the circuit. This value probably was intended to address potential high-speed networks of the future, as it was an over-engineered value at the time. At 100Mbps, a maximally sized packet would take five milliseconds to enter the circuit, which is a far more reasonable time span.

All hosts and routers must pass packets of up to 576 octets in length without any need to invoke fragmentation. Packets of a larger size may be fragmented by the host or the router.

Fragmentation Control

The Packet Identification, Fragmentation Flags, and Fragment Offset fields compose a 32-bit header segment used to control packet fragmentation. Within the design of the Internet Protocol, every network has a maximum packet size or Maximum Transmission Unit (MTU), and these sizes vary. The MTU is an outcome of the network's design and is a product of the network's bandwidth, maximal diameter, and desired imposed jitter. Given that the path selection is dynamic, the sender is not fully aware of the sequence of MTUs supported on the end-to-end sequence of networks. To address this risk of sending oversized packets, the IP specification allows a router to fragment an oversized packet into smaller units that match the MTU of the next network hop.

Fragmentation may occur more than once within an end-to-end transit, and an already fragmented packet may be further fragmented without change to the fragmentation functionality. To accommodate this and to allow some degree of transit efficiency, no reassembly is attempted within the network. Once fragmented, a packet is reassembled only at the end destination.

Three fields are used in fragmentation control: Packet Identifier, Fragmentation Flags, and Fragmentation Offset Value.

Packet Identifier. The packet identifier is a 16-bit value used to identify all the fragments of a packet, allowing the destination host to perform packet reassembly. Note that the packet identifier value cannot be reused while fragments of a previous incarnation of this identifier value remain within the network. For small- to medium-speed networks, this constraint is not onerous, but at gigabit speeds, the wraparound limitation may prove to be a significant constraint. When using maximal-sized packets, fragmentation identifier wraparound occurs every 32 gigabits. When using the more common 576-byte packet size, the fragmentation identifier wraparound is every 256 megabits. The conclusion from this is that as transmission speeds increase, fragmentation capability may have to be dropped as an available option for IP routers.

Fragmentation Flags. The three-bit flag field has the first bit flag reserved. The second bit flag is the *Don't Fragment* flag. When a router attempts to fragment an IP packet with this flag set, no fragmentation occurs, and an ICMP error message is sent back to the sender, informing the sender of the delivery error, and the packet is discarded. The third bit flag is the *More Fragments* flag. When a packet is fragmented, all packets except the final fragment have the More Fragments field set. The fragmentation algorithm operates so that only the final fragment of the original IP packet has this field clear. Even when a fragment is further fragmented, this rule remains in force.

Fragmentation Offset Value. This 13-bit value counts the offset of the start of this fragment from the start of the original packet. The unit used by this counter is octawords, implying that fragmentation must align to 64-bit boundaries.

The fields altered by fragmentation are indicated in Figure 3.8. Here, a 1,300-byte IP packet has been fragmented into two 532-byte packets and a 276-byte packet. The IP packet length has been altered to reflect the fragment size, and the Fragmentation Offset Value field has been set to 0, 16, and 32, respectively. The final fragment has the More Fragments flag cleared to indicate that it is the final fragment of the original packet.

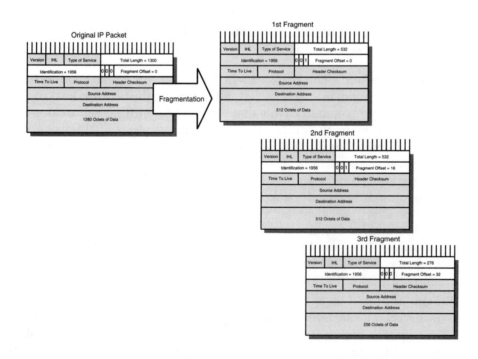

Figure 3.8   Fragmentation of an IP packet.

Fragmentation is not completely transparent. If one fragment is lost within the network, the entire packet is discarded by the receiver, as retransmitting the lost fragment is not an option. This process has performance implications, which is why fragmentation is often avoided. TCP can use a path MTU discovery algorithm [RFC 1191] to allow the TCP session to proceed without the use of fragmentation.

Time To Live (TTL)

This field originally was intended to specify the interval of time a packet could remain in transit within the Internet before being discarded. The unit of the counter was in seconds, and the 8-bit field allowed a 256-second lifetime. However, given that the header contains no timestamps and that the router clocks are not synchronized, the only design option available to the router is to decrement the packet's TTL field by one, irrespective of the elapsed time the packet has been in transit. This field has, by default, become a maximum hop count, preserving the original semantics of ensuring that a packet does not loop endlessly within the network. The default initial value for the TTL field is 64.

Protocol Identifier

This field is used to identify the protocol carried within the Internet packet. Currently assigned values are listed in [RFC 1700].

Header Checksum

This checksum covers only the IP header and is a simple 16-bit 1s complement sum of the IP header. Given that the TTL is adjusted on a hop-by-hop basis, this checksum must be recalculated incrementally each time it is passed through an IP gateway.

Source and Destination Addresses

The Source and Destination fields are 32-bit quantities that are the addresses of the sender and intended recipient of the IP packet. One of the quite remarkable aspects of the original design is the use of such large fields for the address, and the intention to use globally significant address values, rather than locally significant addresses. Remember that when using low-speed transmission lines, every bit of protocol overhead impacts the data transmission efficiency. Other protocols in use at the time IP was designed used 8-bit address values, or, as a bold initiative, included 16-bit values, ascribing them local corporate or campus network significance. The adoption of an address space encompassing 4 billion addressable entities, when the original requirement of connectivity appeared to be in the hundreds or low thousands, was either an act of inspired genius or outlandish optimism. Either guess is correct. We will cover the structure of the IP address in the next section.

IP Options

Base IP packet headers are 20 octets long and contain no further fields. However, the protocol design does allow the addition of a variable number of options to the IP packet. These options are appended to the base IP header and precede any IP data payload.

Options are specified in a variable length syntax, using a (*type*, *length*, *field*) triplet, although a number of fixed length options also are used. The *type* is divided into three fields, as indicated in Figure 3.9. The first bit is a *don't copy on* fragmentation flag, followed by a 2-bit class, in which 0 is defined as control and 2 bits are for debugging and measurement, and a 5-bit option value. The values defined are indicated in Figure 3.10.

Most options are rarely used these days, and, with two exceptions, are essentially obsolete within the public Internet. The loose source routing and strict source-routing parameter are used in operational networks as a valuable debugging tool. You should note that these options have been used to launch various security attacks, so many parts of the Internet, and many enterprise internets, disallow such options to be used.

LOOSE SOURCE-ROUTING OPTION

The loose source-routing option enables the sender of the packet to specify a number of addresses in sequence according to where the packet must be passed before being delivered to its final destination. This is another way of expressing *landmark source routing*, in which the packet must be routed to each landmark in turn before reaching its final destination.

This routing option allows the user to assist the normal routing behavior by effectively informing the local routing environment where the next routing step is in the destination path. However, loose source routing is far more useful as a routing debugging tool. A network operator can attempt to replicate a reachability event by specifying the customer interface as a loose source route point, so that the packet is passed first to the customer interface point and then routed to the destination. Loose source-routing options have been used

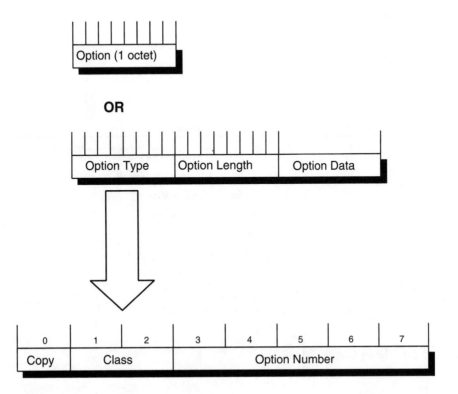

Figure 3.9 IP options.

to exploit various security weaknesses in many networks. A common mode of exploiting such weaknesses is to generate packets with a source address of a trusted host, and use a loose source-routing option that includes the address of the attacking host. If the security mechanisms simply check on the source address of the packet, such attacks may result in successful penetration of the secure environment. Consequently, many networks choose to block datagrams that contain this option due to this perceived risk of intrusion.

Option Type: Copy Field

0	Copy on fragmentation
1	Don't Copy on fragmentation

Option Type: Class Field

0	Control
2	Debugging and Measurement

Option Type

Copy	Class	Number	Length	Description
0	0	0	-	End of Option List. This option is 1 octet, and is used to mark the end of all IP options
0	0	1	-	No Operation. This option is used for padding
1	0	2	variable	Basic Security Option
1	0	3	variable	Loose Source Routing
0	2	4	variable	Internet Timestamps
1	0	5	variable	Extended Security Option
0	0	7	variable	Record Route
1	0	8	4	Stream Identifier
1	0	9	variable	Strict Source Routing

Figure 3.10   IP option values.

STRICT SOURCE-ROUTING OPTION

This routing option is more specialized in its application, because this option specifies a complete path from the source to the destination, listing each hop in the path in strict sequence. This hop-by-hop path must be followed by the packet.

Outside of a network debugging tool, this option has found little real use in the Internet, because applications do not normally attempt to completely specify an end-to-end path through the Internet, and the security risk considerations apply equally to this option.

Header Fields Summary

The header fields provide the following functionality to IP:

- ◆ Version to allow header interpretation
- ◆ Header length to frame the header and the payload

- Identification, Flags, and Fragmentation Offset to support datagram fragmentation
- TTL to prevent infinite looping of packets
- The Protocol field to specify the protocol handler at the destination to which the packet is to be passed
- The source address to determine where delivery failure messages should be directed
- The destination address to determine to where the packet should be delivered
- The total packet length to assist in packet framing

Of more significance in looking at the IP protocol is looking at what is missing from the protocol rather than what is there. Most notable is any form of local labels or context fields. An IP packet could be injected into the network at any location and still be correctly delivered to the same destination. The packet contains no notion of how the packet should be delivered in terms of which path to choose but contains only a global destination identifier, which the local router must translate into a local forwarding decision.

ICMP

Within a datagram regime, failure to deliver a datagram is not in itself an error condition. Some losses are the result of local congestion, where a part of the network is overloaded. Some losses are the result of errors in the packet header, where the packet is undeliverable by the network under any circumstances. In this latter case, the IP architecture makes some provision to notify the sender of this error condition. The Internet Control Message Protocol (ICMP) is used for this error notification.

A nonintuitive design choice, ICMP is a protocol layered above IP and uses IP as its network layer protocol. The packet format is as indicated in Figure 3.11. If ICMP messages are generated in response to certain IP packets that encounter an error condition and if ICMP packets are themselves IP packets, what is to stop a recursive loop of ICMP messages from saturating the network? ICMP messages are generated in specific circumstances, and ICMP messages are not generated as a result of processing an ICMP error message, an IP datagram addressed to or from a broadcast or multicast address, or a noninitial IP fragment. These guidelines are intended to prevent the occurrence of ICMP storms.

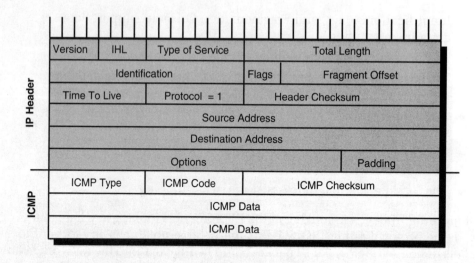

Figure 3.11   ICMP packet format.

IMCP Destination Unreachable.   Messages are generated by a router when the destination address cannot be located in the router's forwarding table. In such a situation, the header plus the first section of the IP payload are returned to the source address as an ICMP Destination Unreachable message. Hosts also may return ICMP Destination Unreachable messages when the port or protocol is undefined at the destination host.

ICMP Redirect Messages.   Messages are sent by a first hop router to the sending host to inform the host that a better router choice than the one it has selected is available. This redirection is based on an Internet architectural model, which proposes that hosts do not need to participate in Internet routing. A host requires only three items of information to be completely functional within this model:

◆ The IP address of the host's interface to the local network

◆ The subnet mask associated with the network

◆ An address of a default gateway that connects the local network to the broader Internet

When the local network has two or more gateways, the selected default gateway responds with ICMP Redirect Messages to inform the host of those destination addresses in which an alternate first hop gateway is more appropriate.

ICMP Source Quench.   Messages may be generated by a router when a packet is discarded due to local buffer congestion. As a flow-control method, ICMP Source Quench has not had wide acclaim nor widespread acceptance. This method of flow management is very indirect and ineffectual because it increases the amount of traffic at the point in time when traffic already has reached overload conditions. No guarantee is made to ensure that the ICMP Source Quench will be sent to the system sending at the highest data rate, nor is any guarantee given to ensure that the sending system will respond to the ICMP Source Quench message. Flow-control mechanisms that attempt to ensure that the router does not enter the state of buffer space exhaustion in the first place appear to offer greater promise at present, and mechanisms that use Random Early Deletion (RED) are now being deployed as a more stable method of undertaking network flow control and congestion management.

ICMP Time Exceeded.   These messages encompass two error conditions. The first is a router encountering a packet whose TTL field is decremented to 0. In this case, the actual error is *TTL Exceeded*. The router must discard the packet and may inform the sender that the TTL has been exceeded. This event usually is the outcome of a routing loop within the Internet, but with an ever-expanding network diameter, the typically chosen TTL default value of 64 may be too small for some environments. The second condition is the destination host exceeding its fragmentation reassembly timer. When a fragment of an IP packet arrives at the destination, a timer is initialized so that all fragments of the packet must be assembled within the allotted time. If the timer expires, the partially assembled packet is discarded, and an ICMP Time Exceeded message is generated back to the sending host. This error signal is used in the traceroute tool to expose the per-hop choices being determined by the routing system.

ICMP Parameter Problem.   Messages are sent when the header field is badly formatted in some fashion, and the packet is discarded.

ICMP Echo Request and ICMP Echo Reply. These messages are not sent in response to an IP error condition. Instead, they form a request/response pair so that a source can send an echo request to a destination, which, in turn, should exchange the source and destination fields, change the request to a response code, and then return the packet back to the original sender. The packet format enables identifier and sequence numbers to allow mapping between requests and responses and can have a variable length payload that is carried in both the request and response packets. This format is used in the *ping* program to undertake basic probes for connectivity, delay, and reliability of a path between two points on the network. *Ping* takes an IP address as an argument and directs an ICMP Echo Request datagram to the address. The program sets off a timer and awaits the corresponding ICMP Echo Reply message. The fact that a reply was received indicates that the remote system is operating and that the network path is functional. The delay between sending the packet and receiving its response can be used in a series of repeated measurements to deduce some information regarding current load on the network path. Accordingly, *ping* and ICMP Echo Request/Reply play a central role in practical networks operations management.

ICMP Information Request and Reply. This message is not an error diagnostic message but was intended to allow systems to be assisted in initial configuration. Protocols such as Reverse ARP, BOOTP, and DHCP have assumed this area of functionality, and this message format is unused today.

ICMP Timestamp and Timestamp Reply. This information message was intended to assist in the synchronization of real-time clocks on various network components. This function has been superseded by the use of the Network Time Protocol (NTP) that provides this clock synchronization function and provides clock accuracy using a mechanism of time distribution from authoritative time servers.

ICMP Address Mask Request and Reply. This bootstrap option is intended to assist in the self-configuration of hosts on a network. Its function has been largely superseded by the BOOTP and DHCP protocols.

ICMP Router Advertisement and Solicitation. Messages are intended to be used by hosts to dynamically discover routers on the local network. Again, this function was intended to form part of a self-configuration environment and has been largely superseded by BOOTP and DHCP, both of which attempt to offer a more complete configuration function within a small set of network transactions.

UDP

UDP is a protocol layered above IP that offers end-to-end functionality between a pair of host systems. The format of a UDP packet is indicated in Figure 3.12.

The end-to-end address used by UDP includes *source* and *destination ports* that are 16-bit values. The 96-bit, 4-tuple of source address, source port, destination address, and destination port is used by the destination system as an index into the process table to identify the correct process to which the datagram is to be delivered.

- ◆ The *length field* refers to the UDP component of the packet and explicitly omits the IP prefix.
- ◆ The *UDP checksum* is computed over a synthesized header indicated in Figure 3.13.

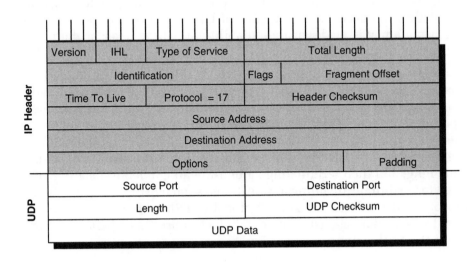

Figure 3.12   UDP packet format.

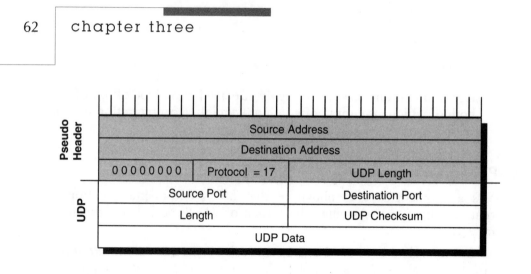

Figure 3.13   UDP packet for checksum computation.

The UDP checksum is optional, and a value of 0 indicates that no checksum exists. However, omission of the checksum can allow corrupted data to be passed through the network without detection, and this has led to incidents of corruption of the DNS in the past.

UDP is effectively a null protocol. It offers port addressing and header checksums, but no other functionality other than that provided within IP itself. Within the network, a sequence of UDP packets may be reordered or lost. No guarantee is made for the reliability of data transfer or the preservation of order on an end-to-end basis.

UDP has been used to support the Trivial File Transfer Protocol (TFTP), Domain Name System (DNS) query protocols across the wide area network, and network file systems across local networks. UDP also has been used to support authentication applications in which a remote authentication server is queried by local agents. In this context, the attributes of UDP are efficiency in minimal protocol transmission overhead and no overhead in establishing, maintaining, and then terminating an end-to-end connection state. UDP also is used for real-time streaming applications, such as voice or video transport protocols, and the Network Time Protocol (NTP), where the ability to time packet transmission against an external clock source is of paramount importance to the application.

TCP

TCP is the embodiment of the end-to-end architecture in the overall Internet architecture. All the functionality required to take a simple base of datagram delivery and impose upon this an end-to-end signaling model that implements reliability, sequencing, flow control, and streaming must be embedded within TCP.

TCP is a bilateral duplex protocol, which admits only two parties to the connection. However, TCP allows both parties to send and receive data within the context of the single TCP connection. Rather than impose a state within the network to support the connection, TCP uses synchronized state between the two end points, and much of the protocol design ensures that each local state transition is communicated to and acknowledged by the remote party.

Like UDP, TCP provides a communication channel between processes on each host system. The channel is reliable, serialized, and full duplex. The stream of octets generated by the process at one of the connections will be passed across the Internet by TCP so that it is presented to the remote process as the same sequence of octets, in the same order as that generated by the sender. However, TCP is a true streaming protocol, and application-level network operations are not transparent. Some protocols explicitly encapsulate each application transaction; for every *write*, there must be a matching *read*. In this manner, the application-derived segmentation of the datastream into a logical record structure is preserved across the network. TCP explicitly does not preserve such an implicit structure imposed on the datastream, so that there is no explicit pairing between *write* and *read* operations within the network protocol. A TCP application may *write* three data blocks in sequence into the network connection, which may be collected by the remote reader in a single *read* operation. This is termed a *streaming protocol*.

The only stream formatting permitted within TCP is the concept of *urgent data* in which the sender can mark the end of a data segment that the application wants to bring to the attention of the receiver. The TCP segment that carries the final byte of the urgent data segment can mark this data point, and the TCP receiving process has the responsibility to pass this mark to the receiving application.

TCP allows data to be passed in both directions simultaneously. The TCP connection is identified by the hosts at both ends by a 96-bit, 4-tuple of source IP address, source port, destination IP address, and destination port, in which the port identifier is a 16-bit value. Note that the same port number can be associated with a number of distinct connections, because a connection includes the local and remote address fields, rather than only the port identifiers. A number of low numbered ports are considered *well-known* and are associated with defined services, and higher numbered ports are associated with dynamic use.

The abstraction used here is that of a *socket*, which acts as the interface between the process and the network. The socket is bound to a TCP port address. TCP uses the mechanism of a synchronized state between two sockets. The process expects to direct the socket to *open* a connection to the remote socket, and following a success indication from the open operation, to *send* and *receive* data blocks and query the *status* of the socket. When the transaction is complete, the process must be able to *close* the connection, or in the event of an abnormal condition, *abort* the connection (see Figure 3.14).

The TCP header structure is indicated in Figure 3.15. The header structure uses a pair of 16-bit source and destination *port addresses*. The next field is a 32-bit sending *sequence number*, which identifies the sequence number of the first data octet in this packet. The sequence number is not an absolute value, and the selection of an initial sequence value is critical. The initial sequence prevents the misinterpretation of delayed data from an old connection being incorrectly interpreted as being valid within a current connection. The sequence field is necessary to ensure that arriving packets can be reordered into the sender's original order. This field is also used within the flow control

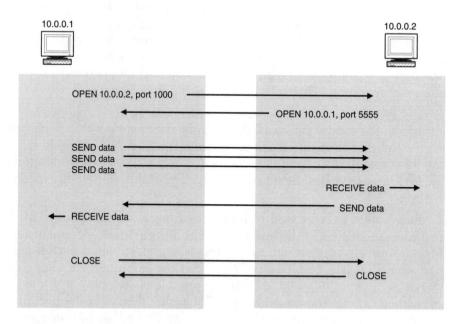

Figure 3.14   TCP control operations.

structure, as it allows each side of the connection to estimate the current round-trip time across the network.

The next field is the *acknowledgment number*, used to inform the remote end of what data has been successfully received. The acknowledgment sequence number is actually one greater than that of the last octet correctly received at the local end of the connection. The *data offset* field indicates the number of 4-octet words within the TCP header. Six single *bit flags* are used to indicate various conditions. *URG* is used to indicate whether the *urgent pointer* is valid. *ACK* is used to indicate whether the acknowledgment field is valid. *PSH* is set when the sender wants the remote application to push this data to the remote application. *RST* is used to reset the connection. *SYN* is used within the connection startup phase, and *FIN* is used to close the connection in an orderly fashion. The *window field* is a 16-bit count of available buffer space. The window field count is added to the acknowledgment

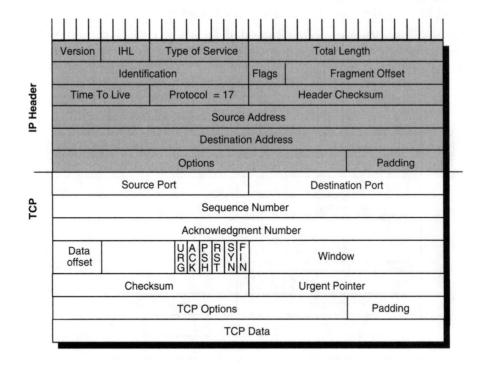

Figure 3.15   TCP packet header structure.

number to indicate the highest sequence number the receiver can accept. As with UDP, the *TCP checksum* is applied to a synthesized header that includes the source and destination addresses from the IP datagram (as indicated in Figure 3.16). The final field in the TCP header is the *urgent pointer*, which when added to the sequence number, indicates the sequence number of the final octet of urgent data.

A number of options can be carried in a TCP header.

The Maximum Receive Segment Size option is used when the connection is being opened. This option is intended to inform the remote end of the maximum segment size, measured in octets, that the sender is willing to receive on the TCP connection. This option is used only in the initial SYN packet (the initial packet exchange that opens a TCP connection). This option sets both the maximum possible receive segment size and the maximum possible size of the advertised TCP window, passed to the remote end of the connection. This option should be used with MTU discovery to establish a segment size that can be passed across the connection without fragmentation.

The Window Scale option is intended to address the issue of the small maximum window size in the face of paths that exhibit a high-delay bandwidth product. This option allows the window size advertisement to be right-

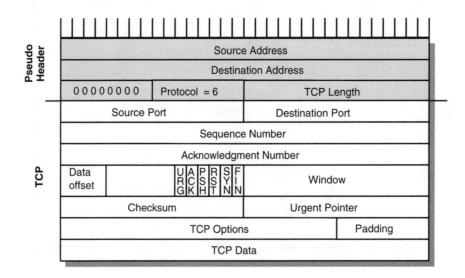

Figure 3.16 TCP packet for checksum computation.

shifted by the amount specified. Without this option, the maximum window size that can be advertised is 65,535 bytes (the maximum value obtainable in a 16-bit wide field). The limit of TCP transfer speed is effectively one window size in flight between the sender and the receiver. For high-speed, long-delay networks, this limitation is arbitrary, given that the TCP send buffer memory in excess of 64K in today's hosts is not an economic factor. Also, if network capacity is available, the sender should be able to use the network resource. Use of the window scale option allows TCP to effectively adapt to high bandwidth delay network paths, by allowing more data to be held in flight. The maximum window size with this option is 2^{30} bytes, or 1G. This option is negotiated at the start of the TCP connection and can be sent in a packet only with the SYN flag. Note that while an MTU discovery process allows optimal setting of the Maximum Receive Segment Size option, no corresponding bandwidth delay product discovery allows the reliable automated setting of the window scale option.

The SACK Permitted option and SACK option alter the acknowledgment behavior of TCP. (*SACK* is an acronym for selective acknowledgment.) The SACK Permitted option is offered to the remote end during TCP setup and is available to a SYN packet. The SACK option permits selective acknowledgment of permitted data. The default TCP acknowledgment behavior is to acknowledge the highest sequence number of in-order bytes. This default behavior is prone to cause unnecessary retransmission of data, which can exacerbate a congestion condition that may have been the cause of the original packet loss. The SACK option allows the receiver to modify the acknowledgment field to describe noncontinuous blocks of received data, allowing the sender to retransmit only what is missing at the receiver's end.

The TCP Echo option and TCP Echo Reply option provide similar functionality to the ICMP Echo Request and Response used in the *ping* probe (described within the ICMP Echo Request and Reply options). This option allows a four-byte identifier to be attached to a TCP packet and allows the receiver to return the identifier as an Echo Reply option. Therefore, the packet delay can be measured within the TCP session. TCP delay is not the same as end-to-end packet propagation delay, given that the remote end TCP protocol may delay an ACK response to ensure efficient use of the network. This option is not commonly used as a network probe device.

TCP Operation

The setup of TCP requires a three-way handshake, ensuring that both sides of the connection have an unambiguous understanding of the remote side's sequence number. The operation of the connection is as follows:

1. The local system sends the remote end an initial sequence number to the remote port using a SYN packet.

2. The remote system responds with an ACK of the initial sequence number and the remote end's initial sequence number in a response SYN packet.

3. The local end responds with an ACK of this remote sequence number.

4. The connection is then opened.

The operation of this algorithm is indicated in Figure 3.17.

A number of special cases exist regarding the handling of SYN packets and the selection of the initial sequence number designed to ensure the establishment of reliable connections.

Following the connection's establishment, the TCP protocol manages the reliable exchange of data between the two systems. In the same way that IP provides no specification of how routing and forwarding is undertaken within the specification of the IP packet and the semantics of the IP header fields, the TCP packet specification provides no predetermined method of data flow control and reliable data transfer management. The algorithms that determine the various retransmission timers have been redefined many times, and the refinement of flow control TCP algorithms remains an active area of IETF activity. The general principle of flow control is based on the management of the advertised window size and the management of retransmission time-outs.

The overall majority of TCP protocol stacks in use on the Internet today do not use state-of-the-art flow control mechanisms and suffer performance degradation as a result. Tuning a TCP protocol stack for optimal performance over a very low-delay, high-bandwidth LAN requires different settings to obtain optimal performance over a dial-up Internet connection, which in turn is different from the requirements of a high-speed wide area network. Although TCP attempts to discover the delay bandwidth product of the connection and to optimize its flow rates within the estimated parameters of the network paths, some estimates will not be accurate, and the corresponding efforts by TCP to optimize behavior will not be completely successful.

One other critical aspect of TCP flow control behavior is that TCP is an adaptive flow-control protocol. TCP uses a basic flow-control algorithm of increasing the data flow rate until the network signals that some form of saturation

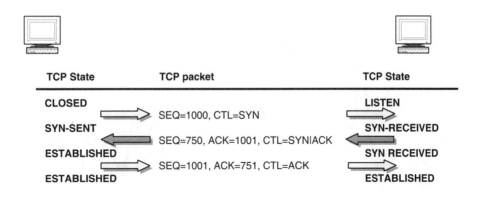

Figure 3.17 TCP three-way handshake.

level has been reached (normally by packet loss). At this stage, the TCP flow rate is reduced, and if reliable transmission is reestablished, the flow rate slowly increases again. If no reliable flow is established, the flow rate backs further off to an initial probe of a single packet, and the entire flow control process starts again.

This process has a number of outcomes relevant to service quality. First, TCP behaves adaptively, rather than predictively. The flow-control algorithms are intended to increase the data flow rate to fill all available capacity but also quickly back off if the available capacity changes due to interaction with other traffic or if a dynamic change occurs in the end-to-end network path. A single TCP flow across an otherwise idle network attempts to fill the network path with data, optimizing the flow rate. If a second TCP flow opens up across the same path, the two flow-control algorithms will interact so that both flows will stabilize to use approximately half of the available capacity per flow. This behavior is indicated in Figure 3.18. The objective of the TCP algorithms is to adapt so that the network is fully used whenever one or more data flows are present. A design tension always exists between the efficiency of network use and enforcing predictable session performance. With TCP, you give up predictable throughput but gain a highly utilized, efficient network.

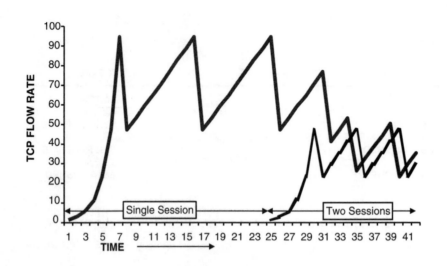

Figure 3.18   Idealized TCP flow behavior.

IP Address Structure

Within any communications system, the underlying structure of addressing is a critical part of the design and its subsequent deployment. In this section, we describe the structure of IP addresses and the interaction between addresses and routing.

An IP address is used to uniquely identify a service point located on the network. Accordingly, IP addresses must be unique to ensure that the particular service point described by the address is not ambiguous. The IP address also is used to locate the service point on the network. In the same way that a postal address of city, suburb, street name, and street number is an address structure that contains an implicit location algorithm, an address normally contains some level of internal structure, which embeds an implicit location algorithm. Accordingly, an IP address serves two functions simultaneously: identification and location.

In the Internet Protocol, every network interface of every host connected to the Internet is identified by a unique IP address. Many other network protocols, however, identify a host by a single protocol-specific address. In IP, a host has as many different IP addresses as network interfaces attached to the host. From the outset, every IP address was globally unique. This assignment of addresses required coordination from the beginning, and the address allocation function remains one in which considerable attention is devoted to ensuring that this attribute is preserved across the public Internet. We'll look at the implications of this attribute when we examine the role of the Internet Address Registries within the role of address allocation.

An IP address is a 32-bit value. This choice of a fixed-length value is certainly one that is revisited from time to time within the area of protocol design. Fixed-length designs may be quite wasteful in overheads, given that the designers must at the outset specify the fundamental restriction on the network's size, and an optimistic view here leads to large address fields that can add significantly to the protocol overhead of data transmission. Variable length address structures normally take greater processing resources to extract and manipulate the address.

*D*efining an address structure can occupy most or very little of the design time of protocol definition. In the case of IPv4, the choice to use fixed 32-bit address structures within the protocol was said to be the outcome of the flip of a coin! It has also been said that the choice between fixed- and variable-sized addresses was the outcome of a single implementor claiming that the implementation of variable address sizes was too complex to code up. (Enough time has passed by that it is getting harder to verify the exact facts, and such observations are already entering the hazy realm of Internet folklore.) In the case of IPv6, the choice to use 128-bit address structures was the outcome of some years of intense debate within the IETF and elsewhere.

Class-Based Network and Host Addresses

The structure of the IP address was initially a network and host delineation. The initial implementations of IP used a division of 8 bits as a network identification field and 24 bits of per-network host identification. The Internet environment used the 8-bit network identifier as the routing element and used the 24-bit field to carry the lower layer network media address to allow final hop per-network delivery. The initial structure, therefore, took a flat address space of 4,294,967,296 possible address values and divided it into 256 networks, each capable of holding up to 16,777,216 hosts. This early structure suffered from the limit of no more than 256 constituent networks. The per-network host part was also found to be inadequate with the advent of Ethernet, which, with its 48-bit media addresses, could not be carried in the 24-bit host identifier field.

Various refinements of IP have imposed an evolutionary structure on the IP address. The refinement adopted was to move to three classes of network addresses: Class A, Class B, and Class C.

◆ Class A addresses retained the original 8-bit network identifier and 24-bit host identifier fields.

◆ Class B addresses used a 16-bit network identifier field and a 16-bit host identifier.

◆ Class C addresses used a 24-bit network identifier and an 8-bit host identifier field.

A block of unstructured address space also was reserved for multicast use, termed Class D addresses, and a final block was reserved for future use, termed the Class E space. This structure of the address space is indicated in Figure 3.19.

The convention used in describing an IP address value is to use *dotted quad* notation, in which the 32-bit value is expressed as a sequence of four decimal values, corresponding to the sequence of the four 8-bit values. Using such a

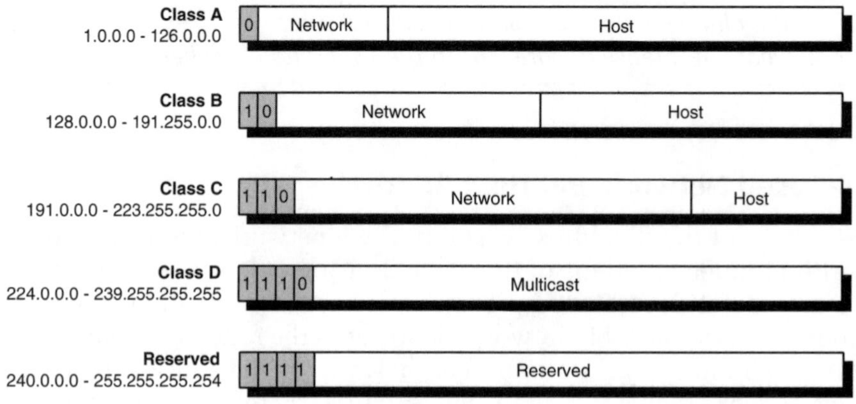

Figure 3.19   IP class-based address structure.

nomenclature, the address 10001011100000101101000000001000 can be expressed as 139.130.204.8 in *dotted quad* notation. Using this notation, the class address structure can be described as follows:

- The Class A address space uses network identifiers from 0–127 and addresses from 0.0.0.0–127.255.255.255.
- The Class B address space uses network identifiers from 128.0–191.255, and addresses from 128.0.0.0–191.255.255.255.
- The Class C address space uses network identifiers from 192.0.0–223.255.255 and covers IP address values from 192.0.0.0–223.255.255.255.
- The Class D multicast address space uses IP addresses from 224.0.0.0–239.255.255.255. No network and host identifier structure is imposed on the multicast address space.

A number of addresses are reserved for special use within this structure. The zero-valued address is used to refer to *this host connected to this network*, and a zero network address together with a non-zero host identifier implies *the identified host connected to this network*. The address that uses the value of 127 in the first 8 bits refers to the internal host loopback function. The address also uses all 1s as a broadcast address format. The address 255.255.255.255 refers to all hosts on the local network. Replacing the leading field by a valid network identifier is a *directed broadcast* and refers to all hosts on a specific network.

This two-level structure of addresses was further refined by the introduction of the concept of a *subnet*. The subnet allows a connected set of networks to share a common externally visible network identifier, but then divide the host identifier into a subnet identifier and a host identifier. The allocation of the number of bits assigned to the subnet identifier is a local administrative decision. Normally, this is a fixed allocation throughout the collection of subnets so described. The major design consideration within this architecture was that the collection of subnets sharing a common external network identifier had to maintain complete internal connectivity. The external Internet cannot be used to repair any breakage within the subnet environment.

Classless Network and Host Address Structure

This address structure was placed under considerable stress in the early 1990s. The 128 Class A networks were too large to be used efficiently by even the largest of Internet-connected entities, and the 254 host limit of the Class C space made the 2,097,152 Class C networks too small to be of any practical use. The 14,284 Class B networks were absorbing most of the growth of the Internet, and the signs were visible that this space would be exhausted quickly. The Class B space was too big, because 65,536 hosts in a network was simply too high a number to use efficiently, and the Class C space was too small, because 256 hosts per network was well less than the number of host computers within most enterprise networks. The adopted direction was to provide a mechanism that addressed the immediate issues, while also looking at an evolutionary version of the IPv4 protocol. The immediate mechanism was intended to provide a means to use the upper and lower areas of the address space (the old Class A and Class C addresses) without creating undue pressure of explosive growth of the Internet routing tables.

The CIDR World

The resulting structure of Classless Inter-Domain Routing (CIDR) is used today in the Internet. This structure is an evolution of the subnet concept, in which local connectivity structure is effectively hidden when outside of the local area. Within the CIDR view of the IP address space, every routing entry is expressed as a network identifier prefix and an associated prefix length. In this structure, the old Class A network 10 is now expressed as 10.0.0.0/8, indicating that the network address prefix is described in the first 8 bits. This allows a contiguous collection of old Class C networks to be expressed as a single entity, so that the four Class C networks—222.1.16.0, 222.1.17.0, 222.1.18.0, and 222.1.19.0—can be represented as the single entity 222.1.16.0/22. The immediate outcome of using CIDR-based routing tools is the ability to use the old Class C space without a consequent explosion in routing space entries.

To minimize the pressure caused by the size of the Internet's routing table, further structure of the address space is necessary. If every local network is addressed using a randomly assigned network prefix value, each network prefix must be routed across the entire public Internet as a distinct routed entity. Considering that the number of such network prefixes is in the hundreds of thousands today and soon will be in the millions and considering that the current state of the art in routers and routing protocols can manage some tens of thousands of routing entries, this random address structure is not an address management structure that can support the Internet.

The current IP address structure and allocation policies are intended to provide some form of solution to this problem. The environment can be described as CIDR with ISP address allocation. The intent is to align, in a general sense, the address allocation with the prevailing topology of the network. This alignment enables ISPs to receive a CIDR block of addresses and to allocate subblocks to their customers. The local routing structure within the subblock is constrained to the network internal to the ISP. The ISP announces to its external connections only the aggregate CIDR address block, masking local details of the inter-customer routing structure within these aggregate address announcements. The benefits of such an approach are seen in a linear growth of the routing table during the past four years this policy has been in use, while the network itself has continued to grow linearly. A plot of the routing table size is shown in Figure 3.20. The disadvantage is the necessity for customers of ISPs to be prepared to shift address blocks if they choose to shift providers. For larger customers, this task can be an extremely significant logistical problem, not without attendant expense and disruption.

T wo major engineering issues were involved within the scope of this activity surrounding the IP address structure. The most immediate was the pressure on the allocation of Class B address space. Evident in 1991 was the fact that the 14,284 Class B networks would be entirely allocated within a few years. A need existed for an immediate solution to address this looming issue of address exhaustion and a longer-term solution to create a larger address space. The second issue was the increasing size of the forwarding table for the Internet. This increase had performance implications when attempting to undertake high-speed forwarding, coupled with a lookup within a massive forwarding table.

CIDR was an attempt to address both of these requirements, although CIDR has not been without some element of controversy. Local deployment of CIDR has no immediate tangible benefit to the local network that offsets the costs of using what can be a more complex routing structure. The benefit lies in the more global conservation of address space through greater efficiency. The more contentious issue is that of CIDR addressing within the ISP environment. To maximize the benefits of CIDR, clients of an ISP use subaddress blocks of an ISP's CIDR address block. Changing providers implies changing local IP addresses, which is never an easy task for networks of any size.

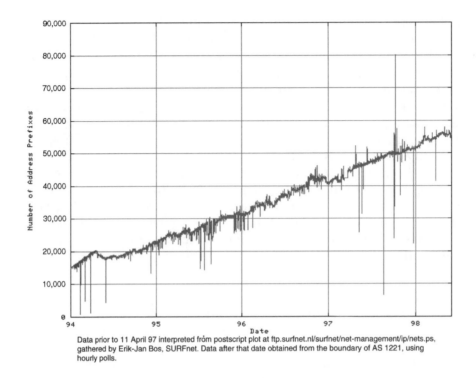

Data prior to 11 April 97 interpreted from postscript plot at ftp.surfnet.nl/surfnet/net-management/ip/nets.ps, gathered by Erik-Jan Bos, SURFnet. Data after that date obtained from the boundary of AS 1221, using hourly polls.

Figure 3.20   Internet routing table growth.

The address structure now on the Internet has returned to the original two-level structural partitioning. This structure uses a network prefix or a routed prefix and a host part, in which the internal structure of the host part is not visible to the routing structure at this point in the network. The change to the original 8-bit/24-bit partitioning is twofold. First, the partition point is variable within the address, admitting different network prefix lengths for different networks. Second, the partition point is variable within the network, so that a partition visible in the routing system at one point in the Internet may be abstracted into a more general routing entry at another point.

The Evolution of Names and the Domain Name System

The original Internet application environment used the dotted quad form of address values as a user-level means of referencing a remote system. To connect to a remote system, the user would need to specify a command of the form *telnet 10.20.1.15* or direct electronic mail to an address where the two components of the address were the remote user name and the remote IP address. Today, in e-mail, this syntax is expressed as *user@[10.20.1.15]*. This format is unwieldy and unnatural for people to use. Numeric addressing systems, such as the telephone, have a massive directory architecture available for telephone users so that we do not have to attempt to remember thousands of seemingly random digit sequences. Computer networks offer the potential to craft this directory system into the network itself, so that users need only to specify names and leave the network to negotiate numerical addresses at a level invisible to the user.

Before the Domain Name System

A very early refinement to the model of numeric addresses was to use a local data structure that allowed a text string, or name, to be mapped into an IP address locally. This way, the user could reference a remote host by name and then have the application use a local routine to translate the name into an IP address to hand to the TCP or UDP Application Programming Interface (API). This translation mechanism was easy to implement and, in local terms, easy to maintain. This mechanism also was not novel for IP, and many protocols of the time also used local translation tables to undertake this same common function. Some protocols attempted to carry names within the protocol architecture, introducing limitations on name lengths and allowable characters as a byproduct of the protocol data structures. The base IP architecture does not carry names in protocol data structures. All translation between names and numbers is a strictly local function, which allows a relatively free format over what constitutes a valid name, while preserving a certain economy and efficiency of the protocol data structures by omitting the carriage of names from the protocol.

Of course, the immediate problem with this is the fragmentation of the name space. Although a name may translate to one IP address value on one host, the same name may translate to a completely different address on another host. To introduce coherency into the name space, the role of a central registry of names is a critical step. This registry acts as the authoritative source of mappings used on individual hosts. For an update to the mappings to be promulgated through the network, inform the central registry of the addition or deletion, and the registry then will confirm the transaction and distribute a new mapping table following the completion of the transaction.

Forming the Domain Name System

For the Internet, the task of coordinating a master file of mapping host names to IP addresses was undertaken by the Network Information Center at SRI. Updates to this master file were undertaken on a first-come, first-served basis, and the resulting file, the *hosts.txt* file, was distributed both over the Internet and via magnetic tape. Names were simple character strings of up to 30 characters. Although the simplicity of the local translation mechanism was maintained, a single point undertaking periodic flooding of the entire translation table to every host on the Internet was always prone to problems of scale. The distributed file was always incomplete, and the process of name selection became increasingly challenging as the name space started to fill. As the file increased in size, the operation of flooding new versions of the entire translation table to every host on the Internet was also increasingly unwieldy. The size of the file increased; the frequency of updates increased; and the number of recipients increased.

In considering this, the specifications for an Internet name scheme were drafted. This system, the Domain Name System (DNS) has a number of critical features:

◆ A hierarchical name structure with variable depth. Such hierarchical name systems are common in wide-scale name environments as they allow distribution of administrative control into successively localized control points and reduce name clash from a global clash to such localized points of administration.

◆ A distributed database in which each element of the distribution conforms to the hierarchical structure of the name space.

◆ A uniform and simple mechanism of data caching allowing for efficient operation through the local storage of remote information.

◆ A generic translation mechanism that can be used to return other forms of answers, in addition to a name, to address translation.

◆ A mechanism intended to provide translations to applications, rather than a user-level mechanism.

The DNS name space uses a *label tree*. Each label is a string of no more than 63 characters. A domain name is an ordered list of the node labels encountered on the path between the named node and the root node of the tree, using the reserved "." character as the indicator of a transition from a node to its parent as the path. For example, the name FOO.BAR.COM.ZZ corresponds to the domain tree, as indicated in Figure 3.21. In this example, COM.ZZ is a subdomain of ZZ, and BAR.COM.ZZ is a subdomain of COM.ZZ.

The name space described here is incomplete without being able to associate a set of properties with each name. This process is accomplished through the use of resource records (RRs); a number of RRs can be associated with a name within the name space. Each RR is held as a 4-tuple of Type, Class, TTL, and Data.

> The Type field indicates the type of the resource. A number of common fields are described in Table 3.1.

> The Class field indicates the protocol family for which this record applies. IN is the value used for Internet RRs.

> The TTL field indicates the anticipated period of data validity. TTL specifies a period, in seconds, for which the RR can be cached and used before the primary source should be queried for a new instance of

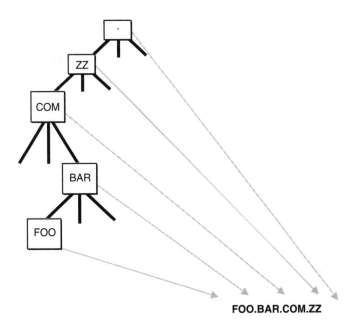

FOO.BAR.COM.ZZ

Figure 3.21   DNS name structure.

the RR. Caching can be disabled by specifying a 0 value for TTL. Highly volatile data should use a short TTL to allow changes to be promulgated quickly, and more static data should use a longer TTL to reduce the level of query traffic.

The Data field has a format dependent on the Type and Class fields. For example, for an "A" type RR, the data is a 32-bit IP address, and in the case of a CNAME record, it contains a domain name.

Table 3.1 DNS Type Field

DNS Type	Value	Meaning
A	1	IPv4 host address
NS	2	An authoritative name server
MD	3	A mail destination (obsolete—use MX)
MF	4	A mail forwarder (obsolete—use MX)
CNAME	5	The canonical name for an alias
SOA	6	Marks the start of a zone of authority
MB	7	A mailbox domain name (EXPERIMENTAL)
MG	8	A mail group member (EXPERIMENTAL)
MR	9	A mail rename domain name (EXPERIMENTAL)
NULL	10	A null RR (EXPERIMENTAL)
WKS	11	A well-known service description
PTR	12	A domain name pointer
HINFO	13	Host information
MINFO	14	Mailbox or mail list information
MX	15	Mail exchange
TXT	16	Text strings
RP	17	for Responsible Person
AFSDB	18	for AFS DataBase location
X25	19	for X.25 PSDN address
ISDN	20	for ISDN address
RT	21	for Route Through
NSAP	22	for NSAP address, NSAP style A record
NSAP-PTR	23	
SIG	24	for security signature
KEY	25	for security key
PX	26	X.400 mail mapping information

Table 3.1 *continued*

DNS Type	Value	Meaning
GPOS	27	Geographical Position
AAAA	28	IP6 address
LOC	29	Location information
NXT	30	Next domain
EID	31	Endpoint Identifier
NIMLOC	32	Nimrod Locator
SRV	33	Server selection
ATMA	34	ATM Address
NAPTR	35	Naming Authority Pointer
KX	36	Key eXchanger
CERT	37	CERT
TKEY	249	TKEY
TSIG	250	Transaction signature
IXFR	251	Incremental transfer
AXFR	252	Transfer of an entire zone
MAILB	253	Mailbox-related RRs (MB, MG, or MR)
MAILA	254	Mail agent RRs (Obsolete—see MX)
*	255	A request for all records

Querying the DNS

Queries made to the DNS specify a name as the query, and the query is qualified by query type and query class. The query is resolved by starting at the root and follows a chain of referrals to locate the server that holds the desired RR. To find the Internet address of FOO.BAR.COM.ZZ, the DNS resolver would do the following:

1. Initially query the root servers, who in turn would return a referral to the set of DNS servers for the domain ZZ.
2. The query then would be repeated to these servers, and the response would be a referral to the set of name servers for COM.ZZ.
3. Again, the query is repeated to these servers, and the response would be a referral to the servers for BAR.COM.ZZ.
4. The final query is to these servers for the matching RR for the entry FOO.BAR.COM.ZZ, and an A RR would be returned.

Obviously, if this strict resolution model were followed across the Internet, this would make the 13-root name servers sink under an impossible load. Caching of responses to each of these steps allows subsequent queries to be resolved without the need to repeat the request to the authoritative servers. The responses can be held locally for the associated TTL period and then can be reused for related queries without the need to repeat the network query.

Responses to the query are either a matching RR, an error indicating that the RR does not exist, or a temporary error indicating that no answer was found at this point.

The outcome of this process is a distributed system that supports a hierarchy of administration. The importance of a central point to ensure synchronization and uniqueness within the name space is replaced by a distributed system. The advantage of the DNS is its function distribution, where local names are administered locally, and uniqueness becomes a local administrative issue rather than a global one. The disadvantage is that complete synchronization of the name space is not possible, and old cached data is held within the namespace even after the original data is updated in some form. This is a relatively well-understood tension in any data design. The more information is cached locally, the greater the time required to distribute changes to the system. Accordingly, the period of transition increases, in which new information is attempting to supplant older cached information. One of the major design attributes of the DNS is to use a dynamic self-defined caching model, where each point in the hierarchy can define a cache strategy for the data maintained at that point in the DNS name structure. Highly volatile data can have short cache periods, which will allow rapid promulgation of dynamic changes. However, this happens at the expense of increased DNS traffic. More stable data can have longer TTL values and reduce DNS query traffic, but at the expense of slower distribution of changes.

Of course, the practice is some distance away from the theory, and there is no doubt that functionally correct implementations of the DNS are not as common as they could be. Too many implementations allow the recirculation of old cached data with incorrectly refreshed TTL values. Also, too many implementations allow corruption of the caches by accepting nonauthoritative cache updates rather than updates originating from the duly delegated point of authority. The security model has only recently been addressed. Today, many implementations do not implement reasonable trust models, so corruption of the DNS is a continual problem.

The DNS Delegation Model

The delegation model in the DNS today commences with 13 so-called *root name servers*. These systems are located in high-utility locations around the globe and provide the origin of the hierarchy of the name database. The data in these systems is provided and authorized by the Internet Assigned Numbers Authority (IANA). Delegations in these root name servers use a mix of two approaches. The first, and original, approach is to use a number of generic classifications, place organizations within such classifications, and then place host system entries at some delegated level within the organization. In this model, the original delegations were EDU for educational and research institutions, GOV for governmental agencies, and MIL for military establishments. A number of others have been subsequently added, including NET for network service providers, ORG for various organizations, INT for international bodies, and, of course, COM for commercial entities. Subsequent expansion of the breadth of this name space included the ISO 3166 two-letter country codes as points of access for delegated national name administration. This structure is indicated in Figure 3.22.

Although the technical model of the DNS as a name hierarchy is one that attempts to ensure continued scaling through distribution, the DNS did not address the social aspects of names. For the same reasons that similar commercial businesses have naturally clustered physically within a dedicated area long before the function of a town planner was ever dreamed of, the name space has seen natural clustering at critical hot spots within the namespace. The efforts at increasing the breadth of the first level set of names has not relieved the quite substantial pressure for names within the COM space in particular. The generic pressure is to heavily populate only a very small subset of the complete name space.

The current perception is that names are valuable Internet assets, and a shorter name is a better name. Such a perception has led to intense pressure towards the root of the name hierarchy to service this demand for a broader set of short domain names. Consideration of this has led to a number of efforts intended to ensure the broader availability of names outside of the national country codes, some of which have resulted in a set of specific proposals in recent years. Although this debate began within the traditional Internet circles, the current situation of Internet name administration is now including national and international bodies. Some form of long-term resolution to this area does appear to be somewhat elusive at present, given such a broad spectrum of

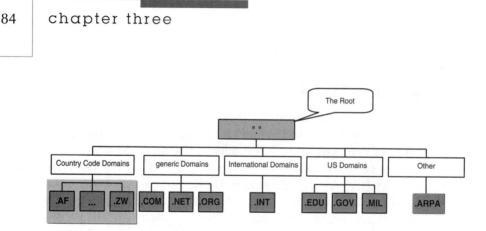

Figure 3.22   The DNS delegation structure.

players and motivations. Internet governance has become an increasingly critical issue within this space. Unfortunately, as the number of governance players increases, the chances of achieving a widely accepted, stable, and sensible refinement of the DNS name environment are less likely.

Internet Bodies

Let's shift focus within this final area of Internet architecture to briefly examine the bodies that play a role in the maintenance and evolution of this architecture. The bodies involved within the Internet Standards process are indicated in Figure 3.23.

The Internet Engineering Task Force

At the working end of the spectrum is the Internet Engineering Task Force (IETF). The IETF is a volunteer organization, with a small full-time Secretariat. The Secretariat function was until recently the subject of a U.S. federal grant but has now undergone a financial restructuring to be a body funded by the IETF.

The IETF is organized into working groups, in which working group membership is open, and the group is chaired by one or two individuals. The working group's activities are not so open-ended. The overall majority of working groups are not formed until the IETF has reached a basic level of comfort regarding the proposal. This includes the acceptance of a valid constituency for the group, so that a sufficient number of individuals wish to contribute to working in this area. The proposal also must provide a description of the intended scope of activity of the working group, the specific material the working group will develop, and the anticipated timetable for the group's activity. The document that describes these aspects of the working group is termed the *working group charter*, and the group is not created until the charter has been adopted by the IETF. The timetable is normally quite rapid. Two years would be a long-lived working group; one year would be a more typical timetable within a working group's charter.

Much of the working group's activity is undertaken through e-mail. A major requirement of the IETF process is openness, and within this requirement, the mailing lists are open to any individual who wishes to join. Likewise, all documents under study or development by the group are placed in publicly

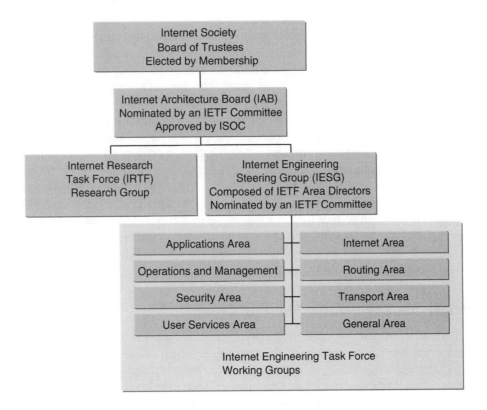

Figure 3.23   The bodies involved in the Internet standards process.

accessible archives. These electronically mediated activities are complemented by three face-to-face meetings a year, in which all the active working groups of the IETF meet to review progress and refine further direction.

Working groups operate in a fashion not used by many other standards bodies. As Dave Clark of MIT explained it in 1992, when the operation of the IETF was under close introspective scrutiny, "We reject kings, presidents, and voting; we believe in rough consensus and running code." Within the IETF hallways, this quote has been a popular T-shirt adornment ever since. The IETF has concentrated on undertaking functional decisions based on technical merits. Imposed authority models of either external imposition or even by election do not sit cleanly within such a framework.

IETF working groups do not vote. Given the open nature of working group membership, the effort within the group is to strive for peer consensus as a means of acceptance. Of course, consensus is not the same as unanimous agreement, and in its most questionable state, consensus could be characterized as equal levels of disagreement. The rough consensus referred to here is one of reasonable peer acceptance of a proposal as being technically functional and, preferably, technically elegant. The process of consensus does not always arrive at single outcomes, and some situations result in different views on technology, where the respective proponents produce different proposals. A single consensus cannot always span the difference. In such a case, the running code is the ultimate test of relevance. A critical step within the IETF standards process is the production of more than one implementation based on the draft standard. The test of the draft standard is based on the functional interoperation of these implementations. A further step to an Internet standard is the adoption of the technology by the market, so that the Internet standard is seen as being relevant and useful within a working network. In this sense, running code is seen as the test of relevance of the IETF to work in areas where technology standards make useful sense.

The Internet Engineering Steering Group

Each working group is located within an *area*. An area is a collection of similarly focused working groups under the supervision of one or two area directors. Currently, the IETF is organized into eight areas: Internet, transport, routing, security, applications, operations and management, user services, and general. The Internet Engineering Steering Group (IESG) is a body composed of the area directors. This group is responsible for approving the charter of working groups and to review their progress and output. When documents are created by the working group, the IESG advances the document through the Internet standards process, ensuring that the document is appropriately reviewed and that the document has been used as the basis for multiple independent working interoperable implementations within this process of adoption. The members of the IESG are dedicated volunteers, and their workload is typically at the extreme edge of voluntary effort, given the extent of the workload IESG membership entails.

> T he IETF Web pages are located at www.ietf.org. The Web pages provide information on current IETF working groups, draft documents, and proceedings of previous meetings.

The Internet Research Task Force

The Internet Research Task Force is a counterpoint to the IETF and is composed of a number of focused, longer-term research groups. The topics under study by these groups are related to Internet protocols, applications, architecture, and technology. Participation is by individual contributors, rather than by representatives of organizations.

The IRTF Research Group's guidelines and procedures are described more fully in [RFC 2014].

> T he IRTF Web pages are located at www.irtf.org/irtf. The Web pages provide information on current IRTF research groups.

The Internet Architecture Board

The IESG develops Internet standards within a process. The process used by the IESG has been adopted by the Internet Architecture Board (IAB). This group of individuals attempts to ensure the continued coherency of the Internet technical architecture. This task is undertaken not by virtue of any ability to impose authority over the standards process, the direction of the IESG, or the activities of the IETF, but by virtue of advocacy and active involvement within the IETF meetings and within the IETF working groups. The IAB is also the point of appeal regarding the IESG's interpretation of the Internet standards process and will review the IESG's actions in those cases where a dispute cannot be resolved within the working group, the area, and the IESG itself. As with the IESG, the IAB's membership is composed of volunteers. Although IESG or IAB members go through no election process, the task of selecting individuals to serve on these two bodies is undertaken by the IETF membership. Each year, ten individuals are drawn at random from a self-nominated pool of active IETF members. Their task is to review approximately half of the IESG and IAB members and ensure that the positions are filled by the best-qualified individuals from the IETF membership.

T*he IAB is described at www.iab.org/iab. The Web page contains an overview of the IAB and minutes of IAB meetings.*

The Internet Assigned Numbers Authority

The Internet Assigned Numbers Authority (IANA) is the central coordinator for the assignment of unique parameter values for Internet protocols. The parameter values assigned in this way were most recently documented in STD-2 [RFC 1700], published in October 1994.

The body was historically chartered by the Internet Society and the United States Federal Networking Council and has been historically funded to undertake its activities though U.S. federal agency program activity grants. IANA has been the subject of considerable attention within the overall area of Internet governance and self-regulatory functions, and some changes in its organizational structure to reflect an industry self-regulatory stance are an inevitable part of the transition of the Internet from a research program into a significant communications service activity. At the time of this writing, IANA is anticipated to be evolving into an incorporated body, drawing on an industry self-regulatory model as the basis of its authority and funding.

ISPs typically interact with areas coordinated through IANA in the tasks of DNS name registration and IP address block allocation. Generally, the interaction is not directly with IANA. The task of DNS allocation is delegated into the various top-level domain name administrative bodies, as described in the preceding section. The task of IP address allocation and AS number allocation is coordinated through the three regional registries: ARIN in the Americas and sub-Saharan Africa; RIPE in Europe, the Middle East, and Northern Africa; and APNIC in the Asia Pacific region.

The IANA Web pages are located at www.iana.org/iana.

For Internet address assignments to ISPs, the most common course of action is to become a member of the relevant regional registry and receive IP address allocation and AS number assignment services from that registry.

- ◆ ARIN, the Americas Registry, is located on the Web at www.arin.net.

- ◆ RIPE, the European and Middle East Registry, is located on the Web at www.ripe.net.

- ◆ APNIC, the Asia Pacific Registry, is located on the Web at www.arin.net.

The Internet Society

The organizational framework of this process is carried within the Internet Society. The Society provides the organizational home for the Internet Standards and assumes any liabilities that may occur within the process. The body also acts as the ultimate point of appeal in the Internet standards process, where a party can appeal on matters pertaining to the process itself, rather than its application to a particular case or incident.

The Internet Society is described in the Web pages at www.isoc.org.

Summary

In many ways, the Internet architecture and the associated framework of bodies has followed a structure characterized more by establishing a perspective radically different from the more conservative established communications industry. From the perspective of the Internet, the effort was one in which much needed to be proved about the utility of the Internet architecture, contrasting it to the proprietary nature of alternative solutions and to the heavily encumbered and overly ponderous movements of other international standards bodies.

From a purely Internet perspective, for the last decade we have been concentrating in slaying the giants of the old communications world by practicing a utilitarian form of technology—if it can work as software, then it's of far greater value than nonworking paperware. We worked hard. We enjoyed the challenge to do it faster and to do it better. It felt good, and we did it. And, in this area of communications technology, this approach has achieved success—overwhelming success. But, the prize of such a victory is to become the mainstream of the technology industry, and the price, like it or not, is to recreate all the institutions and their associated ponderous weight and political awareness that we so vehemently criticized in a past lifetime. The IETF may yet be described as the last great push from the technology pragmatists to sweep all aside with the compelling force of good ideas and utilitarian engineering. During the next few years, we will be presented with the critical test of whether we can continue to advance this approach. Increasing external pressure will be felt to embrace the encumbrances and ponderous movements of bodies who now see their only future in terms of an Internet communications world. We will have to address these pressures in some way as we continue.

chapter four

Internet Architectures

In this chapter, we examine the design of Internet service networks. The first aspect to be examined is the architectural principles of the design, highlighting the relationship between design simplicity and ease and effectiveness of operation. These principles then are translated into a network design. The elements of the design are examined, looking first at the interface to the client and examining how this interface can be constructed. The internal infrastructure of the network then is examined, looking at various design options available to construct the internal carriage component of the network. We then look at several different ISP profiles and examine designs suited to each type of ISP. The chapter concludes with a look at possible futures in this area of network design. Some of the material covered here refers to routing protocol configuration; return to this chapter after reading Chapter 6, "Managing Routing," to review the material describing the routing configurations.

Today, the Internet is composed of more than 60,000 constituent networks. Each network is operated autonomously, and the only common factors shared by all these networks are the use of a common protocol, the adherence to a common address management structure, and the adherence to a common name structure. No center can be found to this mesh of connectivity. No single landmark proudly proclaims "This *is* the Internet. Connect here." Instead, every point on the Internet can be extended and can offer further connectivity. This network has no center—only an expanding circumference.

The service architecture is similarly dispersed. Inside the network are no service points. The interior of the network contains a collection of stateless packet switches and a set of transmission circuits. No content factories are in the center of the network. Instead, every host system connected to the Internet can offer useful services, if the users of that system so choose. And, such services are available to all other users connected to the Internet, if they choose to avail themselves of such services.

Many communications networks have been constructed as distribution networks. Radio networks, television networks, cable networks, and newsprint networks all operate on the principle of a unidirectional network that uses a core content factory and a system that efficiently distributes the content to a set of receivers. The telephone network is a different architecture from this distribution model. The telephone architecture is a bidirectional unicast network, with fixed service elements. Any handset may initiate a connection to any other handset. The connection is a fixed service element, based around the real-time bidirectional transfer of voice signals between two parties. The connectivity services and fixed service management are operated by the service network, and the handsets are peripheral interface devices to a fixed-function network.

The Internet architecture is a progressive refinement to this model, which develops the telephony model by pushing control functionality out of the network onto the host computers. The service model of the network is variable, and no connection element exists. Host computers may establish connections on a one-to-one basis as per traditional unicast bidirectional communications. The network also can support one-to-many broadcast models of distribution and support many-to-many multicast communication models.

Inside all of the service model's flexibility is the additional variable of tens of thousands of independent network operators whose interconnection effectively provides the connectivity mesh supporting the Internet. Some structure is discernible within these networks. Within an idealized structure end users of the Internet connect into local Internet Service Providers within the scope of a retail service structure. These local ISPs connect to regional ISPs on a wholesale basis. The regional ISPs connect to transit service providers, who collectively provide the backbone connectivity services for the Internet. This structure is indicated in Figure 4.1.

Reality is not so well ordered. Every service provider appears to indulge in some sector of the end user retail market, and the delineation between wholesale and retail is highly unclear. Service contracts also are not exclusive, so that ISPs make multiple service arrangements to increase their resiliency and reduce their overall costs. Connectivity is not just provider-to-provider but also includes various forms of exchange points in which multiple providers can exchange traffic. The resulting structure of the Internet Service Provider architecture could be refined, as indicated in Figure 4.2.

Of course, even this view does not adequately capture the full diversity of interaction in today's Internet; ISPs interact in both bilateral arrangements as 1:1 connections but also participate in multilateral arrangements that are

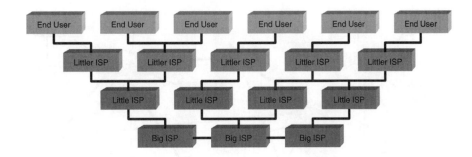

Figure 4.1   The hierarchical view of Internet structure.

typically undertaken at exchange points. Figure 4.3 may best express the architecture of the Internet today, which includes the diversity of end-user connectivity, the mix of retail and wholesale environments, the ability to undertake multiple upstream services, and the existence of exchange points at various locations within the Internet.

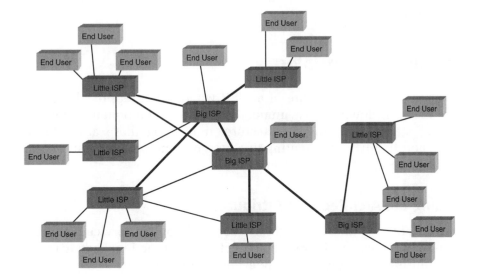

Figure 4.2   The nonhierarchical view of Internet structure.

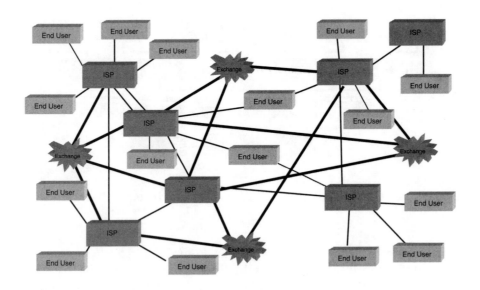

Figure 4.3 The current view of Internet structure.

In this chapter, we examine the typical architecture of one of these constituent networks.

Architectural Principles

In looking at the architecture of an ISP we adopt an approach designed to break the task down into a number of discrete components: defining the essential attributes of the architecture, translating these attributes into a design, and finally implementing this design as an implementation plan and associated operational support structures.

Defining the Architectural Attributes

When considering the architectural aspects of a public service network infrastructure, we must consider simplicity of design, functional adequacy, affordability, the ability to implement, relevance, and scalability as key components of the architecture.

Simplicity

In terms of network architecture the most critical aspect is structural simplicity. Simplicity is a key principle in that it effectively imposes the minimum of constraints and allows each client of the service to readily interface its infrastructure and service environment into that of the ISP. Simplicity of design also allows the ISP to adapt to changing technologies and changing service requirements that may be imposed by the client base in the future without the necessity for complete, and costly, rebuilding of the entire network.

The principle of simplicity is perhaps the key attribute of any large ISP service architecture. The issue here is that by its very nature a major service infrastructure is cast in the role of providing services to a diverse and distributed client base. Architectures that are effectively developed in an environment of ad hoc engineering, and architectures that are in themselves diverse and complex, present the implementation engineer and the operational service group with a set of complex problems, which are typically very expensive to address. In addition, such complex architectures often exhibit metastability, so that subsequent incremental engineering efforts intended to enhance the service may prove either highly expensive, or at times impossible, to undertake. For example, networks that use a chaotic mixture of ATM virtual circuits, IP tunneling, route filtering, and static routes to meet a diversity of client requirements on a one-by-one basis are creating a chaotic environment that will prove expensive to operate and highly resistant to further incremental change.

Simple uniform architectures for a communications service may prove cumbersome in terms of obtaining the initial levels of consensus, which enable the project to proceed. When specifying a uniform simple service structure, the sum of the potential client requirements may have to be factored in to arrive at a common denominator of requirements. However, this initial effort will result in a network far more robust, scalable, useful, and efficient to operate.

Functional Adequacy

The second critical architectural principle is that of functional adequacy. Therefore, the architecture should meet the basic client service objectives without imposing additional qualifications or constraints. Providing multiprotocol functionality in the network makes little sense if the protocols do not scale to the scope of the network and if there is no demand from the target client population. Providing a network service that only addresses part of the clients' requirements is also a pointless exercise. The network architecture should provide a functional base that allows the clients' service needs to be efficiently addressed.

Affordability

Affordability is perhaps implied within any such architecture. Note that any network architecture not affordable within available resources of the ISP's business plans should never be implemented.

In the ISP business, a very common business plan is to use return on cash flow as the basis for incremental investment in network infrastructure. This move is sound because it makes little sense to use initial investment capital to purchase a large, but idle, inventory of equipment and transmission resources. The alternative approach is to adopt a more flexible position, purchasing additional inventory when there is user demand. If the business plan has been prepared correctly, such user demand will be accompanied by revenue levels that will ensure a corresponding return on the additional investment.

Ability to Implement

The ability to implement, or the technical feasibility, is also a principle that is effectively implied within any architecture. If a network architecture relies on technologies that cannot be purchased and deployed today, then the architecture cannot be realized, and accordingly, such an architecture specification is functionally irrelevant for any other purpose than a vision statement of potential future service objectives.

Also note that there are essential differences between operating a research experiment, operating a technical feasibility trial, and operating a production service. Customers expect reliability in a communications service, and this reliability can be provided by taking a conservative approach to the architecture, using components and systems that have been proved in such environments, and combining them in ways that are well understood. This is not the characteristic of a research experiment, or a feasibility trial.

Relevance

Networks are service structures, and the architecture of a network should accordingly be designed to meet actual end client needs, rather than to impose a different methodology on the client base. A network should provide service to the end-user application services and protocols that are being deployed by the user base, rather than to implement a service environment that forces clients to deploy new services and protocols. One of the many lessons learned from the Open Systems Interconnection (OSI) effort of the late 1980s was that clients are loathe to incur additional cost to migrate their service environment simply to match their technology with that of the external communications service provider. Clients are far more interested in purchasing an external communications service that uses the same technology suite as their local in-house service. The seamless interaction of local area network services and wide area network services is absolutely critical to the acceptance and relevance of the service to the end-user population.

Scalability

Across the world, the Internet service market currently grows somewhere between 5 to 20 percent per month. That level of growth corresponds to situations in which the network doubles in size in a period of between every 6 to 20 months. Any architecture needs to have a period of applicability in a period of years rather than months. The result of these two observations is that the chosen network architecture itself should be able to scale in size significantly. If, for example, we wanted to use a single architecture for four years, across a period in which the network doubles in size every ten months, we need to ensure that the architecture will be able to withstand a growth factor of 80 in order to meet the design criteria.

This type of growth is perhaps the most significant hurdle for any Internet architecture. Recognize that scale has many dimensions. Scale is where the number of connected customers continually grows, where the number of new locations to build Internet infrastructure grows, where the amount of traffic to be carried grows, where the number of dynamic changes to the network grows, and where the equipment at each location takes up more and more rack space.

Managing scale in all these dimensions simultaneously is not possible if the architecture is constantly under stress. You should consider how the architecture expands to handle more customers, more locations, and greater traffic volumes and at what point the chosen architecture reaches a natural limit.

Network Design

After architectural principles have been agreed upon, the subsequent step is to translate such general principles into a specific engineering design for the network. As a general rule, ISP network services are not implemented within an environment of access to limitless resource and funding. Accordingly, the major design objectives are to minimize long-term operational costs and to maximize service capability. Obviously, these two objectives work together in a trade-off, as a richer service capability typically implies higher operational cost, while reducing the service portfolio can offer associated cost reductions. The engineering input is to attempt to match available resources to client expectations within the overall environment as defined by the architecture.

The ISP service profile can be very broadly characterized as access services and carriage. Within the area of carriage, the most significant long-term operational cost is the lease of bandwidth services, both as domestic circuit leases and, where appropriate, international circuit leases. Although routing equipment represents a potentially large initial capital outlay, bandwidth costs dominate recurrent expenditure profiles for the carriage component of the ISP activity profile.

Therefore, within the engineering of the network design, the unit cost of leased bandwidth becomes the major parameter in the cost and capability trade-off.

A number of additional design considerations must be factored into the overall design. The first consideration is the *trade-off between various cost factors*. Within the cost factors are considerations related to initial implementation costs and consequent recurrent operational costs. Within certain limitations there are a number of trade-offs between these two cost areas. Making a large initial capital outlay and creating an infrastructure that does provide some economies of scale of operation is possible. However, the preceding discussion about the dominance of the bandwidth's recurrent costs within the total network cost structure implies that other cost elements are not generally such a major concern.

The second of these design considerations is that of *network performance*, which in terms of the design phase, is a consideration of anticipated end-to-end network load patterns, the timescale of growth in load, and matching such load against planned network capacity provision. Effectively, this covers the area of congestion management (or avoidance) and instantaneous burst performance capabilities within the network. Additional performance parameters include end-to-end delay factoring. Here, topology choice, carrier mode choice, possible packet reframing, and data reformatting, such as payload compression, may impact the end-to-end latency timings on various paths through the network. In terms of carrier choices, satellite paths for intercontinental links may provide significantly reduced unit costs for the circuit lease, but the penalty is one of performance, in which the end-to-end delay is raised from some 50–150ms for undersea cable paths to some 320-ms for a corresponding single satellite-hop satellite path. Given that end-user performance is sensitive to delay, this choice point is critical. Where high-bandwidth, high-delay circuits are used in conjunction with host systems with small TCP buffers, the host systems are effectively incapable of achieving full-bandwidth end-to-end performance on an unloaded circuit.

The next design consideration is that of *operational reliability*, in which the desire is to design a system that is operationally stable. This area encompasses design considerations, such as meshed internal topologies, and the need to avoid single points of criticality within the network. This area also may include the use of communications technologies that are well proven within the environment of deployment in order to reduce the risk of extended periods of unavailability. Finally, this area also encompasses issues, such as routing protocol management design, in which the overall management approach is intended to provide the highest possible operational integrity and overall system reliability.

The next consideration, *manageability*, means that the network system must be designed so that it can be managed in an operational sense and can conform to various managerial policies as and when necessary.

The final consideration is that of *extensibility*, which is a reasonable reflection of the dynamic levels of growth of the Internet itself and the associated Internet technology base. To design a system within parameters of fixed capacity and a fixed service portfolio effectively implies high future cost in a reengineering effort to include larger scale-of-service operations in whatever format they may assume. The design must provide some capability for extension in size, in terms of the customer population; the number of provided access services; the volume of traffic carried; and the number of external connections to peer and upstream ISPs.

A Design Strategy

We now have a number of architectural principles for the design of the ISP network and a number of additional considerations relating to cost trade-offs, performance, reliability, manageability, and extensibility.

The overall strategy within the design is to integrate the considerations described within an overall framework of cost and capability. The major guideline within overall design strategy is that affordable capacity will determine the quality of the delivered service. Although very high-speed networks can offer either high levels of burst load capacity or service very large user populations, often affordable networks have to compromise within these parameters, and anticipating such design compromises from the outset is only reasonable.

Within a finite resourcing environment, the optimal design strategy is to ensure that areas identified as current service requirements are addressed within the network's intended service portfolio, before attempting to integrate other services. This strategy can be interpreted in a number of ways, including the following:

> **Supported protocol families**. The network service provider should concentrate on supporting protocols for which a real current demand for connectivity services exists. Supporting little-used protocols often results in underresourcing of core service activities and increases the operational cost of the network.

> **Supported application services**. Similar arguments apply to the supported application set. Again, the service provider should avoid resourcing support of application sets for which there is little demand and should be willing to offload elements of support of experimental application efforts to those clients who are in a position to take part in the experiment.

The overall strategy is to maintain a good focus on the relevance of services to the client population, and be in a position to devote resources to providing a service to meet these current requirements. Only once such requirements have been met can future needs be assessed and potentially addressed.

The core components of the network design can be classified within two broad areas: the client access architecture and the network infrastructure architecture. The customer access elements are the design of dedicated access ports into the network, shared access to modems and ISDN channels, and use of soft partitioned channels of a shared access service, which include Frame Relay PVC's, ATM PVC's, and timeslots of a channelized common bearer. The area also includes the definition of the demarcation between the customer's facilities and the edge of the ISP service network. The core network design elements are the transmission elements, the router or switching elements, and the design of how routing information is carried within the network.

The model used here to review ISP architecture is that of a breakdown into the two major design areas: the client access architecture and the infrastructure of the network (see Figure 4.4).

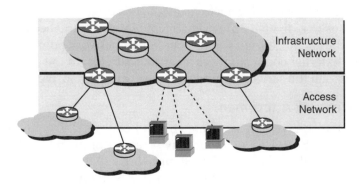

Figure 4.4   ISP architecture.

Client Access Architecture

Two means exist for providing access to ISP service networks, and the decision as to which model is used in any particular case is largely determined by the nature of the client. If the client is a corporate entity, a university campus, a government agency, or similar, then typically the client is already operating some form of service network internally within the organization. In this case, the access design is concerned with the issues of creating a stable networking peering model in which the ISP network and the client's network interoperate smoothly. This client can be characterized as a *network access client*. If the client is a single system, such as a residential PC or a small office PC, and the connection is established on an intermittent basis, then the model of access is typically that of a dial-access environment. Here, the ISP must extend additional services to the client to support the single attached host. This client can be characterized as a *dial access client.*

We look at both models in this section, starting with the network access client.

The Network Access Client

The client interface is the interface between the ISP's network service structure and the client's network. This interface is specified both in a physical sense, in terms of equipment interconnection, and in terms of delineation of protocol and service operational responsibility. The following sections examine this interface in more detail.

An ISP can provide access services to clients in a broad diversity of ways. This variability maps to a diversity of environments in which ISP access services are marketed, and they range from the self-contained network environment, which requires only external connectivity as a carriage service, to the single-user environment, in which the service requirement is far more intensive.

Models of Network Attachment

The client network exists on a private site and is typically some form of LAN or connected set of LANs. The client may be a corporate enterprise, a university campus, or an ISP. The provider ISP network exists as a collection of common access points, interconnected by a WAN. How do these networks interconnect to allow the ISP to extend service to the client?

The major issue here is the determination of the boundary between the ISP and the customer. *Clear demarcation* of respective responsibilities for equipment and services is essential for an effective operation. Having an unclear physical demarcation, or an unclear responsibility demarcation for the provision of services, leads to a service environment prone to duplication, inconsistency, and operational confusion. As important as clarity of demarcation is *uniformity of demarcation*. A demarcation policy should be as uniform as possible for all customers of the service. Having customized service boundaries defined on a per-customer basis does not scale cost effectively into a large service provision operation. No general operational processes and service management structures will accommodate such diversity within the service environment.

So where should the ISP network end and the client network commence? The typical structure of connectivity for client and ISP networks is indicated in Figure 4.5. The structure is that of three components:

- The client boundary router
- A connecting transmission circuit
- The ISP access router, commonly referred to as a Point of Presence (PoP) router

The client boundary router typically exists on the customer site and interconnects to the customer's local network. The client boundary router typically undertakes client-specific functions, including firewall functions and associated traffic filters, control of directed broadcast, and source address filters, all intended to implement some level of security integrity for the client site as well as implementing the client's external connectivity policies.

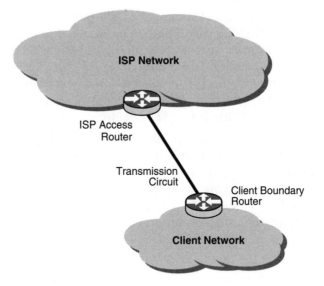

Figure 4.5   Network access architecture.

The connecting transmission circuit is a dedicated circuit, which may be leased from the carrier or may be some form of switched circuit, such as an ISDN circuit, a Frame Relay virtual circuit, or an ATM virtual circuit.

The PoP router typically undertakes the function of network routing control and has the responsibility for managing access into the client's network. The router must advertise the network routes that correspond to the client's address blocks to the remainder of the network. The PoP router is the point where route filters are installed to ensure integrity of route advertisements. Any network ingress or egress traffic control, monitoring, accounting, or filtering by the network also would be normally undertaken on this router, because it is the logical boundary of the ISP management domain.

A number of variations of this model are examined here. The simplest is that of a client network, which connects to a single service provider. Refinements of this model include the use of multiple separate attachments to the same service provider and separate attachments to different service providers.

Single-Homed Network Clients

The most appropriate starting point is the network client who connects exclusively to the ISP using a dedicated access port. The connection can be any one of a number of forms, such as a leased circuit, a radio link, private cable, or a permanent PSTN modem call. The model of interaction from the perspective of a routing service is that the ISP offers the client a *default route*, and the ISP has the exclusive responsibility for announcing the client's routes to all other clients of the ISP and to all external connections. This connection model is relatively straightforward; the ISP dedicates an access port to the customer and associates the network routes that correspond to the customer's address blocks to the access port. This form of connection in illustrated in Figure 4.6.

In terms of protocol interaction for Internet services, the client interface is a routing interface, in which routing information is passed, either administratively or encapsulated within routing protocols, in both directions across the interface. Reachability information concerning the addresses of the client's networks is passed to the network service provider, and the network service provider passes to the client information concerning the reachability of other networks via the provider's infrastructure.

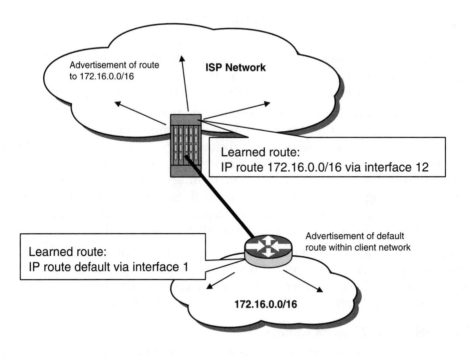

Figure 4.6 Single-homed network access.

The provider should explicitly set up an exclusion filter in client-originated routing advertisements, which ensures that only those networks that the client and provider agree are to be advertised by the client are passed into the provider's internal routing tables for advertisement throughout the network. Not only does this routing configuration ensure that the client can advertise only those networks on which it has agreed are the basis of the service consumer role, but this effectively isolates any routing faults on the client side from causing havoc within the provider's routing space.

The question is: What is the appropriate way to carry this information across the interface? You may wish to review this section after reading Chapter 6, which examines routing protocols in greater detail.

The first approach considered here is to use a dynamic routing protocol to carry this routing information. The initial potential choice for this task could be the use of RIP as the routing protocol. The attributes of RIP include simplicity of configuration and operation and the wide implementation base. This effectively confers RIP with the status as the lowest common denominator of routing protocols, and in many client/provider interface configurations, the limited capabilities of RIP are potentially adequate for the task required. In considering the use of the RIP protocol, this is very poor advice from the Internet perspective. As long as the Internet used Class A, B, and C addresses or aggregates of Class C addresses, the use of RIP in this context as an interface protocol between service provider and client was not particularly dangerous. It was inefficient, but also it was readily configured and reliable to operate in such a configuration. However, with the increasing use of provider-based address hierarchies, in which clients are assigned fragments that are not aligned to the old Class boundaries, this historical assessment of RIP as a candidate routing protocol no longer holds. Caution: The use of RIP in this context relies on three major premises, all of which may be wrong now or in the future!

- The first premise is that the policies the client wishes to represent to the Internet through the ISP are exactly aligned to the service provider's default case policies. Therefore, place the client's network within a distinct policy domain and present the client's routes as being qualified by that domain.

- The second premise is that the client either wishes to present a small number of routes to the service provider or that the link between the client and the provider is of sufficient bandwidth that the bandwidth used by the RIP protocol is not a significant proportion of the total tail loop bandwidth.

◆ The third premise is that the network provider and the clients are all routing within an environment that can be mapped into a class-based routing structure. Thus, supporting addresses based on address prefixes that historically could be interpreted as subnets of Class A or B networks is not possible. This final premise is perhaps the most telling and weakest of the set of premises that underlies the use of RIP as an interface protocol.

The use of other dynamic protocols for this task is possible. The RIPv2 protocol is a refinement of RIP to allow the use of address masks within route advertisements, so that the protocol can be deployed within a classless routing environment. This is a potential choice within a small-scale environment, but additional cautionary notes on the use of RIPv2 are addressed in Chapter 6. Alternatives also include EIGRP, the classless variant of the earlier IGRP routing protocol. These two protocols, IGRP and EIGRP, are proprietary protocols of Cisco Systems, and the client and the ISP may not be using this vendor's routers for the connection and may not want to support these routing protocols. OSPF, a link state protocol, also supports classless routing environments.

All of these protocols suffer from the constraint of being an interior routing protocol and are intended to carry topology information in association with routing information. The problem space of the client/ISP connection interface is not a topology discovery problem, in that the client does not want to expose the client-side topology to the ISP and other clients of the ISP, and similarly, the ISP does not want to expose the topology of the ISP to the client. In the deployment environment under consideration, that of a singly connected client, topology discovery is unnecessary. The environment under consideration is therefore one of reachability maintenance rather than topology discovery, which in turn, indicates that it is quite feasible, indeed preferable, to use *static routes* to support this form of client interface. In a statically routed environment, the networks to be advertised by the client are passed to the ISP by some administrative process. The ISP then creates static routing entries within the PoP router, which directs traffic for the client to the relevant interface. This mechanism is very robust in that it cleanly delineates the routing environment of the client from that of the ISP and can manage classless routing environments with ease. Some issues exist with scaling of the administrative processes to manage a large client set, but this client connection architecture for single-homed permanent clients is highly robust.

Within this model of single-homed clients, the provider can advertise to the client the default route and not provide an explicit enumeration within the routing interface of the exact composition of this default route. Indeed, within a structure of static routes, the client can direct the default route to the interface leading to the ISP and eliminate the need for a dynamic route completely. In many ways, this configuration is preferred for this connection environment, as the inclusion of any form of dynamic routing is unnecessary in this case.

The cumulative result of these two measures is a radical simplification of the boundary between the client and the ISP. The static routes loaded onto the ISP router, which describe the client's networks, ensure that any routing errors and any instance of routing instabilities within the client network are not propagated beyond the client boundary into the broader Internet environment and that the Internet is only aware of those routes that the client has approved to fall within the client's policy relating to broader Internet visibility. The use of a single external default route within the client network ensures that no extraneous routes are carried within the client network. An example configuration is indicated in Figure 4.7. In this case, an additional static route has been added to the configuration, creating a lower preference route pointing to the null interface. This works in single-homed configurations and is intended to reduce the amount of dynamic route changes further into the core of the Internet. This configuration always asserts a route to the customer network, irrespective of the status of the interface.

The overall guideline in such situations is that the network architecture should strive to realize the simplest routing environment with the greatest possible level of isolation between the two environments.

Network Clients with Multiple Connections

The architecture proposed for the connection of single-homed clients can be replicated when the client connects to the same ISP using more than one connection. In its simplest case, the PoP side of each connection is used to announce the client's complete set of routes, and the client side of each connection is used to promulgate a default route into the client network.

The outcome of this configuration is a case of *closest exit*, where traffic passes to the other network at the closest possible point, as indicated in Figure 4.8. Of course, this configuration is not entirely robust, and in many cases, the outcomes of this configuration do not match the client's expectation of the service model. The flow can be asymmetric, taking a different path from the a client host into the ISP from the return path from the ISP to the same client

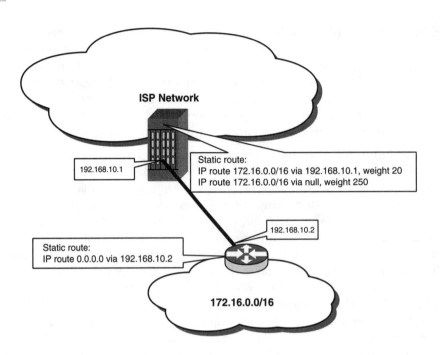

Figure 4.7 Static routes for network access.

host. In such a situation route discovery tools, such as *traceroute*, give a misleading view of traffic flow, and performance reporting tools also may give erroneous results as a consequence of this asymmetry. The other observation is that multiple connections are often made in an attempt to increase the robustness and reliability of the external connection, whereas this particular configuration may reduce this robustness. If the client network suffers some internal break in connectivity, the statically routed closest exit arrangement continues to use the closest exit, which leads to traffic discard at the point of the internal break with the client network.

If greater levels of robustness are required, then the interface between the client and the provider should use some form of dynamic routing protocol. Again, the precise details of the topology of the client network are not relevant to the ISP, so that a peering based on an interior routing protocol peering is not considered a stable solution. Static routes do not naturally lend themselves to dynamic adjustment based on the current network topology state. Accordingly, a finer level of reachability is required in this situation than can be provided with simple static routes, and interior routing protocols operate at a

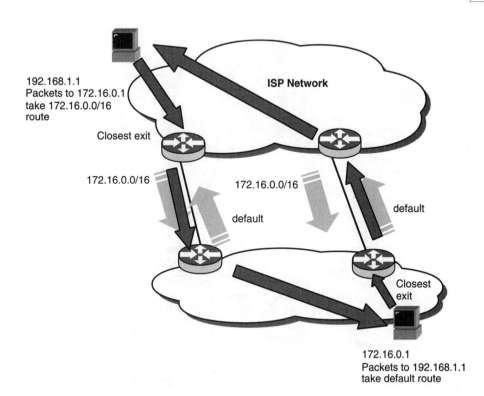

192.168.1.1
Packets to 172.16.0.1
take 172.16.0.0/16
route

Closest exit

ISP Network

172.16.0.0/16

172.16.0.0/16

default

default

default

Closest exit

172.16.0.1
Packets to 192.168.1.1
take default route

Figure 4.8   Multiple connections for network access.

level of detail that makes them inappropriate to use in this configuration. The preferred configuration is to use an exterior routing protocol, and BGP4 is a highly logical choice in this context.

The general configuration of a BGP-based interconnection between client and ISP is indicated in Figure 4.9. The client uses internal BGP (iBGP) peering sessions to interconnect all the client edge boundary points and uses external BGP (eBGP) peering sessions to the respective ISP routers. In this case, the client must carefully control the way in which internal routes are passed from the internal routing tables into the BGP route tables to ensure that the correct routes are announced at each point of connection at all times. In this scenario, if internal connectivity within the client network fails, then the respective BGP announcements will, if correctly configured, announce only locally reachable routes to the ISP, allowing the ISP's routing system to choose the correct ingress point into the client network. The client will, by default,

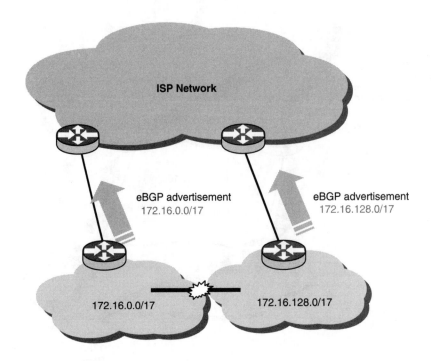

Figure 4.9 Partitioned BGP-based multiple connections for network access.

now use the external default routes to reach parts of the network that were previously reachable through the client networks. In effect, the client's break of internal connectivity will be restored through the ISP.

Multihomed Network Clients

The next refinement to this architecture is the client's use of multiple exterior connections. This refinement is undertaken for numerous reasons, including optimization of service charges from multiple service providers, attempts to improve the reliability of external connectivity, or the matching of policy and security requirements with multiple service providers.

Again, the physical aspects of the connection follow the same model as that outlined previously for single-homed clients, in which each connection involves a client edge router, a common transmission circuit, and an ISP PoP access router. This general configuration is indicated in Figure 4.10. The area of greatest attention is to configure the routing environment to conform to the policies and expectations of the clients and the set of ISPs who share the client.

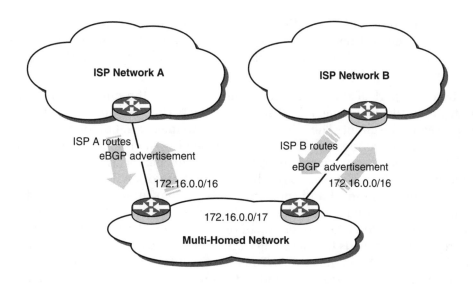

Figure 4.10   Multihomed network client.

Two basic configuration issues need to be resolved: How does the client choose an external path for traffic being passed to the Internet and to what extent can the client affect the choice of inbound ISP for traffic being passed from an Internet location into the client network? Of course, do not overlook the overall objective of the configuration: performance, coherency, manageability, and reliability of the resulting environment, which in some configurations may prove totally elusive.

The choice of an external path for a host within the client network can be either based on local constraints within the client network or on the destination of the traffic, or a combination of the two. Using local constraints allows each ISP to effectively advertise a default route to the client, and the outcome of propagation of these multiple defaults within the client network determines which ISP will be used by any particular host on the client network. Careful manipulation of default route metrics can lead to a variant of this approach where multiple ISPs can be used in a primary/backup structure, so that an alternative default is preferred only when the primary default route is unavailable. If the choice of the external ISP is to be based on the destination of the traffic, then significantly greater levels of routing information need to be imported into the client network. The client's routing environment must now be aware of the complete set of routes that are reachable from each provider and be able to use a local policy setting to make a choice between two ISPs when the same destination is reachable via multiple ISP route advertisements. This is a task for a BGP route configuration, which supplants the use of a simple default route configuration.

The other part of this is the management of how the client advertises its routes to multiple connected ISPs, which affects the way Internet traffic will be passed to the client. The client can choose to make a set of identical advertisements to all connected ISPs, effectively leaving the issues of performance and transit policy management open. From the perspective of the remote Internet host, the path taken to reach the client network will be determined as an outcome of the local and inter-ISP route system interaction, and a deterministic choice of path will be taken. In such a scenario, the client network will not attempt to voice any policy of preference for the incoming path, and, as a result, traffic loads for incoming traffic may not match the installed capacity of the client-ISP connections. The client can take a more active stance in determining and advertising a policy for inbound traffic by use of selective route advertisements to each connected ISP or by manipulating the information associated with the route entries, which is used as a precedence indicator. In the case of the BGP4 protocol, this latter course of action is generally undertaken by a technique commonly termed *AS path stuffing*.

Note that this environment is quite complex, and certainly the outcomes of such exercises in traffic path management in a multiprovider environment are not absolute. Considerable room for dynamic flux still exists, in that the path taken between two hosts on the Internet is the outcome of an interaction between the egress policies of the first network, the transit policies of the set of potential intervening networks, and the ingress policies of the destination network, and one party cannot dictate absolutely and unilaterally the policies of any other party.

The Dial Access Client

The second model of access to the ISP network is termed the *dial access client*. This term may immediately conjure up the picture of a single personal computer and a modem as the client, and the use of an analogue PSTN call to reach an ISP's Network Access Server (NAS). However, this term is intended to cover a larger set of scenarios including LAN dial access, ISDN access, and other dynamic access mechanisms where the connection between the client and the ISP is intermittent rather than permanent.

The support issues of the dial access client include support for authentication mechanisms and user access profiles, accounting record management, and intermittent access support. The elements of the ISP support for dial access clients are the NAS units, authentication support systems, and mail and Web servers to support user functions. This configuration is indicated in Figure 4.11.

The Network Access Server

The NAS units were traditionally a compound device consisting of a set of modems and a protocol-based access server. The modem units were configured into a rotary group so that one access call would select the next available free modem for the call.

A rotary group is a PSTN feature, in which a collection of individual access PSTN lines are addressed by a single access call number. The rotary selector takes the incoming call, which was placed to the rotary number, and selects the next available access line to terminate the call. The advantage of a rotary, as against a pool number, is that if a modem jams or is defective in some fashion, subsequent call attempts will move onto the next access line in sequence, rather than having all subsequent calls placed against the faulty pool access line.

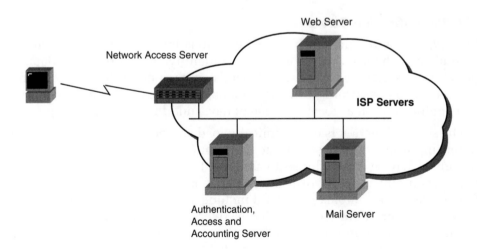

Figure 4.11 Dial access client support systems.

The client modem and NAS modem then would synchronize, and the client computer would be connected to the serial port of the access server. This system was prone to a number of performance reliability issues, stemming from the use of two analogue loops within the call, one for the client end modem and one for the ISP modem, as well as the separation of the modem and the access server function. Where ISDN services exist, using devices that integrate the modem and server function is preferable. This integration effectively eliminates the second analogue loop, allowing greater signal quality and higher modem synchronization speeds. It also reduces the number of hardware components within the ISP configuration, reducing the provisioning cost per available port. The functionality is slightly richer. If the incoming call is an ISDN digital call, switching a digital modem into the call is not needed, because the call can be switched directly to the access server. If the call is an analogue call, a modem is switched in and, when the modem synchronizes against the incoming call, the resulting digital signal is switched to the access server.

In both cases, when the call is synchronized, client-side scripts then undertake authentication of the user. The Point To Point (PPP) protocol then is invoked by the client end to establish the IP access session. The PPP session passes a dynamically assigned IP address to the client system for use on the serial port, and when this is configured the PPP session enters data transfer mode.

The Authentication Server

The authentication phase fulfills two functions for the dial-up user. The first is to identify the user, validate the user's identity against the ISP's data, and permit access. Access permission depends on a match of the offered identify and associated passwords with stored data, as well as factoring environmental conditions, such as location, time of day, and other concurrent logins.

The second function is to dynamically load any per-user NAS-side configuration applicable to the user for the duration of the session. This profile may be null or may be an IP address to assign to the remote side to allow the user to use a constant address irrespective of the port accessed for the call. The profile may be more complex and could include access filters and even QoS profiles. To support Virtual Private Dial Networks (VPDN), it is common to see the authentication profile also include the specification of a layer 2 tunnel to extend the incoming dial access by a tunnel that passes across the hosting ISP network and terminates within the nominated private network. If the access is LAN-based, rather than a single host system, any additional routes that describe the LAN IP addresses have to be loaded into the NAS, also as part of the authentication-based loaded profile.

Resolving the access query locally in the NAS is not required. Commonly used authentication mechanisms, such as Radius, permit the use of Radius proxy agents and Radius servers, so that the original access request can be referred by the proxy to the appropriate remote Radius server This is again of significant use within VPDN environments where the authentication operation is managed within the VPDN and not by the host access network.

Access Support Systems

The major characteristic of dial access is that the systems are not permanently connected to the Internet, yet most Internet service applications assume a model of permanent Internet connectivity. For example, to reliably tell the sender of an e-mail message that the recipient is offline and that the sender should reattempt the delivery at some later time is not possible. Instead, the recipient's ISP must act as a proxy agent for the recipient and undertake to operate the necessary services on behalf of the recipient and locally store the outcomes. When the recipient connects to the ISP, the ISP must be able to download all stored transactions to the recipient.

The most prevalent dial ISP support system is electronic mail, in which the ISP must operate a send-mail host to allow the collection of messages on behalf of the dial user and operate a PoP/IMAP mail host to allow the user to download the stored messages at a later date.

Support services typically also include Domain Name services, Web hosting services, and Usenet access services as a core service portfolio, although this will vary among ISPs. Additionally, Web proxy cache servers, DNS forwarders, games servers, IRC servers, and ftp servers may be part of the service portfolio, again at the ISP's discretion.

Minimally, all these functions can be placed on a single ISP host platform, and with small- to medium-sized ISPs, they commonly are all resident on a single client service host. Such a configuration will not scale, and, as the number of clients increases, these service operations migrate to separate host systems. In the larger operations, this function migrates to multiple server farms, where a number of host systems operate in parallel to service the client population.

Network Infrastructure Architecture

In the design components of the interior of an ISP operation are essentially two components, transmission capacity and switching capacity. The major objective is to ensure that an adequate capacity is available to match imposed load from client traffic without extravagantly overprovisioning capacity to the point of impacting the network's financial performance. Within the Internet capacity, provisioning still remains an imprecise exercise, where the network designer must attempt to set an acceptable compromise between peak demands and average load patterns.

Network Transmission

Network transmission capacity can be constructed in a number of ways, which has some implications on the resulting network design.

Transmission capacity can be provisioned using dedicated circuits. These circuits are synchronous-leased circuits, typically provisioned as a dedicated facility using a synchronized data clock so that data can be transmitted and received at a constant clock rate. Characteristics of the circuit are as follows:

- Clock rate
- Propagation delay
- Transmission error rate
- Error characteristics

The clock rate is the transmission capacity of the circuit, normally expressed in bits per second. The propagation delay is a function of the transmission path distance between the two end points and the transmission medium. Although a radio signal propagates at a speed very close to the speed of light, propagation of a signal through copper is some $3/4$ of the speed of light, and propagation through fiber-optic cable is some $2/3$ of the speed of light. The general intention is to reduce delay to a minimum, within the constraints of cost, of course. Within a domestic network, this factor is not absolutely critical, but delay does become a critical factor in longer international and intercontinental circuits. In such environments, the trade-off between delay and cost is a major determinant in the choice between satellite systems and the often faster submarine cable-based circuits. No single answer exists for such a situation because each ISP is using its own positioning in terms of price and performance. Although one ISP may find the additional delay acceptable given the opportunity to be able to use the reduced lease cost to enter the market at a lower price, another ISP may find the quality constraints imposed by the additional delay an unacceptable compromise. The transmission error rate is normally expressed in the probability of a bit error in transmission. Bit errors normally are detected in the packet checksum, and the packet containing the error is discarded. This process causes a retransmission within the end-to-end protocol, which causes a reduction in the data transfer rate. The error rate should be kept as low as possible. Error characteristics refer to whether the error pattern is impulse-based or a constant level of noise. Again, this process impacts on the protocol performance across the transmission medium. Where feasible, increasing the delay by using a form of forward error correction (FEC) to allow noise-based single-bit errors to be corrected is better than relying on end-to-end packet retransmissions.

An alternative to leased dedicated capacity is to use some form of switched transmission infrastructure. In parts of the developing world, the choice may well be constrained by what is available to that of X.25 virtual circuits. Other carrier environments may complement this with more recent switched technologies, which include Frame Relay, Switched Megabit Data Service (SMDS), and ATM. The common characteristic of these media is that no precise synchronization of the data clocking rate exists between the sender and receiver. In the case of X.25, this is replaced by a mechanism of hop-by-hop flow control, so that the sender's ingress rate is effectively governed by the available resources within the network and the capacity of the receiver. In the case of Frame Relay, the sender can operate at speeds equal to the network ingress capacity. The network provides a degree of reverse pressure by signaling error congestion to the sender; however, ultimately, the network must protect itself by shedding excess traffic when it is under excessive load. Frame Relay uses a two-step load-shedding mechanism, in which the first pass of load shedding effectively imposes a committed information rate on all senders. If this fails to relieve the congestion, the switch discards frames of the remaining data-streams. SMDS and ATM use a similar mechanism of switches within the network, which does not undertake internal flow control. When the data load exceeds the availability of resources, the switched system will need to undertake some form of load shedding.

When assessing switched services against the use of dedicated leased circuits, a number of salient factors need to be included within the consideration. Switched services may allow overuse of the service, so that the network may burst at data rates in excess of some base commitment. Of course, this also implies that the transmission service will encounter some level of data loss when the sender is operating at data rates in excess of available capacity. In theory, this could allow the ISP to provision circuits at the average level of traffic load and use the switched system's burst capabilities to carry peak traffic. Of course, this expectation requires careful scrutiny, because an ISP's peak load often occurs at the same time as the peak load of other subscribers to the common switched service, so that there may be no available burst capacity at the critical peak times. Switched services can have variable end-to-end latency, and the TCP flow control protocol, which implicitly assumes an environment of relatively constant end-to-end propagation delay and congestion-induced jitter, may operate at suboptimal efficiency as a consequence. Often, switched services are provided with an associated service-level agreement that indicates the expectation of performance and stability provided to the ISP client. The issue of enforceability of the agreement is a critical concern, because switched systems have no inherent technology component that enforces such service-level agreements. The enforceability of the agreement is therefore a contractual matter rather than an intrinsic attribute of the switching technology.

Ultimately, however, these considerations are minor and apply only after the major selection criteria have been addressed. The major criteria are those of *cost* and *availability*, and the ISP's requirements for carriage capacity may be addressed by a single carriage product from the carrier.

Network Topology Design

The other consideration is the internal topology to be used within the network—the leased circuits or switched virtual circuits.

Star Topology

The simplest topology is that of a hierarchical, or star, topology. A simple star topology is indicated in Figure 4.12. A central location is used as the hub of the network, and radial circuits are used to connect in other locations. If the central location is within the major service area, this topology minimizes the costs and provides the greatest efficiency of carriage capacity. However, a star topology suffers from the problem of critical points of failure. If the central location fails, then the entire network fails. If the link between a remote location and the central location fails, the remote location is disconnected. However, an ISP often has as an objective the desire to provision as much carriage capacity as possible, and the star topology may present the combination of a maximum capacity for a minimal cost, together with what may be an

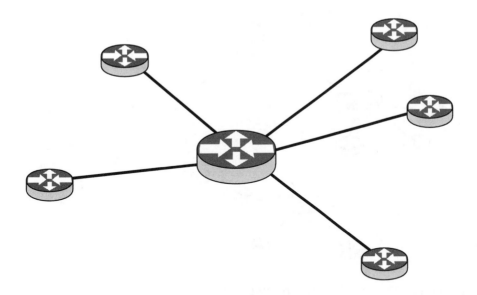

Figure 4.12 A star topology.

acceptable level of operational risk. Many initial academic and research networks were built on this principle of maximizing capacity, and the resulting networks were all variants of the basic hierarchical star topology.

A refinement to this topology is the cascaded star topology, in which a backbone star topology feeds into local concentration points that drive a star to local access calls, as indicated in Figure 4.13. Such topologies often have the enticing aspect of minimal circuit lease cost to provide access to a set of points but do not address any of the issues of critical points of failure. If any link or site fails, the service is unavailable for the duration of the outage.

Backbone Loop Topology

One remedy to the criticality of the central hub of a backbone star is to use a backbone loop configuration, in which every regional hub is connected to two other hubs, and the resulting connectivity forms a ring. Such a topology in shown in Figure 4.14. A ring has the advantage of being resilient to a failure of a single link, or even a single site, and the routing algorithm will repair connectivity. The issue here is that the network topology may be ill-suited to the flows imposed upon the network, and each router on the loop may be faced with a high imposed transit switching load as well as presenting customer

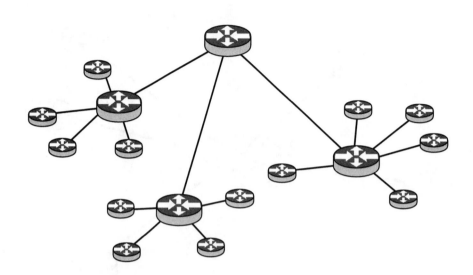

Figure 4.13 A cascaded star topology.

traffic with high propagation delays through the network. In addition, a loop is not always a cost-efficient solution given that smaller (and potentially more remote) regional locations may have to be provisioned with two high-capacity access circuits to manage the backbone transit load, imposing an unnecessary financial and performance impost on the network.

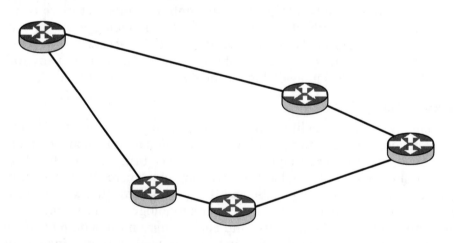

Figure 4.14 Backbone loop topology.

Meshed Topology

An alternative topology is that of a mesh of connectivity. A mesh attempts to link every location to two or more other locations, as shown in Figure 4.15. In this way, if a single link fails, no corresponding loss of connectivity occurs. If an entire location fails, no other location is isolated as a secondary effect. Meshed topologies are more challenging to load efficiently, and as a consequence, are typically less cost efficient than a hierarchical topology but may be better matched to have direct capacity to support major traffic flows than a loop topology. Extreme care also must be taken to ensure that separate circuit paths actually use separate transmission paths. In an environment of leased circuits, this requires close cooperation between the ISP and the carrier to provision each circuit on a distinct set of bearer systems. In a switched network, this is not possible, as the network path taken between two endpoints of the switched network is chosen at the level of the switched system and not under any form of client control. In such a system, a meshed topology of switched virtual circuits may be provisioned on an underlying hierarchical topology, and the benefits of the meshed topology through diverse physical paths may not be achieved using this approach.

Dial Backup

The other alternative topology is a sparse topology complemented by dial backup. When a transmission path fails, the routers can be configured to use a dynamic carriage service to establish a temporary circuit to bridge the point of failure. This may be possible using X.25 services, ISDN, switched virtual

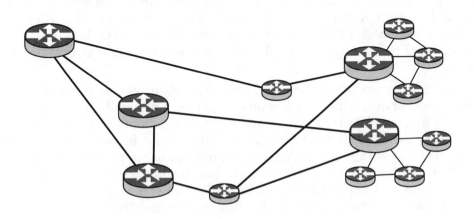

Figure 4.15   Meshed topology.

circuits within Frame Relay, ATM, or modem circuits established across the PSTN. Some simple guidelines should be established to ensure that this operates in a robust fashion.

First, the capacity of the dynamic backup circuit should be within the same order of magnitude as the original circuit. Using a dynamic backup circuit that cannot pass the level of imposed traffic causes chronic congestion problems, and the case of the cure being worse than the initial disease is very relevant.

Second, the backup circuit activation should be correctly damped. Some error conditions cause a circuit to oscillate between available and unavailable states, within a period of some tenths of a second through to tens of seconds. Having a dynamic backup circuit control linked against this availability condition will cause similar oscillation in the routing state, which will cause large-scale routing load. The backup circuit should, once triggered, remain up for a period that will allow the routing to stabilize and traffic flows to be reestablished before allowing the circuit to be torn down and the use of the primary circuit resumed.

In general, dynamic backup is a useful facility for smaller networks. Reliable dynamic systems that can establish circuits of multimegabit capacity or greater are still forthcoming from the carriage providers.

Network Access Point Design

As well as the issue of transmission options, the design of the network also encompasses the design of the network access locations, or Points of Presence (PoPs), for the ISP. Although all of the access functions can be squeezed into a single hardware platform, this direction is not popular, given that while the access locations can be provisioned with minimal cost, the bundling of an entire set of functions onto a single platform creates a highly critical point of failure.

The more common approach is to use a set of dedicated platforms to create the access service, with each component platform undertaking a specialized task. The general breakdown of switching components is to use internal routers to terminate internal transmission links and use access routers to terminate customer circuits. In this fashion, route structures and related configuration required to support customers can be undertaken on the access routers, and the internal routers can be configured as high-capacity switching systems designed for maximal availability and performance.

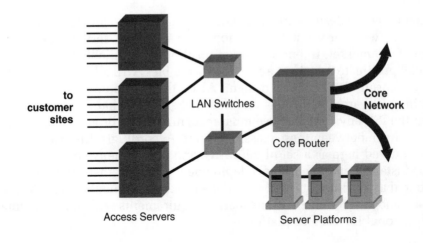

Figure 4.16   Network access point design.

The general organization of a network access location is indicated in Figure 4.16. The access routers typically support high-density shared access services such as ISDN and support other access transmission services, such as Frame Relay, ATM, or other point-to-point transmission services. In addition, the access location also may include a set of dial access Network Access Servers, using either modem banks, or, as outlined, ISDN primary rate access services and digital modems. Other more specialized access services may be terminated in the access location. Digital Subscriber Line (DSL) termination units or a DSL Access Multiplexer (DSLAM) can be added to the architecture, as can terminations for a hybrid fiber/coaxial (HFC) cable data system. The internal routers are typically designed for maximum availability and performance and use a lower port density configuration. The "glue" between the access devices and the internal routers is a local network. Although an Ethernet hub can suffice for low-density locations, many centers now use multiple switched hubs, based on 100Mbps Fast Ethernet switches.

ISP Architectures

We now have enough background to commence examination of the technical design of ISP networks. Before doing so, we must make a number of cautionary comments. These designs are very generic in nature, and any ISP will find that its mileage will vary. Local conditions, the intended service platform, the nature of the market, intended market positioning, available technology, and financial profile, to name but a few of the variables, will all impact on the ultimately chosen deployment design. Also, the taxonomy chosen here in describing ISP architectures is one that makes somewhat arbitrary divisions within the ISP environment; we must recognize that a broad spectrum of ISP profiles sits in between these classified roles. Accordingly, these architectures are not offered here as a set of definitive and comprehensive blueprints that will be instantly mappable into a deployment program. Instead, these designs are offered as an illustration of how the various components of an ISP service can be combined to meet various market requirements within the parameters of a functional ISP service platform.

The Access ISP

The assumption here is that the access ISP concentrates the service into the dial access market, offering dial-intermittent Internet access into the residential, community, and small enterprise sector. The service function assumes a client profile of a single PC and an analogue or ISDN modem. The local focus of the ISP allows it to position itself into a local niche market provider, using local presence and a service-rich operational profile as its market discriminator. For the access ISP, this local positioning of service combined with access is a measure of insulation against the very highly competitive market of the access function undertaken by the larger regional and national providers. Notwithstanding this business positioning, cost containment of the service platform is a key aspect of the ISP design, intended to allow the ISP to offer the service within a price point that is competitive with other local ISPs.

The predominate ISP platform architecture of such providers is that of a distributed set of dial access services in local offices and a central office to house the service-management functions.

The illustrated topology of an access ISP in Figure 4.17 uses a simple star topology as the underlying transmission design. This topology is intended to minimize circuit lease costs, accepting the risk of service failure to the outlying dial access service locations.

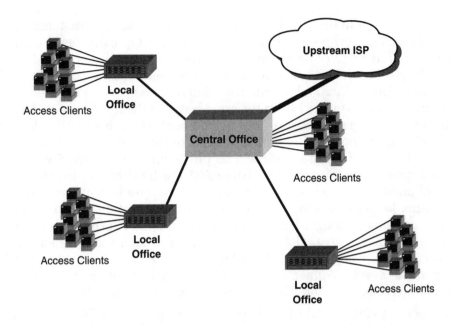

Figure 4.17 The access ISP.

The Access ISP Local Office

In the basic ISP access architecture, the dial access services in the local offices are constructed using a single hardware chassis. This architecture incorporates both the function of termination of incoming dial calls and termination of the circuit to the central office. Where available, ISDN primary rate access services should be used for termination of dial access services. This technology decision to use ISDN allows for the elimination of a bank of separate modems and an associated rotary group of access PSTN numbers, greatly simplifying the operational management task and allowing savings in operational expenditures. The decision to use ISDN as the dial access technology also allows the access ISP to offer the most recent analogue access services, which operate at speeds of up to 56Kbps. This market factor is competitive within a client population that is eager to increase the speed of access to the Internet. It also allows the access ISP to service both analogue access clients and ISDN clients using a single access number and single service platform.

The data circuit to the central office has no particular requirements, so the choice of carriage technology and carrier offering is typically based on minimizing the unit price of bandwidth and operating at an acceptable level of availability and reliability. The relationship between the capacity of the circuit to the central office and the number of dial access ports is a price/quality decision to be made by the ISP, in the same way that the number of dial access ports provisioned per number of contracted clients is a price/quality decision by the ISP. Given that the maximum data rate of any individual access port is 64Kbps, the central office circuit can be provisioned with capacity equal to the aggregate access capacity provisioned at the local office. However, this mode of provisioning access is an extravagant exercise in a highly cost competitive marketplace, and more aggressive traffic aggregation measures should be factored into the design. Traffic aggregation factors of the order of 3:1 to 5:1 are common in this area, although this number is highly dependent on the dial access occupancy levels that the ISP can achieve. With a 5:1 aggregation factor and an average connection rate of 40Kbps, a bank of 96 access modems would be serviced by a 768-Kbps connection to the central office.

In general, a single local office is provisioned in each PSTN local call cell, and expansion of the service is typically through adding ISDN primary rate services and digital modem cards to the server unit.

The Access ISP Central Office

The access ISP central office is used both as the traffic hub for the ISP as well as the service hub. The traffic management components form one part of the central office, and the service and management platforms form the other part. In the central office, a router is used to terminate the local office circuits and provide traffic routing between local offices. This router is the traffic hub switching point for the ISP's network. In the design indicated in Figure 4.18, a second router is used to terminate the connection to one or more upstream transit service providers. This separation of function between local traffic switching and external connectivity is typically undertaken to ease operational management functions. One routing unit uses external routing protocols to undertake policy-based routing with external providers to ensure that external connectivity costs, which are generally a significant proportion of the total carriage cost for the ISP, are minimized. The other unit uses internal routing protocols to ensure internal topology maintenance. The two routers are interconnected by a dedicated channel or a private LAN.

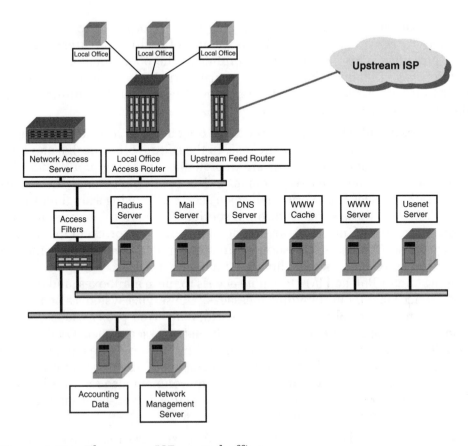

Figure 4.18 The access ISP central office.

External connectivity may be through a combination of connectivity providers and exchanges. Connectivity providers offer a transit service, accepting the access ISP's routes and undertaking to announce these routes so that full and complete Internet connectivity is achieved. In the simplest case, a single external connectivity provider can be used, which does simplify the external connection design considerably. As the traffic volumes grow and the level of local access ISP activity rises, the access ISP may choose to participate in a local exchange structure in addition to maintaining external connectivity. This decision normally is based on cost containment, allowing the access ISP to exchange traffic within the local region without payment to the external connectivity provider. The next step is the use of multiple upstream connectivity providers. This construction complicates the operational environment for the access ISP, but where differing tariff structures exist, this step may result in the access ISP using an external routing policy that minimizes the total connectivity cost for a certain mix of external traffic.

As well as a traffic hub, the central office operates as a service and management center for the network's client base. In the central office design shown in Figure 4.17, the service functions are depicted as operating on distinct platforms. Of course, no strict requirement exists for doing so, and the service configuration ranges from very small scale access ISPs using a single-host system to house all these services through service delineation into distinct platforms, to an emerging need to operate multiple platforms in parallel to manage the service loads. The service functions undertaken typically include mail services, which include holding incoming mail on behalf of clients, allowing clients PoP and IMAP remote access to these mailboxes, and offering relay services for clients' outgoing messages. The service systems also include DNS hosting and resolver functions, World Wide Web proxy caches, World Wide Web hosting for client pages, and a Usenet browser service. On the client operations and management side, the server functions include a client access authentication system, client profile manager, and client accounting and billing systems. The network management environment also requires hosting, including network polling and performance management, fault management systems, and similar operational management tools.

Two local networks are typically used to host these functions: a service access LAN, and a service management LAN. The reason for these two networks is as a basic security measure, intended to separate the management function out of the client-accessible component of the network. Although this is by no means an entire security policy in itself, this basic segregation of traffic into the two security domains is an excellent first step in constructing a useful and robust security environment.

The Regional ISP

While the preceding access ISP model services the individual PC client within the local residential, community, and small enterprise market segments, the service platform changes as the scope of the ISP operation broadens. One of the major characterizations of the service portfolio in this next generic area is the provisioning of permanent access to network clients in addition to dial access. This network-level access generally demands higher access speeds and quality of service and requires varying levels of customization. Such customization of the service may take various forms, such as virtual private network facilities, policy-based routing, or customization of the ISP's mail, Web, or other central services.

The architecture of a regional ISP is typically more complex than that of a simple star or star hierarchy, due to the requirement to increase the robustness of the network service. In addition, the network topology is influenced by the requirement to offer a larger scale of services, so that the feature of multiple service platform locations should be integrated into the design. Indicative generic topology for a regional ISP is illustrated in Figure 4.19.

Here, the central office function is now deployed at two or more locations, as a means of load distribution and mutual backup to improve overall availability. The central offices are interconnected by a primary path and some form of backup path, again as a means of ensuring maximal availability of the services. The interior design of the central office is similar to that of the access ISP central office, although the option of using discrete platforms for each service function is more prevalent within the regional ISP, owing to the greater scale of operation. The major difference here is not in the internal architecture of the central office as such, but in the requirement to operate two or more such facilities, which translates to a load-distributed architecture for each of the services at the service application level.

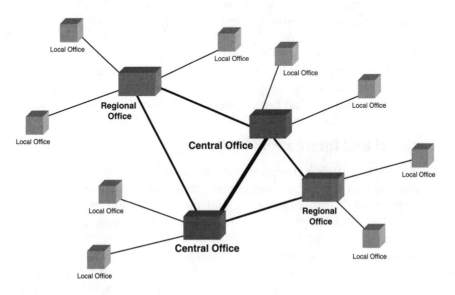

Figure 4.19   The regional ISP.

Regional and Local Offices

This design introduces the architectural component of a regional office as a means of access aggregation. Here, the ISP terminates a set of local office access points into a router hub, and then switches this traffic back to the central offices via some form of load distribution over multiple paths. This is certainly a very robust design from the perspective of resiliency, but other factors, such as carrier bearer topology and transmission costs, may force some level of compromise in this area of design. If the two links to the regional office use precisely the same set of fiber bearers and transmission switches, then the probability of failure in a single access transmission service not affecting the other service is very low indeed. The regional offices carry routers, network access units, and a basic set of local servers, which in turn are linked back to the major central office servers.

The local office is similar in design and function to the local office of the access ISP. The local office is used within this architecture to also serve the requirements of low-bandwidth permanently connected network customers, as well as the dial access requirements. The local office design may be extended from a single Network Access Server to a set of units, as per Figure 4.20. In the configuration considered here, the discrete functions are segregated into multiple routers. As with the access router, the Network Access Server is based on ISDN primary rate access, to allow the unit to service both PSTN and ISDN calls. An additional unit, the access router, is used to terminate permanent connection clients, using available carrier facilities that reach to the customer premises. These services normally would include some form of $n \times 64$Kbps access service, frame relay service, and other low- to medium-speed carriage services. In the design indicated here, a separate router is used for the link to the regional office, allowing a separation of function for ISP internal links to those items of equipment that terminate customer connections.

The National and International ISP

The final generic network design examined here is the large-scale ISP operation. Three major types of very large scale provider enterprises exist: the large-scale commercial ISP operation, operating across one or more national markets; the national telephone service operator, operating across a national market or within the scope of some form of alliance operating across a number of national markets; and finally, large-scale national academic and research facilities in many parts of the world, whose typical mandate is to provide services based on uncommercially, available leading-edge technologies to the academic and research sector.

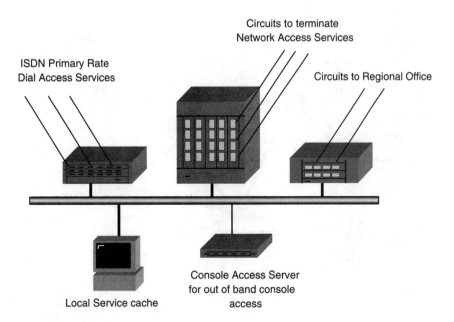

ISDN Primary Rate
Dial Access Services

Circuits to terminate
Network Access Services

Circuits to Regional Office

Console Access Server
for out of band console
access

Local Service cache

Figure 4.20 The local office.

A large diversity of approaches exists within the ISP industry, as the designs tend to concentrate on meeting very specific objectives. Rather than generalize from the type of enterprise operator, we look at a number of different generic approaches to large-scale ISP operations.

The Large Integrated ISP

The first approach is to continue to scale the regional ISP even further, building on the approach of a high-speed inner core network, connecting a set of central offices. Fanning out from these central offices would be a feeder network to a number of regional offices, and from there to local offices, as outlined. This type of approach is indicated in Figure 4.21.

The Outsourced Access ISP

A large-scale access provider may want to outsource the dial access hardware and use a set of local providers for local access services and then transport the traffic back through the access providers' network through to the ISP core network. This outsourcing allows the ISP to extend access locations into more marginal areas of small-market penetration by sharing the access infrastructure

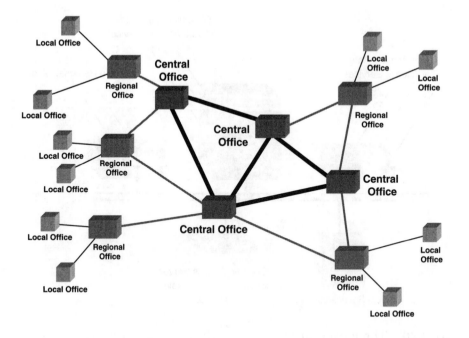

Figure 4.21 The large integrated ISP.

with a number of other clients, while still allowing for economies of scale and offering a comprehensive access service within the chosen market areas. In this design, the ISP operates the central office and associated core network, but outsources the local and regional office access and aggregation functions to the contracted access provider.

This allows the ISP to expand rapidly into a number of markets simultaneously with a massive call on capital, or, often more critically, without a massive Internet design and engineering task to be undertaken by a small core team of design engineers.

The Multimode ISP

The telephone provider approach to the large-scale Internet provision is also varied. Some telephone providers have seen this as a mechanism to maintain market share in related communications products, such as long-distance telephone calls or mobile telephony, and have concentrated on providing Internet access services, which are required by the critical market sector that uses the core telephone communications product.

Other approaches from the telephone carrier sector have intended to provide a more comprehensive service offering, by packaging up a full range of Internet access services, which can be constructed from their carriage infrastructure, offering both a broad range of access services and wide-scale coverage with the service. Such an approach to the market can see an access offering, which covers the more established access mechanisms of PSTN and ISDN dial access, as well as extending the access options to include any one of a number of Digital Subscriber Line (DSL) access mechanisms, Hybrid Fiber Coax (HFC) services, Internet access layered above mobile data services (GSM and PCS technologies), as well as packet radio access services.

The Bearer-Switched ISP

The carrier also may use a carriage architecture for the Internet network that mirrors the underlying bearer service for telephony, using an architecture of major service locations and regional traffic aggregation points, which match the bearer switching and aggregation points. This allows the Internet carriage to be provisioned highly efficiently on the underlying bearer system, enabling the major traffic concentration points to be provisioned at major trunk bearer switching points and enabling the access network to follow the bearer system out towards local switching points.

This alternative is not often possible for a noncarrier, and each logical function of the ISP network has to be provisioned as a customer tail loop from the underlying bearer carriage network, starting with provisioning large-scale PSTN termination points within the customer access network, rather than at the local switch point, and continuing through to having to provision major ISP trunk switches at the end of switched data service access loops, rather than at the switches. Within a completely deregulated market, this may have some cost-efficiency impacts on those large-scale ISPs who do not operate their own carriage and switching infrastructure, and the emerging alignment of carriage providers and large-scale ISP operations is certainly not coincidental, given the trend towards complete deregulation of the communications industry in many national markets.

The Transit ISP

Another design approach is large-volume carriage as a transit ISP operation. Here, the typical architecture and design problem has been to deploy a carriage solution using equipment that is indistinguishable from a beta product test platform. The trunk carriage sector of the Internet continues to grow at a pace that sorely tests the traditional product development process. Current high-volume ISP transit designs use either a switched core using ATM switching, allowing access to trunk carriage speeds of 155Mbps, with a near-term outlook of reliable 622Mbps, or a data link technology that allows IP packets to be placed directly into the payload frames of the Synchronous Digital Hierarchy architecture (SDH, or, in the United States, this is termed the Synchronous Optical Network, or SONET), allowing trunk carriage speeds for Internet trunks of 155Mbps with near-term outlook of reliable 622Mbps and 2.4Gbps without an attendant requirement to shift to a different transmission architecture.

ISP Local Access Office Architectures

The local access office, or Point of Presence (PoP), is one of the major components of the ISP architecture. The PoP is the aggregation point that collects local customers into the common routing and transmission fabric, and the PoP typically also is used as a junction point of the high-bandwidth backbone network. PoPs are major traffic concentration points, and the architecture of these sites is a critical component of the overall ISP architecture.

The architecture of the PoP has evolved in a manner commensurate with the technological evolution of the LAN. The backbone network was a T1-based network (1.5 Mbps) (or E-1, 2Mbps, in other parts of the world), and the access lines were typically at speeds of 56K through to T1 speeds. The PoP switching bandwidth was generally in the order of 3 to 5 Mbps. The PoP architecture of the late 1980s used a LAN to separate the core backbone routers with the customer access routers, as indicated in Figure 4.22. The simplest means of providing such a separation between these two sets of routers was that of a PoP Ethernet, which served as a common communications bus. The LAN also allowed the connection of other devices, including management units, traffic monitors, and application servers. Consequent refinements of this architecture were to divide the PoP LAN into multiple Ethernet segments, in an effort to segregate the major traffic flows into discrete LANs to avoid PoP congestion.

With the adoption of higher-speed trunk circuits, such as T3 (45Mbps) circuits, the Ethernet-based PoP network is inadequate, and the next generation of PoP LANs used an FDDI ring as the PoP LAN. The FDDI ring offers both higher resiliency and more deterministic delay factors, as indicated in Figure 4.23. However, inevitably, this configuration will congest under increasing traffic loads, and the use of segmenting the flows into multiple rings is a useful approach. In general, the segmentation is to allow the core routers to use one ring and to place the customer access routers on a second ring.

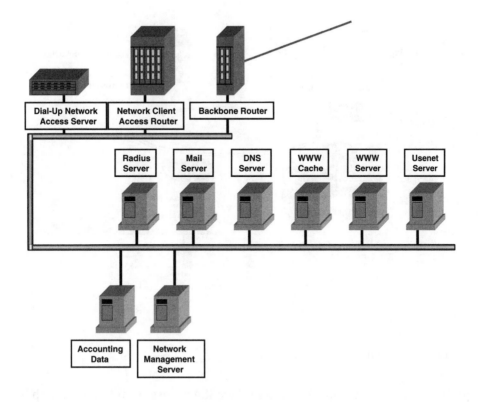

Figure 4.22   The LAN-based PoP.

As the trunk speeds continue to increase, the FDDI rings are inadequate, and the next step is to use a full-duplex Fast Ethernet/FDDI switch in place of the common FDDI ring. This allows increasing volumes of customer traffic to be passed around the PoP. The core router interconnection changes from a single FDDI ring to a full-duplex Fast Ethernet, or even a number of Fast Ethernet connections assembled in parallel.

Scaling the PoP to meet ever-increasing traffic volumes continues to place further pressure on PoP design, and the next generation of PoPs is now being constructed in the larger ISPs. These may use gigabit Ethernet switches in a configuration similar to the Fast Ethernet/FDDI switch architecture, although configurations that use local Packet over SONET framing are also possible. One potential technique is to connect all the core routers on a PoP local SONET ring, replacing the intercore router FDDI with a higher-capacity SONET ring.

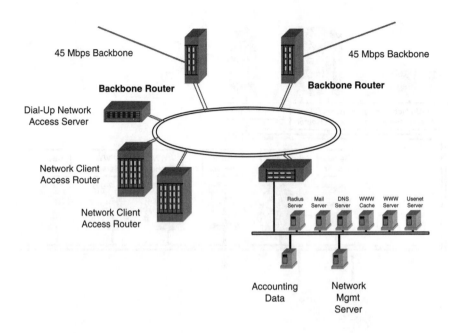

Figure 4.23 The FDDI-based PoP.

Equally possible is the approach to replace the access router switch with a set of fiber connections using Packet over SONET framing to create the connections between the core and the access routers, as indicated in Figure 4.24.

Future Architectures

In a word, scale. A potential future is that a single public Internet data network supplants the existing plethora of private data networks, in the same way that the public switched telephone network supplanted the embryonic private telephone networks that were appearing at the start of the twentieth century. The service model of such a public data network is that of a single access service with multiple service environments, including voice, video, and commercial applications augmenting existing data service environments.

The expectations of the network are also changing quickly in relation to this emerging service model. In 1993, the common expectation of a large ISP operation was an ATM transmission backbone using 155-Mbps virtual circuits. The current expectation, some five years later, is that of a Packet over SONET

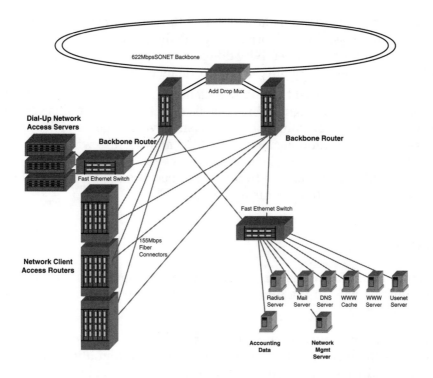

Figure 4.24 The fiber-based PoP.

(POS) network, using data clocking at speeds of 622 Mbps to 2.4 Gbps. Even this approach is being challenged by a view of IP packets placed within an optical network, using dense wave division multiplexing of 2.5–10 Gbps individual bearers, as the mechanism of multiplexing the fiber bearers to different communications services. Similarly, the switching speeds are now at such a point where gigabit-per-second IP switching is now a technically visible future. This should be contrasted to the outlook of 1993, where there was some doubt that IP packet switching at such speeds was going to be feasible at all, and fixed-length cell switching appeared to the only path to very high speed.

Perhaps the greatest change in expectations over the past five years is the way in which multiple virtual connectivity domains with differing quality parameters are now anticipated to be engineered. Whereas this requirement would have been expressed in terms of a collection of ATM virtual circuits five years ago, the expectation is now that that these requirements can be met within a common IP switching fabric, using an adjunct of universe tagging on packets to allow multiple connectivity domains to coexist and allowing applications to negotiate service quality and performance with the network.

Given this expectation that the public data network is an IP-based platform, then the architecture and engineering must be structured within this scenario of allowing both very large volumes of traffic and a very large diversity of traffic profiles. The expectation also exists that the architecture will continue to realize further economies of scale, and as the network infrastructure is engineered to carry higher volumes of traffic, the expectation is that the unit cost of carrying this traffic will continue to decline.

Summary

To support a highly functional and cost-efficient ISP operation considerable attention must be paid to the fundamentals of the network architecture and design.

The architecture must accommodate growth. A suitable architecture enables the creation of a network platform and then allows for rapid and sustained growth of the platform without the need to redesign the network at frequent intervals. Any ISP that is forced to replace the base platform and carriage infrastructure every few months will quickly fall behind, failing to grow at the level of market expectations and rapidly fade out of the market.

The architecture must create a cost-efficient network. Basic Internet carriage is a commodity product, and any provider that creates a network platform that is inefficient in terms of carriage costs compared to data payload volumes will be unable to sustain a suitable competitive price position, and again will rapidly fade out of the market.

The architecture must match the market sector the ISP operates in. Clients of a service want a service architecture that naturally and readily complements their own skills and capabilities. A service architecture that is unwieldy to use or provides services and functions, that are irrelevant to the client will be readily superseded by a service that is attuned to the customers' requirements.

chapter five

Network Infrastructure

In this chapter, we examine the two major technology components of the internal workings of an ISP operation: the IP router and transmission services. The first half of this chapter looks at the operation of the router and its role in network routing and network management. Various types of routers and their roles within an ISP network are examined. This section concludes with some comments about selecting a router for use within an ISP environment. The second half of the chapter examines the carrier structure and the services available within the area of point-to-point digital circuits, frame relay, and ATM. The section concludes with some notes on selecting carriage services.

What Is a Router?

One of the most essential components in an ISP's equipment inventory is the router, so we need to examine the role of the router and its performance and function. In their most basic form routers are a packet-switching device intended to interconnect two networks. However, there is a set of network interconnection devices that can also perform this basic function in a wide variety of ways, so some further elaboration is necessary to distinguish a router from these devices.

The simplest network interconnection device is a *repeater*. A repeater's task is to reproduce data from one network to the other, working at the physical level of bits: 1s and 0s. A repeater is in many ways analogous in function to a signal regenerator in transmission systems, faithfully reproducing the original transmission signal received from one network onto the other, preferably with minimal real-time delay and preferably with no deviation from the original signal. The repeater's capability to undertake this function is based on physical layer functionality, being able to recognize the signal encoding of each medium and faithfully translate the logical signal from one medium to the other.

While a repeater's function is unconditional forwarding, a *bridge* adds a basic level of network topology knowledge to the task. A bridge is a data link device, operating at the data link frame and address level of the protocol stack. In its normal mode of operation, a data link frame is forwarded by a bridge from one network to the other only if the bridge is aware that the destination of the frame is located on the other network, and that the task of forwarding the frame is necessary to ensure successful frame delivery. Source-route bridges and mixed media bridges are refinements of this forwarding function. A bridge operates at the data link layer, creating the appearance of a single network to the network layer.

Routers undertake interconnection of two networks at the level of the network protocol. Routers are active protocol-specific elements that participate in a shared topology discovery algorithm. Protocol packets are addressed to the data link level address of the router. The router strips off this data link layer encapsulation and inspects, and potentially modifies, the network level packet header fields. The protocol-specific information in the header, usually the destination address of the packet, is used as the basis of a forwarding decision to determine the correct next hop network and next hop router on that network. The packet then is encapsulated in the data link information as required by the next hop network and forwarded into that network. The sequence of processing operations internal to the router to achieve this functionality is indicated in Figure 5.1.

Although a router can be constructed as a software process on a general-purpose computing platform, high-performance routers are constructed as specialized items of equipment. This can vary from simple platforms that use a very conventional single processor and memory with a routing software kernel driving a set of interface devices, to a parallel high-capacity platform with multiple special-purpose processors driving particular components of the routing function. The drive to these specialized architectures lies in the increasing scale of network deployment in which the data-switching requirements cannot be hosted on a single processor platform. Current high-performance architectures use techniques of interface processor engines with on-board switching and caching to allow as much switching to be performed within the context of the interface processor without loading the common bus or main switching element. Further refinements in this distributed parallel architecture are anticipated to occur to allow routers to switch gigabit per second trunk circuits and to terminate up to tens of thousands of virtual circuits on a single switching platform.

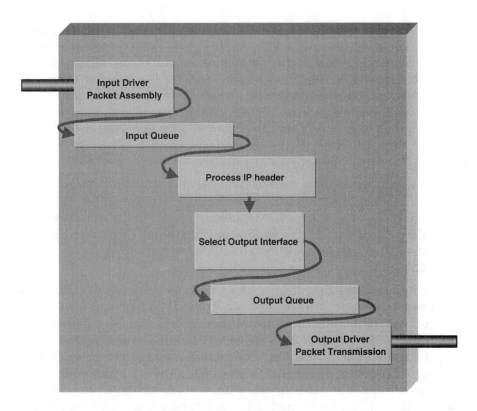

Figure 5.1 The steps involved in routing an IP packet.

Router Functions

Routers undertake three major tasks: packet forwarding between network interfaces, participation in the operation of routing protocols, and the operation of local network management tasks. We examine each of these functions in turn to provide some insight on the internal operation of a router.

Packet Handling

The description of packet handling used here is a very generic description of packet handling within a router. Although the set of tasks described here is common to all routers, the manner in which these tasks are implemented within various router hardware and software platforms varies considerably. These functions make reference to the processing steps indicated in Figure 5.1.

The network interfaces on routers receive packets explicitly addressed to the router. The data link level address of the packet must reference the router interface's data link level address, or the local network's broadcast address, or, if configured, one of the local multicast address groups. After the packet is assembled by the interface driver, the data link encapsulation is stripped off the packet, and the protocol-specific payload is forwarded to the relevant protocol forwarding process within the router. The forwarding process is generally shared between multiple interfaces, so the packet is placed in an input queue while awaiting the processing resource.

The protocol process first decides whether the packet is addressed to this router. The check must involve the protocol addresses for all connected interfaces. If this is the case, the packet will be processed in the same fashion as a host would process a packet addressed to it, stripping off the protocol transport encapsulation and forwarding the payload to the appropriate application process. Otherwise, the packet must be forwarded.

Forwarding involves determining the next hop by looking up the destination address in a local forwarding table. If the IP packet has strict or loose source-routing options enabled, the destination is drawn from the option field of the packet. Otherwise, the IP header destination address is used in the lookup algorithm. The forwarding table contains entries for network address blocks, rather than a comprehensive list of 32-bit host addresses, so the algorithm used locates the entry in the table corresponding to the best match within the table. Here, *best* is defined as *most specific* or *longest match,* referring to the number of bits used in the match of the unmasked bits of the destination address to the corresponding unmasked bits of the table entry's network address. The more bits used in the match, the longer, or more specific, the match. If no match is in the table, no possible forwarding decision exists. In this case, under specific circumstances, the router generates an ICMP error response to the packet, addresses the ICMP packet to the original packet's source address, discards the original packet, and forwards the ICMP packet back to the sender. Otherwise, the packet header TTL field is decremented by 1. If this action brings the TTL field to 0 through this operation, under specific circumstances, an ICMP error response is generated, as per the preceding procedure, and the packet is discarded. If loose or strict source-routing options were used, the option-specific pointers are updated as necessary. At this stage, the packet is ready for forwarding, and the interface selected by the table match is selected as the next hop interface.

The next hop network's maximum transmission unit size is compared against the size of the packet. If the packet is too large, and the packet's header field permits fragmentation, the packet is fragmented to match the maximum transmission unit size. Again, an ICMP error message may be generated if fragmentation is required and if the packet header does not permit such an action.

The packet is then queued for the next hop network interface, using the output queue associated with that interface. If the queue is full, the packet may be discarded. Such a discard operation may emit an ICMP Source Quench message to the sender, indicating that a local congestion condition has resulted in a packet discard. If the sender is using TCP, this message may be interpreted as a signal to reduce the congestion window and slow down the transmission rate. The utility of this action is a matter of some debate, and some routers elect not to generate ICMP Source Quench messages or do so under relatively strict rate control measures. The packet is encapsulated (or segmented, as in the case of ATM) as per the data link layer of the next hop, including generating the date link layer address, and the packet is then transmitted on the next hop network.

Routing Protocols

Routers also participate in the operation of routing protocols. Routing protocols are used to maintain in each router a coherent picture of the current topology of the network and a set of minimum cost paths to every reachable destination address. Two families of routing protocols are in use on the Internet: interior and exterior routing protocols.

An *interior routing protocol* is a distributed algorithm that operates across all the participating routers, in which the basic intention of the algorithm is one of traffic management distribution and synchronization. Here the objective of the protocol is for the routers to distribute local topology information across the entire set of routers and then to ensure that each router makes a local next hop decision consistent with the minimum cost path to reach a destination. Therefore, the collection of such local next hop decisions avoids loops and is consistent with minimal cost end-to-end paths. The intention of an interior routing protocol is to ensure that all local traffic management decisions are based on a current and consistent picture of overall network topology.

In Figure 5.2, the paths to destination A are indicated. The routing protocol has selected a set of paths that correspond to the minimal path cost to reach A. The path cost is determined by the sum of the individual link costs that make up the end-to-end path.

The protocol must ensure that it has an accurate picture of the operational status of all local network interfaces. When the status changes, the router must inform the routing protocol of the change so that any consequent adjustments to forwarding paths can be made.

An *exterior routing protocol* is used as a peering protocol between two or more network domains. The intent of the exterior routing protocol is not to expose the dynamic state of the internal topology of one network domain to the other. Indeed, the intention of an exterior routing protocol is the exact opposite—the functional objective of the protocol is to allow two network domains to exchange information regarding destination addresses reachable from each network without explicitly disclosing the internal paths used from the interconnection point to the destination's location. Exterior routing protocols also provide a means to allow third-party reachability to be described, so that if network domain A is connected separately to network domains B and C, the exterior routing session between A and B can be used to inform B of destinations reachable in domain C, using domain A as a transit (see Figure 5.3).

Exterior domains have explicit need for the ability to *tag* a collection of routes with the identity of the network domain where they originated. As these routes are promulgated from one network domain to the next, the routing protocol must record the sequence of domains through which the route has been promulgated. These network domains are termed *Autonomous Systems* (AS). A multidomain sequence is described as a sequence of these autonomous systems, and the sequence is termed an *AS path*. The role of the exterior routing protocol is to allow the network administrator to express external connection policies through the manipulation of the AS path entries within exterior routing protocols. The policy may explicitly permit or deny

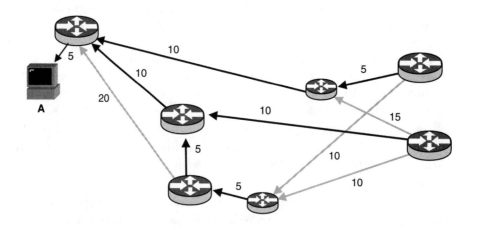

Figure 5.2 Path selection within a network.

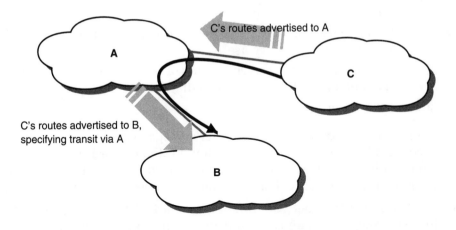

Figure 5.3 Transit routers within an exterior routing protocol.

the routing advertisement of network addresses associated with an AS or AS path. The connection and transit policies of the local network and the network's neighbors are expressed as permitted AS path entries, which are accepted by the local network, and permitted AS path entries that are advertised to neighboring networks.

An IP router is not constrained to operate a single routing protocol, and multiple routing protocols may be active concurrently. No matter what the number of concurrent routing processes, the router maintains a single IP forwarding table to make local switching decisions, so that where multiple sources of routing information exist, including both static and dynamically learned routes, the router requires a set of precedence rules to determine in what order of precedence routing information is loaded into the forwarding table.

This discussion is a very brief overview of the role of routing protocols, intended to introduce the topic within the context of router functions. Routing protocols and their functionality and role are covered in further detail in Chapter 6, "Managing Routing."

Network Management

Routers also can undertake a number of management functions to assist in the task of network management. The router maintains a set of counters that provides an indication of the following performance attributes:

- ◆ Router performance
- ◆ Router resource use (such as queue depth, queue drop counters, CPU load, and router memory use)
- ◆ Link use (transmitter and receiver counts of octets and packets and collision counters for shared access media)
- ◆ Link condition (error counters)

These functions are monitored by the router and aggregated into variables that are polled via a Simple Network Management Protocol (SNMP) network management compliant utility. SNMP traps can be used by the router to generate reports of real-time events, such as link status changes or connection events.

End-to-end integrity of network links is also part of the router management function. The router relies on two indicators of interface integrity:

- ◆ The control lines of the physical interface, which provide an indication of carrier status and clock integrity
- ◆ The use of a lightweight end-to-end integrity monitoring function

For point-to-point circuits, routers normally use a lightweight link monitoring protocol, or keepalive protocol, to ensure that the circuit remains up in both directions, that the circuit has not shifted to a loopback condition, and that the remote router is operational. This is accomplished by a simple counter-reflection protocol undertaken at the link layer. Each router maintains a per-link counter variable and a timer. The counter is passed to the remote router, which responds with a reflection of this counter as well as sending its counter-value. The local router increments its counter and sends this new value to the remote end, together with a reflection of the remote counter. If the router does not see a reflection within a set interval, the link is reset and marked as unavailable.

Additional Router Functions

Although the functions of packet forwarding, router protocol operation, and network management form the core router functions, routers have been considerably refined to adapt to increasing scale and broader utility of operation.

Routers can apply a set of administrative controls (or filters) to modify the basic action of the forwarding process. Filters can specify a number of match criteria, which are applied to packets. These criteria can take the form of particular destination addresses, a range of addresses, a set of source addresses, or a combination of the two. The match criteria also can include specification of the protocol within the IP payload, whether it be TCP, UDP, or ICMP, and the port addresses used by TCP and UDP.

For example, to match mail traffic to the address 139.130.1.1, a filter rule could be specified, as in Figure 5.4.

The actions of the router following a filter match could be to discard the packet (may occur within a firewall function) or to forward the packet onto a particular interface irrespective of the forwarding table entry (policy-based forwarding) or to change the packet's relative priority in the forwarding operation (quality-of-service policies). Essentially, the set of actions available with filters allows the network manager to alter the default router behavior, to ensure that traffic conforms to a set of local policy constraints, using a set of administrative tools and related criteria of applicability.

Routing and Switching

As the network continues to scale, the task of the network manager is to deploy hardware platforms that can manage traffic volume. In recent years, the debate between routing and switching has enjoyed some prominence, and various ISP networks have used both approaches to meet the demands imposed on them.

Routing. Uses a forwarding decision that is local-context free, because a circuit or other soft network state is not required to have been established beforehand in order for the packet to be forwarded. The forwarding decision is based on the destination of the packet, rather than on either the source of the packet or the identity of the preceding router in the packet's path through the network.

Switching. Describes a generic technique in which the local forwarding decision is determined by attributes of the data link layer encapsulation and in which the IP header is not used within the forwarding

Figure 5.4   Router filter specification.

decision. This decision may involve some form of soft network state being set up within the switching fabric to create the appearance of end-to-end virtual circuits at the IP level. This local state is used to generate switching level circuit descriptors that are used to make local forwarding decisions in the interior of the network.

Switching is intended to reduce the time and size of the forwarding function when performing routing at every forwarding point. Switching replaces the hop-by-hop IP destination address lookup with the model that uses a path through the switching fabric, which is selected upon ingress to the first switch. This technique can prove highly efficient in certain deployment environments, because the switching decision uses a smaller selection descriptor space. The size of the switch descriptor space corresponds to the size and complexity of the topology of the switched environment, whereas the IP forwarding descriptor space is the order of size of the number of distinct reachable destinations carried within the network's routing environment.

For example, in the topology in Figure 5.5, the forwarding decision is relatively simple because only two outcomes are possible. If X and Y are large transit networks, the decision at R2 whether to forward the packet to network X and Y involves a lookup into a table of all potential Internet destination addresses in order to make a choice between two outbound paths. Within a switching fabric, encompassing R1 and R2 as switches, the network feeding R1 would make the IP decision as to whether to direct the packet to X or Y at R1, and then the packet would be encapsulated with a switch identification that would allow R2 to undertake a local lookup within a table of two entries and make a switching decision based on this information.

To Switch or Not To Switch . . .

Because a path description is predicative, in that if the topology of the switch fabric changes, the path descriptor may be invalidated, the deployment of switching systems in a robust environment requires some containment of scale. Switching gains its ultimate strength in a high-speed local environment in which end-to-end speed is the ultimate network objective. Switching also is used within the high-speed transmission core of some Internet service provider networks in which speed and scaling are the factors that have led to the decision to switch within the backbone network.

Ultimately, the decision to switch or to route within the network is based on two very common design factors: performance and cost. Switches allow relatively simple high-capacity elements to be used within the core of the transmission network, at the cost of some increased complexity at the periphery of

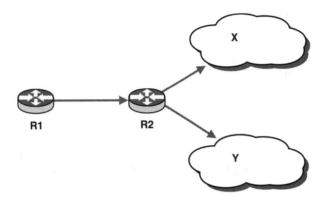

Figure 5.5 Routing and switching example.

the switching fabric, where end-to-end switching fabric state has to be initiated and maintained. Switches also do not necessarily reduce the impact on the total routing complexity. Switching systems add an intermediate layer of switching between the IP systems and the transmission substrate that is not necessarily a cost-efficient additional element to add to the overall network design. Switching can allow other non-IP forms of network traffic to be injected into the network, enabling the network to be used for other purposes as well as IP carriage. Switching also can be used to support multiple IP address families on a single network, supporting various forms of private network domains simultaneously. Such additional functions can provide additional revenue streams that can offset the cost of adding this layer of functionality into the network.

Routing systems allow for higher degrees of flexibility within the choice of transmission elements and network topologies and can allow a single packet-switching regime to operate on the underlying transmission substrate. This, in turn, may allow the network operator to realize some economies of scale of operation.

Some hybrid switching and forwarding mechanisms also are being devised, which attempt to use the outcome of a routing process that computes end-to-end paths, such as OSPF, to create path descriptors, which then are used within a packet encapsulation to allow the packet to be forwarded through a switching fabric. These Multi-Protocol Label Switching (MPLS) techniques are being considered by the IETF for adoption as standards [draft-ietf-mpls-arch 1997].

Router Requirements

The Internet document RFC 1812, Requirements for IP Version 4 Routers [RFC 1812], specifies much of the functional requirements for IP routers. The document describes the Internet architecture and the role of the router within this architecture and then discusses specific router requirements at each layer of the OSI seven-layer reference model.

> **Link layer.** For the Link layer, the document specifies that for point-to-point lines a conformant router must support the PPP protocol. The protocol includes the operation of the PPP Link Control protocol, which can negotiate a number of options, including header compression, asynchronous character maps, Maximum Receive Unit negotiation, Link Quality Monitoring, and link integrity monitoring via magic number exchange.
>
> **Internet layer.** At the Internet layer, the router may support the IP options of IP source routing, record route, and timestamp options. Support for source routing may have implications for the network's security policy, as source routing can be used in conjunction with source address spoofing to subvert simple filter sets. A router must verify the IP checksum and discard packets that fail the check. The router must implement fragmentation, and where required and permitted by the packet, the fragmentation should ensure that the least number of fragments is generated. The router also must check and decrement the TTL field on forwarding. Routers also must support the generation of ICMP messages.

The Router Requirements RFC indicates that routers should not generate ICMP Source Quench messages. In the event that they do originate such messages, they should provide some mechanism for limiting the rate at which such messages are sent. This area is one of continuing research, and mechanisms to inform flow-controlled sessions of the onset of router resource contention and the most effective means of host response to such messages remain an active topic. ICMP Source Quench messages can be regarded as a means of explicit congestion notification and can be used by the sender as a signal to reduce the congestion window.

The document mandates the support of statically entered routes, as well as support for OSPF as a routing protocol for interior routing applications. This document also indicates that if support for exterior routing protocols is provided, BGP must be supported as a candidate exterior routing protocol. Finally, the router must be manageable by SNMP, and all SNMP operations must be supported, with a core set of Management Information Bases (MIBs) included within this support.

ISP Routers

What kinds of routers are typically deployed within the ISP infrastructure? In general, it makes sound operational sense to restrict the number of different units to as small a set as possible and preferably use individual products from a single product stream so that the operational management tasks are similar across the set of units in operation. Such a strategy minimizes the support costs inherent in maintaining a broad range of equipment and allows the ISP to maintain a small inventory of components to allow rapid response to component outage and to respond to expansion requirements in a timely fashion.

Customer Premises Router

If the ISP is supporting end-to-end services that link local network facilities on the customer's site to the Internet, then there is a requirement to terminate the service access transmission line and access the customer's LAN with an onsite router. This option is referred to as Customer Premises Equipment (CPE). For an ISP service model, this is a basic unit that uses the following:

- A local Ethernet interface (or potentially a small multiport Ethernet hub)
- An ISDN Basic Rate Interface (BRI)
- Nonvolatile configuration memory, allowing the unit to operate correctly on power up

This configuration is illustrated in Figure 5.6.

Figure 5.6   CPE router.

Typically, such units use a dial-on-demand configuration so that the call to the ISP is established in response to local onsite activity. The unit also may be able to use multiple B channels in a PPP multilink configuration, using a load condition as a trigger for establishing additional calls. Other features will vary between vendors. The functionality set is required to support the small office environment's external connectivity requirements, and such additional functional components of the CPE router may include DHCP server functions to allow dynamic local host configuration, firewall address translation capabilities, and the ability to define various forms of packet filters. The routing requirements for such devices are not significant: Typically, the CPE router may be used to generate a local default route announcement on the local LAN and may use RIP to undertake this task. The router also may announce local network prefixes to the ISP, although the more typical configuration would use statically configured route advertisements at the service provider's end to achieve this function.

The unit needs to be small and environmentally robust, with enough LED indicators to allow a basic level of fault diagnosis from the LED display.

Network Access Server Device

The NAS, or Network Access Server, is the unit used to terminate incoming PSTN and ISDN calls. The unit is typically designed with the following:

♦ A number of ISDN primary rate interfaces (PRI)

♦ A 10/100 Ethernet interface

♦ One or more administrative control access ports (a multiport configuration would use one port for local access and the second for remote access)

The number of primary rates that can be configured into such a unit has been increasing significantly. Although initial units terminated one or two ISDN primary rates, units that terminate four through to ten primary rates are now available, and there is certainly pressure to increase the number of available ports per unit in an effort to reduce the cost per port in provisioning dial access server banks.

The unit accepts incoming PSTN or ISDN calls.   In the case of incoming PSTN calls, the unit switches in a signal processor onto the circuit to act as a terminating analogue modem for the call. ISDN calls can be handled directly.

The unit typically uses an associated authentication mechanism, such as Radius or a variant of TACACS.   This mechanism allows a centralized account management structure to validate the user, and, optionally, to specify a profile that can be loaded to the NAS to match the user's requirements. Such a profile may be a virtual private dial network configuration, some form of filter list, or any other vendor-supported profile that can be dynamically assigned to the port being used for the call.

The unit is normally housed in a specialized environment.   Therefore, extreme environmental tolerance is not normally a factor, but the unit is a critical point-of-service availability for the ISP, so some level of environmental resilience is useful.

The memory and processor capability of the device is critical.   The dial access servers tend to be the critical performance bottleneck for Internet services, given that the dial link is usually the determinant bottleneck link and consequently the NAS-side driver is the point where performance management is critical. The unit must have adequate buffer memory to serve the number of configured access ports, noting that the buffers which are excessively large will negatively impact on the levels of jitter experienced by the user's applications. The most critical factor appears to be adequate levels of processor capability. The processing load includes buffer management, packet discard selection, and operating performance management measures, such as fair queuing, early discard, and explicit congestion notification. Efficient performance of a dial access system is critically dependent on adequate buffer space and processor capability at the ISP end of the connection.

The unit must support PPP access and multilink PPP.   This support is necessary, both at session startup and as in the model of dynamic call management, where additional calls can be bundled into the existing PPP session. The use of pooled access numbers also implies that the multilink call set may be spread across several NAS units, and some form of distributed multilink is required.

The routing model typically used for the NAS is usually tightly controlled. Single host calls may be handed a single IP address as part of the PPP setup negotiation, and the pool of addresses managed by the NAS is advertised by the NAS to the local PoP LAN. The NAS also may have to manage incoming calls where the remote end is a network rather than a single host. In such cases, the authentication profile may specify the network prefixes to be associated with the call, which must be loaded into the NAS as administratively loaded static routes.

The ISP also may support virtual private dial network access (VPDN). In this case, the NAS should comply with the VPDN technology being used, whether it is dynamically loaded routing and traffic filters or tunnel initiation and associated tunnel authentication and maintenance mechanisms.

The typical architecture of the NAS is a chassis with a motherboard that contains the unit's processor and local network and control ports. Plug-in modules contain ISDN access ports and arrays of digital modems, allowing the unit to be expanded incrementally. The NAS must participate in the routing environment of the ISP and must support the interior routing protocol used by the ISP. Within the NAS, this protocol is typically a set of local route prefixes routed by other local devices reachable over the LAN, and a default route that points to the interface of the local core network routers.

Customer Access Router

Although the NAS is used to terminate intermittent access calls, the customer access router is used to terminate various forms of permanent access arrangements. The model of interaction is to terminate connections that are network peer attachments, and the router must handle a diversity of physical connection technologies as well as providing a rich set of routing tools and administrative control mechanisms.

Connections into customer access routers can use a variety of communications technologies, which can be characterized using a taxonomy of synchronized end-to-end clocking and unsynchronized clocking and dedicated and shared access ports. Synchronized clocked media include Digital Data Service (DDS) circuits; bearer circuits, such as T1 circuits in North America and E1 circuits in many other parts of the world; and larger capacity circuits clocked at 45Mbps (T3), 34Mbps (E3), or 155Mbps (OC-3/STM-1). The characterization of this family of circuits is end-to-end data clocking that ensures that no data is lost in transit within the communications medium. Such circuits are usually terminated using a dedicated interface on the access router. The density factor of such interfaces on the router is a critical factor in the choice of router.

The other communications mechanism is that of a shared switched medium, where end-to-end virtual circuits are configured across the switching fabric. Such communications media include frame relay Permanent Virtual Circuits (PVCs) and ATM PVCs. The characterization of this family of circuits is a decoupling of the sending and receiving data clocks. In this environment the interior switches may experience congestion loads that, in turn, cause transient data loss, due to this lack of end-to-end synchronization of data flow rates. Within the router, a single physical termination is shared across a number of PVCs that are represented within the router as a logical interface. A number of shared access media support synchronized clocking, including ISDN access, framed T1 and E1, and more recently, framed E3 and T3.

The typical architecture of a customer access router is a chassis and an associated set of processor and interface options. These units are a critical item of network infrastructure, and the router may support dual power supplies, dual processors in a hot standby configuration, and hot swap interface modules. Such measures are intended to enhance the operational availability of the unit, which will increase the reliability of the service provided to the ISP's client base. The architecture also should allow for a high density of access connections, enabling the service provider to terminate a large number of customer access connections within a single-access termination device.

The access router forms the boundary of the service provider network and must provide a rich set of functionality to the network operator. The unit must be able to support a large set of traffic and routing filters and provide a wide range of routing options to allow the service provider to interface with a wide range of customer environments. Although the units are not typically under high levels of load stress due to high volumes of traffic throughput, the unit must be able to apply a rich administrative tool set to the access ports, including traffic-shaping admission profiles; quality-of-service profiles; and reachability profiles, including virtual private network support, accounting profiles, routing profiles, and traffic filter profiles. This demands a processor-capable architecture that can undertake a relatively high per-packet processing overhead, while not necessarily being able to manage a very high packet-switching load.

Core Router

The core router presents a different profile in terms of operational requirements. The objective of the core routers is to provide a stable platform that protects the integrity of the core backbone of the network, while ensuring that the trunk transmission systems are used efficiently. Compared to traditional communications models, the distance profile of Internet traffic typically exhibits a higher proportion of nonlocal traffic. Accordingly, the relative load placed on the trunk transmission systems, as a proportion of the amount of total access capacity into the network, is higher. Therefore, Internet systems are typically highly demanding of trunk performance, and core routers must be able to withstand the pressure of switching very high volumes of packets per second between a small number of high-speed local ports and high-volume trunk circuits. The core routers also need a high level of functionality to support the chosen routing architecture and sufficient memory and processing capability to undertake high-speed packet-switching using routing tables that do not contain a default route (or *default free*), and accordingly these high-end routers may represent a significant investment on the part of the ISP.

One potential deployment architecture uses a common router chassis for both the core and access routers. While the access router uses a high-density interface module configuration, the core router uses a smaller number of high-speed interface modules to support the trunk network. This is possible, as many of the attributes of the core router are shared with the access router. These attributes are flexible interface configuration, high-performance route processor capability, high availability requirements of dual power supplies, dual processor configurations, and hot swap interface modules. In addition, this approach of a common router chassis is also supported by the ability to use a common on-site spares pool and a common hot standby capability, common operational support processes and common environmental requirements. For such reasons many ISPs use this approach of a common hardware platform for both access and core routers, using a system configuration of a smaller number of high-speed interfaces for the core routers and a high-density configuration for access routers.

However, the core routers do have to manage increasing levels of high-speed data flows. The larger the ISP, the greater the demand on these routers to scale to a size approaching management of multiple gigabit-per-second trunk lines. The interface technologies required for core routers is that they must support both high-speed transmission media and high-speed local LAN access media. For the high-end ISP market, therefore, the core router requirements are supported for OC-3/STM-1 and OC-3/STM-4 Packet over SONET (POS) frame formats as well as high-speed ATM access at comparably fast line speeds. The packet-switching requirements for this high end of the requirement set is a total switching capability of some tens of gigabits per second, or up to one billion packets per second.

Selecting a Router

Routers form the core of the technology base of the ISP operation. Whatever the purchase price, if the router is operationally inflexible, difficult to configure, or unreliable in operation, the router is no bargain. The cost of ownership of a router is dominated by the cost of operational management within the environment of an ISP operation.

You must ensure that your technology and business requirements are well understood by potential equipment vendors and that the selected vendor is committed to your requirements as a customer. This is not a case of simply choosing the cheapest vendor in the market and hoping that any consequent problems can be addressed without impact to your customers. The capital cost of routing equipment is a small proportion of the overall cost of the ISP operation, and care should be taken to outlay sufficient capital to ensure that the routing platform used is of a quality and has sufficient levels of technical support to meet the current operational and business objectives of the ISP enterprise.

Ultimately, many parameters form part of the selection task for an ISP:

Cost of ownership. Although purchase cost is certainly part of the selection criteria, total cost of ownership is a more relevant metric, taking into account maintenance costs and residual value in addition to capital purchase cost.

Quality of support. A relevant consideration, quality of support includes both hardware support arrangements and software support, in which the ISP requirements are to ensure very high availability of the service.

Availability of system configurations. Also relevant parameters are the system configurations, which match the ISP requirements, in terms of density of interfaces, equipment size, power, and environmental requirements.

Performance. The unit must be able to manage the load level the ISP anticipates will be passed through it.

Options. Options that enhance availability, such as hot swappable interface cards, dual processors, and dual power supplies also may be of interest to the purchaser.

Conformance. Conforming to pertinent Internet and industry standards is also a relevant consideration, and in particular, the router requirements specifications [RFC 1812] are certainly reasonable prerequisite functional requirements.

An ISP cannot afford to operate a wide diversity of router platforms. Careful consideration should be given to using a range of router platforms that share a common configuration and command interface. In this way, the operational overheads of training and the entire operational stability of the ISP can be enhanced considerably.

Carriage Choices: PDH, SDH, and Others

Constructing an IP transmission infrastructure is perhaps still within the realm of being more of an art than a well-understood network engineering task. As many designs for IP transmission capacity exist as there are IP networks, and rather than selecting various carriage options from a rich selection of available alternatives, the approach to date has been characterized by adapting what is available in carriage options to meet the requirements of the IP network.

The basis for this approach is largely historical, in that for the last 50 years the major consumer of the world's communications facilities, both in volume and revenue terms, has been telephony. Not surprisingly, the communications system has been constructed with a primary objective of meeting the requirements of the telephone network. Data transmission services have historically been a smaller-scale activity, and to date, have been provisioned on the margins of voice. Thus, data systems have been constructed as an adjunct to a well-provisioned and much larger voice carriage system. North American 56 K, T1, and T3 leased circuit services, and 64 K, E1, and E3 leased circuit services elsewhere, are the resale of components of the voice carriage hierarchy.

The data market is now growing very rapidly in size, and the sustained exponential growth experienced with data over the past decade is now challenging the far slower linear growth trends of telephony. The differences are, however, quite marked. Telephony systems are provisioned on a peak usage model, designed to offer reliable service at the busiest times of the day, week, and year. To achieve this, the network has a usage profile of a telephone network, which is very bursty, with marked peaks that far exceed average utilization levels. Much of the network is idle within such a usage regime, as it is designed to meet the peak load levels without major congestion. Tariff systems for telephony must reflect this network usage pattern, so that the tariff for a single call may not necessarily reflect the marginal cost of a single call in an idle period, but more typically, the tariff reflects the total costs of the network, with its peak capacity provisions, amortized over the total imposed call volume. Data applications are typically adaptive in nature, adapting their behavior to the changing characteristics of the network. Data applications will attempt to consume a large amount of network resources during otherwise idle periods and back off and consume a fair share of available resources when the network is under contention during peak periods. The corresponding network load profile is far more uniform than telephony, with sustained high-load levels being a common observation. As data systems continue to grow in size, they will start to exert significant levels of pressure on the design of the underlying carriage systems, creating a carriage infrastructure attuned to the requirements of data networks. However, that still remains a future in most parts of the world, and the more common task is to adapt carriage systems which are part of the telephony carriage infrastructure into useful data conduits. This section examines what options are typically available for the ISP in this area of carriage.

Defining Transmission Systems

Transmission systems have three major characteristics: bandwidth, delay, and cost.

Although *bandwidth* is commonly interpreted to mean the capacity of a line, as measured in bits per second, strictly speaking, bandwidth, capacity, and bit rate are different concepts, where bandwidth is the information carrying capacity of a link; capacity is the number of analogue symbols per second; and bit rate is the product of capacity and the mean number of bits per symbol.

Delay is a signal propagation metric. Electromagnetic radiation propagates at a speed of some 3.34 μs/km in a vacuum. The speed of propagation in optical fiber depends on the fire's refractive index and is typically 5.13 μs/km (microseconds per kilometer). This implies that a transcontinental link of some 3900km has a one-way propagation delay of 20μs, while an undersea cable circuit may extend over 8500km of cable and have a one-way propagation delay of 44μs. Geostationary satellite systems have an altitude of 35,784km, which corresponds to a 239μs one-way propagation delay for stations directly under the satellite and a propagation delay of 281μs for a more typical configuration of earth stations, assuming no switching delay within the satellite's switching systems.

The speed of light in a vacuum, or the physical sciences constant c, is probably the most investigated constant in all of science. According to electromagnetic radiation theory, its value, when measured in a vacuum, should not depend on the wavelength of the radiation nor (according to Einstein's postulate relating to the speed of light propagation) on the observer's frame of reference. Estimates of the value of c *have been progressively refined from Galileo's estimate in* Two New Sciences *of 1638, "If not instantaneous, it is extraordinarily rapid," to a currently accepted value of 299,792.458 kilometers per second (with an uncertainty of some 4 millimeters per second). The speed of light in glass, or fiber-optic cable, is significantly slower, at approximately 194,865 kilometers per second (the speed will vary according to the precise composition of the glass fiber, as the addition of impurities into the glass will increase its density and reduce the speed of propagation); whereas the speed of voltage propagation in copper is slightly faster at approximately 224,844 kilometers per second.*

The *cost* of a link is not a physical characteristic but one that nevertheless is very relevant to consideration of carriage choices. In general, link cost is an expression of the original price of infrastructure installation, the level of demand for the facilities, and the anticipated rate of financial return by the original investors in the facility. Infrastructure installation may include more cost factors than the price of the conductor and any required signal amplifiers or regenerators. The cost of right of access for terrestrial systems, the cost of geostationary orbital slots, or the cost of restoration capacity and repair for undersea cable systems also may be a significant factor in the total cost of the infrastructure. In general, the rule of thumb is that the longer the link, the greater the cost, although for some satellite-based systems this is not necessarily the case. Also, generally the higher the bandwidth, the greater the cost, although this is not usually in direct proportion, and the unit cost of bandwidth may decline as link bandwidth increases.

The Carrier Hierarchy

Much of the world's communications system has been constructed on the basic premise that the human spoken word uses a limited range of frequencies and has limited dynamic range. The world's telephone network is attuned to being able to reproduce the spoken word with acceptable clarity, and to do so uses a system that can carry analogue signals of between 350Hz and 3400Hz.

To convert this analogue signal to a digital signal the technique used is Pulse Code Modulation (PCM). The first step is to transform a continuous analogue signal into a sequence of pulses. To undertake this transformation without information loss requires the application of sampling theory. Nyquist's theorem asserts that to undertake a discrete sampling of an analogue signal without information loss, the sampling rate must be no less than twice the highest frequency contained within the analogue signal [Jordan 1985]. For voice signals, the Nyquist sampling rate should be no less than 6,800 samples per second, assuming that the highest frequency is 3400Hz. The voice carriers standardized on a sampling rate of 8000 samples per second to allow for intelligibility of voice reproduction, effectively choosing a network clock base of 125μs. The number of bits used to encode the amplitude of each sample is the next conversion issue. The smaller the number of bits used for this encoding, the greater the distortion of the signal (quantization distortion), while a higher number of bits imposes a greater load on the digital carriage system. The voice carriage industry standardized on an encoding that uses 256 levels, called *quantization levels*. Conveniently, this maps to an 8-bit encoding value. Voice signals have a limited dynamic range, and to reduce the distortion of voice the encoding mechanism from the analogue sample to an 8-bit encoded value is nonlinear. The greatest concentration of encoding levels is within the dynamic range of voice signals. After worldwide adoption of a single time base, and a single quanitization factor, it was probably too much to expect worldwide standardization of the encoding algorithm. The choice of a quantization algorithm is not uniform worldwide, and *μ-law* encoding systems are in use in the United States and Japan while *A-law* systems are common elsewhere. In either case, a voice call is mapped to a 64-Kbps datastream, and this 64-Kbps digital stream is the base building block of the voice carrier hierarchy.

To take these individual 64-Kbps streams and allow them to be carried within larger bearers across the network requires the use of a multiplexing technology. The most common multiplexing technology used in today's carrier networks is Time Division Multiplexing (TDM).

Time Division Multiplexing

The basic problem addressed by Time Division Multiplexing (TDM) is indicated in Figure 5.7.

Multiplexing takes a number of discrete inputs and multiplexes these inputs into a single higher capacity datastream. This stream can be transmitted over a higher capacity link and then demultiplexed back into the original discrete channels. Where the inputs are constant rate signals, the multiplexing creates a single signal whose rate is no less than the sum of the component rates.

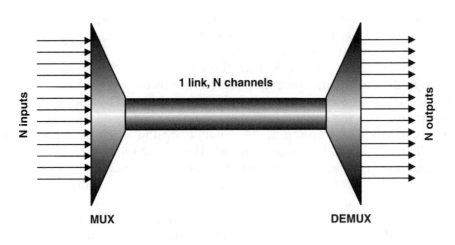

Figure 5.7 Multiplexing.

Time division multiplexing effectively takes a frame of data from each input in turn and transmits these frames across a common link. As the speed of the common link is the sum of the component links, no data is lost in this transmission model. The way in which this is achieved within the multiplexor (MUX) is by using a frame buffer for each input line. Incoming bits are loaded into the frame buffer. At every scan interval, the common line scheduler empties the frame buffer and loads it into the link driver. The common line scheduler scans each frame buffer in turn, where the complete scan of all input lines takes one scan interval. The output operation is similar, in that each frame is assembled in the common input driver and then placed in the link driver buffer for the output line (see Figure 5.8).

The frame buffer can be of any length, although the longer the frame buffer, the greater the latency of the multiplexing operation. The scan interval of the carrier hierarchy is typically based at the sample interval of PCM encoding of voice circuits, which is a scan time interval of 125μs, or 8000 scan intervals per second.

TDM is inherently very simple in its operation, but such simplicity is not without cost. TDM allocates a fixed amount of capacity to each input channel, whether the channel is active in transmitting a data element or not. A simple TDM MUX cannot operate on an adaptive basis where the common channel

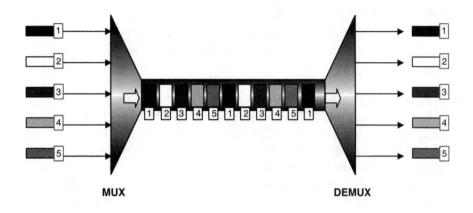

Figure 5.8   Time division multiplexing.

capacity is less than the sum of the input capacities and each channel is allocated resources on the basis of data activity. Nor can a TDM allow uncontrolled clock slippage of any of the input channels. The assumption in a simple TDM model is that each input line operates within a synchronized clocked mode, so that packing the common multiplexed datastream with control information is not required.

TDM systems commonly use a simple framing protocol, in which each scan is terminated with a single frame control bit. This bit alternates on each scan, creating a recognizable bit pattern, "01010. . .", which can be used to synchronize the demultiplexing unit to the input unit, so that the demultiplexing unit can recognize the alignment of each scan frame within the bitstream.

This system is complicated by allowing the various clock sources to drift within certain parameters. There is no single 125μs clock driving the entire voice network, and the system was constructed to allow some level of longer-term clock drift between the various component PCM clocks. This is accommodated within the TDM system by providing overflow space within each scan frame, so that a clock operating at a slightly faster rate can insert additional bits into the overflow space, with an associated timeslot label to indicate which input line has generated the additional bits. This allows the TDM MUX to correct the overrunning source at periodic intervals.

The Plesiochronous Digital Hierarchy

In a TDM digital switched hierarchy, the 64Kbps PCM encoded datastreams are termed DS0 circuits. From this point, the carrier hierarchy is constructed (see Table 5.1).

- In North America and Japan, the first level of carrier multiplexing is to take 24 of these DS0 circuits to create a DS1 circuit, operating with the inclusion of an 8-Kbps framing signal stream at a data rate of 1.544Mbps (commonly termed a T1 circuit). Elsewhere, the first level of the hierarchy uses 30 DS0 circuits to create the CEPT-1 circuit, clocked at 2.048Mbps, here allowing for 128-Kbps framing and control signal streams in addition to the 30 PCM streams (commonly termed an E1 circuit).
- The next level of the hierarchy, DS2, is four multiplexed DS1 streams. This point in the hierarchy is not used in most carrier systems.
- The next level is that of a DS3 bearer. In the North American system, this takes 28 DS1 groups and maps them into a 44.736-Mbps bearer, termed a T3 circuit. In the CCITT bearer system, a CEPT-3 is a mapping of 16 E1 circuits, which is a 34.368-Mbps bearer, termed an E3 circuit.

The additional space allocated in these higher order points of the carrier hierarchy are used to allow for slightly different clocking speeds of the individual streams, so that space is allocated for stuff bits to allow for clock alignment at the start of every frame. This is why this hierarchy is termed a *plesiochronous digital hierarchy* (PDH), (where plesiochronous means "almost

Table 5.1   The Plesiochronous Digital Hierarchy

Hierarchical Level	North American DS-x (Kbps)	European CEPT-x (Kbps)	Japanese (Kbps)	International (Kbps)
0	64	64	64	64
1	1,544	2,048	1,544	2,048
2	6,312	8,448	6,312	6,312
3	44,736	34,368	32,064	44,736
4	139,264	139,264	97,728	139,264

synchronous") because the different DS1 bearers are not tightly time synchronized with each other. If one stream is running slightly faster than the other multiplexed streams, it can overrun into the overflow bits. This technique spreads each component stream over the entire aggregate frame, and the task of extracting or inserting a single component stream into a multiplexed group without disturbing the remainder of the multiplexed streams is not commonly undertaken. Every voice switch within the PDH carrier hierarchy must demultiplex the trunk signal down to the level of DS0 streams before a call can be switched.

The PDH carrier system allows for point-to-point DS0 data links operating at speeds of 56Kbps in North America, or at 64K elsewhere, to be used for private point-to-point circuits. Typically, carriers also allow for a number of DS0 circuits to be provided in a composite bundle, normally by provisioning a DS1 bearer and then marking out a number of timeslots that are available for use within the data circuit. The PDH also allows for the provisioning of DS1 point-to-point circuits, at 1.544Mbps or E1 at 2.048Mbps, depending on the locally used hierarchy, and where available, from the carriage operator, DS3 circuits, which operate at 44.736Mbps, or E3 circuits at 34.368Mbps. No composite DS1 circuits are available from the carriage operators, due to the operation of PDH framing, although the use of inverse multiplexors can take a number of DS1 circuits and create composite data rates between DS1 and DS3 speeds.

The Synchronous Digital Hierarchy

These issues of making the hierarchy fit a set of imprecisely synchronized clocks can be eliminated if all component datastreams are synchronized. In a precisely synchronized environment, every component stream will occupy a fixed area of the multiplexed data frame, allowing streams to be added or removed without a complete demultiplexing operation as a prerequisite. This is used in the Synchronous Optical Network (SONET) to define a carrier hierarchy. SONET is the North American standard, and the Synchronous Digital Hierarchy (SDH) standard is used in other parts of the world.

The defined speeds within the hierarchy are indicated in Table 5.2. As these speeds are now synchronous, there is no need to add overflow bits into the multiplexed frames, so that the data rates are now exact multiples of the data rates of the lower speed trunk systems. The frame format remains locked to the constant 8000 frames per second base, or 125µs per frame. The base frame is an OC-1 frame, which is 810 bytes, as formatted in Figure 5.9. Each byte within an OC-1 frame corresponds to one 64-K DS0 stream. Higher order rates are constructed by interleaving OC-1 frames using byte interleaving.

Table 5.2 The Synchronous Digital Hierarchy

Hierarchical Level	North American Designation	International Designation	Data Rate (Mbps)
1	OC-1		51.84
2	**OC-3**	**STM-1**	**155.52**
3	OC-9	STM-3	466.56
4	**OC-12**	**STM-4**	**622.08**
5	OC-18	STM-6	933.12
6	OC-24	STM-8	1244.16
8	OC-36	STM-12	1866.24
9	**OC-48**	**STM-16**	**2488.32**
10	OC-192	STM-64	9953.28

Within the carrier industry, two points on this hierarchy are becoming available as carriage options, namely OC-3 and OC-12, and OC-48 remains a likely option in the very near future.

Digital Modems

As noted in Chapter 2, early endeavors in store-forward message-passing networks made widespread use of modem-based carriage services. The low cost of local modem calls suited the funding nature of such networks, and, as long as total volumes were low, the modem-based systems could keep pace with the total amounts of traffic to be transported.

The task of the modem is to map a digital stream into an analogue signal that can be passed over a voice line. The voice band telephone channel is a bandpass channel, traditionally thought of as operating from about 300Hz to 3400Hz. Modems have to operate within this band. Early modems used discrete tones that fell within this frequency band for communicating data, but the information density was not very high, and such modems operated at speeds of 300bps. Quadrature amplitude modulation (QAM) was a significant improvement, modulating a carrier sine wave signal in both phase and amplitude, allowing a number of discrete signals, offering information densities of multiple bits per hertz. Depending on the line quality, the number of symbols per second can be increased to fill the available voice channel spectrum. The V.34 rate, for example, uses a carrier of 1959Hz, and a symbol rate of 3429 symbols per second, giving a bandwidth from about 244Hz to 3674Hz. This

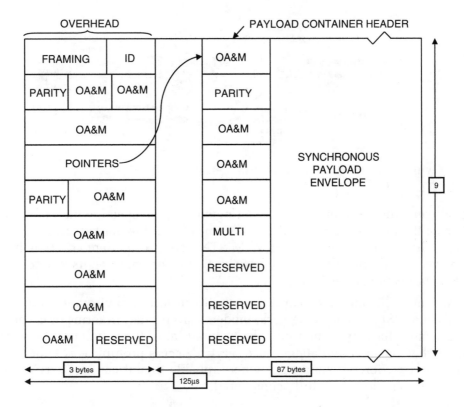

Figure 5.9 Base SDH frame.

bandwidth is effectively the theoretical maximum spectrum space available on a voice system.

However, digital telephony, such as ISDN, allows the use of 56-Kbps modems to operate, using pulse amplitude modulation (PAM) from the network to the client modem, while using QAM on the return path. This allows a 56-Kbps data rate from the network to the modem and a 33.6-Kbps rate in the reverse direction, as indicated in Figure 5.10. The standard for this form of modem operation is V.90, adopted as a communications standard in February 1998.

For many millions of Internet access subscribers, V.90 will play a central role in connecting to the Internet for many years to come. This is in spite of variable connection speeds, variable connection success rates, long coding latencies, modem connection scripts that remain overly complex and

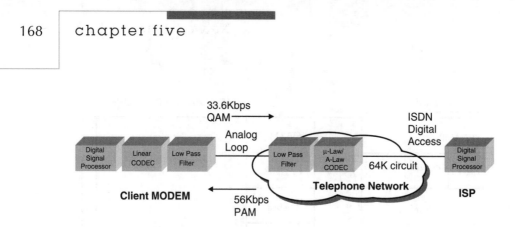

Figure 5.10   V.90 modem access method.

sometimes trouble-prone, and a resulting connection speed, which falls well short of the processing capability of current PCs on the market. The observation is that across a widely deployed PSTN network, modem access is inexpensive, and, despite these shortcomings of cumbersome use, its low cost is a very significant market factor.

Modems will play a strong role in Internet access environments, but in terms of an ISP's carriage network, modems are limited in terms of capacity, delay, and reliability, which must be factored in. In those parts of the world where there is no other data carriage service, or it is prohibitively expensive, this may be a forced choice, but where reliable digital carriage services do exist, they should be carefully considered.

Digital Circuits

A number of point-to-point digital carriage services were introduced to the market following the introduction of digital infrastructure into the telephone network. The earliest of these services is the Digital Data Service (or DDS). DDS services are point-to-point 56-Kbps circuits (in some networks it is a 48-Kbps circuit). DDS services are provisioned as 64-K digital circuits within the digital transmission network. On the copper loop, the loop is groomed to remove loading coils, taps, and other sources of unwanted noise and distortion. The encoding used on DDS systems is an alternate mark inversion (AMI), in which each 1 bit is represented alternatively by a positive and a negative voltage pulse. The properties of this encoding include a net zero DC voltage, and relatively easy detection of impulse noise. However, no inherent clocking of 0 bits takes place, and the two end points may loose clock synchronization with a long sequence of 0 bits. The clock signal uses 1 bit in every 8 as a 1 bit to ensure the maintenance of clock synchronization. The DDS data rate is therefore 7 bits of every 8-bit frame, or 56-Kbps.

A variant of the encoding system addresses the potential loss of clock synchronization on long strings of 0 bits by the use of bipolar 8th zero substitution (B8ZS) line encoding, to offer clear channel capacity at 64Kbps. The encoding system requires slightly greater complexity, in which every sequence of eight 0 bits is encoded with a pair of bipolar pulses on the 8th 0. This preserves net DC voltage and preserves sufficient pulse density to maintain synchronous clocking at both ends.

Higher speeds are based on a T1 (or E1) connection. Commonly available carrier services use a number of 64-K frames from a framed T1 (or E1) and use a Customer Service Unit (CSU) to aggregate these framed segments and present them to the customer as a single-clocked service. Carrier services also typically include the provision of clear channel T1 (or E1) circuits, which allow the customer to use CSU equipment to clock at the effective data rate of the circuit.

Yet higher speeds are available using a number of hybrid methods. Inverse multiplexing is commonly used to bond together a number of parallel T1 (or E1 circuits) and present an aggregate data rate to the routing equipment. Inverse multiplexors currently on the market can bond up to eight T1 (or E1) circuits and present a data clock rate of 16Mbps to the router's data port. Some care must be taken when using this approach so that the propagation times of each component circuit are not in wide variance.

Within typical carrier pricing structures, the unit cost of data circuits decreases for each 64-K increment from 64-K to the T1 or E1 point. Using inverse multiplexing, the unit cost of multiple T1 or E1 circuits increases again, as the capital cost of the inverse multiplexor has to be factored into the total costs of the carriage service. The next price point in many carrier's portfolios is in the T3 or E3 service point, where lower unit costs are again realizable. Such higher speed services are not universally available, but where provisioned, they are normally of a form of *clear channel* services. Framed T3 or E3 services are not a common feature of the typical carrier service portfolio.

These circuits are all based on the PDH carrier hierarchy, as discussed in the previous section. They offer an end-to-end synchronized data clock, which preserves bit-level and packet-level clocking between the sender and receiver.

SONET and SDH

We have described the use of a tightly synchronized clocking environment to create a digital carriage hierarchy that does not distribute framed data across the frame in order to compensate for clock drift within the various constituent circuits. This allows for the construction of high-speed digital carriage hierarchies that can be easily combined or split. Individual circuit groups can be peeled off the aggregate circuit or readily inserted into a vacant circuit slot.

The SONET Add/Drop Multiplexor (ADM) undertakes the insertion of a data flow into a SDH stream and can perform the removal of a data flow. This does not remove the requirement to set up a channel within an SDH bearer system manually, but it does allow the use of individual channel manipulation without the need to demultiplex the entire circuit hierarchy. In addition, SDH systems are typically configured in a dual ring structure, using the architecture of a working and a protection ring. The ADM automatically switches data into the protection ring in the event of failure of the working ring.

The synchronized clocking also allows the carrier speed to be increased well beyond the 34-Mbps or 45-Mbps speeds, which are the typical ceiling of carriage services provided from the PDH hierarchy. The services emerging from the SDH bearer system are STM-1 at 155Mbps and STM-4 at 622Mbps. These services already are being used within large capacity Internet backbone systems, and interface equipment is available from router vendors to operate at these carriage speeds. With the continuing growth of the Internet, use of STM-16 circuits at 2.5Gbps is confidently anticipated.

The use of SDH within the carriage service environment assumes that there are a number of data circuit streams that are multiplexed on a single fiber and that high-volume IP datastreams are but one high-volume use of the underlying fiber system.

ISDN

The digital circuit services discussed share a second common attribute, as well as synchronized data clocking. The services are statically assigned on an end-to-end basis. If the customer wants to change the location of either end of the circuit, the carrier must reconfigure the digital circuit service network to relocate the circuit. This administrative overhead is a contributory factor to the cost of operating digital circuits. The architecture of the Integrated Services Digital Network (ISDN) is a carrier effort to combine the utility of digital end-to-end circuits with the switching systems used in the PSTN environment, allowing digital calls to be dynamically created and torn down by the customer.

The ISDN system is part of the switched telephone network and uses the same switching services. Telephone and data services can be accessed via ISDN. The difference is that in the ISDN architecture, the local loop is not an analogue signal; the local loop is a collection of 64-K data channels, which are effectively an extension of the internal digital channels used to carry voice circuits within the PSTN.

Two access services are defined within the ISDN architecture; a Basic Rate Interface (BRI), and a Primary Rate Interface (PRI). A BRI uses three separate channels into the network: a 16-Kbps signaling channel, the *D channel*, and two independent 64-Kbps data channels, *B channels*, that can be used for data or voice. The D channel is used to control the B channel connections, using a set of call control messages (the format of these messages is defined in the ITU-T standard Q.931) to initiate and terminate B channel calls. Each B channel call is a clear channel 64-Kbps clear channel circuit. In this architecture, the customer equipment is more complex than the equipment used to terminate digital end-to-end circuits, as the customer equipment now has to manage the three circuits and use Q.931 to manage calls on the two B channels. ISDN BRI interfaces can be used to initiate calls or answer incoming calls.

A PRI uses a configuration of 23 B channels (in North America, or 30 B channels elsewhere) and a 64-Kbps D channel. Again, the D channel is used to control the calls made on the B channels, and the operation is similar to that of the BRI.

The use of ISDN for infrastructure carriage is dictated by the prevailing carrier tariff. The use of the service may entail a slightly greater investment in equipment, but this may be offset by slightly lower tariffs for the service. ISDN is not a high-speed carriage system. The ISDN service network treats each 64-K circuit as an independent call, and it is the responsibility of the customer equipment to use inverse multiplexing (or *bonding)* to group together bundles of B channel calls and create the functional equivalent of a larger capacity aggregate channel.

The major current use of ISDN within the ISP domain is to terminate modem and ISDN-based access calls from ISP clients. The use of V.90 high-speed modems is predicated on the assumption that the service provider end of the call uses a digital interface to the PSTN network. This is often implemented using an ISDN PRI, and the dial-in Network Access Server terminates the incoming access calls using onboard digital signal processors.

X.25

From the synchronously clocked end-to-end digital circuits, our overview of carrier technologies and services moves into switched services. These services do not provide end-to-end synchronous clocking of data. These services operate in a manner similar to IP itself: carrying discrete packets of data through a switching environment. The carriage usually emulates a circuit-switching environment, in that a *call* creates an end-to-end sequence of switching decisions, which is set up as the call is initiated, and the data packets then are carried along this circuit for the duration of the call.

X.25 is a specification of an interface into a packet-switched transport technology developed by the telephony carriers in the 1970s. The technology model used for the protocol was a close analogy to telephony, using many of the well-defined constructs within telephony networks. X.25 supports switched virtual circuits, in which one connected computer can establish a point-to-point dedicated connection with another computer (equivalent to a *call* or a *virtual circuit*). Accordingly, the X.25 model essentially defines a telephone network for computers.

The X.25 protocol specifies the interface between the network and the client. The network boundary point is the *Data Communications Equipment* (DCE), or the network switch, and the Customer Premise Equipment (CPE) is the *Data Termination Equipment* (DTE), where the appropriate equipment is located on the customer premises.

X.25 specifies the DCE/DTE interaction in terms of framing and signaling. A complementary specification, X.75, specifies the switch-to-switch interaction for X.25 switches within the interior of the X.25 network. The major control operations in X.25 are *call setup*, *data transfer*, and *call clear*. Call setup establishes a virtual circuit between two computers.

Call setup refers to the creation of a virtual circuit between two DTEs. The circuit operates as a reliable flow-controlled circuit. *Data transfer* then takes place across this reliable network transport protocol, so all data frames are sequenced and checked for errors. X.25 switch implementations are flow controlled, so each interior switch within the network does not consider that a frame has been transmitted successfully to the next switch in the path until it explicitly acknowledges the transfer. The transfer also is verified by each intermediate switch for dropped and duplicated packets by a sequence number check. Because all packets within an X.25 virtual circuit must follow the same internal path through the network, out-of-sequence packets are readily detected within the network's packet switches. Therefore, the X.25 network switches implement switch-to-switch flow control and switch-to-switch error detection and retransmission, as well as preserve packet sequencing and integrity. This level of network functionality allows relatively simple end-systems to make a number of assumptions about the transference of data. In the normal course of operation, all data passed to the network will be delivered to the call destination in order and without error, with the original framing preserved.

In the same way as telephony uses simple peripheral devices (dumb handsets) and a complex interior switching system (smart network), X.25 attempts to place the call- and flow-management complexity into the interior of the network and creates a simple interface with minimal functional demands on the connected peripheral devices. The Transmission Control Protocol (TCP) implements the opposite technology model, with a simple best-effort datagram delivery network (dumb network) and flow control and error detection and recovery in the end-system (smart peripherals).

This level of reliability within the network itself comes at a price. X.25 networks are generally slow-speed networks, as the reliable, flow-controlled hop-by-hop protocol is not conducive to high-speed switching. This functionality is also unnecessary for IP networks, as the end-to-end control algorithms in the IP protocol are more than adequate for high reliability and performance.

Frame Relay

Frame Relay is described as an "industry-standard, switched data link-layer protocol that handles multiple virtual circuits using HDLC encapsulation between connected devices. Frame Relay is more efficient than X.25, the protocol for which it is generally considered a replacement." [Cisco 1995] Frame Relay removes the switch-to-switch flow control, sequence checking, and error detection, and correction from the X.25 protocol, while preserving the connection orientation of data calls. This allows for a lighter-weight transport protocol that can support higher data transfer rates with less hop-by-hop handling of data.

A set of frame relay technical specifications is at the Frame Relay Forum Web site, located at www.frforum.com.

Frame Relay's origins lie in X.25, but were influenced by the development of Integrated Services Digital Network (ISDN) technology, in which frame relay originally was seen as a packet-service technology for ISDN networks. The frame relay rationale proposed was the perceived need for the efficient relaying of HDLC framed data across ISDN networks. With the removal of the X.25 protocol features of data link layer error detection, retransmission, and flow control, Frame Relay uses a model of unreliable frame delivery, leaving these error and flow control functions to be performed by end-to-end upper layer protocols (it is reasonable to suggest that the similarity to IP protocols is not entirely accidental).

Frame relay standards contain a specification of the interface between the client and the frame relay service network, termed a User-to-Network Interface (UNI). Switches that implement the frame relay service network may use any form of switching technology, including the commonly used ATM cell switches, or dedicated circuits with HDLC-framed packets. Whereas interior frame relay switches have no requirement to undertake error detection and frame retransmission, the frame relay specification does state that frames must be delivered in their original order, which is most commonly and efficiently implemented using a connection-oriented interior switching structure.

Current frame relay standards address only permanent virtual circuits (PVCs) that are administratively configured and managed in the frame relay network; however, frame relay forum standards-based work currently is underway to support Switched Virtual Circuits (SVCs). Additionally, work recently was completed within the Frame Relay Forum to define frame relay high-speed interfaces at HSSI (52Mbps), T3 (45Mbps), and E3 (34Mbps) speeds, augmenting the original T1/E1 specifications.

FRAME RELAY CONNECTIONS

Frame Relay supports the engineering notion of a *bursty connection*. Frame Relay defines this type of connection using the concepts of Committed Information Rate (CIR) and traffic bursts and applies these concepts to each Virtual Circuit (VC) at the interface between the client (DTE) and the network (DCE). (Frame Relay could never be called acronym-light!) Each VC is configured with an administratively assigned information transfer rate, or *committed rate*, which is referred to as the CIR of the virtual circuit. The interface allows the client to pass traffic into the network at rates in excess of this base rate, with the proviso that all traffic transmitted in excess of the CIR is marked with a Discard Eligible (DE) bit in the corresponding frame.

The first-hop frame relay switch (DCE) has the responsibility of enforcing the CIR at the ingress point of the frame relay network. When the information rate is exceeded, frames are marked as exceeding the CIR. This allows the network to subsequently enforce the committed rate at some point internal to the network. This is implemented using a rate filter on incoming frames. When the frame arrival rate at the DCE exceeds the CIR, the DCE marks the excess frames with the discard eligible bit set to 1 (DE = 1). The DE bit instructs the interior switches of the frame relay network to select those frames with the DE bit set as discard eligible in the event of switch congestion and discard these frames in preference of frames with their DE field set to 0 (DE = 0).

This mechanism of using the DE bit to discard frames as congestion is introduced into the frame relay network provides a method to accommodate traffic bursts while providing capacity protection for the frame relay network. It can be regarded as a *soft partitioning* of the network, in which clients' traffic may exceed the base levels allocated to them if there is no contention for the network resource. Under conditions of contention, each client is allocated its respective CIR rates.

FRAME RELAY CONGESTION MANAGEMENT

There is more to congestion management than the single response of CIR rate enforcement. Frame relay congestion control is handled in two ways: congestion avoidance and congestion recovery. *Congestion avoidance* consists of a Backward Explicit Congestion Notification (BECN) bit and a Forward Explicit Congestion Notification (FECN) bit in the frame header. The BECN bit provides a mechanism for any switch in the frame relay network to notify the *originating* node (sender) of potential congestion when queued traffic builds up in the switch's queues. The sender is notified that the transmission of additional traffic (frames) should be restricted. The FECN bit notifies the *receiving* node of potential future delays, telling the receiver to use possible mechanisms available in a higher-layer protocol to alert the transmitting node to restrict the flow of frames. The avoidance mechanism does not explicitly call for the switch to discard packets, nor does it explicitly notify only those clients whose transfer rates exceed their CIR. The ECN mechanism is advisory and informs the current senders that the frame network is under stress and that CIR rates may be enforced. An appropriate response for a sender may be to back off the transmission rate to the CIR level, because if the sender backs off to the CIR, the consequent packet loss rate will be minimized. *Congestion recovery* is the enforcement of the CIR rates for each sender.

These mechanisms traditionally are implemented within a frame relay switch so that it uses three queue thresholds for frames held in the switch queues, awaiting access to the transmission-scheduling resources. When the frame queue exceeds the first threshold, the switch sets the FECN and BECN bits of all frames. Both bits are not set simultaneously; the precise action of whether the notification is *forward* or *backward* is admittedly somewhat arbitrary and appears to depend on whether the notification is generated at the egress from the network (FECN) or at the ingress (BECN). The intended result is to signal the sender or receiver on the UNI interface about congestion in the interior of the network. No specific action is defined for the sending or receiving node on receipt of this signal, although the objective is for the node to recognize that congestion may be introduced if the present traffic level is sustained and that some avoidance action may be necessary to reduce the level of transmitted traffic. If the queue length continues to grow past the second threshold, the switch then discards all frames that have the Discard Eligible (DE) bit set. At this point, the switch is functionally enforcing the CIR levels on all VCs that pass through the switch in an effort to reduce queue depth. The intended effect is for the sending or receiving nodes to recognize that traffic has been discarded and subsequently to throttle traffic rates to operate within the specified CIR level, at least for some period before probing for the availability of burst capacity. The higher-level protocol is responsible for detecting lost frames and retransmitting them and for using this discard information as a signal to reduce transmission rates to help the network back off from the congestion point. The third threshold is the queue size itself, and when the frame queue reaches this threshold, all further frames are discarded.

WHY USE FRAME RELAY?

The two main attractions for using frame relay circuits within an ISP network are as follows:

♦ The tariffs for frame relay services often reflect the ability for the frame relay provider to oversubscribe the network in terms of total access rates provisioned into the network. The subscriber to frame relay pays a tariff based on the CIR, and the traffic levels may peak to levels equaling the access speed. In the case of dedicated circuits, the ISP must provision sufficient capacity within the circuit to handle peak loads, and within the frame relay environment, the ISP may offer this peak capacity without attracting a comparable tariff.

◆ A single physical access service can be configured within multiple virtual circuits, allowing for multiple logical links to be provisioned with the single local access circuit. This ease of provision of multiple circuits is also reflected in advantages in the frame relay service tariff.

An example ISP configuration using frame relay is indicated in Figure 5.11.

Of course, some issues surround the use of frame relay circuits. Frame relay adds a layer of switching and queuing, further increasing the delay, and possibly the jitter level of data packet transit, which may have negative performance implications for application traffic. The queuing structures within the frame relay switches congest from time to time, and CIR levels are enforced through the frame relay switch undertaking packet discard on marked frames. The burst capabilities of frame relay may not be available when required by ISP traffic behavior, and accordingly, the opportunities presented by this form

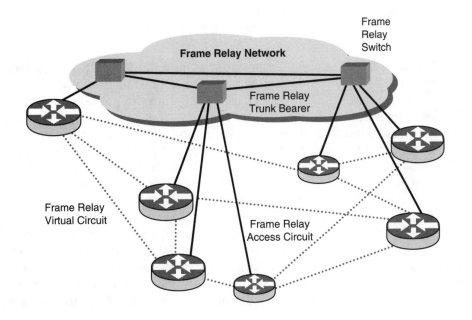

Figure 5.11 Frame relay ISP network.

of carriage sharing using soft partitioning may not be achievable by the client. Beyond CIR are no guarantees within frame relay, and even CIR is not a technologically enforced guarantee, but rather a universally enforced first level of load shedding. If the network remains overcommitted, load will continue to be shed until the switches regain a state of dynamic equilibrium between load and capacity.

ATM

Asynchronous Transfer Mode (ATM) has been described, possibly unfairly, as the chainsaw massacre of the data carriage industry! This depiction refers to the method of data carriage within ATM, in which, on ingress to the ATM network, each data packet is segmented into a series of small cells, each of which contains a 5-byte header and a 48-byte payload, and on egress from the ATM network, the cell sequence is reassembled into the original packet.

The majority of information in this section is condensed from the ATM Forum Traffic Management Specification Version 4.0 [AF 1996a] and the ATM Forum Private Network-Network Interface Specification Version 1.0 [AF 1996c].

Like X.25 and frame relay, ATM provides an alternative multiplexing technology to TDM. The antecedents of ATM lie in the TDM technology, in which the initial refinement to TDM was to expand the time slot period and then tag each TDM time slot component with a header fragment. This refinement allowed asynchronous time division multiplexing. (ADTM describes the technology base, but ATM was adopted as the name for the set of international standards based on this ADTM activity.) This technology was further refined to allow the use of switches within the common TDM bearer, which swapped the timeslot tags at the same time as the timeslot frame was swapped from one bearer to another. A set of such timeslot tag swaps can form a virtual circuit through a timeslot switching fabric, in which an input circuit can be mapped to an output circuit in a fashion very similar to TDM but with the additional flexibility of being switched within the bearer framework as a timeslot frame. Therefore, switching of circuits does not require the complete devolution of the aggregated high-speed bearers back into their individual circuits at every switch.

These circuits now form a *soft partitioning* of the network, as distinct from the fixed partitioning undertaken by TDM. Each stream is not synchronously clocked, and each stream is not necessarily allocated a fixed amount of resources from the underlying common platform. The asynchronous, switched timeslot now was mapped to a circuit through the set of timeslot switches, termed a *virtual circuit*. These concepts were first proposed in 1974 by Fraser, at Bell Labs [Fraser 1974]. When this technology was presented to the telephone operating companies as a scalable switching architecture that had far greater flexibility and efficiency than TDM-based architectures in the mid-1980s, the response was positive, and an expectation of migration to ATM was anticipated to be completed by 2020!

The computing industry had a different response. Having just completed a transition from Ethernet to FDDI, the prospect of requiring a new generation of LAN technology for every new generation of processor was not an inviting prospect. The promise offered by ATM was a scalable architecture that was not constrained to any particular bandwidth or distance limitation. With this impetus, ATM was rapidly thrust upon the IT industry, and from there, ATM was reintroduced into the carrier world with a new sense of urgency.

THE VIRTUAL CIRCUIT

The basic concept within ATM is that of the virtual circuit. In the datagram model of switching, the sender places the destination address in the datagram and passes the datagram into the network. Each switch must undertake a match of the datagram destination within a table of all possible destinations, creating a switching complexity that scales as the size of the network grows, irrespective of the complexity of the topology. Within the virtual circuit model, the initial phase is similar to the datagram model, in which a setup message is passed to the destination. The return message accepting the call has the additional function of setting up a circuit state within the network. Subsequent packets reference the circuit identifier rather than the destination address. The lookup space at each switch now scales back to the number of active circuits that traverse this switch, which is generally considerably less than the number of possible destinations within the network.

The task of assigning unique circuit identifiers across the network, which has switching significance for those switches along the chosen path, is one that is not sufficiently stable or robust. Instead, a local label is used, and the end-to-end path is constructed using a technique known as *label swapping*. In label swapping, each virtual circuit label has only local significance, and the same label can be used elsewhere in the network with impunity. Each switch

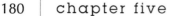

operates a translation table in which the incoming interface and circuit identifier of a cell determine a mapping to an outgoing interface, together with the allocation of a new circuit identifier, which has significance for the next switch in sequence. The new circuit identifier is written into the cell header, and the cell is forwarded on the selected output interface.

This switching algorithm is very simple and can be readily constructed using fast switching hardware. Proponents of ATM argue that the datagram switching algorithm cannot operate as efficiently due to the issue of size of the routing table lookup undertaken on a per-datagram basis, whereas proponents of a datagram-based switch argue that the VC identifiers are a slower and more cumbersome version of a datagram router's switching cache. One way to increase the speed of certain types of VC setup is to use the concepts of virtual paths and virtual circuits. A *virtual path* (VP) is a set of hops and associated label swaps that traverse the switching fabric from an entry point, the source, to a egress point, the destination. A VC in this structure is a logical end-to-end channel on a path, so that many VCs can be delivered on a single VP. Multiple traffic paths can be delivered across a single switching fabric, and the overhead of path creation is limited to some extent through the segregation of an end-to-end state into paths and logical flow circuits. The mapping of a path through the network can either be performed statically by the network administrator or dynamically via an interswitch protocol that has a similar function in the discovery of the minimal cost path to that of the interior routing protocols in the IP domain. The switch also can generate additional state information on a per-VC basis, including various quality-of-service parameters, which can be used to create various service characteristics that apply to the VC as a complete entity.

The primary purpose of ATM is to provide a high-speed, low-delay, low-jitter multiplexing and switching environment that can support virtually any type of traffic, such as voice, data, or video applications. ATM segments and multiplexes user data into 53-byte cells. Each cell is identified with an 8-bit VP Identifier (VPI) and a 16-bit VC Identifier (VCI), which indicate how the cell is to be switched from its origin to its destination across the ATM switched network.

Frame-based data traffic, such as IP packets, is segmented into a sequence of 48-byte cell payloads by the ingress switch and switched through the ATM network. The egress router has the task of collecting the cells and reassembling the original packet, which then is passed out of the ATM switching environment. The ingress segmentation and egress reassembly (commonly termed Segmentation and Reassembly, SAR) processes require substantial computational resources. In modern router implementations, this process is done primarily in silicon on specially designed Application Specific Integrated Circuit (ASIC) firmware.

Why 53 bytes per ATM cell? The 53 bytes are composed of a 5-byte cell header and a 48-byte payload. The original engineering refinement effort came up with two views. One view proposed 16 bytes per cell payload, in keeping with the original use of ATM as an evolutionary refinement of synchronous time division multiplexing, which at its base level, uses 1-byte timeslots. The other view proposed 128 bytes per cell payload as a minimum useful payload for various data applications. The small payloads allowed for low jitter within the network and also reduced the amount of signal loss upon single cell drop. The larger payloads provided for increased network efficiency by increasing the payload size in relation to the header and were sufficiently large to allow for the potential of direct mapping of upper level protocol units into cell payloads. At this stage, committee activity took control over technology considerations, and the proposals were refined to 32-byte and 64-byte payloads, respectively. At this point, neither set of proponents were willing to compromise, so the outcome was an adoption of a median value of 48 bytes per cell payload. Like many compromises, it allowed for equal displeasure for both sides: The value chosen was too large for simple voice encoding and too small for data use. This value has resulted in the adoption of costly tecnologies for the adaptation of the ATM switching fabric for voice and data, and the rationale for widespread adoption as a sucessor to the current TDM carrier hierarchy is by no means as clear as it once was.

ATM CONNECTIONS

ATM networks essentially are connection oriented; a virtual circuit must be set up and established across the ATM network before any data can be transferred across. The two types of ATM connections are *Permanent Virtual Connections* (PVCs) and *Switched Virtual Connections* (SVCs). PVCs generally are configured statically by some external mechanism—usually, a network-management platform of some sort. PVCs are configured by a network administrator. Each incoming and outgoing VPI/VCI, on a switch-by-switch basis, must be configured for each end-to-end connection.

Obviously, when a large number of VCs must be configured, PVCs require substantial administrative overhead. SVCs are set up automatically by a signaling protocol, or rather, the interaction of different signaling protocols.

ATM ADAPTATION LAYERS

ATM Adaptation Layers (AALs) were originally intended to provide an end-to-end carriage platform that applications could interface to directly. Much of the functionality observed in other higher level protocols, therefore, including flow control, error detection, and presentation, would be performed at the AAL layer. Although this approach was much in evidence in the definition of AAL1, most of the data use of ATM today uses AAL5, a much more lightweight framework used to host higher level protocol data units.

- ◆ AAL1 was intended to service constant bit rate traffic, in which the clocking rate of incoming data was preserved within the ATM network and reproduced on egress from the ATM network.

- ◆ AAL2 has not been defined, nor at this stage is it likely to be defined.

- ◆ AAL3/4 carries data frames of variable size (less than 64K), allowing for detection of corrupted, resequenced, and lost packets. To achieve this, the adaptation must use a SAR function to map the protocol data units into a sequence of calls. The mapping function used in AAL3/4 takes 4 bytes from every cell payload to achieve this.

- ◆ AAL5 is a lightweight SAR that exploits the basic property of ATM that no cells are resequenced in transit. The segmentation consists of adding a trailer to the protocol data unit, which includes length information and a 32-bit checksum and then transmitting the extended unit in 48-byte units. The final cell has an end indicator set in one bit of the call header. Reassembly is triggered by the end-of-packet bit, and the length and checksum are used to check for integrity of the received protocol data unit.

ATM TRAFFIC-MANAGEMENT FUNCTIONS

Certain architectural choices in any network design may impact the success of a network. The same principles ring just as true with regard to ATM as they would with other networking technologies. The primary responsibility of traffic-management mechanisms in the ATM network is to promote network efficiency and avoid congestion situations so that the overall performance of the network does not degenerate. A critical design objective of ATM is that the network utilization imposed by transporting one form of application data does not adversely impact the capability to efficiently transport other traffic in the network. It may be critically important, for example, that the transport of bursty traffic does not introduce an excessive amount of jitter into the transportation of constant bit rate, real-time traffic for video, or audio applications.

To deliver this stability, the ATM Forum has defined the following set of functions to be used independently or in conjunction with one another to provide for traffic management and control of network resources:

Connection Admission Control (CAC). Actions taken by the network during call setup to determine whether a connection request can be accepted or rejected.

Usage Parameter Control (UPC). Actions taken by the network to monitor and control traffic and to determine the validity of ATM connections and the associated traffic transmitted into the network. The primary purpose of UPC is to protect the network from traffic misbehavior that can adversely impact the QoS of already established connections. UPC detects violations of negotiated traffic parameters and takes appropriate actions—either tagging cells as CLP = 1 or discarding cells altogether.

Cell Loss Priority (CLP) control. If the network is configured to distinguish the indication of the CLP bit, the network selectively may discard cells with their CLP bit set to 1 in an effort to protect traffic with cells marked as a higher priority (CLP = 0). Different strategies for network resource allocation may be applied, depending on whether CLP = 0 or CLP = 1 for each traffic flow.

Traffic shaping. ATM devices may control traffic load by implementing leaky-bucket traffic shaping to control the rate at which traffic is transmitted into the network. A standardized algorithm called Generic Cell Rate Algorithm (GCRA) is used to provide this function.

Network-resource management. Allows the logical separation of connections by Virtual Path (VP) according to their service criteria.

Frame discard. A congested network may discard traffic at the AAL (ATM Adaptation Layer) frame level, rather than at the cell level, in an effort to maximize discard efficiency.

ABR flow control. You can use the Available Bit Rate (ABR) flow-control protocol to adapt subscriber traffic rates in an effort to maximize the efficiency of available network resource utilization. You can find ABR flow-control details in the ATM Forum Traffic Management Specification 4.0 [AF 1996a]. ABR flow control also provides a crankback mechanism to reroute traffic around a particular node when loss or congestion is introduced or when the traffic contract is in danger of being violated as a result of a local CAC (connection admission control) determination. With the crankback mechanism, an intervening node signals back to the originating node that it no longer is viable for a particular connection and no longer can deliver the committed QoS.

The major strengths of any networking technology are simplicity and consistency. Simplicity yields scalable implementations that can readily interoperate. Consistency results in a set of complementary capabilites. The preceding list of ATM functions may look like a grab bag of fashionable tools for traffic management without much regard for simplicity or consistency across the set of functions. This is no accident. Again, as an outcome of the committee process, the ATM technology model is inclusive, without the evidence of a filter of consistency. The network operator has to take a subset of these capabilities and create a stable set of network services.

ATM ADMISSION CONTROL AND POLICING

Each ingress ATM switch provides the functions of admission control and traffic policing. The admission-control function is called Connection Admission Control (CAC) and is the decision process an ingress switch undertakes when determining whether an SVC or PVC establishment request should be honored, negotiated, or rejected. Based on this CAC decision process, a connection request is entertained only when sufficient resources are available at each point within the end-to-end network path. The CAC decision is based on various parameters, including service category, traffic contract, and requested QoS parameters.

The ATM policing function is called Usage Parameter Control (UPC) and is performed at the ingress ATM switch. Although connection monitoring at the public or private UNI is referred to as UPC, and connection monitoring at a Network-to-Network Interface (NNI) can be called network parameter control (NPC), UPC is the generic reference commonly used to describe either one.

UPC is the activity of monitoring and controlling traffic in the network at the point of entry.

The primary objective of UPC is to protect the network from malicious, as well as unintentional, misbehavior that can adversely affect the QoS of other, already established connections in the network. The UPC function checks the validity of the VPI and/or VCI values and monitors the traffic entering the network to ensure that it conforms to its negotiated traffic contract. The UPC actions consist of allowing the cells to pass unmolested, tagging the cell with CLP = 1 (marking the cell as discard eligible) or discarding the cells altogether. No priority scheme is associated with ATM connection services. However, an explicit bit in the cell header indicates when a cell may be dropped, usually, in the face of switch congestion. This bit is called the Cell Loss Priority (CLP) bit. Setting the CLP bit to 1 indicates that the cell may be dropped in preference to cells with the CLP bit set to 0. Although this bit may be set by end-systems, it is set predominantly by the network in specific circumstances. This bit is advisory and not mandatory. Cells with the CLP set to 1 are not dropped when switch congestion is not present. Cells with CLP set to 0 may be dropped if there is switch congestion. The function of the CLP bit is a two-level prioritization of cells used to determine which cells to discard first in the event of switch congestion.

ATM SERVICE CATEGORIES

Currently, five ATM Forum–defined service categories exist (see Table 5.3):

- Constant Bit Rate (CBR)
- Real-Time Variable Bit Rate (rt-VBR)
- Non-Real-Time Variable Bit Rate (nrt-VBR)
- Available Bit Rate (ABR)
- Unspecified Bit Rate (UBR)

The basic differences among these service categories are described in the following paragraphs.

Constant Bit Rate (CBR).   The CBR service category is used for connections that transport traffic at a consistent bit rate, in which an inherent reliance is placed on time synchronization between the traffic source and destination. CBR is tailored for any type of data for which the end-systems require predictable response time and a static amount of bandwidth continuously available for the lifetime of the connection. The

Table 5.3 ATM Forum Traffic Services [AF1997]

ATM Forum Traffic Management ITU-T I.371	Typical 4.0 ATM Service Category	ATM Transfer Capability Use
Constant Bit Rate (CBR)	Deterministic Bit Rate (DBR)	Real-time, QoS guarantees
Real-Time Variable Bit Rate (rt-VBR)	(For further study)	Statistical mux, real-time
Non-Real-Time Variable Bit Rate (nrt-VBR)	Statistical Bit Rate (SBR)	Statistical mux
Available Bit Rate (ABR)	Available Bit Rate (ABR)	Resource exploitation, feedback control
Unspecified Bit Rate (UBR)	(No equivalent)	Best-effort, no guarantees
(No equivalent)	ATM Block Transfer (ABT)	Burst-level feedback control

amount of bandwidth is characterized by a Peak Cell Rate (PCR). These applications include services, such as video conferencing; telephony (voice services); or any type of on-demand service, such as interactive voice and audio. For telephony and native voice applications, AAL1 (ATM Adaptation Layer 1) and CBR service is best suited to provide low-latency traffic with predictable delivery characteristics. In the same vein, the CBR service category typically is used for circuit emulation. For multimedia applications, such as video, you might want to choose the CBR service category for a compressed, frame-based, streaming video format over AAL5 for the same reasons.

Real-Time Variable Bit Rate (rt-VBR).   The rt-VBR service category is used for connections that transport traffic at variable rates, traffic that relies on accurate timing between the traffic source and destination. An example of traffic that requires this type of service category is variable rate, compressed video streams. Sources that use rt-VBR connections are expected to transmit at a rate that varies with time (e.g., traffic that can be considered bursty). Real-time VBR connections can be characterized by a Peak Cell Rate (PCR), Sustained Cell Rate (SCR), and Maximum Burst Size (MBS). Cells delayed beyond the value specified by the maximum Cell Transfer Delay (CTD) are assumed to be of significantly reduced value to the application.

Non-Real-Time Variable Bit Rate (nrt-VBR).   The nrt-VBR service category is used for connections that transport variable bit rate traffic for which no inherent reliance is placed on time synchronization between the traffic source and destination, but for which no required guarantees of bandwidth or latency exist. An application that might require an nrt-VBR service category is frame relay interworking, in which the frame relay CIR is mapped to a bandwidth guarantee in the ATM network. No delay bounds are associated with nrt-VBR service.

You can use the VBR service categories for any class of applications that might benefit from sending data at variable rates to most efficiently use network resources. You could use Real-Time VBR (rt-VBR), for example, for multimedia applications with *lossy* properties, applications that can tolerate a small amount of cell loss without noticeably degrading the quality of the presentation. Some multimedia protocol formats may use a lossy compression scheme that provides these properties. You could use Non-Real-Time VBR (nrt-VBR), on the other hand, for transaction-oriented applications, such as interactive reservation systems, in which traffic is sporadic and bursty.

Available Bit Rate (ABR).   The ABR service category is similar to nrt-VBR, because it also is used for connections that transport variable bit rate traffic for which no reliance is placed on time synchronization between the traffic source and destination, and for which no required guarantees of bandwidth or latency exist. ABR provides a best-effort transport service, in which flow-control mechanisms are used to adjust the amount of bandwidth available to the traffic originator. The ABR service category is designed primarily for any type of traffic that is not time sensitive and expects no guarantees of service. ABR service generally is considered preferable for TCP/IP traffic, as well as other LAN-based protocols, which can modify their transmission behavior in response to the ABR's rate-control mechanics.

ABR uses Resource Management (RM) cells to provide feedback that controls the traffic source in response to fluctuations in available resources within the interior ATM network. The specification for ABR flow control uses these RM cells to control the flow of cell traffic on ABR connections. The ABR service expects the end-system to adapt its traffic rate in accordance with the feedback so that it may obtain its fair share of available network resources. The goal of ABR service is to provide fast access to available network resources at up to the specified Peak Cell Rate (PCR).

Unspecified Bit Rate (UBR).   The UBR service category also is similar to nrt-VBR, because it is used for connections that transport variable bit rate traffic for which no reliance is placed on time synchronization between the traffic source and destination. However, unlike ABR, no flow-control mechanisms exist to dynamically adjust the amount of bandwidth available to the user. UBR generally is used for applications that are very tolerant of delay and cell loss. UBR has enjoyed success in the Internet LAN and WAN environments for store-and-forward traffic, such as file transfers and e-mail. Similar to the way in which upper-layer protocols react to ABR's traffic-control mechanisms, TCP/IP and other LAN-based traffic protocols can modify their transmission behavior in response to latency or cell loss in the ATM network.

These service categories provide a method to relate traffic characteristics and QoS requirements to network behavior. ATM network functions, such as VC/VP path establishment, CAC, and bandwidth allocation are structured differently for each category. The service categories are characterized as being real-time or non-real-time. The two real-time service categories are CBR and rt-VBR, each of which is distinguished by whether the traffic descriptor contains only the Peak Cell Rate (PCR) or both the PCR and the Sustained Cell Rate (SCR) parameters. The remaining three service categories are considered non-real-time services: nrt-VBR, UBR, and ABR. Each service class differs in its method of obtaining service guarantees provided by the network and relies on different mechanisms implemented in the end-systems and the higher-layer protocols to realize them. Selection of an appropriate service category is application specific.

ATM AND IP

The basic differences in the design of ATM and IP are readily apparent. The prevailing fundamental design philosophy for the Internet is to offer coherent end-to-end data delivery services that are not reliant on any particular transport technology and indeed can function across a path that uses a diverse collection of transport technologies. To achieve this functionality, the basic TCP/IP signaling mechanism uses two very basic parameters for end-to-end characterization: a dynamic estimate of end-to-end Round Trip Time (RTT) and packet loss. If the network exhibits a behavior in which congestion occurs within a window of the RTT, the end-to-end signaling can accurately detect and adjust to the dynamic behavior of the network.

ATM, like many other data link layer transport technologies, uses a far richer set of signaling mechanisms. The intention here is to support a wider set of data-transport applications, including a wide variety of real-time applications and traditional non-real-time applications. This richer signaling capability is available simply because of the homogenous nature of the ATM network, and the signaling capability can be used to support a wide variety of traffic-shaping profiles that are available in ATM switches. However, this richer signaling environment, together with the use of a profile adapted toward real-time traffic with very low jitter tolerance, can create a somewhat different congestion paradigm. For real-time traffic, the response to congestion is immediate load reduction, on the basis that queuing data can dramatically increase the jitter and lengthen the congestion event duration. The design objective in a real-time environment is the immediate and rapid discarding of cells to clear the congestion event. Given the assumption that integrity of real-time traffic is of critical economic value, data that requires integrity will use end-to-end signaling to detect and retransmit the lost data; hence, the longer recovery time for data transfer is not a significant economic factor to the service provider.

The result of this design objective is that congestion events in an ATM environment occur and are cleared (or at the very least, are attempted to be cleared) within time intervals that generally are well within a single end-to-end IP round-trip time. Therefore, when the ATM switch discards cells to clear local queue overflow, the resulting signaling of IP packet loss to the destination system (and the return signal of a missing packet) takes a time interval of up to one RTT. By the time the TCP session reduces the transmit window in response to this signaling, the ATM congestion event is cleared. It is a design challenge to define the ATM traffic-shaping characteristics for IP-over-ATM traffic paths in order for end-to-end TCP sessions to sustain maximal data-transfer rates. This, in turn, impacts the overall expectation that ATM provides a promise of increased cost efficiency through multiplexing different traffic streams over a single switching environment; it is countered by the risks of poor payload delivery efficiency.

SMDS

X.25, frame relay, and ATM are packet-switched virtual circuit environments, in which packet flows are supported by the imposition of a dynamic circuit state and in which the packet headers reference the circuit, rather than the identity of the ultimate destination point. The next carriage service, SMDS, retains the packet-switched structure, but eliminates the imposition of a circuit state from the carriage environment.

The Switched Multimegabit Data Service (SMDS) is a carrier offering that in many markets has played the role of a precursor to the introduction of ATM. The design intent of SMDS was to provide a switched high-speed carriage system with the economies of a large public data service offering, with the transmission properties that resembled a high-speed LAN.

The core service is a central hub, intended to serve a metropolitan area. The switching hub is a connectionless switching system, rather than a virtual circuit switching environment. Packets, of a length up to 9188 bytes, can be addressed to any other connected interface, or, using a multicast group address, packets can be addressed to a group of interfaces. Closed user groups are implemented through packet filters, which define the set of interface locations that can address packets to the customer egress port.

Connection speeds to the central hub can vary from 64Kbps DS0 circuits to 45Mbps DS3 access circuits, and the media can vary from twisted-pair copper loops to fiber access tails. The central hub uses an internal cellular switch, which switches 53 octet cells; however, the internal formatting of these cells is different from ATM, in that the cellular format is a 7-byte header, a 44-byte payload, and a 2-byte trailer.

The major application of SMDS appears to be in servicing the market for LAN-level interconnection of metropolitan offices. It is unclear whether SMDS will enjoy significant investment by carriage providers, given that other high-speed carriage services, based on ATM and SONET technologies, provide a broader solution space.

Wavelength Division Multiplexing

In contrast to the switching systems, which attempt to impose end-to-end virtual circuits that span multiple media segments and share the medium between multiple uses by using some form of time division multiplexing, Wavelength Division Multiplexing (WDM) appears to be a return to a frequency division multiplexing. Current modulation of signals into fiber-optic cable is undertaken at 622Mbps, 2.5Gbps, and 10Gbps. One approach to increase the capacity of the fiber and multiplex a number of datastreams is to use WDM.

In WDM, each signal is encoded into a different *color*, and different, highly stable, lasers inject each signal into a common fiber. The signals are passed through the fiber together, using optical amplification with Erbium Doped Fiber Amplification (EDFA), which provides equal gain to all optical wavelengths. At the remote end, the light is passed through a grating to separate each wavelength.

A spate of WDM capacity announcements have been made, with some announcements quoting a capability to support 32 wavelengths, each of which supports a 10-Gbps datastream. Although it is unlikely that the data service carriage market will see the retail offering of a complete WDM channel to each customer, it does offer the interesting opportunity to shift into supporting high-capacity trunk IP systems using optical multiplexing. The potential of optical switching can be added to this scenario to introduce an all-optical trunk carriage switching system.

Selecting a Carriage Service

Selecting a carriage service is perhaps the most critical choice for an ISP, because the recurrent costs of carriage are often the major cost of the entire ISP operation. The ISP must be able to use a carriage service that scales with the ISP operation and allows the ISP to achieve a consistent reliability and quality of service.

In many situations, the task of selecting a carriage service for an ISP operation becomes a task of identifying what is available to match the capacity and location requirements of the ISP, rather than selecting a particular carriage service option from a wide range of possibilities. In such cases, it becomes the task of the ISP to optimize the use of the carriage service, ensuring that routers at either end are configured to match the transmission characteristics.

Ultimately, the major parameters of consideration of a carriage service are *availability, reliability,* and *unit cost.* If a service is not available, then it is difficult, to say the least, to deploy the service. Reliability is critical, because without a reliable carriage structure, creating a service operation that is reliable is impossible. Unit cost is the cost of carriage divided by the amount of data delivered without error by the system. This unit cost will be the major determinant of the ISP's actual cost of carriage and is a major factor in the pricing regime adopted by the ISP.

chapter six

Managing Routing

Routing is one of the key components of the technical infrastructure of every ISP operation and perhaps one of the more time-consuming activities in operational management. In this chapter, we examine the role of routing and the associated routing protocols within the Internet architecture and then examine a number of specific routing protocols and their applicability in the ISP environment. This chapter examines the role of routing protocols and then looks at the operation of interior and exterior routing protocols. The chapter also examines a number of routing configurations that assist the ISP in supporting a stable operational base for the service.

Why Is Routing Necessary?

Let's take a very simplified view of the operation of a router. Each router in an Internet has a number of interfaces to connected networks. Each interface has an interface IP address and an associated network mask. The router also possesses a forwarding table, which contains a number of elements per entry, including a destination IP network and mask, the next hop address, and an interface index, as indicated in Figure 6.1.

When a router receives an IP packet, it performs a number of tasks:

1. The data link encapsulation is stripped off the packet.
2. The destination IP address of the packet is checked against the interface addresses of the router. If an exact 32-bit match is made, the packet is passed to the router's internal processor for local handling, as the packet is addressed to this router.
3. The destination address is compared against the entries in the forwarding table, using a match determined by using the entry's mark

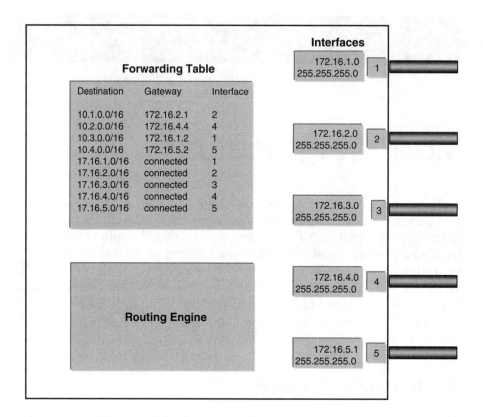

Figure 6.1 The internal elements of a router.

to match the masked bits of the destination address against the masked bits of the entry's network address. The match continues through the table, looking for the *best match*. Here, a best match is defined as the match with the longest mask (or a match on the greatest number of bits used, which is termed the *most specific* match). The corresponding next hop IP address and interface index from the forwarding table is selected, and the packet is passed to the indexed interface driver process.

4. If the interface is busy, the packet is held in a local queue awaiting its turn for transmission. The packet then is encapsulated with the

appropriate data link encapsulation and transmitted out the interface.

Today's routers use a number of techniques to improve the speed of this algorithm, such as caching the outputs of various parts of this algorithm to reduce the processing time for subsequent packets with the same destination address, and using a number of forwarding processors to allow parallel processing of forwarding decisions. Routers also have a number of allowable control mechanisms to enable the operator to modify the behavior of the routing algorithm. Packet filters can be used to describe the generic form of packets that should be discarded. Control mechanisms can override the forwarding table in certain cases, and mechanisms can even direct the router to rewrite parts of the packet header.

The crucial component in this generic router design is the *forwarding table*. The forwarding table is essentially a local view of the scope and technology of the network. The forwarding table defines the scope of the network in that if a destination is not matchable within the forwarding table, the packet is discarded by the router. The forwarding table defines the topology of the network, because the forwarding decision is intended to pass the packet closer, in a network sense, to the destination location. Therefore, it is critical that every forwarding table in an Internet environment must adopt a consistent interpretation of the network's scope and topology, in order to avoid inconsistent local decisions that may result in inefficient network use, looping paths, and improper packet discards. The role of a routing protocol is to distribute topology and scope information throughout the network to ensure that the set of forwarding tables is populated in such a fashion that the network operates with coherency and efficiency.

The Role of Routing Protocols

The role of the routing protocol is to effectively discover both the topology of the network and to enumerate the set of reachable networks from each of the points of egress of the network. If the network were a fixed and absolutely reliable system, this discovery would need to be undertaken at system initiation, and then the forwarding tables could be maintained without further intervention. Of course, such an environment never exists. Individual circuits or routers may drop out and reappear at a later date. The network changes with the addition of new circuits and routers, or with the removal of components from the network. The network also may be affected by dynamic changes in remote networks, so that the set of network destinations that is visible at each egress from the network may change as neighboring network systems change.

Within this dynamically changing environment, the imperative is to ensure that the collection of forwarding tables accurately reflects the network topology and network address reachability at all times, responding to changes in either of these situations as quickly as possible after they occur.

The role of a routing protocol is to maintain a coherent picture of the network's topology and address domain, and to distribute this information so that the forwarding tables of all controlled routers are populated with entries which are entirely consistent with this topology and address domain. In this way the routing protocol creates a set of paths that transit the network, mapping network ingress points to destination-specific egress points.

These virtual paths, which are a by-product of a sequence of forwarding table entries, are generally further constrained so that the paths selected by the routing protocol are *optimal* paths. The selection of such optimal paths within the network topology is defined by using a set of comparative metrics that can be applied to individual hops, so that an optimal path between any two points is a sequence of hops that minimizes the cumulative sum of the chosen metric. The metric itself can be protocol specific, can be input by the network operator, or, under some limited circumstances, can be dynamically calculated by the adjacent routers.

The example network shown in Figure 6.2 indicates a set of internal connections and the metric value of each connection. Each router selects a first

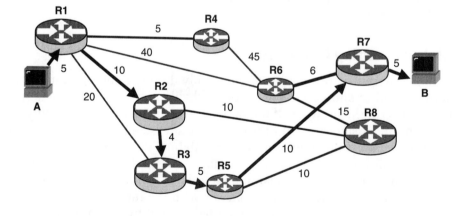

Figure 6.2   An example network topology.

hop for a path to B, based on the total metric of each potential path to B. R1, for example, selects a first hop to R2, on the basis that a path of cost 35 to B passes through R2, which is the minimum cost path available to R1. R2 also selects a first hop to B and selects the hop to R3, on the basis that this selects a path of cost 25, which is the minimal cost path from R2. The outcome of eight independent selection decisions, on routers R1 through R8, selects the path (A, R1, R2, R3, R5, R7, B) as the path from A to B. Every router computes a next hop decision for each destination, and the collection of eight next hop decisions based on the indicated metrics is shown as arrows in Figure 6.2.

Other major constraints are placed on the routing protocol in addition to functional accuracy in its task or optimal path selection. The routing protocol should converge (finish the computation relating to the topology change and discover the current topology) quickly to a new state of equilibrium following any dynamic changes in the topology of the network. If the example network were to lose the connection R5 to R7, then, as indicated in Figure 6.3, the routing system must make the necessary adjustments to recompute a new set of paths. Almost as a contradictory constraint, the protocol should seek to maintain a stable view of the network topology and avoid a situation in which selected forwarding paths undergo continued rapid alteration. As a nongoal, selecting a set of forwarding paths within the network topology that are symmetric is not necessary. The optimal path chosen from point A to point B in the forwarding tables is not strictly required to be the same path as that chosen from point B to point A. Just as many circuits are symmetric in their behavior, the circuit's comparative metric used by the routing protocol often

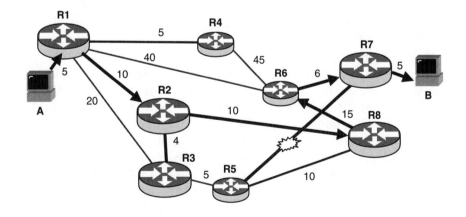

Figure 6.3 Realignment of path selection following topology change.

is identical in both directions. In such a case, the computation to discover the minimal metric path between two points is not dependant on the direction of the path, and symmetric paths are a common outcome of the routing protocol computation. However, the circuits may not all be symmetric in nature, or a comparative metric is used which is direction-related, and as an outcome the computed paths in each direction may be different.

As a basic model, the role of the routing layer in an Internet is as follows:

◆ Routers make forwarding decisions based on a local lookup of the packet's destination address in a forwarding table.

◆ The routing protocol must load and maintain this forwarding table within each router, maintaining an overall consistent view of the topology of the network and reachability within the network.

◆ The routing protocol must respond to dynamic changes in the network's topology or in reachability state.

◆ The routing protocol must select optimal paths, based on a consistent interpretation of a per-hop cost metric.

Class-Based and Classless Routing Protocols

The original model of the Internet environment was that of a local network and an Internet environment. Within the local network environment, every connected host could communicate with every other host connected to the network without the explicit assistance of Internet routing tools. Within the Internet environment, explicit routing was the only mechanism that allowed one network to communicate with another. The structure of an Internet address was a two-part structure: an 8-bit network prefix and a 24-bit per-network host address.

As discussed in Chapter 3, this simple model was refined into three different address structures: the original 8- + 24-bit address structure (Class A), an additional 16- + 16-bit (Class B), and 24- + 8-bit address structure (Class C). The structure within the address was implicitly defined by the network value. Network addresses corresponding to network values from 1 through 126 were designated Class A networks and used an 8-bit network identifier and a 32-bit host identifier (network addresses 0 and 127 were reserved for self-reference purposes). Network addresses of 128.0 through 191.255 were termed the Class B space. Network addresses of 192.0.0 through 223.255.255 were termed the Class C space. Within the Internet environment, routing elements could be handled as simple 32-bit values, with the set of hosts referred to by the routing element implicitly defined by the class to which the element belonged. This route entry of 189.34.0.0 implicitly referred to all addresses within the range 189.34.0.0 through 189.34.255.255, and an entry of 222.10.20.0 referred to all addresses within the range from 222.10.20.0 through 222.10.20.255. Routing implementations had to be revised to allow this implicit interpretation of a class-based mask to be associated with each routing entry, but changing the protocol itself was not required, as long as the protocol used 32-bit fields to carry routing entries.

As local networks grew in number, increasing pressure was being placed on the Internet routing system to carry a collection of routing entries to describe reachability to the separate networks located on a single campus or corporate network. The subsequent refinement to the simple class-based address structure was to allow local Internet routing environments to be routed within the host part of the class-based structure. Each network could determine a per-network mask, termed a *subnet mask*, which was an additional element within an address structure.

For example, the Class B network 172.16.0.0 could be further divided within the network to define 253 subnets, using a network mask of the 24 bits 255.255.255.0 (253 because the 0-valued subnet and the all-1s subnet are best reserved for network-wide broadcast functions). This would allow the address 172.16.10.5 to be interpreted as network 172.16, subnet 10, host 5, as indicated in Figure 6.4. Note that this interpretation is contextual, so that from a remote network the same address is interpreted as network 172.16, host 10.5.

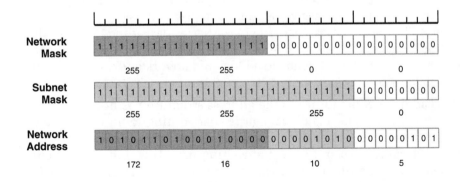

Figure 6.4   Subnetting a network address.

The subnet routing structure was constrained to be locally defined, so that all subnets of a network had to be fully internally connected within the network, as the Internet itself would not carry subnet routes, only class-based routes, so all subnets had to be summarized at the boundary of the local network environment and the Internet. Ensuring that the mask used be constrained to be constant across the network was the safest course of action, because the routing protocols did not carry the subnet mask associated with each entry, so the subnet mask was derived from the mask used on local interfaces which belonged to the network.

Again routing implementations had to be revised to allow this implicit interpretation of a routing entry within the context of a subnet environment and be able to draw the distinction between a subnet address and a network address. However, no changes to the routing protocol were required to support this changed interpretation of an address, which could include a subnet value.

The subnet structure allows a hierarchy of detail, in that within the network, the internal structure of subnet connectivity is carried within the routing table, while outside the network all the subnets are collapsed into a single network routing entity. This address structure is referred to as a *class-based* address structure.

Due to pressure on the Class B space, which many new Internet sites were using in the late 1980s and early 1990s, a generalization of the implicit structure of an IP address was defined as a means of alleviating this pressure without creating massive pressure on the number of entries in the Internet routing table.

The change was to drop the implicit address mask defined by the context of the address and the address value in favor of explicit use of a mask with every address. The explicit mask is defined as a series of leading bits, and the mask notation indicates the number of bits used in the mask. For example, the network entry 172.16.0.0/17 refers to a block of network addresses with the leading 17 bits in common, namely 172.16.0.0 through 172.16.127.255.

This additional flexibility in the address structure has not been without its attendant issues. The major change is that routing table entries now must include both a network prefix and an associated network mask, both of which are 32-bit values. Accordingly, the routing protocols and, in particular, the defined protocol structure to carry routing entries must make explicit provision to carry 64-bit-long routing entries. The routing algorithm also must be altered to allow for the explicit summarization of a collection of routing entries into a single aggregate entry. In a classless world, this summarization was implicit, and it occurred at the boundary of the local subnetted network to the larger Internet. In a classless address environment, there is no such point of implicit functionality, and the network administrator has to determine at which point summarization may occur.

In Figure 6.5 a local network uses three internal networks, which are explicitly summarized at the service provider boundary into a single aggregate routing advertisement.

Having multiple entries describing a full 32-bit address is possible. For example, the address 172.16.10.1 is encompassed within the network addresses 172.16.0.0/16 and 172.16.10.0/24. The implicit assumption within classless addressing is that the precedence is given to the longer mask, so in this case the entry 172.16.10.0/24 is taken as the preferred entry for the full address 172.16.10.1. This addressing does allow for some flexibility in explicit

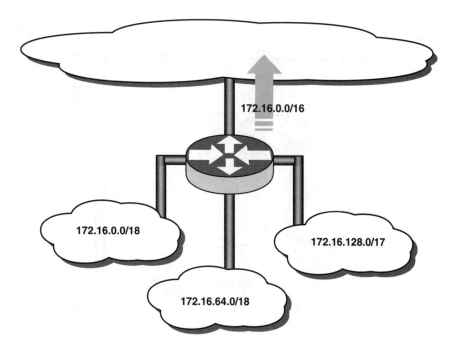

Figure 6.5 Variable length network masks and aggregation.

aggregation, in which some specific entries can coexist with the aggregate route (see Figure 6.6).

This variable structure of addresses is referred to as a *classless* address structure, and we refer to this in relation to the various routing protocols we examine in this chapter.

Interior and Exterior Routing Protocols

RIP, IGRP, OSPF, and IS-IS are termed *interior* routing protocols (the commonly used term is *Interior Gateway Protocol*, IGP). BGP is an *exterior* routing protocol. To understand the distinction between interior and exterior routing protocols, you need to understand the overall architecture of the Internet and the role of routing protocols.

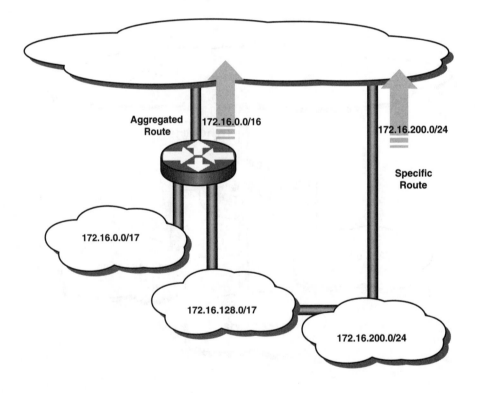

Figure 6.6   Aggregate and specific router.

An interior routing protocol is one that has as its major functional objective the task of discovering the current topology of the network over which the routing protocol is operating and then calculating optimal hop-by-hop paths across the network for every known destination network address. The routing protocol is presented with a set of addresses and their associated locations and a collection of point-to-point connections and associated metrics (or *cost*). The protocol operates as a shared computation within the set of routers that manage the traffic flows within the domain.

The interior routing protocol operates as a distributed process across this set of routers and attempts to derive a stable set of paths, which minimize network cost for every possible path. This set of paths then is translated into local forwarding decisions at each router, and these are loaded into the routers' forwarding tables. Interior routing protocols are therefore highly attuned to optimizing traffic flows within a defined domain and are intended to react to changing network topologies with a rapid convergence into a new set of forwarding paths.

Exterior routing protocols are not intended to manage such a fine level of detail. Exterior routing protocols are intended to manage the space of interconnectivity between interior routing domains. (These protocols are commonly termed *Exterior Gateway Protocols*, EGPs.) The task of an EGP is also explicitly not to expose the current state of the internal topology of one routing domain to another. Instead, the task of an EGP is to communicate reachability between two routing domains, allowing one routing domain to inform its peer which networks are reachable within the domain. The task of the EGP is to allow a large set of routes to be maintained across the peering session and to do so in an efficient and robust fashion. The general method of implementation of EGP is to allow the transfer of a large set of routes at the commencement of the peering session and then send only updates to this set as a smaller set of additional network entries and networks, which should be removed.

The other major aspect of the function of exterior routing protocols is the ability of the network administrator to manage which routes are advertised to peer networks and which routes are to be accepted from peer networks. The issue here is the control of external policy constraints, to align traffic flows to service contracts executed by the network.

The Operation of Interior Routing Protocols

The essential operation of a routing protocol is invariant. Each router has the responsibility to initiate dissemination of local status information through the network, and each router must interpret this information in a consistent and uniform fashion. The objective of the routing protocol is to identify a *best* path through the network from any point in the network to any reachable destination. The term *best* can have many different interpretations for different network administrators, and much of the effort in routing design is to choose a link metric that adequately encompasses the network design objectives relating to path selection.

This dissemination of topology information can be achieved in two major ways, both of which are examined in this section: distance vector protocols and link state protocols. Each approach has a number of strengths and weaknesses, which also are highlighted.

Choosing a Link Metric

Whether a distance vector protocol or a link state protocol is chosen to manage interior routes, the design decision faced by the network engineer is to choose a structure for network metrics that creates traffic flows, which match the chosen network topology and availability of capacity.

The simplest metric is to assign a unitary cost to every link. Under such a scheme, the outcome of the routing protocol will be to select paths that minimize the number of hops, irrespective of the capacity of each of the hops. This may be adequate for some simple networks, but in larger networks where there is a core high-speed backbone network and a set of lower speed access networks, the optimal path may be one that maximizes the available bandwidth, rather than simply looking for a minimal hop count.

A refinement of this metric is to use one based on the inverse of the link bandwidth. Here, the outcome of the routing search for lowest path cost will attempt to maximize the bandwidth of the path. However, this routing algorithm behavior is actually maximizing the sum of the individual link bandwidths as its path selection process; whereas the true available bandwidth of a path is the minimum bandwidth of all links on the path. This difference can lead to anomalous path selection in certain cases, where the minimal sum of these per-hop inverse bandwidth metrics actually selects a path that has a low path bandwidth. The configuration in Figure 6.7 shows such a situation, in which the link metric is derived using 2048Kbps divided by the link bandwidth. Such inverse bandwidth metrics imply that the path from A to D is selected to transit B and C, with a path cost of 14, and the path (A, E, F, G, H, I, J, D) has a path cost of 17, despite the fact that the larger metric path has three times the path bandwidth.

The issue here is that inverse bandwidth is not an additive metric, and the operation of routing protocols that use a link cost metric is to choose paths with a minimum metric sum.

Another candidate per-hop metric is propagation delay for a constant size packet. Delay can include both bandwidth and distance components. Bandwidth is relevant to delay given the observation that a packet of size P bytes will take D seconds to be transmitted, where

```
D = Propagation delay + ((Packet size x 8) / Bits per second)
```

Here, the action of a routing protocol that uses an additive metric will attempt to choose paths which minimize total path delay. This metric is very relevant given that protocols work most efficiently when end-to-end delay is minimized, so that network efficiency is promoted within such a metric. Network cost normally has a significant distance component, and selecting paths that minimize network distance promotes cost-efficient network paths.

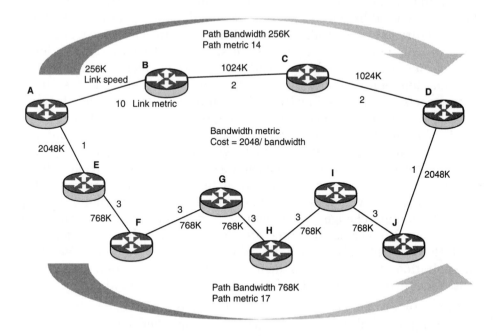

Figure 6.7   Bandwidth link cost metric.

Of course, the issue with any of these three metrics (hop count, inverse bandwidth, and delay), or any statically fixed set of metrics, is that the resulting network flows are insensitive to dynamic network load. The consideration arises whether a dynamically adjustable metric would allow the network to adjust path selection to enable the network to adapt to changing flow patterns. Attempts to use a dynamically calculated hop metric are by no means recent. The Hello protocol [RFC 891] used a link-polling mechanism to measure the delay of each link and generate a metric derived from these measurements. As the traffic load increases on the link, the queue depth increases, which in turn increases the measured delay. As this delay increases, the routing protocol may locate a better path, in which case the protocol then will converge, resulting in a new set of forwarding tables, which results in a shift in traffic loads towards more lightly loaded links where feasible.

The cautionary observation is that using a dynamically calculated metric that is load sensitive effectively creates a negative feedback path back from the outcome of the routing protocol to the input to the protocol. The term *negative feedback* is used because the feedback loop does not reinforce the outcomes of the routing protocol but works in the opposite sense. As traffic flows across the paths selected by the routing process, the dynamic path metrics increase, which in turn may force traffic to use a different path. The same situation may occur on this new path, leading to the situation of routing oscillation and other forms of path instability. Dampening this feedback mechanism is an essential component of any dynamically calculated path metric, so that the metric reacts in very small metric units to traffic shifts. Even this damping is not an optimal solution, given that routing protocols effectively have a fixed set of stable states. When the dynamic metrics vary by degrees, no immediate shift occurs in selected paths. The change happens when the change in the metric value exceeds the allowable variance in the current state, and the routing protocol then converges to a new state. If this causes a reverse traffic movement, the network may immediately revert back to its original state upon the next quantum change in link metrics, and so on. An alternative damping mechanism is to increase the time interval over which the metric is held constant. However, this also may not produce a desirable outcome given that, at the expiration of each interval, the network may shift to a new state, with the consequent disruption to traffic flows that such a shift entails.

Most networks are constructed with administratively determined metrics. The setting of a link metric is normally accomplished with the objective of managing the major traffic flows within the network with the greatest possible

A s a general observation on dynamically calculated metrics, it is perhaps overloading the routing protocol to expect the protocol to undertake dynamic load management tasks as well as topology management and optimal path selection.

performance and efficiency and at the lowest cost to the network provider. In general, this implies that metrics should be set to prefer paths with higher capacity in which large volume flows have to be supported and to prefer paths in which the path delay is minimized. Given a base topology that provides adequate capacity between the major traffic concentration points within a network, picking a set of metrics that makes efficient use of the underlying topology is relatively straightforward. When the base topology is not well attuned to the traffic flows that are imposed on the network, there is little hope of being able to determine a set of path metrics that will alleviate this basic mismatch between installed capacity and traffic flow.

Link metrics should be aligned to ensure that traffic flows pass over paths that have maximal capacity and minimal delay. Thus, low-delay, high-bandwidth links should be assigned a low link cost metric, and higher delay paths and lower capacity links should be assigned correspondingly higher link cost metrics. It is typical for the entire set of links and their metrics to be manually examined to ensure that the major traffic flows use links, which were provisioned for the purpose, and that individual link failure will not cause the network to converge to an unstable or poor configuration. Note that this is not a task which can be undertaken at the time of the initial network design and subsequently ignored. The network administrator should be aware that link metrics will allow a certain amount of fine-tuning of traffic flows over a network topology, and link metrics should be adjusted from time to time on the basis of ensuring continued efficient use of the network. Traffic loads should be closely monitored, and link metrics altered to adjust traffic flows to match available capacity. It is somewhat optimistic to expect that any form of standard algorithm to calculate a link metric, whether static or dynamic, will produce optimal outcomes for every network topology under all possible load conditions.

The observation is that link metrics are too critical a task to leave completely to automated algorithms, and some level of administrative oversight of link metrics and the behavior of the chosen routing protocol is necessary. The network administrator should be prepared to make manual adjustments to link metrics to ensure that the routing protocol generates forwarding paths, which ensures that traffic flows are efficiently handled within the network.

Distance Vector Protocols

This family of routing protocols uses a Bellman-Ford distance vector approach to topology maintenance. They are termed Bellman-Ford as they are based on a shortest path selection algorithm described by Bellman [Bellman 1957] and a distributed version of this algorithm described by Ford and Fulkerson [Ford Fulkerson 1962].

A number of protocols use this approach, most notably the RIP protocol, and a refinement to this, RIPv2, and IGRP and a refinement here as well, the EIGRP protocol.

The protocol is best described by examining the way in which it bootstraps itself into operation:

1. Each router initially generates a local forwarding table, based on the local knowledge of the status and IP address and mask (network address) of every local interface, and is assigned a distance metric of 0 to each entry in the table.

2. This table is broadcast to each adjacent router, using the local interface address as the broadcast source.

3. The recipient of the broadcast increments the distance metrics of the received table by 1. The entries then are checked against the locally stored *best entries* for each network address, and if the received metric is lower than the stored value, the entry is updated. The source of the broadcast is used as the next hop address, and the entry for this network address is updated. If the received update matches an entry in the forwarding table (where a match is that of a matching network address and next hop address), the entry is updated with the received metric. Otherwise, the entry is discarded.

4. The node ages each entry in the forwarding table, and entries that have not been updated for a specified period are removed from the table.

5. The forwarding table is broadcast to each adjacent router, as per the second step, and the algorithm continues at this step.

An Example of Distance Vector Routing

To assist in understanding the operation of this protocol, we look at a small network configuration consisting of seven nodes, and an associated internal topology of connectivity, as indicated in Figure 6.8.

BUILDING THE ROUTING TABLES

Initially, each node can validly make the assumption that it can reach itself, with 0 hops.

The protocol will broadcast this information on all active links, allowing neighbors to receive this information. Upon receipt of the message, the distance metrics are augmented by the cost of the link, which, as RIP uses uniform unitary cost, is an increment of the distance metric and integrates the resulting update into its local forwarding table.

Hence, looking at node A in Table 6.1, after one iteration of the broadcast phase, node A will receive an update from both of its adjacent nodes, B and E, and as an outcome, A now has entries in its forwarding table for B and E, as indicated in Figure 6.9.

Similarly, B will receive updates from A, C, and E and have entries for these destinations, and E will receive updates from A and B and have corresponding forwarding entries. The other node tables also will be populated similarly.

At the next iteration, A will receive copies of the forwarding table from B and E. The result of integration of these two tables into A's forwarding table is the addition of information relating to the reachability of C, using a path via node B. Node A's table now contains data, as indicated in Table 6.1.

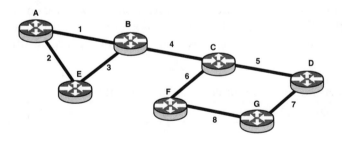

Figure 6.8   Example network.

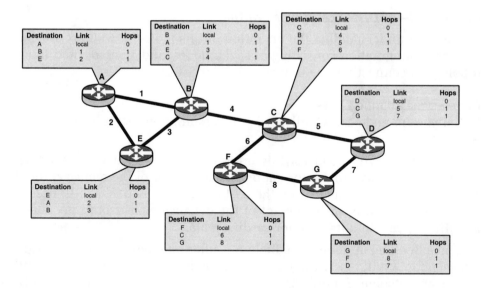

Figure 6.9 After a single iteration of the distance vector exchange.

In the third iteration, B's update contains information relating to reachability of nodes D and F, and by the fourth iteration, node G will be added to A's forwarding table, resulting in a forwarding table for A, as indicated in Table 6.2.

The fifth and subsequent updates will make no further changes to A's forwarding table, nor to any other node's forwarding table, and the algorithm is said to have converged, and topology of the network has been discovered. The final set of forwarding tables is indicated in Figure 6.10.

Note that A does not know precisely how a packet will reach G, and in particular, whether the packet will traverse links 5 and 7 or traverse links 6 and 8. The decision as to which path will be selected where multiple shortest

Table 6.1 Forwarding Table for Node A after Two Iterations

A	Destination	Link	Hops
	A	local	0
	B	1	1
	C	1	2
	E	2	1

Table 6.2 Forwarding Table for Node A after Four Iterations

A	Destination	Link	Hops
	A	local	0
	B	1	1
	C	1	2
	D	1	3
	E	2	1
	F	1	3
	G	1	4

paths exist is not a deterministic one within the scope of this algorithm. Whichever of nodes D and F first provide to C an update that includes reachability to G will be the node C uses for transit to reach G.

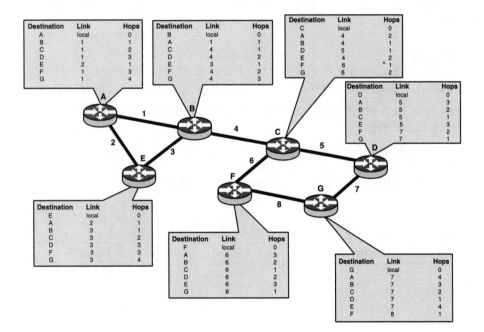

Figure 6.10 Final result of the distance vector exchange.

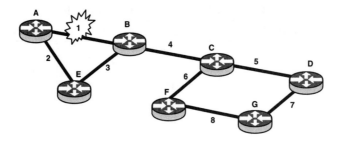

Figure 6.11   Link failure.

Note that the theoretical maximal time for the algorithm to converge from initial startup is the diameter of the network, given that from any segment of the network, only the shortest paths ever promulgate outwards. However, this is not the most useful result, in that the real question is the maximum time to converge when it is necessary to purge incorrect information out of the routing tables.

LINK FAILURE

To illustrate the issue surrounding the time taken for the protocol to converge, it is useful to examine what happens in the case of a simple link failure.

Let's look at node A again and examine what happens when link 1 fails, as indicated in Figure 6.11.

The algorithm requires node A to reassign the costs of all nodes that were reachable through link 1 to be *infinite*. Node A's table will now be as indicated in Table 6.3, where - indicates an unreachable destination or infinite cost.

Table 6.3   Forwarding Table for Node A after Failure of Link 1

A	Destination	Link	Hops
	A	local	0
	B	-	-
	C	-	-
	D	-	-
	E	2	1
	F	-	-
	G	-	-

Node E's table is unaltered by the link failure, and when this table is sent to A at the next iteration of the distance vector protocol, A picks up the routes from E. Within one update, interval connectivity for node A will be restored across the network. However, it will take three more update intervals to completely converge to the state indicated in Figure 6.12. These subsequent three updates do not change the topology of this network in any way, but do update the hop count to reach A for nodes C, D, F, and G.

This then is the *best case* failure for this type of routing protocol, where a backup path is available, and convergence to the backup path is quite rapid.

COUNT TO INFINITY

Certain link failures are not so well handled by a distance vector protocol, and these typically involve situations in which the link failure results in the network segmenting into two or more isolated components. If, in the example network, link 3 breaks (in addition to the previous break of link 1), the resulting topology is as indicated in Figure 6.13.

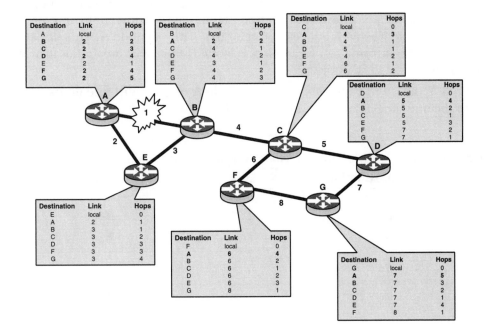

Figure 6.12   Converged forwarding state after link failure.

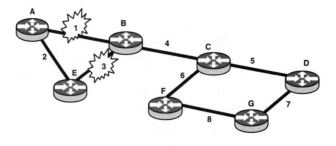

Figure 6.13 Further link failure.

Immediately, prior to the link 3 break, node A had the routing entries as indicated in Table 6.4.

E knows link 3 has failed and has marked all nodes that were reachable via link 3 as unreachable. Now if A sends an update to E before E sends an update to A, E will receive new information, which will allow it to update the unreachable entries with entries that refer to a path via node A. This update is effectively the information in Table 6.4. Node E then will create the forwarding table indicated in Table 6.5.

Node E then will send this update to node A, which will update its tables, with the outcome as indicated in Table 6.6.

Table 6.4 Forwarding Table for Node A prior to Failure of Link 3

A	Destination	Link	Hops
	A	local	0
	B	2	2
	C	2	3
	D	2	4
	E	2	1
	F	2	4
	G	2	5

Table 6.5   Forwarding Table for Node E at First Iteration

E	Destination	Link	Hops
	E	local	0
	A	2	1
	B	2	3
	C	2	4
	D	2	5
	F	2	5
	G	2	6

Table 6.6   Forwarding Table for Node E at First Iteration

E	Destination	Link	Hops
	A	local	0
	B	2	4
	C	2	5
	D	2	6
	E	2	1
	F	2	6
	G	2	7

This state will not converge within the operation of the distance vector algorithm, and the hop count for nodes B, C, D, F, and G will continue to rise without any convergence. In implementations of this algorithm, it is necessary to assign a finite value to this notion of *infinity* and assume that any metric equal to, or higher than, this finite value should be interpreted so that the metric indicates that the node is unreachable. A commonly chosen value for *infinity* is 16, with the side effect that any network which uses this form of routing protocol must have a longest path diameter of less than 16.

During the period while these nodes are counting up to this infinity value, the state of the routing tables is inconsistent. In the preceding example, node A believes that node G is reachable via node E, and node E believes that node G is reachable via node A. Any IP packet sent from A to G will bounce between nodes A and E until the packet's TTL expires. The general observation is that during the phase when the routing protocol is seeking a new converged state, the forwarding tables may contain various routing loops and inconsistencies, which may lead to intermediate states of network congestion during this period. If the routing protocol uses a UDP transport implementation, such as that used by the RIP protocol, this congestion may lead to packet delay and ultimate packet drop levels increasing, further hindering the protocol from quickly converging to a new stable network state.

SPLIT HORIZON AND POISON REVERSE

A number of modifications to the basic operation of the algorithm can prevent some forms of behavior, which lead to the protocol attempting to count to infinity. One such modification is that of *split horizon*, in which the update messages transmitted by the protocol are modified on a per-link basis so that any forwarding tables which refer to the link are omitted from the update transmitted on that link. In the preceding example, where the two nodes A and E were forwarding each other updates which referred to the same link, split horizon would prevent this.

Split horizon does result in certain situations where old information must time-out rather than being explicitly updated, and one potential response to this is to augment split horizon with *poison reverse*. Rather than omit the entries that refer to routes received over this link, poison reverse is more aggressive and changes the metric of such entries to the infinity value, so that the remote end will never attempt to use a router to this path, which traverses this node. Split horizon with poison reverse will still not completely eliminate all potential count to infinity situations, particularly where the loops that are engaging in the count to infinity are three or more nodes in size.

UPDATE TIMERS

Considerable design tension exists between the objective of rapid promulgation of changes in network topology and the need to ensure that the network transitions smoothly from one stable state to another. These objectives are engineering within the timers associated with each entry in the forwarding table. An entry is not automatically removed if an update fails to occur to the entry within the next update interval. The update packet may have been delayed or even discarded, and the routing protocol should not react to such transient events and interpret them as topology changes within the network. Therefore, it is necessary to have route table entries exhibit some level of persistence, so timers are used to ensure that a route is not removed from the tables until a suitable period has elapsed. Typically, this period is six times the update interval, so that the route remains in operation within all reasonable operational parameters of packet delay and loss.

TRIGGERED UPDATES AND HOLD DOWNS

Waiting for the next update interval to transmit an update that includes information relating to a link state change causes undue delays in the convergence of the protocol to a stable state following a change in topology.

A mechanism to address this is the use of *triggered updates*, in which a node that makes a change to the local routing table immediately undertakes the transmission of updates to its neighbors. The objective with this measure is to ensure that changes caused by topology shifts within the network are rapidly promulgated throughout the network, and, as the count to infinity cannot be completely eliminated by split horizon and poison reverse, to attempt to get the count completed as quickly as possible.

Hold downs are used to prevent the rapid fluctuation of a routing table entry between available and unavailable. After a route has been removed from the routing table (or in effect, after the metric of the route has reached the infinity value), the route will be marked for a further fixed interval as being down, irrespective of any updates that may occur within this interval. This mechanism also assists in the prevention of some of the circumstances which trigger the count to infinity problem, in that if the problem is caused by a route withdrawal within the potential loop, the loop interval where the count is happening must be greater than the hold-down time in order for the loop to become established. In conjunction with poison reverse, if a router loses its primary route and then receives a poison reverse from a neighbor, the poison reverse will cause the route to be placed in a hold-down state.

RIP, Version 1

This terminology for the RIP protocol is perhaps somewhat revisionist, in that RIP was never qualified with a version number until version 2 was developed, but as it is necessary to distinguish the two versions, we refer to the original version of RIP as *RIP, Version 1* here.

RIP, Version 1 is documented in RFC 1058 by Charles Hedrick [RFC 1058]. The protocol is aligned well to the generic description of distance vector protocol operation as described. The protocol remains in common use, despite the IETF moving the protocol description to the status of historic. The default values of the RIP protocol actions are as follows:

- ◆ RIP updates are sent every 30 seconds.
- ◆ The update timer is set to 180 seconds.

- Hold-down time is commonly set to 240 seconds.
- *Infinity* is set to the metric of 16 or higher, so that valid distances within RIP are from 1 to 15.

RIP, Version 1 is a class-based routing protocol, as masks are not carried within address prefixes within the protocol. The address prefix value is used to generate a class-based mask.

Within this structure of class-based routing, the major design issue is one of subnet management. RIP, Version 1 assumes that the subnet mask of a class-based network value is a constant value throughout the network, and that the local subnet mask used on local interfaces can be used to compute routes for all subnet routing entries. The algorithm first separates the network part from the subnet + host part, using a class-based mask. If the subnet + host part is null, then RIP, Version 1 assumes that this refers to the entire network. Otherwise, the subnet + host part is split, using a subnet mask derived from the mask used on local interfaces within this same network. If the host part is null, then RIP, Version 1 assumes that the route refers to a subnet; otherwise RIP, Version 1 assumes that the route refers to a host route. Subnet routes are only advertised to interfaces, which are addressed within the same network; otherwise, only the network route is advertised, using a metric of 0 indicating that the network is locally reachable.

RIP, Version 2

Within the increasing deployment of classless routing protocols, and the complementary move to adopt a policy of allocation of addresses within a classless structure, RIP, Version 1 was showing some signs of its age in attempting to manage within a classless environment. Even if the local network's used address space were aligned on class-based boundaries, the use of classless address prefixes in other parts of the network may impact into the local environment, and the use of RIP, Version 1 is really suitable only in very controlled circumstances. It is certainly not an option for an ISP to support the interior network routing environment.

RIP, Version 2 is a reasonably compatible upgrade to the version 1 specification, which adds support for classless network addresses into the RIP protocol. The effort was intended to address the observation that while RIP is a very commonly deployed routing protocol, its inability to support a classless routing environment was a matter of serious concern. RIP, Version 2 uses one of the previously unused per-network fields in the RIP packet format to carry a network mask and a next-hop address per network entry. Also, protocol header fields that were previously zero were assigned to carry a routing domain selector and a route tag attribute. The packet extravagance of RIP, Version 1 is certainly remarkable. To carry a 32-bit network address and a metric that was no more than the value 16, the packet format reserved 128 bits, which is some 91 bits more than could be achieved in a tightly compressed format.

The use of the address plus mask in the network descriptor field of the protocol packet allows RIP, Version 2 to carry classless routes within the protocol. In a homogenous RIP, Version 2 environment, this is adequate to allow the protocol to participate within a classless address environment. The next hop field, as well as the addition of a routing domain flag, allows multiple autonomous domains to use a common local broadcast network, and the route tag field allows routes learned by an exterior routing protocol to have their external attribute preserved.

The other major change to RIP, Version 2 is the introduction of authentication into the routing protocol. RIP, Version 1 listened to UDP port 520 without qualification, and any adjacent host sending packets to port 520 of a router would be configured into the routing environment as a peer router. The authentication field allows the route exchange to be predicated by the successful transmission of an authentication field. This is admittedly not the most robust mechanism of protecting the routing environment but is certainly an improvement over the simple trust model used by RIP, Version 1.

Why ISPs Should Not Use RIP

In spite of these improvements in RIP, Version 2, a number of critical shortfalls of the RIP protocol still make it a very poor choice of interior routing protocols for an ISP.

As the number of networks in the route table increases, the number of UDP packets to carry the router's forwarding table to its neighbors increases. Each entry in the routing table takes 16 bytes. To carry a full routing table of 55,000 routes would take 880,000 bytes. A bandwidth of 235Kbps is needed to ensure that the table can be transmitted within 30 seconds, and this bandwidth overhead would need to be extracted from every single link within the RIP routing domain. The conclusion is that RIP simply does not scale to serve large networks.

RIP also causes a UDP packet storm in that the default implementation generally sends its forwarding table as a sequence of back-to-back UDP datagrams. Where a high-capacity router is sending to a lower-speed router, the smaller router is more likely to exhaust its input resources, causing a loss of connectivity. Large routing systems using RIP need to carefully manage the interpacket delay of RIP updates to ensure that all the routers can manage the RIP update load, while at the same time, ensuring that the process completes within 30 seconds, to allow the next update to be processed. Also, RIP has no form of acknowledgment, in that the receiver cannot understand whether the lack of an update for a network entry is due to transient network factors of delay or drop, or whether the entry has now been removed from the sender's routing table, and no further updates are forthcoming. RIP also cannot be deployed in arbitrarily complex network topologies. The infinity metric of 16 limits the diameter of the network to no more than 15 hops.

RIP also has no knowledge of link capacity. RIP, in its basic form, assumes that every link adds a cost of one unit and makes no distinction between a 45-Mbps T3 connection and a 33.6-Kbps dial link. The metric space is also sparse enough that any attempt to create a number of link costs, which are bandwidth-related, has a savage effect on the allowable diameter of the network.

RIP is also prone to induced resonance, in which a number of routers start to work in synchronization, sending updates at the same time. This not only causes a periodic traffic surge across the network but also causes a periodic surge in router processor usage. As the network grows and the number of routes held within the network grows, this problem becomes more evident to network quality, where the 30-second synchronized routing load causes elevated delay and even packet drop. The RIP update interval needs to be allowed to randomly vary between 15 and 45 seconds to break this pattern. This decision, if adopted by the network operator, forces the routing updates to be transferred within a 15-second interval, which is a limiting factor in the number of routes that can be carried within a RIP network.

RIP is a protocol that is simple to set up, but the operational aspects are simply too significant to make this protocol useful within the ISP environment.

IGRP

In the late 1980s, the choice of an internal routing protocol was effectively limited to RIP, and the networks were growing to the size where RIP's limitations were painfully obvious. IGRP was Cisco Systems' response to these demands for a more capable routing protocol. Like RIP, IGRP is a distance vector protocol that carries class-based routing information. Unlike RIP, IGRP is a proprietary protocol and is not available on a wide range of vendor equipment.

The refinements to the RIP protocol include a lower default update interval, extending the period to 90 seconds, but the major refinements lie elsewhere in the protocol. One of the major changes is the link metric. Where RIP uses a unitary metric, IGRP uses a combination of four basic link metrics:

♦ A 24-bit delay (D) value, measured in units of 10^{-5} seconds. This encompasses link delays that range from 10 microseconds to 167 seconds.

♦ A 24-bit bandwidth (B) value, measured using an inverse scale of 10^7 / link speed in Kbps. This maps to data rates from some 1.2Kbps through 10Gbps.

♦ An 8-bit reliability (R) value, expressing the probability that the packet will be delivered across the link without error, as measured by the router. The value 255 is mapped to 100 percent.

♦ An 8-bit link load (L) value, expressing an average link utilization level as measured by the router.

The metric used by IGRP can be weighted to give greater preference to any of these basic link characteristics.

The second refinement is to explicitly allow two paths of equal cost to be used by a router in a round-robin basis, effectively load sharing across two paths if the metrics are equal. This mechanism is provided by keeping track of alternate paths within the IGRP routing tables, a technique that also allows rapid failover to the next lowest cost link in the event of failure of the selected link. A refinement to equal cost load sharing allows the use of unequal metric load sharing, in which the load sharing is intended to distribute the load in accordance with the difference in metrics, so that if one path is twice the cost of the other, then it will be loaded with half the traffic levels of the other. This feature should be used with some caution to ensure that the alternate path selected does not loop back through this router.

IGRP's mechanism to break the count-to-infinity problem of distance vector routing protocols is based on the technique of a hold-down. Here, when a route is marked as unreachable, the route will not be reinstated by a new availability message for a period of time. The design intention is to keep this hold-down period sufficiently long to allow the original link status update to have been flooded across the network, avoiding transient states in which incorrect reachability information is passed through the network. IGRP also implements split horizon updates to prevent simple loops being created. Poison reverse is used by IGRP when a route's metric is increased by a value greater than 1, and, in conjunction with hold-down, the effect is to prevent the count-to-infinity loop from being established.

Although these refinements offer some improvements to the stability of the routing protocol over RIP, Version 1, some problems are still outstanding. These problems relate to the support of a variable subnet environment, support for the more general classless routing environment, and addressing the issue within IGRP that the mechanisms used to prevent transient count-to-infinity loops impose an extended period of outage for a route through the use of the hold-down.

EIGRP

Enhanced IGRP, or EIGRP, offers a number of refinements to the IGRP protocol to address these shortcomings and to introduce a number of additional functions. EIGRP is also a proprietary protocol of Cisco Systems. One of the major changes introduced in EIGRP is the use of a *diffusing update algorithm* (DUAL) [Garcia-Luna-Aceves 1989]. This algorithm is intended to remove transient loops within the routing space, by undertaking different behaviors when the best path metric to a destination is decreased as compared to when the update attempts to increase the metric. If the update attempts to decrease the metric associated with the best path, the update is immediately accepted. If the update attempts to increase the metric associated with the best path, the router will look for an adjacent router with a best path metric lower than that of the router generating the update and use that path. If no such adjacent router exists, the router will hold its routing table in a fixed state while undertaking a so-called diffusion process. This process involves querying all adjacent routers, with the exception of the router providing the update, providing the proposed new metric to the destination, and requesting a response of the path metric as seen by this router. If the adjacent router can use a path that is not passing through the querying router, then the router will respond immediately; otherwise, it has to hold the routing table and initiate its own diffusion query in order to respond to the original query.

The diffusion process requires each router to maintain the path metrics of each neighbor, and to ensure that the algorithm operates reliably, the updates must be sequenced and positively acknowledged. Given that updates are acknowledged, there is no requirement for periodic full updates, and the result is that updates are generated only in response to events that alter a path metric and are bounded in terms of promulgation to where a path change is necessary.

Attempts to correct the deficiencies of the earlier distance vector protocol implementation have not been without impact on the simplicity of the protocol's operation. The router must maintain the current state of all neighbors' distance vector tables, which is a comparable overhead to maintaining the link state database within a link state protocol. The protocol is a functional peer of a link state protocol like OSPF. The decision for an ISP to use EIGRP, or any other interior routing protocol, is normally a technical evaluation of the suitability of EIGRP against other routing protocols within the intended operational environment. For EIGRP the evaluation is as much an issue of determining whether it is acceptable for the network to use a proprietary protocol as any technical factor. The choice of a proprietary protocol may imply some restriction on the choice of vendor of routing equipment used by the ISP.

A Review of Distance Vector Protocols

Distance vector protocols rely on a model in which local topology descriptions are processed as they flood outwards. From any segment of the network, the routes that emanate from the segment are the shortest paths within the segment. This can be viewed as a distributed serial processing environment, in which calculating the complete set of shortest paths across the entire network requires each component to perform shortest path selection and then flood these selected paths to all adjacent components. This process is iterative, which does not have an explicit completion signal. A complete collection of shortest paths is not derived immediately, but after a process of iteration in which the boundaries of local discovery of shortest paths are progressively widened until a coherent topology is discovered and each local table is configured to be aligned to this topology. There is no indication of when this process completes within the algorithm, and the promulgation of updates is prone to long delays. Meanwhile, updates flood across the diameter of the network while any count-to-infinity loops are exhausted and while any holddown timer is in effect. While the routing protocol is in an intermediate state, the forwarding tables may contain incorrect information, and traffic may be misdirected and delayed or lost.

Link State Protocols

The alternative approach is to use a simultaneous computation, where, in the steady state of operation, a change of link status is rapidly flooded, and every router simultaneously computes a new forwarding table using the same algorithm and the same set of link metrics.

Each router maintains a description of the locally connected links. This link table is periodically flooded throughout the network using a flooding algorithm. Any change in link status is immediately flashed through the network as a link status update. When a link status update is received, the local copy of the link is updated, and an SPF algorithm is applied to the link database. This algorithm discovers the shortest path from this node to all other nodes, using a commonly defined administrative set of metrics. Given that each node is using the same link state database, the outcome of the SPF algorithm within each router yields a consistent set of forwarding tables. The size of the computation is of the order of the number of nodes.

The basic operation of a link state protocol is relatively simple:

1. Each router learns the identity of all adjacent routers.
2. Each router constructs a message containing the identity and cost of the link to each neighbor. This message is termed a Link State Packet (LSP) in IS-IS or a Link State Advertisement (LSA) in OSPF.

Two major link state protocols have been deployed in operational networks: the Intermediate System to Intermediate System protocol (IS-IS) and the Open Shortest Path First protocol (OSPF). Not surprisingly, these two efforts often used different terminology to describe the same concept. Here, we will use the term LSA as a generic term for a flooded link status message and indicate specifically when one protocol or the other is being referred to.

3. The LSA is flooded to all routers in the network.
4. Each router saves the most recent LSA from every other router.
5. Each router now has a complete description of the current topology of the network and can now compute shortest routes.

The algorithm used in this computation is the Shortest Path First selection algorithm, as described by E. W. Dijkstra [Dijkstra 1959].

Neighbor discovery is undertaken by means of a Hello protocol. This protocol is a packet exchange, which ensures that each router reliably tracks the status of all adjacent neighbors and uses a set of agreed timers for polling intervals. Additional fields are used for LAN configurations, where, to reduce

Edsger W. Dijkstra was a professor of mathematics at Eindhoven University of Technology in the 1960s and worked as a research fellow with Burroughs Corporation in the 1970s. In 1984, Dijkstra left the Netherlands to accept the Schlumberger Centennial Chair in the Department of Computer Sciences at the University of Texas at Austin. Dijkstra published papers on many aspects of the computer programming field. Most notably (for network engineers, at any rate), Dijkstra, in 1959, formulated what now is commonly referred as the Dijkstra algorithm, *which is a single-source, shortest-path algorithm that computes all shortest paths from a single point of reference based on a collection of link metrics.*

the potential complexity, one LAN-attached router is configured as the designated router and that device maintains the status of the LAN as a special link.

A router generates an LSA periodically, as well as in response to the discovery of a new neighbor, a link, when a neighbor changes state from up to down or vice versa, or when a link metric changes value. An LSA contains four fields, as indicated in Figure 6.14. The source identifier is the router identifier generating the packet. The sequence number and age field are used in the flooding distribution algorithm. The list of neighbors is used in the shortest path calculation.

The flooding distribution algorithm is one that has been refined considerably since the initial ARPANET Link State algorithm of the early 1980s, in

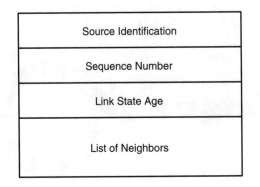

Figure 6.14   The link state advertisement.

order to make this most critical part of the algorithm more robust. Updates must be flooded quickly, but equally important, to ensure that the network does not revert to a state of uncontrolled flooding of bad information.

The sequence number is a large linear number space (at least 32 bits) with two possible uses of this number space. Within OSPF, the number space uses a *lollipop sequence space*, in which the number range varies from $-N + 1$ to 0 using a normal comparison and from 0 to $N - 2$ using a circular comparison: If two OSPF LSA sequence numbers a and b, are both positive, and b is greater than a, then if $(b - a) < ((N - 1)/2)$, b is *circularly greater* than a; otherwise, a is *circularly greater* than b. This is indicated in Figure 6.15. IS-IS uses a simple linear number space, and when two IS-IS LSPs are compared, the one with the greater LSA is considered the most recent. LSAs expire after a certain amount of time (typically configured as one hour).

In OSPF, the age field is initially set to 0 and is incremented on forwarding. The age field is incremented by one every second while being held in memory. When the age field reaches *Max Age* (typically one hour), the record is considered retired, and is not used in the SPF calculation. In IS-IS the age field is set to an initial TTL of one hour. The age field is decremented before the LSP is forwarded, and also decremented at regular intervals while it remains current. When a router expires an LSP, it floods the 0-valued LSP to commence the purging of the LSP. In either case, as the link state record ages out only after one hour, the periodic update of a link state record to ensure it remains current need only happen within intervals also of one hour.

When a router is booted, it can commence flooding LSAs with an initial sequence number of 0. If any LSAs from the router are still active, the receipt of the new LSA causes a reflooding of the old LSA. When this is received at the originating router, the router increments its sequence number to a value greater than the old LSA and refloods the update.

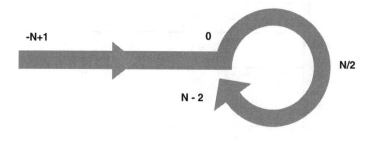

Figure 6.15 The lollipop sequence space.

The Dijkstra algorithm operates over the most recent LSA from every router. The algorithm uses three sets, one for the set of evaluated routers (or nodes), and the remainder of the nodes are placed in the other set. A set of currently unevaluated paths is stored in set P. The algorithm operates as follows:

1. The set of evaluated nodes, E, is initially set to contain the local source node S. All other nodes are placed in the other set, R. The set of paths, P, is initialized to the set of links from S. P is sorted in order of increasing metric.

2. If P is empty, mark all remaining nodes in R as unreachable and terminate the algorithm.

3. Select the first (shortest) path in P and add the final node, N, to set E if N is not already in E. Add the path cost (S, N) to all paths originating from N and add these new paths to P.

4. Sort P by increasing path cost and loop at step 2.

This algorithm is perhaps best viewed by looking at its operation in the same example network used in the distance vector metric analysis, in which the link costs are as given in Figure 6.16.

The operation of the algorithm is indicated in Figure 6.17. At each step, the shortest path is selected, and all adjacent hops to the selected node are added into the consideration set. When the consideration set is empty, the forwarding table can be generated.

Link state protocols offer rapid loopless convergence because the network does not transition through intermediate states when a partial update to the

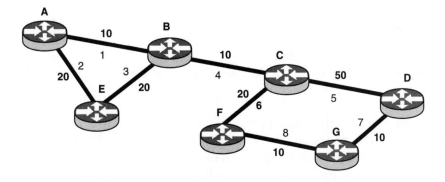

Figure 6.16   Link state network.

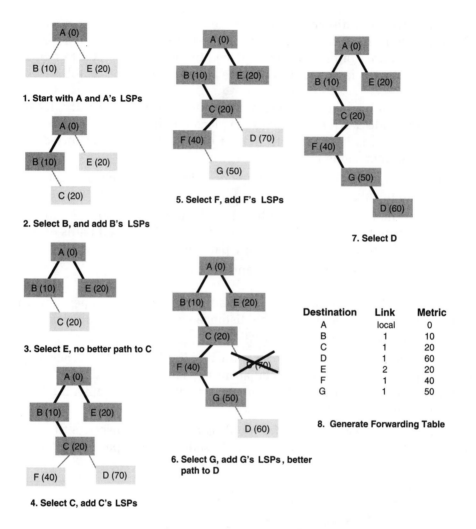

Figure 6.17 Operation of the link state algorithm.

topology occurs. In a link state protocol, you do not need to undertake a count to infinity or hold-down updates in an intermediate state. The outcome of the link state calculation is a new loop-free topology. Link state protocols support a much greater potential metric range without altering the time to undertake the computation across the topology, and theoretically, using a number of different metrics applied to the same base topology is possible. Therefore, routing decisions may be undertaken based on various quality-of-service attributes, such as delay, available throughout, or reliability. However, quality-of-service metrics have never been deployed in any significant sense in the Internet to date. The issues preventing this include ensuring that the varying views of the metrics create local topologies, which are consistent with the larger Internet environment, and that each packet can be matched unambiguously with a particular metric.

OSPF

OSPF is a relatively standard link state protocol, using neighbor discovery, a distributed link database, and LSA flooding. OSPF allows external routes that are learned in our routing domains to be transported across the OSPF routing domain.

One of the issues with link state algorithms is to identify a stable and consistent behavior in non-link-based networks. Broadcast networks, such as Ethernet, Token Ring, FDDI, or radio networks, with multiple attached routers, present a particular problem to a link state protocol, because if N routers are connected to the network, $N^2 - N$ directional adjacencies are in the link state database. OSPF attempts to reduce the number of adjacencies by electing a designated router (DR) for the broadcast network. All routers initiate an adjacency with this DR. The DR announces the links on the network by representing the LAN as a virtual router with N adjacencies, as indicated in Figure 6.18.

For resiliency, the election of a DR also elects a Backup Designated Router (BDR), and all routers initiate an adjacency with the BDR as well as the DR. If the DR fails, the BDR can announce the network adjacencies, so that the time to resume the announcements is minimized, and the impact of the change to the remainder of the network is minimized.

OSPF also supports the concept of external routes, which are passed into the OSPF routing domain by a border router. Of course, if the OSPF routing domain has just one external border, it would be more efficient to announce a default route into the OSPF routing domain and not pass the external routes. This is useful only when there are multiple border routers, and the OSPF domain is required to make an efficient choice of the minimal cost exterior gateway. The border router can initialize the metric of the external route to a metric that reflects the cost of the external route and then pass these external

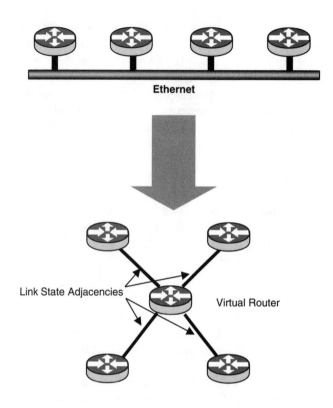

Link State Adjacencies

Virtual Router

Figure 6.18 A virtual router LAN in OSPF.

routes into the network using *gateway link state records*. These routes are then promulgated through the network and are used by OSPF to assist in the selection of an optimal border router to reach an external destination. The external routes can carry a tag field, which can carry some form of identification of the external origin of the route. Care should be taken in injecting large sets of external routes into OSPF, as implications are reflected in memory usage in the OSPF tables in each router.

The major issue of link state databases, and OSPF is no exception, is that of scaling into management of complex and dynamic topologies. The most effective response to such pressures is to use a structure of routing that matches a general logical structure of connectivity. The typical structure of connectivity for large networks is the use of a backbone network and a set of local distribution systems. This situation has a direct analogy within OSPF, which uses the concept of a *backbone area*. The backbone area is effectively the common backbone core of the network and a set of a connected regions, which are simple *areas*. An *area* in OSPF is a contained flooding domain where flooding of LSAs is limited to area boundaries and all Shortest Path First computation is undertaken within the confines of the area. Each interface of every router is a member of a single area. A router may have all interfaces contained within the same OSPF area, in which case the router is termed an *interior router*. To allow the network to link these OSPF areas together, a number of routers must belong in two or more areas. The router may have interfaces in different OSPF areas, in which case the router is termed an *area border router*, as indicated in Figure 6.19.

Interface link state messages within OSPF manage this hierarchical concept. Per-interface LSAs are flooded by a router to all interfaces on the router that share the area of which the interface is a member, and the router collects all LSAs that describe the state and cost of every link within the area to undertake per-area SPF calculations. Area border routers also generate *summary record* messages for all routes announced within other areas and pass these into the area. In Figure 6.20, area border router R1 generates summary records for areas 0 and 2 and announces these into area 1 and then generates summary records for areas 1 and 3, and announces them into area 0.

Area 0 is always the *backbone area*. This backbone area has a special and exclusive role in supporting connectivity between all other OSPF areas, as OSPF uses a strict two-level hierarchy of area connectivity. All areas should

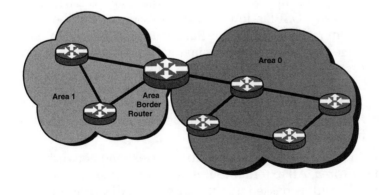

Figure 6.19   Areas in OSPF.

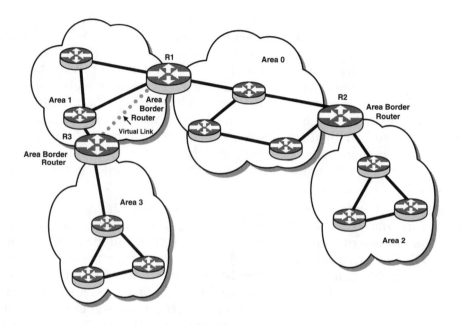

Figure 6.20 Area border routers.

maintain connectivity with area 0 through the deployment of a common area border router. OSPF does allow for an exception to this through the use of manually configured virtual links, which link an area border router to a backbone-connected area border router, as indicated in the R3–R1 link in Figure 6.20. This model manages to cope with split areas that maintain backbone connectivity relatively easily. OSPF allows the area to segment and become two logical areas for the duration of the split. Backbone splitting is more challenging for the protocol to handle and requires manually configured virtual links to be tunneled across an area to repair the break. Such a configuration is indicated in Figure 6.21. When designing an OSPF network, one area has to be configured as the backbone area. Good design practice indicates that a network should start with all routers configured into area 0 and then expand into other areas on the basis of growth.

An area with a single router gateway to the backbone network can be represented by a *stub area*. All external routes are summarized into a single default route, and this default is passed into the stub area. All OSPF routes from other areas are still passed into the stub area as summary routes. Some vendors' implementations, notably Cisco's, implement an extension of *totally stubby*

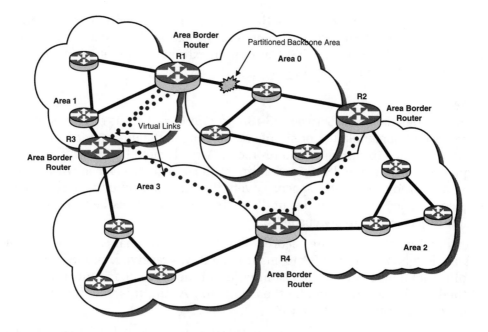

Figure 6.21 Repairing backbone area partition.

areas, in which all external routes and all summary routes are condensed into a single default route, and the only routes present within the area are area-local routes. OSPF also supports *not so stubby areas* [RFC 1587] in which certain external routes can be imported into the area, and other external links are summarized as a default route.

OSPF also supports *on-demand circuits* [RFC 1793], in which periodic hellos are suppressed, and the periodic refreshes of link state advertisements are not flooded over the on-demand circuit. These packets bring up the circuit only when they are exchanged for the first time or when a change occurs, but otherwise, the circuit can be closed while the topology remains stable and there is no data traffic.

In terms of design guidelines with OSPF, configuring 40 to 50 routers per area is a good upper limit. More can be added to the area, but the risk of instability does increase. Where multiple LANs with interconnecting routers are present, care should be taken to ensure that the same router does not get elected as the designated router on every connected LAN. In the same fashion, avoid loading a router with more than four or five area border routing functions. The Internet routing table contains in excess of 50,000 entries. It is unwise to inject this into an OSPF area as an external route set, as the memory demands will be overwhelming.

IS-IS

Many similarities exist between IS-IS and OSPF, and what differs is often a difference of nomenclature or simple reshuffling of the bits rather than significant difference in design of the protocol. Already noted is the difference in sequence space, where IS-IS uses a direct linear sequence space while OSPF uses a lollipop sequence space. Given that the periodicity of the linear sequence space is of the order of 60 years, the differences between the two number spaces are largely cosmetic.

In flooding the link state records, OSPF uses a mechanism of a positive acknowledgment of each LSA to ensure that it was received, and IS-IS uses an implicit acknowledgment via examination of the sequence number of copies of the LSP that are received by the originator. Again, this falls into the relatively cosmetic area of difference.

Perhaps the most visible difference is in the use of areas. First, there is a difference in nomenclature. In IS-IS the *area 0* backbone area is referred to as the *Level 2 network*, and the other *areas* of OSPF are referred to as *Level 1 networks* in IS-IS. More significantly, IS-IS Level 1 networks are managed in an analogous fashion to *totally stubby areas* of OSPF. Accordingly, in IS-IS, packets destined to nonlocal addresses are forwarded to the closest Level 2 boundary router, rather than being able to use additional information to allow the packet to be forwarded to an area boundary router that lies on the shortest path to the destination.

The second area of difference is in the size of the metrics used to describe each link. OSPF uses a 16-bit field, and IS-IS uses a 6-bit field. For complex topologies in which there is a desire to establish a system of primary paths and a set of potential backup paths, this limited metric set of 31 discrete values may prove insufficient. However, the differences between the two protocols are not that great. Although the majority of ISP networks use OSPF as their IGP, some large ISP networks use IS-IS very successfully.

A Review of Link State Protocols

The major issues that affect distance vector protocols within the Internet environment are largely addressed by link state protocols. In looking at OSPF, note that it offers the following capabilities to the network engineer:

- No limitation on the hop count within the network
- No restriction on the use of variable length subnet masks, nor on the application of classless address deployment
- OSPF uses multicast to send the link state updates, ensuring that the updates are directed to relevant listeners.
- Routing updates are sent only when changes occur. The periodic update period is extended from 30 seconds as the default RIP update interval to one hour in OSPF.
- OSPF (and indeed any link state protocol) will converge quickly.
- OSPF can calculate a collection of paths of equal or similar metric and allow the router to subsequently load-balance.
- OSPF (and IS-IS) includes explicit use of routing hierarchies to limit the span of the link state domains.

Although a distance vector routing protocol is often easier to set up, it generally does not produce an accurate, readily manageable, and highly stable routing environment. Link state routing protocols take more effort in the initial design to ensure that the network is sensibly partitioned into routing areas. The size of each area in terms of number of links and number of routing entries is within the processing and memory capabilities of the routers. After this initial design work is undertaken, a link state routing protocol offers greater stability, with almost immediate convergence to backup paths in the event of component failure. With a richer metric space, the network engineer has a greater ability to represent various path characteristics with precision.

The Operation of Exterior Routing Protocols

Routing the entire Internet via a single instance of an interior routing protocol is not possible. The network is simply too large to promulgate detailed local structure and its dynamic behavior to all parts of the network, nor is it necessary to do so. There is no requirement to make local changes in the next hop decision for any given destination, given some change in topology of some remote network, and the network will benefit in terms of stability of operation by bounding the promulgation of local topology changes. In effect, this bounds the scope of operation of each instance of an IGP, and to connect these together, the network uses exterior gateway protocols.

*E*GP is both an abbreviation of a generic exterior routing protocol and the name of an exterior routing protocol that was widely deployed prior to the common adoption of BGP. In this book, we adopt the conventional use of the term EGP as a generic exterior routing protocol.

EGPs do not have to carry topology information across the network, but they do carry reachability information and associated policy information and have to manage very large reachability data sets. An EGP is an interautonomous system routing protocol.

Autonomous Systems

The model used in the Internet to implement this hierarchy is termed an *Autonomous System* (AS). While we've been using this term for some time already, it's now an appropriate point to provide a more detailed definition, as the AS is an integral part of the EGP routing environment. An AS is a bounded, internally connected segment of the Internet that has a single exterior routing policy.

*S*ome definitions of an AS include the operation of a single technical and managerial domain that spans the AS; however, in a routing sense, which is where the AS is most prevalent, this definition is not relevant, nor it is necessarily that accurate a characterization.

The exterior view of an AS is an area of the network whose interior details are masked, which announces to its adjacent AS a collection of destination network addresses reachable within that AS. The announcement has a single associated policy applied to all routes within the AS announcement. The AS also may announce its capability to act in a transit capacity on behalf of other autonomous systems. Each AS has an identifying label, which is a unique 16-bit value, normally assigned by the relevant Regional Internet Registry. Routing between autonomous systems does not refer to dynamic topology changes within each AS, but instead refers to reachability of network addresses, and the dynamic behavior is the addition and withdrawal of such addresses in the bilateral peering. Each AS can operate its IGP as an independent routing domain. A number of generic characterizations of AS configurations have routing implications for BGP, described in the following sections.

Single-Homed Stub AS

A single-homed stub AS has a single exterior connection to an upstream provider AS. In stub configuration, it is not necessary to operate a BGP session between the two domains, because routing independence can be achieved through the use of a synthesized default route within the stub AS (pointing the default route to the provider AS), and for the provider AS to use a set of static routers describing the routers within the stub AS. BGP may be used as an alternative to such static route configurations where there is a large set of routes to maintain and the operational overhead of such static route management is cumbersome. Stub autonomous systems do not normally qualify for a Registry-allocated AS number, and when the use of BGP is desired, the provider typically assigns the stub AS an AS number from the private AS pool (AS 65412–AS 65535) for use in these situations. In this configuration, the routes learned by the provider AS would be mapped back into the provider's IGP and announced to external peers as part of the provider's local routes with the provider's AS as the originating AS. A single-homed stub AS is indicated in Figure 6.22.

Multihomed Stub AS

If the stub AS purchases access services from more than one provider AS, then the AS is said to be *multihomed*, as its routes are announced by multiple autonomous systems. The use of the term *stub* here is retained to indicate that the AS does not provide connectivity services to any entity outside of the bounds of the AS, and it advertises only those routes associated with its AS to its providers. It is not strictly necessary to operate an EGP across the AS peering session, although this will introduce some significant complications for the AS in determining capacity and reachability policy. The AS cannot use a simple exterior default exit path in this configuration, as there are multiple exterior paths. The AS must make some form of policy decision as to which exterior provider to use, and under what circumstances for outgoing packets. The AS may want to specify a simple primary default path and use the other upstream provider as a backup default path. If the AS wants to undertake some form of load-balancing across all the connections, the AS must import routes from the upstream autonomous systems and then manipulate the preference associated with these routes in order to implement an outgoing traffic

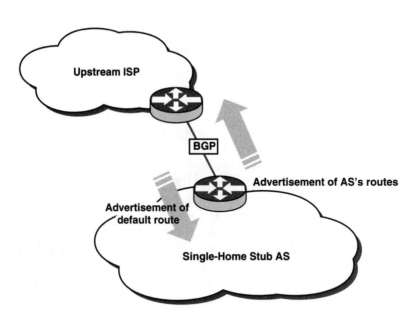

Figure 6.22 A single-homed stub AS.

policy. Similarly, the AS should advertise its routes to all upstream autonomous systems and use BGP policy mechanisms to bias incoming traffic
flows to match the desired connection policy. A multihomed stub AS configuration is indicated in Figure 6.23.

Multihomed Transit AS

A multihomed transit AS has multiple AS connections, and, unlike the stub
AS, it also provides transit services for some or all of the adjacent autonomous
systems. This transit service allows an AS to reach a nonadjacent AS via this
network, using the local network purely in a transit capacity. This environment presents similar issues to that of the multihomed stub AS in terms of
management of routes. The AS must undertake routing exchanges with each
of its neighbors in a manner that is mutually agreed and must publish its transit policies in a way that other providers can utilize. The transit AS should, as
permitted, announce routes learned from one AS to all other autonomous systems and ensure that the integrity of the route announcements is preserved.
The transit AS does need to be designed carefully to ensure that external
routes are carried on the transit component of the network, and other areas of

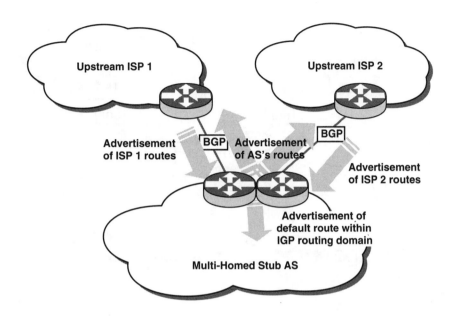

Figure 6.23 A multihomed stub AS.

the network use simpler IGP structures with an associated default routing arrangement to reach the transit core. Normally, a transit AS will have dispersed exterior connections, so such autonomous systems typically include iBGP in their BGP configuration to link these external gateways to each other. A multihomed transit AS configuration is indicated in Figure 6.24.

BGP

Although a number of protocols have undertaken this function, the current protocol used across the Internet is the Border Gateway Protocol (BGP). BGP has undergone a number of refinements over its operational life. BGP was originally described in RFC 1105, in June 1989 [RFC 1105]. BGP-2 was described in RFC 1163 [RFC 1163], in June 1990, and BGP-3 was described in RFC 1267 in October 1991 [RFC 1267]. The current version, Version 4, was deployed on the Internet in 1993, while the RFC describing this protocol, RFC 1771, was published in March 1995 [RFC 1771]. The protocol has been stable for some years now and managed the Internet routing domain which, at the start of 1998, was of the order of 56,000 routing entries.

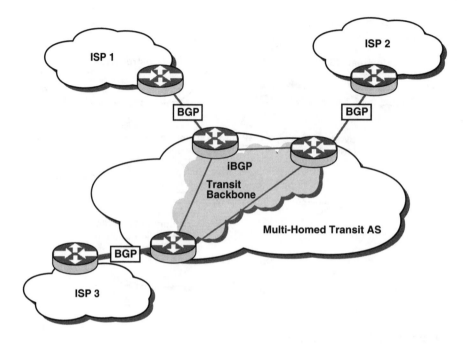

Figure 6.24   A Multihomed transit AS.

BGP binds together the concept of destination network addresses and autonomous systems into a path vector-based routing technology. Every route object represented within a BGP-4 route database carries a network address and an associated path vector of AS values, as indicated in Figure 6.25.

In Figure 6.25, AS1, originating the route to network 10.0.0.0/8 associates a path vector of AS1 with the route advertisements passed to AS2 and AS3. AS2 prepends AS2 to the routing vector and announces a route to network 10.0.0.0/8 with an associated path vector of (AS2, AS1) to its peers, AS1 and AS4, and so on. AS5 receives two announcements of 10.0.0.0/8, one with a path vector of (AS4, AS2, AS1) and the other with the path vector (AS3, AS1). AS5 then makes a policy decision as to which route path to accept. The general behavior of a BGP transit AS is to select a candidate path to use for a given destination address, prepend the local AS value to the associated path vector, and then to advertise this route, with the new vector, to its adjacent AS peers. Loops are avoided by the simple measure of refusing to accept a route object that already includes the local AS in the object's path vector. In this example,

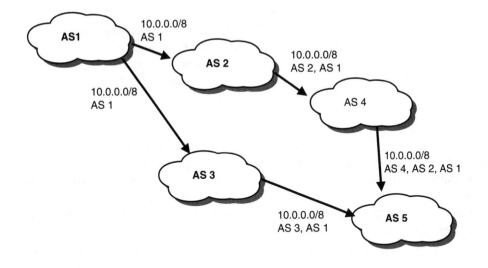

Figure 6.25   Multiple autonomous systems and AS paths.

AS1 can detect the AS2 announcement as a loop due to the fact that its AS value already appears in the path vector.

One of the most important path attributes is the AS-PATH. As reachability information traverses the Internet, this information is augmented by the list of autonomous systems that have been traversed thus far, forming the AS-PATH. The AS-PATH allows straightforward suppression of the looping of routing information. In addition, the AS-PATH serves as a powerful and versatile mechanism for policy-based routing.

BGP-4 enhances the AS-PATH attribute to include sets of autonomous systems as well as lists. This extended format allows generated aggregate routes to carry path information from the more specific routes used to generate the aggregate.

BGP uses an algorithm that cannot be classified as either a pure distance vector or a pure link state. Carrying a complete AS path in the AS-PATH attribute allows you to reconstruct large portions of the overall topology. That makes it similar to the link state algorithms. Exchanging only the currently used routes between the peers makes it similar to the distance vector algorithms.

> *To conserve bandwidth and processing power, BGP uses incremental updates, in which, after the initial exchange of complete routing information, a pair of BGP routers exchanges only changes (deltas) to that information. The technique of incremental updates requires reliable transport between a pair of BGP routers. To achieve this functionality, BGP uses TCP as its transport [RFC 1774].*

In the operation of BGP, note that many of the issues about reliable operation of the network protocol are addressed through the decision to use TCP as the platform for BGP communication. TCP is, of course, a stream protocol rather than a record-oriented protocol, so BGP uses a 16-byte marker format to delimit BGP messages. The marker is followed by a 2-byte length and a 1-byte type field, making the minimum BGP message 19 bytes.

Because the communication between the BGP routing peers is a reliable channel, the protocol can use a behavior that loads a complete routing table as part of the initial session activity and then sends incremental *updates* for the remainder of the session lifetime.

In addition to triggered *updates*, BGP uses an explicit *keepalive* message to ensure that the connection remains open. This message is sent every 60 seconds by default, and in a stable configuration without updates, BGP consumes slightly less than three bits/second to maintain the connection. BGP sessions use a *hold time* as the maximum amount of time between successive *keepalive* or *update* messages that can elapse before declaring the peering session inoperative and attempting to reinitialize the session. This value is commonly set to 180 seconds. The keepalive interval is generally set to one-third of the hold-time interval.

BGP operates via a set of update messages. Each update message contains a set of routes that are unreachable, a set of path attributes for a path, and a set of network addresses, which are associated with that set of path attributes. Path attributes are where BGP has most of its capabilities, and defined path attributes are as follows:

Origin.   Indicating whether the origin is from an IGP, via EGP (the protocol), or incomplete

AS_Path.   Describing the AS path associated with the destination

Next_Hop.   Describing the IP address of the border router to be used as the next hop to reach the listed destinations

Multi_Exit_Disc.   Multiple exit discriminator is used by the source AS to inform the target AS of a preference between multiple boundary points between the two autonomous systems.

Local_Pref.   Local preference is used to inform other BGP routers in the local AS of the originating BGP session's degree of preference for an advertised route.

Atomic_Aggregate.   Informs other BGP routers that the local system selected a less specific route without selecting a more specific route which is included in it.

Aggregator.   Indicates the last AS number that formed the aggregate route and the IP address of the BGP router within the AS.

In addition to these standard-defined path attributes are a number of additional path attributes that have been added by vendors and network operators. Of some note are the following:

Community.   Used to carry a set of locally defined attributes about a path.

Destination Preference.   Used to bias the preference of a remote AS to a particular path.

AS Paths

AS paths are normally an ordered sequence of AS values, which describe the sequence of autonomous systems that a packet must transit to reach the destination using this path. However, BGP allows the use of aggregation to combine a number of specific routing entries into a more general aggregate single routing entry that encompasses the specific routes. Within this operation, some path detail may be lost, which could admit the possibility of routing loops forming. At the point of this route aggregation, the local AS forms an initial AS path for the new route, which contains a single element, an AS set. This set is constructed by forming the union of the AS paths used in all the component route entries, and the resulting set is an unordered collection of AS values.

Figure 6.26 indicates AS4 aggregating the route 10.1.0.0/17 originating within AS1 with the path (AS2, AS1) with a second route, 10.1.128.0/17, originating within AS3 with the path (AS3). The resulting AS path of the aggregate route, 10.1.0.0/16, is the union of these two paths, {AS1, AS2, AS3}, and the path advertised to AS5 is (AS4, {AS1, AS2, AS3}).

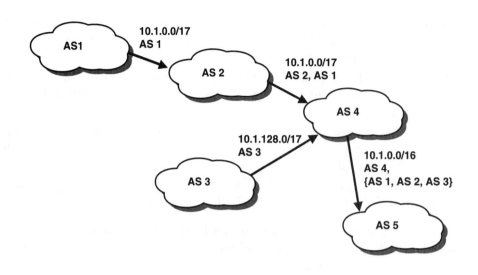

Figure 6.26 Aggregating routers and AS sets.

iBGP and eBGP Multihop

The most straightforward method of connecting two boundary BGP routers is via a direct physical connection between the two devices. This connection can be a point-to-point circuit, or it can take the form of a peering across a local broadcast network. The latter is the common case for Internet exchanges and similar peering constructs.

This connection is not always possible to achieve, for configurations in which the external connection is load-shared over a number of parallel circuits or in which intervening routers are not boundary BGP routers. In such situations, vendor-specific extensions are provided with the Cisco implementation of BGP, which allow the use of a multihop IP connection between the two boundary routers. This configuration is indicated in Figure 6.27.

iBGP

The preceding configurations are termed eBGP and eBGP multihop (external BGP), to distinguish these from iBGP (internal BGP). In a simple stub AS configuration, there is a single exterior boundary router that supports all eBGP sessions. The interior routing protocol directs a default route to this boundary point. Such a configuration can support simple transit between the two external autonomous systems across the boundary router.

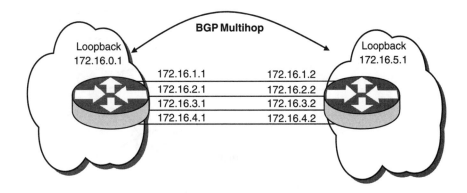

Figure 6.27 eBGP multihop.

However, if the external connections are terminated in separate boundary routers, and the AS is a transit AS, the destination routes and associated path attributes must be passed between the two boundary routers. Using a redistribution of the routes into an interior routing protocol will cause the path attributes to be discarded, so the only alternative is to set up an internal peering between the two boundary routers. Such an internal BGP session is termed an *iBGP session*. No particular distinction exists between directly connected and multihop iBGP configurations. A typical application of iBGP is indicated in Figure 6.28.

Sound network design dictates that redistribution of externally learned routes into the local IGP is most unwise. Accordingly, it is good sense to use iBGP as a mechanism to carry exterior-routing information along all transit paths between external boundary router peers within the same AS. A default route should be injected into the interior routing system from the backbone transit-path routers, and the interior routing system can undertake the redistribution of this default route to the lower portions of the network hierarchy. In this way, packets bound for destinations not found in the interior-routing table are forwarded automatically to the backbone, where a recursive route lookup would reveal the appropriate destination (found in the BGP table) and forwarding path for the destination. At this point, internal traffic can use the exterior-routing information to make a more informed decision on how to forward traffic bound for external destinations. This deliberate omission of redistribution of BGP routes into the interior routing domain also allows for a higher degree of routing stability.

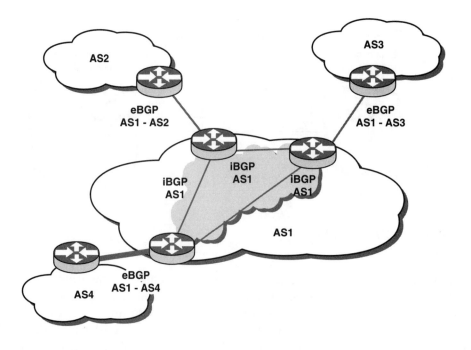

Figure 6.28 iBGP configuration.

The path vector construct is inadequate to detect routing loops that may arise across the iBGP sessions within the AS, so there is a simple restriction on iBGP that addresses this: Routes learned via an iBGP peer session are not advertised to other iBGP peers. The corollary of this constraint is that every BGP router must form a 1:1 iBGP peering session with every other BGP router within the AS. That is, all BGP speakers within a network must directly iBGP peer with all other BGP speakers.

This requirement for an N^2 peering mesh leads to one of the major scaling issues with autonomous systems and BGP. This mesh of BGP peering sessions can exceed the capabilities of the component routers, and when the iBGP mesh becomes sufficiently large, then alternative iBGP structures should be deployed. Quantifying *large* can be difficult and can vary depending on the characteristics of the network. The network operator should monitor the resources on routers on an ongoing basis to determine whether scaling the iBGP mesh is starting to become a problem.

To address this BGP load, it is necessary to introduce some refinements to the configuration of iBGP. The most effective method is to introduce *iBGP route reflectors*, which dilute the strict requirement for a complete mesh of peering sessions. The typical deployment structure is to create a small iBGP core mesh and configure these core iBGP routers as route reflectors. Other iBGP peers are configured as local reflector clients from the closest core reflector. Alternatively, the AS can be internally segmented into a number of sub-autonomous systems (typically using AS values from the private AS number space) with a BGP confederation to create the external appearance of a single AS. This segmentation may have implications for any nontransitive path attributes that may be deployed, and it is less disruptive to use iBGP route reflectors as the mechanism to address iBGP scale issues. These configurations are indicated in Figure 6.29.

BGP Synchronization

Where there are multiple BGP boundary routers in a transit AS, the BGP advertisements must be synchronized to the IGP within the AS. Figure 6.30 indicates that AS1 learns the route 10.0.0.0/8 from AS2. This router is learned

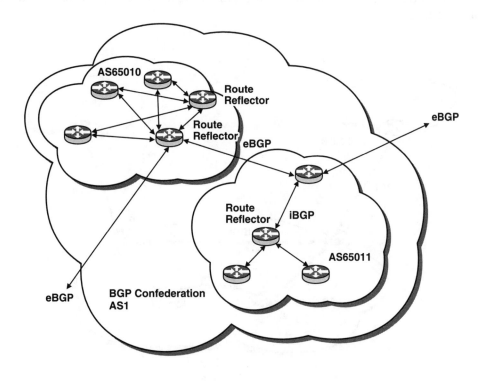

Figure 6.29   iBGP route reflectors and BGP confederations.

at boundary router A. If AS1 is acting as a transit for AS2, then this router will be passed via the iBGP session from router A to router B, which will announce the route to AS3. When AS3 passes a packet addressed to a host within network 10.0.0.0/8, router B will pass the packet towards router A, and from the IGP, will learn that the first hop towards A is via E. As E is not participating in any iBGP sessions, it has no route to this address and will discard the packet.

In this situation, A should inject the routes learned from AS2 into AS1's IGP, Router B should wait until E redistributes the routes to B via the IGP before announcing the routes to AS3 via the eBGP session. Thus, the interior routing protocol promulgation of the route is synchronized with the TCP-based iBGP route update.

As a cautionary note, redistribution of exterior routes into the interior routing protocol should be avoided whenever possible. Rather than burden the IGP with the massive load of carrying a large external route set, design a transit backbone and link the routers on this backbone using iBGP. In this way, redistribution of external routes into the interior routing protocol can be avoided.

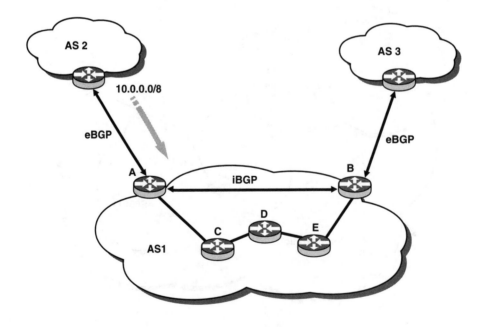

Figure 6.30 iBGP route synchronization.

BGP Route Selection Process and Routing Policies

The base BGP route selection process is to prefer a path with the most specific network address that matches the destination address. This is a generic classless matching algorithm, in which the longest prefix is the preferred match. When comparing two advertisements of the same prefix with differing AS paths, the default action of BGP is to prefer the path with the lowest number of transit AS hops; the preference is for the shorter AS path length.

However, a number of approaches can be used to alter this path selection process. Some of these approaches are local mechanisms that can be undertaken only by the network administrator, affecting the path taken for traffic leaving the AS. Other mechanisms are passed to a remote AS and are attempting to bias the remote egress path selection policy to match with the preferred AS path ingress policy.

These tools may not necessarily have definitive outcomes, because a remote AS can indicate a preference only to the local AS as to which egress path should be selected. The local AS may choose to implement local path selection policies, which may override such remote indications. Because of the relative complexity of the transit structures used within the Internet today, such efforts of exerting control at a distance involve not only the two autonomous systems attempting to negotiate an agreed policy, but also involve the consideration of the path selection policies of all autonomous systems positioned on a potential transit path between these two autonomous systems. Consequently, inter-AS routing has often been described as an art rather than a science, and a black art at that!

AS PATH FILTERING

Of course, one of the most obvious ways to bias the BGP path selection process is to omit those paths that do not conform to the policy of the local AS via some filter mechanism. If a route is not seen for a particular destination from a particular peer, traffic will not be forwarded along that path.

For example, in the network of Figure 6.31, AS3 normally would pick a path to AS2 of the form (AS1, AS2), preferring it to the longer path of (AS5, AS4, AS2). However, AS3 may have negotiated a better transit price from AS5 and does not want to use AS1 as a transit. Instead, AS3 wants to present all traffic destined to AS2 through AS5 as the first hop AS. In this case, AS3 could filter all incoming paths of the form (AS1, AS2) from AS1's routing advertisements to AS2, to allow AS2 to conform to its routing policy.

The filtering can be done on an inbound (accept) or outbound (advertise) basis, based on any variation of the data found in the AS path attribute.

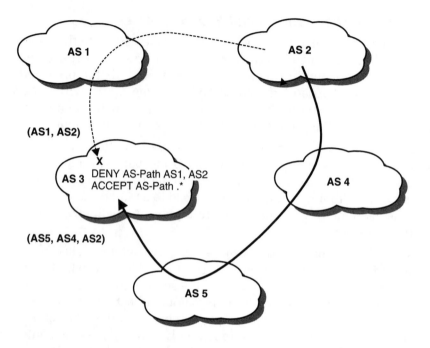

Figure 6.31   AS path filtering.

Filtering can be done on the origin AS, any single AS, or any set of autonomous systems found in the AS path information. This provides a great deal of granularity for selectively accepting and propagating routing information in BGP. By the same token, however, if an organization begins to get exotic with its routing policies, the level of complexity increases dramatically, especially when multiple entry and exit points exist. The downside to filtering routes based on information found in the AS path attribute is that it really provides only binary selection criteria; you either accept and propagate the route, or you deny and do not propagate the route. This does not provide a mechanism to define a primary and backup path.

AS PATH PREPENDING
In referring back to the network in Figure 6.29, inbound routing filters have had the result of causing AS3 to direct its outgoing traffic to AS1 via AS5. However, traffic flow in the opposite direction may not obey the same policy. AS2 will see for AS3 a path of (AS1, AS3) compared to an alternative path of

(AS4, AS5, AS3) and will, by default, select AS1 as transit to reach AS3. Can AS3 affect the path selection properties of AS2 to bias it to select the longer path?

The AS paths can be manipulated to achieve this outcome using a mechanism called *AS path prepending*, which is the practice of inserting additional instances of the originating AS into the beginning of the AS path prior to announcing the route to an exterior neighbor. If AS3 inserted two additional instances of AS3 into the AS path advertised to AS1, then AS2 would be faced with selecting a path between (AS1, AS3, AS3, AS3) and (AS4, AS5, AS3), and the desired result would be achieved. This outcome is indicated in Figure 6.32.

How much of today's Internet traffic load engineering and interconnection policy is held up by this technique of AS path prepending is a source of concern. When used in isolated instances, it can produce the desired result, but when used in a more widespread fashion, prepending can cause constant adjustment rippling across the network. In this example network, if AS4, in

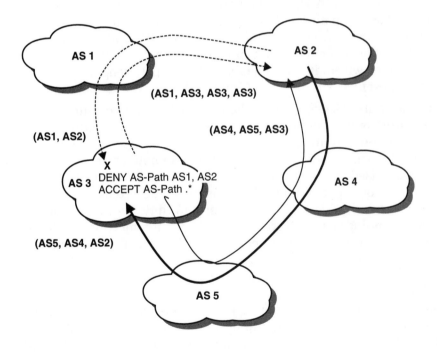

Figure 6.32   AS path prepending.

order to satisfy a local policy requirement of its own, decides to perform AS path prepending on all routes announced to AS2, then AS2 may be presented with a choice between (AS1, AS3, AS3, AS3) and (AS4, AS4, AS4, AS5, AS3), and the path selection will flip back to transit AS1, without AS3's knowledge.

Similar to AS path filtering, AS path prepending is a negative biasing of the BGP path-selection process. The lengthening of the AS path is an attempt to make the path less desirable than would otherwise be the case. This mechanism commonly is used for defining candidate backup paths. AS path prepending cannot positively bias the path selection process.

SPECIFIC ROUTE INJECTION

BGP always will prefer more specific routes, irrespective of the relative AS path lengths of the specific and more general route objects. This preference can be used to bias path selection and to undertake primary and backup paths for particular routers without having to undertake AS path prepending.

In the example network indicated in Figure 6.33, if AS3 wanted AS2 to use the path (AS4, AS5, AS3) for the network address 10.0.0.0/8 and use (AS1, AS3) as a backup path for this network address, then AS3 could advertise 10.0.0.0/8 to AS2 and advertise the routes 10.0.0.0/9 and 10.128.0.0/9 to AS5. AS2 will use the longer path as its preferred path due to the existence of more specific routes within its routing table. The AS path length is examined only if identical prefixes are advertised from multiple external peers.

Specific route injection should be used with extreme caution. One of the major scaling issues the Internet faces as a whole is the continued growth in size of the Internet routing table. Widespread use of specific route injection as a means of biasing routing policy would cause new pressures on the size of the devices used to carry Internet routes. Already, some backbone transit providers enforce entry filters that block specific routes from well-defined ranges of network addresses, in an attempt to limit the amount of fragmentation in the routing space. Overuse of specific route injection would cause further measures to be adopted to ensure that the global routing table remains within a workable size.

BGP COMMUNITIES

Another method of making routing policy decisions using BGP is to use the *BGP community* attribute to group destinations into communities and apply policy decisions based on this attribute instead of directly on the prefixes. A number of defined communities have a determined outcome, and others can be defined by network operators.

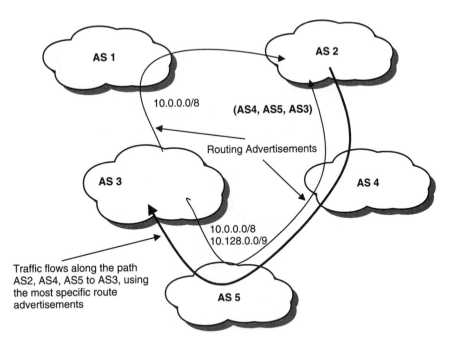

Figure 6.33   Specific route selection.

The most well-known (and widely used) community is that of *No_Export*. When a path attribute includes this community, the route cannot be advertised to peers outside of the local confederation. In the network of Figure 6.34, another way to ensure that AS2 does not transit AS1 to reach AS3 is for AS2 to mark the BGP advertisements to AS1 with the No_Export community attribute. This attribute prevents AS1 from advertising the routes to AS2.

Communities provide a useful and convenient mechanism for an AS to place tags on routes. Consequently, this mechanism has grown in popularity because it provides a simple and straightforward method with which to apply policy decisions relating to the treatment of routes.

As indicated in Figure 6.35, AS1 has a customer, AS2, and participates in two peering exchanges, in which it peers with AS3 and AS4. The policy requires that AS1 does not want to act as a transit for AS3 to reach AS4, but does act in a transit capacity for its client, AS2. AS1 could place all routes received from AS2 into a community 1:10, all routes received at the peering

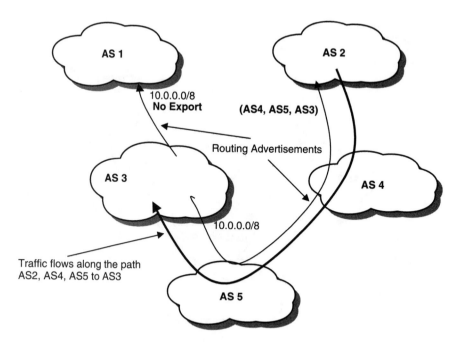

Figure 6.34   BGP communities.

exchanges into a community 1:20, and nonannounced routes into the community 1:30. At the exchange, AS1 announces only routes that include the community attribute 1:10, thereby not announcing routes that would make AS1 act as an unfunded interexchange transit operator.

BGP communities are very flexible tools, allowing groups of routing advertisements to be grouped by a common attribute value specific to a given AS, as the community value has two parts: a two-byte AS number and a two-byte value. The community can be set locally within the AS or remotely to trigger specific actions within the target AS. The community value can be defined by a provider to allow remote autonomous systems to label advertised routes as primary or backup or to allow the default path selection process to be weighted by a community attribute. Community values can trigger actions that encompass more than path selection and manipulation and can be defined to modify any of the actions of the BGP routers.

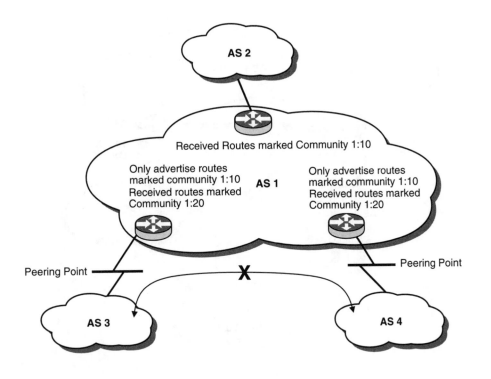

Figure 6.35   BGP communities and peering.

BGP LOCAL PREFERENCE

BGP local preference is a local path attribute (local to the immediate AS), which indicates the preference given to the route object by the AS. BGP local preference is carried only within iBGP sessions, so it applies across the entire AS, but the attribute is nontransitive, or rather, not passed along to neighboring autonomous systems.

An example of the use of the local preference attribute is indicated in Figure 6.36. Both AS2 and AS3 are advertising a route to 10.0.0.0/8, as AS4 is multiply homed. AS1 can make a decision to prefer the path via AS2 by setting the local preference attribute to 20 at boundary router A for the 10.0.0.0/8 route being presented by AS2 and by setting the local preference attribute to 10 at boundary router B for the incoming 10.0.0.0/8 route. The iBGP sessions ensure that these local preference settings are promulgated throughout the BGP routers within the AS, ensuring that they will select the path directed towards AS2.

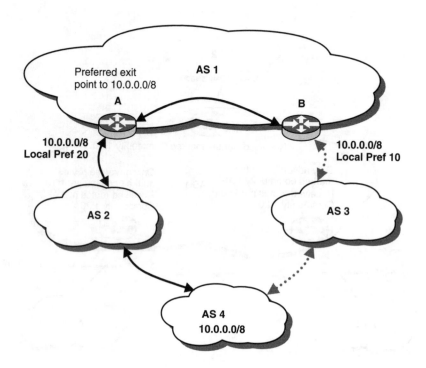

Figure 6.36 BGP local preference.

THE MULTI-EXIT DISCRIMINATOR (MED) ATTRIBUTE

Another BGP tool that can be used to bias route selection policies between autonomous systems is the *Multi-Exit Discriminator* (MED) path attribute. The difference between a MED and a local preference attribute is that while the local preference attribute is a local tool to select an outgoing path, the MED is an exported attribute to inform adjacent autonomous systems of a preferred ingress path to the AS. The MED attribute is passed to the neighboring AS and no further.

The primary use of the MED path attribute is to allow the network administrator to inform an adjacent AS of a preferred ingress path for the route when multiple links exist between the two autonomous systems, with each link advertising the same length prefix. MED is a route-specific tie-breaker in such cases and can be used on a route-by-route basis to allow the network administrator to load-balance incoming traffic across multiple links. In Figure 6.37, AS1 has two connections to AS2 and wants different links used for particular route objects. For incoming traffic addressed to network 10.0.1.0/24, AS1 prefers that path A is used by AS2, and for network 10.0.2.0/24, AS1 prefers that path B is used by AS2. Check to ensure that the adjacent AS honors the advertised MED, as the AS may use a local export policy that may override the MED attribute setting, before extensive setting of MED values to implement load-balancing.

BGP ROUTE DAMPENING

One of the major performance issues within the BGP environment is the level of route change. Within the core of the Internet, every route change in the periphery that causes a destination prefix to be withdrawn, or reannounced, causes an update to be propagated into the core of the network. The resulting

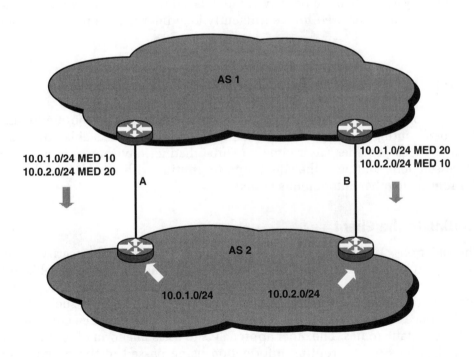

Figure 6.37   BGP Multi-Exit Discriminator.

router load in computing consequent changes to the routing table within the Internet core can be overwhelming, particularly when a route entry starts to *flap*. A *flap* is a rapid oscillation of route withdrawal followed by route re-announcement. It can be caused by route instabilities elsewhere in the network or by faulty circuits that have an error rate, which is just marginal to support the operation of BGP. Route selection, and indeed route-entry promulgation should take into account a route entry's history of flapping and attempt to avoid the use of routes that are exhibiting instability.

Some vendor implementations of BGP allow the network operator to remove route entries from consideration while the entry is flapping and will reconsider the route entry for inclusion in the route selection process only after it has remained available for a sufficiently long period. The Cisco Systems' implementation assigns the route a penalty value upon each flap, and when the penalty exceeds a threshold value, the route is suppressed, no longer considered in path selection, and no longer propagated to neighboring autonomous systems. In the absence of further flaps, the penalty value exponentially decays. When the penalty value falls below a reuse threshold, or the route has been suppressed for a sufficiently long interval, the route is reconsidered.

Designing a Routing Environment

This section applies the general principles of management of routing to outline some routing design guidelines, which are critical to the stable operation of the service provider environment. Three distinct environments must be addressed here: routing to the client, interior routing within the AS, and exterior routing to other autonomous systems.

Routing to the Client

The major objective when routing to the client is stability and integrity of the routing environment. The goal is to avoid fate sharing, in which instabilities or inaccuracies within the client's routing environment are not promulgated into the provider's routing environment. One way to implement such a routing interface is to omit dynamic routing from the client interface completely and to use static routes. The other approach is to use some form of routing, but to apply filters on the routing information being passed to the provider to ensure that it fits within the announced set of routes and route attributes upon which the provider and client have agreed. A number of client connection mechanisms exist, and the routing interface in each of these scenarios is examined here.

The Dial-Up Host

The typical dial configuration is the use of provider address pools and dynamically assigned addresses. A pool of addresses is assigned to a Network Access Server (NAS) for use in dynamic assignment. When the dial call is answered, the subsequent authentication and connection phase assigns a single host address to the remote end, as part of the PPP LCP operation. The LCP options also include the notification of a gateway address and an address mask. The entire address pool is statically configured in the NAS as a static announcement into the IGP, which then is carried through the service provider network (see Figure 6.38).

Where the client has a requirement for end-to-end address-based authentication, or wants to operate services such as Web publishing or ftp archives from a constant address, assigning a constant address to the client system each time it connects to the network may be appropriate. If the customer is mobile, this address assignment must be matched by a corresponding dynamic installation of a route into the NAS and the subsequent advertisement of this router into the interior of the network.

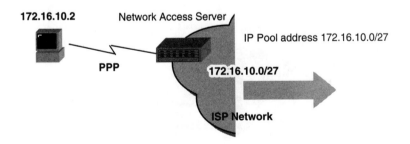

Figure 6.38 The dial-up host.

The Dial-Up Network

With the increasing penetration of computers into the residential and small-business market, the model of a single system using dynamic dial-up connectivity is being complemented by a model of dynamic dial-up connectivity of a small network of host systems, in which a number of LAN-attached hosts use the dial host as a gateway for external access. This model of connectivity is typically a fixed location model, and the NAS configuration must be able to announce a route to the client's network once the connection is made. One way to achieve this is to associate a fixed address to the dial-up connection and then configure the NAS with a static route to the client network that uses the assigned dial-up address as the target of the route (see Figure 6.39).

An alternative approach is to use vendor-specific extensions to the Radius authentication profile [RFC 2138] and place the routes to be loaded into the NAS into the Radius user profile. When the dial-up client is authenticated, the routes associated with the client's network can be loaded into the NAS.

The Permanently Connected Client

This is a common form of client connection in which the client of the network service is itself a network, whether a corporate, campus, or enterprise network. The connection to the ISP uses a leased line or a similar form of permanent connection. A number of variations within this connection regime call for different routing policies, the most common of which are outlined here.

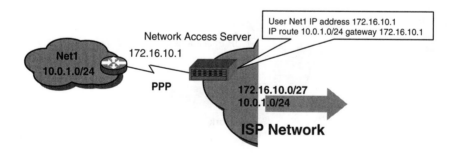

Figure 6.39   The dial-up network.

THE SINGLE-HOMED CLIENT

The simple form of this connection is where the client uses the ISP exclusively for its exterior connectivity requirements and uses a single connection to the ISP. In this case, the routing configuration is most readily supported using static routes on both sides of the connection. Within the client network, the client generates a default route in the boundary router, with the default path pointing to the router interface used to connect to the ISP. The client network promulgates this default route through the local network using the chosen interior routing protocol. Within the ISP network, the ISP configures a set of static routes, which describes the network addresses used by the client into the access router that terminates the client connection, and directs these routes to the relevant interface used by the client connection (see Figure 6.40).

Some explanation of this approach is necessary. The design philosophy is an application of Occam's Razor to the problem, devising a solution, which is simple, but no simpler than it must be. The design separates the two routing

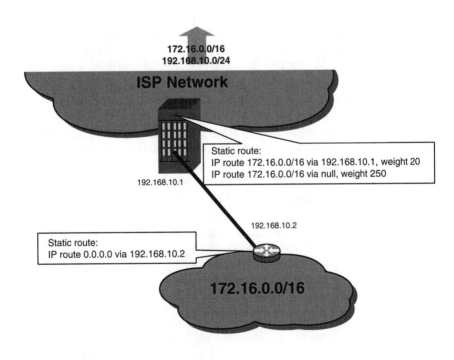

172.16.0.0/16
192.168.10.0/24

ISP Network

Static route:
IP route 172.16.0.0/16 via 192.168.10.1, weight 20
IP route 172.16.0.0/16 via null, weight 250

192.168.10.1

192.168.10.2

Static route:
IP route 0.0.0.0 via 192.168.10.2

172.16.0.0/16

Figure 6.40   The single-homed client.

domains to ensure that nether domain can subvert the integrity or stable operation of the other. The client uses a static default to describe the ISP network, and the ISP network uses a collection of static routes to describe the addresses used within the client network. The additional administrative overhead required to operate processes to add and remove static routing entries is a small burden to ensure this form of route domain independence. Many ISPs that use a link from the client into the ISP's interior routing domain can relate the story of an inadvertently generated default route leaking from a client network into the ISP network, subverting the ISP's exterior connections and sending all exterior traffic to the hapless client.

THE MULTICONNECTED CLIENT

This single-homed client may be a corporate entity with a distributed operation or a client ISP with its own network and may augment the single connection with connections in other locations. The client is still using the ISP exclusively for exterior connectivity, but some policy issues arise with the use of multiple connections. You need to understand the objectives of the client in order to design a routing environment to support this configuration.

The approach outlined previously for the single connection can be replicated for each connection, as indicated in Figure 6.41. In this case, each network uses closest exit routing. Such a configuration does allow for mutual backup of the various client connecting links, so that if one link fails the other links will immediately absorb the displaced traffic load. However, this simple approach may not match the client's expectations. The closest exit routing system will produce asymmetric paths through the network for certain pairs of communication systems. Such asymmetry will confuse various network probe tools, such as traceroute and ping, and the network operators do need to be aware of the possibility of such asymmetry when addressing operational issues. More critical is the problem of loss of traffic if the client network internally segments due to some form of internal outage on the network. If the client network segments, the static routing structure will not adjust to the event, and traffic will be misdirected as a consequence.

In some cases, the client wants an alternative routing policy that minimizes the internal transit load on the client network, termed *closest entry routing*. In this configuration, the client wants the ISP to use the entry point closest to the destination address. This type of client routing configuration can be undertaken using a combination of specific and aggregate static routes linked to each client interface. Each connection has a number of specific static routes that correspond to destinations within the client network, which are close to

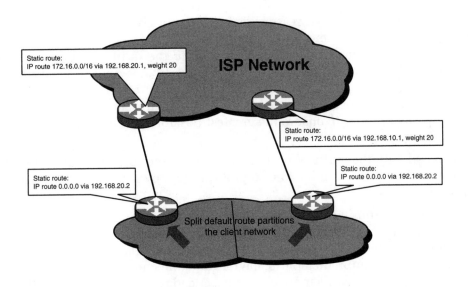

Figure 6.41   The multiconnected client.

the ISP connection, and a set of generic aggregate routes, which describe the customer's complete set of routes. In the normal course of operation, the closest entry points will be used by virtue of the specific routes. If the client network segments, the specific routes will ensure that connectivity is maintained across the client network. If a single connecting link fails, the aggregate routes will ensure that the other links assume a backup role for the duration of the link failure.

There are other motivations behind a client ordering multiple connections to an ISP. The general observation is that rather than attempt to apply a single routing structure to all such connections, it is often productive to take the time to understand these motivations and then engineer a solution that preserves the essential attributes of decoupling the two routing domains but simultaneously achieves as much of the client requirements as possible.

THE MULTIHOMED CLIENT

The multihomed client is connected to a number of service providers. The motives for so doing are quite varied. For many clients, it is a desire to improve the reliability of Internet connectivity, in the expectation that if connectivity fails through one service provider, the other provider will still provide connectivity. Other reasons may be financially based and stem from a desire to minimize cost by attempting to set traffic ingress and egress policies on each exterior connection that are attuned to the tariff structures of each provider, with the anticipated outcome that the total service costs are minimized. For content providers, this may stem from a desire to reach as many potential clients as possible with minimal hop lengths and minimal provider transit paths in order to ensure the greatest possible performance in delivery of content.

As noted with the multiconnected client, you need to understand the motivation of the client in order to design a routing environment that can meet these objectives.

The simplest routing structure is to replicate the static routes of the single-homed client. Here, this simple structure is too simple and consequently inadequate for the task. The conflicting default route paths within the client network lead to unpredictable behavior, and the multiple announcements of the client's networks by more than one AS leads to some unpredictability of exterior path selection to reach the client. The multiprovider asymmetry of traffic flows does not assist when attempting to diagnose operational faults, and some instability of the client's connectivity is a potential outcome of this arrangement.

The deployment of BGP will assist here, using a configuration in which the client is a multihomed stub AS, as illustrated in Figure 6.23. The client has two eBGP sessions, one to each ISP, and advertises its routes to each ISP with an AS path that references its local AS. If multiple exterior boundary routers are used, they will need to be interconnected via iBGP sessions, with an iBGP routed transit core. For egress traffic, the client network has a number of options. The client can use a primary default route to point to one provider and import a set of routes from the other providers, together with the use of a hierarchy of default routes to ensure that external connectivity remains available during outages of the primary egress link. If the client wants to make a finer grained decision about which provider to use for a broader set of routes, the client can receive a full set of routing entries from each provider and then apply local policy considerations to select paths for each destination. For ingress traffic, the client can use the various BGP techniques to describe path preferences for incoming traffic.

The use of BGP in this connection now introduces a coupling of the routing environments of the client and the service provider, and the service provider now must use a different mechanism to limit the routing interaction to an administratively agreed set of routes and route attributes. The typical mechanism is to pass all announced routes through an input filter, to ensure that the client network announces only those network destinations that have been notified as belonging to the client. An additional filter may be applied to ensure that the client advertises only associated AS path information, which conforms to an administratively provided AS path template, again to ensure that a configuration error within the client does not propagate further out into the Internet environment. The service provider also may apply a community attribute to the routes to ensure that subsequent handling and advertisement of the route conforms to the service contract with the client.

THE TRANSIT CLIENT

The transit client is a form of the transit AS, in which the client is itself a provider to third-party clients. The client may be single-homed to the ISP, or may be multihomed. In either case, as this client has third-party clients, which themselves can be assumed to be multihomed, the ISP needs to use an eBGP session with the client to ensure integrity of routing and associated policy.

Here, similar policy principles apply as to the multihomed stub client network. The ISP should use some form of administrative filter on announced routes to ensure that the client does not inadvertently announce routes that do not form part of the client's reachable domain. Perhaps more critically in this environment, the ISP should agree with the client on a means of operating an ingress filter on AS path sequences being passed into the ISP network, to ensure that the AS announcements correspond to policy of both the client and the ISP, but also are in broad conformance with the policy requirements of the third-party clients.

The ISP also will need to agree on an advertisement policy with the client for routes advertised to the client network. The client may want to receive only advertisements for routes, which are within the ISP's AS. Of course, it must be noted that it is often easier for the client to use ingress filters at the client boundary router, rather than have the ISP perform this filter action at a distance on the client's behalf. The general principle in such cases is that control is best exercised locally rather than at a distance.

Interior Routing

Interior routing structures are of course strongly influenced by the interior architecture of the network itself, the service role of the network, its size, and the way in which routing policy is implemented.

A typical transit ISP uses a structured hierarchy inside the network, using a core network as the interior backbone. Attached to this core system is a distribution system. Within this level of the hierarchy are boundary routers that service exterior peer connections and routers that act as aggregation and local switching points for client-facing access routers. At the next level of the hierarchy are the access routers, which terminate connections to clients, either as permanently connected clients, or NAS-connected dial-up clients (see Figure 6.42).

The core network forms the backbone area (or Level 2 area in an IS-IS context) of a link state routing protocol, although each access distribution node and its collection of local access routers form nonbackbone areas (or Level 1 areas if using IS-IS). This allows the locally managed networks to be routed across the interior fabric of the network across paths determined by the metrics of the network's component links. Careful design is necessary to ensure that the metrics used create flow volumes that make rational use of the backbone network and that backup paths exist to provide resiliency in the event of failure of any of the network's components. Careful design also is required to ensure that the routing areas do not become so large that the routing protocol saturates and fails. Considering that most ISPs experience very aggressive growth rates in which the network doubles in size in periods of between 6 to 18 months, this consideration of scale factors is very relevant.

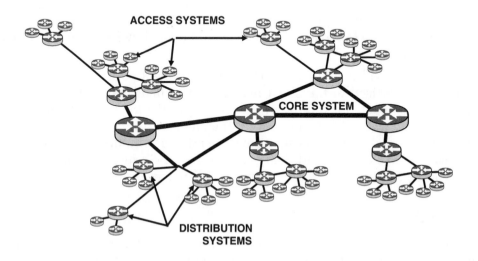

Figure 6.42 Interior network structure.

The backbone area should generate a default route that points to the network of core transit routers used within the backbone and promulgate this default route into the nonbackbone routing areas. Because the internal IGP is carrying all the routes explicitly within the routing domain, the default is used to point to exterior routes learned from external BGP sessions, as these routes are not promulgated into the interior routing domain.

The external boundary routers are interconnected by a set of transit core routers. These routers are configured with iBGP, so that exterior transit does not pass into the distribution or access network and no route redistribution into the interior routing protocol is required. As a rule of thumb the maximum number of BGP sessions supported in any router is between 50 and 100, although this will vary depending on local load conditions. If the load levels do become excessive and start affecting the stability of the BGP peering sessions, the fully meshed iBGP environment should be rationalized with the use of BGP route reflectors.

The interior routes need to be redistributed into the BGP environment, which should be undertaken with a view to maximize the amount of route aggregation that takes place, so that the provider's announced destination addresses are passed into the inter-AS routing space with a minimal impact on the Internet-wide routing tables.

Exterior Routing

Routing to exterior networks is similar to the routing considerations that apply to transit client networks. The service provider announces both interior routes and client-advertised routes to exterior networks. By default, the route announcement uses a simple preprending of the local AS number before announcing the route objects to the exterior BGP peer network. Route advertisements may be modified by any of the route policy modifiers described to ensure that local policy constraints are fulfilled, so that the advertisement may include AS path prepending, MED values, and community attributes, in order to meet the local policy objectives.

The local AS accepts the route advertisement from the exterior BGP peer, and promulgates this external route within the local internal BGP subnetwork.

External route promulgation should be designed to match the service provider's business objectives and policy constraints. The external entities can be divided into three generic functional groups:

- ◆ Clients, who contract the ISP to provide connectivity services
- ◆ Upstream service providers, who are contracted by the ISP to provide connectivity services
- ◆ Peer service providers, in which the two networks may exchange client traffic on a bilaterally negotiated basis

Figure 6.43 indicates the normal routing flow between these entities. Client routes are advertised to clients, upstream service provider networks, and to peer service providers. Routes learned from peer service providers are not advertised to upstream service providers, nor are they advertised to any other peer service provider. The routes form part of the default route provided to clients, and if the client requires the ISP to pass explicit routes to the client, such routes would be passed to the client. Routes learned from upstream service providers are not advertised to other upstream or peer service providers, and form part of the default route provided to clients. Again, such routes may be explicitly provided to a client network.

Routing Registries

The major challenge with manipulation of the policy control mechanisms of exterior routing protocols is to define a local AS configuration that has a predictable outcome in terms of local policy regarding reachability and traffic management. At the same time, it is necessary to accommodate the policy

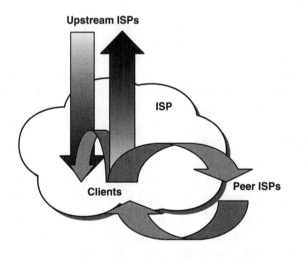

Figure 6.43   Exterior routing flows.

desires of other autonomous systems, where they intersect or impact upon local policy objectives. Policy interaction within the inter-AS environment is a very imprecise art form, considering the topological complexity of the interconnection environment, and the relatively crude level of the available tools of AS path prepending and BGP transitive path attributes. One cannot but wonder that it works at all!

Having this environment automatically establish the points of maximal match to each party's policies remains an elusive objective, and in this vein a number of bodies have been active in constructing tools to assist ISPs to publish their routing policies, and collecting these descriptions into a single repository. These descriptions can then be manipulated to assist in generating specific configurations for routers that effectively construct filter sets which match the prescribed policy constraints and the published policies of other ISPs.

Réseaux IP Européens (RIPE), a collaborative organization of European Internet providers, developed a number of routing registry tools and published a database language [RIPE 181] in which providers could describe their policies and connectivity in a common schema. The National Science Foundation of the United States funded a Routing Arbiter Project to develop these tools, which operated a routing arbiter database and associated route servers based on the manipulation of route objects described using the RIPE-181 syntax. The effort is continuing with the Route Server Next Generation (RSng) project, which, within the forum of the Routing Policy System Working Group of the IETF, is developing a new policy specification language. This policy specification language is termed *Routing Policy Specification Language* (RPSL). The project also requires the definition of a distributed registry model to allow ISPs to publish their external policies and an associated set of analysis tools that will allow for checking of global consistency, diagnosing operational problems, and generating configurations, which can be loaded directly into routers.

So far, this is still work in progress. The existing routing registries can allow an ISP to publish their external routing policies, but the utility of so doing is not as broad as it could be. Interestingly, the IETF effort in this area is moving onward from the specification of a sufficiently powerful language and associated constructs to express routing policies, into the area of authentication of routing policy.

Summary of Routing Considerations

The heart of the operational environment of an ISP is the routing system. Careful design of the routing environment will provide a stable and reliable service platform that can support the various requirements of the client base. The routing system is the critical element to provide connectivity, as well as undertaking the detailed control of which paths traffic will utilize within the network.

The choice of a routing structure and the associated definition of link metrics will allow the network administrator to match traffic flows to available carriage capacity, and accordingly, to ensure that the service delivered to clients is of a high quality, both in terms of performance and robustness.

Where the network interconnects with other service provider networks, the routing system will be the vehicle for determination of the policies of external traffic flows to and from the network. The careful definition of objectives of the external routing system, and the consequent configuration of the exterior routing protocol, is a critical task that ensures not only the stability of the local network but also the stable operation of adjacent networks.

This chapter has presented a very brief overview of a relatively complex area of network design and engineering. Although the general principles of operation of routing protocols have been explored, the network engineer will need to relate these general principles to the specific conditions of the deployment environment.

chapter seven

Network Management

"Yes, we manage our network. We bought one of those network
management packages. We're still not sure how it works."
"Yes, we manage our network. We don't need any fancy software with
green and red flashing icons. If there's a problem, we get to know about
it, and our technical person fixes it."

Network management is more than running a network management software
package or operating a script of ping routines on a workstation. In order to
operate a reliable service, the network must be managed according to a determined discipline, using a coherent structure of information management.

A generalized structure of network management uses a network monitoring
platform, which includes agents that gather information from various managed network elements, and an operational platform that can present various
views of the operational status of the network derived from this information.
This view forms a part of a fault-desk function that can match the operational
status of the network to fault reports submitted by clients of the network,
allowing the fault manager to coordinate remedial responses to service outages while keeping clients informed as to the status of the activity. Fault
reports and collected network management information are stored, allowing
subsequent analysis relating to fault history, service reliability, network element reliability, network accounting, performance trends, capacity forecasts,
and similar information, all of which allow the network manager to make
informed decisions regarding the overall management of the ISP service.

In this chapter, we examine the structure of network management as it
relates to the ISP operation. Using the terminology adopted by the ISO
Network Management Forum, five major functional areas of network management need to be discussed:

- ◆ Fault management
- ◆ Configuration management
- ◆ Security management
- ◆ Performance management
- ◆ Accounting management

We examine security management in Chapter 9, "Security," and the other areas of network management are examined in this chapter.

Before examining each of these areas in further detail, let's look at the various basic tools and techniques available to the network operator to manage the network.

ICMP-Based Network Management Tools

The technical aspects of network management are based on a number of elements within the IP protocol suite. The basic set of network tools is structured on the ICMP protocol, most notably *ping* and *traceroute*, while more structured network management tools are based on the SNMP network management structure. Within the IP protocol suite, the ICMP protocol is used to form the base functionality for the most commonly used and pervasively deployed network management tools.

The Power of Ping

The most common of these tools is the ICMP Echo Request and corresponding ICMP Echo Reply packets, which form the functionality of the ping utility. In its basic form, ping takes a target IP address as an argument, directs an ICMP Echo Request packet to that address, and awaits a matching ICMP Echo Reply response.

A ping response indicates that the target host is connected to the network, is reachable from the query agent, and is in a sufficiently functional state that it can respond to the ping packet. This behavior is indicated in Figure 7.1. In itself, this response is useful information, indicating that a functional network path to the functioning target host exists. Failure to respond is not so informative, because it cannot be absolutely inferred that the target host is not functional. The ping packet, or its response, may have been discarded within the network due to transient congestion, or the network may not have a path to the target host. In this latter case, as the ICMP protocol does not allow the generation of ICMP host unreachable messages in response to a nonroutable ICMP packet, no network error indication can be generated back to the query agent.

Further information can be inferred by ping with some basic modifications to the behavior to the ping algorithm. If a sequence of labeled *ping* packets is generated, the elapsed time for a response to be received for each packet can be recorded, as well as the count of dropped packets, duplicated packets, and packets that have been reordered by the network. Careful interpretation of the response times, and their variance, can provide an indication of the load being experienced on the network path between the query agent and the target. Load will manifest a condition of increased delay and increased variance, due to the interaction of the router buffers with the traffic flows along the path elements as load increases. When a router buffer overflows, the router is forced to discard packets, and under such conditions, increased ping loss is observed. In addition to indications of network load, high erratic delay and loss within a sequence of ping packets may be symptomatic of routing instability, with the network path flapping between a number of states.

A typical use of ping is to regularly test a number of paths, to establish a baseline of path metrics, allowing a comparison of a specific ping result to these base metrics to provide an indication of current path load within the network.

Of course, it is possible to infer too much from ping results, particularly when pinging routers within a network. Many router architectures use fast

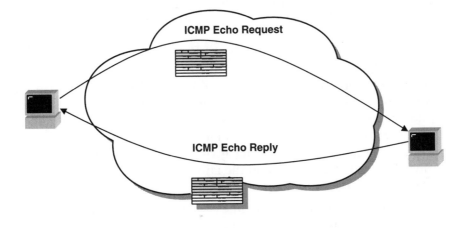

Figure 7.1 The ping function.

switching paths for data packets, and the router's central processing unit is used to process ping requests. The ping response process may be given a low scheduling priority, because the routing protocol operation is a more critical router function, so it is possible that extended delays and loss may be related to the load of the target router processor rather than the condition of the network path. Ping sequences do not necessarily mimic packet flow behavior of applications. Typical TCP flow behavior is prone to cluster bursts of packet transmissions on each epoch of the round-trip time, and routers may optimize their cache management, switching behavior, and queue management to take advantage of this behavior. Ping packets may not be clustered, and instead, use an evenly spaced pacing, in which case the observed metrics of a sequence of ping packets may not exercise such router optimizations, and accordingly, the ping results may not necessarily reflect an anticipation of application performance along the same path. Note that packet delay variance and some small level of loss are not necessarily indicative of imminent congestion-induced collapse along the network path. Adaptive flow protocols, such as TCP, use a flow-control algorithm in which the TCP flow rate is increased to the point where a router buffer overflows and packet loss occurs. Therefore, some background level of packet delay variance and loss is not unusual within normal operational conditions of the network.

With these caveats in mind, monitoring a network through regular ping tests along the major network paths can yield useful information regarding the status of the network, indicating as a base the operational status of the network's routers and service platforms. Analysis of round-trip times and loss rates is also a basic indicator of network load, although care must be taken not to infer too much into such data. An instance of such a report is indicated in Figure 7.2.

Variants of Ping

A number of refinements to ping can extend its utility. Ping can use loose source routing to test the reachability of one host to another, directing the packet from the query host to the loose source-routed host and then to the target host, and back via the same path (see Figure 7.3). However, many networks disable support for loose source routing, given its capability to be exploited in some forms of security attacks, so that the failure of a loose source-routed ping may not be a conclusive indication of a network fault.

Ping also can be used in a rudimentary way to discover the provisioned capacity of network links. By varying the packet length and comparing the ping times of one router to the next hop router on a path, the bandwidth of the

Example text Ping Report

```
> ping -c 100 172.16.1.1
100 transmitted, 100 received, 0.00% packet loss.
128.841 seconds elapsed, throughput = 0.78 packets/sec; 521.574  bps.
round-trip (ms) min/ avg/max = 286.538/298.482/552.258
          var  /sdev/skew/ kurt = 1463.964/38.262/5.115/29.251
```

Graphed Report of regular Ping samples

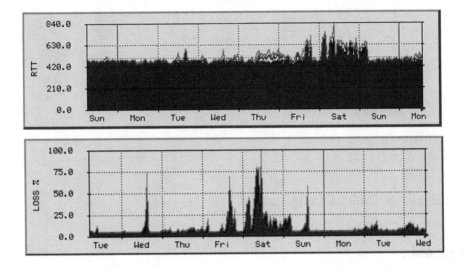

Figure 7.2 Ping reports.

link can be deduced, within a reasonable degree of approximation. The *bing* tool is an implementation of this technique of bandwidth discovery through advanced interpretation of ping results.

A more sophisticated variation of ping is to pace the transmission of packets from the received packets, mimicking the behavior of the TCP flow-control algorithm with slow start and subsequent congestion avoidance. *Treno* is such a tool, in which the transmission of ping packets is managed by the TCP Reno flow control algorithm. Such a tool can indicate available flow rate managed capacity on a chosen path, although this is a relatively intrusive network probe.

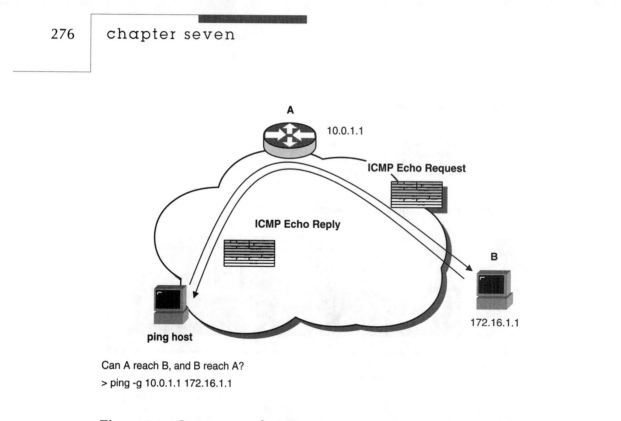

Figure 7.3 Source-routed ping.

Traceroute

The second common ICMP-based network management tool is based on the ICMP Time Exceeded message. Here, a sequence of UDP packets is generated to the target host, each with an increased value of the TTL field in the IP header. This will generate a sequence of ICMP Time Exceeded messages, sourced from the router where the TTL expired. The sequence of such source addresses is the addresses of each of the routers in turn on the path from the source to the destination. This is the traceroute tool, devised by Van Jacobson. Like ping, traceroute also measures the elapsed time between the packet transmission and the reception of the corresponding ICMP packet, so that the complete output of a traceroute execution exposes not only the elements of the path to the destination, but also the delay and loss characteristics of each partial path element. Traceroute also can be used with loose source route options, to uncover the path between two remote hosts, and of course, the same caveats relating to the deployment of support for loose source routing apply. Traceroute operation is illustrated in Figure 7.4, and the modification to a loose source routing option with traceroute is indicated in Figure 7.5.

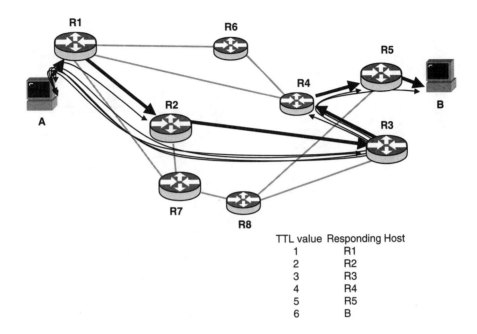

TTL value	Responding Host
1	R1
2	R2
3	R3
4	R4
5	R5
6	B

Figure 7.4   Traceroute.

Traceroute is an excellent tool for reporting on the state of the routing system and operates as an excellent sanity check of the match between the design intent of the routing system and the operational behavior.

The caveat when interpreting traceroute output is that of the issue of asymmetric routes within the network. While the per-hop responses expose the routing path taken in the forward direction to the target host, the delay and loss metrics are measured across the forward and reverse paths, which is not explicitly visible to traceroute.

The Simple Network Management Protocol

The Simple Network Management Protocol (SNMP) is a protocol and an information structure designed to support the detail of network element management. The overall intent of SNMP is to provide a standard way of querying the status of network elements and a standard way that network elements can report on their operational status. This allows a vendor-independent network

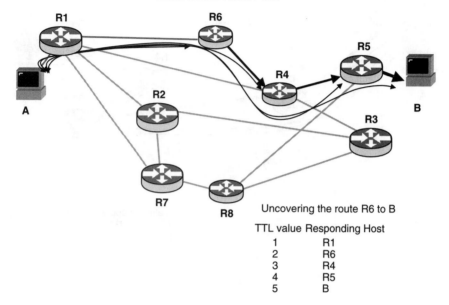

Figure 7.5 Source-routed traceroute.

management environment to be operated by the network manager. The architecture of SNMP is based on a query-response model, in which a management system generates a query within an SNMP-defined query structure, and the query is passed to the managed network element via a UDP network transaction. The network element responds, also via UDP, with an SNMP-formatted response, in which the response corresponds precisely to the query. SNMP also can generate traps, which are managed-element initiated SNMP messages directed to a management host, informing the host of an exception or alarm condition that may require attention.

The security model provided with SNMP, both in the initial version 1 and in version 2, is relatively basic, relying on simple password-based access mechanisms. SNMP version 2 was intended to have a more robust security architecture, but the effort within the IETF Working Group fragmented, and subsequently, the IETF Network Management Area was disbanded, and the outcome, as far as SNMP was concerned, was far from ideal.

The *Structure of Management Information* (SMI) defines the structure of the data objects manipulated by SNMP, and this is termed a *Management Information Base* (MIB). MIB is defined using the ISO-defined *Abstract Syntax Notation One* (ASN.1) notation.

I *cannot help but quote from Marshall T. Rose in* The Simple Book, *published in 1991, in which, in an admittedly nontechnical commentary, Marshall notes:*

> *The official reason for using ASN.1 is to ease the eventual transition to OSI-based network management protocols. The actual reason is that the Internet research community got caught napping on this one, having never spent much time dealing with application-layer structuring. . . . Fortunately, ASN.1 is destined, for better or worse, to become the network programming language of the 90s, just as the C programming language is largely seen as having been the systems programming language of the 80s. So, the choice of ASN.1 is a good one.*

Fortunately, for the world of programming, this foreboding prediction was never to eventuate in the 1990s, and the pain of ASN.1 is largely confined to the world of SNMP data objects.

In addition to the data objects, ANS.1 is used to define the specification of the set of *Basic Encoding Rules* (BER) for SNMP, which allow for a standard method of the transmission of queries and responses within the SNMP protocol.

SNMP data objects are constructed from a simple set of atomic data types (integer, octet string, and object identifier) and compounding operators to allow arrays and records. Objects themselves are identified by a sequence of integers that corresponds to selection of a sequence of edges in a tree of data objects. The system description object can be referred to as an SNMP object by the string .1.3.6.1.2.1.1.1, or, as indicated in Figure 7.6, by the selection of the edges that lead to the sequence of labeled nodes *iso.org.dod. internet.mgmt.mib.system.sysDescr*. The MIB used in SNMP, MIB-II, is an Internet-standard database of objects, together with an extension area, which allows for equipment vendors to provide additional objects. Data objects are transported within a standard tag, length-value triplet.

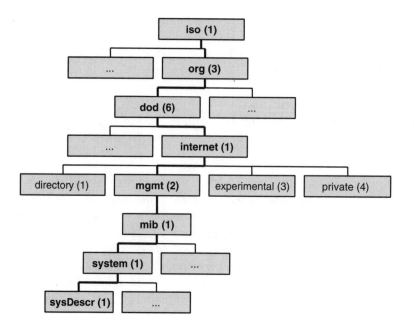

Figure 7.6   SNMP object identifier structure.

SNMP is a simple UDP-based protocol, using UDP port 162. SNMP allows for two query commands, *GetRequest*, which retrieves the current value of the specified MIB object, and *GetNextRequest*, which allows the network management station to return the next MIB object in a depth-first traversal of the MIB-defined object tree. In addition, there is a *SetRequest* message, which allows the network management station to specify an MIB object and a new value for the object. All three messages elicit a *GetResponse* from the managed entity, which is used to return the specified value, or an indication of why the requested action could not be performed by the entity. As well as query-response interactions, SNMP allows for a trap message to be generated by the managed entity, in which the network management station can be informed of a number of standard events that include a power-up start, a restart, interface status change, SNMP access failure, or a vendor-defined event.

As already noted, the security model for SNMP is relatively basic, allowing for *communities of access*. These provide access to the managed entity using a simple password-based mechanism, which is sent in the clear with an accompanying query. Multiple communities can exist, each with a different access mode, allowing some communities read-only access to the managed entity and allowing read and write access to other communities.

SNMPv2 adds the *GetBulkRequest* to the operator set to allow large blocks of data to be retrieved efficiently and adds the *InformRequest* operator to allow management station to management station notification. SNMPv2 also adds to the basic SNMP data set, allowing for 64-bit integer values complementing the original 32-bit integer values. The pressing need was for a more robust security architecture, which was not forthcoming in this refinement effort. In spite of this, with careful filtering, SNMP does provide the platform for the overall preponderance of management functions within the Internet platform world, and is used today within all areas of operational management, performance management, and accounting management.

Fault Management

No network system operates perfectly. As trite as this observation sounds, the corollary is perhaps more significant: equipment will fail, systems will go down, and services will be interrupted. Indeed, when the ISP has to accommodate growth rates in which the network operation doubles in size at regular intervals, simple expansion activity may well be the dominate cause of network service interruptions!

For an ISP, there is an additional issue of expectation setting. The general customer expectation is that the system outage level is on a par with other mature public communications services, such as public telephony, in which outages are isolated events with well-contained impacts. Indeed, this expectation of fault occurrence and management is such that many clients do not anticipate having to notify their ISP of faults when they occur. Many clients have the expectation that the ISP operation is permanently monitoring the operational status of every element of the system and will be in a position to instantly respond to a fault as soon as it occurs. With this very high customer expectation level, customer satisfaction levels fall very quickly when faults are not rectified immediately, and the customer satisfaction levels are very low indeed when it reaches the point of the customer reporting a fault to the ISP.

A high degree of pressure is on the ISP to manage a thoroughly competent approach to fault management, with the attribute that the fault management process enables the following activities:

- Identifies faults within the service platform
- Enables accurate isolation of the fault
- Allows rapid response to such faults
- Enables rapid resolution of the fault

The fault management process also should ensure that clients are well informed as to the nature of the fault, the impact of the fault on the service operation, the status of resolution, and anticipated time to restore full operational status.

The ISP should be aware that customers see the ISP as providing complete end-to-end services and will, therefore, log faults that may relate to the operations of a remote ISP. The arrangements relating to external peering arrangements between ISPs should cover both the process and detail of trouble ticket referral, in which a trouble ticket can be referred across to an adjacent ISP's fault management process for resolution.

Identifying and Responding to the Fault

In addition to driving the response process to individual faults, the fault management process should assist in preventing the recurrence of faults. The overall fault management process must include analysis of the fault history, to allow the ISP to identify systemic faults, indicative of design error or a point of criticality, and to identify element failure, in which a service element is being operated at a level beyond its inherent capability.

A fault management system can be as simple as a set of documented processes used by the ISP operations staff, or it can encompass a fault management system that allows for a large set of staff to perform specialized functions, with the overall management of the response to the fault being tracked by the fault management system. Although a simple set of processes is adequate for very small ISP operations, the critical nature of fault management within the overall activity of service delivery implies that the use of a more robust and disciplined management system is a relatively early addition to the ISP operational management environment. Such systems are variously called fault management systems, fault-desk systems, and trouble ticket management systems, or they can be tied into the technical support role and fall within extended functionality help-desk systems.

Entered tickets are the outcome of all network outage events as reported by a network monitoring system, as well as all customer calls and all scheduled activity that impact on service availability or performance. Tickets are passed to the service manager, who is responsible for assigning a priority in response to the fault, by assessing the impact of the fault. A record of the fault may be passed to an outage reporting system, to allow clients to be informed of the problem, its impact, and the status of the fault response. A typical ticket is indicated in Figure 7.7. As the response is undertaken, the ticket is annotated by the service technicians, allowing individual technicians to assume control of an active fault ticket and rapidly understand the background and current status of the fault.

Rapid Fault Detection

Rapid fault identification is often achieved through network management platforms using regular polling of network elements.

Monitor polling is used to detect error conditions, such as a device not responding, or an active interface transitioning to down. This polling can be as simple as a set of ping routines, which trigger a fault alarm for the target host when the ping fails for a number of successive ping polls, or the polling system can be a monitor to trap SNMP trap messages, or it can be a syslog

```
From ispnet-ops-request@net.isp Sun Jun 14 13:17:23 1998
Date:    Sun, 14 Jun 98 13:05:22 EST
From: ops@net.isp
Subject:  Note #5 on Ticket #15234
To: ops@net.isp, isp-outages@net.isp

Ticket #15234
Original Problem Description:
    Circuit from Blue to White POP has been flapping since 13 June 1998, and line errors are
    rising
Note #5
Author:    tech-a
Date/Time: 13:03 14 Jun 1998
Note:
    After Blue personnel worked along with tech-a team, the problem with this circuit was found to be a
    configuration mismatch in the inverse   mux. Tech-A is currently working to fix the problem, which is now causing
    downtime to the Blue router.  They are expected to finish with the repair by 13:30.  Blue ticket #2015 applies.
Comment:
    For a complete history of this ticket, do "finger ticket-15234@net.isp".
```

Figure 7.7 Example trouble ticket.

interpreter, reacting to remote log messages being generated by the routers and remote platforms. Such faults can be considered hard faults, in that they refer to a network element that has gone out of service, and an alarm can be generated. These alarms should generate fault tickets and initiate a fault response from the network operations area. This could be via the ticket entry or by direct alarms generated to pager systems, describing the nature of the monitor poll that detected the fault.

Threshold polling is intended to detect fault conditions that manifest as a gradual condition, rather than the device or circuit undertaking an immediate transition to unavailable. A circuit may show an increasing number of transmission errors, significantly degrading service, without ever generating an SNMP trap. Threshold polling is normally undertaken within an SNMP polling system, polling the per-interface SNMP error counters. The operator can nominate a number of target hosts and a number of MIB variables that are indicative of potential errors of this sort. An initial polling sequence can be used to establish a baseline value and anticipated variation in the polled value. This allows a threshold alarm value to be set, normally at some 10–20 percent larger than the observed maximum value. If the polling system sees the polled value exceed the threshold for a specified interval, a network exception can be generated. Generally, an immediate response is not required to threshold exceptions, and a second-level fault (or soft fault) can be generated, indicating a condition which, if left unattended, may escalate into a hard fault.

Typically, this forms the basis of the network management platform, where the constant monitoring of the network status yields very timely generation of fault alarms. The platform also can associate with the generated fault alarm an identification of the failing network element, and, of course, the platform can monitor the operational status of hundreds and up to thousands of network components.

Fault Isolation

Isolation of the fault is the first manual step of the process of fault response and involves confirmation of the reported condition, then initial diagnosis as to the cause of the condition. This activity involves an understanding of the configuration of the network, in its design and operational configuration, in order to be able to relate a condition to a component or locality.

> *One of the major problems in many large sites is the practice of never screwing in the connectors. The screws are considered a waste of time as the plug and socket are normally a tight fit. Of course, in a large site with many technicians working on installing services, it is inevitable that the connector will be knocked and displaced from the socket. Generally, such faults, when they occur, are the hardest to isolate, as each component appears to be functioning perfectly well, but the combination does not.*

At this stage, the impact of the fault should be assessed, and those clients whose service is affected by the condition should be notified of the problem.

Fault Response and Resolution

At this stage, the resolution process can be invoked to direct resources to resolve the condition. This is a priority scheduling issue, in which a finite set of technical resources must be deployed against a varying workload. Therefore, the fault resource scheduler must have a clear concept of the priority of the fault and an estimate of the resources required to bring the fault to a conclusion. Such priorities can be adjusted dynamically throughout the resolution process. However, the essential input at this stage is an operational decision as to where to concentrate resources to maximize the effectiveness of the service resources and to maximize overall availability of the ISP platform.

Fault management also may include explicit technical and managerial escalation at determined intervals, so that a long-standing fault receives both additional technical input and management attention within a determined period.

When faults are resolved, the fault closure should trigger a number of programmed events, including notification to the original fault reporter of the resolution of the fault. A number of other actions, including the recording of the generic nature of the fault, the time to resolve the fault, and the way in which it was originally notified, are essential in tracking service quality. The ISP should maintain a number of fault performance metrics, such as faults per 100 services in operation per month, mean time to repair, and mean availability, all of which allow the ISP to identify when faults start to have a negative impact on overall service levels.

The intended outcome of the design, equipment selection, deployment, and operational management processes of the ISP operation is that service-based faults are infrequent, of low impact, and readily isolated and repaired. If these outcomes are not being achieved, the fault management process and the process operators should be audited to ensure that the process is efficient and attuned to the task. The outcome of such an audit may point to inherent weaknesses in the fault management process or its operation. The audit may illustrate a systemic set of faults caused by the design parameters of a system or a component being exceeded. Indeed, the overall design of the system will have an associated total load factor, and fault levels will increase as this load factor is approached.

Configuration Management

Configuration management is the process of maintaining information relating to the design of the network and its current configuration. Configuration management also is the associated inventory of network elements and the role and configuration of each of these elements. Undertaking these activities within an overall discipline of configuration management allows the network engineer to operate the equipment without having to start from a position of having to rediscover the original design and the translation of this design into an operational configuration. The configuration management environment should offer rapid access to the configuration data for every network element and offer indications about why particular configuration options were selected.

Network State

The areas within the broad topic of configuration management include management of the network state information. At a base level, this is a maintained record of the current topology of the network, providing a comprehensive list of the component elements of the network and their means of interconnection. This is the more static component of the state information, in that it is an outcome of the deployment process to maintain a record of what is deployed, where it is deployed, and how it is attached into the network. There is also a dynamic component of network state, which is the operational status of the network elements. At a basic level, such an operational status report may be a simple up/down availability report for each network element. However, this report normally extends to qualify simple availability into a metric of resource use, allowing the metric to indicate whether the network element is idle, operating under conditions of normal design load, or whether the element is overloaded, and the load is impeding the element's ability to undertake its role effectively. In addition to the topology and operational status of network elements, the network state information should include a description of the current operational configuration of each element. This description should include the physical configuration of processor, memory, interfaces, power supply, and such, as well as the software configuration. This may be a router configuration or the configuration settings for a Web server or mailer host.

The configuration management area draws a distinction between physical and logical views of a network. A physical view may see a single application server platform, and a logical view may draw a distinction between the mail server, ftp server, and other functions that may reside on a common platform. Such distinctions are helpful to maintain, given that the pressures of scaling the service often imply a need for flexibility as to which logical service functions are assigned to particular host platforms.

Operational Control

This area of operational management extends to the control of network elements. At a basic level, the operator requires the capability to start and stop individual components of the network, although it often extends to a rich set of operational management tools that enable the operator to control the service and its attributes.

Such control normally is exercised by the ability of the operator to connect to a command port of the managed device and to perform a set of control tasks through this port. Such tasks typically include the capability to alter the configuration of the device, to load and save versions of the configuration, and to load and save versions of the control platform for the device. *Telnet* access generally is used, as it makes relatively minor assumptions about the characteristics of the operational management environment.

This is often more challenging than it sounds, as the command interface is often complemented by the ability to reset the device through a power reset. Where the device is located at an unstaffed remote location, some means of remote power control must be devised to provide such support. SNMP-controlled power packs are often used in this situation. The SNMP *SetRequest* command can be used as a power switch to undertake a power reset of the remote equipment.

Robust operational control mechanisms must not assume that there is always in-band network connectivity to the remote device, so some form of out-band control access is also necessary to support control management. One such design is indicated in Figure 7.8, in which a remote location is configured with power management as well as console port management. A terminal server is configured with the console ports of every managed device, allowing the operator to establish a console connection with any device by a telnet connection to the terminal server. Robust access is provided through the use of an attached modem to the terminal server to allow dial access to the system when primary in-band access is unavailable. Such a configuration allows operational control of software state and power resets from the operations center.

Configuration management also extends to configuration modification. For example, a router may have interfaces added to the unit, or the software

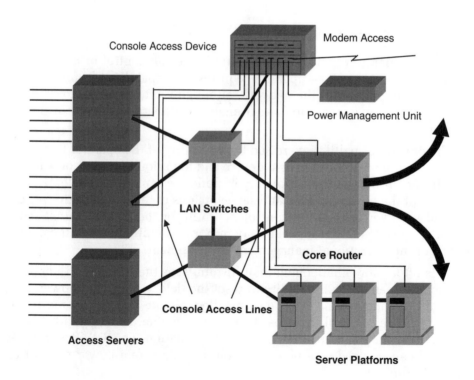

Figure 7.8   Management control access.

configuration may be altered to enable router performance features in response to evolving requirements.

Generally, configuration management is undertaken within a regime of off-site configuration control. The processes involved in configuration management require careful control to ensure that the changes are made to the current configuration, rather than to some previous version of the configuration, and that the new configuration is loaded into the network element.

Inventory Control

This activity also includes inventory management, which maintains a database of network elements, their current configuration, location, in-service history of changes, and fault history. Such an inventory is not only essential from the business perspective of asset tracking, but also can be a valuable source of information in fault management, allowing the service record of a network element to be assessed as part of the process of fault isolation and resolution.

In an Internet network, configuration management also includes the roles of name and address management. It is a major advantage to have a name structure that associates a systematic name to every interface of every router and every service platform. Ideally, the name, in the case of a router, should associate the location of the router, its functional role (whether core, distribution, or access, for example), its location within the site, and the interface type with the name structure. This allows probe tools, such as ping and traceroute, to provide report output that is meaningful in terms of the network's topology. In the case of application platforms, a similar systematic name structure sees the platform's location, type, and application service being integrated into the generated name.

Change Management

The underlying reality of the ISP business is one of constant change, and the configuration management task can best be described in terms of change management. A number of useful practices are intended to minimize the impact of such constant change.

Maintain accurate and detailed records of all physical connections. This includes circuit identification numbers and interfaces, so that any end-to-end path within the network can be identified as a sequence of physical connections and circuits. Accompanying these records should be change logs, indicating which elements have been added or removed from the network configuration, who undertook the change, when, and for what reason. Although such change records need not be retained indefinitely, they are often the best mechanism to expose the likely cause of equipment faults. Equipment that is delivered in a marginal state of stability, or faults that are caused by poor quality installation or the removal of a critical component, should be readily identified from such records.

Plan changes, rather than waiting to see what happens.   Where appropriate, changes should be rehearsed and tested to ensure that the changes on the production platform can be executed cleanly and quickly, with a high confidence in the outcome.

Use locally held configuration copies as the basis of configuration updates.   Routers and application platforms allow the network operator to undertake in-situ changes to the active configuration, or to upload an entire configuration to replace the current settings. Local configuration management allows the imposition of additional rigor into the process, allowing for changed histories to be maintained, together with version control of the incremental changes that have been made to the configuration state. For ISP networks, where there is a constant pressure to adjust the configuration to accommodate more interfaces and more routing performance features, such a discipline of tracking configuration changes allows the manager to back out of unstable configurations. The local configuration database also should include a commentary of the rationale for each change to be stored with the change, to allow for more efficient debugging of the configuration in order to track down instability issues. Such disciplines are well understood in the area of software engineering, but its application to router management is not often appreciated.

Review the change.   Configuration changes are made with some objective in mind. It is a good discipline to describe the specific intent of the change and then review this once the change has been installed to confirm that the objective has been met.

Performance Management

Managing performance is one of the more challenging aspects of network management. It is necessary to define the set of metrics of performance, which have some relevance and bearing to the network and its services, and then match such service-orientated metrics to the data collected from the various managed network elements.

The generic tasks within this area of management fall into four areas:

- Data collection
- Analysis of data for current performance metrics and trends
- Set performance thresholds
- Capacity planning and deployment

The objective of this area of activity is to assist the network manager to reduce levels of network congestion and service degradation and to provide a consistent base level of performance to all users. Using performance management utilities, the network operator can monitor the service performance of the network's transmission, switching, and service delivery platforms. The data gathered here can be used by operations management to see current performance problems.

For example, a user fault concerning slow access to the ISP's mail server may be a result of high congestion levels on one of the circuits on the path between the user and the mail server, or abnormal load on the server itself. An accurate picture of the current performance of the network will assist in rapid primary diagnosis of the fault. Performance data also can use statistical analysis to see longer-term trends as an input into the capacity planning process.

Data Collection

The primary source of data for performance management is SNMP polling for performance metrics. Performance polling gathers data over time that can be analyzed to determine trends and to aid in capacity planning. First, the network manager should determine what MIB variables to poll for, which network elements to poll, and what polling time interval to use. Figure 7.9 indicates a set of SNMP variables that can provide useful input for performance polling of a router.

Polling intervals should bear in mind that high-speed interfaces may see counter wrap-around in a scale of minutes, so that polling intervals of 60 to 120 seconds may be appropriate for very high-speed interfaces. Other variables may be polled at 5-minute intervals without any significant loss of data, or even longer intervals may be used where fine resolution is not required. To keep the data sets to a manageable size, the raw data should be aggregated periodically, storing average and peak intervals for the aggregated time interval.

Overall System Performance Polling

..mib.system.sysuptime	Period of time the system has remained up

vendor extension MIB variables:

..cisco.local.lsystem.freeMem	Amount of free buffer memory
..cisco.local.lsystem.avgBusy1	1 minute average CPU load
..cisco.local.lsystem.avgBusy5	5 minute average CPU load
..cisco.local.lsystem.avgBusyPer	current CPU LOad

Router Interfaces

..interfaces.ifTable.ifInOctets	Total octets received from the interface media
..interfaces.ifTable.ifInUcastPkts	Total unicast packets received
..interfaces.ifTable.ifInNUcastPkts	Total broadcast and multicast packets received
..interfaces.ifTable.ifInDiscards	Total input packets discarded due to local resource limits
..interfaces.ifTable.ifInErrors	Total packets discarded due to error
..interfaces.ifTable.ifOutOctets	Total octets sent to the interface media
..interfaces.ifTable.ifOutUcastPkts	Total unicast packets sent
..interfaces.ifTable.ifOutNUcastPkts	Total broadcast and multicast packets sent
..interfaces.ifTable.ifOutDiscards	Total packets discarded due to local resource limits

vendor extension MIB variables:

..cisco.local.lifTable.locIfInputQueueDrops	Input Buffer queue drop count
..cisco.local.lifTable.locIfOutputQueueDrops	Output Buffer queue drop count
..cisco.local.lifTable.locIfresets	Total number of interface soft resets

Figure 7.9   SNMP variables for performance polling.

For a more detailed view of traffic flows within the network, Cisco has introduced a mechanism it terms "Netflow accounting" into its router platform. This mechanism allows the network operator a different view of the network, based on the number and type of flows being passed across the network at the point of measurement. This profile information can provide useful input in the performance measurement process as to the nature of the traffic flows.

Data Analysis

Data analysis is predicated by a thorough understanding of the system being analyzed, and an ISP network does behave differently than many other network systems. Unlike a telephony network, in which a call takes a fixed amount of resources from the network, a data network has a variable traffic load arising from each end-to-end transaction. The overall majority of traffic, up to some 90 percent of the total traffic, is carried within the TCP protocol. It is necessary, therefore, to understand the behavior of TCP and the interaction of the protocol with the network.

TCP attempts to adapt its load to the characteristics of the network using a flow-control algorithm. In the initial startup phase, termed *slow start*, TCP transmits one segment and then awaits an ACK from this segment from the receiver. Upon receipt of the ACK, the transmitter sends two segments, which in turn will elicit two ACKs from the receiver, and the transmitter continues to send two segments for every ACK received. This exponential rate increase continues until the transmit window exceeds the transmitter's available buffer space. In this case, the transmitter is sending at its maximum rate, and will attempt to continue to do so for the duration of the session. Alternatively, the network loses a packet prior to transmit buffer exhaustion. Upon packet loss, the sender collapses its transmit window by one-half and then adopts a more conservative transmission rate increase, increasing the transmission window by one segment every round-trip time. The flow behavior of TCP is indicated in Figure 7.10. This adaptive behavior is intended to probe and then occupy the maximal level of available end-to-end capacity. The flow rate of any individual flow is limited only by the local transmitter buffer size, corresponding to a maximum flow rate of a buffer every round-trip time, and a "fair share" of the available capacity on the end-to-end path. As end host buffers increase in size, and the TCP window scaling option is widely deployed, the former limit tends to disappear, and the latter limit is more critical. In this model, the optimal operating point is one in which the TCP protocol stack interacts to cause the network to operate at maximum efficiency. One TCP session attempts to operate at the maximum path bandwidth, and two parallel TCP sessions interact so that they stabilize with each session consuming approximately one-half of the path bandwidth, and so on.

At what point is a network link operating at maximum efficiency? The answer is not exactly 100 percent utilization, but it is not far from this in an ideal world. In an ideal world, the buffer absorbs most of the speed variations due to slow start for new sessions and congestion avoidance in the steady state. The buffer queue depth oscillates quite markedly between a full queue and packet overflow and an empty queue. Irrespective of the number of concurrent TCP sessions across the circuit, a single circuit network should have an average utilization of close to 100 percent while there is any form of network activity.

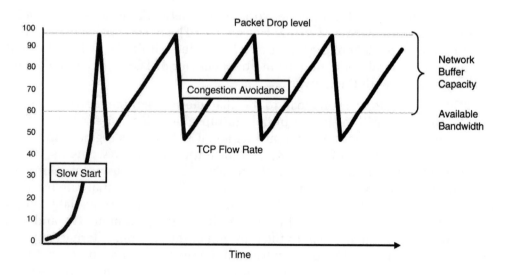

Figure 7.10   TCP flow behavior.

Of course, networks do not replicate this theoretical homogeneity, and a number of factors tend to reduce this point of maximum efficiency:

◆ The diversity of the concurrent active paths
◆ The diversity of round-trip times
◆ The mix of UDP and TCP traffic
◆ The mix of short and long volume traffic flows

These factors all indicate that maximum attainable circuit load is closer to 90–95 percent than 100 percent. Circuits with sustained load levels at or above this level should be carefully examined, as it is likely that the associated router is operating in a mode of buffer exhaustion, and the only remedy at this stage is to augment the capacity of the circuit or reconfigure the routing of the network to relieve the traffic load on the link.

Internet traffic exhibits a day/night traffic pattern. This pattern is not as marked as the telephone system, in which both parties need to be awake to complete the call. In the Internet, only one party needs to undertake the trans-

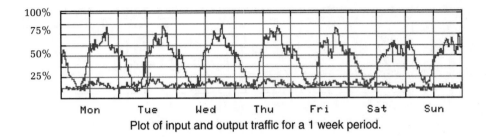

Plot of input and output traffic for a 1 week period.

Figure 7.11   Normally operating link.

action, because the server is likely to be an automated platform. The overall performance threshold is to position the peak load on each circuit at some 85–90 percent of the available capacity. Figure 7.11 indicates the load patterns for an optimally loaded link. As the link takes more traffic, the peak periods start to saturate the link, and a *plateau* load signature commences, in which the line is held at near saturation levels for an extended period, as indicated in Figure 7.12. As the load increases, the plateau effect is more marked, as indicated in Figure 7.13.

Setting Performance Thresholds

This analysis of what is considered acceptable performance can yield threshold points for remedial action. One metric may be phrased in terms of peak

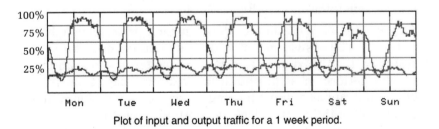

Plot of input and output traffic for a 1 week period.

Figure 7.12   Overloaded link.

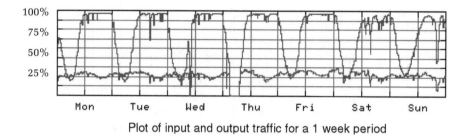

Plot of input and output traffic for a 1 week period

Figure 7.13   Saturated link.

load, so that a link is considered saturated when load exceeds 85 percent of available capacity for more than 10 percent of the time within a week-long analysis window. A metric also may be phrased in terms of overall average load, which will be more helpful in the business cost analysis. A metric may be that a link is saturated when the average weekly line occupancy in the direction of the heaviest traffic load exceeds 55 percent.

However, if a slightly worse peak performance were considered acceptable, higher traffic thresholds might be used as a mechanism to decrease the average unit cost of traffic passed through the circuit. The reason why unit cost decreases with more traffic is that the cost of the circuit is assumed to be fixed for a certain capacity. The more traffic that can be passed across this circuit for a fixed price, the lower the unit cost of data transmission for a fixed unit of data. Equally lower thresholds also can be applied to produce an outcome of superior performance characteristics, at a price of a higher unit cost of traffic. Further analysis of the situation can yield a more generic relationship between overall performance quality and the unit cost of data transmission, indicated in a general fashion in Figure 7.14.

The real question is: Who should set the general performance threshold for an ISP network? The answer is that within the bounds of technically acceptable thresholds, the decision is a marketing matter and not an engineering problem. The performance threshold has a direct bearing on transmission costs, which in turn has a direct bearing on the price position of the ISP service product. In the ISP marketplace, a continuum of price and performance positioning is visible. In general, where higher pricing is associated with higher service performance, a relatively direct relationship exists between price and performance, as indicated in Figure 7.15. Precisely where each ISP positions itself within the competitive market is a business decision, not a technical decision. When a range of acceptable performance threshold values has been determined as an outcome of network engineering, the decision to use a particular set of threshold values is a marketing decision.

Planning

Too commonly, the lead time for ordering transmission capacity is proportional to the capacity ordered. Large transmission systems require a long lead time from order to deployment. Therefore, getting the planning process to give accurate outcomes is a critical business success factor. Not including adequate lead time, and waiting until the need is already established before ordering additional capacity, implies that the network will be running under performance stress for the lead time of the order. The clients may not be so forgiving or patient, and such a situation may lead to loss of market due to poor service quality. Ordering too early implies that the ISP may be paying for idle capacity, effectively increasing operational costs without any increase in matching revenue. Again, this makes for poor business performance.

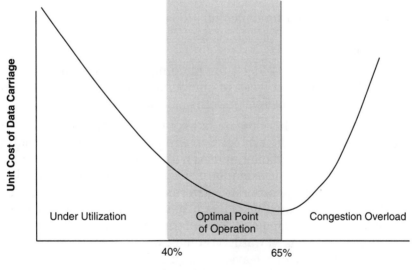

Figure 7.14   Relationship between line load and unit cost.

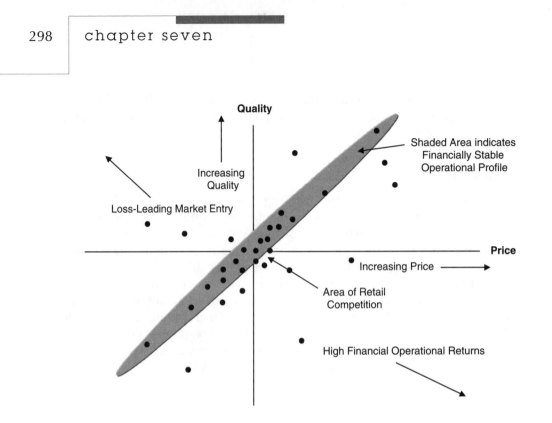

Figure 7.15 Price performance relationship.

Accordingly, it is essential to get the planning process producing accurate results, not only for the next week of operation, but in terms of forward projections of requirements that span months, quarters, and years.

One way to undertake this process is by a market demand model. Such a model attempts to predict the average demand per-client type, segmenting the market into a number of segments, and then looking at the average demand for services from each type. For example, this may be residential, small enterprise, medium enterprise, corporate, government, educational, and Internet service, although such coarse segments usually are broken further into more tightly bounded market segments. The Internet service profile for each segment is estimated in terms of traffic volumes, demand for mail and Web services, and similar metrics of the average segment profile. The total number of entities who fit within each segment within the area of activity is estimated, and the number of such entities who already have undertaken service contracts is estimated, together with an estimation of the ISP's own current market share. The market growth model than attempts to forecast uptake by the remainder of the market and the likely market share of this sector for the ISP, as well as factoring in the net result from any churn of the existing market base. The outcome of this model is a total demand for services that can be translated into a capacity projection. This, in turn, can be used as input to the planning process. Such projections do have their uncertainties, relating to a highly dynamic competitive position within the ISP industry and a poorly understood demand model, which is highly susceptible to technology evolution.

Another planning model is that of forward extrapolation. Here, trend analysis is undertaken in historical data, and this trend analysis is used as the basis of forward projections. The assumption underlying such trend analysis is that the various market factors will average out and the net result will be a sustaining growth level, which is equal to the historical position. Of course, this model is equally insensitive to competitive market factors and technology inputs, and as a result is also quite poor at longer-term predictions. A projection model is indicated in Figure 7.16, which uses forward exponential trend analysis to arrive at a capacity projection.

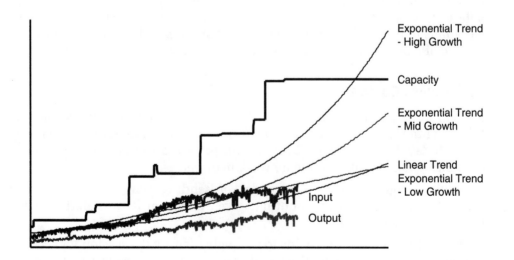

Figure 7.16   Capacity projections through trend analysis.

The optimal approach is to undertake both forecasting activities and analyze the assumptions and risk inherent in each forecast. This should be undertaken at regular intervals, to allow the previous predictions to be matched against actual performance to ensure that the underlying assumptions in each model are refined to match the current situation. It should be recognized that the larger the capacity requirement, the greater the lead time required to secure the capacity, and the larger the associated capital investment. At the final point, it is a business decision as to how to conduct this activity, and the role of the network manager is to ensure that the data provided from the network is an accurate and up-to-date picture of the network's capacity and usage levels.

Accounting Management

Here, we will examine the set of tools and processes that allow ISPs to account for, and invoice, the use of the network and associated services. The most obvious application for such data is in billing systems, in which accounting data is accumulated within the network and a rating algorithm is applied to this data, with the output being a set of customer identifiers and invoice amounts. This table can be passed to a finance system for invoicing and credit management. The structure used here is to examine the accounting requirements for various forms of customer connection and the way in which this data can be accessed and recorded. Following this basic framework, some variations to this will be examined. These variations allow for accounting for the use of a particular service or resource located within the network.

Dial Access Customers

Accounting is the third part of the *AAA* customer management environment, following *authentication* and *authorization*. Two common AAA systems are in use today, *Radius* and *TACACS+*. Both present a similar view in terms of accounting functionality to the network manager.

Radius accounting uses the model of sending start and stop session accounting records to an accounting server. A typical Radius start packet is indicated in Figure 7.17.

The start packet uses two fields to uniquely identify the session for accounting purposes: the NAS identifier and the accounting session identifier. The NAS server generates a corresponding Radius stop packet, as indicated in Figure 7.18.

User-Name = "geoff"
NAS-Identifier = 139.130.204.1
NAS-Port = 20435
Acct-Status-Type = Start
Acct-Delay-Time = 0
Acct-Session-Id = "22"
Acct-Authentic = RADIUS
Framed-Protocol = PPP
Framed-Address = 10.0.0.2

Figure 7.17   Radius start packet.

TACACS+ is very similar, in that there is a comparable use of attribute value pairs, and the same architecture of issuing a start and stop accounting record is used. The attributes of a session that can be used as input into an accounting process include the start and stop times of the session (and the derived connection time), the byte counts for the session, and the packet counts for the session. The essential attributes used within the accounting process are the time fields, the IP address used by the client, and the octet and packet counts that relate to the session.

User-Name = "geoff"
NAS-Identifier = 139.130.204.1
NAS-Port = 20435
Acct-Status-Type = Stop
Acct-Delay-Time = 0
Acct-Session-Id = "22"
Acct-Authentic = RADIUS
Acct-Session-Time = 10
Acct-Input-Octets = 13459
Acct-Output-Octets = 33484
Acct-Input-Packets = 256
Acct-Output-Packets = 750
Framed-Protocol = PPP
Framed-Address = 10.0.0.2

Figure 7.18   Radius stop packet.

The issue with both Radius and TACACS+ is the implicit assumption that individual sessions occur within time periods that can be accommodated within the accounting time window. However, if the accounting is undertaken weekly, and the client has established a long-held session, which extends over several weeks, then the accounting for the session is accumulated within the NAS until the session stops. Some ISPs elect to directly poll the NAS session statistics from the NAS, using vendor extensions to the standard MIB to allow this to occur within the SNMP framework. The advantage of this approach is that it allows uniform processing for dial access and permanently connected clients. The accounting stop record is used to ensure that the session closure is accurately accounted. A typical accounting record for a session is indicated in Figure 7.19.

The advantage of this kind of approach is that it can be used across a variety of environments of both short- and long-held calls; it is compatible with the accounting mechanisms used for permanently connected clients, so that a single accounting and performance reporting system can be used; and it provides a perspective of the performance of the connection, as well as simply recording the totals associated with the entire session.

Permanently Connected Customers

Permanently connected clients do not generate accounting records on creation of the connection, nor on disconnection, as such events are highly infrequent (or at least the expectation is that such events are highly infrequent), and certainly less frequent than the accounting cycle. Also, authentication and authorization often are not used on permanently leased circuits, as the ISP and the client both trust the carrier to implement the circuit in a manner that ensures the circuit is secure and the integrity of the connection is maintained.

Time	NAS	Session	Octet Counters		Data Source
89363670	139.130.204.1	22	0	0	Radius Start
89363800	139.130.204.1	22	240	680	SNMP
89364300	139.130.204.1	22	2364	5367	SNMP
89364800	139.130.204.1	22	4943	10235	SNMP
89364956	139.130.204.1	22	5356	13344	Radius Stop

Figure 7.19   Session accounting entries.

Instead of being able to use accounting start and stop records, the accounting system must be able to poll the point of connection at regular intervals and report back to the accounting system on the status of the customer connection. Given that a customer is connected to a physical port on a router in the simplest form of this model, a viable approach is to regularly poll the counter interfaces using SNMP, retrieving the current value of the packet, octet, and error counters. This information can be stored, with a timestamp, for later analysis. A typical snapshot of a router is indicated in Figure 7.20.

The packet counters may not be collected in this process, as a tariff that has a component based on packet counts or packet rates is uncommon. Accordingly, the minimal set of per-port SNMP counters to collect for accounting purposes would be the interface input and output octet counters and the input error counter.

Timestamp	Interface	Input Octets	Output Octets	Output Errors	InQueue Drops	Interface Name
897747297	I1	2743178883	2081000986	297099	2589	FastEthernet0/0/0
897747297	I2	997448829	3518258030	1643	224416990	Hssi4/0
897747297	I3	4219733489	60459786	0	4241898	Hssi6/0
897747357	I1	2887592138	2393878769	297099	2589	FastEthernet0/0/0
897747357	I2	1236920940	3647419956	1643	224416990	Hssi4/0
897747357	I3	4283217664	60460849	0	4241898	Hssi6/0
897747417	I1	3027536071	2718977088	297099	2589	FastEthernet0/0/0
897747417	I2	1480030909	3772072808	1643	224416991	Hssi4/0
897747417	I3	60109082	60461893	0	4241898	Hssi6/0
897747477	I1	3163387570	3034458667	297099	2589	FastEthernet0/0/0
897747477	I2	1716122973	3892334246	1643	224416991	Hssi4/0
897747477	I3	129753968	60463300	0	4241898	Hssi6/0
897747537	I1	3297014206	3341533971	297099	2589	FastEthernet0/0/0
897747537	I2	1948599952	4011987302	1643	224416991	Hssi4/0
897747537	I3	195596108	60464497	0	4241898	Hssi6/0
897747597	I1	3433145515	3647380738	297099	2589	FastEthernet0/0/0
897747597	I2	2179959595	4133750827	1643	224416991	Hssi4/0
897747597	I3	261023195	60466008	0	4241898	Hssi6/0
897747657	I1	3570082119	3957994287	297099	2589	FastEthernet0/0/0
897747657	I2	2417684622	4255817106	1643	224416991	Hssi4/0
897747657	I3	324198021	60467472	0	4241898	Hssi6/0

Figure 7.20   SNMP log file extract.

The major issue in this technique is to map a customer back to a port. In the Radius and TACACS+ models, the user name is used as the key to the customer database, allowing the accounting records to be placed against a specific customer. In the environment of the permanent connection, a similar functional mapping must be devised. The SNMP-based query returns a variable termed the *interface index*, which is the index into a table of interface-specific SNMP variables. Using a simple mapping from a customer identifier to a SNMP vector or router identifier and interface number in this form of accounting is possible. However, this process is not without some attendant issues, principally as an outcome of the constant growth pressure that the network is subject to. This pressure implies the addition of new interface cards to routers, and the use of replacement higher density interface systems, as a constant feature of the ISP environment. The SNMP interface numbers are not fixed across system reboots, and the mapping between customer connections and router interface numbers requires constant manual maintenance.

An alternative mechanism is to use an IP address uniquely associated with a customer. The customer identifier is now associated with a router and an IP address. The query process polls the forwarding table MIB for the interface associated with the IP address. This interface number then is used to poll the SNMP variables associated with the accounting and performance of the customer's connection. This does extend the time taken to undertake the polling and relies on a strict regime of allocation of IP addresses, but such a strict regime is a prerequisite of IP management in any case.

Alternatively, if the router attempts to preserve the interface description field of SNMP (*ifDescr*) of the interface across reboots, the interface description can be used with the router identifier to describe a customer. This implies that the polling process needs to record the interface description as well as the accounting and performance variables, and this interface can be used to map the values to a particular customer.

The next issue is to determine how often to poll the router for SNMP performance variables. How frequently depends on the performance analysis interval and on the maximum speed of the interfaces being polled. A 100-Mbps interface can increment the octet count variable at a rate of up to 12,500,000 octets per second. At the maximal data transfer rate this corresponds to an increment of 1 billion every 80 seconds, or a cycle of the 32-bit counter every six minutes. To ensure that at least two data points exist per cycle of the counter, use a polling interval of every 120 seconds. For a large network, this interval can generate a very large volume of polling data, and it is a useful planning exercise to ensure that the polling interval corresponds to the maximum interface bandwidth and that the polling system has sufficient data storage to hold the polled data.

Using the standard MIB to poll for interface values is not always possible. When using shared interfaces such as timeslots in a channelized access bearer, Frame Relay Virtual Circuits and ATM Virtual Circuits, technology-specific MIBs, need to be used to access the appropriate variables that describe the performance of the virtual interface. Here, the customer interface is a subinterface of a physical interface, so the identification model of router and interface descriptor can be extended into a triplet of router, interface descriptor, and channel or circuit identifier.

Permanently connected customers also may use multiple parallel connections, with either MPPP as a framing protocol or some form of load-balanced routing intended to evenly spread the traffic across the parallel connections. How do we ensure that the per-interface counter records produced by the accounting system can be added together in a meaningful way? The essential attribute is to ensure that all the measurements are synchronized at the same moment in time. This is not possible to undertake within a large polling system, because you cannot request many thousands of variables across many hundreds of routers at the same precise moment in time. The polling system would suffer "clock tick overload." The alternative is to record accurate time-stamps with each polled item of data, and then, in the initial data analysis, use linear interpolation of the data points to infer the data values at precise clock chime points. For example, the raw data samples may be undertaken at 130-second intervals. The data analysis system uses linear interpolation to generate data points that correspond to clock chimes at precise five-minute intervals. This allows data points from a number of interfaces to be added together to produce an aggregated view of the line's performance and volumes transferred.

The next question is where to collect these data points. The most logical choice is to use the customer-facing interface of the access router as the data collection point. This router is physically secure, as it is located on the ISP's premises, and good connectivity exists between the access router and the ISP network management unit, which is undertaking the polling. When a synchronous access circuit is used between the client and the ISP, no significant difference exists between the traffic profile as measured on the access router and the traffic profile as measured on the client network's edge router. However, when using a switched access media, such as Frame Relay or some ATM service types, this direct data clock relationship does not hold, and the traffic profile may be changed by the access network. The traffic profile as measured at the egress of the ISP network is not necessarily the same as the profile measured at the ingress of the customer network when using such switched access media. Where the ISP operates the CPE, it is a good suggestion to use CPE-based polling for accounting purposes, so that the accounting operation is undertaken in such a way that it reflects the traffic volumes passed to the client at the client demarcation point.

Variations of Accounting Methods

The variations to this accounting model are largely based on marketing models in which there is a desire to separately account for the use of a particular service in order to present the customer with a separate tariff for such services.

The base model of interface-based metrics is that of a distance-independent, application-independent accounting model, in which the distance that a packet has traveled through the network or the service that generated the packet is not recorded by the network, and therefore, not collected by the accounting system. This may not be a sufficiently good fit for an ISP who wants to operate a set of distinguished services at tariffs that are not part of a common Internet carriage tariff. What systems may require separate accounting? This may be a voice gateway, a Web cache, a Usenet news feed, or even a satellite path, where there is a need to associate a differentiated tariff for the use of the service, without establishing a completely independent access overlay across the basic Internet carriage service.

Attaching a packet-level encapsulation, which could record such accounting data, is possible, but to date, such systems have not been seen by the industry as a feasible technical direction. The alternative is to undertake accounting at interior points in the network and collect sufficient information to allow the data to be attributed unambiguously to a client.

One potential mechanism is to use an accounting system that records the source and destination addresses of every packet from a nominated service and the packet size and accumulate this data using a granularity of source and destination address. This is a long-standing area of activity within the IETF, currently being refined within the RTFM Working Group. By analyzing the packet headers, we can re-create the traffic flows, including identification of the initiator of the flow, as well as the duration and volume of the flow, together with the application port associated with the flow. A similar accounting structure is undertaken within Cisco's Netflow accounting structure, where records of the source and destination addresses and port numbers, as well as the packet and byte count associated with the flow, are generated by the router.

In this model of accounting, each packet must be assigned to a client, and to do so requires a match of the source or destination address to those addresses routed by each client. This interior accounting allows for accounting of all kinds of services, as indicated in Figure 7.21, where accounting for the use of a satellite service, a Usenet feed, and a Web cache is indicated. Such an accounting system could be used to disaggregate transit tariffs, undertaking a split accounting of international and domestic carriage.

However, consider three strong caveats before the marketing euphoria takes over:

◆ Interior accounting does not take into account that the packet may not be delivered to the destination in the header. The packet may be dropped by the ISP, or the packet may use loose source routing options that actually direct the packet to a different egress point than that specified in the destination field. The packet also may have been passed to the ISP from a different ingress point than that

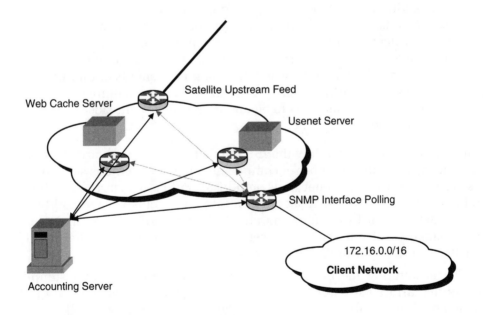

Figure 7.21   Interior accounting in a network.

indicated in the source field. Interior accounting is not completely robust.

◆ The assumption being made here is that each address is uniquely advertised by only one client. This is not the case, and as a client multihomes to a number of ISPs, the same address may be advertised by a number of ISP clients of the upstream ISP. In the case of a multihomed address, the necessary information to capture is both the destination address and some indication from the routing system of the egress port that the routing system has selected. Cisco provides a mechanism to snapshot both packet flow accounting and the next hop AS of the destination IP address in its proprietary Netflow accounting product, which is a reasonable mechanism to address this issue, subject to the caveat regarding loose source routing. Robust interior accounting mechanisms require a simultaneous indication from the routing as to the client identity.

◆ For a large-volume service, packet-based accounting can generate very large amounts of data, because the number of discrete accounting buckets is the cross-product of the source and destination addresses, and local storage and primary analysis are necessarily undertaken at a point in the network very close to the accounting data collection point. The requirement to deploy remote accounting platforms adds to the operational cost of the operation, which may outweigh the marginal benefits of internal richness of the tariff structure. Interior accounting requires primary storage and analysis to be undertaken at a point close to the interior accounting point.

Interior accounting can allow the ISP to create a structured tariff that breaks Internet access into a number of components. It allows various services, such as Web cache access, Usenet feeds, and local traffic, to be tariffed at different rates, allowing the ISP to break out of a standard inclusive commodity tariff. Such selective tariffing offers the client greater ability to tailor its service requirements, outsourcing various service activities to the ISP where the ISP's tariffs present opportunities for the client.

The accounting mechanism needs to make relatively few assumptions about the tariffing structures that the ISP may deploy, as some agility in this area, noted by the ability to quickly set tariff structures in a rapidly evolving market, is a marked advantage for the ISP. The use of a relatively fine-grained accounting mechanism, which undertakes data collection at intervals on the order of five minutes, allows the ISP to amass detailed information about network usage patterns and also structure a tariff, which can make use of peak 5-minute data rates, sustained data rates, ingress data volumes, and egress data volumes and can do so within a set of time periods reflecting peak, shoulder, and off-peak zones.

The use of service-specific interior accounting mechanisms is one that should be exercised with considerable care. Although it does allow for service-differentiated tariff structures, and for a crude level of distance-differentiated tariffs within the overall ISP tariff structure, the caveats regarding the high cost, technical challenges, and risks of inaccuracy of the accounting data act as dampening factors on deployment. Considerable care has to be exercised to create a tariff structure here that is tolerant of such higher margins of accounting inaccuracy.

Summary

Network management encompasses more than operational management of network faults. Network management encompasses a management role which ensures that the network provides the level of service quality that matches the design intent, bringing together the roles of operational management, configuration management, performance management, and accounting management in order to focus on the primary objective of service excellence.

In small ISP operations, these several roles may be undertaken by one or two engineers. The temptation to respond to each set of faults without bringing any systematic process to bear onto the activity is all too often overwhelming. However, the strategic objective of every ISP is to expand its client base and its revenue base, and such expansion is inevitably realized within the management domain. At this stage, any earlier devised processes will come into their own, allowing additional operational staff members to quickly assume a productive role within the operational group. Larger ISP operations, such as those within a larger communications enterprise, generally have a very strong reliance of robust management processes, allowing a very large service division to operate the Internet service, within a set of design criteria specified by a smaller set of specialist Internet engineers.

The major task of any ISP is that of managing growth and ensuring that growth of the management role can be achieved realizing efficiencies of scale as a critical strategic objective of the ISP.

chapter eight

Quality of Service

Acknowledgment is given to Paul Ferguson, who co-authored the material in this chapter.

The Internet historically has offered a single level of service, that of "best effort," in which all data packets are treated with equity in the network. However, the Internet itself does not offer a single level of service quality. Some areas of the network exhibit high levels of congestion and consequently poor quality, but other areas display consistent levels of high-quality service. Customers are now voicing a requirement to define a consistent service quality they wish to purchase, and ISPs now must seek ways in which to implement such a requirement. This effort is happening within the umbrella called *Quality of Service* (QoS).

Of course, this phrase has now become overused, often in vague, nondefinitive references. QoS discussions currently embrace abstract concepts and varying ideologies; moreover, these discussions lack a unified definition on what QoS actually is and how it might be implemented. Subsequently, expectations regarding QoS have not been appropriately managed within the Internet community at large regarding how QoS technologies might realistically be deployed on a global scale. A more important question is whether ubiquitous end-to-end QoS is even realistic in the Internet, given the fact that the decentralized nature of the Internet does not lend itself to homogeneous mechanisms to differentiate traffic. This chapter examines the various methods of delivering QoS in the Internet and attempts to provide an objective overview on whether QoS in the Internet is fact, fiction, or a matter of compromise.

Quality of Service Defined

Dismissing the entrepreneurial nature of the Internet today is hard to do—this is no longer a research project. For most organizations connected to the global Internet, it's a full-fledged business interest. Having said that, it is equally hard to dismiss the poor service quality the users frequently experience; the rapid growth of the Internet and increasing levels of traffic make it difficult for Internet users to enjoy consistent and predictable end-to-end levels of service quality for Internet transactions.

What causes poor service quality within the Internet? The glib, and rather uninformative, response is *localized instances of substandard network engineering which is incapable of carrying the impressed traffic load.* Perhaps the more appropriate question is, "What are the components of service quality, and how can they be measured?" *Service quality* in the Internet can be expressed as the combination of network-imposed *delay, jitter, bandwidth,* and *reliability.*

> **Delay.**　The elapsed time for a packet to be passed from the sender, through the network, to the receiver. The higher the delay, the greater the stress that is placed on the transport protocol to operate efficiently. For the TCP protocol, higher levels of delay imply greater amounts of data held *in transit* in the network, which in turn places performance stress on the counters and timers associated with the protocol. TCP is a *self-clocking* protocol. The sender's transmission rate is dynamically adjusted to the flow of signal information coming back from the receiver, via the *reverse direction acknowledgments* (ACKs), which notify the sender of successful reception. The greater the delay between sender and receiver, the more insensitive this feedback loop becomes. With long delay, the protocol becomes more insensitive to short-term dynamic changes in network load. For interactive voice and video applications, the introduction of delay causes the system to appear unresponsive.

> **Jitter.**　The variation in end-to-end transit delay (in mathematical terms, jitter is measurable as the absolute value of the first differential of the sequence of individual delay measurements). High levels of jitter cause the TCP protocol to make very conservative estimates of *round-trip time* (RTT), causing the protocol to operate highly inefficiently when it must revert to time-outs to reestablish a data flow. High levels of jitter in UDP-based applications are unacceptable in situations

where the application is real-time based, such as an audio or video signal. In such cases, jitter causes the signal to be distorted, which can be rectified only by increasing the receiver's reassembly playback queue. This, in turn, affects the delay of the signal, making interactive sessions very cumbersome to maintain.

Bandwidth. The maximal data transfer rate that can be sustained between two end points. Bandwidth is limited not only by the physical infrastructure of the traffic path within the transit networks, which provides an upper bound to available bandwidth, but also by the number of other flows that share common components of this selected end-to-end path.

Reliability. Commonly conceived as a property of the transmission system. In this context, reliability can be thought of as the average error rate of the medium. Reliability can also be a by-product of the switching system. A poorly configured or poorly performing switching system can alter the order of packets in transit, delivering packets to the receiver in a different order than that of the original transmission by the sender, or even dropping packets through transient routing loops. Unreliable or error-prone network transit paths also can cause retransmission of the lost packets. TCP cannot distinguish between loss due to packet corruption and loss due to congestion, and packet loss invokes the same congestion avoidance behavior response from the sender. This causes the sender's transmit rates to be reduced by invoking congestion avoidance algorithms, even though no congestion may have been experienced by the network. In the case of UDP-based voice and video applications, unreliability causes induced distortion in the original analogue signal at the receiver's end.

Accordingly, when we refer to differentiated service quality, we are referring to differentiation of one or more of these four basic quality metrics for a particular category of traffic. Now that we have defined some basic parameters of service quality, the next issue is: How is service quality implemented within an Internet environment?

Implementing Service Quality

This environment is composed of a collection of routers and transmission links. Routers receive an incoming packet, determine the next hop interface, and place the packet on the output queue for the selected interface. Transmission links have characteristics of delay, bandwidth, and reliability. Poor service quality is typically encountered when the level of traffic selecting a particular hop exceeds the transmission bandwidth of the hop for an extended period of time. In such cases, the router's output queues associated with the saturated transmission hop begin to fill. This process causes additional transit delay (increased *jitter* and *delay*), until the point where the queue is filled, and the router then is forced to discard packets (reduced *reliability*). This situation forces adaptive flows to reduce their sending rate to minimize congestion loss, reducing the available *bandwidth* for the application. Poor service quality can be generated in other ways as well. Instability in the routing protocols may cause the routers to rapidly alter their selection of the best next hop interface. This causes traffic within an end-to-end flow to take divergent paths, which in turn induces significant levels of *jitter* and an increased probability of out-of-order packet delivery (reduced *reliability*).

When we refer to the quality of a service, we are looking at these four metrics as the base parameters of quality, and a variety of network events can affect these parameter values.

Also, in an attempt to take a uniform "best effort" network service environment and introduce structures that allow some form of service differentiation, the tools that allow such service environments to be constructed are configurations within the network's routers designed to implement one or more of the following:

◆ Signal the lower level transmission links to use a different transmission servicing criteria for particular service profiles.

◆ Alter the next hop selection algorithm in order to select a path whose characteristics match the desired service levels.

◆ Alter the router's queuing delay and packet discard algorithms so that packets are scheduled to receive transmission resources in accordance with their relative service level.

◆ Alter the characteristics of the traffic flow (or its shape) as it enters the network, to conform to a contracted profile and associated service level.

The "art" of implementing an effective QoS environment is to use these tools in a way that can construct robust differentiated service environments.

QoS, as opposed to service quality, can be interpreted as a method to provide preferential treatment to some arbitrary amount of network traffic, as opposed to all traffic being treated as "best effort." In providing such preferential treatment, the network is configured to increase the quality level of one of more of these basic metrics for this particular category of traffic. Several tools are available to provide this differentiation, ranging from preferential queuing disciplines to bandwidth reservation protocols, and from ATM-layer congestion and bandwidth allocation mechanisms to traffic-shaping, each of which may be appropriate depending on what problem is being solved. We do not see QoS as being principally concerned about attempting to deliver *guaranteed* levels of service to individual traffic flows within the Internet. Although such network mechanisms have a place within smaller network environments, the sheer size of today's Internet effectively precludes any QoS approach that attempts to reliably segment the network on a flow-by-flow basis, offering the customer guarantees regarding the performance of the environment. The major technology force that has driven the explosive growth of the Internet as a communications medium is the use of stateless switching systems, which provide variable best-effort service levels to intelligent peripheral devices. Recent experience has indicated that this approach has extraordinary scaling properties. The stateless switching architectures can scale easily into scales of gigabits per second, preserving a continued functionality in which the unit cost of stateless switching has decreased at a level close to the basic scaling rate.

If a network cannot provide a reasonable base level of service quality, then attempting to provide some method of differentiated QoS on the same infrastructure is virtually impossible. This is where careful application of engineering, design, and adherence to a set of network architectural principles plays a significant role.

QoS and Network Engineering, Design, and Architecture

Before examining methods to introduce QoS into the Internet, we must examine methods of constructing a network which exemplify sound network engineering principles—scalability, stability, availability, and predictability.

Typically, this exercise entails a conservative approach in designing and operating the network, undertaking measures to ensure that the routing system within the network remains stable and ensuring that peak-level traffic flows sit comfortably within the bandwidth and switching capabilities of the network. Unfortunately, some of these seminal principles are ignored in favor of maximizing revenue potential. For example, it is not uncommon for an ISP to oversubscribe an access aggregation point by a factor of 25:1, especially in the case of calculating the number of subscribers compared to the number of available modem ports. Nor is it uncommon to see interprovider exchange points experiencing peak packet drop rates in excess of 20 percent of all transit traffic. In a single-quality, best-effort environment, the practice of oversubscription allows the introduction of additional load into the network at the expense of marginal degradation to all existing active subscribers. This practice can be very dangerous, and if miscalculated, can result in seriously degraded service performance (due to induced congestion) for all subscribers. Therefore, oversubscription should not be done arbitrarily.

Engineering Considerations for QoS

Network engineering is arguably a compromise between engineering capabilities for the average load levels and engineering capabilities that are intended to handle peak load conditions. In the case of dimensioning access ports, close attention must be paid to user traffic characteristics and modem pool port usage, based on time-of-day and day-of-week, for an extended period prior to making such an engineering commitment. Even after such traffic analysis has been undertaken, the deployed configuration should be closely monitored on a continuing and consistent basis to detect changes in usage and characteristics. It is very easy to assume that only a fraction of subscribers may be active at any given time, or to assume average and peak usage rates, but without close observation and prior traffic sampling, a haphazard assumption could dramatically affect the commercial viability of your ISP business.

Also, it is necessary for the ISP network operator to understand the nature, size, and timing of traffic flows that are carried across the network's transmission systems. Although a critical component of traffic analysis is the monitoring of the capacity on individual transmission links, monitoring the dispersion of end-to-end traffic flows allows the network operator to ensure that the designed transmission topology provides an efficient carriage for the data traffic. It also attempts to avoid having major traffic flows routed suboptimally across multiple hops, incurring additional cost and potentially imposing a performance penalty through additional routing points through the transit.

The same can be said of maintaining stability in the ISP's network routing system. Failure to create a highly stable routing system can result in destinations being intermittently unreachable and ultimately frustrating customers. Care should be taken on all similar infrastructure and critical service issues, such as *Domain Name System* (DNS) services. The expertise of the engineering and support staff will be reflected in the service quality of the network, like it or not.

The Role of Good Design in QoS

Understanding that poorly designed networks do not lend themselves to QoS scenarios is not difficult. If acceptable levels of service quality cannot be maintained, then it is quite likely that adding QoS in an effort to create some level of service differentiation will never be effective. Granted, it may allow the network performance to degrade more gracefully in times of severe congestion for some applications operated within the group of elevated QoS customers. However, limiting the impact of degradation for some, at the cost of increasing the impact for the remainder of the customer base, is not the most ingenious or sensible use for QoS mechanisms. The introduction of QoS differentiation into the network is only partially effective if those customers who do not subscribe to a QoS service are adversely impacted by those who do choose to subscribe to such a service. After all, if non-QoS subscribers are negatively impacted, they will seek other service providers for their connectivity, or they will be forced to subscribe to the QoS service to obtain an acceptable service level. This last sentence requires a bit of unconventional logic, because not all subscribers can realistically be QoS subscribers; this violates some of the most fundamental QoS strategies.

The design principles necessary to support effective QoS mechanisms can be expressed in terms of the four base service quality parameters noted in the previous section: delay, jitter, bandwidth, and reliability. To minimize delay, the network must be based upon a transmission topology that reflects the pattern of end-to-end traffic flows and a routing system design that attempts to localize traffic so that minimal distance paths are always preferred. To minimize jitter, the routing system must be held in as stable a state as possible. Router queue depths also must be configured so that they remain within the same approximate size as the delay bandwidth product of the transmission link fed by the queue. Also, unconditional preferential queuing mechanisms should be avoided in favor of weighting or similar fair access queue mechanisms, to ensure that all classes of traffic are not delayed indefinitely while awaiting access to the transmission resources. Selection of *maximum transfer unit* (MTU) sizes also should be undertaken to avoid MTUs that are much greater than the delay bandwidth product of the link—again, as a means of minimizing levels of network-induced jitter.

An Architecture for QoS

In terms of overall reliability, the onus is on the network architect to use transmission media that have a very low intrinsic bit error rate and to use router components that have high levels of availability and stability. Care should also be taken to ensure that the routing system is configured to provide deterministic outcomes, minimizing the risk of packet reordering. Transmission capacity, or bandwidth, should be engineered to minimize the level of congestion-induced packet loss within the routers. This is not so straightforward as it sounds, given that transmission capacity is one of the major cost elements for an Internet network service provider, and the network architect typically has to assess the trade-off between the cost performance of the network and the duration and impact of peak load conditions on the network. Typically, the network architect looks for average line utilization and *busy hour* to *average hour* utilization ratios to provide acceptable levels of economic performance. The network architect simultaneously must examine busy-hour performance figures to ensure that the network does not revert into a condition of congestion collapse when usage is at a maximum.

Only after these basic design steps have been undertaken and a basic level of service quality achieved within the network can the issue of QoS (or service level differentiation) be examined in any productive manner. The general conclusion here is that you cannot introduce QoS mechanisms to salvage a network that is delivering very poor levels of service. To be effective, QoS mechanisms need to be implemented in a network that is soundly engineered and that operates in a stable fashion under all levels of offered load.

QoS Tools

Given this definition of QoS and an associated framework for engineering QoS, several mechanisms (and architectural implementations) can provide differentiation for traffic in the network. We break these mechanisms into three basic groups, which align with the lower three layers of the OSI reference model: the physical, link, and network layers, as indicated in Figure 8.1.

Physical Layer QoS Mechanics

The physical layer (also referred to as L1 or Layer 1) consists of the physical wiring, fiber optics, and the transmission media in the network itself. Asking how Layer 1 physical media figures within the QoS framework is reasonable, but the time-honored practice of constructing diverse physical paths in a network is, perhaps ironically, a primitive method of providing differentiated service levels. In some cases, diverse paths are constructed primarily for use by network layer routing to provide for redundant availability, should the primary physical path fail for some reason. However, the temptation to share the load across the primary and backup paths is often overwhelming and can lead to adverse performance. For example, having more than one physical path to a destination can result in some arbitrary amount of network traffic taking the primary low-delay, high-bandwidth path, while the balance of the traffic takes a backup path, which may have different delay and bandwidth properties. In turn, such a configuration leads to reduced reliability and increased jitter within the network, unless the routing profile has been carefully constructed to stabilize the traffic segmentation between the two paths.

Alternate Physical Paths

Although the implementation of provisioning diverse physical paths in a network is usually done to provide for backup and redundancy, this can also be

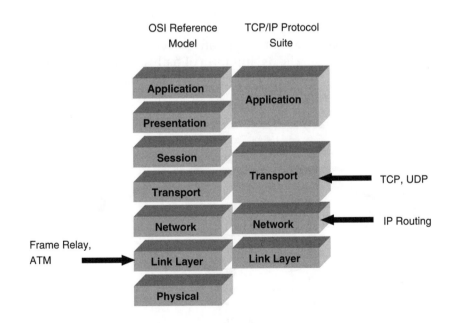

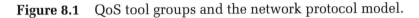

Figure 8.1 QoS tool groups and the network protocol model.

used to provide differentiated services if the available paths each have differing characteristics. In Figure 8.2, for example, best-effort traffic could be forwarded by the network layer devices (routers) along the lower speed path, while higher priority (QoS) traffic could be forwarded along the higher speed path.

Alternatively, the scenario could be a satellite path complemented by a faster terrestrial cable path. Best-effort traffic would be passed along the higher delay satellite path, while priority traffic would be routed along the terrestrial cable system. Certainly, this type of approach to differentiation is indeed quite coarse and not without its pitfalls, which we will examine in the following sections.

DESTINATION-BASED ROUTING AND PATH SELECTION

The method in which IP packets are forwarded in the Internet is based on the destination contained in the packet header. This is termed *destination-based routing*. IP packets generally are switched based on a local decision of the best path to the IP destination address contained in the IP packet header. The by-product of this mode of packet forwarding is that the mechanisms that do exist to forward traffic based on its IP source address, as distinct from its destination address, are not very robust. Accordingly, it is difficult, and operationally unstable, to perform outbound path selection based on the characteristics of the traffic source. The default form of path selection is based on the

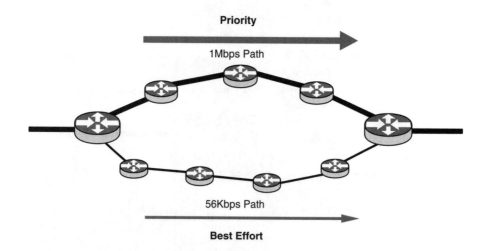

Figure 8.2   Alternate physical paths.

identity of the receiver. This implies that a QoS differentiation mechanism using path selection would be most efficiently implemented on the selection of incoming traffic to the host, while outgoing traffic would adopt the QoS parameters of the receiver. A destination-based routed network cannot control the QoS paths of both incoming and outgoing traffic to any particular location. Each QoS path will be determined as a destination-based path selection. Therefore, in a heterogeneous QoS environment, asymmetric quality parameters on incoming and outgoing data flows will be observed. This is a significant issue for unidirectional UDP-based traffic flows, in which the receiver, not the sender, controls the quality level of the transmission. This issue also is significant for TCP, in which the data flow and the reverse ACK flows may take paths of differing quality. Because the sender adapts its transmission rate via signaling, which transits the complete round trip, the resulting quality of the entire flow is influenced by the lower of the two quality levels of the forward and reverse paths.

TCP AND SYMMETRIC PATH SELECTION

Reliable traffic transmission requires a bidirectional data flow; sessions that are initiated and established by a particular host (sender) generally require control traffic (for example, explicit acknowledgments or the notification that acknowledgments were not processed by the receiver) to be returned from the destination (receiver). This reverse data flow is used to determine the transmission success, out-of-order traffic reception at the receiver, transmission rate adaptation, or other maintenance and control signals, in order to operate correctly. In essence, this reverse flow allows the sender to infer what is happening along the forward path and at the receiver, allowing the sender to optimize the data flow rate to fully utilize its fair share of the forward path's resource level. Therefore, for a reliable traffic flow transmitted along a particular path at a particular differentiated quality level, the flow will need to have its return traffic flow traverse the same path at the same quality level if optimal flow rates are to be reliably maintained. (This routing characteristic is also known as *symmetric paths*.) Asymmetric paths in the Internet continue to be a troubling issue with regard to traffic that is sensitive to induced delay and differing service quality levels, as they are prone to effectively distorting the signal being generated by the receiver. This problem is predominantly due to local routing policies in individual administrative domains through which traffic in the Internet must traverse. It is especially unrealistic to expect path symmetry in the Internet, at least for the foreseeable future.

The conclusion is that path diversity allows for differentiated service levels to be constructed from the different delay, bandwidth, and load characteristics of the various paths. However, for reliable transmission applications, this differentiation is relatively crude.

Link Layer QoS Mechanics

Some believe that traffic service differentiation can be provided with specific link layer mechanisms (also referred to as L2 or Layer 2). Traditionally, this belief in differentiation has been associated with *Asynchronous Transfer Mode* (ATM) and Frame Relay in the *wide area network* (WAN) and predominantly with ATM in the *local area network* (LAN). A brief overview is provided here of how each of these technologies provide service differentiation, and additionally, we provide an overview of the newer IEEE 802.1p mechanics that may be useful to provide traffic differentiation on IEEE 802–style LAN media.

QoS and ATM

ATM is one of the few transmission technologies that provides data-transport speeds in excess of 155Mbps. As well as a high-speed, bit-rate clock, ATM also provides a complex subset of traffic-management mechanisms, *Virtual Circuit* (VC) establishment controls, and various associated QoS parameters for these VCs. We need to understand why these underlying transmission QoS mechanisms are not being exploited by those ISPs using ATM as a data-transport tool for Internet networks in a wide area. The predominate use of ATM in today's Internet networks is because of the high data-clocking rate and multiplexing flexibility available with ATM implementations. Few other transmission technologies provide a high-speed, bit-rate clock. It is helpful to briefly review the ATM VC service characteristics, described in Chapter 5, "Network Infrastructure," and examine their potential applicability to the Internet environment.

The Constant Bit Rate service category. Here there is an inferred time synchronization between the traffic source and destination. This service category is useful when end-systems require predictable delay characteristics and a fixed amount of bandwidth continuously available for the lifetime of the connection. The CBR service category typically is used for circuit emulation.

The Variable Bit Rate service categories. These categories generally are used for any class of applications that might benefit from sending data at variable rates to most efficiently use network resources. The *Real-*

Time VBR (rt-VBR) *service category* is used for connections that transport traffic at variable rates—traffic that relies on accurate timing between the traffic source and destination. An example of traffic that requires this type of service category is variable rate, compressed video streams. Sources that use rt-VBR connections are expected to transmit at a rate that varies with time (for example, traffic that can be considered bursty) but are delay sensitive. The *Non-Real-Time VBR* (nrt-VBR) *service category* is predominantly used for transaction-oriented applications, in which traffic is sporadic and bursty. The nrt-VBR service category is used for connections that transport variable bit rate traffic for which there is no inherent reliance on time synchronization between the traffic source and destination, but there is a need for a guaranteed bandwidth or latency. An application that might require an nrt-VBR service category is Frame Relay interworking, in which the Frame Relay CIR (*Committed Information Rate*) is mapped to a bandwidth guarantee in the ATM network. No delay bounds are associated with nrt-VBR service.

The Available Bit Rate service category.   This category is similar to nrt-VBR and is used for connections that transport variable bit rate traffic. The service provides a best-effort transport service, in which flow-control mechanisms are used to adjust the amount of bandwidth available to the traffic originator. The ABR service category is designed primarily for any type of traffic that is not time-sensitive and expects no guarantees of service. ABR service generally is considered preferable for TCP/IP traffic, as well as other LAN-based protocols, which can modify transmission behavior in response to the ABR's rate-control mechanics. However, there is some doubt that the profile of ABR rate adaptation and the TCP rate adaptation are that compatible, with the conclusion that ABR is a relatively inefficient circuit platform, compared to CBR.

The Unspecified Bit Rate service category.   This is similar to nrt-VBR and ABR. Unlike ABR, no flow-control mechanisms exist to dynamically adjust the amount of bandwidth available to the user. UBR generally is used for applications that are very tolerant of delay and cell loss. UBR has been deployed as a TCP/IP transport substrate, and while the protocol can modify its transmission behavior in response to latency or cell loss in the ATM network, the match between the protocol dynamics and the cell transport dynamics is sufficient to admit a significant level of operational inefficiency in the carriage of TCP/IP packets.

THE MISCONCEPTIONS ABOUT ATM QoS

Several observations must be made regarding the value of ATM QoS and its associated complexity. This section attempts to provide an objective overview of the problems associated with relying solely on ATM to provide QoS in the network. However, quantifying the significance of some issues is sometimes difficult because of the complexity involved in the ATM QoS delivery mechanisms and their interactions with higher layer protocols and applications. In fact, the inherent complexity of ATM and its associated QoS mechanisms may be a big reason why many network operators are reluctant to implement those QoS mechanisms with an ATM network.

Although the underlying recovery mechanism of ATM cell loss is signaling, the QoS structures for ATM VCs are excessively complex. When tested against the principle of Occam's Razor (a popular translation frequently used in the engineering community for years, which is "All things being equal, choose the solution that is simpler"), ATM by itself would not be the choice for QoS services. This is simply because of the complexity involved, compared to other technologies that provide similar results. However, the application of Occam's Razor does not provide assurances that the desired result will be delivered—instead, it simply expresses a preference for simplicity.

ATM enthusiasts correctly point out that ATM is complex for good reason—in order to provide predictive, proactive, and real-time services, such as dynamic network resource allocation, resource guarantees, virtual circuit rerouting, and virtual circuit path establishment to accommodate subscriber QoS requests. ATM's complexity is unavoidable. The underlying model of ATM is a heterogeneous end-to-end ATM client population in which the real-time service models assume simple ATM client applications that are highly intolerant of jitter. The adaptive models of data networking assume very highly sophisticated clients within a heterogeneous networking environment. Here the applications must opportunistically tune their data rates to variations in available capacity that may fluctuate greatly within time frames well inside normal end-to-end round-trip times.

Higher layer protocols, such as TCP/IP, provide the end-to-end transportation service in most cases. Although it is possible to create QoS services in a lower layer of the protocol stack (namely ATM in this case), such services may cover only part of the end-to-end data path. This gets to the heart of the problem in delivering QoS with ATM, as we are working within the Internet in this context, where the true end-to-end bearer service is not pervasive ATM. Such partial QoS measures as ATM provides often have their effects masked by the effects of the traffic distortion created from the remainder of the end-to-end path in which they are not present. Hence, the overall outcome of deployment of a partial QoS structure often is ineffectual. In other words, if ATM is not pervasively deployed end-to-end in the data path, efforts to deliver QoS using ATM can be unproductive. Traffic distortion is introduced into the ATM landscape by traffic-forwarding devices that service the ATM network and upper layer protocols, such as IP, TCP, and UDP, as well as other upper layer network protocols. Queuing and buffering introduced into the network by routers and non-ATM-attached hosts skew the accuracy with which the lower layer ATM services calculate delay and delay variation (jitter).

On a related note, some people think that most traffic on ATM networks would be primarily UBR or ABR connections, because higher layer protocols and applications cannot request specific ATM QoS service classes, and therefore cannot fully exploit the QoS capabilities of the VBR service categories. A cursory examination of deployed ATM networks and their associated traffic profiles reveals that this is indeed the case, except in the rare instance when an academic or research organization has developed its own native "ATM-aware" applications that can fully exploit the QoS parameters available to the rt-VBR and nrt-VBR service categories. Although this certainly is possible and has been done on several occasions, real-world experience reveals that this is the proverbial exception and not the rule.

Note the observations published by Jagannath and Yin [Jagannath 1997], which suggest that "it is not sufficient to have a lossless ATM subnetwork from the end-to-end performance point of view," especially in the case of ABR services. This observation is due to the fact that two distinct control loops exist—ABR and TCP, as indicated in Figure 8.3. Although ABR can effectively control the congestion in the ATM network, ABR flow control simply pushes the congestion to the edges of the network (i.e., the routers), where performance degradation or packet loss may occur as a result. Jagannath and Yin also point out that "one may argue that the reduction in buffer requirements in the ATM switch by using ABR flow control may be at the expense of an increase in buffer requirements at the edge device (e.g., ATM router interface, legacy LAN-to-ATM switches)." Because most applications use the flow control provided by TCP, one might question the benefit of using ABR flow control at the subnetwork layer, because UBR (albeit with Early Packet Discard) is equally effective and much less complex. ABR flow control also may result in longer feedback delay for TCP control mechanisms, and this ultimately exacerbates the overall congestion problem in the network.

Aside from traditional data services that may use UBR, ABR, or VBR services, circuit-emulation services, which may be provisioned using the CBR service category, certainly can provide the QoS necessary for telephony communications. However, this becomes an exercise in comparing apples and oranges. Delivering voice services on virtual digital circuits using circuit emulation is quite different than delivering packet-based data found in local area and wide area networks. Providing QoS in these two environments is substantially different; it is more difficult to deliver QoS for data, because the higher layer applications and protocols do not provide the necessary hooks to exploit the QoS mechanisms in the ATM network. As a result, an intervening router must make the QoS request on behalf of the application, and thus, the ATM network really has no way of discerning what type of QoS the application may truly require. This particular deficiency has been the topic of recent research-and-development efforts to address this shortcoming and investigate methods of allowing the end systems to request network resources using RSVP as a request protocol, and then map these requests to native ATM QoS service classes as appropriate.

The QoS objective for networks similar in nature to the Internet lies principally in directing the network to alter the switching behavior at the IP layer. In this way, certain IP packets are delayed or discarded at the onset of congestion or delay, in order to mitigate, or completely avoid, the impact of congestion on other classes of IP traffic. When looking at IP-over-ATM, the issue (as we will

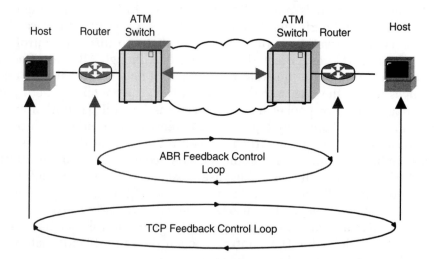

Figure 8.3 ATM and TCP control loops.

see with IP-over-Frame Relay) is that no mechanism is provided for mapping such IP-level directives to the ATM level, nor is it desirable, given the small size of ATM cells and the consequent requirement for rapid processing or discard. Attempting to increase the complexity of the ATM cell discard mechanics to the extent necessary to preserve the original IP QoS directives by mapping them into the ATM cell is arguably counterproductive.

The default IP QoS approach is best suited to IP-over-ATM. If the ATM network is adequately dimensioned to handle burst loads without the requirement to undertake large-scale congestion avoidance at the ATM layer, the IP layer does not need to invoke congestion-management mechanisms. The discussion comes full circle to an issue of capacity engineering, and not necessarily one of QoS within ATM.

Frame Relay

Frame Relay's origins lie in the development of *Integrated Services Digital Network* (ISDN) technology, in which Frame Relay originally was seen as a packet-service technology for ISDN networks. The Frame Relay rationale proposed was the perceived need for the efficient relaying of HDLC framed data across ISDN networks, addressing some of the aspects of the X.25 protocol that were seen as inhibitory factors in looking for higher speed packet-switched networks. With the removal of data link-layer error detection, retransmission, and flow control, Frame Relay opted for end-to-end signaling at the transport layer of the protocol stack to undertake these functions. This allows the network switches to consider data-link frames as being forwarded without waiting for positive acknowledgment from the next switch. This, in turn, allows the switches to operate with less memory and to drive faster circuits with the reduced switching functionality required by Frame Relay.

FRAME RELAY RATE MANAGEMENT CONTROL STRUCTURES

Frame Relay allows a basic level of oversubscription of basic point-to-point virtual circuits. Here, individual flows can increase their transfer rate, with the intent of occupying otherwise idle transmission capacity that is not being used by other virtual circuits that share the same transmission paths. Frame Relay is a link layer protocol that attempts to provide a simple mechanism for arbitration of this deliberate network oversubscription. When the sender is not using all of the committed rate within any of the configured virtual circuits, other VCs can use the transmission space with discard eligible frames. Frame Relay decouples the characteristics of the network access link from the characteristics of the virtual circuits that connect the access system to its group peers. Each virtual circuit is configured with a traffic *committed information rate* (CIR), which conforms to a commitment on the part of the network to provide traffic delivery. However, any virtual circuit can also accept overflow traffic levels—bursts that may transmit up to the rate of the access link. Such excess traffic is marked by the network access gateway using a single bit indicated in the Frame Relay frame header, termed the *Discard Eligible* (DE) bit.

The interior of the network uses three basic levels of threshold to manage switch queue congestion. At the first level of queue threshold, the network starts to mark frames with *Explicit Congestion Notification* (ECN) bits. The implied semantics of this congestion notification signaling are to notify senders and receivers to reduce their transmission rates to the CIR levels, although this action is not forced upon them. At the second level of queue threshold, the switch discards packets marked as DE, honoring its commitment to traffic, which conforms to committed information rates on each circuit. At the third level, the switch discards packets within the CIR levels. The basic premise within Frame Relay networks is that the switching fabric is dimensioned at such a level that it can fulfill its obligations of committed traffic flows. The third level of packet discard is reached rarely, if at all.

FRAME RELAY AND INTERNET QoS

Frame Relay is certainly a good example of what is possible with relatively sparse signaling capability. However, the match between Frame Relay as a link layer protocol and QoS mechanisms for the Internet is not a particularly good one.

Frame Relay networks operate within a locally defined context of using selective frame discard as a means of enforcing rate limits on traffic as it enters the network. This is done as the primary response to congestion. The basis of this selection is undertaken without respect to any hints provided by the higher layer protocols. The end-to-end TCP protocol uses packet loss as the primary signaling mechanism to indicate network congestion, but it is recognized only by the TCP session originator. The result is that when the network starts to reach a congestion state, the method in which end-system applications are degraded matches no particular imposed policy. In this current environment, Frame Relay offers no great advantage over any other link layer technology in addressing this.

In a heterogeneous network that uses a number of link layer technologies to support end-to-end data paths, the Frame Relay ECN and DE bits are not a cure-all; they do not provide for end-to-end signaling, and the router is not the system that manages either end of the end-to-end protocol stack. The router is more commonly performing IP packet into Frame Relay encapsulation. A more functional approach to user selection of DE traffic is possible: one that uses a field in the IP header to indicate a defined quality level via a single discard eligibility field and allows this designation to be carried end-to-end across the entire network path. With this facility, it then is logical to allow the ingress IP router (which performs the encapsulation of an IP datagram into a Frame Relay frame) to set the DE bit. This setting of DE would be in accordance with the discard preference bit setting indicated in the IP header field. The ingress router then passes the frame to the first-hop Frame Relay switch, which then confirms or clears the DE bit in accordance with locally configured policy associated with the per-VC CIR.

The seminal observation regarding the interaction of QoS mechanisms within various levels of the model of the protocol stack is that without coherence between the link layer transport signaling structures and the higher level protocol stack, the result, in terms of consistency of service quality, is completely chaotic.

A n interesting set of proposed enhancements is being reviewed by the IEEE 802.1 Internetworking Task Group. These enhancements would provide a method to identify 802-style frames based on a simple priority. A supplement to the original IEEE MAC bridges standard [IEEE 1993], the proposed 802.1p specification [IEEE 1997] provides a method to allow preferential queuing and access to media resources by traffic class, on the basis of a priority value signaled in the frame. The IEEE 802.1p specification, if adopted, will provide a way to transport this value (called user_priority) across the subnetwork in a consistent method for Ethernet, Token Ring, or other MAC-layer media types using an extended frame format. Of course, this also implies that 802.1p-compliant hardware may have to be deployed to fully realize these capabilities.

The current 802.1p draft defines the user_priority field as a three-bit value, resulting in a variable range of values between 0 and 7 decimal, with 7 indicating the highest relative priority and 0 indicating the lowest relative priority. The IEEE 802.1p proposal does not make any suggestions on how the user_priority should be used by the end-system or by network elements; it suggests only that packets may be queued by LAN devices based on their relative user_priority values.

> *Although the 802.1p* user_priority *may indeed prove to be useful in some QoS implementations, it remains to be seen how it will be most practically beneficial. At least one proposal exists [ID 1997a] that suggests how the 802.1p* user_priority *values may be used in conjunction with the* Subnet Bandwidth Manager (SBM), *a proposal that allows LAN switches to participate in RSVP signaling and resource reservation objectives [ID 1997b]. However, keep in mind that the widespread deployment of RSVP in the global Internet is not wholly practical; it remains to be seen how QoS implementations will use this technology.*

Network and Transport Layer Mechanics

In the global Internet, the common bearer service is the TCP/IP protocol suite. Therefore, IP is indeed the common denominator. This thought process has several supporting lines of reason. The common denominator is chosen in the hope of using the most pervasive and ubiquitous protocol in the network, whether it be layer 2 or layer 3 (the network layer). Using the most pervasive protocol makes implementation, management, and troubleshooting much easier and yields a greater possibility of successfully providing a QoS implementation that actually works.

This particular technology operates in an end-to-end fashion, using a signaling mechanism that spans the entire traversal of the network in a consistent fashion. IP is the end-to-end transportation service in most cases. Therefore, although we can create QoS services in substrate layers of the protocol stack, such services only cover part of the end-to-end data path. Such partial measures often have their effects masked by the signal distortion, which may be created from the remainder of the end-to-end path in which they are not present. The overall outcome of a partial QoS structure is generally ineffectual.

When the end-to-end path does not consist of a single pervasive data-link layer, any effort to provide differentiation within a particular link-layer technology most likely will not provide the desired result. In the Internet, for example, an IP packet may traverse any number of heterogeneous link-layer paths, each of which may (or may not) possess characteristics that inherently provide methods to provide traffic differentiation. However, the packet also inevitably traverses links that cannot provide any type of differentiated services at the link layer, rendering an effort to provide QoS solely at the link layer an inadequate solution.

The Internet today carries three basic categories of traffic, and any QoS environment must recognize and adjust itself to these three basic categories:

♦ The first category is *long-held adaptive reliable traffic flows*, in which the end-to-end flow rate is altered by the end points in response to network behavior. Here, the flow rate attempts to optimize itself in an effort to obtain a fair share of the available resources on the end-to-end path. Typically, this category of traffic performs optimally for long-held TCP traffic flows.

♦ The second category of traffic is a boundary case of the first category, *short duration reliable transactions*. The flows are of very short duration, and the rate adaptation is not established within the lifetime of the flow, so the flow sits completely within the startup phase of the TCP adaptive flow control protocol.

♦ The third category of traffic is *externally controlled load unidirectional traffic flows*, which are typically a result of compression of a real-time audio or video signal. The peak flow rate may equal the basic source signal rate; the average flow rate is a by-product of the level of signal compression used; and the transportation mechanism is an unreliable traffic flow with a UDP unicast flow model.

Within most Internet networks today, empirical evidence indicates that the first category of traffic accounts for less than 1 percent of all packets, but as the data packets are typically large, this application accounts for up to 20 percent of the total volume of data. The second category of traffic is most commonly generated by World Wide Web servers, using the HTTP/1.0 application protocol. This traffic accounts for some 75 percent of all packets, and a comparable relative level of volume of data carried. The third category accounts for some 10 percent of all packets, and as the average packet size is less than one-third of the first two flow types, it currently accounts for some 5 percent of the total data volume.

To provide elevated service quality to these three common traffic flow types, three different engineering approaches must be used:

♦ Ensuring efficient carriage of long-held, high-volume TCP flows requires the network to offer consistent signaling to the sender regarding the onset of congestion loss within the network.

♦ Ensuring efficient carriage of short-duration TCP traffic requires the network to avoid sending advance congestion signals to the flow end-points. Because these flows are of short duration and low transfer rate, any such signaling will not achieve appreciable load shedding but will substantially increase the elapsed time that the flow is held active. This results in poorly delivered service without any appreciable change in the relative allocation of network resources to service clients.

♦ To ensure efficient carriage of the externally clocked UDP traffic the network must be able to, at a minimum, segment the queue management of such traffic from adaptive TCP traffic flows and possibly to replace adaptation by advance notification and negotiation. Such a notification and negotiation model could allow the source to specify its traffic profile in advance and have the network respond with either a commitment to carry such a load or indicate that it does not have available resources to meet such an additional commitment.

As a consequence, no single transport or network layer mechanism will provide the capabilities for differentiated services for all flow types. A QoS-enabled network will probably deploy a number of mechanisms to meet the broad range of customer requirements in this area.

TCP Congestion Avoidance

There are two major types of traffic flow in the Internet today. One is an adaptive-rate, reliable transmission, control-mediated traffic flow using TCP. The other is externally clocked, unreliable data flows that typically use UDP. Here, we look at QoS mechanisms for TCP. To preface this discussion, we must briefly describe the behavior of TCP itself in terms of its rate-control mechanisms.

TCP uses a rate-control mechanism to achieve a sustainable steady-state network load. The intent of the rate-control mechanism is to reach a state in which the sender injects a new data packet into the network at the same time as the receiver removes a data packet. However, this is modified by a requirement to allow dynamic rate probing, so that the sender attempts to inject slightly more data than is being removed by the receiver. When this rate probing results in congestion, the sender will reduce its rate and again probe upwards to find a stable operating point. This is accomplished in TCP using two basic mechanisms.

The first mechanism used by TCP is *slow start*, in which the connection is initialized with the transmission of a single segment. Each time the sender receives an ACK from the receiver, the *congestion window* (cwnd) is increased by one segment size. This effectively doubles the transmission rate for each *round-trip time* (RTT) cycle; the sender transmits a single packet and awaits the corresponding ACK. A TCP connection commences with an initial *cwnd* value of 1, and a single segment is sent into the network. The sender then awaits the reception of the matching ACK from the receiver. When received, the cwnd is opened from 1 to 2, allowing two packets to be sent. When each ACK is received from these two segments, the congestion window is incremented. The value of cwnd is then 4, allowing four packets to be sent, and so on (receivers using delayed ACK will moderate this behavior so that the rate increase will be slightly less than doubled for each RTT).

This behavior will continue until the transfer completes or until the sender's buffer space is exhausted. In the latter case, the sender is transmitting at its maximum possible rate across the network's selected path, given the delay bandwidth product of the path, or an intermediate router in the path experiences queue exhaustion, and packets are dropped. Because the algorithm tends to cluster transmission events at epoch intervals of the RTT, such overload of the router queue structure is highly likely when the path delay is significant.

The second TCP rate-control mechanism is termed *congestion avoidance*. In the event of packet loss, as signaled by the reception of duplicate ACKs, the value of cwnd is halved, and this value is saved as the threshold value to terminate the *slow start* algorithm (*ssthresh*). When cwnd exceeds this threshold value, the window is increased in a linear fashion, opening the window by one segment size in each RTT interval. The value of cwnd is brought back to 1 when the end-to-end signaling collapses, and the sender times out on waiting for any ACK packets from the receiver. Because the value of cwnd is below the ssthresh value, TCP also switches to *slow start* control mode, once more doubling the congestion window with every RTT interval.

The responsiveness of the TCP congestion avoidance algorithm is measured in intervals of the RTT, and the overall intent of the algorithm is to reach a steady state in which the sender injects a new segment into the network at the same point in time that the receiver accepts a segment from the network. This algorithm works most efficiently when the spacing between ACK packets as received by the sender matches the spacing between data packets as they were received at the remote end. Note that the algorithm works optimally when congestion-induced packet loss happens prior to complete queue exhaustion. The intent is to signal packet loss through duplicate ACK packets, allowing the sender to undertake a fast retransmission and leave the congestion window at the ssthresh level. If queue exhaustion occurs, the TCP session will stop receiving ACK signals and retransmission will occur only after time-out. At that point, the congestion window is brought back to a single segment, and the slow start algorithm is recommenced.

An equal performance problem is network congestion events that occur within very short time intervals compared to the RTT, as may be the case in a mixed traffic load across a common ATM transport substrate, in which short ATM switch cell queues may lead to very short interval cell loss events. In this case, a TCP session may switch from the aggressive window expansion of *slow start* into a much slower window expansion of *congestion avoidance* at a traffic rate well below the true long-term network availability level.

One major drawback in any high-volume IP network is that when there are congestion hot spots, uncontrolled congestion can wreak havoc on the overall performance of the network to the point of congestion collapse. When a high volume of TCP flows is active at the same time, and a congestion situation occurs within the network at a particular bottleneck, each flow conceivably could experience loss at approximately the same time. This creates what is known as *global synchronization*. (*Global* refers to all TCP flows in a given network that traverse a common path.) Global synchronization occurs when hundreds or thousands, or perhaps hundreds of thousands, of TCP flows back off their transmission rates and revert to TCP slow start mode at roughly the same time. Each TCP sender detects loss and reacts accordingly, going into slow start mode, shrinking its transmission window size, pausing for a moment, and then attempting to retransmit the data again. If the congestion situation still exists, each TCP sender detects loss once again, and the process repeats itself, resulting in a network form of gridlock [Zhang 1990].

Uncontrolled congestion is detrimental to the network: Behavior becomes unpredictable, system buffers fill up, packets ultimately are dropped, and the by-product is a large number of retransmits that could ultimately result in complete congestion collapse.

Preferential Congestion Avoidance at Intermediate Nodes

Van Jacobson discussed the basic methods of implementing congestion avoidance in TCP in 1988 [Jacobson 1988]. However, Jacobson's approach was more suited for a small number of TCP flows, which is much less complex to manage than the volume of active flows in the Internet today. In 1993, Sally Floyd and Van Jacobson documented the concept of *Random Early Detection* (RED). This concept provides a mechanism to avoid congestion collapse by randomly dropping packets from arbitrary flows in an effort to avoid the problem of global synchronization and, ultimately, congestion collapse [Floyd 1993]. The principal goal of RED is to avoid a *queue tail drop* situation in which all TCP flows experience congestion at the same time, and subsequent packet loss, thus avoiding global synchronization. RED also attempts to create TCP congestion signals using duplicate ACK signaling, rather than through sender time-out, which produces a less catastrophic rate backoff by TCP.

RED monitors the mean queue depth, and as the queue begins to fill, it begins to randomly select individual TCP flows from which to drop packets, in order to signal the receiver to slow down. This behavior is indicated in Figure 8.4. The threshold at which RED begins to drop packets is generally configurable by the network administrator, as well as the rate at which drops occur in relation to how quickly the queue fills. The more it fills, the greater the number of flows selected, and the greater the number of packets dropped. This results in signaling a greater number of senders to slow down; thus resulting in a more manageable congestion avoidance.

The RED approach does not possess the same undesirable overhead characteristics as some non-*FIFO* (First In, First Out) queuing techniques (for example, simple priority queuing, class-based queuing, and weighted-fair queuing).

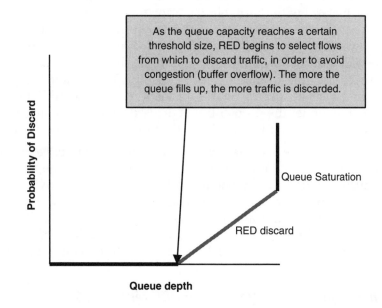

Figure 8.4   RED queue discard behavior.

With RED, it is simply a matter of who gets into the queue in the first place; no packet reordering or queue management takes place. When packets are placed into the outbound queue, they are transmitted in the order in which they are queued. Queue-based scheduling mechanisms, such as priority, class-based, and weighted-fair queuing, however, require a significant amount of computational overhead due to packet reordering and queue management. RED requires much less overhead than these non-FIFO queuing mechanisms, but then again, RED performs a completely different function.

RED can be said to be fair: It chooses random flows from which to discard traffic in an effort to avoid global synchronization and congestion collapse, as well as to maintain equity in which traffic actually is discarded. Fairness is all well and good, but what is really needed for differentiated QoS structures is a tool that can induce unfairness—a tool that can allow the network administrator to predetermine what traffic is dropped first (or last, as the case may be) when RED starts to select flows from which to discard packets. You can't differentiate services with fairness.

Several proposals in the IETF have suggested using the IP precedence subfield of the *Type of Service* (TOS) byte contained in the IP packet header to indicate the relative priority, or discard preference, of packets and to indicate how packets marked with these relative priorities should be treated within the network. As precedence is set or policed when traffic enters the network (at ingress), a weighted congestion avoidance mechanism implemented in the core routers determines which traffic should be discarded first when congestion is anticipated due to queue-depth capacity. The higher the precedence indicated in a packet, the lower the probability of discard. The lower the precedence, the higher the probability of discard. When the congestion avoidance is not actively discarding packets, all traffic is forwarded equally.

Of course, for this type of operation to work properly, an intelligent congestion-control mechanism must be implemented on each router in the transit path. A least one currently deployed mechanism is available that provides an unfair, or weighted, behavior for RED. This deviation of RED yields the desired result for differentiated traffic discard in times of congestion and is called *Weighted Random Early Detection* (WRED). A similar scheme, called *enhanced RED*, is documented in a paper authored by Feng, Kandlur, Saha, and Shin [Feng 1997].

Scheduling Algorithms to Implement Differentiated Service
Other approaches to implement differential QoS within the network use the routers' queuing algorithm (or *scheduling discipline*) as the enabling mecha-

nism. Considering that queuing is perhaps the optimal point to introduce QoS differentiation mechanisms, this is an area of considerable interest.

FIFO QUEUING

The base of best effort, single quality network environments is that of a FIFO queue, in which there is no inherent differentiation undertaken by the router's transmission scheduler (see Figure 8.5). Every packet scheduled to be transmitted on an output interface must await all previously scheduled packets before transmission. All such packets occupy slots in a single per-interface queue, and when the queue fills, all subsequent packets are discarded until the queue becomes available again. As with the basic RED algorithm, this is a fair algorithm, because it allocates the transmission resource fairly and imposes the same delay on all queued packets. For differentiated service levels, it is necessary to alter this fairness and introduce mechanisms to trigger preferential outcomes for classes of traffic.

The basic modification of the single-level FIFO algorithm to enable differentiated QoS is to divide traffic into a number of categories and then provide resources to each category in accordance with a predetermined allocation structure, implementing some form of proportional resource allocation.

Of course, the *Law of Conservation* holds here, so that the sum of the mean queuing delays per-traffic category, weighted by their share of the resources they receive, is limited. The corollary is that reducing the mean queuing delay for one category of traffic will result in the increase in mean queuing delay for one or more of the remaining categories of traffic [Kleinrock 1975]. Accordingly, you can't improve the performance profile of one class of traffic

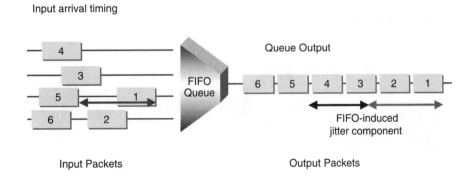

Figure 8.5   FIFO queuing.

without adversely affecting the performance profile of one or more of the other classes of traffic. The level of degradation will be similar in quantity to the level of improvement that was effected.

PRIORITY QUEUES

A basic modification to the FIFO structure is to create a number of distinct queues for each interface and associate a relative priority level to each. Packets are scheduled from a particular priority queue in FIFO order only when all queues of a higher priority are empty. In such a model, the highest priority traffic receives minimal delay, but all other priority levels may experience resource starvation if the highest precedence traffic queue remains occupied. To ensure that all traffic receives some level of service, the network is required to use admission policies to restrict the amount of traffic admitted at each elevated priority, or the scheduling algorithm needs to be adjusted to ensure that every priority class receives some minimum level of resource allocation. Accordingly, this simple priority mechanism does not scale well, although it can be implemented with relatively little cost, and more sophisticated (and more robust) scheduling algorithms are required within the Internet for QoS support. (See Figure 8.6.)

GENERALIZED PROCESSOR SHARING

The ideal approach is to associate a relative weight (or precedence) with each individual traffic flow. At every router, traffic should be segmented into an individual FIFO queue and the scheduler configured to service all queues in a bit-wise round-robin fashion, allocating service to each flow in accordance

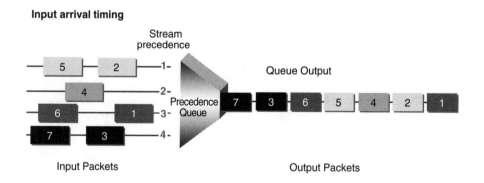

Figure 8.6 Precedence queuing.

with the relative weight. This is an instance of a *Generalized Processor Sharing* (GPS) discipline [Keshav 1997].

WEIGHTED ROUND-ROBIN AND DEFICIT-WEIGHTED ROUND-ROBIN

Various scheduling techniques can approximate this GPS model in which packets are used rather than bytes. A basic approach is to use a packet's marked precedence to place the packet into a precedence-based queue and then use a *weighted round-robin* scheduling algorithm to service each queue. If all packets are identically sized, this practice is a relatively good approximation of GPS. When packet sizes vary, this algorithm can exhibit significant deviation from a strict relative resource allocation strategy. This can be partially addressed using a *deficit-weighted round-robin* algorithm [Keshav 1997] that modifies the round-robin algorithm to use a service quantum unit. A packet is scheduled from the head of a weighted queue only if the packet size minus the per-queue deficit counter is less than the weighted quantum value. If this is the case, the next packet in the queue is tested using a weighted quantum value that has been reduced by the size of the scheduled packet. When the test fails, the remaining weighted quantum size is added to the per-queue deficit counter and the scheduler moves to the next queue. This algorithm performs with an average allocation that corresponds to the relative weights of each queue. However, it still exhibits unfairness within time frames that are commensurate to the maximum packet service time.

WEIGHTED FAIR QUEUING

Weighted Fair Queuing (WFQ) [Demera 1989] attempts to provide fairer resource allocation measures that protect "well-behaved" traffic sources from uncontrolled sources. WFQ attempts to compute the finish time of each queued packet as if a bit-wise weighted GPS scheduler had been used and then schedules for service the packet with the smallest finish time that would have been receiving service in the corresponding GPS scheduler model. The operation of a WFQ scheduling system is indicated in Figure 8.7. WFQ is both a scheduling and packet-drop policy, in which packet drop is based on a preference for dropping packets with the greatest finish time in response to an incoming packet that requires a queue slot. Although WFQ requires a relatively complex implementation, it has a number of desirable properties. The scheduling algorithm does undertake fair allocation, which ensures that different categories of traffic cannot resource starve other categories. The algorithm also bounds the queue delay per-service category, which also provides a lever to create delay-bounded services without the need for resource reservation.

Traffic-Shaping Nonadaptive Flows

One of the more confounding aspects of providing differentiated services at the network and transport layers of the TCP/IP suite is dealing with non-adaptive flows, or, in other words, traffic flows that do not adapt their transmission rates in response to loss in the network. The most offensive of this category appear to be applications that use UDP as their transport protocol. This is somewhat ironic in that long-standing traditional thinking has assumed that applications that use UDP are generally thought to be designed to be intelligent enough to recognize loss, because UDP does not provide any error correction itself. The resulting observation is that this is a fundamentally flawed assumption, because applications that use UDP are generally not very network friendly in terms of their ability to adapt to changing network conditions.

The subsequent action is to rate-shape UDP flows as they enter the network, limiting their transmission rate to a specified bit rate. This method is arguably a compromise; it's not pretty, but we understand how to do this, and it works.

Bits from each service class are serviced in rotation, weighted by relative weight

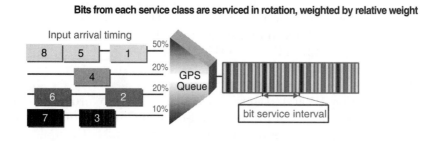

Packets from each service class are serviced in accordance with an equivalent bit-wise service model

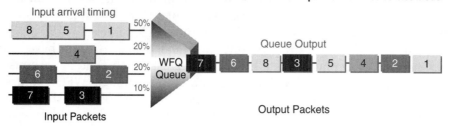

Figure 8.7   WFQ queuing.

There are, however, a couple of proposed methods to enhance the basic RED mechanism to provide some relief in the face of nonadaptive flows; however, the validity and practicality of these schemes are still being evaluated. One such proposal is discussed in [Lin 1997].

Integrated Services and RSVP

The Integrated Services architecture [RFC 1633] and RSVP [RFC 2205] are excessively complex and possess poor scaling properties. This suggestion is undoubtedly prompted by the existence of the underlying complexity of the IP layer signaling requirements. However, RSVP also is no more complex than some of the more advanced routing protocols. An alternative viewpoint might suggest that the underlying complexity is required because of the inherent difficulty in establishing and maintaining path and reservation state information along the transit path of data traffic. The suggestion that RSVP has poor scaling properties deserves additional examination, however, because deployment of RSVP has not been widespread enough to determine the scope of this assumption.

As discussed in [RFC 2208], several areas merit concern regarding the wide-scale deployment of RSVP. With regard to concerns of RSVP scalability, the resource requirements (computational processing and memory consumption) for implementing RSVP on routers increase in direct proportion to the number of separate RSVP reservations, or sessions, accommodated. Therefore, supporting a large number of RSVP reservations could introduce a significant negative impact on router performance. Likewise, router-forwarding performance may be impacted adversely by the packet classification and scheduling mechanisms intended to provide differentiated services for reserved flows. These scaling concerns tend to suggest that organizations with large, high-speed networks will be reluctant to deploy RSVP in the foreseeable future, at least until these concerns are addressed. The underlying implications of this concern also suggest that without deployment by Internet service providers, who own and maintain the high-speed backbone networks in the Internet, the deployment of pervasive RSVP services in the Internet will not be forthcoming.

Another important concern expressed in [RFC 2208] deals with policy-control issues and RSVP. Policy control addresses the issue of who is authorized to make reservations and encompasses provisions to support access control and accounting. Although the current RSVP specification defines a mechanism for transporting policy information, it does not define the policies themselves, because the policy object is treated as an opaque element. Some vendors have indicated that they will use this policy object to provide propri-etary mechanisms for policy control. At the time of this writing, however, the IETF has chartered a new working group, the *RSVP Admission Policy* (RAP) working group [IETF RSVP], to develop a simple policy-control mechanism to be used in conjunction with RSVP. Several mechanisms have already been proposed to deal with policy issues. However, it is unclear at this time whether any of these proposals will be implemented or adopted as a standard.

The key recommendation contained in [RFC 2208] is that given the current form of the RSVP specification, multimedia applications run within smaller, private networks are the most likely to benefit from the deployment of RSVP. The inadequacies of RSVP scaling, and lack of policy control, may be more manageable within the confines of a smaller, more controlled network envi-ronment than in the expanse of the global Internet. RSVP may provide gen-uine value and find legitimate deployment utility in smaller networks, both in the peripheral Internet networks and in the private arena, where these issues of scale are far less critical. Therein lies the key to successfully delivering QoS using RSVP. After all, the purpose of the Integrated Services architecture and RSVP is to provide a method to offer quality of service, not to degrade the ser-vice quality.

Service Level Agreements

From a marketing perspective into this area of performance engineering, the obvious question to ask is whether it is possible to support *Service Level Agreements* (SLAs) with clients of the service, and if so, in what form could such SLAs be phrased?

For some clients, the service environment of best-effort delivery places too much performance risk with the client, and none with the ISP. The most direct way for an ISP to increase the earning potential of the network service is to increase the traffic levels on the network without a corresponding augmenta-tion of carriage capacity. The outcome to the ISP is certainly a reduction in traffic-based unit costs of the network, as more traffic is being passed over a network infrastructure that has constant cost. However, the side effect of this ISP business strategy is declining levels of service offered to each client, and the increased load will increase the frequency and severity of congestion events occurring within the network.

The SLA is an attempt by the customer to impose some limit on the extent to which the ISP can indulge in oversubscription of carriage and switching capacity. The SLA imposes some minimum level of service level, or performance, which the ISP must meet under the terms of the access contract. Although the intent is eminently sensible and prudent from the perspective of both parties, it presents issues in the implementation which are not so readily answered, and these issues are related to QoS considerations.

The first consideration is how to phrase an acceptable service level or how to define a base level of quality within the ISP's network. Of course, an entire network does not exhibit a certain level of quality at any particular instant. Instead, individual traffic flows encounter various quality conditions through the lifetime of the flow, and these quality conditions can be considered an expression of the quality of the network. Phrasing a quality constraint in terms of the complete absence of packet loss makes little sense in an environment where a background-level packet loss is a natural outcome of TCP flow behavior. However, specifying an average packet loss metric is open to a wide variety of interpretations. The underlying observation is that in an environment of opportunistic traffic flows, in which each TCP flow dynamically adjusts its behavior to occupy as much of the available network as possible, the outcome is one of variable-flow performance. In a variable-flow environment, each flow continually attempts to balance its performance with those flows competing for the same resource. Gross limits can be expressed on packet loss, jitter, delay reliability, and path stability within an SLA. However, it is likely that the SLA will be able to encompass only some instances of a large level of oversubscription, while the finer aspects of quality metrics may well prove elusive to any form of a realistic SLA.

The second consideration is how to measure an SLA. Once an SLA is specified in terms of a measurement technique, the ISP will divert attention away from the overall delivery of a service quality level and concentrate most on achieving those specifications as drawn up within the SLA, even at the expense of quality of service. Accordingly, the measurement of the SLA must be specifically generic so as not to create highly specific network tuning, but at the same time, the measurement must not be so generic that the technique and the reported outcomes become the subject of dispute. The scope of the measurements is also relevant. For example, an ISP would find unacceptable an SLA measurement specification consisting of a set of end-to-end flow quality measurements in which the paths transited other parties' networks and in which the end system platforms exhibited variable performance due to other load factors. If the measurement is via a mechanism that loads a network with traffic, then the measurement itself has a detrimental effect on available network capacity. On the other hand, network probe mechanisms, such as ping clusters, tend to produce outcomes in terms of reported round-trip loss and jitter, which are not well correlated to concurrent TCP and UDP flow performance.

Currently, the use of SLAs as a tool to enforce base levels of service quality within the Internet environment has questionable outcome. Consistent poor service is still most effectively addressed by client churn, in which clients move to other competitive providers in response to poor service experiences, and a consistent effort to achieve high-quality service has outcomes in high levels of client loyalty to the service. Attempts to codify this into an SLA through financial penalty, to force an ISP into a certain mode of operation, are not always as successful as either party would hope.

QoS Observations

A number of dichotomies exist within the Internet that tend to dominate efforts to engineer possible solutions to the quality of service requirement. Thus far, QoS has been viewed as a wide-ranging solution set against a very broad problem area. This fact often can be considered a liability. Ongoing efforts to provide "perfect" solutions illustrate that attempts to solve all possible problems result in technologies that are far too complex, have poor scaling properties, or simply do not integrate well into the diversity of the Internet. By close examination of the issues and technologies available, some very clever mechanisms are available. Determining the usefulness of these mechanisms, however, is perhaps the most challenging aspect in assessing the merit of any particular QoS approach.

In the global Internet, however, implementing QoS within the most common denominator becomes an issue—this is clearly the TCP/IP protocol suite—because a single link-layer media will never be used pervasively end-to-end across all possible paths. What about the possibility of constructing a smaller network of a pervasive link-layer technology, such as ATM? Although this is certainly possible in smaller private networks, and perhaps in smaller peripheral networks in the Internet, it is rarely the case that all end-systems are ATM-attached, and this does not appear to be a likely outcome in the coming years. In terms of implementing visibly differentiated services based on a quality metric, using ATM only on parts of the end-to-end path is not a viable answer. The ATM subpath is not aware of the complete network layer path, and it does not participate in the network or transport layer protocol end-to-end signaling.

The simplistic answer to this conundrum is to dispense with TCP/IP and run native cell-based applications from ATM-attached end-systems. This approach is certainly not realistic in the Internet, though, and chances are that it is not very realistic in a smaller corporate network, either. Very little application support exists for native ATM. Of course, in theory, the same could have been said of Frame Relay transport technologies in the recent past and undoubtedly will be claimed of forthcoming transport technologies in the future. Link layer technologies are similar to viewing the world through plumber's glasses; every communications issue is seen in terms of point-to-point bit pipes. Each wave of transport technology attempts to add more features to the shape of the pipe, but the underlying architecture is a constant perception of the communications world as a set of one-on-one conversations, with each conversation supported by a form of singular communications channel.

One of the major enduring aspects of the communications industry is that no such thing as a ubiquitous single link layer technology exists. Hence, there is an enduring need for an internetworking end-to-end transport technology that can straddle a heterogeneous link layer substrate. Equally, there is a need for an internetworking technology that can allow differing models of communications, including fragmentary transfer, unidirectional data movement, multicast traffic, and adaptive data-flow management.

ATM itself, or any other link layer technology, may be an appropriate technology to install into a network. Surely, ATM offers high-speed transport services, as well as the convenience of virtual circuits. However, what is perhaps more appropriate to consider is that any particular link layer technology is not effective insofar as providing QoS in the Internet for reasons that have been discussed thus far.

To quote a work in progress from the Internet Research Task Force, "The advantages of [the Internet Protocol's] connectionless design, flexibility, and robustness, have been amply demonstrated. However, these advantages are not without cost—careful design is required to provide good service under heavy load" [Braden 1997]. Careful design is not exclusively the domain of the end-system's protocol stack, although good end-system stacks are of significant benefit. Careful design also includes consideration of the mechanisms within the routers that are intended to avoid congestion collapse. Differentiation of services places further demands on this design. In attempting to allocate additional resources to certain classes of traffic, it is essential to ensure that the use of resources remains efficient and that no class of traffic is totally starved of resources to the extent that it suffers throughput and efficiency collapse.

For QoS to be functional, all the nodes in a given path need to behave in a similar fashion with respect to QoS parameters. At the very least, do not impose additional QoS penalties other than conventional best effort into the end-to-end traffic environment. The sender (or network ingress point) must be able to create some form of signal associated with the data that can be used by downstream routers to potentially modify their default outbound interface selection, queuing behavior, and/or discard behavior.

The insidious issue here is attempting to exert *control at a distance*. The objective in this QoS methodology is for an end-system to generate a packet that can trigger a differentiated handling of the packet by each node in the traffic path, so that the end-to-end behavior exhibits performance levels in line with the end-user's expectations and perhaps even a contracted fee structure.

This control-at-a-distance model can take the form of a *guarantee* between the user and the network. This guarantee is one in which, if the ingress traffic conforms to a certain profile, the egress traffic maintains that profile state, and the network does not distort the desired characteristics of the end-to-end traffic expected by the requestor. To provide such absolute guarantees, the network must maintain a transitive state along a determined path, where the first router commits resources to honor the traffic profile and passes this commitment along to a neighboring router closer to the nominated destination and capable of committing to honor the same traffic profile. This is done on a hop-by-hop basis along the transit path between the sender and receiver, and yet again from receiver back to sender. This type of state maintenance is viable within small-scale networks, but in the heart of large-scale public networks, such as the global Internet, the cost of state maintenance is overwhelming. This mode of operation of RSVP presents some serious scaling considerations and is inappropriate for deployment in large networks.

RSVP scaling considerations present another important point, however. RSVP's deployment constraints are not limited to the amount of resources it might consume on each network node as per-flow state maintenance is performed. As the number of discrete flows increases in the network, the more resources it will consume. Of course, this can be somewhat limited by defining how much of the network's resources are available to RSVP—everything in excess of this value is treated as best-effort. What is more subtle, however, is that when all available RSVP resources are consumed, all further requests for QoS are rejected until RSVP-allocated resources are released. This is similar to how the telephone system works, in which the network's response to a flow request is commitment or denial, and such a service does not prove to be a viable method to operate a data network on which better-than-best-effort services arguably should always be available.

The alternative to state maintenance and resource reservation schemes is the use of mechanisms for preferential allocation of resources, essentially creating varying levels of best-effort. Given the absence of end-to-end guarantees of traffic flows, this removes the criteria for absolute state maintenance, so that *better-than-best-effort* traffic with classes of distinction can be constructed inside larger networks. Currently, the most promising direction for such better-than-best-effort systems appears to lie within the area of modifying the network layer queuing and discard algorithms. These mechanisms rely on an attribute value within the IP packet's header, so these queuing and discard preferences can be made at each intermediate node. First, the ISP's routers must be configured to handle packets based on their IP precedence level or similar semantics expressed by the bit values defined in the IP packet header. First, you need to consider the aspect of using the IP precedence field to determine the queuing behavior of the router, both in queuing the packet to the forwarding process and queuing the packet to the output interface. Second, consider using the IP precedence field to bias the packet discard processes by selecting the lowest precedence packets to discard first. Third, consider using any priority scheme used at Layer 2 that should be mapped to a particular IP precedence value.

Several methods have been proposed within the IETF, which may yield robust mechanisms and semantics for providing these types of *differential services* (diffserv).

A *good Web reference for differentiated service models is at diffserv.lcs.mit.edu/.*

The generic diffserv deployment environment assumes that the network uses ingress traffic policing, in which traffic passed into the network is passed through traffic-shaping profile mechanisms, which bound their average and peak data rates and their relative priority and discard precedence in accordance with the traffic profile and the administrative agreement with the customer. These ingress filters can be configured to either discard out-of-profile packets, or the ingress filter may mark them with an elevated discard priority so that they are carried within the network only when there are adequate resources available. Within the core of the network, WFQ (or similar proportional scheduling algorithms) can be used to allocate network resources according to the marked priority levels, allowing the high-speed and high-volume switching component of the network to operate without per-flow state being imposed.

The cumulative behavior of such stateless, local-context algorithms and corresponding deployment architectures can yield the capability of distinguished and predictable service levels and hold the promise of excellent scalability. You still can mix best-effort and better-than-best-effort nodes, but all nodes in the latter class should conform to the entire QoS selected profile or a compatible subset (an example of the principle is that it is better to do nothing than to do damage).

Summary

In summary, QoS is possible in the Internet, but QoS does come at a price of compromise; there are no perfect solutions. In fact, one might suggest that expectations have not been appropriately managed, as service performance guarantees are simply not possible in the Internet, at least not for the foreseeable future. What is possible, however, is delivering differentiated levels of best-effort traffic in a manner that is predictable, fairly consistent, and provides some level of capability to offer discriminated service levels to different customers and to different applications.

chapter nine

Security

The Internet is a hostile environment. As an ISP, you and your clients will be the subject of security incidents, including attempted intrusion and denial-of-service attacks. Some of these attacks may succeed. To respond to these incidents, you need to be aware of security considerations, formulate policies as to how to minimize the risks of such incidents, and plan how to respond when they occur.

There is always an opening caveat when discussing security issues, and this chapter is no exception: when dealing with matters concerning security there are no absolutes. It is a foolhardy claim, and one that invites undue attention when made in public, that a system, or a network, is absolutely secure. No system possesses such an attribute, particularly when the totality of the system includes the component service platforms, the network elements, the operational staff, and the business processes. Instead of absolutes, the best an ISP can aspire to in this area is an uncertain set of relativities of risk. Here, the ultimate assessment is one of a probability of a harmful intrusion into the network and its service platforms. Of course, this is of little consolation to the ISP, who, naturally, is seeking clear and unambiguous answers to security-related questions.

Other considerations make the Internet environment an easy target for attempts to breach security arrangements. Millions of entry points into the Internet exist, allowing an individual to conceal his or her identity and location with considerable ease, and each system that is compromised becomes one additional platform in a chain of indirect access, to assist in identity masking for further intrusion attempts. Additionally, the Internet does operate on a level of distributed trust that makes security of operation difficult to maintain in all circumstances. The DNS name system, given its distributed nature of local authority, is vulnerable to various forms of malicious attack, and subversion of the DNS is sometimes used as a springboard for intrusion attempts. In a similar fashion, the Internet routing system relies on a strong level of mutual trust, and subversion of the routing system, and the consequent redirection of traffic flows, can be undertaken without any initial intrusion to trigger the event.

Is the assertion that absolute security does not exist on the Internet sufficient cause for any ISP or client to cease using the Internet? Of course not! Like crossing a road, every activity presents some element of risk. The intent of security-related activities is to minimize such risks, through effective management practices and by staying well informed, in the same way that keeping your eyes open is a reasonable precaution to adopt when crossing roads.

The ISP does need to formulate a security plan for the network and its servers. One general approach is suggested in [Fites 1989]:

1. Identify what you are trying to protect.
2. Determine what you are trying to protect it from.
3. Determine how likely the threats are.
4. Implement measures that will protect your assets in a cost-effective manner.
5. Review the process continuously and make improvements each time a weakness is found.

Of course, it is equally true that the cost of protection should be less than the total cost of what is being protected. Adopted security measures should not make the task of operating the service so expensive that it becomes impossible to compete within the marketplace. However, the cost of a security incident is not just the cost of recovery. The total cost includes business costs relating to the reputation of the ISP to its clients as a secure and reliable enterprise.

A wealth of security-related information is on the Internet. One of the best starting points to access this information is [RFC 2196], The Site Security Handbook, as well as the CERT Web pages, at www.cert.org.

Priorities of Activity

Every ISP has a similar story to tell of a large number of potential activities to undertake and nowhere near enough resources to achieve outcomes in every activity. Part of the business management role is to prioritize such activities to ensure that tasks that are critical to the business receive adequate attention. Of course, for an ISP, the most critical tasks tend to be those that directly generate revenue, and tasks that do not have an immediate positive financial outcome do not receive the same level of attention. Security activities, being preventative in their general nature, typically fall into the latter category, and often do not receive any tangible level of resource from the ISP. Such a business response is short-sighted, because it increases the risk of a successful intrusion and increases the risk of widespread damage as a consequence of the intrusion. The probability of detection of the initial intrusion reduces substantially if systems are left with their security mechanisms unattended. In the aftermath of such events, particularly when a client's credit card details are involved, the outcomes are often catastrophic to the ISP who has been the victim.

Security activity should not be ignored by the ISP. However, all available resources should not necessarily be concentrated on security-related activities. Without due attention to income-generating activities, the ISP may find itself operating a relatively secure, but financially unviable, network service. As with many activities, the answer lies in finding an appropriate balance between security activities and other necessary ISP service activities.

One productive means of establishing such a balance is to understand the priorities that exist for ISPs within the security area.

Integrity of the service. The ISP has to protect the integrity of the network service and must be able to make the operation of the network relatively secure. This extends not only to the routers and switching elements of the network but also to the protection of the integrity of the service delivery host platforms, including DNS servers, mail servers, Web servers, and caches, and any other service platforms operated by the ISP.

Client security. As well as protecting its own service assets from intrusion and disruption, the ISP is expected to assist clients to secure their operation from security incidents. This can take various forms, but normally does not extend all the way to have the ISP assume all responsibility for client network security. However, in certain areas, the client must trust the ISP's integrity of operation in order to implement its own security policy. For example, in the environment of *Virtual Private Networks* (VPNs), the client must trust the ISP to present only valid remote VPN traffic to each client's VPN location.

Incident response. When security incidents occur there is the expectation that the ISP will assist clients and peer ISPs in the tracing of such incidents to their source. Equally, where various forms of denial-of-service attacks are experienced, the ISP should assist in the removal of the attack, either through blocking the traffic or through identification of the source of the attack.

Legal obligations. Underpinning this is the ISP's legal and regulatory obligations, which may include the requirement to report criminal activity and cooperate with law-enforcement agencies in the investigation of such incidents.

It is a business decision as to what level of resources is made available to support the ISP's security activity and a tactical decision as to how to deploy such resources to ensure that an effective security response is forthcoming from the ISP.

The Nature of Security Incidents

The most long-lived method of attack on a system is to gain a password for access to the system and then exploit known platform-specific vulnerabilities of the system to gain control of the platform. Although this activity still takes place on the Internet with alarming frequency, it is now being complemented by other forms of intrusion and disruption.

Today, the types of security incidents on the Internet include the following attributes:

◆ Exploitation of protocol flaws
◆ Use of source listings to identify system flaws
◆ Use of ICMP to launch denial-of-service attacks
◆ Abuse of the anonymous ftp servers
◆ Exploitation of weaknesses in Web servers and e-mail servers
◆ Use of IP source address spoofing

The intent is now not just intrusion, but also the activity of denial of service is becoming more prevalent, in which the attack is intended to disrupt the service without actually intruding into the service platform. Such denial-of-service attacks are a major issue to ISPs, and the sophistication of these attacks is increasing. Prevalent at present are so-called *SYN attacks* in which a system is targeted by a flood of TCP SYN packets, causing system exhaustion through the system's attempt to open discrete connections for each received SYN packet. Denial-of-service attacks also have exploited the remote broadcast mechanism, in which a target system is flooded with packets in response to a trigger packet sent to a network that has remote broadcasts enabled.

Attacks also are being launched against the infrastructure of the Internet, with routers being exploited to launch denial-of-service attacks through the subversion of the routing system. Because many security systems also use name as a primary mechanism of authentication of a remote entity, DNS servers are also under pressure, with the intention of inserting incorrect name bindings. This area is being given an increased amount of attention, because of the widespread impact that can result from such infrastructure attacks.

For these reasons, it is necessary for an ISP to develop a security policy and implement this policy within the areas of service infrastructure design, configuration of service platforms, and operation of incident response processes that can respond meaningfully to security incidents.

ISP Security Policy

A security policy is intended to assist the ISP in responding to security incidents, allowing the ISP to develop proactive processes to minimize security risks and to guide the ISP to handle incidents promptly, efficiently and effectively, reducing the potential impact of an incident through an effective response.

Such a policy should encompass a number of areas of ISP activity:

◆ The policy should provide guidelines relating to the *evaluation of service technology*, to ensure that the equipment does not compromise the current security environment.

◆ The policy should also state the ISP's position with respect to the *privacy of data*.

◆ In a similar vein, the policy should state the process of admitting *access to data* and in what formats.

◆ In general, most ISPs adopt a policy position akin to that of a *common carrier*, in which the ISP undertakes not to inspect or alter in any way client content passed over the network, nor does it accept any liability in the carriage of such content. In terms of *account-abilities*, the client is responsible for the content of data passed across the network.

♦ The ISP should specify in such a policy guideline the process of reporting security incidents, outlining the *responsibility of the ISP and that of the client* in such situations.

The overall intent of the policy is to allow the ISP and its staff to respond efficiently to security incidents, while not compromising client confidentiality considerations, nor exposing the ISP or the client to unwarranted liabilities within the structure of the response. An ISP should obtain legal advice on such a policy, after it is drafted, to ensure that these objectives are adequately addressed from a legal perspective. Further detail in this area is available in [RFC1281], "Guide-lines for the Secure Operation of the Internet."

This general policy should be augmented by a more specific system management policy, covering the system administration role undertaken by the ISP, particularly as it relates to the ISP's responsibilities when operating systems that house client's data. Electronic mail servers and relays, Web publishing platforms, and Web caches are all instances of such systems. The policy should explicitly note the circumstances under which a system administrator could inspect client data and the consequent obligations on the administrator regarding the divulging of this information to any other party.

The security policy also should impact the drafting of the service contract with the ISP's clients, ensuring that the contract includes provision for sensible security provisions and obliging the client to exercise responsible and legal behavior in its use of the ISP's services. The contract should include specific provisions regarding the following:

♦ The misuse of the service
♦ Actions intended to disrupt the service of the ISP or any third party
♦ Breaking into other accounts or services
♦ The access or alteration of third-party data without the express or implied consent of the party involved

The service contract also should cover aspects of disruptive or criminal behavior, such as the launching of intrusion attempts, denial-of-service attacks, or the abuse of the e-mail and Usenet systems through the posting of large volumes of unsolicited messages. Where permitted, the contract should allow the ISP to exercise some ability to cancel the service contract to the client if these provisions of the contract are abused. Finally, the contract should clearly state the liability of the client as a consequence of undertaking such activities.

Securing the Network Infrastructure

The *ideal* secure environment for network infrastructure services is to physically delineate the client service environment from the service control environment. In this ideal environment are two distinct networks, one to route client data and allow client service applications access to the network's service applications and another to manage the service elements. Such an ideal environment is indicated in Figure 9.1. Within such an environment, the individual service platforms are configured to respond on the service plane to requests on the configured service port. For example, a mail relay server would respond only to the mail port (TCP port 25) for incoming requests and initiate connections only to remote mail server ports, a DNS server to port 53, and so on. Routers would explicitly not respond to incoming session requests from the service plane, limiting their actions to switching packets within the service plane and responding to and generating ICMP messages as appropriate. Such a management architecture is termed *out-of-band* management,

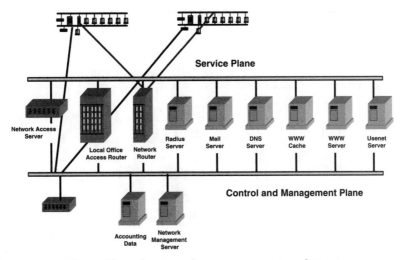

Figure 9.1 Out-of-band network management architecture.

because all control and management functions are performed on a separate management network, physically distinct from the service network.

Such a configuration is generally not constructed precisely along these lines, in that the duplication of the network infrastructure for a separate management and control network does imply additional cost to the ISP. The more conventional construction technique is to use a single network infrastructure for both service and control and management functions, using *in-band* network management, as indicated in Figure 9.2.

In this environment, the effort of designing a security architecture is directed towards emulating the functionality of an out-of-band network management architecture. Here, service elements operate with management access restricted to the network operations center; external access to the network operations center is restricted; and the network operates in a way that attempts to be resilient against attacks which exploit flawed protocol behavior.

Securing the Routers

One of the major attacks undertaken on the network itself is the *denial-of-service* attacks. The intent of this form of attack is to bring the network to a state where it can no longer carry client data. The most common way of undertaking this is to attack the routers themselves, with the intent to cause them to cease forwarding packets or to forward packets to an incorrect destination.

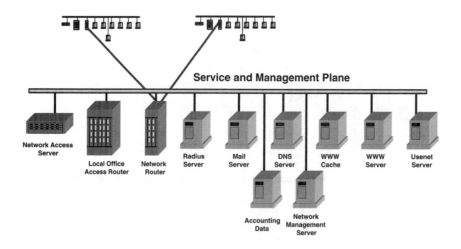

Figure 9.2 In-band network management architecture.

The former may be triggered by intrusion and then deliberate misconfiguration or a flooding attack in which the router is overwhelmed with unroutable data, causing router performance to degrade. The latter may be triggered by the injection of spurious routing updates.

The basic prerequisite for good router security is a robust routing design. It is a high-risk activity to engage in routing peering unless some basic precautions are configured into the design.

◆ Where possible, routing peering should be avoided completely, and static routes used instead. A significantly reduced risk of promulgation of bad routing information leaking across from clients into the ISP's routing environment exists when static routes are used at the boundary between the client and the ISP.

◆ Where peering is necessary, use an exterior routing protocol. Currently, BGP4 is an obvious choice.

◆ To avoid promulgation of bad routing information, pass all learned routes and their attributes through an ingress filter, permitting only those routes where the route prefix and its associated AS path match an administratively maintained filter set.

◆ In this environment, the ISP should use a routing registry to register its routing policies and strongly encourage its BGP peers to do the same.

In this way, the routing information passed across a peering session should conform to a set of published routing policies, minimizing the risk of deliberate or unintended routing corruption. The identity of the routing peers also should be protected, because one mechanism of attack is to spoof the identity of a trusted routing peer. The solution to this type of threat is to protect the routing updates by use of authentication fields within the chosen routing protocol. These can be either of the form of authentication fields within every update or the use of encryption of the entire routing protocol updates, using checksums and sequence numbers to protect against replay attacks. Widespread adoption of secure routing protocol updates is still not a feature of today's Internet, and the consequent vulnerability of the network routing environment remains a source of significant concern. Flooding is harder to protect against, and the mechanisms to address such incidents remain in the realms of packet flow tracing to identify the source of the flood.

Extreme care should be taken with allowing access to routers. A common vulnerability is to use readily guessable SNMP community names, coupled with SNMP community write access to the router. SNMP access should be restricted to source addresses used by the NOC and should ignore SNMP access attempts using loose source routing. Routers' interactive access should be carefully controlled, with access logs generated and inspected regularly. There also is risk in allowing interactive access to the command interface of routers unless it is coupled with a strong authentication mechanism, such as Kerberos, to ensure that passwords are not sent across the network in an unencrypted form. As with SNMP access, the router should reject access attempts from source IP addresses other than those used by the NOC for access and should explicitly prevent source-routed access attempts. Router configurations should be uploaded from the router to the NOC at very regular intervals, and the current configuration checked against the NOC master copy for unauthorized changes. Ideally, configuration changes should be made at the NOC, using a source code control system to ensure that every configuration change is logged against a NOC operator. All changes should record the data and time of the change and comments relating to the reason for the configuration change. The change itself should be downloaded to the router from the NOC.

Routing configurations also can assist in providing some level of resiliency against host-based attacks, and a number of router options are typically supported on router platforms, which can be used in this area:

No source routing. Many attacks use a mechanism of enabling loose source routing in an attempt to circumvent site security mechanisms. Here, the identity of a trusted host is placed in the source field, and the attacking host is referenced within the loose source–routing option. Although it is normally a client network responsibility to disable loose source routing at the Internet boundary, some ISPs also disable this IP packet option within the network infrastructure as an added precaution. Some debate over the utility of this measure has existed, because source routing is a useful tool for the *Network Operations Center* (NOC) to debug some forms of routing and performance problems. Source routing allows the NOC to direct diagnostic packets through a particular location and then deduce the network routing conditions at that point. If an ISP chooses to leave source routing enabled within the infrastructure, clients should be explicitly informed of this decision and advised of actions they should take if they want to disable it from their network.

No directed broadcast. By default, in an Internet environment, it is possible to generate a directed broadcast packet addressed to all hosts connected to a remote network. This form of packet is commonly used to launch denial-of-service attacks, in which a single packet is directed to the directed broadcast address. If it is an ICMP Echo Request packet, it will generate a cascaded response to the source address from every host connected to the network. The attack uses a packet in which the source address is the address of the target host. A sequence of such packets directed to the remote broadcast address causes the remote network to act as an unwitting amplifier of the packets, which are then sent to the target system. Where the ISP manages client edge routers, and where there is an internal network used to house a set of service platforms, directed broadcast should be disabled in the network's boundary router.

Ingress source address filtering.   Many forms of attack use invented, or *spoofed*, source addresses in the packets, as a means of hiding the identity and location of the attacker, or, as with directed broadcast attacks, as part of the mechanism of the attack. In many cases, defining a set of ingress packet filters on the ISP network is possible so that the source address of a received packet must match the set of routes advertised from the associated network port. Widespread deployment of such filters will make source address spoofing more challenging in the wider Internet. Some side-effects to this are possible, notably with mobile IP, where the application relies on using source addresses that do not match the corresponding state of the routing system, in order to operate correctly. The technique of ingress source address filtering is described in more detail in [RFC 2267].

The preceding measures do not in themselves create a secure Internet environment, but they do assist in increasing the resiliency of the network to instances of attempted abuse and attempt to make the task of tracing an attack somewhat easier.

In some regulatory regimes, the ISP may need to allow law-enforcement agencies the ability to insert tap points into the network and intercept network traffic. Due account of the local regulatory requirements should be taken by ISPs, both in the design phase and in the operational environment. Where the requirement is present to allow traffic interception, this should be designed so that the tap points operate in a highly secure fashion.

Securing Service Platforms

In an out-of-band network management environment, each service platform presents to the network only an entry point, which is associated with a service port. This does minimize the points of vulnerability but still allows the platform to be the subject of intrusion and denial of service through exploiting weaknesses in the service application and the platform. In a more conventional in-band network management, the avenue of potential exploitation of the service platform widens, and the desire for a robust service environment does include very careful consideration of security issues.

Two parts exist to securing service platforms in a conventional in-band network management architecture: the access to the server environment should be carefully controlled, and the platforms themselves should be carefully managed.

Where possible, server environments should be located on a dedicated service network, distinct from the client access networks and distinct from the NOC network. A typical architecture of deployment is indicated in Figure 9.3, in which a dedicated network is used to host network service platforms, with

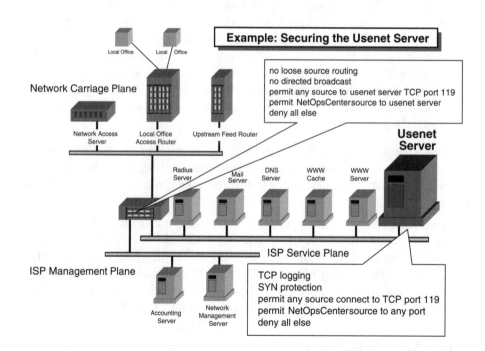

Figure 9.3   Service platform architecture.

access mediated by an entry router, which effectively functions as a basic filtering firewall. The firewall permits general access to the service ports of each platform and permits control and management access only to the NOC address.

Depending on the desired robustness of the service architecture, the NOC access could be replaced by an encrypted tunnel from the NOC to the service entry router.

Such an access architecture should be further backed up with service platform-based connection filters, which implement a similar access regime for each host. This more general security architectural approach attempts to avoid reliance on a single mechanism of defense. Using both router and host access filters does provide a robust means of mutual support for implementing a security environment. The access mechanisms also implement another important generic approach to security, that of explicit permission, using a default of denial of access.

The second part of the server security architecture is to secure the host itself. This area, that of host-specific security mechanisms, is a well-documented area, and the ISP is well-advised to research the topic thoroughly within the context of the host operating system that is used by the ISP. Here, we will highlight just the major issues that should be addressed.

A reasonable checklist of server host security mechanisms should include the following:

◆ Keep access accounts up-to-date and regularly change passwords.

◆ Use host connection filters, or *wrappers*, which are configured to explicitly permit certain connection types while denying access to all other connection attempts.

◆ Use up-to-date platform software and application software images. Many updates are the outcome of increasing the resiliency of the platform or the application, and operating out-of-date images is a widely exploited mechanism of effecting intrusion into server systems.

◆ Log all server access events as a means of detecting intrusion attempts and potential back-tracing of any incidents.

◆ Use strong checksums of the system and application images to allow detection of attempts to install Trojan horse versions of system components. (A Trojan horse is a deliberately manipulated version of a utility that preserves its original functionality but also contains a mechanism to admit access to an intruder upon entering some form of command sequence.)

♦ Maintain a remotely held and secure copy of the system software and critical data sets to ensure that a rapid recovery of the server is possible.

♦ Consider using nonwritable media, such as CD, for read-only system images and information data sets.

♦ Where sensitive information is held on the server, use encryption of the data to minimize the damage in the event of intrusion.

♦ Strip all nonessential service and system components off the server platform. Such stripping may include sendmail, remote access servers (the Unix r-* servers), the finger daemon, compilers, system configuration files, and similar nonessential system components.

♦ Consider using end-to-end encryption for control access, either using an encrypted tunnel to the firewall router or using an encrypted access session, such as the secure shell, ssh. One-time passwords also should be considered for secure server access.

♦ Use available systems' security tools to monitor the integrity of the server environment.

In addition, a number of other measures are relevant to particular server platforms.

For Web server platforms:

♦ Do not configure interactive user accounts on the server. Allow clients the ability to upload data sets into the server into a dedicated server area.

♦ Carefully manage the use of user-provided CGI programs and test these programs most scrupulously prior to staging the program onto the server.

For DNS server platforms:

♦ Use server software that loads only authoritative data into the DNS cache.

- Use server software that throttles response rates to repeated requests from the same query point, to prevent denial-of-service attacks.

For ftp servers:

- Avoid using writeable directories, or, if a writeable guest account is necessary, set the directory to nonreadable and constantly monitor downloading activity into the area.
- Use a stripped ftp-specific file root to avoid grabbing of the system access and configuration files.
- Use a dedicated platform for ftp access where possible, avoiding colocation of the ftp service with any other service delivery operation.

For e-mail servers:

- Use e-mail configuration files that explicitly prevent use of the server as a relay by unauthorized clients.
- Where POP/IMAP access is implemented, restrict such access to the associated accounts to a basic shell that permits only POP and IMAP access activity.

And, perhaps most importantly, for all platforms:

- Check for intruder activity in system logs, accounting files, and the file system. Given the copious quantities of such information generated on a busy server, consideration should be given to scripting such checks to generate management alarms in which anomalous information is detected in such records.

This may appear to be a daunting checklist, and many ISPs implement only a partial set of these measures on their server platforms. As noted at the outset of this chapter, security activity is one of risk assessment, rather than absolute outcomes, and risk assessment should be applied to this activity as a business and strategic judgement. However, the environment of deployment of ISP service platforms is a hostile environment, in which no effective external control mechanisms exist to moderate behavior, as law enforcement processes within a global network are not as timely or as effectual as many would hope. In response to this threat, good security mechanisms, diligently applied, are intended to produce a robust and reliable service environment, which translates to a valuable business asset in a highly competitive marketplace.

Securing Client Access

The ISP should be aware of its limitations in this area for managing the entire client network environment and the potential liabilities in undertaking contractual obligations that may not be possible for the ISP to fulfill. Care should be exercised to ensure that any service contract that includes security considerations, or warranties of ISP performance related to security of the client's network, includes conditions that the ISP is confident of being able to meet.

Aside from the security of the client network itself, the ISP can take a number of actions that assist the client in securing its environment. The access routers that terminate a client network connection can be configured with loose source routing disabled (although this is noted as a debatable measure), and egress packet filters can be configured, which prevent any packets that have a client's address in the source field of the packet from being passed to the client. In addition, ingress packet filters can be used, which permit only packets with a source address from within the client's address block to be passed into the network. Such mechanisms are indicated in Figure 9.4.

A common denial-of-service attack on clients is to flood their access lines with traffic. Such attacks place considerable strain on the ISP operational support staff, who are often requested to install custom filters on the client's access port for the duration of the attack. Consideration should be given to allowing a secure mechanism for the client to add filter entries to the egress filter of the access router without the need for direct involvement of the ISP's operational staff. If such a tool is considered, care should be exercised to ensure that this is implemented using a robust authentication mechanism, and that the filter lists do not reach a level of complexity, which compromises the operation of the router itself. Consideration also should be given to implementing an interface to the tool that attempts to create a simple paradigm of router filters, to ensure that the customer can create the desired effect without compromising the normal operation of its service.

One of the most important tasks for the ISP in this area is to inform clients of the existence of a hostile Internet environment and ensure that clients are making an informed decision as to how they want to respond to security, both in terms of security measures they want to install and the way in which the client wants to respond to security incidents.

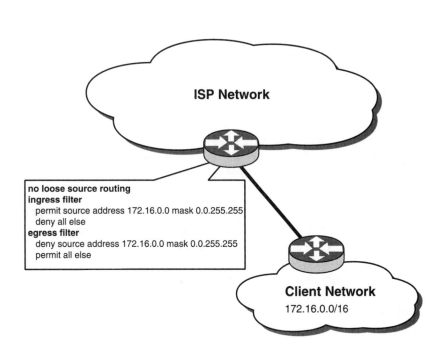

Figure 9.4 Client access configuration.

Responding to Incidents

The first time an ISP really engages in a security policy and substantially addresses security considerations is commonly after the first intrusion. Unfortunately, by then the levels of confidence in the service provider may have been eroded to the extent that it is simply too late to recover the business. It is prudent for the ISP not only to prepare and execute a security plan, as a set of defensive mechanisms to deter intrusion episodes, but also to plan for a response to intrusion episodes. The plan should identify the available responses and work with these resources to address the intrusion, recover from any damage, and analyze the event in a timely and effective manner. The domain that an intruder typically works from is a well-organized area of activity, which communicates effectively internally, and responds quickly after a breach is made into a system or network environment.

A timely and efficient response is necessary to ensure that critical assets are not compromised, that the systems are not used as a springboard for further intrusion into other systems within the network or within client networks, that essential data is not corrupted, and that confidence in the integrity of operation of the ISP is not compromised. Planning a response should address a set of objectives that are intended to identify what has happened, establish how to prevent a recurrence of exploitation of the same vulnerability, and prevent the intrusion from escalating further, as a primary set of tasks. The subsequent step is to recover from the event and update policies and procedures if there is a weakness within these processes which has been exposed. As appropriate, the ISP should present the evidence of the incident to law-enforcement agencies and work with such agencies to determine the identity of the attacker.

The plan should nominate how an incident response is to be managed so that the response can be coordinated effectively within the organization, rather than having multiple fragmentary efforts underway. Management of the response should be handled by a single point of contact, who is then responsible for coordinating the response effort within the organization. The plan also should include escalation mechanisms, so that internally, the coordination responsibility may change hands if the event is not being effectively addressed in a timely manner or if the intrusion has resulted in uncovering greater levels of damage and intrusion.

The first part of the plan should be to establish how the plan is activated. Clients should be aware of a process to report suspected security incidents, as should peer ISPs, as well as the Internet security response groups. The reporting point should allow both secure e-mail as well as a 24-hour phone contact to an appropriate operational staff member. This external reporting mechanism should be complemented by internal alarms, which are raised by the ISP's security defense mechanisms. These mechanisms should indicate a security incident on discovery of anomalous logged data or through the triggering of a trip wire defense within the system.

When an incident is reported by any of these mechanisms, the primary task is to verify the report as one which is relevant to the ISP and pertains to a current incident. The ISP often receives security reports that refer to client networks, and the ISP does need to have a relevant client contact to pass the security report toward in a reliable fashion. Reports may be inaccurate, or the alarm may trigger a false call. It may be necessary to collate the reports, collected logs, and current system status to confirm the event.

The second step is to initiate a response, which should be aware in advance of its priorities of activity. As always, human safety should be the primary priority of activity. A second level of priority should be to protect confidential and sensitive data, which in the case of the ISP, often relates to credit card information and other forms of client data held by the ISP. The next level of priority is to protect other data and the integrity of the system platforms. Finally, the response should minimize disruption to the service environment.

With these priorities in mind, incident response typically follows a sequence of activity. The initial objective is to identify the scope of the incident. Many environments use circles of mutual trust, in which other systems may become highly vulnerable to intrusion if one system within the trust circle is breached. Where uniform software and hardware platforms are used within an ISP, which is a common method of operational management of a large ISP operation, the vulnerability exploited on one system may be shared with other systems. As breached systems are identified, the four levels of priority should be assessed in relation to the system, identifying threats to human safety, sensitive data, other data and system resources, and whether the service platform should continue in operation or be isolated from the network. If the scope of the activity extends to other sites, it is a sensible and prudent action to inform these sites through their security incident reporting channels. Although the sharing of information relating to an incident may be subject to various legal and business considerations, the primary responsibility is to inform other sites which appear to be affected of the nature of the incident.

The next step is incident containment and removal of vulnerability. Containment may involve the off-lining or shutdown of affected systems or a close monitoring of activity. Typically, this should follow a predetermined plan of action, which can be executed in a timely fashion, as this step is intended to protect the data assets held on the system. The system then should be reviewed to identify and remove the vulnerability. This may be detecting and removal of virus codes, hidden files, Trojan horse software, and similar artifacts left from the intrusion. Evidence of the intrusion should be held safely and analyzed at a later date, as it will assist in determining the initial nature of the intrusion and may assist law-enforcement authorities in their investigation of the incident.

The next action is to recover the system state. Where system and application software images are affected, use restoration from a trusted media source. Given uncertainties of the original point of intrusion, it may be necessary to revert to the original vendor-supplied media in this step to ensure that a clean system and application image is loaded onto the platform.

The final step is to report on the incident and the method of response. This step is an essential part of reviewing the overall security policy and its effectiveness and reviewing the incident response plans and the way in which they operated. Such reviews ensure that the ISP, as an organization, can assemble resources to respond effectively and efficiently to minimize the impact of such security incidents.

Summary

The Internet is not a secure environment. Every ISP can confidently expect to be the target of various attacks intended to gain access to the network and server platforms, as well as to be the victim of attacks intended to disrupt the services provided. The ISP also can expect such attacks to be launched against its clients, and, possibly, be the victim of an attack launched by a client.

Good security is an outcome of an effective planning process. The process should identify the risks and generate a security policy, which states achievable objectives for the organization. Such objectives should document the assets that the ISP wants to protect through the adoption of design architectures, which support protection of the ISP's assets, the deployment and operation of security defense mechanisms, and the incident response processes. The policy also should state the objectives.

Careful attention to security will create a robust and relatively secure service environment that translates into a valuable business asset for the ISP.

PART THREE

ISP Engineering and Business Strategies

chapter ten

Servicing Internet Markets

The Internet presents a different view of a communications service market than many more established communications services markets. The twentieth century has seen the pervasive development of the service network architecture. This architecture assumes that the network is engineered to undertake the delivery of a specified service, and that different services require the support of discrete networks. Thus, the radio broadcast network uses a different infrastructure than that of the telephone service network, and so on. The network is attuned to the characteristics of the service it supports. As an example, telephony is broken down to a service requirement for the real-time, bidirectional exchange of 3.5-kHz bandwidth analogue signals for an average duration of some 250 seconds. In looking at the architecture of today's telephone networks, we can see that a considerable level of engineering input allows the transmission and switching of such signals. Such service networks define the service within the characteristics of the network itself, and the units that terminate the network are relatively simple. The outcome of this is that the bulk of the investment lies in the interior of the network, rather than at the telephone network's periphery. The market model for such a service network allows the network operator to set a retail price based on the utility and value to the client of access to the service. Setting the price on the basis of the marginal cost of supporting the service within the network is not strictly necessary. This architecture often has been referred to as a *smart* network with *dumb* peripherals.

The architecture defined by the Internet is almost the reverse of this service-based network. The network is not attuned to any particular service characteristic. The assumptions made by the Internet architecture of the underlying transmission service are so minimal that it is tempting to assert that the underlying network may be unsuitable for any service at all. The most fundamental of these assumptions is the omission of per-call states within the network. A network that must maintain a per-call state within each of its switches incurs a significant operational overhead, not only in the performance of call setup and tear down, but in the memory state within the switched network to maintain the concept of an active call state. A connectionless network has no such requirement to maintain state, and the switching fabric is not burdened with the requirement to maintain per-call information. This simpler system scales with less incurred overhead. In the architecture of the Internet, the service definition occurs in the host platforms at the periphery of the network, and the service being supported has no meaning to the interior of the network. In this model, the bulk of the investment occurs outside the network, within the periphery, and the network itself is a simple stateless switching fabric. This architecture can be summarized as a *dumb* network with *smart* peripherals.

What is the relevance of this to the examination of the Internet market? Unlike access to a service-oriented network, access to an Internet service provider is not of itself an intrinsically high-value proposition to the client. The investment on the part of the client has already been made in the form of the purchase of the host computer and software, and the value lies in the end-to-end services that can be supported as a result. Consequently, in its basic form, the Internet access market is not a high-margin or high value service. Neither is the Internet an intrinsically expensive service in terms of the incremental cost over the basic transmission costs. Indeed, the increase of efficiency of transmission within an Internet environment is typically a greater offset than the cost of the Internet switches, so that the Internet service competes directly with basic leased carriage services in terms of cost. This is not overly good news for those seeking high margins in the Internet access market. Internet access and switching is simply not an intrinsically highly complex task that requires massive investment with huge risk, and therefore, this activity cannot sustain high margins in an open competitive market.

Accordingly, the objective of the ISP in this market is to push higher levels of value into the service proposition made to the client. In this chapter, we examine some of the options available to the ISP to achieve this within the area of network services. In the following chapter, we look at additional value-added services in the area of application support provided by the ISP.

Internet Access Services

The basic ISP market offering within the Internet market is, of course, Internet access. Internet access can take many forms, ranging from permanent wired connectivity to various forms of support for client mobility.

The Business Market

The value proposition within this form of basic access is easily stated in engineering terms, but is perhaps more ambiguous in contractual terms. The value proposition in engineering terms is indicated in Figure 10.1. The ISP advertises the default route to the client, indicating to the client that packets destined to any valid Internet destination address will be delivered by the ISP towards the destination. The client advertises a set of routes to the ISP, who in turn, undertakes to ensure that these routes are reachable throughout the Internet. It should be noted that the ISP is in no position to guarantee actual delivery of all packets to their ultimate destination. The ISP can only indicate that it will pass the packet correctly through its own network and pass it through the correct egress port to the next network in the routing path. This is quite different to the typical end-to-end service models of other communications services.

The issue that this basic service model presents to the customer is that the service client is assumed to be technically proficient in terminating such a service and then generating a service environment on the client side of the connection that can effectively and productively exploit the opportunities

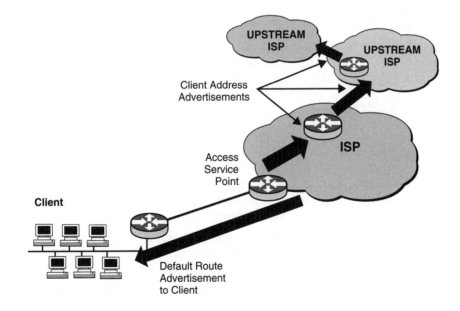

Figure 10.1   Basic Internet access service.

presented by the Internet service environment. Few communications service environments probably are as forbidding to enter as the Internet, within the structure of this form of service:

- The client has to lease a circuit from the client's premises to the ISP's point of attachment, designing the circuit to meet the anticipated load demands and performance expectation of the client.
- The client has to be able to transact for services with the address registries to obtain an IP address block to the client network, and potentially an autonomous system number if multihoming is contemplated.
- The client must configure a routing environment that interfaces with the ISP's routing structure.
- The client must secure a domain name or names from the relevant domain name registrars and then deploy DNS servers for these names so that the delegation of the name to the servers yields a functioning name environment.
- The client must manage electronic mail services and determine how those services will interface to the Internet environment, and create and manage various forms of Web servers and other service interfaces to the network.
- Of course, this environment has to be conducted in a manner that is adequately secure, so that the client's network is not unduly compromised from the risk of external attack.

The more complete picture of an Internet access environment is indicated in Figure 10.2.

From this perspective, it may not be so surprising why basic Internet access is relatively inexpensive compared to the client's total cost of connectivity, as most of the tasks and most of the client expenditure lies in constructing and maintaining a complete service environment rather than in the exchange of packets and bytes between the ISP and the client.

It is also not surprising why uptake of Internet services, particularly within the small- to medium-business enterprise sector remains very low. Many of the larger corporations may either have the technical expertise within the entity to undertake such tasks or have the means to externally source such expertise. All other enterprises are looking for a more comprehensive solution set from

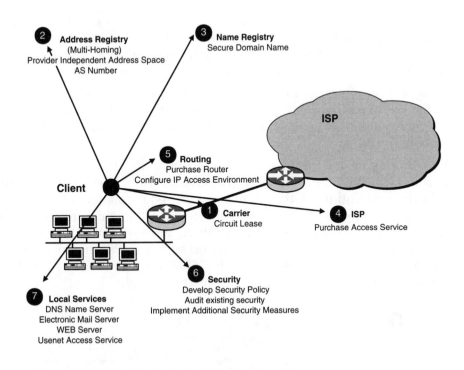

Figure 10.2 Internet access environment.

the service provider, removing many of the expertise requirements and decision points from the process and operating to a functional specification of the desired service.

Extending the Access Service

Various Internet access market offerings that encompass more than simple attachment services are common. These offerings attempt to broaden their market reach by covering this gap between required capability and actual capability and resources on the part of the client.

One of the more common form of refinements is to offer a LAN attachment service. Here, the service offered by the ISP includes the provision and management of the tail loop to the customer's premises and the provision of interface equipment at these premises. The on-site equipment (commonly referred

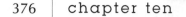

to as *Customer Premises Equipment*, or CPE) undertakes attachment to the client's local network and is configured with network address translation functions and access filters to ensure a basic level of integrity of customer security. Such a service environment is indicated in Figure 10.3

The operation of services on the customer's premises normally does not allow the ISP to realize any significant economies of scale of operation, and remote service management always presents issues of robustness and reliability for both the ISP and the business client.

The next step for the ISP to add further value to the service contract is to support services within the ISP's service infrastructure, effectively providing an outsourcing solution for the client's service requirements. Into this environment can be placed an outsourced solution for domain name operation, security monitoring, electronic mail operation, and Web publishing, to name a few options. The options on how to support such an environment are examined in further detail in Chapter 11, "The ISP Service Profile," in which the ISP solutions for the service environment are examined.

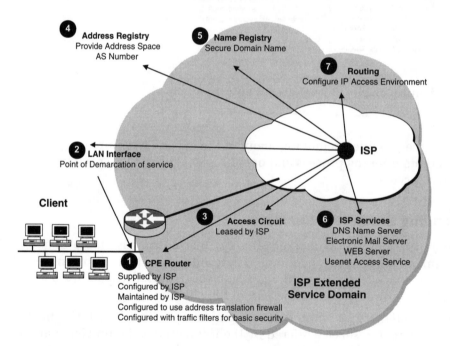

Figure 10.3 Managed access services.

Further value can be added for medium enterprises by offering a virtual private network domain, offering the capability to link multiple locations and multiple ISP access points into a single virtual corporate network, with associated operational characteristics of security of privacy and assurance of performance. Issues associated with virtual private networks are examined in further detail in Chapter 12, "Virtual Private Networks."

The progression of value in this sequence of market offerings can be indicated as follows:

- The base service is that of a *basic access service*. This service connects the client's network to the Internet and casts the ISP in the role of a carriage provider for IP packets.

- This offering can be refined to a *managed access service*. Here, the elements of access are outsourced to the ISP, so that the ISP undertakes the lease of the access circuit and the provision of on-site routers. The ISP also manages and maintains the access configuration for the client.

- Further services can be provided by the ISP to support the client's Internet presence. Such support includes DNS servers, e-mail servers, and Web servers operated by the ISP for the client. This service is a *managed Internet presence*.

- Additional value can be added by supporting the client's internal communications needs as well as the external Internet access requirements. This *managed communications environment* includes support for Virtual Private Networks, roaming access, and the so-called *extranet* services, which are managed by the ISP for the client.

- This can be further augmented by the provision of *business solutions*, which combine communications and commerce to create managed network commerce services that assist the client to conduct business over the Internet.

Such a service environment is indicated in Figure 10.4.

The overall endeavor of this effort is to create an environment that spans a greater extent of the market. The lever to achieve this is the ISP's expertise and scale of operation, directed to provide cost-effective technology solutions to clients who do not have the resources to construct such a service environment within their enterprise. At the same time, the ISP increases the value proposition offered to the client. This allows the ISP to migrate out from a low value-

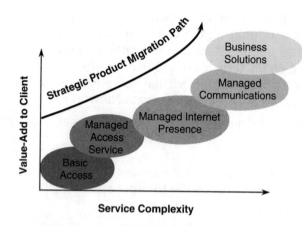

Figure 10.4 Business solution services.

added commodity market of basic access, into a market in which the solutions service places the relationship with the client on a more strategic and higher valued footing.

The competition to such enterprise positioning on the part of the ISP stems from two major sources: IT solutions enterprises, and software vendors. The IT solutions provider enterprises who have traditionally provided data center-type solutions to large enterprises are now seeing viable markets being created within the small- to medium-enterprise market sector. The software vendor is perhaps the strongest area of competitive pressure to the ISP, as the software market is attempting to bridge these same gaps in capability through software-based solutions. The objective here is to attempt to encapsulate the expertise required to construct such service environments within the software itself and present a simple control interface to the operator. Although the efforts to date have perhaps worked in the favor of the ISP, due to the visible shortfalls in packaged software solutions, this market undoubtedly will have competent software solutions available as a capital purchase for the client, as an alternative to a recurrent service fee from an ISP in the not too distant future.

The Personal Market

It would perhaps be more conventional to label this market as the *residential*, or *dial-up market*, but the use of the term *personal market*, is deliberately chosen here. The market space is to service individuals' requirements for Internet access, concentrating on support for intermittent access of a single host. Although offering only access services in this market is possible, this option is somewhat limiting for the ISP, because it forces the client to make separate arrangements for electronic mail access, access to Usenet browse servers, and access to other service delivery platforms that are conventionally provided within an ISP contract. This marketplace is highly competitive, and the market expectation of a base level of services provided with a dial-access account certainly includes more than the basic capability to dial the ISP's modem banks and have your identification accepted. The base expectation now includes a local mailbox, access to a Usenet browse server, and local Web caches where appropriate.

We can approach this market from a service provision perspective in two ways:

- Identification of the access service at the remote end
- Identification of the user at the remote end

The traditional telephony model is one in which the access instrument attracts usage charges, irrespective of the individuals who use the instrument. With the increasing deployment of calling line identification being used within telephone networks, it is possible to undertake a similar structure for ISP access. This structure is based on an authentication service using the identity of the remote access service, rather than on the identity of the user, so that the access and charges are accounted to the remote access line. A number of ISPs have constructed access services using this mechanism. In such cases, the local telephone service operator often undertakes this approach as a means of adding value to the local telephone service and using the existing service structures to provide a cost-effective entry into the ISP market.

However, the mainstream ISP dial-access market does not use the remote end access line identification as the means of authentication, but instead, uses a username and password. In this form of access, the individual undertakes an authentication phase with the ISP, and if the access is permitted, the individual is billed, irrespective of the access line or access device that the individual may be using. This forms the basis of a personal access account, because the user can use any method to access the ISP's service, albeit with additional access carriage cost when the client moves out of the local access call zone. The mobility of the client is a significant marketing asset within this market, particularly where the ISP also can provide a wide geographic coverage.

Accordingly, locality is not a strict limitation to this market, nor is dial access itself. Within this market, the dial component of the service is not strictly a prerequisite, as the same service elements are extended to all other forms of session-based individual access, including access from hybrid cable systems or various forms of Digital Subscriber Line (DSL) access. The marketing offering here is the creation of *virtual presence* service for the individual, where the ISP acts as a proxy agent for the purposes of sending and receiving messages, hosting Web pages or related content publication services, or supporting electronic transactions. Such a service offering is indicated in Figure 10.5.

The major inhibitory factor to this market is similar to that of the business market, in which the expertise levels expected of the user to negotiate the Internet can be a very forbidding factor. Such a service offering is considerably more complex than the ten-digit interface of a telephone handset, and the computer literacy factor is a significant market inhibitory factor. In this case, the market inhibitory factor is shared with the software industry. Much of the advances in computing power in the past decade, particularly in the desktop market, have not gone into speed of applications as much as into the

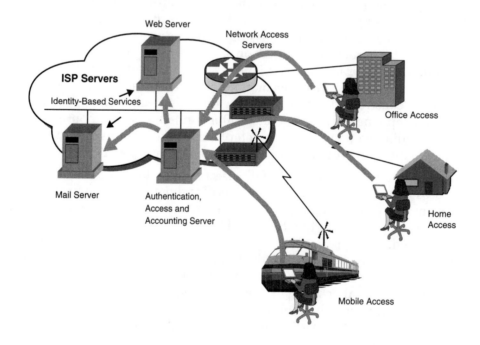

Figure 10.5 Personal Internet services.

human engineering factors of look, feel, and intuitive behavior of service applications.

Access Technologies

A continuing and highly expensive source of frustration to the entire ISP and software industry is that the process of using a modem that will interface to the local telephone system and consistently and reliably establish a high quality access session to a local Internet service provider remains an elusive target. Into this market, the hybrid cable and DSL technologies offer the potential of removing the often troublesome step of converting the digital stream into an analogue signal, which uses the same audio spectrum as the human voice, and then converting it back to an identical digital stream at the other end.

Cable TV infrastructure offers permanently connected high-bandwidth Internet access into a large residential market space. The typical configuration of these systems is a shared communications bus, using a 27-Mbps common forward data path and a 768-Kbps common return path. A deployment structure for a hybrid fiber coax network is indicated in Figure 10.6. The major advantage of this approach is the capability of supporting permanent access using a *plug-n-play* approach in which Internet systems can be plugged into a wall socket for connectivity. However, a number of inhibitory factors have proved significant barriers in a mass market rollout. The cable systems were not conditioned for digital data streams, and noise levels of the return path often seriously impair the performance of any bidirectional data system. The shared system progressively degrades with additional usage, and the capability to incrementally provision additional data bandwidth is not a readily exercised option for cable systems. For users, the performance of cable systems can be highly variable. For ISPs, the cable system can be a barrier to direct access to clients. The cable systems do not readily admit a model of competitive access to cable clients, and in many parts of the world, competitive cable access is implemented by installing multiple parallel cable systems. In a commodity Internet access market, no financial margin for such extravagance exists in provisioning cable infrastructure.

The alternative approach to addressing the post-modem access market is to exploit the available spectrum of the copper pairs in the tail loop of the fixed telephone network. Modulation, equalization, and error-control techniques can support speeds of up to some 6Mbps over 12,000 feet of access copper pairs. The technology to support such speeds is termed *Digital Subscriber Line* (DSL). A variety of DSL technologies are available, including Asymmetric DSL (ADSL), Symmetric DSL (SDSL), High bit-rate DSL (HDSL), Very high bit-rate

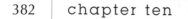

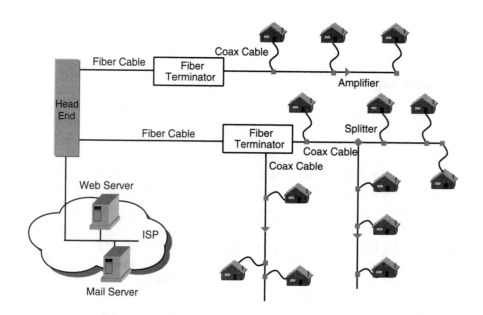

Figure 10.6 Hybrid Fiber Coax (HFC) deployment.

DSL (VDSL), Universal DSL (UDSL), and ISDN DSL (IDSL). The common property of these technologies is the use of a digital encoding technique, which exploits the available signal spectrum space on the copper loop, while avoiding encoding techniques that accumulate voltage on the wire pair or generate excessive crosstalk. The characteristics of each variant are indicated in Table 10.1.

Table 10.1 DSL Comparison

DSL Scheme	Downstream Bit Rate (Kbps)	Upstream Bit Rate (Kbps)	Voice Support
IDSL	144	144	Active
UDSL	1,000	300	Splitterless
SDSL	160–1,168	160–1,168	No
HDSL	2,048	2,048	No
ADSL	1,500–8,000	64–800	Passive
VDSL	1,500–25,000	1,600	Passive

Compared to cable systems, the key difference here is that cable is a shared medium, and DSL is not. The DSL line is used exclusively by a single client, and no contention for bandwidth exists on the local loop. As the network loads, DSL offers the potential for more consistent service levels. The DSL architecture is an overlay of a permanent data delivery system on the existing telephone local loops. A DSL deployment design is indicated in Figure 10.7.

At this stage it is unclear whether competitive ISP access will be provided within the DSL environment. Some regulatory regimes allow the client to sign over the copper loop to a competitive local carrier, in which case, ISP competition will be part of the competitive access to the copper loop. Other regulatory regimes appear to be heading in the direction of implementing competitive service access via client-to-service provider virtual circuits, implemented potentially by ATM virtual circuits. Such an architecture reproduces the essential architectural elements of the modem-based competitive ISP access market.

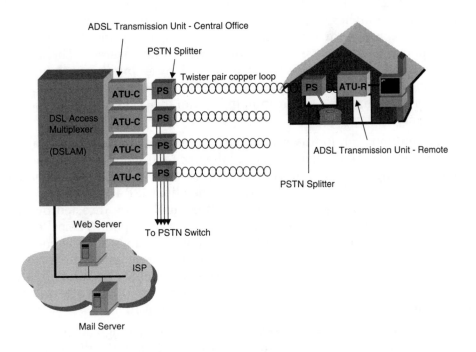

Figure 10.7   DSL deployment architecture.

Both these access technologies offer a number of persuasive advantages to the client: increased speed of access, permanent plug-in access, and an end to modem configuration woes. It is likely that this will prove to be a significant enabling factor to the Internet, allowing more sophisticated applications to make more use of network capabilities, and potentially unleashing a second wave of plug-in Internet-enabled consumer devices. The unresolved issue is whether the widespread use of high-speed permanent access technologies, such as cable and DSL, will still permit a highly competitive overlay Internet access market. The alternative scenario is that the Internet access will be an integral part of the transmission access, in which case competition will be via competitive provision of local loop and local cable services.

Roaming and Mobility

The extension to the Internet access service is to offer access services to a highly mobile workforce, allowing identical access across a wide geographic coverage. The demographic sector that makes extensive use of the Internet includes a highly mobile workforce, and matching the service offering to this sector allows a higher value solution to be proposed to the client. The brute force approach to providing solutions in this space is for the ISP to have access points spread across a very broad geographic coverage. The user may use a constant access number, which is mapped by an *Intelligent Network* (IN) telephone network feature to the closest available local access point, or the user may use a directory application to look up the access number associated with the closest access point.

Such solutions call for investment into access systems on a large scale, and such extensive coverage can be beyond the financial scope of many dedicated ISP business operations. One wide area access solution is for the carrier to use a shared access pool structure, in which the client ISP is assigned a unique national number, and clients calling on this number are directed by the IN telephone network to the closest carrier modem access pool. The called number then triggers ISP-specific authentication mechanisms, and the creation of some form of an access tunnel from the access server to the ISP's network interface to the carrier. This allows the ISP to outsource a solution for a wide geographic coverage while paying the carrier access pool provider on a usage basis. Such a roaming solution is indicated in Figure 10.8.

The lowest cost solution is to use a set of reciprocal agreements between ISPs, allowing the client to dial the local ISP provider and authenticate itself using the home provider's authentication mechanism. The reciprocal agree-

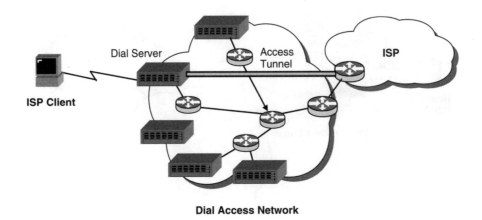

Figure 10.8 A shared dial-access network.

ments effectively allow the home provider to bill the client for the remote access and the home provider to pay the peer provider for the access session at an agreed settlement rate. In this solution, the client must maintain a directory of locations and access numbers, and greater stress is placed on the client's expertise to configure its system to successfully access different ISPs' access systems. In this environment, the client's view of the Internet changes when accessing the network via a remote service provider, and the IP address and host names assigned to the client's access host will be locally assigned, rather than assigned from the home provider. This access structure is indicated in Figure 10.9.

The other form of value-added access service is that of *mobility*. The difference between roaming and mobility is that the roaming service allows the client to re-establish static connectivity at various locations; whereas mobility allows the client to remain connected while being mobile. This service does have immediate application for laptop connectivity, mimicking the functionality of the cellular telephone service.

One means of accomplishing this is by direct use of a mobile telephony solution using a modem that attaches to a cellular telephone, or a so-called cellular data modem. The limitations of this approach lie in the restricted bandwidth available within the cellular telephone environment, which already uses extensive compression of the analogue signal in order to maximize the

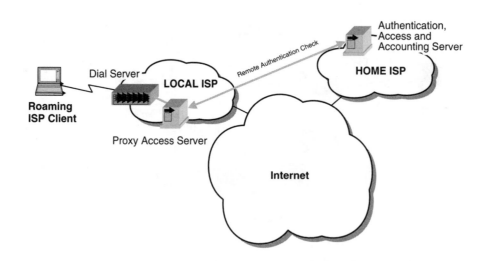

Figure 10.9 Roaming solutions.

spectrum efficiency of cellular communications, and also lie in the cellular service pricing structure, which is conventionally based on a premium service price structure for mobile voice. These limitations can be prohibitively high to all but a very small sector of the potential market for mobility services. The user is charged for the duration of the call, rather on the traffic interactions with the service network. Spectrum is consumed for the duration of the call, irrespective of activity levels. This access model can be taken one step further (as always) by integrating the functions of the laptop computer into the cellular phone, creating a single device that is both a voice and a data device, or integrating the functions of the cellular phone into the laptop, creating a mobile device with a more usable keyboard!

The alternative is to use a packet radio solution, in which the mobile device registers its presence within a radio cell, and the cellular packet data service network then directs packets to the device to the appropriate base station. Such a packet-based solution admits a more flexible model of service, because no connection needs to be made or broken. The mobile device and the cellular service network maintain a basic interchange to ensure that location information is kept up-to-date. This is indicated in Figure 10.10. This model is used by the CDPD services in the United States.

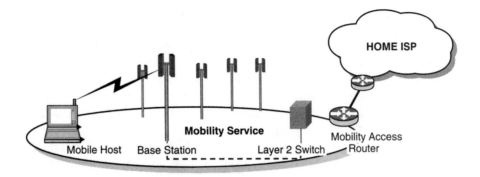

Figure 10.10   Mobility services.

The CDPD activity is sponsored by the Wireless Data Forum, an industry body whose aim is to promote interoperable standards for wireless access. The Web page for this body is www.wirelessdata.org.

The model of this service is an *always on* model, in which the device is always known to the network, but the radio spectrum is only used when there is data. The interesting corollary is that this service lends itself readily to the emerging Internet device market, in which devices such as pagers, alarm systems, and others, can exploit the potential of the Internet service environment to create highly capable mobile devices. Oddly enough, this approach has come full circle in terms of identification of the end entity, in which the device is the object identified by the network, rather than the user. The advantage of such an *always on* model for mobility is that the issues of interfacing equipment to cellular data modems and establishing modem connectivity to a service provider are circumvented, and in so doing, a simpler usage paradigm can be constructed in which connectivity is established to the mobile support network when the device is powered on.

The drawback is that while the current access ISP market is an overlay to the underlying service networks, allowing different operators to operate ISP services from the operators of the underlying carriage service, this form of service binds the carriage service with the Internet access service, so that one operator must undertake both functions.

The CDPD standards support mobility through link layer mobility support. An alternative approach is to use IP directly to support mobility. This approach has been the subject of considerable research in recent years, and the standards for IP-level mobility are documented in [RFC 2002]. The functional objective within this architecture is to support true IP-level mobility, so that a host with a fixed IP address will continue to be able to send and receive IP datagrams as it leaves its home base and transits through a mobility environment. As yet, this technology has not been the subject of widespread deployment, but the concepts and approaches to mobility used in this approach do have the potential for creating systems that provide a smooth transition between fixed and mobile connectivity [Perkins 1998].

Extending Internet Services

It is tempting to describe this section as an oxymoron, because the base Internet service, that of unreliable datagram delivery, is not inherently extensible. However, this section also can be described as a tautology, because the upper application service levels of the protocol stack are completely flexible and can support transmission over any medium that can be encoded into a digital information stream. However, the context used here is to examine what other base Internet services can be offered within the structure of an ISP's service portfolio, to both expand the potential market for the ISP's services and add value to the service portfolio.

One of the more effective means of extending the market reach of the Internet is to increase its utility by allowing Internet users to interact with other communications services from within the Internet service environment.

GSM Messaging

As a simple example, the Global System for Mobile communications (GSM) supports a message service (the short message service, or SMS), allowing messages of up to 150 characters to be transmitted to a GSM phone using a reliable transfer. Where GSM is widely deployed as a mobile telephony technology, it is common for ISPs to provide a gateway allowing for e-mail messages to be addressed to a GSM phone alias (using an address of the form *phone_number@sms.provider*, for example), creating a mobile messaging service. Recent experiments with Internet-wide GSM gateways have led to significant stress on the inter-carrier settlement arrangements for GSM messaging, and while local service gateways will enjoy considerable popularity as hybrid paging systems, deployment of larger scale gateways will probably await further refinement of the GSM SMS inter-carrier agreements.

Radio Paging

Radio paging is also another readily accessible area of Internet service extension. Although it is possible to deploy an electronic mail gateway to access a radio paging service using a similar form of user functionality to that of the GSM SMS interface, a number of aspects to a paging protocol are not completely suited to an electronic mail interface. Electronic mail is not always delivered in a timely fashion, and when delivery is stalled within the mail delivery network, there is no notification to the sender of this deferred delivery condition. RFC 1861 documents a Simple Network Paging Protocol (SNPP), which allows an application to interface to a paging service and deliver the page messaage directly, with an immediate notification of the message delivery status.

Fax Services

Of perhaps more intrinsic interest is the Internet interface to fax services. Fax transmission plays a large role in existing communications systems, and various studies have indicated that a significant portion of long-distance minutes within the telephone network are composed of fax traffic. The increasing penetration of e-mail access does present a lower cost alternative to simple messaging. Here, the widely adopted functionality of MIME mail attachments includes the capability to send working documents, rather than the fax functionality of transmitting a picture of the document.

However, the fax system possesses a number of attributes that support its continued use. The fax system offers the capability to transmit signatures, allowing a basic means for the receiver to validate a document. Without some form of electronic signature, which is still not widely promulgated, electronic mail does not offer any reasonable means of authenticating the sender of a message. The fax system also offers the capability to confirm delivery of the document to the remote printer, so that the sender has a record of successful delivery. In its basic form, electronic mail does not offer confirmed delivery of a message, and although there are extensions that request the recipient to inform the sender, their use is not mandated within a mail system.

The Internet can offer a number of functional alternatives to the limited fax model of scanner to remote printer connectivity. The TPC.INT fax service implements a distributed hybrid service that allows electronic mail messages to be delivered to remote fax servers, similar to the functionality of a remote printer. This service, documented in RFC1528 and described at www.tpc.int, uses a mechanism of delivery via the Internet to a server that is local to the destination fax phone number. The choice of a local server is made by the means of embedding the full international format of the destination phone number into the mail domain address. By using a reverse number notation within the domain address, the operation of the DNS can be exploited to provide the correct local fax delivery server. The server then converts the mail body to a format compatible to a fax printer and then uses the mail header to extract a destination phone number to undertake the call and deliver the fax. The operation of this system is indicated in Figure 10.11. This particular system is operated at no incremental cost to the sender of the fax. The destination's remote server undertakes the last hop delivery on the basis that the server operator can use the cover page to provide some form of message or advertising to recover the costs of the local server and the local calls.

The current objective within this area of fax support is to extend this existing Internet-based functional model to a more general method to link the fax scanner with the fax printer over the Internet packet network, carrying the distance fax traffic using Internet tariffs rather than telephony tariffs. One solution is to use a store-and-forward set of fax servers, in which the sender dials

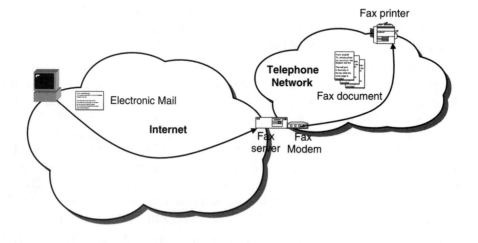

Figure 10.11   TPC.INT fax delivery.

a local server access number and then adds digits that correspond to the remote location. The fax is transmitted to the local server via a local PSTN call. The server then passes the fax, as an Internet data file transfer, to the remote fax server, which then can spool the file for a local PSTN call to the destination fax printer. In this system, the sender will not receive immediate notification of delivery, and the server system may need to be configured to offer a confirmation faxback on completion of the transaction.

The further refinement of this functional model is to use tighter levels of integration of Internet carriage with the fax signaling specifications to create a functional analogue of the fax environment, while undertaking the carriage of the long-distance component of the fax signaling using a TCP connection. This calls for an adaptation phase that answers the access call and then accepts additional call digits corresponding to the remote fax number. This number then triggers a TCP connection to a remote fax server, which then makes the remote local call to the fax printer. The local server extracts the digital signaling sequence from the fax sender and transmits this information to the remote server. This then reproduces these signals to the fax printer, passing back all received signals in the same fashion. With careful control of the fax protocol timing within the hybrid end-to-end signal path, such a system can offer the same level of reliability as the telephone-based fax connection, while allowing the fax client to use Internet-based services. Such a configuration is indicated in Figure 10.12.

This service architecture offers greater carriage efficiency for fax services. Here, the digital fax data is transmitted through the long-distance communications network at a rate precisely matching the data content. This is achieved without the overheads of analogue modulation of the digital signal and then an additional PCM modulation of the analogue signal, nor with the overhead of circuit space inefficiency that is inherent in a voice circuit. The service architecture also can present superior accuracy of signal transfer, because the TCP connection provides reliable server-to-server transfer of the fax data. Despite the advantages of this hybrid solution for fax services, the market is still exhibiting a high level of inertia to shift from the model of fax as an overlay service on the telephone network. Certainly, the hybrid solution requires equipment investment into technology and requires extensive coverage within a single ISP's domain, probably complemented by the execution of bilateral service agreements with other ISPs to provide fax gateway peering.

From the user's perspective, the interface to the fax service may require customized interface equipment on the client's premises to map the dialed destination number into a call to the local gateway server followed by

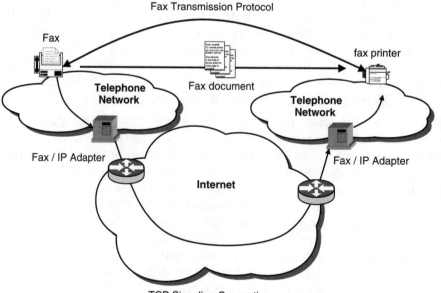

Figure 10.12 Internet-based fax services.

authorization and presentation of the dialed number. Alternatively, the dial operation must use an initial access number, followed by authentication digits and the destination number, making the dial operation more involved. At this stage, the marketing opportunities offered by servicing part of the fax market are secondary to the greater opportunities being presented by an ever-expanding access market. When this primary market growth factor shows signs of market saturation, a reasonable prediction is that the ISP service market will move into the opportunities presented by secondary markets. One example of this is the fax long-distance service sector, as a means of driving continued market growth. In the face of such competition, we can predict that existing long-distance carriers also will show strengthened levels of interest in such solutions as a means of preserving current market share in an increasingly competitive fax market.

Voice Services

Sending voice through the Internet has been an application that has been around for some time. Using a host's speaker and microphone there are many host applications that allow the user to open an application connection to a peer-speech application and then use this connection to transfer voice. This connection is a UDP-based connection, in which the analogue microphone signal is digitized (using any one of a number of digitizing algorithms) and then wrapped into a sequence of UDP packets and transmitted to the receiver across the Internet. The receiver removes the UDP wrapping and decodes the digital signal, applying various timing modifications to the signal stream to recreate the original timing of the sender. The resulting analogue signal then is fed to the host's speaker. Oddly enough, the network operator needs to do very little to achieve acceptable audio quality from such a configuration. If a UDP flow is sustained within a network, the adaptive TCP flows will back off their sending rates if there is congestion at a critical point in the UDP flow path, ensuring the UDP flow of a relatively high throughput.

Such a configuration is certainly an interesting item of technology, but it does not include many of the artifacts that contribute to the value of the more traditional telephone world. As with the fax application, the real market opportunity offered by the Internet is to undertake distance carriage of the voice call, allowing handset-to-handset connections using an Internet-based transport. Also, as with the fax application, the opportunities presented by this model of operation are the use of digital compression and packet carriage to achieve high efficiencies within the underlying carriage, particularly in a mixed traffic environment in which the Internet voice traffic is carried in conjunction with other Internet traffic.

The technical makeup of such a service is one that is readily conceived and operates in a manner similar to calling card services. An Internet voice gateway is attached to the phone network, which answers access calls and then authenticates the calling party through the use of a Personal Identification Number (PIN). The calling party then enters the destination number to the local gateway. The number is translated to a remote Internet voice gateway, which then completes the call using a remote end local call. The voice signal is converted into a UDP packet flow at each gateway and passed through the Internet network. Such an architecture is indicated in Figure 10.13.

Voice Challenges

A number of issues in this area of activity present a large set of technical and business challenges. Although a number of Internet voice services are available on today's Internet, their capacity to carry large volumes of calls and the associated traffic levels is yet to be established. Scaling, which is a challenge in so many aspects of the Internet environment, is readily apparent when

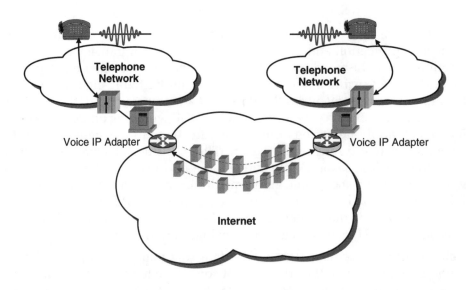

Figure 10.13 Internet voice service architecture.

applied to this area. Although voice services using UDP flows can be adequately handled on a high-quality network that has a relatively small voice load in comparison to TCP flows, the issues relating to service quality when UDP voice flows start to fill larger proportions of the carriage capacity become challenging. When the relative level of adaptive traffic starts to decrease, the network itself must assume the role of resource arbiter to preserve the quality of UDP flows, calling for technology solutions at a scale that stresses existing quality-of-service architectures. Call quality is not a readily manageable attribute in the Internet environment, even though this is a well-understood concept within the traditional telephone architecture. Issues of monitoring call quality and providing a service to customers that allow for the potential variation of call quality is also a service challenge. For the ISP, the issue is one of significant capital investment in technology solutions that are attuned to a particular service. The extent to which existing investment in service infrastructure can be leveraged is limited. Equally of significance for the ISP is the issue of compliance with the existing regulatory environments. Since the value-added service environment is one that has seen significant deregulation over the previous decade, public voice carriage remains an area that in many countries is still subject to various levels of regulatory control.

Voice Potential

The Internet appears to offer some longer-term potential for more efficient carriage of voice services compared to circuit switching technologies. However, this statement must be made with some care, as the carriage efficiency of voice over the Internet is not obvious at first glance. The overheads of encapsulation of the compressed voice signal data, together with timing information added by a real-time signaling protocol, plus the overhead of UDP and IP headers, adds significant carriage overheads to the encoded voice signal. The cumulative outcome is that voice over the Internet does not produce any significant carriage efficiencies over compression of a voice signal within a PSTN network. If carriage cost opportunities exist, they are realizable in the margins of silence suppression and switching cost. It is not obvious that there is a large shift in the cost base for voice services when moving into an Internet-based voice carriage environment.

However, current retail prices for PSTN services are not necessarily exclusively based on the marginal costs of carriage and switching to support the call. The current pricing position for voice carriage reflects a service quality that is often termed *carrier quality*. This operational requirement for availability, quality, and reliability within the telephone system is set at some of the highest levels within the communications industry. The ISP may not be exposed to the same cost profile, as the ISP voice service may be constructed without the expenditure elements designed to consistently offer the highest levels of service quality.

Accordingly, in offering Internet-based voice carriage services, the potential exists to offer these services to the retail market at a lower price than currently prevails from the established communications service sector. However, a widespread transition of large segments of the voice market into the ISP sector is by no means a certain outcome of this observation. The size of the current market, and the well-established position of the current voice providers throughout the globe, implies that this market will be vigorously defended by the incumbent providers. Many established voice carriers are actively engaged in trials of various Internet voice solutions. Such trials may service a number of purposes, such as a means of gauging the market response to such a product, in looking at alternative methods of interprovider interconnection to support end-to-end calls that transit across multiple providers, or as a means of gaining operational experience in the technologies required to provide this service. One potential reaction to this perceived longer term market threat is for the incumbent providers to offer a competitively priced Internet-based voice carriage product. However, some considerable elasticity exists in the

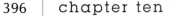

current voice market, which has yet to be tested. The capacity of this industry to respond to price-based incursions of a competitive technology will be visible in the coming years, and it may be a potential outcome that the scale of the circuit-based carriage deployment can offer pricing responses that set it at levels which directly compete with an Internet-based service.

At present, the voice market does not appear to be a major market sector objective for most ISP operations. As with the considerations concerning the fax market, the primary access market for ISP services is growing at a rate that stresses the service delivery capabilities of most established ISP enterprises. It is only when this primary market growth activity shows signs of market saturation will these secondary markets become the object of significantly greater levels of competitive activity.

Service Futures

A very strong pointer here cannot be ignored in terms of the evolution of the Internet market. Taking a second look at Figure 10.13, it is apparent that in this service environment, neither party need be aware that the long-distance carriage supporting the call is an Internet infrastructure. In this architecture, the Internet has broken out of a traditional service environment in which the terminating units are computers with screens and keyboards. The service model proposed in this architecture uses an embedding of the Internet technology into interior gateways, so that the user is unaware of its existence. Ultimately, it is not inconceivable that the voice over IP gateway function is embedded directly into the handset, so that the handset itself becomes the device attached to the Internet. This device view of the Internet has numerous applications already, ranging from Internet-attached surveillance cameras to remote managed power boards. Given a continuance of real unit price decreases in communications services, it is likely in the future that this device-service market will dwarf the currently established market of personal computer-mediated communications.

Multimedia Services

A number of critical factors are required to support the combination of services required for the multimedia environment: access bandwidth, performance of the Internet network, critical mass of clients with capable service platforms, and sustainable business models.

A *pologies are offered for the use of the word* multimedia. *If only two words are to be chosen as having been completely abused by the communications industry, and abused to the point where they no longer offer any residual semantic value, the top candidates must be* convergence *and* multimedia. *The only excuse that can be tendered here is that* multimedia *is easier to type than* voice and video and data.

Already, the streaming media technologies can offer very acceptable audio and video performance, using a small-frame format video session and a 28.8-Kbps modem connection. The quality improves with 64-K ISDN services and still further with 128-K two-channel ISDN services. The potential for the ISP in assisting this market include a richer content environment for users as well as increased use of ISP services by the client population. Indeed, the point of pressure at present appears to be the adoption of sustainable business models to support this environment rather than Internet technology issues.

From the ISP's perspective, the multimedia market implies a large growth in the traffic volumes that must be presented to each client. In the same way that the widespread shift from ASCII text to the graphical browser model of interaction in the first half of the 1990s was a major contributory factor in infrastructure demands, the widespread adoption of multimedia services will herald another sharp increase in the resource requirements demanded of the ISP, lifting the unit costs of servicing clients. In the face of such changes are a growing number of ISPs who see flat-rate access pricing as unsustainable and are moving to usage-based metering of the ISP's services. Similarly, the access costs for content providers is becoming a significant barrier to content publication of multimedia services. The reaction from many ISPs is to adopt multimedia content hosting services within the network infrastructure as a means of increasing the performance of multimedia content delivery, while simultaneously removing a significant barrier to content provision. This latter aspect of performance of delivery is critical, because the multimedia service market is one that is critically influenced by reception quality.

Summary

The ISP market continues to take a very conservative view of the market, working within a market sector that has concentrated heavily within the static access markets for both corporate and personal access services. Although the market has proved to be extraordinarily dynamic to date, with levels of demand far exceeding many service providers' capacities to respond, it also is being fueled by an increasing sophistication of applications and an increasing capability of the access platforms that will quickly overrun currently deployed access systems.

The business market will require further sophistication of services on the part of the ISP provider to shift from basic network access services to the business sector to a position of providing solutions to business imperatives, using the leverage of economies of scale and technology expertise to add value to the relationship. Business solutions also require increasing levels of resilience and quality within the provided service, and access on a best-effort basis with no performance undertakings is increasingly an inadequate response to evolving business market requirements.

In the personal service market, the heavy reliance on low-speed modem dial access is creating a critical bottleneck of pressure, and the operational clumsiness of modem access is perhaps best likened to an electricity system that reticulates gasoline and places an electricity generator in each household. The overlay model of the ISP industry, using existing voice-based access services as the means of servicing the market, is a service model that has a built-in obsolescence factor within the demands of an ever-evolving technology base. The access market will seek higher speed access solutions, not only to fuel faster access to richer content, but also to realize some of the social objectives promised by technology refinement. In particular, the promise of support for effective collaborative environments offers the capability to recruit a dispersed workforce, allowing each member of a work team the ability to use telecommuting facilities as a partial or complete substitute for the daily commute to the office. At the same time, this allows ISPs to make a significant incremental jump in the value of the access service to the client and their employer. This can be complemented by roaming services, which, as with mobile telephony, is a significant value addition to basic access.

The next level of market extension is into related areas of communication services, and solutions that push the Internet service environment into the area of messaging and paging that already exist in today's Internet. The Internet market also presents cost-effective alternative distance services for fax and voice services, allowing, where the regulatory environment permits, the Internet to provide packet-based transmission services in competition with the established circuit-based services. As the market grows in size, further changes to the service operator makeup will be made, as the larger telephone providers take on a strong position to defend their existing share of this market space and its associated level of value.

chapter eleven

The ISP Service Profile

In the early phases of the development of the Internet, the network service provider operated in a fashion little distinguished from the underlying carriage services. The service provider leased carriage capacity, terminated this carriage capacity with IP routers, and then resold this capacity as an Internet access service by selling access ports on the routers. The assumption within this admittedly very simple service model was that the clients of the service were university campus and research institute networks, both of which were self-sufficient with respect to the upper level Internet service environment. The network was positioned as a Layer 3 service (referring to the OSI protocol architecture) providing protocol-based carriage, through the management of carriage and routing technologies.

This service profile of the network service provider has evolved considerably in the past decade, and now a typical profile encompasses a rich set of application service elements. These services are positioned as value-added components to the carriage service. For the dial-up client, such services act as surrogate facilities, providing a permanent network point of presence to complement the intermittent client access. For corporate clients, such services are a means of outsourcing a number of IT services and offer a way to publish services on the Internet without compromising the security of the corporate network. In this chapter, we examine such value-added services provided by ISPs and examine the technical issues associated with their operation.

The task for the ISP is to provide such services cost effectively, within an environment of limited support resources. If any service requires large levels of consultancy services with a high level of expertise, then the ISP is faced with the choice of separately tariffing for the consultancy load, not offering the service, or creating an alternative interface to the service that alleviates the direct consultancy load. These aspects are explored as each service is described.

In this chapter, we look at Internet Mail services, Domain Name services, Web-based services, Usenet services, and other services that an ISP may consider as part of its service offering to its customer base. We examine both the technology models that support these services as well as the business issues in supporting such services within an ISP operation.

Electronic Mail Services

The most prevalent value-added service for clients is that of electronic mail services. A decade or so ago, many public mail universes existed, encompassing Internet-based Simple Mail Transfer Protocol (SMTP) mail delivery services, X.400 services, BITNET mail, UUCP mail, FIDO messaging, and various vendor-based mail systems. The emerging ISP industry commonly took on the role of manager of mail-relay gateways, translating from one mail universe to another. The widespread deployment of Internet-based mail delivery services has all but eliminated the need to operate large-scale mail gateways, and this is no longer a role that ISPs undertake in the 1990s. The ISP mail service role is now commonly providing mailboxes, mail relay services, and mail list hosting.

The basic protocol for transmitting messages within the Internet environment is the Simple Mail Transfer Protocol (SMTP), originally documented in RFC 821.

An Overview of Internet Mail Delivery

A number of documents define the format of Internet mail messages and their handling by mail agents.

◆ RFC 822, *Standard for the Format of ARPA Internet Text Messages*, defines the division of the mail message into header and body portions, the syntax and order of header entries, and the form of addresses used as mail addresses.

◆ RFC 821, *Simple Mail Transfer Protocol*, defines the protocol used to pass mail from one host to another using a TCP connection.

A number of documents extend this specification in various ways. RFC 1123, *Requirements for Internet Hosts—Application and Support*, amends and clarifies some of the original specification, and a number of RFC documents outline a set of specifications collectively termed Extended Simple Mail Transfer Protocol (ESTMP).

To deliver an item of mail to an Internet address the following steps are executed:

1. The domain part of the address is extracted (in a simple address of the form *fred@acme.com.au*, the domain part is *acme.com.au*, or the left part following the @ character).

2. The Domain Name System (DNS) is queried with this domain name for the Mail Exchange (MX) resource record with the lowest preference value. Continuing this example, if the DNS contained the following entry, then this indicates that all mail intended to be delivered to the domain *acme.com.au* should, by preference, be passed to the host *mailgate.isp.net.au*:

```
acme.com.isp.        IN    MX    20    mailgate.net.isp.
                     IN    MX    50    backupmail.net.isp.
```

   The mail delivery system then translates this domain into an IP address by generating a query for a corresponding *A* record, yielding an IP address for the delivery of the mail item:

```
mailgate.net.isp.    IN    A             172.16.10.20
```

3. The mail delivery system then attempts a TCP connection to port 25 of the host addressed by the lowest valued MX record, to commence mail delivery. In the example here, this is a connection request to the IP address 172.16.10.20.

4. If the TCP session cannot be established, the sender will attempt to connect to a system with a higher valued MX (referred to as secondary MX servers), in the order of increasing MX preference values.

5. When a TCP session is established, the mail is transferred. A simple ASCII protocol is used, using a format of query-response. The base SMTP exchange to deliver a message is indicated in Figure 11.1.

The mail exchange protocol has four components.

- The *HELO* command is used to identify the sending host to the receiver.
- The *MAIL* command is used to identify the sender of the message.
- The *RCPT* command is used to identify the receiver of the message.
- The *DATA* command is used to pass the message body to the receiver.

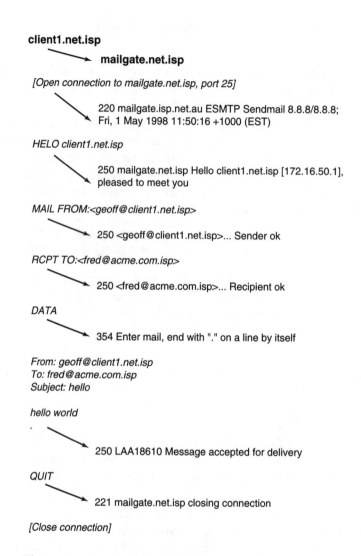

client1.net.isp

mailgate.net.isp

[Open connection to mailgate.net.isp, port 25]

220 mailgate.isp.net.au ESMTP Sendmail 8.8.8/8.8.8;
Fri, 1 May 1998 11:50:16 +1000 (EST)

HELO client1.net.isp

250 mailgate.net.isp Hello client1.net.isp [172.16.50.1],
pleased to meet you

MAIL FROM:<geoff@client1.net.isp>

250 <geoff@client1.net.isp>... Sender ok

RCPT TO:<fred@acme.com.isp>

250 <fred@acme.com.isp>... Recipient ok

DATA

354 Enter mail, end with "." on a line by itself

From: geoff@client1.net.isp
To: fred@acme.com.isp
Subject: hello

hello world

.

250 LAA18610 Message accepted for delivery

QUIT

221 mailgate.net.isp closing connection

[Close connection]

Figure 11.1   SMTP mail delivery exchange.

As can be seen from this brief overview of SMTP, mail delivery normally operates on an end-to-end basis. The question is: What services can an ISP provide its clients to assist in meeting their messaging needs?

Secondary MX Servers

The basic mail support service is that of a secondary MX mail server, that accepts mail addressed to the client's domains when the client's primary mail server is unavailable. This is achieved by using one (or possibly two, for greater resilience) mail server that is explicitly configured to act as a relay for the delivery of mail to the nominated domains. Explicit configuration of allowed domains to use the server is related to the consideration of unsolicited commercial e-mail (UCE, these days commonly referred to as *spam,* and those who generate such bulk mailings are referred to as *spammers*), in which an open mail relay is invariably abused by spammers in an attempt to both conceal their identity and offload the mail delivery task to an unwitting victim. Therefore, when configuring secondary MX mail servers, you should use a configuration in which the domains accepted by the server are explicitly added to the system, resulting in a server which accepts mail for the configured domains, while mail to all other domains is rejected. This structure implies a level of administrative overhead to maintain the configuration of domains for which the relay server will accept relayed mail. However, a Web-based customer interface to add, list, and delete domains from the secondary mail servers will assist greatly in this area. Typically, this configuration is structured along the lines of a four-day retention on the secondary server, with hourly attempts to redeliver to the primary server.

The most prevalent architecture for this service within the ISP sector is a Unix-based operating platform, configured with mail server software. *Sendmail* is very commonly used as the mail server software, although a number of other software platforms also exist to undertake this mail relay function.

A refinement of the service is to lock the service against the DNS and the customer database, so that the client's domain will be relayed as long as the client is a current client of the ISP, and the DNS lists the server as a secondary MX server.

Mail Accounts

The secondary MX service works well when the client has a fully functional mail environment and the secondary system is used as a backup resource. Dial-up clients, whether individual clients or small business clients, typically have no such local mail service infrastructure. They may not have the necessary resources to operate an STMP server nor have the expertise in house to configure such a facility. In addition, the intermittent connectivity may not be adequate to allow senders to initiate their mail connection when the user is dialed in. In such cases, considerable value can be placed in the ISP operating a mail service for the client. The three components to such a mail service are the mail account, mail retrieval, and mail delivery, as indicated in Figure 11.2.

The Mail Server

The first function is that of accepting incoming mail addressed to the client and storing it on a local server. To achieve this, the ISP must operate a mail server that is configured as the primary MX for the domain used by the client. Resiliency of this service is paramount. The drop in confidence levels by the client population if the mail server loses incoming mail is dramatic, and the engineering of robustness into this area of service provision is one that cannot be overstressed. The ISP may use its own secondary mail servers to improve the resiliency of the service and may use a configuration of a number of mail servers within an environment of a mail server farm in order to improve the

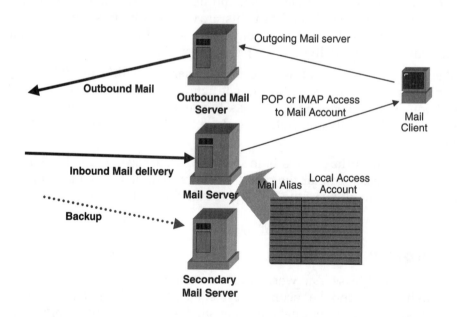

Figure 11.2   Components of an ISP mail service.

performance and resiliency of the mail system. Disk storage systems that incorporate resiliency, such as disk arrays using RAID technology, and a frequent backup process, both intended to ensure rapid and complete recovery from component failure on the server system, are also highly advisable features of the mail server systems architecture.

The simplest configuration is to operate all client accounts as distinguished usernames from a single common domain name operated by the ISP. The corollary is that all usernames must be unique, which, for well-populated systems requires large amounts of ingenuity on the part of the users. This simplifies the operational configuration of the mail server through the use of a single domain name. Also, an astute choice of a common mail domain name is perceived as a marketing channel, given its widespread promulgation by the ISP's clients into the broader Internet community. Many thousands, or even millions, of e-mail addresses of the form *user@isp-name.net* combine to form a powerful way to circulate an ISP's name in the retail market. There also is a certain element of churn constraint that this mechanism places on the client. If the client moves to a new ISP, the original ISP's e-mail service may no longer be accessible or even configured to service the ex-client's messages, so a change of provider entails a change of mail address on the part of the client.

The alternative name-management environment is to use fully qualified names, in which the client is provided with the ability to create a domain name of the client's choice. Then the client can nominate one or more user names, which are unique only within the confines of the selected domain name. The ISP operates both the domain name servers for the selected domain as well as the primary and secondary MX mail servers. Incoming mail directed to the client's domain is mapped by the mail alias file to an internal account on the primary mail server and stored in the client's mail box for subsequent collection. Such a configuration involves more processes to set up, as it includes domain name registration, domain name activation, and configuration of the mail server's aliases for each mailbox to map the fully qualified mail address (*user@domain*) into a local account mail stop.

In terms of addressing real customer requirements, this latter approach is certainly more in tune with emerging expectations. This approach can be compared to the telephone domain, in which customers are voicing a desire for single *numbers for life*; the telephone number is associated with the individual, not the location of a particular handset. Within the electronic mail domain, the emerging customer requirement is for a constant e-mail address that can be operated by the selected ISP, as an agent of the client, for the duration of the service contract. The customer, on reassignment of the service contract with another ISP, wants to transfer the e-mail address and enjoy transparent continuity of mail functionality.

Mail Retrieval

The second component of the service is to allow the client to retrieve the stored mail. The requirement here is that the client needs dedicated access to the client's mail account on the server and then have the ability to upload the mail onto the client's system. This is accomplished through the use of the Post Office Protocol (POP) or the Interactive Mail Access Protocol (IMAP). The ISP requirement is to operate a POP/IMAP server for use by the clients of the service and also operate an account management system to allow the clients to undertake rudimentary management tasks associated with their account (such as a change of password). Such a server can be configured onto the same system that operates as the mail host and for small-scale ISP operations, this is quite adequate. Larger ISP operations typically split the two functions onto different servers and use dedicated POP/IMAP servers or server farms.

The ISP needs to decide at the outset whether to restrict access to the client's mail to access undertaken directly to the ISP's service network, or whether the mailbox access can be undertaken through any provider's Internet access. If the decision is taken to restrict mail access to ISP client access mechanisms, then the mail system should be configured with access filters so that access is permitted using only a source IP address, which is part of the ISP's provider address block or part of an address block that the ISP has agreed to route for a client. A lower overhead solution, which is comparable in functionality, is to configure the mail server into an address block only announced as a route to clients of the ISP. This ensures that the server's address is not announced at exchanges or other peering interconnections and is not announced to upstream providers. Such a restriction ensures that the mail service is a value-added component of the ISP's Internet access service, and if there is no distinct tariff for use of the mail service, this is a prudent precaution. Of course, this does not permit roaming access to the mailbox and may be unduly restrictive for certain client requirements. If an open access is required to the mail system, then it is prudent to tariff for the mail service as a distinct service.

Operating with distinct service models for local and roaming clients is possible. Such a scenario places the responsibility for checking the access type upon the mail access system itself, and some alteration of the mail access software is necessary. As a part of the mail access authentication, the mail access server has to first ascertain the type of client. The server then applies either an

ISP-access filter to the source address, if the service is bundled into the access product, or activates an accounting entry if the mailbox is a separately tariffed service. The costs in developing a robust system to implement such a model should not be underestimated, however.

POP SERVERS

The Post Office Protocol, Version 3 (POP3 [RFC 1725]) is a very simple downloading protocol, using TCP for reliable transmission, with the client listening on TCP port 110. The client connects and identifies itself to the server. This identification is either in the form of a clear transmission of a username and password, or a name and an encrypted exchange using an MD5 digest string that includes a shared secret between the client and the server. Once authorized, the server places the maildrop in an exclusive access state and allows the POP client to scan the number of messages in the mail drop, upload messages from the maildrop, and delete messages from the maildrop. When the client quits, the updated maildrop is recombined with any new incoming mail as the new maildrop state.

The anticipated model of deployment of the POP protocol is in a mode in which the maildrop is uploaded to the client's mailer, and filtering and processing of the mail is managed by the client. Client POP agents can use an alternative model of selective retrieval and message identification so that the maildrop becomes the permanent mail repository, and the client is configured as a browsing mail reader. However, this is more efficiently and reliably supported using IMAP-based client mail tools. Of course, if mail is allowed to accumulate in the maildrop, the size of the maildrops becomes larger, and the operation of the POP3 servers becomes less efficient when manipulating such large compounded mail objects. The ISP may want to implement a number of policy constraints over the retention of messages and message deletion polices or use a set of tariffs, which encourages rapid turnaround of mail messages. These measures are intended to avoid exhaustion of POP server resources through large-scale mail retention on the server.

POP contains no mechanism to send mail from the client system. The client is expected to use the SMTP protocol to access a local mail relay for outgoing mail. The relay can be the same server as the POP server, or it may be a different host.

IMAP SERVERS

The Interactive Mail Access Protocol: Version 4, rev1 (IMAP4 [RFC2060]) is a more powerful protocol than the POP protocol and addresses a variety of client/server interaction environments. The three basic contexts of client/ server interaction are offline, online, and synchronized use. IMAP4 can be used in any one of these three contexts.

1. The offline context is that of the POP environment, in which the mail is uploaded onto the client, and the local mail processing and storage is performed autonomously by the client, with any generated mail being locally queued until the next online event.

2. The online model uses a client that manipulates messages, which remain on the server system. No assumption can be made that the client can store messages, and therefore, the client operates in a mode likened to a browser function.

3. The synchronized mode is a hybrid of these two models, in which the client uploads a set of messages from the server and manipulates them locally, as in an offline context. At a later date, the IMAP client informs the server of the locally performed changes, which are then synchronized on the server's copy of the mail environment.

IMAP originally was specified as an online protocol, allowing remote manipulation of a set of mailboxes, using a protocol that was attuned to mailbox operations. It was intended to be a more efficient and faster mode of remote operation than using a network-distributed filestore, such as NFS. IMAP has evolved to support all three operational contexts, allowing IMAP clients to readily switch between online and synchronized contexts. In online mode, the client can load data on demand, as compared to an offline mode of operation in which the entire maildrop is uploaded to the client before the user can commence with the mail function. Not only does IAMP allow the client to only load messages on demand, the client can request only a section of the message. This is a significant improvement in responsiveness of remote mail operations over a slow link, or when manipulating large messages. To further improve responsiveness, the server can perform MIME attachment processing, allowing the client the option of viewing large attachments.

IMAP does not necessarily associate the user state with the mailbox. The association of which mail messages in the mailbox have been read may be held with the client, rather than the server. This is a powerful construct, as it allows IMAP to be used as a protocol for browsing shared public mailboxes. The model of a message browsing client with client-held state is precisely the same model as that used by Usenet news browsers. Considerable power exists in a client model that allows the user access to messaging-based information, using the same client to read personal mail, mailing list items, and Usenet items.

IMAP can demand more resources from the server when managing personal mail accounts. If the model of both online and synchronized services is used, the IMAP server plays a critical role, and the server's storage and processing resources are deployed in an on-demand model to support interactive transactions.

IMAP OR POP?

Which service model should an ISP support, IMAP or POP? If the IMAP server is configured so that it operates in a mode that enforces offline context of operation, then there is no significant difference in either model. However, the simpler form of the POP protocol allows for highly efficient server implementations, and as a consequence POP is the predominant deployed server environment.

The IMAP processing model is more commonly deployed within a corporate environment, in which an effective and robust messaging environment is considered a corporate asset. ISPs that want to enter the outsourcing market may see some strategic advantages in operating a more comprehensive mail service, rather than a simple client upload facility, supporting the messaging requirements of both office and remote corporate employee access requirements.

Outbound Mail Delivery

The third component is to allow the client to post outbound mail. Most client mailing systems are not configured to act as a standalone mailer, undertaking the full functionality of correctly processing outbound mail requests, and instead use the concept of a mail *helper*, which will accept all outbound mail and process it correctly. This helper is functionally little different from the secondary MX server relay—it can be seen as an outbound relay server, and it can be co-located on the same server platform with minor adjustments to the mail configuration. The task of the outbound relay server is to expand the destination mail addresses into a set of delivery actions. For each address, the target domain name is resolved into a set of MX records, and delivery is attempted to each of these servers in increasing order of preference. If the destination address is invalid, or the mail cannot be delivered within a reasonable period of time, the mail is returned to the sender with an error notification.

Offering a Mail Service

It is necessary to provide explicit additional service conditions on such a service, given that the client's mail is seen as being critically important to the client, and the complete set of conditions under which the mail service is operated must be included in the client's expectations.

It is highly unlikely that a mail service provider will accept the responsibility for holding an arbitrarily large amount of mail for a user for an indefinite period of time. The uncertainties in resource requirements and load levels are simply too great to allow the ISP to offer a high-quality robust mail service. Some form of resource usage control is required. The resource control may be administrative, or it may be based on tariff incentives. A common service constraint is for mail to be stored only for a certain period until the service provider removes it. A limit may be placed on the amount of mail stored on the server in terms of the total size of the maildrop, and further mail for the user may not be accepted by the server until mail is drained. Alternatively, the stored mail may attract an incremental storage service charge, designed to provide the client with a strong incentive to upload the mail onto the local system at regular intervals. The service provider may make a distinction between mail that has been read, and unread mail, implementing a smaller retention period for mail which has been read and left on the server, as compared to unread mail on the server.

For an ISP to explicitly state the disposition of stored messages when a client service contract is terminated is a prudent precaution. The ISP may wish to delete the mail, or forward the mail to a client-nominated mail address. The client also may have the ability to execute a new contract with the ISP, relating only to the provision of electronic mail services without the explicit provision of carriage services.

With the increasing use of spam mailers, ISPs need to have an explicit policy regarding clients who generate spam. The policy must be widely promulgated and actively implemented. The Internet community considers it inappropriate for an ISP to absolve itself from responsibility in this area. The community does expect each ISP to have a policy, which they are prepared to implement, that makes it a breach of the service contract to generate and send bulk unsolicited e-mail.

You should not assume that a single access contract will be uniformly associated with a service requirement for a single mail service. In a residential context, the single access contract may cover user access by a number of individuals. In the enterprise and educational sector are a number of distinct mail accounts. The ISP needs to cater to such diversity, allowing a client access contract to have a variable number of associated mail service contracts. Some clients may want to have a nominated administrator, who can create and remove additional mail services, as well as set up access passwords for these controlled mail services. Other clients may want the service provider to provide management services for each mail account individually. Such contracts may be associated with incremental tariff components.

A Comprehensive Mail Service Environment

The Mail account environment typically has the ISP acting as a message delivery agent, and the client's system is the mail host. With the pervasive presence of Web browsers and scripting tools, together with the use of IMAP as mail server protocol with greater functionality in this area, ISPs now can offer an environment in which messaging functionality is distributed between the client and the server. This distribution allows the ISP to create a more comprehensive messaging environment that includes message filtering and sorting on inbound mail; multiple mailboxes; integration of various office functions, such as fax and voice messaging; and document management, including document life-cycle management and document archival.

At this stage, the developmental effort in this area is still relatively new, and whether the market for this style of service will achieve critical mass is unclear. The competition in the market to this managed mail service are mail management software environments that are implemented as host software. The typically low capital purchase cost of such software and the ever-increasing local host processing capability set a very ambitious price performance point with which these more complex distributed functionality environments compete. At this stage, the area of message processing and the functionality of the distributed office environment appear to be an integral part of the software vendor marketplace. Crafting a richer functional environment is a task in which the software vendors appear to have taken the lead, coupled with continued aggressive sales of fully functional PC platforms into the residential and corporate markets.

However, richer functionality may enter the market from the ISP sector. If the sector succeeds in widespread deployment of high capacity to the residential market, then a number of possibilities are revealed. Such deployment will, in all probability, rely on the Digital Subscriber Line technologies (termed *xDSL*, to indicate the generic Digital Subscriber Line approach). If this high-capacity access is combined with lightweight residential Internet access devices that concentrate functionality to a capable browser, then we can assume that the service environment will be provisioned by the ISP.

The tensions between these two views of the market, that of a capable software environment and an ISP-provisioned encompassing service, have yet to be resolved. The development effort appears to be directed towards simple paradigms, which will map effectively into a comprehensive messaging environment, rather than widespread deployment of a well-understood service suite.

The current offerings in the ISP area are predominately directed towards supporting a rich client host software environment, with servers that act as maildrop hosts managing local mail accounts and a simple upload client access model.

Mail Lists

The final section regarding mail services is that of mail list management. The ISP can offer the client the ability to manage a mailing list, using a number of list management techniques. Although a mailing list can be set up within the Mail Transport Agent directly (such as via entries in the *sendmail* configuration file), using a list management software package to manage mailing lists is preferable. The most popular freely available packages are *Majordomo* and *ListProcessor*, although other freely available and commercial list management packages are available to the ISP.

The administrative tasks associated with mailing list management can be quite onerous, particularly when the list starts to accumulate out-of-date mail addresses that generate bounce messages. Issues may relate to the ISP's liability regarding content mailed to the list. The overall intent in structuring such a service is as follows:

- To minimize the ISP's administrative input
- To ensure that the legal liability regarding content is duly addressed
- To attempt to simplify the list management processes so that lists can be readily managed by the client who is the list host
- To operate a list processing environment that is efficient at handling the mail volumes associated with managing what could potentially be a significant number of large mailing lists.

ISPs commonly regard mailing list hosting as a value-added service and potentially allow for a separate tariff to host such a list on behalf of the client. The provision for a tariff component allows for the greater levels of support and use of mail resources that a mail list typically consumes.

The normal approach is to use the model in which the client is the list owner and has the responsibility for list maintenance. This includes approving list subscription if so desired, providing the welcome message, determining the list type (whether it is operated as a digest or a mail list), and operating the list moderation policy. *Majordomo* allows this function to be undertaken via mail transactions between the majordomo host and the list owner, although this interaction should be complemented with the ability for the list owner to use a browser to control the list. From the ISP's perspective, mailing list support can be managed relatively efficiently, with a set of processes that are implemented as scripts associated with Web pages. The client also should be able to configure a bounce policy, so that list addresses, which generate delivery errors, are notified to the client, with the option of list removal. The ISP also should offer a list archival capability, with a Web-accessible archive and search capability. Access policy to this archive should be managed by the list host, so that the list host undertakes overall responsibility for content and access to the list.

Mail lists are an excellent marketing asset in the competitive dial access ISP market place. Not only do mail lists generate traffic and stimulate Internet usage by the client list owner, but they also provide a means for other clients to directly involve themselves within Internet communities of interest, as mailing lists tend to be a greater stimulus to active involvement than the counterpart, the Usenet mailing list, due to the more personal aspect of mail. Further information on managing a mailing list is documented in [RFC1211].

Domain Name Services

The original approach by ISPs to the domain name issue was to group all services and all client-related systems operated by the ISP within a single name structure, using the ISP's domain name as the common root of the service names. For example, if the ISP used the domain name *isp.foobar*, then mailboxes for clients might be named *client@mail.isp.foobar,* and Web pages hosted on the ISP's Web server may be named by the somewhat obtuse name structure of *www.isp.foobar/~client.*

Part of the attraction for the client of operating in-house Internet systems was to break out of this imposed name hierarchy, which labeled the client's services implicitly within the ISP's domain name. From a corporate customer perspective, this second-level name structure of *client@mail.isp.foobar* and *www.isp.foobar/~client* was perceived as being second class. Not only did it imply that the corporate entity did not have the wherewithal to operate its own Internet service environment, it also implied that a change of provider required a change of service point names, which is always an expensive and cumbersome process.

The requirement being voiced by the corporate client sector, and by an increasingly sophisticated sector of the individual client base, was for the ISP to assist the customer in operating services, which used the client's domain name as the name of the service point. Four major components of the name system compose such a service from the ISP's perspective, which we will examine here.

Obtaining a Domain Name

Domain name registries are, in general, not well-geared towards assisting the neophyte user to obtain the services appropriate to the user's requirements. Rather, their typical processes are geared towards high volumes of transaction processing. The registry's business model does not normally accommodate an educational and consulting component to explain to potential clients what a domain name is, how it can be used, the policies regarding domain name eligibility, and the differences between various domain name types (such as the difference between a name within a generic top-level domain and a domain name within a country hierarchy).

The preferred business model of the name registries is to act in a simple, uniform, process-driven mode, using a single transaction fee for all transaction types, allowing little latitude for lengthy individual consultation with neophyte users who require further assistance. This stance by the registries effectively leaves the task of educating and consulting to the user's service provider, the ISP. Such consultation may well be part of the initial connection services.

The typical service offered by the ISP in this area is to consult with the client regarding the client's expectations in terms of the desire to operate on the Internet using its own domain name and clarify the associated costs and support services that such a decision implies, as well as assisting the client in determining which name is appropriate for the client. This is an area that has potential liabilities in terms of infringement of intellectual property rights or trademark infringement, so the ISP is well advised to ensure that the advice offered to the client is suitably qualified to ensure that the client is fully aware of the potential liabilities in this area. It is prudent to ensure that the staff involved in this aspect of service delivery are fully trained as to the ISP's obligations to correctly inform the client.

After the client has made a decision as to a preferred domain name, the ISP typically acts as an agent of the client in approaching the name registry and requesting the name. Many registries offer high-volume ISPs a streamlined process to achieve this, recognizing that the larger ISPs use specialized staff to generate these requests, that the error and resubmission rate of applications submitted by such staff are low, and that the registry processing overheads can be reduced in recognition of this. Indeed, with the evident trend of the late 1990s to move the area of domain name registries into commercial undertakings, there is a strong likelihood that the ISP may assume the role of a franchised retailer of domain names.

Secondary Name Servers

To ensure that a domain name is well defined and readily accessible across the entire Internet, a domain zone should be supported by one or more secondary name servers in addition to the primary name server. One secondary name server is generally considered to be a mandatory requirement, and additional secondary servers make good operational sense.

The secondary name servers are intended to provide continuity of service, so that when the primary name server is unreachable, the secondary name servers can provide consistent and current answers to DNS queries. Secondary name servers also absorb some of the query load, as the parent name server usually rotates the list of name servers on each NS query, allowing each name server to absorb an equal proportion of the query load.

Secondary name server configuration requires the insertion of information in four points of the DNS to complete the operation:

- The parent domain configuration should list all the name servers, both primary and secondary, of the domain.
- The primary name server should list the secondary name servers in Name Server (NS) resource records in the primary zone file, and the fields in the Start of Authority (SOA) record should be set appropriately.
- The primary name server should list itself as the primary server for the domain and permit TCP access from the secondary server to undertake zone transfers.
- The DNS configuration file of the secondary name server should be configured with the zone name for which it is operating a secondary name service and the IP address of the primary server.

This is indicated in Figure 11.3.

The basic DNS service that an ISP can offer the client is the provisioning of a secondary name server service for client domains. The ISP can operate one or more secondary name server systems, with an application interface that allows the domain name and the IP address of the primary server to be specified to the server for automatic inclusion into the secondary server configuration files. Typically, this function is hosted on a Unix-based platform, using the BIND software releases, although releases of name server software are available on other software platforms. The easiest administrative interface for DNS services is one that allows the client to operate the DNS environment via a set of client-accessible Web forms. Such forms should explain the function undertaken by a secondary name server and allow the client to enter the details of the domain and the primary server. The processing associated with the Web form can check the integrity of the DNS configuration and update the ISP name server with this additional information at its next scheduled restart.

Having explicit deletion of secondary name servers is not necessary; instead, a system of warning followed by automatic removal may be adequate. Even if explicit deletion of the secondary function is permitted, automatic

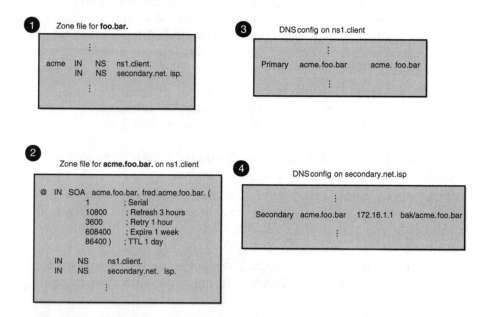

Figure 11.3   DNS configuration.

scanning of secondary entries for integrity is a reasonable course of action. The typical errors a secondary server may encounter are as follows:

◆ Poor configuration of the primary name server, in which the SOA values are inappropriately set, or the authoritative flag is not set in response to queries relating to the domain. Within the SOA fields, the refresh interval should be normally no less than one hour (a value of 3600); the retry interval should be no less than one minute (a value of 60); the expire interval normally should be no less than one day (86,400); and the TTL interval should be no less than 3600 (one hour).

◆ Missing primary reference to the secondary server, in which the primary name server is not referencing the secondary server in its NS resource records for the zone.

◆ Missing delegation reference to the secondary server, in which the delegation record does not include explicit mention of the secondary server.

◆ Inability to undertake a zone transfer from the primary server, due to filtering, which prevents the secondary server from making TCP connections to the DNS port of the primary server to complete the zone transfer.

One name management process that can be used is to regularly check each secondary entry. If an error is encountered, a warning message is issued to the client's contact address. If the error persists over a reasonable period, a second warning can be issued, and the entry can be automatically removed thereafter. Such a process allows DNS secondary servers to be managed on a highly automated basis, with the transactions being applied to the server triggered by the client, without the active intervention of ISP operational or customer service staff. It is also advisable to create mutual secondary agreements with other ISPs so that the service offered to the client is one in which a single request with the local ISP can result in a secondary record installed on a number of robust, topologically distributed servers.

Secondary name servers are an instance of an ISP value-added service, which, if well organized as a client-driven service, makes minimal calls on ISP operational management resources. It simultaneously provides a valuable service to the client and is a service that is not easily undertaken by the client alone.

Primary Name Servers

For the service provider to take a more active role in managing the domain name for the client is possible, by operating the primary name server for the client. This service is requested by clients for two common reasons:

- The client is permanently connected to the Internet but does not want to devote operational management resources to manage a domain name server on site, and instead wants to outsource this activity to the ISP.

- The client wants to outsource its Internet *presence* to the ISP and have the ISP operate services using the client's domain name.

In the latter case, in which the ISP is configuring the domain name as an ISP-operated presence on the Internet, the domain name is typically deployed as a client mail address and a Web server. In this case, the ISP can use simple standard templates to configure the primary name server and use the existing secondary name servers to create secondary servers for the domain.

The other case is where the client wants to outsource the operation of the primary and secondary name servers but also wants to retain control over the contents of the primary zone file. If the ISP wants to support such an operational configuration, the challenge is to devise a management interface for the primary zone file, allowing the client to modify the zone file. At the same time, the interface must provide sufficient support to the client so that errors in the zone file are minimized, and the client can undertake the desired name configuration tasks easily. The risk with this activity is that the ISP drastically increases its consulting load in assisting clients to configure their domain correctly, yet derives no real benefit from the activity, either in increased revenue or in customer loyalty. In such a case, the activity is undertaken at an overall loss to the ISP. The purpose of the specialized interface to the primary zone file is to relieve this consulting load by creating an interface that guides the client to enter the correct data and provide information as to the function of the name system and the entered data. If the system can be configured as a client self-managed system, then the service can be provided with little overhead to the ISP.

DNS Forwarders

The final DNS service, which an ISP can provide to its clients, is a DNS forwarder. A DNS forwarder is intended to act as a proxy agent in the resolution of DNS names. The forwarder builds up a rich cache of DNS information, which can be applied to subsequent queries, so that the forwarder speeds up DNS name resolution. The forwarder is a normally configured DNS name server. No special configuration option exists for turning a DNS server into a forwarder, although some care is required in managing its performance.

A name server's operation is altered if it is configured to use a forwarder. If the requested information is already in the local database of authoritative data or cached data, the server will answer the request using the local information. If the information is not available locally, then the server will direct the query to the forwarder and pause for a short period for the forwarder to respond. If the forwarder fails to respond within the period, the server will contact the remote servers itself and resolve the query in the normal fashion.

Well-managed ISP-provided forwarders will speed up DNS name resolving for clients considerably. However, considerable care must be taken in their configuration and management, as there are a number of problems that can affect forwarder performance. A number of misbehaving DNS query applications slip into a looping state and start to send a rapid sequence of queries for the same nonexistent name. If the application uses the forwarder, then the forwarder will be swamped with such queries and forwarder performance will plummet quickly. The common resolution of this is to patch the name resolver algorithms to use a local cache of recent queries, using the name and the source IP address of the query as the cache index. When the cache is hit the request is ignored by the forwarder.

Forwarders within a large ISP operation can be placed under very high levels of load. It is common to observe the name-resolution process start to consume larger amounts of memory and then start to generate an excessive number of page faults. The short-term remedy is to monitor the memory size of the name server. When it exceeds a threshold, the monitor should automatically restart the process. The long-term remedy is to increase the capacity of the forwarder.

Forwarders are prone to suffer from a success disaster. After a critical level of referrals have been passed to the forwarder, it will be able to generate rapid responses to a very large proportion of the queries passed to it. This increased performance will attract other clients to use the forwarder, resulting in the design capacity of the forwarder being exceeded at some point. In such a situation, disaster strikes, with a large number of clients configured to use the forwarder, and the forwarder's performance plummets under the excessive load.

Fortunately, a number of solutions exist to this problem. Although one solution is simply a larger platform, solutions that are potentially more cost effective and scalable can be deployed. One is to exploit the UDP-based trans-

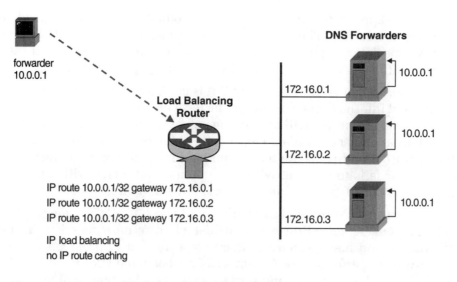

Figure 11.4 Load-balanced DNS forwarders.

actions of the DNS and use parallel forwarders with router-based load balancing, as indicated in Figure 11.4. Another is to distribute forwarders across the network, using the routing system to direct each client request to the closest DNS forwarder.

Web Caching

DNS forwarders can provide enhanced performance to clients through reuse of cached data. The forwarder also can reduce the amount of DNS traffic passed out of the ISP's network by having the forwarder answer a significant proportion of DNS queries without passing queries outward. This technique of caching can also be applied to Web traffic.

The Benefits of Web Caching

The same benefits of improved performance and reduced outbound traffic loads can be realized for World Wide Web traffic through the deployment by the ISP of Web caches. In a basic sense, Web caches operate in a standard fashion for any form of cache. The request is passed through an agent, which makes the request to the original source as a proxy agent. The response then is passed

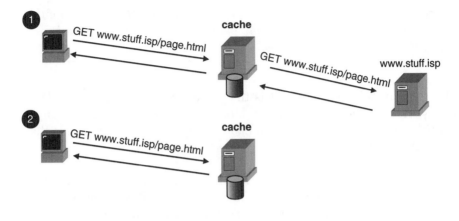

Figure 11.5   A Web cache.

back to the original query point as well as retaining a copy in the cache. If the same request is passed to the cache soon after the original request was serviced, the response can be generated from the cache without further reference to the original source. The operation of a Web cache is indicated in Figure 11.5.

Measurements of ISP traffic profiles indicate that some 70 percent of a typical ISP's traffic is Web-based traffic. An analysis of Web requests indicates that the typical level of similarity of requests (for the same object as one previously requested) can be as high as 50 percent of all Web-based traffic. For many ISPs, particularly those operating outside of North America, transmission costs dominate the cost profile of the ISP's operation. If the cache came to even 50 percent of a theoretical maximum caching performance, the ISP can reduce its external traffic volume requirements by some 17 percent. When the costs of caching are compared to the costs of transmission, this can be a significant difference.

If the average cost of transmission is $150 per gigabyte, and the ISP has a typical carriage profile of purchasing 1000 gigabytes per month from an upstream ISP, then a cache operating at a 25 percent hit rate can save the ISP a recurrent expenditure of $25,500 per month. If the cache costs $100,000 as a capital expenditure and $10,000 per month in operational costs to support the service, then the business case *analysis would see the cache activity return some $10,000 per month to the business, allowing for complete depreciation of the capital expenditure within 24 months.*

The other benefit to the client is that of an increase in speed of Web page delivery. As the cache is generally closer to the client than the target Web page, the download time from the cache can, in general, be faster than performing the download form the original source.

The average size of a Web transaction is some 16 data packets within the TCP flow. Within a TCP slow-start flow-control process, the first cycle will transmit one packet and wait for an ACK. The reception of the ACK will trigger transmission of a further two packets in the second cycle, and then the sender will await two ACKs. Reception of these two ACKs will trigger a further four packets in the third cycle and eight in the next cycle, and the remaining single packet in the fifth cycle. Therefore, allowing for optimal behavior of the TCP slow-start algorithm, this takes some five round-trip times. If a user is located some distance away from the Web page, and the round-trip time to the source is 300ms, the propagation delay of the page load will be 1.5 seconds. In comparison, if the round-trip time to the local Web cache is 2ms, then the propagation delay of the page load will be 10ms. These latency figures assume an uncongested network in both cases. In this case, as long as the Web cache search can complete within one second, the cache will be faster to the user.

A slightly different analysis is possible when comparing the performance of a cache configured at the head end of a cable-IP system versus the performance of direct access. The difference in latency in this case is due both to the closer positioning of the cache to the user and in the greatly increased effective bandwidth from the cache to the user, in which the cache download can operate at speeds of megabits per second, as compared to kilobits or tens of kilobits per second when using dial-up analogue or ISDN services. For a 100K image download, the dial user may experience a 60-second delay, and the same delivery from a local cache via cable-IP may take less than one second.

The trade-off with caching is that of the cost of carriage capacity, both in terms of monetary cost of the carriage and the performance cost of the application's transaction time, versus the cost of the use of caching, in terms of capital cost and functionality cost. For non-North American ISPs in which there is a large cache hit rate against North American locations, the benefits of widespread caching are quite substantial. For cable-IP operators, the benefit of local cache operation is the ability to exploit the benefits of the very high-speed final hop from the head end to the end user. For other ISPs, the benefits of caching are less dramatic, but nevertheless, there are tangible positive outcomes of caching in terms of performance and cost that can be exploited.

Web-Caching Models

A number of models demonstrate how to perform effective Web caching. Some systems are deployed as a user-invoked option, in which the user nominates a Web cache to the browser as a proxy helper, and the browser then directs all Web requests to the proxy cache. At any stage, the user can instruct the browser to turn off the use of the proxy cache. If the ISP operates in this mode, the benefits to the user in using the cache need to be clearly stated and understood by both the client and the ISP.

Some ISPs, notably in the smaller dial-up provider sector, in which the providers operate in a highly cost-competitive market, operate in a *forced cache mode*. Here, all Web traffic on TCP port 80 is blocked from direct outbound access, and the ISP's clients are forced to configure their browsers to use the provider's cache for external Web access.

The use of a cache for all Web traffic also can be undertaken by the ISP, without the explicit configuration of the cache into the user's browsers. Irrespective of precisely how this is engineered, this technique is termed *transparent caching*, in which the user may not be explicitly aware that caching is being undertaken to the user's requests. It should be noted that no mechanism to date of forced or transparent caching is completely transparent to both the Web client and the Web server. Where the Web server uses an end-to-end security access model, the transparent cache may fail, as the cache will present the cache's address as the source of the request, rather than that of a client. This may result in a page denied error to the cache request, whereas the client could have completed the transaction. While this may not affect a large proportion of total Web traffic, in those situations where the use of the cache is mandated, either through filters and a force function, or through transparent network redirection, there is no user-visible workaround to the error, and the level of user frustration with the entire cache service rises dramatically.

If the sole benefit to the client is improved speed of response, then the ISP must understand that the performance of the Web cache systems must be continually tuned to be highly responsive to Web requests under all load conditions experienced by the ISP. Performance of cache hits must be maintained at a level consistently faster than the alternative of direct client access to the original client site. Performance of cache misses must be at a level that is not visibly slower than that of direct access to the original site. If the user's perception of performance of the cache drops, the benefit to the user also drops. In the case of user-optioned caching, the users will turn off the cache option in their browser and return to a mode of direct access. If the ISP is operating forced or transparent caching, the user may consider moving to a different ISP.

The business model of a cache is that the capital and operational costs associated with localizing traffic to the cache result in cost reductions to the ISP when compared to the operation of a non-cached network. These cost reductions can be passed on to all users through operation at a lower price point or passed on to those clients who make use of the cache. The generic model of applying the cost reduction to a general price determination for the ISP's services is certainly an advantage in a price-competitive marketplace. However, unless the performance of the cache is consistently very high, and the transparency of the cache is close to perfect, each individual user will attempt to use direct access methods.

The alternate business model is to pass on the marginal cost savings to those clients who make use of the cache, and at a level that corresponds to the client's use of the cache and its effectiveness in operating at a high cache hit rate. If, for example, the ISP uses a charging model that includes a tariff component based on the amount of data delivered to the client for the accounting period, this tariff component could be adjusted by the amount of use the client made of the cache system and the relative operating efficiency of the cache in generating cache hits.

As an example, if traffic is tariffed at $100 per gigabyte as delivered to the customer, a discounted value can be derived for traffic delivered from the Web cache. If the average cache hit rate is 30 percent of the delivered volume (which is a slightly different measurement to hits as a percentage of total Web requests), then after factoring in the costs of capital equipment and operational support, the traffic from the cache could be tariffed at $50 per gigabyte. Here, the benefit of using the Web cache is passed directly to those clients who make use of the cache, who enjoy both lower tariffs in direct proportion to their use of the cache and derive superior performance through using the cache. The accounting for this marketing model is certainly a more involved process, involving additional accounting systems and processing to undertake an accurate per-client view of cache usage.

It is becoming increasingly evident that a robust business model associated with discretionary use of a Web cache is that of access to a lower unit price of traffic. In this way, the user sees the incentive of immediate financial benefit in choosing to use the cache system. Where the provider deploys transparent or forced caching, translating the benefits of caching into an overall reduced tariff structure for all clients makes some sense.

Web Cache Systems

Cache systems can take a variety of forms. The original Web server from CERN, the original location of the development of Web software, allowed a mode of proxy behavior. This cache server model was developed significantly in the *Harvest Project*, a research project at the University of Colorado. As an evolutionary path, the cache server is being further developed within the scope of the development of the *Squid* cache server software and the associated Internet Caching Protocol (ICP).

Currently, the most widely deployed package of this form is the Squid system, although a number of cache systems are available commercially. Some of these systems are software packages that operate on a conventional operating system platform, and some use a customized platform kernel, which is optimized for the demands of a cache delivery environment. The difference between the use of freely available software and vendor-supported software lies in the levels of support offered to the ISP and the level of local expertise required to operate the cache service.

Some ISP business profiles may prefer a model of purchase of a caching system where the capital purchase costs are low, and the continuing operational support load may be higher. The advantage of such an approach lies in the consequent ability of the ISP to refine the behavior of the cache systems to match quite precisely the performance criteria desired from the cache systems. The alternative is to purchase a supported caching environment from a vendor. This may result in quite acceptable outcomes without the need to make considerable investments in developing in-house expertise in this area. It is matter for each ISP to determine where the most critical engineering support activities lie, and invest in expertise in the most critical of these areas.

Some ISPs may take the deliberate step to invest expertise into caching, while other ISPs may see market opportunities being created from other activity domains.

There are a number of characteristics of Web caching systems which are relevant to the performance of the caching environment.

◆ The first is the *size of the cache.* The relationship between the size of the cache and its hit rate is not a linear relationship. For typical patterns of Web use generated from a relatively large user population, a cache of one gigabyte or so will yield very good hit rates. Further increase of the cache size will yield incremental improvements in the cache hit rate, which are best described by a negative exponential relationship. Thus, caching systems with 10 gigabytes of storage do not produce markedly different performance characteristics than larger 100-gigabyte caching systems. No objective *best* size of cache system can be determined, as local environments differ, but every environment exhibits the law of diminishing returns, in which the addition of further cache capacity yields progressively smaller tangible differences in the cache effectiveness. The larger the cache, the greater the time taken for the cache to search its local database for a hit or a miss. Generally, larger caches perform more slowly on the initial Web reference search than smaller cache systems. Also, large caches take some time—days or even weeks—to build up a sufficiently large repository of cached data to produce an improved cache hit rate.

◆ The next parameter is the *number of simultaneous cache requests* that the cache server can manage efficiently. Note that this is a different metric to the number of requests per second that the cache server can manage. The number of simultaneous sessions that the cache server can support is related to the amount of resources allocated to the cache request and the total resource capacity of the box.

◆ The environment of deployment is very relevant to the performance of the cache environment. The related metric to the number of simultaneous requests that can be managed is the *average time to process a request.* Combining these two metrics provides the number of requests per second, which the cache system can process. The same unit will have a different performance metric of requests per second when deployed in different parts of the Internet. If the cache system is deployed with a satellite-based feed, then the average time to process a cache miss is considerably longer due to the higher latency of the satellite path. This leaves the process managing the original request open for a longer period, blocking other requests from using this process slot. If the same unit is deployed in a location where cache misses take fractions of a second to process, the process slot can be quickly reused.

Cache Hits versus Web Page Hits

One of the biggest tensions is the balance between the cache operator's desire to maximize the hit rate of the cache system and the desire of many Web page publishers to maintain an accurate count on the number of hits of the page and from where those hits occur. In the overall majority of cases, it is the requests that are of interest here, rather than the control of delivery of the content. The Web publisher is not necessarily interested in absorbing the hits for Web content. Indeed, many Web publishers see value in distributing the load of content delivery of fixed content material further out towards the client base, rather than the Web publisher bearing the cost of the distribution load from the local site.

Static pages, composed of plain text and images, are readily cached. As a consequence, the original page publisher may not obtain an accurate count of the number of times the page was displayed by users if the Web server's log was analyzed. Some Web page designers place information in the Web page directives that direct the Web cache server not to reuse a cached page. The most common way of doing this is to set the *Expires* Web page information header to the current date and time, so the next time the page is referenced, a new fetch will be undertaken. One of the more common hacks to cache servers to attempt to improve the hit rate is to allow this directive to be ignored.

However, the most effective answer deployed by Web page designers is to include a dynamic component in the page, in the form of a CGI script. The CGI script records the hit and interrogates the entity who has downloaded the page. This solution is a compromise, because it slows down the delivery of the page to the end user, but it does allow the Web page publisher to real-time data regarding hit rates on the page, which is a vital component to Web publishing.

Web Cache Deployment Models

The simplest deployment model is that of deployment of a simple cache system as a browser selectable resource. This system can be deployed within a POP with a TCP port 80 interface opened for client access. Such a deployment model is indicated in Figure 11.6.

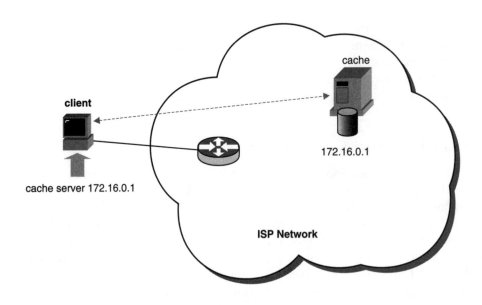

Figure 11.6 A selectable Web cache.

Scaling Web Caches

Scaling this deployment model can prove challenging. One scaling solution is to deploy a server at each POP and use the same IP address for each server. This solution allows the ISP to provide a consistent configuration to all clients and to augment capacity at any location seamlessly. The total system also can allow failover recovery mode, in which failure of a single server will automatically recover to other servers deployed in the network. This deployment model is indicated in Figure 11.7. Such servers can be configured as a set of local satellite systems to a larger caching core, using an ICP configuration to set up a caching hierarchy.

Another scaling measure is to alter the single server to multiple servers, using a TCP-based, load-sharing mechanism in the switching system to ensure that the servers are evenly loaded. This is indicated in Figure 11.8.

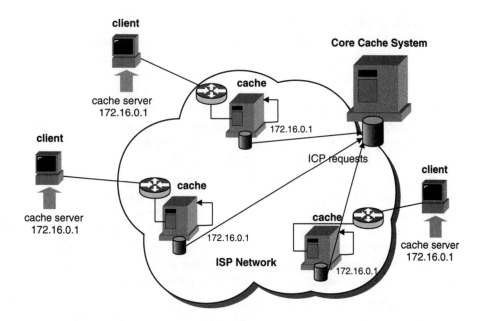

Figure 11.7   Replicated Web caches.

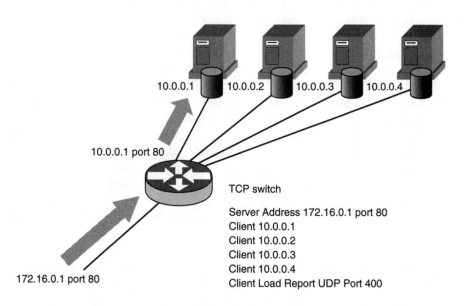

Figure 11.8   Load-balancing Web caches.

Accounting for Web Cache Use

These deployment systems allow for user optional cache configuration. If the ISP wants to account for the use of the cache, then the cache server or the switch that feeds the cache server must play an active role in accounting collection. If every network address is uniquely advertised to the ISP by a particular client, then the task of accounting for cache use can be performed using the logged records of the cache system itself. Because every IP address can be uniquely mapped to an ISP client, it is possible to also associate the volume of bytes delivered by the cache to the identified client.

Unfortunately, two factors make this supposition of address uniqueness somewhat weak. First, dial-in address assignment implies that the association of an IP address to a client is held only within dial-up accounting records in the first instance, and the binding is valid only between the times referenced in the start and stop records. This can be configured into an accounting model by simultaneously processing the dial accounting records when attempting to associate a particular IP address at a particular time to a client.

The second factor is slightly more challenging. For an ISP that offers permanent access transit services, the potential exists that any particular IP address may not be uniquely routed. Normally, such multiple access environments are part of a BGP-based interaction with multiple clients. Knowing the IP address of the query agent is not enough. As indicated in Figure 11.9, ascertaining the next hop AS number as well as the IP address is now necessary to make a determination of the client, who is using the cache. The implication is that the accounting records now need to be generated on a router, which is the entry point to the cache. In addition, the router must participate in the iBGP core mesh to maintain current AS path selection choices. Given the considerable overheads that such an engineering design entails, various restrictions may be placed on the use of a cache server that offers a lower access tariff. A common measure is that the lower tariff is available only to customers who singly home with the ISP. Not only is this a strong market incentive for customer loyalty, it also allows simple engineering solutions for cache accounting, as the lookup from the IP address in the cache log to a customer account is then relatively straightforward. Such measures allow a cache-use tariff to be very competitively positioned in the market.

Although the temptation exists to devise an engineering solution for every issue an ISP encounters, a marketing-based solution may offer better leverage at a lower cost. Although within a small ISP, the lines of communications between the engineering and marketing groups are highly functional, as the ISP grows, such paths of communication

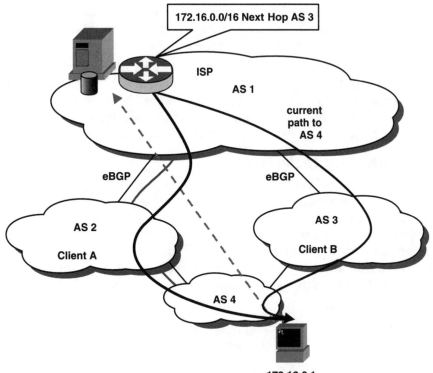

Figure 11.9 Mapping an IP address to a client.

*start to become less functional. Alternative solutions, which span mar-
keting measures as well as engineering solutions, may not be so readily
apparent to larger ISPs, and the temptation to indulge in engineering of
cost-inefficient solutions is always a constant risk in such cases.*

Domain of Access to the Cache

As well as accounting issues, another component for the consideration of
optional use Web caches is that of the necessity of restricting the use of the
cache to clients of the ISP. The motive for so doing is to ensure that the cache
is available only to clients of the service and not to clients of peer ISPs. It may
not be an issue worth the effort of solving, and the first question ISPs should
ask is, "To what extent does this happen, and what impact does it have on the
operation of the Web cache systems?" In the majority of cases, the accounting

of cache usage may reveal that this is an issue of negligible proportions, and any effort expended in devising an engineering solution would far outweigh the loss to the ISP through such use of the service.

If the measurement of such usage is considered sufficient to warrant engineering solutions, then the mechanisms available to the ISP are to ensure that the Web cache access is filtered at the edges of the ISP network and to ensure access is possible only by ISP clients, or that the address of the cache is not exported in the routing system to peer ISPs or upstream ISPs.

Further Deployment Challenges

Transparent and forced caching presents some further deployment challenges, in addition to those related to scaling, accounting, and access domain. The requirement is to pass all Web requests through a cache server. A number of techniques exist to achieve this, including an *inline* cache, in which all traffic is passed through the cache server (see Figure 11.10). This configuration allows the cache server to extract Web requests and pass them through a cache. A technique that does not place the cache as a critical point of poten-

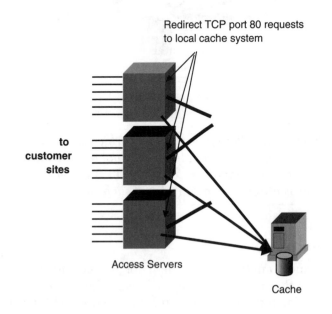

Figure 11.10 Inline transparent caching.

tial failure is to use policy redirection within the router, redirecting all port 80 traffic to the attached cache.

The first challenge of transparent caching is to devise a fail-safe mechanism, so that if the cache server fails for any reason, the caching redirection is disabled. One cache vendor's solution is to use a redirection function within the router, in conjunction with a Web cache management protocol that performs the function of informing the redirecting router of the availability of adjacent Web caches. Alternative nonproprietary solutions center around using policy-based redirection on the ISP's distribution routers to redirect all port 80 traffic to an address announced by the cache system by the local core router at a lower routing priority. Failure of the cache system will result in the Web traffic bypassing the cache and being routed by the core.

The second major challenge is to process cache misses at a speed comparable with normal non-cached Web retrieval. A process of pulling the document into the cache and then serving the document to the original requestor does not meet that objective. The transparent cache has to feed the document to the requestor while simultaneously creating a stored copy for subsequent cache serving.

However, the largest challenge to the transparent cache is that the transparent cache can serve only documents that are not dependent on the identity of the requestor being preserved. Web servers that use an end-to-end model of access, based on source address identification, or Web servers that attempt to present different documents to the client based on the client's source address, do not fit within the transparent caching model. The operator of the transparent cache server must recognize that the transparency is strongly conditional, and some clients may be disadvantaged when these systems are deployed.

It is highly likely that further development will occur with cache servers in the near future. Large-scale backbone IP networks that use T3 or OC-3 transport cores may carry tens of thousands of requests per second. Designing transparent caches that fit within the transport core does present scaling issues in terms of cache system performance. This factor continues to elude many of today's products available on the market. The generic architecture today is to use a cache network that attempts to place the cache systems closer to the access edge of the network, where the Web request volumes are within the scale of today's cache systems. Transparency of the cache remains an issue, and it is perhaps an area of further refinement within the specification of the underlying *http* Web server protocol. A potential implementation within Web browsers may allow the user to state the acceptability of using a cache to complete a request, and allow non-cache Web page retrieval attempts on cache failure, in the same way that the provider can use page expiration directives to direct a cache not to store the presented data.

Web Hosting

One of the other very common functions performed by ISPs as a value-added service to clients is that of hosting clients' Web pages. For dial-up clients, this mechanism is essential to provide an enduring presence on the Internet without the need to maintain a permanent connection. For other clients, this mechanism provides a means of outsourcing to the ISP a value-added service that may not be supportable within the resources available to the client. The value proposition is very similar to that of a maildrop service, although the interaction with the ISP service is somewhat different.

The Multiuser Web Host

The first form of the client Web publishing model used by ISPs is to use a multiuser host as the Web publishing platform and to provide each client of the service with a local account and associated storage space to place Web pages for publication (see Figure 11.11). The use of Web pages of the form

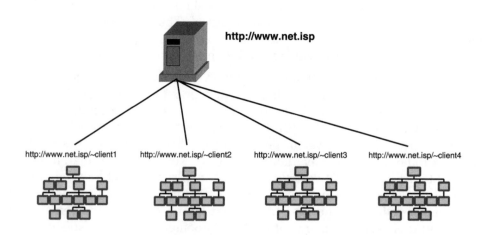

Figure 11.11   The shared Web host.

www.server/~account is indicative of this type of approach. For simple Web publication, which is tied with provision of mail accounts, this can be achieved as an additional service to the account, extending the mail account to allow storage of Web content through the server account. The model works effectively for low-volume support of static Web pages, in which the client is agreeable to have its content placed under the domain name of the operating ISP. Like mail servers, a concurrent quota or charging regime usually exists, in which the essential metric of resource usage is the amount of storage space available to each client to load with Web pages.

For the ISP, such a model does present policy issues of incurred liability of content hosted on the ISP's common Web server, and the ISP is responsible for developing a service contract that allows the ISP to ensure that it discharges its own obligations under law. The ISP also should ensure that the clients are aware of their own liabilities in publishing material. Administering such policies is not without cost, and the ISP should be in a position to respond to content issues in a responsible and consistent fashion. The ISP also should determine how the client will load content into the server. If the ISP chooses to run a multiuser interactive access server, the client needs interactive accounts and a supported interactive environment. This interactive environment must allow the client to manipulate local file structures, edit files, operate data transfers, and undertake similar local functions. The support cost of such an environment may be prohibitive for the ISP. A preferred mechanism is to allow the client to upload entire directory structures into the corresponding account on the server.

For the client, this model of Web publication presents some limitations. Many clients see the use of a name of the form www.*name*.com as an essential prerequisite for Web publication, and this model of hosting does not allow for such a naming scheme. The ISP also may limit the publication to simple static pages, inhibiting the use of CGI scripts and other forms of server-side computation. The issues in operating a single shared CGI environment across multiple client accounts do pose a number of system management questions, which are not readily answered in a stable scalable fashion. The common response is that if the client wants to use elements of dynamic content, the client must embed these within the Web page using some form of scripting or applet inclusion, which may be a more complex publication model. The system does scale well, in that a large server platform can accommodate some thousands of accounts. This model often is used to support basic Web publication capabilities for base retail dial-up services.

Virtual Web Hosts

The refinement to the common server is to create virtual Web servers, in which each client is distinguished with a distinct server name (see Figure 11.12). The server can take two approaches to support such an access structure:

- Configure the server to respond to multiple IP addresses and to associate each IP address with a different virtual Web server environment. Each server DNS name uniquely resolves to the matching IP address, and packets directed to that address are passed to the matching server process.

- Use a single IP address and use the DNS to map multiple domain names to this shared IP address. The Web server associated with this address uses the host part of the http protocol requests to process the request within the context of the virtual Web server.

The two approaches are functionally similar. Compared to the user account mechanism, the segmentation of the entire Web server environment allows each virtual engine to have its own processing environment, with a private CGI processing environment that allows server-based processing. As with any multiuser processing environment, the use of multiple accounts with processing capability does require careful and attentive system management.

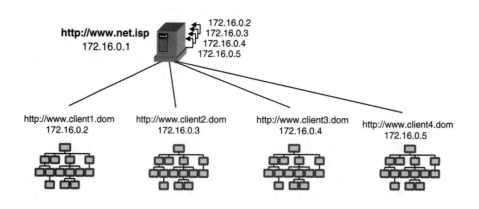

Figure 11.12   Virtual Web hosting.

This ensures the coherence and integrity of the system as a whole and the integrity of each virtual processing environment. The value proposition to the client is the provision of an Internet Web server using the client's name and identity. As with client-based mail domain names, the client has greater mobility of ISP services, a considerable asset to the client. The client also can outsource the publishing platform, offloading the access and server traffic from the client's Internet access facility, as well as outsourcing the server platform management role. Such a service is an excellent example of adding value to the base ISP access service and provides a good match to the service requirements of the small- to medium-enterprise market.

Dedicated Web Hosts

The next refinement of the hosting model is to provide dedicated Web server platforms to each client. A number of dedicated Web server systems are available on the market, which use a micro kernel and provide Web services, as well as an administrative access channel to allow remote management of the unit. Such an environment alleviates the ISP's requirement to operate a common multiuser system management environment, which can be a significant workload factor. One potential model is that the client leases exclusive use of an ISP-hosted server unit and is granted administrative control of the server environment. The client has the ability to load content, configure access rules, and define a CGI environment to allow dynamic delivery of content and local processing within a standalone environment. The value proposition to the client is the use of a Web server platform operated under the client's chosen identity. Again, the server traffic load is removed from the client's access service, and the client has administrative control of the operational environment. From the ISP's perspective, the choice of a standard Web server platform allows the ISP to configure equipment requirements, in terms of rack space, power requirements, and environmental demands with reasonable uniformity, bringing down the costs of housing the equipment. The use of ISP equipment dedicated exclusively to the client also allows the ISP to offer a solution that has no capital cost component to the client, allowing the costs to be recouped within the recurrent service costs.

Co-location of Web Hosts

The final step for the ISP in offering Web server solutions is to simply offer co-location facilities, in which the client leases space within the ISP's equipment housing facility. The ISP provides a secure and conditioned environment, and the client provides the equipment and manages it remotely. The value proposition to the ISP is perhaps a minimal one, because the client is not required to use the access ISP for the co-location service. The client generally is looking for an environment that is well-located in terms of proximity to the major anticipated readership and offers competitive co-location pricing within the bounds of the client's operational needs. This may result in a co-location environment being chosen that is hosted by another ISP, and the location may be in another city or in another country, where the location and cost are optimally matched with client requirements. Often, the service of co-location of content servers is provided as a more specialized service and may be provided by an exchange or NAP operator, allowing a content provider to maximize the reachability and service performance.

Usenet Services

Usenet (or Netnews) is a long-standing Internet application service. The original implementation was undertaken at Duke University and the University of North Carolina in 1979. The rationale for the effort was based on the observation that mailing lists are a very inefficient way of disseminating a message to a large community. The mailing list *explodes* the message into as many copies as list recipients and then transmits each copy through the network. The Usenet model attempts to minimize the network load associated with large public mailing lists by placing a copy of the message into a number of server locations, where local readers then can browse the message database.

Usenet is essentially a public medium, in which the message poster exercises no direct control over the reader community. The similarities of this model of publication of messages to that of the World Wide Web are quite apparent. If this application were developed in the mid-1990s, it would have been a Web application environment (and indeed, there are a number of Web browser Usenet reading tools and a number of Web applications that implement a similar function). However, the Internet of 1979 was a hybrid environment of permanent connections, intermittent connections, and store-forward messaging relay systems, with no ensured ability for a reader in a local network to directly access a remote message center. The design adopted to create this functionality in a hybrid environment was to use a collection of loosely synchronized message centers, or Usenet servers, each of which served a local readership population. The model allowed for any server to accept a posted message, and the servers then would cooperate to relay the posting to all other servers as a subsequent background task.

The Usenet system encompasses many thousands of separate discussion streams, termed *newsgroups*. These newsgroups are named within a hierarchical structure, with a relatively small number of primary groupings, and an increasingly specific set of named hierarchies. For example, the newsgroup name *news.software.readers* exists within a general set of newsgroups that relate to the Usenet environment (*news*), and a second grouping of newsgroups that discuss Usenet software (*software*) and in particular, the client reader applications (*readers*).

Usenet messages are posted into one or more newsgroups by a reader client. The message header format is formed into a correctly formatted Usenet message (this format is documented in RFC1036), which has a very similar format to SMTP mail messages. The message is passed to the local article database for inclusion and to the relay system to be flooded across the Usenet server network. This is indicated in Figure 11.13. The figure shows the two models of a browser, a local reader accessing a local news database, and a remote browser client, which uses a network link to the server. Distribution of Usenet is undertaken though the NNTP protocol, which is also the protocol used by the remote browser.

The Usenet distribution is undertaken by means of a statically configured overlay network of NNTP server peering sessions. Each server has a set of

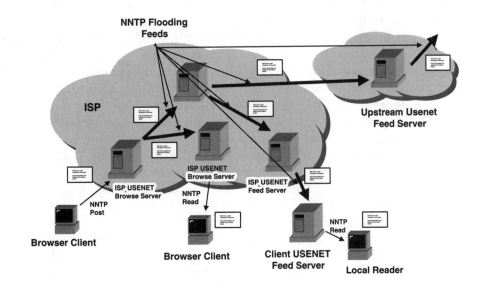

Figure 11.13   Usenet feed model.

local peer servers and an associated set of newsgroup hierarchies that will be fed to that peer and a number of feed qualifiers. Each message posted to the local server is offered to all peers who have indicated that they accept feeds for the newsgroups referenced in the posting. Each message accepted from another server may be offered to the other peer servers, as determined by the configuration of accepted hierarchies and qualification conditions. Of course, such flooding algorithms are prone to looping. The Usenet architecture uses two header fields to assist in loop prevention. Every message has a *Path:* header, which is a list of server names. The Path: header is the reverse ordered list of servers that have relayed the message from the posting host to the local server. If the server sees itself referenced in this header, it has good grounds for not accepting the message. When attempting to feed a message to a local server peer, if the peer already is listed in the *Path:* header, then the feed should not be undertaken. In a rich mesh of server peering, this is inadequate to detect duplicate messages, which arrive via different relay paths, and a second header, the *Message-ID:* header, is used here. This header contains a unique text string (uniqueness is typically obtained by including the name of the original posting server and some field that is unique within the server), which is stored in a local server database. When an article is passed to the server, it checks the local database and rejects the message if there is a match.

Usenet is a very large message stream. Tens of thousands of newsgroups exist. (It is impossible to give an accurate number here, as a server will typically have a set of the so-called *mainstream* Usenet newsgroups and a set of regional, local, and custom newsgroups.) The volume of messages that a typical server, which receives the major set of newsgroups, will be processing is some 8.5 gigabytes per day (as of early 1998), with more than 900,000 articles per day. A single feed of such a volume is some 850Kbps, assuming an even feed across 24 hours. An ISP planning to offer a large set of Usenet newsgroups should plan carefully to ensure that the communications capacity can be met. This situation can be compounded by the pressure from folk dubbed by the Usenet traditionalists as "The Church of Instantaneous Propagation" [Spencer 1998]. Here, the requirement was expressed, loudly, that Usenet propagation should exhibit very short delays, and the pressure on providers was not only to have the posted article, but to be first with the article. This has manifested as a configuration environment in which each site uses a number of upstream feed sites, and this increase in the denseness of the Usenet peering mesh does have its associated operational costs. This amount of data is significant to force flow through a server system, and some care is necessary to engineer the server to successfully manage this load and allow for the inevitable growth of the Usenet environment. The server configuration must encompass large storage space, filestore efficiency, database efficiency, and processor and memory capacity requirements. But, it is only Usenet news, and, as has been pointed out frequently, much of the volume of postings are spam and other forms of unsolicited, or off-topic, material. Usenet can be seen, perhaps somewhat uncharitably, as the sewerage of the Internet. On a cost and revenue basis, the additional effort in engineering such support for rapid propagation of Usenet material, which on a per-user basis generates only a marginal revenue stream, may not be justified. This observation may provide a more pragmatic ISP an appropriate response to such user imperatives for instantaneous Usenet propagation.

Types of Usenet Services

There are a number of services associated with Usenet news that an ISP may offer its client base. For some network clients, this may take the form of a feed of some, or all, Usenet newsgroups to the client's news server. For other clients, this is commonly a browse server, from which a client can direct its news browser to the ISP's browse server.

The Usenet Feed

To offer any service, the ISP must first gather a Usenet feed. One way, and perhaps the most straightforward, is to include provision for such a feed into the service contract with the upstream provider. Of course, a single feed may not meet any imposed requirements for timeliness or reliability, so that additional feeds must also be contemplated. Either all feeds can be *full feeds*, attempting to gather in the entire range of Usenet newsgroups, or some segmentation can be applied to the feeds in order to allow for some local optimization.

Usenet news exhibits strong bimodal size characteristics, in which a large number of small-sized articles interacts with a much smaller number of larger articles (alt.binaries is a typically cited hierarchy in which large postings abound). Some 90 percent of all articles are less than 8K in size, while the same 90 percent of all Usenet articles account for only 10 percent of the total volume of the typical full Usenet feed. A potential exploitation of this bimodal characteristic is to segregate feeds, so that groups where larger articles tend to concentrate could be managed more appropriately. One approach for smaller news articles is to use multicast transport systems, in which a single feed site can place small articles directly into a single multicast IP packet. and then multicast the article to the multicast group.

Experiments with a Multicast Network News Protocol are described at www.va.pubnix.com/ietf-mnnp/).

Multicast transmission is normally backed by a reliable information exchange to confirm article transmission. A functionally similar alternative is to use a satellite-based distribution system, in which a single uplink news feed is broadcast on the downlink, so that multiple simultaneous receivers can tap into a unidirectional Usenet feed. Again, a more conventional reliable information exchange would be used to catch up on lost articles.

Feeding ISP Clients

A client may request a Usenet feed as part of the contracted service. Accommodating this request is a case of configuring a local server to set up a Usenet peering with the client's server. This server configuration task is relatively straightforward, although some additional issues reside within the details:

♦ The client should specify the newsgroup hierarchies to be fed to the client. Enabling the client to control its service configuration information dynamically allows for more efficient control over such feeds.

♦ The bandwidth of the connection to the client and the acceptance speed of the client's server should be matched against the size of the Usenet feed. Servers that are slow to accept articles can impact on the entire efficiency of operation of the feed server, and mechanisms to ensure that an excessive feed backlog is alarmed are a sensible operational management precaution.

♦ The number of simultaneous feeds configured on a single server should be carefully monitored to ensure that the server can maintain a timely feed that is being quickly dispatched.

♦ Retention periods for articles stored on feed servers should be quite small, and the overall feed server configuration is to undertake a rapid turnaround of articles with minimal local retention.

♦ Feed servers will stress the disk bandwidth and memory bandwidth of the platform. Much of the issues of server performance centers around the history database of message identifier values. Some care also should be taken with the selection of server software to ensure that the software as well as the hardware can handle the Usenet loads.

Feeds can be set up as *push* or *pull*, in which feed clients are handed new items in configured newsgroups that they then can integrate into their Usenet database (push) or in which the clients determine which newsgroups and articles they want passed to them (pull). *Pull* feeds extract a higher workload on the local feed server, and for a large feeding hub ISP, the use of *pull* feeds is generally discouraged on the grounds of efficiency. *Push* feeds will operate with lower server overhead, but a higher administrative overhead reacts to the changing requirements from feed clients regarding which newsgroups they want to receive via the *push* feed.

Client Browse

The second potential ISP service is to offer browse capability to an ISP Usenet server. Browsing is normally a retail-based ISP service, distinct from a more wholesale-oriented feed service, and does require a somewhat different server configuration in order to deliver a well-managed service. The typical requirement for a browse server is to support a large storage system to allow retention of a feed for some days. Obviously, the size of the storage space is dependent on the size of the feed and on the retention policies that may be applied on a per-newsgroup basis or across the entire Usenet hierarchy. A careful choice of retention settings will construct a service that meets the client's expectations.

Browse servers are considered open targets by less than scrupulous individuals who want to send off-topic advertisements or something similar. Some care should be taken to ensure that the ISP's browse server does not add to the level of abuse of the Usenet system. The ISP needs a clear policy of what constitutes such abuse of Usenet and should ensure that the service contract allows for the policy to be enforced. The browser also should be protected by access filters to allow only client browse access. It also may be prudent to filter all browse-generated postings before acceptance, ensuring that the posting is not massively cross-posted to hundreds of newsgroups and that the headers are valid (checking for forged approvals when posting to a moderated group, for example). In terms of the ISP's posting policy, an ISP may want to insert extension headers into the posting to provide a way to match a posting with client access logs at a later date. Of course, it is only reasonable to inform the clients that such actions are being taken, within the scope of the service contract.

Browse servers need careful consideration of access policies and service charges. Allowing access to a browser to clients who want to then pass this access to their end users, allowing multiple browse sessions from a single client, can quickly overwhelm any form of browser platform. The consequent cost of providing additional capacity into the server environment may not be recouped by the ISP through normal service charges. It often is observed that transit ISPs do not offer browse access to their clients and that policy is often reflected in an access mechanism in which access to the browse server is restricted to individual dial-up sessions.

The Usenet Distribution Model

The underlying issue with Usenet is that the distribution model is one that can be paraphrased as *just in case*. Here, large amounts of data are transferred to a local server and held for a period, just in case a client wants to access the data. The efficiencies that originally were envisioned in the design of Usenet, in terms of a distribution model that has altered only slightly in the subsequent two decades, depend strongly on the assumption that each article will be accessed locally multiple times by local clients. With the explosion in content volumes, this assumption does need to be questioned, and the overall volumes of data movement and cost of local retention, as compared to the actual volumes passed to readers, indicate a falling efficiency that tends to make the entire proposition increasingly questionable. The asset of the news distribution model is that the summaries of available information (the list of locally available newsgroups and the current articles available within the groups) also are held locally and that the reader has a reasonably well-understood means of being informed as to what content is available at the time.

The World Wide Web model is one of the assumption of a large volume of content with a sparse readership. This model can be paraphrased as *just in time*, in which delivery of the content to the reader is based on an explicit reader request for the content, and the delivery is effected in real time. The Web-caching architecture does not alter this model to any great extent—it locally retains a copy of information delivered in response to an explicit request in order to intercept any following request for the same information and deliver it just in time to the next reader. The weakness of this model is the absence of the summary of available information, and the proliferation of various search and indexing engines on the Web attempts to provide summaries of information that mimics the function of a Usenet directory.

This leads to a number of thoughts on the future of Usenet and conjecture on the next wave of architectures that provide greater efficiency of Usenet environment operation. Flooding references to the original data, rather than the data itself, may be a viable approach, in which the reader has access to local content indexes. However, the request for the article itself is made to the original server, which holds the posting. The delivery mechanism is similar to the Web model and allows for the imposition of caches, and even caching hierarchies, to enable the dynamically driven local storage of commonly accessed content. This may well prove to be a productive direction to accommodate further expansion of the Usenet environment.

The catch cry of the imminent death of the Usenet environment through explosive growth is one that continually echoes throughout the Usenet, summarized by the slightly cynical comment, "Imminent death of Usenet predicted, news at 11." The reality has been that Usenet has proved to be quite amazingly resilient to date, and, despite some doubt as to the value of every single Usenet posting, Usenet forms an important core of the service environment of the Internet.

Specialized ISP Services

ISPs provide a wide variety of services to their clients as a means of differentiation in the market, and as a means of servicing particular niche markets with services that are attuned to the characteristics of the target market sector.

Such services are almost limitless in their scope and extend through news wire services, stock quotes, and similar business services, which are provided across the Internet at a price premium. An ISP may elect to purchase a multiuser license from the content provider and then integrate the content into the service portfolio provided to the ISP's clients. A significant service sector is based on multiuser real-time network games, in which game servers are placed into the ISP's server environment, and the ISP's clients can access these servers within a retail access package. Internet Relay Chat (IRC) servers and the related area of MUD and MOO chat servers also are part of this server set, allowing support for distributed real-time chat services. Such game and entertainment systems do enjoy passing popularity, and after a strong burst of popularity in the mid-1990s, the chat servers are waning. In their place, the multiuser real-time game servers are enjoying a surge of popularity, reflecting the increasing requirement on the part of the user for services that are more engrossing in terms of the user environment.

Of course, a cynical observation here is that in this market sector still dominated by per-hour charging access arrangements, any service that encourages longer session connection times on the part of users is a high-value proposition to the ISP!

Scaling the Service Environment

Content service platforms, such as Web servers, news browser services, ftp servers, and similar servers, which are well recognized by a distinguished domain name, are prone to the problem of inexorable growth in usage levels. Although the immediate response from the service provider may be to augment the size of the server and increase the network bandwidth from the server into the network switching fabric, it is often the case that the usage levels require more drastic solutions, which allow for dramatic levels of scaling.

One of the more powerful tools for scaling is parallel servers, spreading the service load over multiple servers. The servers can be replicated in a single location, using parallel load-sharing techniques, or they can be distributed across the ISP's network, allowing the server to be positioned closer to a local user population. The requirement for parallel servers is that they share a common DNS identity. In this way, clients of a service can be informed that the name of the service is a constant name, and this single server name can be configured into their local host. Having multiple server names, with qualifications as to which name is applicable in which situations, leads only to confusion both on the part of the client and the ISP's support staff. In this case, any tangible level of load sharing may not be achieved. The service constraint is that although parallel server architectures offer significant advantages in scaling the server capability for a user service, the servers must be configured in such a fashion that all servers can respond to a single service domain. The intent of the engineering is to ensure that one system, and precisely one system, responds to each service request, that successive requests elicit responses from different services in a load balancing manner, and that the selected server system remains constant for the life of each service transaction. The ways in which this can be achieved are outlined here.

Load Sharing Servers

Where it is required to augment the server capacity using parallel servers in a single location, the techniques to support such configurations are dependent on the nature of the service. Where the client/server transaction is undertaken using a single UDP query response model, the servers can be configured using conventional router load balancing. A configuration for three parallel DNS forwarders is indicated in Figure 11.14. The DNS resolvers use a common loopback address, which is the advertised address for the forwarder service. The router will attempt to load balance packets being sent to the common IP address; thereby balancing the load across the multiple servers. If the server needs to undertake its own query, it will use the IP address of the local network connection, ensuring that the response will be sent to the correct server.

One method of load sharing parallel TCP-based servers requires more specialized local switching support. Again, the parallel servers share a common loopback address, and the router will see parallel routes to the same IP address. Here, the router is required to load share across TCP sessions, which

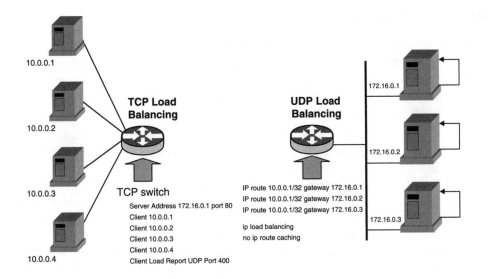

Figure 11.14   Local load sharing.

requires the forwarding cache within the router to remember the entire four-tuple of the TCP session to ensure that all packets within the same TCP flow are forwarded along the same routing path. This approach is indicated in Figure 11.14. This is not a conventional router structure, and typically, a customized load-sharing switch is required. With this customized environment, a more accurate form of load sharing can be used, combining TCP-based flow selection with a keepalive protocol to ensure that the switch correctly will identify when servers are added and removed from the server farm. The protocol also may use load reporting, allowing the switch to select the server with the lightest resource load for each new TCP connection. This has been referred to as a *Layer 4 switch* by some vendors.

A form of local load sharing between parallel servers, which does not require custom switching equipment, exploits DNS server behavior. When a resource is listed with multiple A resource records, the order of the records will be rotated on each response. Each time the server's DNS is queried, each server will be referenced in rotation. This somewhat rudimentary form of load sharing relies on any particular answer not being cached within the DNS for long periods of time. However, this approach can be used to implement a reasonable form of parallel server TCP-based load sharing.

Distributed Servers

The other means of addressing scaling load on servers is to place a number of servers in a distributed fashion across the network. The intent of such a configuration is not only to distribute server load across a number of systems but also to perform topologically based server loading, in which all clients within a local region of the network use a common local server.

One way of achieving this is to use the routing system, as indicated in Figure 11.15. In this configuration are multiple servers, each with the same service IP address. For a server transaction, the DNS query for the server name responds with this constant server IP address. The client then generates a packet to this address and passes it to the ISP's network. The routing system selects a minimum cost path to the IP address, which, in a conventional routing environment, should follow a path to the local server. Not only does this allow server load to be distributed across the network, removing traffic hot spots that a large central server farm creates, it also allows the client to reach

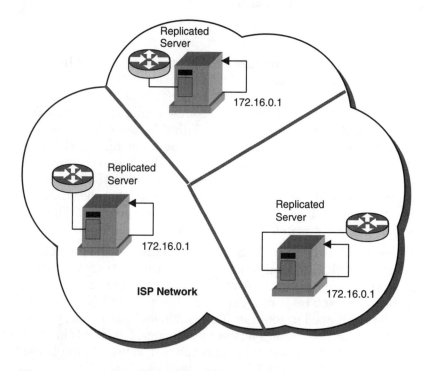

Figure 11.15 Distributed load sharing via routing.

a server that has the characteristics of minimal delay to the client. Minimizing delay is an essential component of enhanced performance, so that the quality of the service transaction also can be improved by using this strategy.

A rudimentary form of load balancing can be undertaken by manipulation of the advertised route metric within the routing systems. Here, an increased initial metric can reduce the radius metric of client selection, and a reduced initial metric can increase this metric.

Routing-based server load distribution also has the attributes of support for dynamic addition and removal of servers, as well as being capable of supporting automatic failover where a server fails. Addition of a server entails the announcement of the server's IP address from a new location within the network, thereby attracting local client traffic to the server. Removal of the server is simply a case of route announcement withdrawal, allowing the routing system to be redirected to the next closest server. In a TCP server environment that uses long-held TCP sessions, such as news browsing, care should be taken in exercising this feature too regularly. The change in server IP address routing will cause the active TCP sessions to be directed to a different server, causing TCP resets and session aborts.

The stability of the ISP's routing system is an essential attribute of this form of design, as any instability in the routing associated with the service IP address will cause all service access TCP sessions within the radius of routing instability to be reset, causing a service outage. Because the servers remain operational, and the routing instability is a localized phenomenon, identifying the cause of such service access faults will provide a challenging task for any operational service support team.

Distributed servers can span more than a single ISP, and the same technique of localizing access to a local server resource using the routing system can be extrapolated to the larger inter-AS routing environment. Again, the same caveats regarding the suitability of this technique to UDP-based query response services and short TCP-based transactions are recommended, because any form of routing instability will cause the service sessions surrounding the instability to break. Because today's Internet has relatively significant levels of instability within the inter-AS routing environment, this system of transparent server load distribution does have its caveats regarding general applicability—despite the strong incentive for vastly improved server performance through localization of client/server traffic within the larger Internet.

An alternative method of localization of traffic, which is not so prone to routing instability, is to use the DNS as the localization tool. In this environment, replicated DNS servers for the server's domain are hosted on, or close to, each distributed server. Each DNS server has the same IP address and always responds with the IP address of the local server. This configuration is indicated in Figure 11.16. In the normal sequence of events, a client first will use the DNS to translate the common service name to an IP address, which will occur on the local instance of the DNS server, and then the client will be directed via the DNS response to use the local server. After the client has a service address, any network routing instability will not affect the service transaction, so that this is a more resilient method for supporting long-held client/server transactions. Of course, caching of responses and the use of forwarders may frustrate the selection of locality of the server in every case, but the overall outcomes of server load distribution and reasonable localization of client/server traffic are achievable using this approach. Alternatively, a single DNS host is used, and the response value is computed on the basis of the source address of the query.

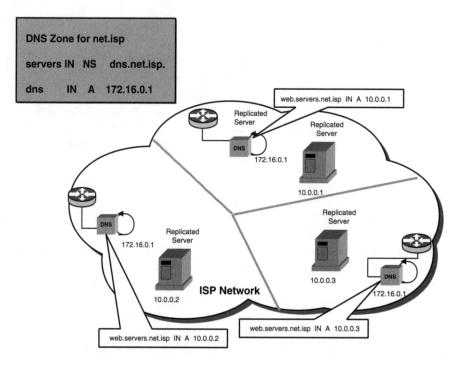

Figure 11.16   Distributed load sharing via the DNS.

Web Hosting Revisited

One of the engineering questions faced by the ISP engineer is: "How do you create a set of Web host servers that distributes the Web server load and offers superior server performance to clients?"

Localized servers are of significant interest to content providers, in which a desire exists to provide highly responsive servers to local client populations or to distribute a larger server load for high-volume popular Web sites. Some Web sites allow the user to indicate its geographic location, and the Web server then will point the client's browser to a new location. At best, this location is an imprecise approximation, because the possibility always exists that the network path from the client to the geographically closer server mirror site may be longer and slower than the network path to the major server.

Use of the routing system to automatically select the network-based closest server is a very good approach in terms of having the network select the *best* path at the time. The routing system will drive a path selection that reflects minimization of the distance metric at all times. However, routing instability, as noted, may affect the quality of the service.

Within the larger inter-ISP environment, using a DNS-based approach is possible, which does offer reasonable stability and reasonable accuracy of server selection. The technique is to periodically collect the BGP tables from the points in the network where each server is located, and, using AS paths as the distance metric, for each routing prefix in the BGP tables, calculate the closest server. This information is used with a DNS server, so that for each query, the source address is looked up in the table, and the matching server address is returned to the DNS query point. This combines the essential attribute of server transaction stability with reasonable accuracy of the selection of a local server instance.

One of the major performance factors within the Internet is that of delay, and minimizing end-to-end delay is a major influence on the quality of the client/server transaction. One of the significant ISP service opportunities in the emerging content market is for groupings of ISPs to offer a client a distributed hosting service. Such a service replicates the client's primary content on ISP virtual Web hosting servers, using a cache update protocol to ensure that the replicated data is kept current. Using the technique of a single DNS that uses routing information to determine the *closest* local server, the client is referred to a local ISP-operated server in a completely transparent fashion.

Such mechanisms are becoming increasingly important to the Internet as a whole as it continues to scale. The reliance on a continuing supply of large amounts of bandwidth to fuel a content environment, which has no intrinsic capability to undertake rational use of the communications system, is one that is inherently inefficient and, therefore, needlessly expensive to operate. Use of caching technologies, coupled with network services that undertake local server selection, allows the network to assist in the localization of content transactions. This measure both improves the speed of such transactions through reduced delay, server load sharing, and reduction of traffic concentration and reduces the carriage cost of such transactions. The ability to deliver such performance improvements to content publishers and to deliver cost efficiencies to all network users is an important value discriminator for ISPs who are anxious to identify value-added opportunities in a market place that is rapidly assuming the characteristics of a commodity marketplace.

Summary

The ISP access and transit market is quickly turning into a commodity marketplace. The price of the service is being driven down by competitive pressure to equate to the margin cost of service provision. Any ISP business operating in this basic market will offer relatively low returns on invested capital, and the business risks will increase as the larger ISP enterprises bring economies of scale to bear on the market.

Adding value to the basic ISP service, through the provision of additional services, allows the ISP to break out of the base commodity environment to provide services to its client base that add value to the basic access service. Such a role assists each client to achieve its individual objectives in terms of its expectations of requirements from the Internet. The more the ISP can attune these services to the clients' needs, the greater the ability to price the service at a level that reflects the value of the service application, rather than the marginal cost of the elements of service provision.

This type of service entails a high level of customer focus on the part of the ISP, understanding the service expectation of the clients, and understanding the value to the client in meeting such expectations. If these attributes are matched with engineering excellence in service provision, the total package the ISP can offer its clients is one of direct relevance, and, more critically, direct value to the client.

chapter twelve

Virtual Private Networks

*Acknowledgment is given to Paul Ferguson, who
co-authored the material in this chapter.*

The term *Virtual Private Network* (VPN) has become almost as recklessly used in the networking industry as has *Quality of Service* (QoS) to describe a broad set of problems and solutions, when the objectives themselves have not been properly articulated. This confusion has resulted in a situation where the popular trade press, industry pundits, vendors, and consumers of networking technologies alike, generally use the term VPN as an offhand reference for a set of different technologies. This chapter attempts to provide a common-sense definition of a VPN, an overview of different approaches to building them, and the role of the ISP in supporting VPNs.

What Is a VPN Anyway?

The wonderful thing about virtual private networks is that its myriad definitions give every company a fair chance to claim that its existing product is actually a VPN. But no matter what definition you choose, the networking buzz-phrase doesn't make sense. The idea is to create a private network via tunneling and/or encryption over the public Internet. Sure, it's a lot cheaper than using your own frame-relay connections, but it works about as well as sticking cotton in your ears in Times Square and pretending nobody else is around.

Wired Magazine, *February 1998, Wired's "Hype List—Deflating this month's overblown memes." Ironically, number 1 on the* Hype List *is Virtual Private Networks with a life expectancy of 18 months.*

As *Wired Magazine* notes in this quotation, the myriad definitions of a Virtual Private Network are less than helpful in this environment. Accordingly, it makes sense to begin this examination of VPNs to see whether it is possible to provide a common-sense definition of a VPN. Perhaps the simplest method of attempting to arrive at a simple definition for VPNs is to look at each word in the acronym individually and then tie each of them together in a simple, common sense, and meaningful fashion.

A Common Sense Definition of Virtual Private Networks

Let's start by examining the word *network*. This term is perhaps the least difficult for us to define and understand, because the commonly accepted definition is fairly uncontroversial and generally accepted throughout the industry. A network consists of any number of devices that can communicate through some arbitrary method. Devices of this nature include computers, printers, routers, and so forth and may reside in geographically diverse locations. The methods in which they may communicate are numerous, because there are countless electronic signaling specifications, and data-link, transport, and application layer protocols. For the purposes of simplicity, let's just agree that a *network* is a collection of devices that can communicate in some fashion and can successfully transmit and receive data among themselves.

The term *private* is fairly straightforward and is intricately related to the concept of *virtualization*, insofar as VPNs are concerned, as we'll discuss in a moment. In the simplest of definitions, *private* means that communications between two (or more) devices is, in some fashion, secret—that the devices which are not participating in the private nature of communications are not privy to the communicated content and that they are indeed completely unaware of the private relationship. Accordingly, data privacy and security (data integrity) are also important aspects of a VPN that need to be taken into consideration when considering any particular VPN implementation.

Another means of expressing this definition of private is through its antonym, *public*. A public facility is one that is openly accessible and is managed within the terms and constraints of a common public resource, often via a public administrative entity. By contrast, a private facility is one in which access is restricted to a defined set of entities, and third parties cannot gain access. Typically, the private resource is managed by the entities who have exclusive right of access. Examples of this type of private network can be found in any organizational network, which is not connected to the Internet, or to any other external organizational network, for that matter. These networks are private because no external connectivity exists, and thus, no external network communications exists.

Another important aspect of privacy in a VPN is through its technical definition. For example, privacy within an addressing and routing system means that the addressing used within a VPN community of interest is separate and discrete from that of the underlying shared network and from that of other VPN communities. The same holds true for the routing system used within the VPN and that of the underlying shared network. The routing and addressing scheme within a VPN should, for all intents and purposes, be self-contained, but this scenario degenerates into a philosophical discussion on the context of the term *VPN*. Also, it is worthwhile to examine the differences between the *peer* and *overlay* models of constructing VPNs—both of which are discussed in more detail in the section "Network Layer VPNs."

Virtual is a concept that is slightly more complicated. The *New Hacker's Dictionary* (formerly known as the Jargon File) [Raymond 1993] defines *virtual* as

> **virtual /adj./** [via the technical term "virtual memory", prob. from the term "virtual image" in optics] **1**. Common alternative to {logical}; often used to refer to the artificial objects (like addressable virtual memory larger than physical memory) simulated by a computer system as a convenient way to manage access to shared resources. **2**. Simulated; performing the functions of something that isn't really there. An imaginative child's doll may be a virtual playmate. Oppose {real}.

Insofar as VPNs are concerned, the definition in the second of the two definitions is perhaps the most appropriate comparison for virtual networks. The virtualization aspect is one similar to what we briefly described as private, but the scenario is slightly modified—the private communication is now conducted across a network infrastructure that is shared by more than a single organization. Thus, the private resource actually is constructed by using the foundation of a logical partitioning of some underlying common shared resource, rather than by using a foundation of discrete and dedicated physical circuits and communications services. Accordingly, the private network has no corresponding private physical communications system. Instead, the private network is a virtual creation that has no physical counterpart.

The virtual communications between two (or more) devices is due to the fact that the devices which are not participating in the virtual communications are not privy to the content of the data, and that they are also unaware of the private relationship between the virtual peers. The shared network infrastructure could, for example, be the global Internet, and the number of organizations or other users not participating in the virtual network may literally number into the thousands or even millions.

A VPN also can be said to be a *discrete* network, in the sense of separate or distinct. The discrete nature of VPNs allow both privacy and virtualization. Although VPNs are not completely separate, intrinsically, the distinction is that they operate in a discrete fashion across a shared infrastructure, providing exclusive communications environments that do not share any points of interconnection.

The combination of these terms produces *VPN*—a private network, in which the privacy is introduced by some method of virtualization. A VPN could be built as follows:

- Between two end-systems or between two organizations
- Between several end-systems within a single organization
- Between multiple organizations across the global Internet
- Between individual applications
- Any combination of the preceding

In the public network infrastructure context, almost every service is virtual in one sense or another.

No such thing as a nonvirtual network exists, when you consider the underlying common public transmission systems and other similar public infrastructure components as the base level of carriage of the network. What separates a VPN from a truly private network is whether the data transits a shared versus a nonshared infrastructure. For instance, an organization could lease private line circuits from various telecommunications providers and build a private network on the base of these private circuit leases. However, the circuit-switched networks owned and operated by the telecommunications companies are actually circuits connected to their Digital Access Cross-Connect Systems

(DACS) network and subsequently their fiber optics infrastructure. This infrastructure is shared by any number of organizations through the use of multiplexing technologies. Unless an organization is actually deploying private fiber and layered transmission systems, any network is layered with virtualized connectivity services in this fashion.

A VPN doesn't necessarily mean communications isolation, but rather the controlled segmentation of communications for communities of interest across a shared network infrastructure.

The common and somewhat formal characterization of the VPN, and perhaps the most straightforward and strict definition, is:

A communications environment in which access is controlled to permit peer connections only within a defined community of interest, and is constructed though some form of partitioning of a common underlying communications medium, where this underlying communications medium provides services to the network on a nonexclusive basis.

A simpler, more approximate, and much less formal description is:

A private network constructed within the public Internet.

Although VPNs may be constructed to address any number of specific business needs or technical requirements, a comprehensive VPN solution provides support for private dial-in access; support for multiple remote sites connected by leased lines (or other dedicated means); the ability of the ISP, as VPN service provider, to host various services for the VPN's customers (for example, intranet Web hosting); and the ability to support not just intra-, but also inter-VPN connectivity, including connectivity to the global Internet.

VPN Motivations

Several motivations exist for building VPNs, but a common thread in each is that they all share the requirement to *virtualize* some portion of an organization's communications—in other words, make some portion (or perhaps all) of the communications essentially invisible to external observers, although taking advantage of the efficiencies of a common communications infrastructure.

Economics

The base motivation for VPNs lies in the economics of communications. Communications systems today typically exhibit the characteristic of a high fixed-cost component, and smaller variable cost components that vary with the transport capacity, or bandwidth, of the system. Within this economic environment, it is generally financially attractive to bundle a number of discrete communications services onto a common high-capacity communications platform, allowing the high fixed-cost components associated with the platform to be amortized over a larger number of clients. Accordingly, a collection of virtual networks implemented on a single common physical communications plant is cheaper to operate than the equivalent collection of smaller physically discrete communications plants, each servicing a single network client.

Therefore, if aggregation of communications requirements leads to a more cost-effective communications infrastructure, why not pool all these services into a single public communications system? Why is there still the requirement to undertake some form of partitioning within this common system, which results in these virtual private networks? The answer to this question lies in the desire for enhanced privacy.

Privacy

The second motivation for VPNs is that of communications privacy, in which the characteristics and integrity of communications services within one closed environment are isolated from all other environments that share the common underlying plant. The level of privacy depends greatly on the risk assessment performed by the subscriber organization—if the requirement for privacy is low, then the simple abstraction of discretion and network obscurity may serve the purpose. However, if the requirement for privacy is high, then there is a corresponding requirement for strong security of access and potentially strong security applied to data passed over the common network.

VPNs and the Public Data Network

This chapter cannot do justice to the concept of VPNs without some historical perspective, so we need to take a quick look at why VPNs are an evolving paradigm, and why they will continue to be an issue of confusion, contention, and disagreement. This is important, because you will indeed discover that opinions on VPN solutions are quite varied, and everyone seems to be deeply religious about how they should be approached.

Historically, one of the precursors to the VPN was the *Public Data Network* (PDN), and the current familiar instance of the PDN is the global Internet. The Internet creates a ubiquitous connectivity paradigm, where the network permits any connected network entity to exchange data with any other connected entity. The parallels with the global *Public Switched Telephone Network* (PSTN) are, of course, all too obvious—where a similar paradigm of ubiquitous public access is the predominate characteristic of the network.

The public data network has no inherent policy of traffic segregation, and any modification to this network policy of permitting ubiquitous connectivity is the responsibility of the connecting entity to define and enforce. The network environment is constructed using a single addressing scheme and a synchronized routing hierarchy. This allows the switching elements of the network to determine the location of all connected entities. All of these connected entities also share access to a common infrastructure of circuits and switching.

However, the model of ubiquity in the *Internet PDN* does not match all potential requirements, especially the need for data privacy. For organizations that want to use this public network for private purposes within a closed set of participants (for example, connecting a set of geographically separated offices), the Internet is not always a palatable possibility. A number of factors are behind this mismatch, including the following issues:

◆ Quality of service (QoS)
◆ Availability and reliability
◆ Use of public addressing schemes
◆ Use of public protocols
◆ Site security
◆ Data integrity (admitting the possibility of traffic interception)

In addition, a corporate network application may desire more stringent levels of performance management than are available within the public Internet or indeed may want to define a management regime that differs from the underlying Internet PDN.

Service Level Agreements

It is worthwhile at this point to briefly examine the importance of *Service Level Agreements* (SLAs) in regard to the deployment of VPNs. SLAs are negotiated contracts between VPN providers and their subscribers; they contain the service criteria to which the subscriber expects specific services to be delivered. The SLA is arguably the only binding tool at the subscriber's disposal with which to ensure that the VPN provider delivers the service(s) to the level and quality as agreed. It is in the best interest of the subscribers to monitor the criteria outlined in the SLA for compliance. However, Service Level Agreements present some challenging technical issues both for the provider and the subscriber.

For the subscriber, the challenge is to devise and operate service measurement tools that can provide a reasonable indication as to what extent the SLA is being honored by the provider. Also, a subscriber may use an SLA to bind one or more providers to a contractual service level, but if the subscriber's VPN spans multiple providers' domains, the SLA also must encompass the issue of provider interconnection and the end-to-end service performance.

For the VPN provider, the challenge lies in honoring multiple SLAs from a number of service clients. In the case of an Internet PDN provider, the common mode of best-effort service levels, using host protocol-mediated resource sharing, is not conducive to meeting SLAs, given the unpredictable nature of the resource allocation mechanism. In such environments, the provider either has to ensure that the network is very generously engineered in terms of the ratio of subscriber access capacity to internal switching capacity, or the provider can deploy service differentiation structures to ensure that minimum resource levels are allocated to each SLA subscriber. The former course of action tends to reduce the benefit of aggregation of traffic. This, in turn, has an ultimate tariff implication. The latter course of action does have implications in terms of operational management complexity and scalability of the network.

Alternatives to Internet VPNs

The alternative to using the Internet as a VPN today is to lease circuits, or similar dedicated communications services, from the public network operators (the local telephone company in most cases) and create a completely private network. A layering convention allows us to label this as *completely private*, as these dedicated communications services are (at the lower layers of the protocol stack) again instances of virtual private communications systems constructed atop a common transmission bearer system. Of course, this is not without precedent, and the majority of the early efforts in data networking and many of the current data networking architectures do not assume a deployment model of ubiquitous public access.

Many network architectures do not assume a deployment model of ubiquitous deployment. This is quite odd, when you consider that the inherent value of an architecture lies, ultimately, in ubiquitous public access. The alternative, a chaotic collection of closed private networks, is ultimately worthless. The value of ubiquity has been conclusively demonstrated in the telephony marketplace since the start of the twentieth century. While the data communications industry appears to be moving at a considerable technological pace, the level of experiential learning and consequent level of true forward progress, as distinct from simple motion, still leaves much to be desired!

Instead of a public infrastructure deployment, the deployment model used has been that of a closed (or private) network environment in which the infrastructure, addressing scheme, management, and services were dedicated to a closed set of subscribers. This model matched that of a closed corporate environment, where the network was dedicated to serve a single corporate entity as the sole client. This precursor to the VPN can be called the private data network and was physically constructed using dedicated local office wiring and dedicated leased circuits (or private virtual circuits from an underlying switching fabric such as X.25) to connect geographically diverse sites.

However, this alternative has an associated cost, because the client now has to manage the network and all its associated elements, invest capital in network switching infrastructure, hire trained staff, and assume complete responsibility for the provisioning and on-going maintenance of the network service. Such a dedicated use of transport services, equipment, and staff is often difficult to justify for many small-to-medium-sized organizations. Although the functionality of a private network system is required, the expressed desire is to reduce the cost of the service through the use of shared transport services, equipment, and management. A number of scenarios can address this need, ranging from outsourcing the management of the switching elements of the network (managed network services), to outsourcing the capital equipment components (leased network services), to outsourcing of the management, equipment, and transport elements to a service provider.

An Example VPN

In the simple example illustrated in Figure 12.1, network A sites have established a VPN across the service provider's backbone network, and VPN network B is completely unaware of its existence. Both VPN network A and VPN network B can harmoniously coexist on the same backbone infrastructure.

This type of VPN is, in fact, the most common type of VPN, where geographically diverse subnetworks belong to a common administrative domain, interconnected by a shared infrastructure outside of their administrative control (such as the global Internet or a single service provider backbone). The principle motivation in establishing a VPN of this type is that perhaps the majority of communications between devices within the VPN community may be sensitive in nature (again, a decision on the level of privacy required rests solely on a risk analysis performed by the administrators of the VPN), yet the total value of the communications system does not justify the investment in a fully private communications system that uses discrete transmission elements.

On a related note, the level of privacy a VPN may enjoy depends greatly on the technology used to construct the VPN. For example, if the communica-

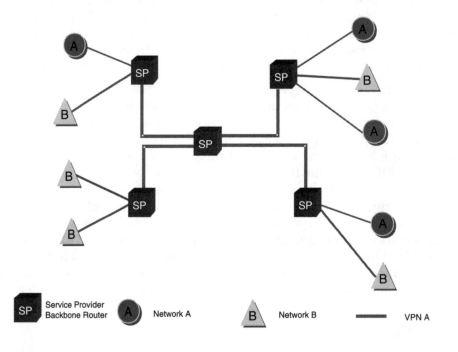

Figure 12.1 Basic VPN example.

tions between each VPN subnetwork (or between each VPN host) are securely encrypted as the VPN transits the common communications infrastructure, then the privacy aspect of the VPN is relatively high.

The granularity of a VPN implementation can be broken down further to a single end-to-end, one-to-one connectivity scenario. Examples of these types of one-to-one VPNs are single dial-up users establishing a VPN connection to a secure application, such as an online banking service, or a single user establishing a secure, encrypted session between a desktop and server application, such as a purchasing transaction conducted on the World Wide Web. This type of one-to-one VPN is becoming more and more prevalent as secure electronic commerce applications become more mature and further deployed in the Internet.

It is interesting to note that the concept of virtualization in networking also has been considered in regard to deploying both research and production services on a common infrastructure. The challenge in the research and education community is one in which there is a need to satisfy both network research and production requirements. VPNs also have been considered as a method to segregate traffic in a network so that research and production traffic behave as *ships in the night*, oblivious to one another's existence, to the point that major events (for example, major failures, instability) within one community of interest are completely transparent to the other. This concept is further documented in MORPHnet [Aiken 1997].

VPNs may be constructed to span more than one host communications network, so that the *state* of the VPN may be supported on one or more VPN provider networks. This scenario is perhaps at its most robust when all the providers explicitly support the resulting distributed VPN environment, but other solutions, which do not necessarily involve provider knowledge of the overlay VPN, are occasionally deployed, with mixed results.

Engineering VPN Solutions

The confusion factor comes into play in the most basic discussions regarding VPNs, due principally to the fact that actually several different types of VPNs exist. Depending on the functional requirements, several different methods of constructing each type of VPN are available. The process of selection should include consideration of the following:

◆ What problem is being solved
◆ Risk analysis of the security provided by a particular implementation
◆ Issues of scale in growing the size of the VPN
◆ The routing model of the interaction between the client networks and the VPN provider
◆ The complexity involved in both implementing the VPN, as well as ongoing maintenance and troubleshooting

To simplify the description of the different types of VPNs, they have been broken down in this chapter into categories that reside in the different layers of the TCP/IP protocol suite.

Network Layer VPNs

The network layer in the TCP/IP protocol suite consists of the IP routing system—how reachability information is conveyed from one point in the network to another. A few methods exist to construct VPNs within the network layer, and each is examined in the following paragraphs.

A brief overview of the differences in the *peer* and *overlay* VPN models is appropriate at this point. Simply put, the *peer* VPN model is one in which the network layer forwarding path computation is done on a hop-by-hop basis, in which each node in the intermediate data transit path is a peer with a next-hop node. Traditional routed networks are examples of peer models, in which each router in the network path is a peer with its next-hop adjacencies. Alternatively, the overlay VPN model is one in which the network layer forwarding path is not done on a hop-by-hop basis. Rather, the intermediate link layer network is used as a *cut-through* to another edge node on the other side of a large cloud. Examples of overlay VPN models are ATM, Frame Relay, and tunneling implementations.

Having drawn these simple distinctions between the peer and overlay models, we can see that the overlay model introduces some serious scaling concerns in cases in which large numbers of egress peers are required. The number of virtual adjacencies increase in direct relationship with the number of peers. That is, the amount of computational and performance overhead required to maintain routing state, adjacency information, and other detailed packet forwarding and routing information for each peer becomes a liability in very large networks. If each egress node in a cut-through network become peers, in an effort to make all egress nodes one Layer 3 hop away from one another, this limits the scalability of the VPN model quite remarkably.

For example, as the simple diagram in Figure 12.2 illustrates, the routers surrounding the interior switched infrastructure represent egress peers, because the switches in the core interior could be configured so that all egress nodes are one Layer 3 hop away from one another, creating what is commonly known as a *cut-through*. This is the foundation of an overlay VPN model. Alternatively, if the switches in the interior were replaced with routers, then the routers positioned at the edge of the cloud now become peers with their next hop router nodes, not other egress nodes. This is the foundation of the peer VPN model.

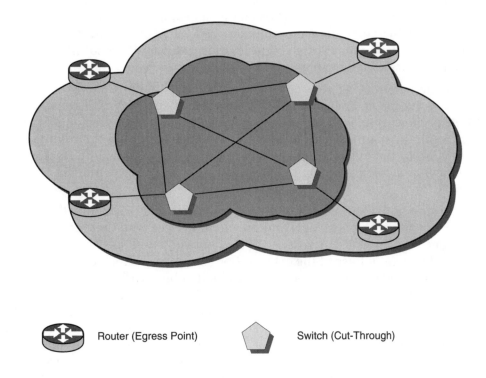

Router (Egress Point)   Switch (Cut-Through)

Figure 12.2   Cut-through VPN architecture.

VPN Routing Models

The other perspective on the network layer VPN architecture is that of the routing model presented to each client network. The VPN is not always transparent to the client at the routing level, and the VPN provider needs to understand the implications of various VPN approaches as they impact on the client's subnetworks, particularly with respect to the level of routing complexity that each model passes back to the client.

The cut-through model is illustrative of a routing model where the VPN host network is replaced by a virtual LAN, as each egress node undertakes a network-layer peering with every other egress node. This can be extended to the client network through the use of egress nodes which participate with the customer's network routing environment, through either use of an egress node dedicated to a customer network, or through the use of an egress node that supports multiple *virtual routers* per node, using a dedicated routing context per egress port. Here the VPN takes on the appearance of a LAN, and the customer's VPN-wide routing environment can be managed by the customer through the deployment of a single Interior Gateway Protocol (IGP) routing domain across all client subnetworks.

An alternate routing view is to explicitly combine the VPN peering of the egress ports (or dedicated egress routers) into a single *virtual router*, using OSPF as the customer access routing interface to enable the creation of the virtual router to span this emulated LAN. This does simplify the routing view presented to the customer of the VPN host as being a single virtual router, although at a cost of forcing the customer networks into deploying OSPF as their IGP within the VPN client subnetworks.

The alternative to the LAN or virtual router view is to separate the routing environments of the host VPN and the client networks so that the client cannot operate a single IGP across all VPN client subnetworks. This can be constructed by explicit use of the exterior Border Gateway Protocol (eBGP) as the peering routing protocol between each client subnetwork and the host VPN. This model creates the VPN host network as an explicit routing domain, and also forces each client subnetwork to be distinct IGP routing domains. This can be a more complex architectural model for the client, and the resulting VPN is one that, in a routing sense, is jointly operated by the client and the VPN provider. The most common routing model for VPNs today is a simplification of this separated routing domain model, supported by the explicit configuration of static routes on each VPN egress port, and the absence of any dynamic routing peering with the client subnetwork. The VPN host operates its distinct routing domain, and each client subnetwork operates its IGP routing domain independently. While this creates a very simple routing model for the client, the lack of any form of dynamic routing exchange between the client and the VPN host can lead to its own forms of operational complexity, particularly relating to the manual handling of client address blocks and explicit customer control of routing metrics.

Controlled Route Leaking

Controlled route leaking (or *route filtering*) is a method that also could be called *privacy through obscurity*, because it consists of nothing more than controlling route propagation to the point that only certain networks receive routes for other networks within their own community of interest. This model can be considered a *peer* model in a routing sense, because the edge VPN subnetworks (clients) establish a routing relationship with the first upstream VPN provider's router, instead of an edge-to-edge route peering relationship with VPN subnetworks (other VPN clients) that comprise the remainder of that VPN. Although the common underlying Internet network generally carries the routes for all networks connected to it, this architecture assumes that a VPN is effectively formed by taking a subset of these routes. The routes associated with this set of clients are filtered so that they are not announced to any other connected client subnetwork, and that all other non-VPN routes are not announced to the client members of the VPN. For example, in Figure 12.1, if the service provider (SP) routers only *leaked* routing information received from network A subnetworks to other network A subnetworks, then sites not in network A (for instance, sites in network B) would have no explicit knowledge of network A, nor would network A have explicit knowledge of any other networks that were attached to the service provider's infrastructure. This is indicated in Figure 12.3. Given this lack of explicit knowledge of reachability to any location other than other members of the same VPN, privacy of services is implemented by the inability of any of the VPN hosts to respond to packets that contain source addresses from outside the VPN community of interest.

This use of partial routing information is prone to many forms of misconfiguration. One potential problem with route leaking is that it is extremely difficult, if not impossible, to prohibit the subscriber networks from pointing default to the upstream next-hop router for traffic destined for networks outside of their VPN. From within the VPN subscriber's context, this may be a reasonable action, because *default* for the VPN is reachability to all other members of the same VPN, and pointing a default route to the local egress path is, within a local context, a reasonable move. However, it does allow a

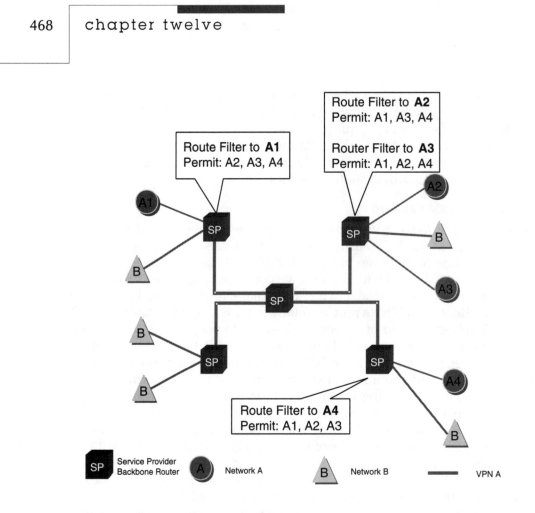

Figure 12.3   Route-managed VPN.

VPN customer to generate traffic into another VPN, with potential consequences of denial of service, or other forms of a breach of inter-VPN security.
It should be no surprise to learn that this implied *default* route is a common
occurrence in VPNs where the customer configures and manages the customer
premise equipment (CPE) routers. If the service provider manages the configuration of the CPE routers, then this potential for misconfiguration can be
managed. Otherwise, it may be wise on the part of the service provider to
place destination address filters and source routing filters on first-hop VPN
ingress routers, where the destination address filters effectively match the
VPN routing filters, in order to prohibit the VPN from accepting any traffic
destined for networks outside of the defined VPN.

Also, this environment implicitly assumes a common routing core. A common routing core, in turn, implies that each VPN must use addresses that do not clash with those of any other VPN on the same common infrastructure and cannot announce arbitrary private addresses into the VPN. Another, perhaps less obvious, side effect of this form of VPN structure is that it is not possible for two VPNs to have a single point of interconnection, nor is it possible for a VPN to operate a single point of interconnection to the public Internet in such an environment. This so-called *gateway*, where all external traffic is passed through a control point that can both enforce some form of access policy and record a log of external transactions, cannot be constructed in the basic form of a route filtering VPN. The common routing core uses a single routing paradigm, based solely on destination address.

This requirement highlights one of the dichotomies of VPN architectures. VPNs must assume that they operate in a mutually hostile environment, where any vulnerability that exposes the private environment to access by external third parties may be exploited in a hostile fashion. However, VPNs rarely are truly isolated communications environments, and typically all VPNs do have some form of external interface allowing controlled reachability to other VPNs and to the broader public data network. The trade-off between secure privacy and the need for external access is a constant feature of VPNs.

To implement an external interconnection requires the network to route externally originated packets to the VPN interconnection point. If they are admitted into the VPN at the interconnection point, then the same packet may be passed back across the VPN host network to the ultimate VPN destination address. Without the use of Network Address Translation (NAT) technologies at the interconnection point of ingress into the VPN, this kind of communications structure is effectively insupportable within this architecture, as indicated in Figure 12.4.

In general, the technique of supporting private communities of interest simply by route filtering can at best be described as a primitive method of VPN construction, that is prone to administrative errors and admits an undue level of insecurity and network inflexibility. Even with comprehensive traffic and route filtering, the resulting environment is not totally robust. The operational overhead required to support complementary sets of traditional routing

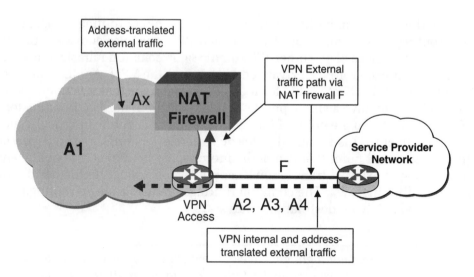

Figure 12.4   Address-translation VPN.

and traffic filters is a relevant consideration, and this approach does not appear to possess the scaling properties desirable to allow the number of VPNs to grow beyond the bounds of a few hundred, using today's routing technologies.

Having said that, however, a much more scalable approach is to use BGP communities [RFC 1997] as a method to control route propagation. The use of BGP communities scales much better than alternative methods insofar as controlling route propagation and is less prone to human misconfiguration within manual VPN management administrative processes. Briefly, the use of a BGP community attribute allows a VPN provider to *mark* BGP NLRIs (Network Layer Reachability Information) elements with a community attribute, so that configuration control allows route information to be propagated in accordance with a community profile, as indicated in Figure 12.5. Routes within a single VPN can be marked with a single community attribute using this approach, allowing the edge filtering function to be controlled by the community attribute, rather than through the deployment of multiple instances of a per-VPN route filter.

Because traffic from different communities of interest must traverse a common shared infrastructure, there is no significant data privacy in the portion of the network where traffic from multiple VPNs share the infrastructure.

BGP Communities

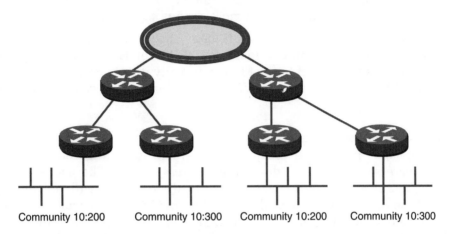

Community 10:200   Community 10:300   Community 10:200   Community 10:300

Figure 12.5   BGP community-based VPN.

Therefore, although connected subnetworks—or rather, subscribers to the VPN service—may not be able to detect the fact that there are other subscribers to the service, multiple interwoven streams of subscriber data traffic pass unprotected in the core of the service provider's network.

Tunneling

Sending specific portions of network traffic across a tunnel is another method of constructing VPNs; some methods are more effective than others. The most common tunneling mechanisms are *Generic Routing Encapsulation* (GRE) [RFC 1701] tunneling between a source and destination router; router-to-router, or host-to-host, tunneling protocols such as *Layer 2 Tunneling Protocol* (L2TP) [ID 1997d]; *Point-to-Point Tunneling Protocol* (PPTP) [ID 1997e]; and *Distance Vector Multicast Routing Protocol* (DVMRP) [RFC 1705] tunnels.

Tunneling can be considered as an overlay VPN model, but the seriousness of the scaling impact relies on whether the tunnels are point-to-point or point-to-multipoint. Point-to-point tunnels have fewer scaling problems than do point-to-multipoint tunnels, except in situations where a single node begins to build multiple point-to-point tunnels with multiple end points. Although a linear scaling problem is introduced at this point, the manageability of point-to-point tunnels lies solely in the administrative overhead and the number of tunnels themselves. On the other hand, point-to-multipoint tunnels use cut-through mechanisms to make greater numbers of end points one hop away and subsequently introduce a much more serious scaling problem.

Although the Multicast Backbone (Mbone) itself could quite literally be considered a global VPN, and although DVMRP tunnels are still widely used by organizations to connect to the Mbone, it really is not germane to the central topic of VPNs, as the focus of VPNs today remains an issue of managing unicast traffic.

TRADITIONAL MODES OF TUNNELING

GRE tunnels, as mentioned previously, generally are configured between a source (*ingress*) router and a destination (*egress*) router. The packets designated to be forwarded across the tunnel, already formatted with an encapsulation of the data with the normal protocol-defined packet header, are further encapsulated with a new header (the GRE header), and placed into the tunnel with a destination address of the tunnel endpoint (the new next-hop). When the packet reaches the tunnel endpoint, the GRE header is stripped away, and the packet continues to be forwarded to the destination as designated in the original IP packet header (see Figure 12.6).

GRE tunnels are generally point-to-point; that is, a single source address exists for the tunnel and usually only a single destination tunnel endpoint exists. However, some vendor implementations allow the configuration of point-to-multipoint tunnels; that is, a single source address and multiple destinations. Although this implementation is used in conjunction with Next-Hop Routing Protocol (NHRP) [ID 1997e], the effectiveness and utility of NHRP is questionable and should be tested prior to deployment. It is also noteworthy that NHRP is known to produce steady-state forwarding loops when used to establish shortcuts between routers.

Tunnels, however, do have a number of very compelling attractions when used to construct VPNs. The architectural concept is to create VPNs as a collection of tunnels across a common host network. Each point of attachment to the common network is configured as a physical link that uses addressing and routing from the common host network and one or more associated tunnels. Each tunnel endpoint logically links this point of attachment to other remote points from the same VPN. The technique of tunneling uses a tunnel egress address defined within the address space of the common host network, and the packets carried within the tunnel use the address space of the VPN. This, in turn, does constrain the tunnel endpoints to be co-located to those points in the network where the VPN and the host network interconnect.

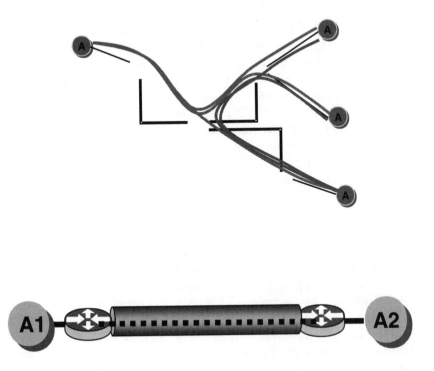

Figure 12.6   Tunnel-based VPN.

The advantage of this approach is that the routing for the VPN is isolated from the routing of the common host network. The VPNs can reuse the same private address space within multiple VPNs without any cross impact, providing considerable independence of the VPN from the host network. This requirement is key for many VPNs because private VPNs typically may not use globally unique or coordinated address space. Often, the consequent requirement is to support multiple VPNs that independently use the same address space. Such a configuration is not supportable within a controlled route leakage VPN architecture.

The tunnel also can encapsulate a number of different protocol families, so that it is possible for a tunnel-based VPN to mimic much of the functionality of dedicated private networks. Again, the need to support multiple protocols in a format that preserves the functionality of the protocol is a critical requirement for many VPN support architectures. In this requirement, an IP common network with controlled route leakage cannot provide such services, whereas a tunneling architecture can segment the VPN private protocol from the common host network. The other significant advantage of the tunneled VPN is the segregation of the common host routing environment with that of the VPN. To the VPN, the common host network assumes the properties of a number of point-to-point circuits, and the VPN can use a routing protocol across the virtual network, which matches the administrative requirements of the VPN. Equally, the common host network can use a routing design that matches the administrative requirements of the host network (or collection of host networks) and is not constrained by the routing protocols used by the VPN client networks.

Perhaps these advantages would be sufficient to conclude that GRE tunneling is the panacea for VPN design. However, several drawbacks exist to using GRE tunnels as a mechanism for VPNs, mostly in regard to administrative overhead, scaling to large numbers of tunnels, and quality of service and performance. Since GRE tunnels must be manually configured, there is a direct relationship between the number of tunnels that must be configured and the amount of administrative overhead required to configure and maintain them; each time the tunnel endpoints change, they must be manually reconfigured. Also, although the amount of processing required to encapsulate a packet for GRE handling may appear to be small, a direct relationship exists to the number of configured tunnels and the total amount of processing overhead required for GRE encapsulation. Of course, tunnels can be structured to be triggered automatically, but a number of drawbacks are evident with such an approach. These drawbacks dictate careful consideration of related routing and performance issues. The worst end-state of such automatic tunnel generation is that of a configuration loop in which the tunnel passes traffic over itself. It is important, once again, to reiterate the impact on the VPN client network of a large number of routing peering adjacencies that result from a complete mesh of tunnels; this scenario can result in a negative impact on routing efficiency.

An additional concern with GRE tunneling is the capability of traffic classification mechanisms to identify traffic with a fine enough level of granularity, and not become a hindrance to forwarding performance. If the traffic classification process used to identify packets (which are to be forwarded across the tunnel) interferes with the router's capability to maintain acceptable packet-per-second forwarding rates, then this becomes a performance liability.

Privacy of the network remains an area of concern because the tunnel is still vulnerable; privacy is not absolute. Packets that use GRE formatting can be injected into the VPN from third-party sources. To ensure a greater degree of integrity of privacy of the VPN, it is necessary to deploy ingress filters that are aligned to the configured tunnel structure, further adding to the administrative overheads of VPN management.

It is also necessary to ensure that the CPE routers are managed by the VPN service provider, as the configuration of the tunnel endpoints is a critical component of the overall architecture of integrity of privacy. However, most VPN service providers are reluctant to add CPE equipment to their asset inventory and to undertake remote management of such CPE equipment, due to the high operational overheads and poor capital efficiencies typical of CPE deployment. Arguably, one might suggest that having a dedicated CPE router to support the VPN attachment defeats one of the basic premises of constructing a VPN, which is the use of shared infrastructure as a means of reducing overall network service cost.

VPNs can be constructed using tunnels without the explicit knowledge of the host network provider, and the VPN can span numerous host networks without any related underlying agreements between the network operators to mutually support the overlay VPN. Such an architecture is little different from provider-operated VPN architectures; the major difference lies in the issue of traffic and performance engineering and the administrative boundary of the management of the VPN overlay. Independently configured VPN tunnels can result in injection of routes back into the VPN in a remote location, which can cause traffic to traverse the same link twice—once in an unencapsulated format and again within a tunnel. This can lead to adverse performance impacts.

This form of overlay VPN also has no control over which path is taken within the common host network, nor the stability of that path. This scenario can lead to adverse performance impacts on the VPN. Aside from the technology aspects of this approach, the major issue is one of whether the VPN management is outsourced to the network provider, or undertaken within administrative functions of the VPN.

One of the more serious considerations in building a VPN on tunneling is that there is virtually no way to determine the cost of the route across a tunnel, because the true path is masked by the cut-through nature of the tunnel. This situation could ultimately result in highly suboptimal routing, meaning that a packet could take a path determined by the cut-through mechanism, which is excessively suboptimal, although native per-hop routing protocols might find a much more efficient method to forward the packets to their destinations.

Virtual Private Dial Networks (VPDNs)

Although several technologies (vendor-proprietary mechanisms as well as open, standards-based mechanisms) are available for constructing a virtual private dial network (VPDN), there are two principal methods of implementing a VPDN that appear to be increasing in popularity—L2TP and PPTP tunnels. From a historical perspective, L2TP is the technical convergence of the earlier L2F protocol specification and the PPTP protocol. However, one might suggest that because PPTP is now being bundled into the desktop operating system of many of the world's personal computers, it stands to be quite popular within the VPN market.

At this point it is worthwhile to distinguish the difference between *client-initiated* tunnels and *NAS-initiated* (Network Access Server, otherwise known as a dial access server) tunnels. The former is commonly referred to as *voluntary* tunneling, whereas the latter is commonly referred to as *compulsory* tunneling. In voluntary tunneling, the tunnel is created at the request of the user for a specific purpose; in compulsory tunneling, the tunnel is created without any action from the user, and without allowing the user any choice in the matter.

L2TP AND PPTP

L2TP, as a compulsory tunneling model, is essentially a mechanism to *off load* a dial-up subscriber to another point in the network or to another network altogether. In this scenario, a dial-up subscriber dials into a NAS, and based on a locally configured profile (or a NAS negotiation with a policy server) and successful authentication, a L2TP tunnel is dynamically established to a predetermined endpoint, where the subscriber's PPP session is terminated, as indicated in Figure 12.7.

PPTP, as a voluntary tunneling model, on the other hand, allows end-systems (for example, desktop computers) to configure and establish individual discrete point-to-point tunnels to arbitrarily located PPTP servers, without the intermediate NAS participating in the PPTP negotiation and subsequent tunnel establishment. In this scenario, a dial-in subscriber dials into a NAS; however, the PPP session is terminated on the NAS as in the traditional PPP model. The layered PPTP session then is established between the client end-system and any arbitrary upstream PPTP server that the client desires to connect to. The only caveats on PPTP connectivity are that the client can reach the PPTP server via conventional routing, and that the user has been granted the appropriate tunnel access privileges on the PPTP server, as indicated in Figure 12.8.

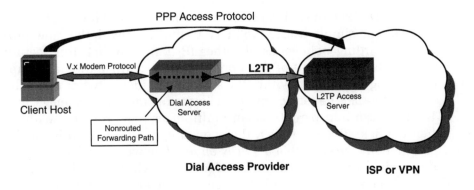

Figure 12.7 L2TP-based VPDN.

While L2TP and PPTP may sound extraordinarily similar, there are some subtle differences that deserve further examination. The applicability of either protocol is very much dependent on what problem is being addressed. It is also about control: Who has it, and why it is needed.

With PPTP in the voluntary tunneling implementation, the dial-in user can choose the PPTP tunnel destination (the PPTP server) after the initial access PPP negotiation has completed. This feature is important if the tunnel destination changes, as no modifications are necessary to the client's view of the base PPP access following a change in the PPTP server, or following a change of the transit tunnel path from the client to the server. It is also a significant advantage that the PPTP tunnels are transparent to the service provider, and no advance configuration is required between the NAS operator and the

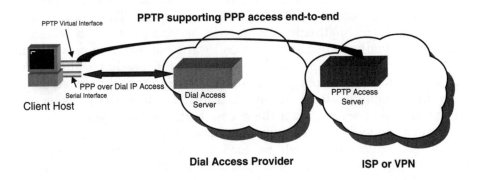

Figure 12.8 PPTP-based VPDN.

overlay dial access VPN. In such a case, the service provider does not house the PPTP server and simply passes the PPTP traffic along with the same processing and forwarding policies as all other IP traffic. In fact, this feature should be considered a benefit of this approach. The configuration and support of a tunneling mechanism within the service provider network would be one less parameter that the service provider has to operationally manage, and the PPTP tunnel can transparently span multiple service providers without any explicit configuration. However, the economic downside to this for the service provider, of course, is that a *VPDN-enabled* network service could be marketed and yield an additional source of revenue. Where the client undertakes the VPDN connection, there is no direct service provider involvement and no value added to the base access service.

From the subscriber's perspective, this is a win-win situation, because the client is not reliant on the upstream service provider to deliver the VPDN service—at least no more than any client is reliant on an ISP for basic IP-level connectivity. The other win is that the subscriber does not have to pay a higher subscription fee for a VPN service. Of course, the situation changes when the service provider takes an active role in providing the VPDN service, such as housing the PPTP servers, or if the subscriber resides within a subnetwork in which the parent organization wants the network to make the decision concerning where PPTP tunnels are terminated. The major characterization of PPTP-based VPDN is one of a roaming client base, where the clients of the VPDN use a local connection to the public Internet data network and then overlay a private data tunnel from the client's system to the desired remote service point. Another perspective is to view this approach as *on-demand* VPDN virtual circuits.

With L2TP, in a compulsory tunneling implementation, the service provider controls where the access PPP session is terminated. This setup can be extremely important in situations where the service provider to whom the subscriber is actually dialing into (let's call it the *modem pool provider* network) must transparently hand off the subscriber's PPP session to another network (let's call this network the *content provider*). To the subscriber, it appears as though the local system is directly attached to the content provider's network, when in fact the access path has been passed transparently through the modem pool provider's network to the subscribed content service. Very large content providers, for instance, may outsource the provisioning and maintenance of thousands of modem ports to a third-party provider, who in turn agrees to pass the subscriber's traffic back to the content provider. This setup is generally termed *wholesale dial*. The major motivation for such L2TP-based wholesale dial lies in the typical architecture of the PSTN network. The PSTN network is constructed in a hierarchical fashion, in which a local PSTN exchange directly connects a set of PSTN subscribers, which is in turn connected via a trunk bearer to a central office or metropolitan exchange that may be connected to a larger regional office or major exchange. A very efficient means of terminating large volumes of data PSTN calls is to use a single common call termination point within the local or central exchange to terminate all local data PSTN calls, and then hand the call data over to a client service provider using high-volume data transmission services. The cost efficiencies that can result from adoption of this architecture form a large part of the motivation for such L2TP-based VPDNs, so a broad characterization of the demand for this style of VPDN can be characterized as a wholesale/retail dial access structure. Another perspective is to view this approach as *static* VPDN access.

Of course, if all subscribers connecting to the modem pool provider's network are destined for the same content provider, then there are easier ways to hand this traffic off to the content provider's network. This could take the form of simply aggregating all of the dial access traffic in the local Central Office, and handing the content provider a single aggregate datastream. However, in situations when the modem pool provider is providing a wholesale dial service for multiple upstream next-hop networks, the methods of determining how each subscriber's traffic needs to be forwarded are somewhat limited. Packet forwarding decisions could be made at the NAS, based on the source address of the dial-up subscriber's computer, allowing for traffic to be forwarded along the appropriate path to its ultimate destination, in turn intrinsically providing a virtual connection. However, the use of assigning static IP addresses to dial-in subscribers is highly discouraged due to the inefficiencies in IP address utilization policies, and the critical success of Dynamic Host Configuration Protocol (DHCP) [RFC2131] has made static IP address allocation to dial-up subscribers essentially a relic of earlier days.

However, some serious scaling issues must be considered when deploying a large-scale L2TP network. These concerns revolve around the issue of whether large numbers of tunnels can actually be supported with little or no network performance impact. Since there have been no large-scale deployments of this technology to date, no empirical evidence exists to support or invalidate these concerns.

In some cases, however, appearances are everything; some content providers do not want their subscribers to know that when they connect to their service, they have instead been connected to another service provider's network and then passed along ultimately to the service to which they are subscribed. In other cases, it is merely designed to be a matter of convenience, so that subscribers do not need to log into a device more than once.

Regrettably, the L2TP protocol draft does not detail all possible implementations or deployment scenarios for the protocol. The basic deployment scenario is quite brief when compared to the rest of the document, and is arguably biased toward the compulsory tunneling model. Nonetheless, there are implementations of L2TP that follow the voluntary tunneling model. To the best of our knowledge, there has never been any intent to exclude this model of operation. In addition, at various recent interoperability workshops, several different implementations of a voluntary L2TP client have been modeled. Nothing in the L2F protocol would prohibit deploying it in a voluntary tunneling manner, but to date it has not been widely implemented. Further, PPTP has also been deployed using the compulsory model in a couple of specific vendor implementations.

In summary, consideration of whether PPTP or L2TP is more appropriate for deployment in a VPDN depends on whether the determination is made that control needs to lie with the service provider or with the subscriber. Indeed, the difference can be characterized as to the client of the VPN, in which the L2TP model is one of a wholesale access provider, who has a number of configured client service providers who appear as VPNs on the common dial access system, whereas the PPTP model is a one of distributed private access in which the client is an individual end user, and the VPN structure is that of end-to-end tunnels. One might also suggest that the difference is also a matter of economics, because the L2TP model allows the service provider to actually provide a *value-added* service, beyond basic IP-level connectivity, and charge its subscribers accordingly for the privilege of using it, thus creating new revenue streams. By contrast, the PPTP model enables distributed reach of the VPN at a more basic level, enabling corporate VPNs to extend access capabilities without the need for explicit service contracts with a multitude of network access providers.

Network Layer Encryption

Encryption technologies are extremely effective in providing the segmentation and virtualization required for VPN connectivity and can be deployed at almost any layer of the protocol stack. The evolving standard for network layer encryption in the Internet is IPSec (IP Security). Although the IPSec architecture and its associated protocols are being finalized in the Internet Engineering Task Force (IETF), there is relatively little network layer encryption being done in the Internet today. However, some vendor proprietary solutions are currently in use.

IPSec is actually an architecture—a collection of protocols, authentication, and encryption mechanisms. The IPSec security architecture is described in detail in "Security Architecture for the Internet Protocol," draft-ietf-ipsec-arch-sec-02.txt, S. Kent, R. Atkinson, November 1997. Additional information on IPSec can be found on the IETF IPSec home page, located at www.ietf.org/html.charters/ ipsec-charter.html.

Although IPSec has yet to be deployed in any significant volume, it is worthwhile to review the two methods in which network layer encryption is predominantly implemented. The most secure method for network layer encryption to be implemented is end-to-end, between participating hosts. This allows for the highest level of security. The alternative is more commonly referred to as *tunnel mode*, where the encryption is only performed between intermediate devices (routers), and traffic between the end-system and the first-hop router is in plaintext. This setup is considerably less secure, because traffic intercepted in transit between the first-hop router and the end-system could be compromised.

As a more general observation on this security vulnerability, where the VPN architecture is based on tunnels, the addition of encryption to the tunnel still leaves the tunnel ingress and egress points vulnerable, because these points are logically part of the host network as well as being part of the unencrypted VPN network. Any corruption of the operation, or interception of traffic in the clear, at these points will compromise the privacy of the private network.

In the end-to-end encryption scheme, VPN granularity is to the individual end-system level. In the tunnel mode scheme, the VPN granularity is to the subnetwork level. Traffic that transits the encrypted links between participating routers, however, is considered secure. Network layer encryption, to include IPSec, is merely a subset of VPN requirements.

Link-Layer VPNs

One of the most straightforward methods of constructing VPNs is to use the transmission systems and networking platforms for the physical and link-layer connectivity, yet still be able to build discrete networks at the network layer. A link-layer VPN is intended to be a close (or preferably exact) functional analogy to a conventional private data network.

ATM and Frame Relay Virtual Connections

A conventional private data network uses a combination of dedicated circuits from a public carrier, together with an additional private communications infrastructure, to construct a network that is completely self-contained. Where the private data network exists within private premises, the network generally uses a dedicated private wiring plant to carry the VPN. Where the private data network extends outside the private boundary of the dedicated circuits, it is typically provisioned from a larger public communications infrastructure, using some form of time-division and/or frequency-division multiplexing to create the dedicated circuit. The essential characteristic of such circuits is the synchronization of the data clock, so that the sender and receiver pass data at a clocking rate, which is fixed by the capacity of the dedicated circuit.

A link-layer VPN attempts to maintain the critical elements of this self-contained functionality, while achieving economies of scale and operation by utilizing a common switched public network infrastructure. Thus, a collection of VPNs may share the same infrastructure for connectivity and share the same switching elements within the interior of the network, but explicitly must have no visibility, either direct or inferred, of one another. Generally, these networks operate at Layer 3 (the network layer) or higher in the OSI reference model, and the infrastructure itself commonly consists of either a Frame Relay or ATM network, as indicated in Figure 12.9. The essential difference here between this architecture of virtual circuits and that of dedicated circuits is that there is now no synchronized data clock shared by the sender and receiver, nor necessarily is there a dedicated transmission path, which is assigned from the underlying common host network. The sender generally has no prior knowledge of the available capacity of the virtual circuit, as the capacity varies in response to the total demand placed on it by other simultaneous transmission and switching activity. Instead, the sender and receiver can use adaptive clocking of data, in which the sender can adjust the transmission rate to match the requirements of the application and any signaling received from the network and the receiver. It should be noted that a dedicated circuit system using synchronized clocking cannot be oversubscribed, whereas the virtual circuit architecture (in which the sender does not have a synchronized end-to-end data clock) can indeed be oversubscribed. It is the behavior of the network when it transitions into this oversubscribed state, which is of most interest here.

One of the nice things about a public-switched wide area network that provides virtual circuits is that it can be extraordinarily flexible. Most subscribers to Frame Relay services, for example, have subscribed to the service for economic reasons; it is cheap, and the service provider usually will throw in a Service Level Agreement (SLA) that *guarantees* some percentage of frame delivery in the Frame Relay network itself.

The remarkable thing about this service offering is that the customer is generally completely unaware of whether the service provider can actually deliver the contracted service at all times and under all possible conditions. The Layer 2 technology is not a synchronized clock blocking technology in which each new service flow is accepted or denied based on the absolute ability to meet the associated resource demands. Each additional service flow is accepted into the network and carried on a best-effort basis. Admission functions provide the network with a simple two-level discard mechanism that allows a graduated response to instances of overload; however, when the point of saturated overload is reached within the network, all services will be affected.

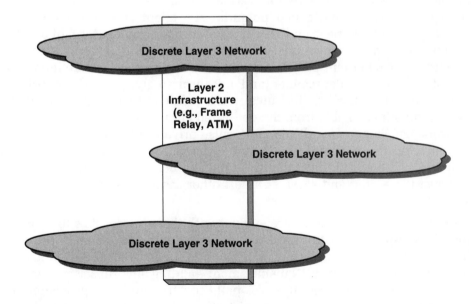

Figure 12.9 Virtual circuit-based VPN.

This situation brings up several other important issues. The first concerns the engineering practices of the Frame Relay service provider. If the Frame Relay network is poorly engineered and is constantly congested, then this may very well be reflected in the service quality delivered to the subscribers. Having said that, the flexibility of PVCs allow discrete VPNs to be constructed across a single Frame Relay network with a very high degree of integrity. And, in many instances, this scenario lends itself to situations in which the Frame Relay network provider also manages each discrete VPN via a telemetry PVC. Several service providers have *Managed Network Services* (MNS), which provide exactly this type of service.

Although the example revolves around the use of Frame Relay as a link layer mechanism, essentially the same type of VPN mechanics hold true for ATM. As with Frame Relay, no data clock synchronization exists between the sender, the host network, and the receiver. Once again, the quality of the service depends on proper capacity engineering of the network, and no inherent guarantee of service quality is given as an attribute of the technology itself.

The generic observation is that the engineering of Frame Relay and ATM common carriage data networks is typically very conservative. The inherent capabilities of both of these link layer architectures do not permit a wide set of selective responses to network overload, so that in order for the network to service the broadest spectrum of potential VPN clients, the network must provide high-quality carriage and very limited instances of any form of overload. In this way, such networks are typically positioned as a high-quality alternative to dedicated circuit private network architectures, which are intended to operate in a very similar manner (and, not surprisingly, generally are priced as a premium VPN offering). Technically, the architecture of link layer VPNs is almost indistinguishable from the dedicated circuit private data network; the network can support multiple protocols, private addressing, and routing schemes, as the essential significant difference between a dedicated circuit and a virtual link layer circuit is the absence of synchronized clocking between the sender and receiver. In all other aspects, the networks are very similar.

Certainly scaling concerns are evident with these approaches to constructing VPNs, especially with regards to configuration management of provisioning new VCs and routing issues. Configuration management still tends to be one of the sore points in VPN management—adding new subscribers and new VPNs to the network requires VC path construction and provisioning, a tedium that requires ongoing administrative attention by the VPN provider. Also, as already mentioned, full-mesh networks encounter scaling problems, which in turn, results in VPNs being constructed in which partial meshing is done to avoid certain scaling limitations. The liabilities in these cases need to be examined closely, because partial meshing of the underlying link layer network may contribute to suboptimal routing (for example, extra hops due to hub-and-spoke issues or redirects).

These problems apply to all types of VPNs built using an overlay model, and not just to ATM and Frame Relay. Specifically, these issues also apply to GRE tunnels within a network layer VPN.

MPOA (Multi Protocol Over ATM)

Another unique model of constructing VPNs is the use of Multi Protocol Over ATM (MPOA) [ATMF 1997], which uses RFC 1483 encapsulation [RFC 1483]. This VPN approach is similar to other *cut-through* mechanisms in which a particular switched link layer is used to enable all Layer 3 egress points to be only a single hop away from one another.

In this model, the edge routers determine the forwarding path in the ATM switched network, because they have the ability to determine to which egress point packets need to be forwarded. After a network layer reachability decision is made, the edge router forwards the packet onto a Virtual Connection (VC) designated for a particular egress router. However, because the egress routers cannot use Address Resolution Protocol (ARP) for destination address across the cloud, they must rely on an external server for address resolution (ATM address to IP address).

The first concern here is a sole reliance on ATM; this particular model does not encompass any other types of data link layer technologies, rendering the technology less than desirable in a hybrid network. While this may have some domain of applicability within a homogenous ATM environment, when looking at a broader VPN environment that may encompass a number of link layer technologies, this approach offers little benefit to the VPN provider.

Secondly, there are serious scaling concerns regarding full-mesh models of connectivity, where suboptimal network layer routing may result because of cut-through. In addition, the reliance on address resolution servers to support the ARP function within the dynamic circuit framework brings this model to the point of excessive complexity.

The advantage of the MPOA approach is the use of dynamic circuits rather than more cumbersome, statically configured models. The traditional approach to supporting private networks involves extensive manual design and operational support to ensure that the various configurations on each of the bearer switching elements are mutually consistent. The desire within the MPOA environment is to attempt to use MPOA to govern the creation of dynamically controlled edge-to-edge ATM VCs. Although this may offer the carrier operator some advantages in reduced design and operational overhead, it does require the uniform availability of ATM, and in many heterogeneous environments, this is simply not the case.

In summary, this model is another overlay model, with some serious concerns regarding the ability of the model to withstand scaling pressures.

The Virtual Router Concept

There have also been *peer* VPN models introduced, that allow the egress nodes to maintain separate routing tables—one for each VPN—effectively allowing separate forwarding decisions to be made within each node for each distinctive VPN. Although this model is interesting, this also introduces concerns about approaches in which each edge device runs a separate routing process and maintains a separate routing information base (RIB, or routing table) process for each VPN community. It also should be noted that the *virtual router* concept requires some form of packet labeling, either within the header or via some lightweight encapsulation mechanism, in order for the switch to be able to match the packet against the correct VPN routing table. If this label is global, the issue of operational integrity is a relevant concern, although if it is a local label, the concept of label switching and maintenance of edge-to-edge label switching contexts is also a requirement.

Among the scaling concerns are the number of supported VPNs in relation to the computational requirements and the stability of the routing system within each VPN (that is, instability in one VPN affecting the performance of other VPNs served by the same device). The aggregate scaling demands of this model are also significant. Given a change in the underlying physical or link layer topology, the consequent requirement to process the routing update on a per-VPN basis becomes a significant challenge. Use of distance-vector protocols to manage the routing tables would cause a corresponding sudden surge in traffic load, which grows in direct proportion to the number of supported VPNs. The use of link-state routing protocols would require the consequent link-state calculation to be repeated for each VPN, causing the router to be limited by available CPU capacity.

Multi-Protocol Label Switching

One method of addressing this scaling issue is to use VPN labels within a single routing environment, in the same way that packet labels are necessary to activate the correct per-VPN routing table. If local label switching is used, then this is effectively the architecture of an MPLS VPN. It is perhaps no surprise that when presented with two basic approaches to the architecture of the VPN—the use of network layer routing structures and per-packet switching, and the use of link layer circuits and per-flow switching—that the industry would devise a hybrid architecture which attempts to combine aspects of these two approaches. This hybrid architecture is referred to as *Multi-Protocol Label Switching* (MPLS).

The architectural concepts used by MPLS are generic enough to allow it to operate as a peer VPN model for switching technology for a variety of link layer technologies, and in heterogeneous layer 2 transmission and switching environments. MPLS requires protocol-based routing functionality in the intermediate devices, and operates by making the interswitch transport infrastructure visible to the routing. In the case of IP over ATM, each ATM bearer link becomes visible as an IP link, and the ATM switches are augmented with IP routing functionality. IP routing is used to select a transit path across the network, and these transit paths are marked with a sequence of labels that can be thought of as locally defined forwarding path indicators. MPLS itself is performed using a label swapping forwarding structure. Packets entering the MPLS environment are assigned a local label and an outbound interface based on a local forwarding decision. The local label is attached to the packet via a lightweight encapsulation mechanism. At the next MPLS switch, the forwarding decision is based on the incoming label value, in which the incoming local label determines the next hop interface and next hop local label, using a local forwarding table indexed by incoming label. This lookup table is generated by a combination of the locally used IP routing protocol, together with a label distribution protocol, which creates end-to-end transit paths through the network for each IP destination.

The major observation here is that this lightweight encapsulation, together with the associated notion of boundary-determined transit paths, provides many of the necessary mechanisms for the support of VPN structure. MPLS VPNs have not one, but three key ingredients:

- ◆ Constrained distribution of routing information as a way to form VPNs and control inter-VPN connectivity.
- ◆ The use of VPN-IDs, and specifically the concatenation of VPN-IDs with IP addresses, to turn (potentially) nonunique addresses into unique ones.
- ◆ The use of label switching (MPLS) to provide forwarding along the routes constructed via constrained routing and VPN-IDs.

The generic architecture of deployment is that of a label-switched common host network and a collection of VPN environments that use label-defined virtual circuits on an edge-to-edge basis across the MPLS environment. It is not the intention to go into any amount of detail on the MPLS architecture here, apart from noting that each MPLS switch uses a label-indexed forwarding table, in which the attached label of an incoming packet determines the next hop interface and the corresponding label. An example is indicated in Figure 12.10, where a table is illustrated indicating how MPLS virtual circuits are constructed.

Numerous approaches are possible to support VPNs within an MPLS environment. In the base MPLS architecture, the label applied to a packet on ingress to the MPLS environment effectively determines the selection of the egress router, as the sequence of label switches defines an edge-to-edge virtual path. The extension to the MPLS local label hop-by-hop architecture is the notion of a per-VPN global identifier (or *Closed User Group* identifier), which effectively is used within an edge-to-edge context. This global identifier could be assigned on ingress, and then used as an index into a per-VPN routing table to determine the initial switch label. On egress from the MPLS environment, the CUG identifier would be used again as an index into a per-VPN global identifier table to undertake next hop selection. Routing protocols in such an environment need to carry the CUG identifier to trigger per-VPN routing contexts.

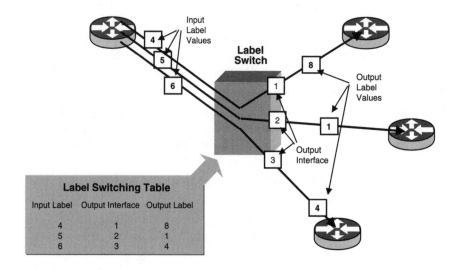

Figure 12.10   MPLS VPN.

It should be stressed that MPLS itself, as well as the direction of VPN support using MPLS environments, is still within the area of active research, development, and subsequent standardization within the forum of the IETF, so that this approach to VPN support is still somewhat speculative in nature.

Link Layer Encryption

As mentioned previously, encryption technologies are extremely effective in providing the segmentation and virtualization required for VPN connectivity and can be deployed at almost any layer of the protocol stack. No industry standards exist, per se, for link layer encryption, thus all link layer encryption solutions are generally vendor specific and require special encryption hardware.

Although this scenario can avoid the complexities of having to deal with encryption schemes at higher layers of the protocol stack, it can be economically prohibitive, depending on the solution adopted. In vendor-proprietary solutions, multivendor interoperability is certainly a genuine concern.

Transport and Application Layer VPNs

Although VPNs certainly can be implemented at the transport and application layers of the protocol stack, it is not very common. The most prevalent method of providing virtualization at these layers is to use encryption services at either layer. For example, encrypted e-mail transactions, or perhaps authenticated Domain Name System (DNS) zones, transfer between different administrative name servers, as described in DNSSec (Domain Name System Security) [RFC 2065].

Some interesting, and perhaps extremely significant, work is being done in the IETF to define a Transport Layer Security (TLS) protocol, which would provide privacy and data integrity between two communicating applications. The TLS protocol, when finalized and deployed, would allow applications to communicate in a fashion designed to prevent eavesdropping, tampering, or message forgery. It is unknown at the time of this writing, however, how long it may be before this work is finalized, or if it will be embraced by the networking community as a whole once the protocol specification is completed.

The significance of a *standard* transport layer security protocol, however, is that once implemented, it could provide a highly granular method for the virtualizing communications in TCP/IP networks, thus making VPNs a pervasive commodity and native to all desktop computing platforms.

Non-IP VPNs

Although this chapter has focused on TCP/IP and VPNs, it is recognized that multiprotocol networks also may have requirements for VPNs. Most of the same techniques previously discussed here also can be applied to multiprotocol networks, with a couple of obvious exceptions—a number of the techniques described here are solely and specifically tailored for TCP/IP protocols.

Controlled route leaking is not suitable for a heterogeneous VPN protocol environment, because it is necessary to support all protocols within the common host network. GRE tunnels, on the other hand, are constructed at the network layer in the TCP/IP protocol stack. However, most *routable* multiprotocol traffic can be transported across GRE tunnels (for example, IPX and AppleTalk). Similarly, the VPDN architectures of L2TP and PPTP both provide a PPP end-to-end transport mechanism, which can allow per-VPN protocols to be supported, with the caveat that it is a PPP-supported protocol in the first place.

The reverse of heterogeneous VPN protocol support is also a VPN requirement in some cases, where a single VPN is to be layered above a heterogeneous collection of host networks. The most pervasive method of constructing VPNs in multiprotocol networks is to rely upon application layer encryption, which is generally vendor proprietary, although some would contend that one of the most pervasive examples of this approach was the mainstay of the emergent Internet in the 1970s and 1980s—that of the UUCP network, which was (and remains) an open technology.

Quality of Service Considerations

As well as creating a segregated address environment to allow private communications, there is also the expectation that the VPN environment will be in a position to support a set of service levels. Such per-VPN service levels may be specified either in terms of a defined service level that the VPN can rely upon at all times, or in terms of a level of differentiation that the VPN can draw upon the common platform resource with some level of priority of resource allocation.

Using dedicated leased circuits, a private network can establish fixed resource levels available under all conditions. Using a shared switched infrastructure, such as Frame Relay virtual circuits or ATM virtual connections, a similar intent is to provide a quantified service level to the VPN through the characteristics of the virtual circuits used to implement the VPN.

When the VPN is moved away from such a circuit-based switching environment to that of a general Internet platform, is it possible for the Internet Service Provider to offer the VPN a comparable service level that attempts to quantify (and possibly guarantee) the level of resources which the VPN can draw upon from the underlying host Internet?

This area is undergoing rapid evolution, and much of this area remains within the realm of speculation rather than a more concrete discussion about the relative merits of various Internet Quality of Service (QoS) mechanisms. Efforts within the Integrated Services Working Group of the IETF have resulted in a set of specifications for the support of guaranteed and controlled load end-to-end traffic profiles using a mechanism that loads per-flow state into the switching elements of the network [RFC 2211, RFC 2212]. There are a number of caveats regarding the use of these mechanisms, in particular relating to the ability to support the number of flows that will be encountered on the public Internet [RFC 2208]. Such caveats tend to suggest that these mechanisms will not be those ultimately adopted to support service levels for VPNs in very large networking environments.

If the scale of the public Internet environment does not readily support the imposition of a per-flow state to support guarantees of service levels for VPN traffic flows, the alternative query is whether this environment could support a more relaxed specification of a differentiated service level for overlay VPN traffic. Here, the story appears to offer more potential, because differentiated service support does not necessarily imply the requirement for per-flow state, so that stateless service differentiation mechanisms can be deployed, which offer greater levels of support for scaling the differentiated service [ID1998j]. However, the precise nature of these differentiated service mechanisms and their capability to be translated to specific service levels to support overlay VPN traffic flows still remain in the area of future activity and research.

The VPN Service Market

In a very generic sense, the preceding descriptions of the ways in which to construct VPNs can be summarized with the observation that there are two approaches to the VPN service market: The VPN is created as a set of end-to-end states without the active involvement of the underlying ISP (or ISPs), or the VPN is created by the ISP itself, as some form of state held within the network.

From the perspective of the ISP, the latter approach is generally the preferred one. Note that Internet carriage services are essentially a commodity service, in which price becomes the dominant market factor. This admits relatively low levels of added value to basic carriage-bit transmission services and leaves the ISP sector operating within a regime where competitive pricing pressure reduces revenue levels down to minimal returns on invested capital. To break out of this mold, the ISP must increase the value proposition that the ISP's service offers to the customer base, and the VPN is certainly one way the ISP can offer value-added services to its corporate clients.

The initial step is to offer cost-effective service alternatives to existing client-operated services. As noted, the essential value proposition of the VPN is one of reducing the operating cost of communications services. The value proposition as proposed by the ISP-operated VPN to the corporate client is to not only provide the opportunity to use shared infrastructure and reap communications cost benefits through the use of such aggregated service platforms, but, in operating the VPN for the client, the VPN is attempting to undertake some of the service role that would normally be done by the client. The preferred position of the VPN is to operate the corporate network services for the client, including carriage services, messaging services, intranet content services, and so on and, indeed, to offer IT-based solutions to the client, which obviate the need for the client to operate networking services in house. The preferred base for the ISP to undertake this service function is via the systems already deployed to support public Internet access, which include services such as carriage, message delivery, content platforms, and support of commerce transactions. The desired approach from the ISP is to undertake a level of VPN support that can provide a *soft partitioning* of these service operations, so that the various VPN client-based services can be operated with both integrity and with predictable (and potentially guaranteed) service levels that match the client's expectations.

In this way, the ISP positions itself as a strategic partner of the client, offering a set of services that extend well beyond the basic carriage service, enhancing the value of the relationship.

From this perspective, the value relationship that underpins the VPN market is one in which the client gains access into a larger scale carriage and IT service operation, and by outsourcing its requirements in this activity area to a VPN provider, the client anticipates reduced cost with no degradation of the quality or integrity of the operation. This may address other issues for the client, such as securing in-house skills to manage such IT services or the deployment of capital to address IT solutions rather than core business needs. From the VPN provider's perspective, the provider gains access into new market sectors, which allows it to increase the value of the offered service, breaking out of basic commodity Internet carriage operations, which is the traditional service model for many corporate clients. This relationship is depicted in Figure 12.11. The size of this VPN service market worldwide is estimated to be valued at some U.S. $1.5 billion in 1998, and various industry projections place this market at between U.S. $8 billion and U.S. $10 billion by 2001.

Another dimension to the VPN market is that of enhancing the reach of the corporate network. This is germane to both the permanent access and dial access markets, in which the client has the desire to use the wide reach of the public Internet to extend the spread of the existing corporate network using the cost efficiencies of Internet-based carriage as the mechanism for such extension. In this environment, it is not necessarily the case that a single ISP will have the span of network coverage to offer VPN services either, and indeed, it is often the case that the reach requirements will extend across multiple ISP service areas.

One means of addressing this requirement is that the client may elect to use client-operated VPN-based technologies, such as end-host–initiated secure tunneling. In each location, the client purchases public Internet access services and then uses secure (and presumably encrypted) end-to-end tunnels to link the remote location back to the corporate network. Here, the savings for the client is the difference between Internet access tariffs and more traditional leased circuit services and call management systems, although this savings is offset by a slightly more complex remote access environment that uses tunnel management as the essential technology. This type of environment is indi-

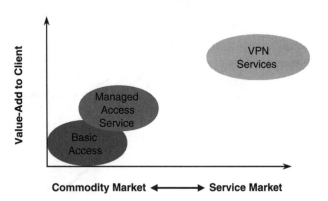

Figure 12.11   VPNs and the service environment.

cated in Figure 12.12. Note that this environment can be made relatively secure, because the tunnel initiation and encryption can use robust security measures to ensure that only trusted end stations can complete connections to the corporate network. The disadvantage of this type of approach is that the client cannot negotiate any form of service quality to support such connections, and although the mechanism may be functionally robust, the end-to-end service quality may be inadequate to support the client's application environment.

Alternatively, the client may elect to use an ISP-based VPN service. To offer the desired range of remote access to the client, the ISP may need to provision a VPN that spans a number of ISPs. Such endeavors of multi-ISP VPNs are currently in the area of active development of the ISP service portfolio. ISPs may use different architectures to support VPN operations, and creating a single robust VPN architecture from often disparate components remains a challenge to network engineers. The current ISP support mechanisms associated with global roaming for dial access could be tuned to support VPDN mechanisms, although the participating ISPs would need to adopt compatible approaches with dial access authentication control and associated dial profiles. These

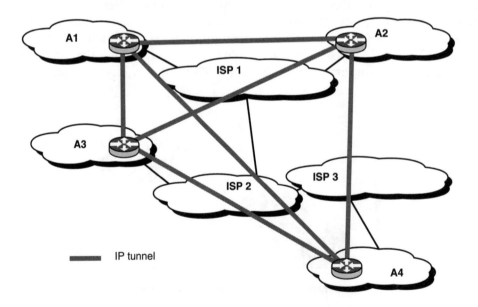

Figure 12.12   Client-managed VPN network extension.

profiles load VPDN support, and ISP consortiums marketing such common VPDN solutions will quickly proliferate over the coming months.

Multi-ISP VPN support has a number of dimensions, and in addition to basic compatibility of VPN support structures, an attendant issue exists regarding managing the resulting quality of the VPN environment across multiple ISPs. A larger issue exists regarding transitivity of quality of service mechanisms across ISPs—both the sense of technical compatibility and the issue of interprovider settlement of quality-distinguished traffic—which will require some form of resolution to allow such consortium-based approaches to extend beyond the VPDN environment to a more embracing VPN range of solutions. The network-mediated VPN also has a deep issue of confidence in trust models, which much be addressed. In a network-initiated VPN, the remote ISP has the capability to initiate access into the client's private network. If no direct contractual relationship between the remote ISP and the client exists, how can the client place any degree of trust in such remote access requests? How can the client validate the bona fides of the remote ISP access request as being a trusted agent of the local contracted ISP and trust that the access request is from a genuine member of the client's VPN?

This area of the multi-ISP VPN likely is one that will receive significant attention over the coming months as the business requirements for each, as well as price performance and service, start to enter into the VPN arena.

Summary

So what *is* a Virtual Private Network? As we have discussed, a VPN can take several forms. A VPN can be between two end-systems, or it can be between two or more subnetworks. A VPN can be built using tunnels, encryption (at essentially any layer of the protocol stack), or both. A VPN can consist of networks connected to a service provider's network by leased lines, Frame Relay, or ATM, or a VPN can consist of dial-up subscribers connecting to centralized services or other dial-up subscribers.

The pertinent conclusion here is that although a VPN can take many forms, a VPN is built to solve some basic common problems, which can be listed as virtualization of services and segregation of communications to a closed community of interest, while simultaneously exploiting the financial opportunity of economies of scale of the underlying common host communications system.

To borrow a popular networking axiom, "When all you have is a hammer, everything looks like a nail." Every organization has its own problem that it must solve, and each of the tools mentioned here can be used to construct a certain type of VPN to address a particular set of functional objectives. More than one hammer can address these problems, and network engineers should know that VPNs are an area in which many people use the term generically; there is a broad problem set with equally as many possible solutions. Each solution has a number of strengths and a number of weaknesses and vulnerabilities. No single mechanism exists for VPNs, which will supplant all others in the months and years to come, but instead, we will continue to see a diversity of technology choices in this area of VPN support.

VPNs will be a significant component of the ISP service offering, designed to extend the ISP service portfolio beyond simple commodity-based services into an area of value-added services. Real synergies exist between corporate clients who are seeking IT solutions that lever price, performance, and skills in operating complex services from the ISP, and ISPs who are seeking solution-based services, which add significant value to the relationship with the client.

chapter thirteen

ISP Business Plans

Although technical capability and an optimistic frame of mind are excellent ingredients for an ISP enterprise, in themselves they are not enough to ensure business success as an ISP. Business success demands the rigor of business planning, understanding how costs are incurred, how products are marketed, how revenue is generated, and ultimately, how financial returns are made on business investments. In this chapter, we examine the business side of the ISP enterprise, looking critically at the area of cost identification and pricing policies within the overall discipline of a business plan.

Some facets of the ISP business profile appear to be constant aspects of this sector. One of the most critical is that of management of growth. In most parts of the world, the Internet activity base is growing at rates of between 6 and 10 percent every month. One of the major risks of market share decline for any ISP is the inability to grow the business at the rate of the growth of the market. Failure to grow at the rate of market growth calls in competitive ISPs, who can establish a strong presence based on filling this unmet demand. Another factor, particularly common in the smaller ISP sector, is the inability to apply good business management principles to the ISP operation, relying instead on a set of technical skills to see the business through. A large number of small businesses fail in their first year of operation, and the ISP sector, despite the promises of robust growth, appears to have no exemption from this general mode of operation, although the rapid market growth for ISP business is perhaps a slightly more forgiving business environment than many. In any case, the major cause of business failure is poor business planning and execution.

The aim of a business plan is not to define a detailed operations plan that must be slavishly followed to every detail. The business plan is intended to describe the viability of the enterprise, chart the likely directions of the enterprise, and identify issues posing business risks to the enterprise. The timeline

497

contained in a business plan is also approximate and is intended more to indicate major milestones in the progress of the enterprise, rather than to set very tight deadlines on activities, particularly those affected by external forces. Obviously, the business plan is not a single one-time document. The plan should be reviewed from time to time and periodically revised to reflect the current state of the enterprise and its current intended direction. This allows various market and service initiatives of the ISP and those of its competitors to be folded into the ISP business plan within a relatively flexible framework. A business plan is not an assured future. A business plan is a guess of a likely future, albeit hopefully a well-structured guess, but nevertheless a guess of a future.

In this chapter, we develop a simple example business plan for an ISP business, highlighting the various steps involved in the process.

The Current ISP Business Climate

The business landscape of the ISP industry is not especially novel in business terms. The business is a service enterprise, purchasing goods and services from various communications and information technology service provider industries, adding a component of technical service and financial competency, and marketing the product into the service marketplace. This business domain is one that is currently characterized by very robust levels of growth in demand, high numbers of enterprises, and quite extraordinary levels of diversity of profiles servicing this demand. The small-business ISP enterprises are competing with very large ISP enterprises, and, increasingly, also competing with large established communications service providers, who are entering the ISP marketplace. Smaller enterprises are often quick to react to market opportunities, and are able to deploy capital and services into emerging markets within a very short time span. In rapidly expanding markets smaller enterprises are often the lead agents in meeting initial demand levels, using their early market leadership as a business asset. Very large established operators are often slow to react to rapidly developing markets. Such enterprises need to address how to redeploy their resources from established lines of business in order to focus on new opportunities. Such enterprises also must address the very uncertain nature of a rapidly changing market, and adequately address the increased level of uncertainties and risks such a shift of activity focus also entails. Typically, the larger players undertake a slower market entry, balancing the relatively higher levels of operational commitment and expertise within their more traditional markets against the opportunities offered by large-scale capital and service investment into the emerging market. The gap between demand and market service levels is filled by smaller operators, who can react very quickly to the opportunities such a situation presents.

Although this represents the picture of the ISP industry in the 1990s, the industry will continue to evolve, probably along lines already well-understood from the evolution of related industry sectors. Ultimately, as the growth in demand tapers off, and as the characteristics of the service model and the value opportunities tend to stabilize, the market itself will start to exhibit some level of stability. In this more stable market of the future, the larger enterprises can bring investment pressure to bear, in order to achieve business cost efficiencies and to secure high levels of competitive market share. The opportunities presented to the smaller players in this second phase are either to rapidly aggregate into larger enterprises in order to compete on approximately equal terms with the larger market entrant, or to realize their market assets by selling off their enterprise to such large market entrants. In most markets, the ultimate outcome of this process is to stabilize the provider industry into a smaller number of large operators, who compete within commonly defined areas of activity, while mutually ensuring that the environment remains a viable area of activity. This is one potential future for the ISP business sector.

However, predictions of market stability within the Internet continue to be confounded by the experience of constant robust growth and evolution in the service models. At what point the ISP market will start to coalesce is still a somewhat open issue. Some observers point to recent ISP consolidation activity in this area as a primary sign that this second phase of business operations has already started. Meanwhile, the continued stream of new ISP enterprises into the ever-expanding market points to continued expansionary activity.

It is within this overall environment that an ISP must phrase a business plan, which offers a desired business outcome for the enterprise, maximizing the opportunities for the enterprise, while attempting to minimize aspects of financial risk.

Step 1—Identify the Objectives

A number of differing objectives exist as to why the ISP is entering the market, and the business plan should reflect such motivations. The business could be positioned as a longer term provider enterprise, looking to establish a significant share of the chosen retail market base. Alternatively, the enterprise could be characterized as a start-up business, looking to develop a market to the point when the business is then in a position to be sold as a viable concern, or to the point where it may be the subject of a public float on the share market. Alternatively, the business may be structured as a stable small-business enterprise, working from a conservative business plan within a well-defined market segment. You must understand the objectives of the enterprise in order to construct a business plan that achieves such desired outcomes.

Competitive Market Entry

It may be that the primary business objective is to rapidly achieve significant market share within a number of nominated market sectors. To achieve this, the ISP may be willing to purchase this market position through leading with a product pricing structure that places the initial operation of the business at an operating loss (loss leading). Generally, one of the major means of determining the ability to operate at a competitive price point is a significant volume of operation. This, in turn, enables economies of scale to be realized within the business. One business plan approach is to enter the market assuming that this position of scale and profitability will be reached in time, and to price the initial market entry of the product according to the longer term business expectation. A business plan along these lines would include the provision for the initial losses, encountered within the startup phase of operation, to be recovered in subsequent trading once critical operational volume has been achieved. This is not unusual within the highly competitive ISP industry, in which loss leading into the market is a very common business practice.

The risk of such a business stance is that the initial growth of the business is at a price that does not cover unit service provision costs. This causes the business loss to multiply, with each new customer placing an additional strain on the initial business capital investment. This situation requires careful management, as investors then are required to take a long-term position of support to the ISP's future outlook. The typical investor position is that such initial operating losses are tolerable, given the opportunity to generate very high rates of return in the future. Unfortunately, the ISP industry outcomes realized so far typically do not appear to possess such rosy hues of shareholder return, and the long-term pricing position within the emerging ISP commodity market is one in which the rates of return are, at best, only marginally positive.

Venture Start-Up

It may be the primary business objective to create a business that is groomed for a future sale of the business, either in the form of a public share float or in the form of a private sale. Again, one of the critical objectives here is rapid growth and the securing of a significant market share or the servicing of a strategically important market sector. Equally important here is the need to secure a particular asset base that provides the enterprise with some inherent value in addition to a basic commodity service operation. This motivation is quite common within the ISP market. However, it is an objective that is not always achieved.

As a broad generalization, very significant acquisitions of ISPs have taken place where the ISP has been able to secure significant proportions of the commercial market sector. Services aimed at this sector need to cover a broad geographic scope and target requirements for value-added services, such as service outsourcing and virtual private networks. Equally important are the services that need to be provided at a price point that results in a positive financial outcome to the ISP business. The frequent outcome is that the highly competitive market forces any ISP attempting to gain strong market share to drop the price into the area of operating loss in order to gain market share. The subsequent challenge, and one that has enjoyed mixed success within the ISP industry, then is to readjust prices to turn the business into a position of positive financial operation while still retaining the customer base.

Cash Flow–Based Growth

The business may be a small-scale enterprise in which the business grows through accumulated cash flow. In this scenario, the financial returns from one operating period are invested back into the business, to allow for business expansion in the next operating period. The growth of the business and the capability to gain economies of scale in such an enterprise is limited by the surplus margins of the business cash flow.

Typically, such enterprises are operated within niche markets with a service portfolio attuned to the niche market's requirements. This is not always a successful strategy, even though it appears to be a financially prudent way to manage a business. If the enterprise is highly successful within the chosen market niche, the business opportunities expand at a faster rate than available investment funds. The business then suffers from undercapitalization and opens the niche market up to competition, through the consequent unmet demand. Such enterprises are also vulnerable to market fluctuations, in which short-term falls in demand make financial calls on the operating reserve and can place the operation into a technically insolvent position, despite a strong activity base. Such vulnerabilities within the cash flow–based operation do make it an ideal fit to the typical fast-growth ISP enterprise.

Evidently, no limit is placed on how small an ISP enterprise can be. One NOC of a major ISP received a call from a mystified user, who complained that he could not reach his local ISP and was appealing for help. The NOC followed up on the fault and finally managed to contact the ISP. The ISP operator's mother answered the call and said that she was sick of the mess in her teenage son's bedroom and had turned off all the equipment in the room. She was not going to turn it back on until he had cleaned up his bedroom!

Step 2—Sizing the Market

The first part of any business planning exercise is to research the size of the potential market within the target areas of operation. For example, an intending residential dial-up provider would examine the number of residences within the target area and their demographic breakdown, including the average disposable income, spending habits, and mean age. For an enterprise looking at services to the commercial sector, a similar study would be undertaken on the number and type of commercial enterprises within the target area. This estimate of total market size then is refined to reflect current levels of demand for the service that currently are being met and the current levels of unmet demand. These numbers provide a benchmark for the immediate levels of opportunity for the enterprise. The planning process also should estimate the growth in demand from this market sector across the period examined in the business plan.

Some five years ago, the figures relating to market size and, more critically, unmet demand were large enough that very little rigor was necessary in this primary research activity intended to identify significant opportunities in the ISP business sector. More recently, the levels of servicing such markets have risen dramatically, and the corresponding outcome is that additional levels of diligence with respect to accuracy are required in the market plan to correctly identify the area of market opportunity for the ISP's product.

This exercise is intended to provide a base level of the size of the target market sector. The next task is to estimate the proportion of this market, which is likely to be gained by this ISP, or market share. This is a business estimate based on competitive positioning and marketing success factors and must include issues such as the following:

- Brand awareness
- Niche marketing (*niche marketing* is defined as marketing to a particular community of common interest or activity, such as healthcare services, educational institutions, and so on)
- Competitive pricing factors
- Additional market entrants
- Level of competitive churn by consumers of the product (*churn* is when an existing client signs over to another service provider)

In general, such estimates of market behavior are the outcome of commercial market surveys. Such surveys should indicate the following:

- Levels of market demand
- Satisfaction with existing service providers
- Activity patterns and related characteristics of the market sector

It is not within the scope of this book to advise how this market research should be conducted, aside from noting that the level of research and the consequent precision of metrics of the target market should be approximately commensurate with the intended level of initial startup capital being sought.

This part of the business plan is best described as modeling the market. The exercise is intended to expose relationships between marketing initiatives, pricing, service portfolios, service performance levels, and the consequent level of market demand for the ISP's services. The model should allow various assumptions regarding price, marketing, and services to be tested against the likely market response. This allows the business to assess the risks and opportunities of various ISP service initiatives, to a first order level of accuracy.

The outcome of the sales and marketing planning process should be a dynamic model of the target market's size and behavior. Applying a service and pricing structure for the intended ISP operation to this model is necessary, and is intended to indicate estimates of revenue streams for the business. However, pricing is not completely elastic. The ISP does incur costs in the provision and use of such services, and identifying how such costs are incurred and how they impact on pricing models is also necessary.

Step 3—Identifying Costs

Using a level of broad simplification, costs for an ISP operation fall into three major categories:

- Service operations costs
- Sales and marketing costs
- Business operations and administrative costs

A number of methods can be used to identify such costs within the structure of a business plan. A useful structure is to attempt to represent costs on a per-unit basis. The most reasonable metric in such a case is the cost per service in operation (SIO), so that the plan can be adjusted to various market models that project differing SIO outcomes for the ISP. We describe one approach to this model of cost identification in this section, looking at each major sector of expenditure within the ISP activity profile.

Service Operations Costs

This area covers the capital and recurrent costs of operating the ISP service and covers the cost of service delivery platforms, network management systems, carriage services, and network access servers.

Generally, costs within an ISP operation follow a step function, as indicated in Figure 13.1. The ISP buys into a certain capacity of service delivery and then resells this as goods and services. At a threshold of sale level, the ISP should reinvest into a larger scale of operation and again can now resell this additional capacity. The article of optimism within this cyclic exercise is that each time the ISP invests in additional servers and carriage capacity, the augmented size of the purchase allows the ISP access to lower unit costs through economies of scale. The overall direction of expenditure divided by sold volume or true unit cost should be generally downward through each cycle of investment. This is indicated in Figure 13.2.

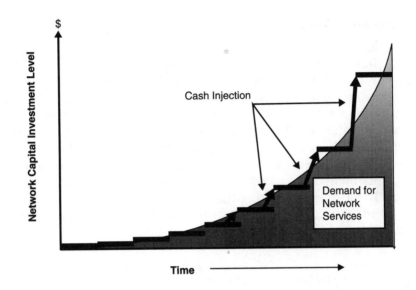

Figure 13.1   ISP cost function.

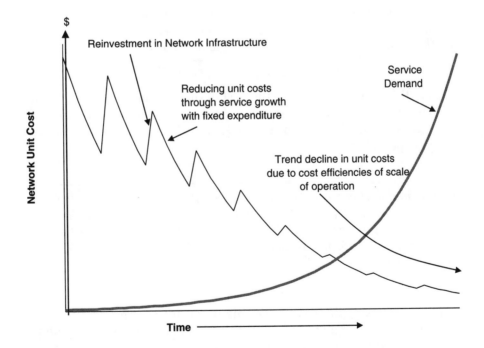

Figure 13.2   ISP unit cost.

Service Delivery Platforms

Equipment has a cost of ownership that can be described by the capital purchase cost, less any recoverable value after the equipment has reached the expiration of its useful service life. This is the *depreciation* of the value of the asset. The business plan can use a *prime cost depreciation schedule*, in which a fixed proportion of the original purchase price is written off the value of the asset at regular intervals. Alternatively, the plan can use a *diminishing value depreciation*, in which a fixed proportion of the residual value is written off the value of the equipment at regular intervals, leaving a new residual value. Added to this depreciation cost is the annual cost of maintenance for the equipment. In terms of translating this cost into a unit cost per SIO, it is necessary to divide this equipment cost by the average number of ISP clients that can be supported on the service platform.

A mail host platform costs $10,000 to configure to support 1000 mail accounts. Assuming a 30 percent prime cost depreciation for the platform, and a $500 per annum maintenance contract, this platform can be configured into the business plan as a recurrent cost to the business of $3500 p.a. with an estimated service life of the platform of 40 months. Assuming one mail account per client service, then the service platform cost per SIO can be estimated to be $3.50 p.a.

Added to this equipment cost is the cost of service operations and customer service. Necessarily, this is an estimate of the system administration tasks to maintain the service, together with the estimate of the number and duration of service calls per client.

The mail host is estimated to cost $8000 p.a. in system administration tasks and is estimated to generate an average of four helpdesk calls per client each year. Each helpdesk call has an average cost of $10. The total platform cost per mail service is estimated to be $51.50 p.a. for each service.

The preceding example is typical of many service operations, in which the major determinant of the cost of the service is the cost of servicing helpdesk calls to answer client queries relating to the service. The service platform itself represents a relatively minor proportion of service costs. The bottom line in terms of service management and cost containment for the ISP lies in the effort to improve unit costs within the business plan. Typically, this is addressed through the attempt to use a management environment that provides self-help to the client through automated interfaces, and positioning a call to helpdesk staff as a last resort.

The total cost of service delivery platforms also should include location costs. Location is typically specified in terms of power budget, air conditioning, and rack unit costs. These need to be converted into a cost per SIO per annum to allow for inclusion within a standard specification of cost within the business plan.

Network Access Equipment

A similar cost exercise can be undertaken for network access equipment supporting dial-in access. The depreciation rate of the equipment must include consideration of a forecast point in time of technical obsolescence of the access modems, so that quite aggressive depreciation rates are often used for such equipment.

The first cost breakdown within a business plan is to arrive at a realistic annual cost per dial access port, using factors of purchase price and depreciation rates for units configured to a particular port configuration. This gives an annual cost per port for dial access. To relate this to a cost per SIO requires the business plan to make a judgment regarding the quality of the service. If the ratio of clients to ports is too high (a ratio of 20:1 is definitely considered unacceptably high in most situations), the clients' perception of service quality declines rapidly. Customer churn is a typical outcome, in which customers actively seek alternate ISPs where the probability of having their dial access calls answered by an available modem port is far higher. A client to port ratio of 1:1 allows each client to have dedicated access to a permanently allocated modem, where the modem port is idle when the client is not connected. This option is relatively expensive for the ISP and does not allow the ISP to compete in the mainstream competitive dial-access market. Typical ratios of clients to modem ports for ISPs sit between 5:1 to 10:1 in most dial access markets.

In this example of costing dial access, a 120-modem port access server costs $80,000 to purchase. Depreciation, using a prime cost method, is set to 33 percent p.a., so that the cost of ownership per server unit is $26,666 p.a. Maintenance is purchased at a rate of 7.5

> *percent of purchase cost, so that the maintenance cost in this case is $6000 p.a., making a total equipment cost of $32,666 p.a. Assuming a SIO ratio of 7:1 in terms of client to modem ports, the cost per SIO is some $39 p.a. in access port costs.*

Access routers for permanent client connection can be similarly costed within a business plan, dividing the annual cost of ownership by the number of configured services to derive an access cost per SIO, using a client to port ratio of 1:1 in the calculation. The depreciation rates are typically less aggressive, given that router ports are not subject to the same rapidly evolving technology refinements of modems.

> *In this example of costing permanent network access, a router with a purchase price of $30,000 has a depreciation rate of 25 percent and a maintenance cost of 7.5 percent of the capital cost. The router has eight dedicated ports for use by SIOs and, therefore, has a cost per SIO of $1219 p.a.*
>
> *The same router can be configured with two channelized E1 interfaces, supporting 120 64-Kbps SIOs, in which the access cost per SIO drops to $81 p.a.*

The overall intent of the access router architecture is to minimize the annual cost per SIO, and the most effective way to do this is to increase the port density. Channelized services, which multiplex a number of services to a single physical interface, are one of the most effective ways to achieve this.

Network access costs also should factor in costs of distribution and core routers, again using a similar technique of deriving an annual cost of ownership, and then examining the scaling properties of the design. Generally, these components of the business plan are not strictly on a per SIO basis, and the typical method of including such costs into the business plan is on the basis of a cost per POP.

Carriage and Communication Costs

A significant component of the cost structure, particularly for transit ISPs, lies in carriage costs or circuit lease costs from the carriers. These costs are derived from the following:

- The cost of provisioning local dial access for each POP
- The cost of internal carriage services within the ISP's network
- The cost of carriage services to connect to peer and upstream service providers
- The service fees levied by upstream service providers

LOCAL DIAL ACCESS

For the purposes of business planning, formulating costs and revenues within a single common metric is necessary. For local dial access services, the typical carrier cost is installation charges, plus periodic access charges, plus call charges. Although the local access bank should not be performing any calls, the first two charges definitely apply to the ISP enterprise.

Considerable care should be taken in purchasing local dial access services to ensure that the price and technical attributes of the service match the desired service characteristics. Analogue lines may be priced at a lower level, but because of the signal distortion effects of the analogue tail loop, such services generally offer inferior connection speeds and inferior line quality as compared to digital access services. For quality access services, the preferred carrier access service is primary rate ISDN or framed T1, feeding the digital signal to onboard digital signal processors, reducing the second analogue loop to insignificant lengths.

As an example, a 30-channel ISDN primary rate service has an installation fee of $3000 and a monthly rental of $800. The per-hour access costs for the ISP are then $0.88 per hour. If the average occupancy level of the 30-modem bank over a month is 10 calls, the per-hour access costs for the ISP are $2.64 per hour.

CARRIAGE SERVICES

If we assume that cost is incurred by the ISP through the carriage of data, the question posed in business planning is, "What is the marginal cost of data carriage?" The answer is a very helpful, "It depends." If the carriage service costs $100 per month and it carries one megabyte of data in the month, then the cost of carriage of that megabyte is $100. If the same carriage service carries 1000 megabytes in the month, then the cost of carriage is $0.10 per megabyte.

An overly optimistic business plan might forecast that every circuit is loaded completely with data, and the plan could compute unit costs of data carriage based on this expectation. This would be most unwise, and 100 percent line occupancy over an extended period is a good signal of catastrophic service quality failure and that the network is very badly overloaded.

To arrive at a reasonable ratio of data volume to carriage capacity, we must examine the typical behavior of circuits within the Internet environment and derive a load *signature*; hence, a target optimal line occupancy figure.

Currently two primary patterns of usage exist:

- The business market, in which the traffic tends to follow the traffic pattern of business hours, peaking in the weekday afternoon time zones
- The residential market, in which the peaks tend to occur in weekday evenings, with a strong weekend use

These traffic patterns are indicated in Figure 13.3. In both cases, a substantial period of idle capacity exists, corresponding to the period from midnight to 8:00 A.M. and shoulder periods in the morning and early evening, as well as the peak load time intervals. Good network design engineering would place the peak load points at 85–90 percent of available capacity. Higher values would invite heavy peak period congestion, which would degrade service performance just at the point in time where there are the greatest number of connected clients. This results in degraded service levels and causes traffic inefficiencies, which in turn exacerbate the peak congestion load. This then indicates that the average daily line occupancy for an optimally loaded circuit should be between 35–55 percent in most cases.

As an example, a 2.048-Mbps circuit lease costs $15,000 per month. What is the unit cost of data?

A 2-Mbps circuit is clocked at 2,048,000 bits per second and can deliver 22,184,400,000 bytes per 24 hours if operated continuously at the data clock rate. Working on a target line occupancy of 45 percent, this equates to a line capacity of 9,982,980,000 bytes of data. The lease cost for 24 hours is $4931.51, which equates to a cost of 5 cents for each 1,000,000 bytes of data, assuming costs are incurred for traffic moving in one direction only. Assuming that the traffic is bidirectional, and is evenly loaded onto the circuit in each direction, this results in a unit carriage cost of 2.5 cents per million bytes.

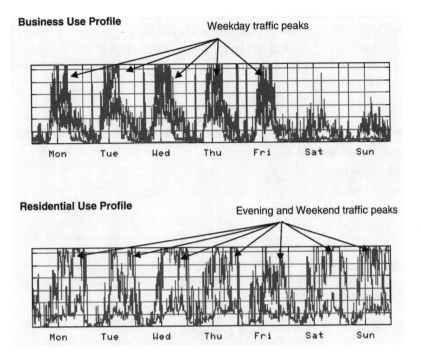

Figure 13.3   Network usage patterns.

This setting of a desired line occupancy level allows an ISP to ascertain the marginal cost of carriage for every circuit, under optimal load conditions.

AVERAGE UNIT CARRIAGE COST

The next exercise is to introduce a model of projected traffic flows to analyze the overall picture of carriage costs for the ISP enterprise. One potential model looks at the average cost of delivering a megabyte of data to a client, by attempting to factor into the cost the various unit costs of each of the circuits in the network, allowing for average traffic flow patterns and allowing for some inefficiency in uniformly loading the network to optimal levels.

In a non-U.S. ISP network, it is quite common to see some 60 percent or more of data to clients being delivered from offshore origins, either through upstream service contracts or international peer structures. The remainder of the delivered data is delivered from local caches, domestic trunking, and local sources. Estimating the proportion of traffic being delivered to the customer is necessary to arrive at an average unit cost of delivered data.

For example, a non-U.S. ISP has unit costs of traffic for various traffic types, as indicated in the following table. The traffic mix delivered to each customer was, on average, according to the proportions indicated in this table.

Traffic Type	Unit Cost per Megabyte	Proportion of Delivered Traffic
Upstream international ISP	50 c	60%
International peers	20 c	8%
Domestic trunks	3 c	5%
Cached	8 c	20%
Local traffic	0.5 c	7%

Multiplying the two values together yields the proportion of cost contribution for each traffic type and enables us to derive the average unit cost of delivered data.

Traffic Type	Cost Component
Upstream international	30 c
International peers	1.6 c
Domestic trunks	0.15 c
Cached	1.6 c
Local traffic	0.03 c

This set of cost components can be added to give the average unit cost of delivered data. In this example, the value of 33 cents per megabyte.

In the example, 90 percent of the unit cost of the carriage service delivered to clients is derived from a single source—the cost of the upstream international ISP connection. The conclusion, for our example ISP, is that managing this single area of cost will have a more significant effect on the business cost of carriage than any other single activity.

The strategy for a non-U.S. ISP is to create an advantaged business position within the chosen market by ensuring that the costs of carriage are minimized, so that the product can be positioned at a level that is priced competitively. Various options are open to the ISP to contain such costs, including the following:

◆ The use of a higher average line occupancy on the offshore circuits, in order to reduce unit costs of these carriage services

◆ The use of aggregation of many offshore upstream purchasing arrangements and consequent multiple traffic flows into single larger flows of higher volumes. Not only does a single large volume flow allow for a higher efficiency of carriage, it also allows the ISP access to lease high-capacity carriage circuits. Both these factors allow the business to achieve lower unit costs of carriage.

◆ The use of satellite circuits may provide a lower cost alternative to undersea fiber-based circuits. This option may have a visible performance impact due to the higher propagation delay of the satellite circuit.

The area of carriage costs is one area of activity where the difference between North American-based ISPs and ISPs operating in other areas of the globe is most evident. In the North American-ISP operation, noncarriage service costs dominate the ISP cost profile, as carriage costs are effectively limited to the components of carriage of domestic trunk costs and local carriage.

Sales and Marketing Costs

Sales and marketing costs are becoming an increasingly critical component of the ISP business profile and are now assuming the same proportions of business expenditure as they consume in any other highly competitive service sector.

The role of sales and marketing activities, from a customer-facing perspective, is threefold:

1. To identify new customers to the ISP and provide a match of the ISP service portfolio to the customer's expectations

2. To encourage churn of customers of competitive ISP operations by indicating the superior attributes of the ISP's operation.

3. To ensure that the ISP's services remain competitive and well matched to the needs of the ISP's clients.

These roles are relatively traditional for the sales and marketing effort, and the roles in this area are intended to provide a constant sales stream to the ISP of new customers and to ensure that the evolving service requirements of existing customers are clearly stated to the ISP's business management area. For an ISP, this area is becoming almost a forced investment, as passive marketing campaigns are now competing against active sales campaigns, making contact with prospective clients and actively identifying the opportunities and benefits of the ISP's services.

However, in this market, another equally valid role exists for marketing, as a feedback channel from the client base to the ISP. In an area that traditionally has been seen as one dominated by technology, the marketing task has been to sell technically oriented products and services. In such an environment, the service client has had to take on a relatively foreign and unforgiving technical set up that was geared to the ISP providing services with minimal additional overhead. Although this was suitable for a marketplace dominated by enthusiasts and the IT sectors of larger academic and corporate enterprises, such a strong technical focus does not make for a mass consumer product suitable for large-scale rollout. This role of marketing is to bring back the service expectations of the potential market to the ISP, to allow the ISP to use the marketing effort as a means of undertaking market research.

The ISP probably will undergo the transformation of roles that has appeared in many other technology-based sectors: Instead of the technology areas producing a particular product, which then is passed to the sales and marketing areas to sell into the market, a more effective direction is for the marketing areas to work closely with the ISP's technical resources in order to construct products and services that are implemented as a much more precise fit to customer expectations. The challenge posed by this approach is to balance the tensions that constantly exist between these two areas of activity. The product specifications phrased from marketing areas often have little regard to feasibility and cost efficiency of the subsequent product and its operation. In contrast, the outcome of a highly technically focused effort often assumes a corresponding base level of technical competency on the part of the customer that is simply unrealistic in a mass-marketed product. (The programming interface of the initial generation of video cassette recorders is often cited as an example of the outcome of such a product development process.) However, the ISP who can successfully manage this product development process will be in a position to create a family of products and services that are well attuned to breaking into new markets for ISP services and exposing the existing customer base to additional services that can enhance the value of their business relationship with the ISP.

Another role of the sales and marketing sector is one of constantly reinforcing to the ISP the view that in the service industry the focus of all activity is to fulfill the customer's service needs. The customer's perceptions of the service levels provided by the ISP will play a large role in customer retention and positive customer referrals, so that emphasizing a focus on customer requirements and promptly responding to customer service needs is a fundamental component of ISP business success.

Business Operations and Administrative Costs

This area encompasses the costs of administrative management of the enterprise, including the costs of support staff, accommodation expenses, and various other business expenditures. These costs normally are a relatively constant proportion of the business activity levels and can be estimated to sufficient accuracy within the scope of planning by a fixed overhead on total financial expenditure.

This area also encompasses the costs of billing and bad debts. Some ISPs adopt a charge in arrears model, where the customer is invoiced for the provision of services after the event. In the telephone world, where this charging model is common, this mode of invoicing certainly increases the costs of the service. In effect, the service provider becomes a credit provider of significant proportions, and the risk of bad debts is quite considerable. Alternatively, ISPs can elect to use advance purchase plans or periodic payment plans, and pass on the saving of the reduced credit risk and reduced operating capital burden to the customer through advance purchase discounts. The cost of this part of the business is often underestimated by many small businesses, and ISP are no exception. The cause of many small business failures is often due to poor billing practices and inadequate credit control, which in turn cause a cash flow crisis within the business, leading to business failure.

Often, ISP enterprises are initiated through an assertion of technical competence in the area of service provision. Although such skills are a core part of the competencies required by any ISP, business management skills are also an essential component of core competencies of any ISP enterprise. The process of business planning should draw upon such skills in the preparation of the plan and should certainly accommodate the costs of business enterprise management within the total operational profile of the business. The tasks required include business administration, accountancy, financial management, and human resources, and the overall intent is to construct a business platform that will allow the operation of technical services in a stable and cost-efficient manner.

ISP Cost Profiles

The general areas we've covered summarize the nature of ISP costs within the structure of a business plan. Note the typical balance of these costs will vary for certain profiles of ISPs, and will vary within various areas of the world.

The first typical profile is that of the dial service operator within North America. For such an operator, service platform operations and customer support occupy a very significant proportion of the total business costs, balanced only by the cost of provisioning dial access. The carriage costs, either as circuit lease costs or as upstream ISP service costs, do not dominate the business plan. Instead, sales and marketing costs take on a significant role within the overall business profile. A typical cost profile for this operation is indicated in Figure 13.4.

This business profile alters for a non-North American operator. Here, it is very typical that the upstream service carriage costs prove to be the most significant expenditure item, potentially absorbing up to 60 percent of the total business costs, depending of course on the location of the business and the circuit tariffs within the ISP's region. The typical cost profile of such an enterprise is indicated in Figure 13.5.

The business profile is again changed for a non-North American transit operator, who provides both domestic and international transit services. Here,

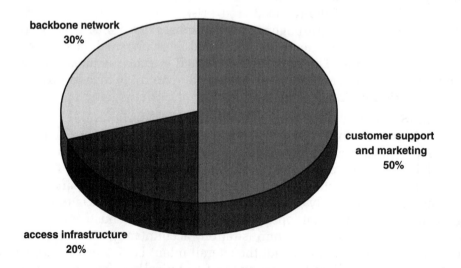

Figure 13.4   Cost profile for a typical U.S. ISP business.

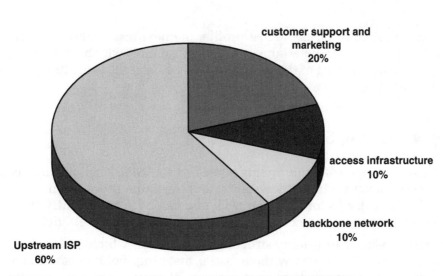

Figure 13.5 Cost profile for a typical non-U.S. ISP business.

the carriage costs dominate the entire profile of the enterprise, and the other business costs have little impact on the overall profile. This cost profile is indicated in Figure 13.6.

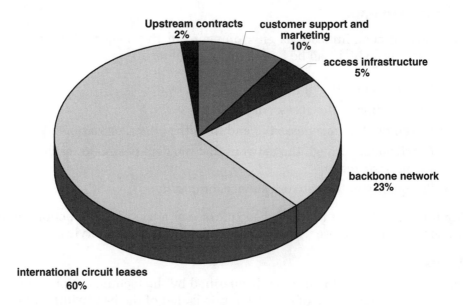

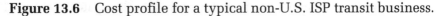

Figure 13.6 Cost profile for a typical non-U.S. ISP transit business.

Given a particular business cost profile, the next task within the business planning process is to determine a pricing structure, which will ensure the competitive positioning of the ISP's services, while at the same time ensuring that the enterprise operates to achieve fiscal objectives.

Step 4—Pricing Structures

In this section, we examine pricing strategies for ISPs. This business is certainly very immature in many respects, and the value proposition presented by the ISP industry sector is still not well understood. Consequently, the value clients are prepared to place on the ISP function is still very elastic.

A wide diversity of pricing structures also exists, which includes hourly charges, fixed-rate charges without usage metering, volume-based charges, and many other forms of charging structures. Of course, one characteristic of a commodity market is that pricing packages become more complex in order to obfuscate direct comparison between competitive service providers, but ISPs also tend to have different objectives to achieve within their approach to the marketplace, and the pricing structure reflects these differing motivations.

Pricing Elements

In a generic communications environment are five major attributes of the access service, which can be folded into a retail tariff:

- The characteristics of the access service, or *access*
- The duration of the access, or *time*
- The amount of data passed to and from the client, or *volume*
- The distance through the network that the data passed to reach the client, or *distance*
- The quality of the network service, or *quality*

Almost any ISP access tariff can be expressed as a compound function involving some, or all, of these five basic attributes of the access service.

Access

The ability to access the Internet is qualified by the technical aspects of such access. The major metric of access circuits is that of the bandwidth of the circuit, as bandwidth of access indicates the peak data flow rates that the client can pass into the network, as well as placing a ceiling on the total volumes of data passed to and from the ISP's network in any period.

Access-based pricing, if used by the ISP as the sole tariff determinant for permanent connections, results in a flat-fee structure, typically indexed by access bandwidth. In terms of administrative cost of operation of such a tariff, this tariff is very efficient to support. Accurately metering a client's use of the ISP's network is not required, and invoicing and payment can be undertaken in advance of service delivery. Such an outcome is favorable for the ISP's business management, particularly in a cash-flow business, as it reduces the risks of bad debt and the amount of credit extended to clients through a metered payment in arrears tariff. The cost of the billing process can be minimized, as the computation of the meter data as input to the billing process is relatively straightforward to implement.

From the client's perspective, a number of advantages are inherent with such an access pricing structure. The client enjoys predictable liability for the service, which, for a corporate client, can be easily incorporated into the client's expenditure budgets. No marginal cost is incurred by the client for access to the service, intended or otherwise. This allows the corporate client to extend Internet access throughout the corporate network without an externally forced requirement to impose access controls or internal metering and cost apportionment to limit the client's service charge liability. For a corporate client, a campus, a public agency, or other medium to large enterprises, such an attribute of the access service tariff is a very powerful incentive, as it is an enabler for administrative efficiencies within the client's network. The client also enjoys an *always on* service with dedicated permanent access. There is no latency to fire up the connection, and the connection is always available. This connection allows the client to house Internet service platforms to extend its scope of business activity into the Internet without incurring unpredictable service charges from the ISP.

Considering these persuasive advantages for flat-rate access-based pricing for permanent connection, it is no surprise that this is a very widely used pricing model in the ISP industry.

However, some weaknesses exist in this pricing model. Given a typical spread of client traffic volumes for any given access speed, the clients see differing unit costs for the service, as indicated in Figure 13.7. The flat fee is effectively an average of the client volumes, and some clients will pass less data than the average. Such clients will be exposed to unit costs of data carriage well in excess of the marginal cost of provision of such carriage, whereas high-volume clients of the same ISP service enjoy unit costs of carriage well below the marginal cost of provision. As is typical within the Internet environment, the ISP's lower volume clients will increase their traffic volumes presented to the ISP, and in a flat-fee structure this will occur without any corresponding change in the ISP's revenues. In an otherwise static environment, the ISP is faced with the issue of increasing data volumes without matching revenue increases. As this additional traffic is placed into the existing ISP carriage infrastructure, this may cause a decline in service level for all clients, decreasing the value proposition the ISP offers to its entire client base. Alternatively, the ISP can augment capacity within the network in response to these increased traffic loads, increasing the ISP's expenditure without any corresponding increase in revenue, decreasing operating margins, and thereby increasing the business risk to the ISP. The only way for the ISP to counterbalance is to increase volumes from existing clients within a flat-fee structure by raising the flat fee to reflect the climbing average usage levels, or com-

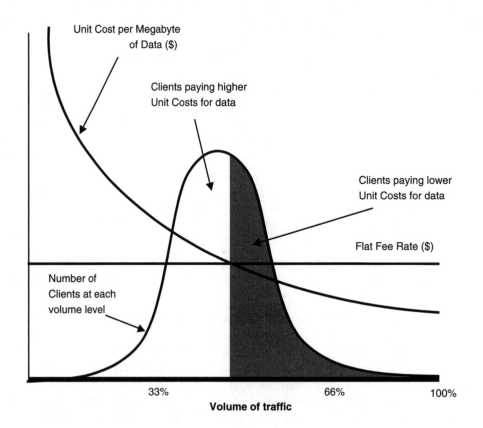

Figure 13.7   Unit costs for a flat-fee service.

plement the flat-fee price structure with a very strong sales and marketing effort to feed new entry-level clients into the business profile, or use the increasing volumes of traffic to attempt to access larger capacity carriage systems that offer the ISP lower unit costs of carriage. Typically, ISPs undertake the latter two actions, although the requirement for a continual stream of entry-level customers to sustain set flat pricing rates is a pricing strategy prone to business failure after market penetration is sufficiently large, and the number of new clients starts to taper down.

Such a flat rate pricing plan also provides no incentive for rational or careful use of the network's resources, because the client's cost is constant regardless of any self-imposed usage profile or usage constraint. To the extent that this pricing mechanism does not provide any incentive for rational use of the network, such a tariff mechanism does not work in the longer term interests of the ISPs. Additionally, this form of tariff does not expose the user to the marginal costs of service provision, and such a pricing strategy may come under longer term pressure in a commodity market, in which the long-term outcome of competitive commodity pricing practices is to expose the customer to the marginal cost of production of the commodity.

Access charges also apply in the context of describing flat-rate dial access pricing, as they effectively replace a unit time tariff with a single access tariff. A flat-fee pricing structure for dial access is typically invoiced in advance on a monthly basis per client. The objective is to generate payment in advance of usage, while effectively committing the client to the ISP for a period covered by the access charge. The advance payment is a strong positive aspect to the ISP and the client, allowing the ISP to receive payment in advance of expenditure, reducing the bad debt levels and positively influencing the business position, while the client enjoys a predictable fixed expense. As with permanent connection fixed fees, dial-up fixed fees do suffer from overuse, which, in the case of dial access, can rapidly escalate into acute access port saturation. Unlimited access accounts for a fixed sum allow a client to operate a pseudo-permanent access service, which quickly extends average connection times for dial access. This shift in usage patterns can have an immediate effect on the modem pools, causing periods of saturation, in which the number of unsuccessful call attempts start to increase. As the number of call attempts rises, the behavior by the client is then to place further pressure on the modem port pool behavior by extending call access times. Having gained an access port the user optimization is not to relinquish it. Where local access dial calls are also untimed, there is no incentive whatsoever to release the call, and indeed there is a strong disincentive, given that the client will incur a call charge to subsequently reestablish the call. This behavior will further exacerbate the pressure on the modem access poll.

Larger dial-access ISPs may provide sufficient modems in their access pools to attempt to avoid modem poll saturation or may resort to more active call management structures, such as idle timeouts, or set up an environment in which an incoming call may be able to usurp a long held existing call. Other larger ISPs offer a two-tier pricing model and use a flat-fee structure as a base entry-level package, which may have lesser parameters of service quality. This allows the product to be differentiated from a premium product, which features superior quality metrics regarding call success rates, modem quality, and service support.

Time

Two dimensions to a time-based pricing structure exist: the use of the time of day for peak/off-peak pricing structures for permanently connected clients and the use of time of day and duration of access for intermittent access dial services. The first structure is applicable when considering volume changes and is considered in the next section; the dial access service is examined here.

A price structure based on the duration of the access and the time of day of the access is very widely used within the ISP business. The base form of charging is that of a per-hour connection price, in which each access is accounted to the customer, and at the end of each billing period, the total access time is calculated. Peak and off-peak pricing structures can be set up by using an *accounting clock* whose speed relative to the real-time varies according to peak and off-peak periods. Although in the peak periods, the usage is accounted on a 1:1 basis, in off-peak periods a number of hours may elapse for an accounting hour to be debited from the client's account. Such a pricing structure has the attribute that increased usage of the network by the client will be accompanied by an increase in connection hours. Increased connections hours will, in turn, result in increased revenue levels. The increased revenue levels will allow the ISP to expand the network, thereby accommodating the increased resource demands without weakening the underlying business model.

The disadvantage of this pricing approach is that a pure usage-based tariff does not have any client loyalty component. The client can readily move between ISPs in order to optimize costs within a strongly competitive price-based market. The marketing response from the ISP industry to this situation is to move to a flat-fee pricing structure for dial access, or an access tariff, as described previously. However, the common response to this potential scenario is to associate a fixed monthly fee with a quota of connection time, and then charge additional connection hours in arrears at a casual rate reflecting overflow of the fixed quota. Marketing responses typically take this and broaden it out, creating a number of time quota points to appeal to various usage profiles, but the general principle is that the cost efficiencies in the dial-access market come to play when the access ports can be accessed by multiple clients. For this to happen, there must be some form of incentive for the client to disconnect from the service, and this is most commonly implemented using a time component within the overall dial service price structure.

Volume

The next potential pricing metric is that of data volumes, in which the total amount of traffic received from the client into the network and the total amount of traffic passed from the network to the client is factored into the tariff schedules.

In some situations, carriage costs absolutely dominate the complete cost structure of the ISP. In a fixed tariff structure, the risk to the ISP is that increased traffic levels with the network do not necessarily imply increased revenue to the ISP. The consequent dilemma for the ISP is whether to maintain the capacity levels within the network and suffer increased congestion levels and consequent drop in service quality levels or to augment capacity in the network and suffer from a decrease in the rate of financial return due to greater levels of expenditure without matching levels of increased revenue.

In such a situation, an alternative response is to use a pricing model in which increased traffic levels in the network are matched by increased revenue, allowing the ISP to augment network capacity and accordingly maintain both service quality levels and financial rates of return. The question this poses is how to devise a price structure based on measured volumes of data passed to and from the client.

If the tariff includes a price component based on the traffic volume passed into the ISP's network, this results in a disincentive for content providers to become clients of the ISP service, as the more popular the content service, the greater the liability incurred by the content provider. Effectively, in this price structure, the information provider is paying for the carriage of information to the receiver, without any mechanisms on the part of the provider to limit its financial liability to the ISP. Also, the data sender is charged for passing the packet into the network, irrespective of whether the network delivers the packet or drops it in flight. The ISP maximizes its rate of return by operating a network that hovers in the area of load congestion, because revenue will be maximized by operating on the limits of acceptable congestion within the network.

The alternative pricing structure is to base the tariff on received traffic volumes, using the amount of traffic passed to the client as the determinant of the ISP charge. Such a pricing structure does offer a superior match to the characteristics of network traffic flows, where up to 70 percent of traffic is passed through the network at the explicit behest of the receiver, who is using such applications as Web pulls, ftp downloads, and receptions of streaming audio and video sources. If volume charges are passed only to the data receiver, the content provider has a significantly reduced overall level of liability, because the receiver pays for the carriage of the content through the network. This is a strong enabler for content provision, which acts as a market stimulus. The other aspect of receiver volumes is that the ISP receives revenue only after the data has passed out of the network to the client. Packets discarded within the ISP's network do not generate revenue to the ISP and have been carried at the ISP's expense to the drop point. There is, accordingly, an incentive for the ISP to ensure that the network does not hover around a state of congestion and that peak rates within the network are both brief and do not cause large levels of packet loss.

Of course, neither pricing structure matches the characteristics of every Internet application. Various refinements have been proposed to this mode, and have been implemented in some areas of the Internet. One approach is to attempt to capture the entire TCP flow and pass the cost for all traffic within the flow, irrespective of its direction to the flow initiator. This approach matches more closely the concept of a *call*, in which the call initiator pays for the entire cost of the call. Because the flow includes knowledge of the port address, this does allow the ISP to potentially charge differential amounts according to the use of well-known application ports, charging Usenet traffic at a different rate from Web traffic, as an example. Of course, there is still no clear *call initiator* for UDP packets, so attribution of UDP volumes to the sender or the receiver remain a somewhat arbitrary judgment. As far as larger ISPs are concerned, the costs of collecting flow data and capturing the flow initiator are very challenging, not only because of the volume of simultaneous flows involved and the number of new flows per second, but also because of the likely use of asymmetric paths within a large ISP, which services in a transit role to other ISPs. Here, a flow collector may only observe one half of the TCP conversation, and the data may not allow efficient matching of the various half-flows that have been assembled.

The volume tariff should be set with three factors in mind: the marginal cost of data carriage on all of the ISP's circuits, the marginal cost of data carriage to contracted upstream providers, and the general characteristics of traffic flows within the network. From this data, we can derive the average cost of data delivery and then set a volume tariff, which is based on this cost of carriage. Of course, such a tariff also opens competitive opportunities, particularly in an international transit context, where the overall price factor is that of the international circuits. In such scenarios charging an average price for all delivered traffic is heavily biased to the international circuits, and specific local transit paths result in being highly overcharged on a true marginal cost of carriage basis. The outcome of such an environment in a highly competitive industry is the creation of local exchanges between local ISPs, passing the transit provider for local traffic flows.

Volume charging also can be indexed against time of day, to allow peak and off-peak pricing mechanisms, creating an incentive for clients to push large volume, non-time-critical transactions into off-peak periods, evening out some components of network load, and increasing overall network carriage efficiency.

The unit of volume also can be set by the ISP to any desired level of coarseness, ranging from megabytes to gigabytes, or even tens of gigabytes. The coarser the tariff steps, the greater the extent of predictability of the tariff, although the price increments are also larger. At a certain level of coarseness the tariff effectively recreates the bandwidth-based access charges. For example, a 20-G-per-month unit of charging corresponds quite accurately to a 64-Kbps increment of access bandwidth, as 64-Kbps circuits can deliver up to 20-G per month at full circuit occupancy.

Distance

The other factor to be considered is whether the pricing structure is used as a mechanism to encourage some form of rational consumption of network resources. The proponents of inclusion of a distance factor within price structures argue that the costs of carriage within the underlying transmission network are distance dependent, due to distance-related cost components in provisioning the transmission network. Following this line of reasoning, exposing the client to the marginal costs of the use of these various systems will result in a rational model of resource consumption, where the client makes a cost-influenced decision as to whether to consume a network resource and undertake a transaction across the network.

Such an economic view of managing resource consumption has been widely promulgated within the telephony industry, where the cost of a call often is related to the distance of separation of the two parties, as well as the call's time of day and duration. Such an economic rationale has yet to permeate the Internet, although some evidence exists that this is changing with the introduction of differential pricing for services that are provided from a point local to the client, such as reduced volume-based tariffs for Usenet traffic flows, or for local cache server-delivered objects.

The TCP/IP protocol is of little assistance here in setting up distance-related tariffs, as the IP packet has no history of its transit through the network, nor is the end user explicitly aware that any individual network transaction involves a particular path that traverses long-haul transit links. Indeed, shifts in the routing state of the network may redirect traffic through longer paths, so that the concept of distance-based charging is one that is at odds with the technology base of the network. Equally, unlike the telephone network where the users are aware of a distance tariff selection through the differences in the dialing sequence, no such user visible difference exists within the Internet environment. Indeed, the effort of the Internet technology has been to compress the distance factor to the point where it is simply not a visible selector within the operation of Internet applications.

Some attempts have been made to introduce distance components into ISP tariffs, most notably through the use of differential tariffs for local traffic, such as Usenet flows and Web caches. For example, the traffic delivered to a client from a local Web cache may attract a lower volume tariff than other traffic, creating an incentive for clients to use the local cache rather than pull traffic from Web sources dispersed throughout the globe. Where carriage costs from upstream ISPs form a significant cost component of overall costs, the provider may choose to charge a different rate for this traffic, as against traffic sources from within the ISP's network. Such scenarios are indicated in Figure 13.8.

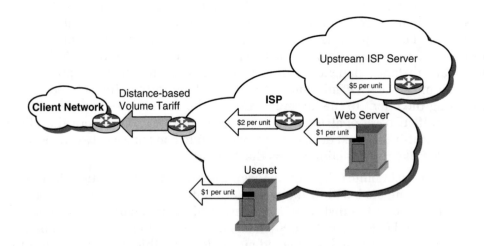

Figure 13.8 Distance tariffing.

The difficulty involved with setting up accurate metering for such a tariff is quite high, particularly in high-volume networks. Identification of the client also can be challenging; in the interior of the network, how do you know which client to charge for a transaction, given that all you have is an extract of the packet header?

As long as the total demand for Internet services continues to exhibit explosive growth, such factors are commonly considered to be of minor importance, and the major objective of most pricing structures is to achieve rapid market uptake of the ISP's services in order to secure a significant long-term market share.

Quality

The common conundrum of the ISP is that within a price/quality space, an ISP platform with a uniform technical and pricing structure creates a single outcome, and the entire network operates within this single price and quality point. Competitors may chose to differentiate by offering services at other points within the price/quality spectrum, while clients attempt to minimize price for a preferred service quality level.

The objective of the ISP pricing strategy in this area is to cover a large spread in the price/quality space, offering a number of differentiated service quality offerings to the market, using differential pricing in conjunction with this measure in order to provide broad market coverage from a single operational network platform.

Although the business theory is sound, using a single service platform, with pricing strategies to reflect differentiated quality of service characteristics, this area is still one where, technically, experimentation predominates over accepted industry practice. An ISP may execute a Quality of Service (QoS) contract with a client and mark all packets received from the client with an indication of elevated priority, in association with some form of tariff premium. This may not provide the best outcome here, as the ISP may have to mark all packets received at any ingress that specifies the client's networks as a destination with an elevated priority. While such filter-based marking is possible for small-scale provider environments, like many other differentiated service mechanisms, it does not scale to larger provider environments, and the large-scale deployment of ingress filters and associated deployment of differentiated service behaviors within the network itself.

A number of very simple QoS structures can be applied to the network to yield simple QoS outcomes and effective QoS pricing at the same time. For international transit networks in which the cost of the international transit components dominates the cost of the entire network operation, engineering

QoS on just these links may provide acceptable business and service outcomes. One potential measure is to use QoS priority elevation at the ingress to the international circuit in the direction of highest traffic flow. The intent is to increase the circuit loading and use differentiated service outcomes by manipulation of the queuing mechanisms on the circuit ingress. The metering for differentiated pricing can be undertaken on the egress side of the link, metering all packets received from the link, which have elevated priority, and accounting them to the target IP address or to the next hop AS if using BGP routing. The intended advantage to the ISP is twofold: It has the potential to raise the line occupancy of the circuit, allowing the ISP to reduce unit costs of the circuit, and it allows the ISP to offer some form of service and price differentiation.

A similar mechanism can be used with path differentiation on international circuits. For example, it may be possible to exploit the lower circuit costs and longer delays for unidirectional satellite circuits to offer a differentiated service that uses a satellite path as compared to an international cable path, and then use quality-based pricing strategies to provide differentiation to the client.

Pricing for Other Services

This section has concentrated on pricing for carriage services. Although carriage costs are the dominant service cost for many other ISPs, the common objective is to add value to the basic carriage proposition and augment carriage with related Internet service offerings.

Some ISPs choose to bundle access to additional services into the basic carriage tariff, arguing that a simple tariff is a better market proposition within a competitive market. In this way, mail accounts, Web hosting, and similar services are provided within the parameters of the basic access service without additional tariffing. No doubt, the cost of metering and invoicing for such ancillary service elements can impose a significant incremental cost to the service operation, and the decision to meter and invoice for such services immediately imposes a cost to the ISP excluding any costs of operation of the service platform itself. Bundling such services into the basic access package does allow for the basic operational unit costs of the service to be transferred into the total ISP product unit costs without having to add the costs of the operation of usage metering of the service or the costs of a second line item within the invoicing operation.

However, some service elements are often the subject of price structures: the operation of an outsourced network service to a corporate client prices service elements as distinct from carriage. This may be as simple as a cost per mailbox in an outsourced electronic messaging solution or the cost per megabyte of hosted Web content, or it may extend to a contracted price to provide operational management to an entire private router network and service elements.

In some cases, the service platform does not assume a physical identity, such as the operation of a virtual private network environment, in which the basic value of carriage is augmented with the addition of a soft-state network segmentation to support the concept of a private network. Here, no matching physical service delivery unit exists, yet the value of the base carriage service has been augmented, and the pricing structure can reflect such value propositions.

Tariff Structures

Within the initial academic and research networks, the common starting position was that of a centrally funded network resource, and no pricing structure was imposed on the end clients of the network service. Although such a mode of operation is a strong catalyst for network growth, given that the service is free of incremental cost to the end user, it is not a longer term sustainable solution, and some form of pricing for the provision of network services is an inevitable step.

When determining a pricing structure, we must consider a number of factors, including risk to the ISP's business, market acceptance, ease of implementation, accuracy of metering, scalability, and competitive position.

Simple pricing structures that offer ease of implementation, acceptable risk to the ISP, and competitive viability are the dominant considerations here.

Where the cost of service operations dominate the ISP cost structure (as against the costs of carriage) a tariff structure of flat-rate access pricing is often chosen, in which the attributes of ease of implementation, simplicity, accuracy, scalability, and competitive pricing far outweigh the business risks to the ISP, which are associated with increased resource consumption without accompanying incremental revenue.

In other contexts, such a tariff may not be the best choice for an ISP. Where carriage costs dominate the ISP's cost structure, a flat-rate tariff approach may present unacceptable business risks, and some form of incremental tariff structure may be more appropriate. Incrementally metered tariffs will present issues in the deployment of meter systems that can measure network usage to an acceptable level of accuracy with acceptable levels of integrity of operation. For dial-access operations, a fixed monthly fee for a fixed amount of access time, plus provision for incremental fees for additional usage, may present an acceptable tariff structure. Such a structure also could be refined with the use of off-peak tariff discounts if so desired, although this is an example of a form of incremental creep of any tariff structure, in which the tariff is modified with the use of volume discounts, off-peak rates, and other features and conditions. In a commodity market where price is the basic market discriminant, such ornate pricing features tend to proliferate, generally as a result of attempting to match a tariff to a whole variety of particular circumstances, and as a means of ensuring the direct price comparisons between provider services are not readily accomplished.

Where metering is undertaken, it is most efficient to perform this at the edge of the network, where the traffic segments to interface to each client. The network context at this point is one that does possess customer attributes, and the association of traffic with a particular customer is undertaken easily. Distance, or service-based, tariffing often requires the ISP to undertake tariffing in the interior of the network, at the point where the service platform interfaces to the network or where the distance carriage element interfaces to the remainder of the network infrastructures. Such deployment scenarios are indicated in Figure 13.9, indicating a potential tariffing structure for the use of a Web cache and a unidirectional satellite circuit. The issues with metering in such an environment are quite involved and center around the translation of recorded packet attributes to a unique association with a particular client account. Accounting of resource use purely in the format of source and destination address matrices is inadequate in many situations, as loose source routing may invalidate the header, or the same address prefix may be announced by multiple clients, particularly in the case of a transit ISP. Linking the accounting information with the forwarding decision of the routing system is necessary in order to undertake an accurate association of address to client. Cisco Systems has used a mechanism called Netflow accounting that can produce accounting records. Such records have the attributes of source and destination addresses, volumes, and BGP next hop AS number, which in a BGP routing environment, can be used to identify the client currently associated with the forwarding decision to implement interior accounting.

Within a price-based commodity marketplace, where the base ISP access market appears to be heading, there is a constant search to differentiate a product by using various pricing components that attempt to break out of a regime of simple price comparison between providers. Accordingly, the tariff options deployed by ISPs will start to exhibit greater levels of internal differentiation, and the complexity of the operation of meter systems (and the related operation of matching meter data to customers) will occupy significant levels of attention within the ISP operation.

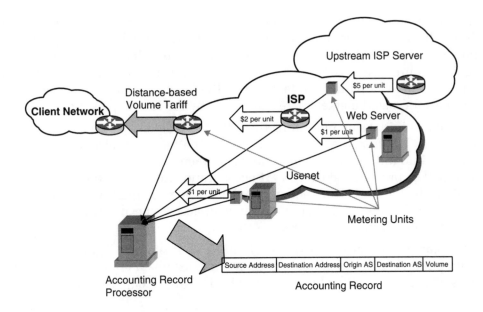

Figure 13.9 Multiple usage metering points.

Step 5—The Complete Business Plan

We now have enough material to develop a reasonably complete business plan for an ISP. We end this chapter by completing an example business plan using the steps described in this chapter.

The example ISP here is a non-U.S. ISP, leasing an expensive international circuit, as well as operating a local retail enterprise. The ISP also attempts to operate a high-quality service, using high levels of modem availability and very liberal carriage provisioning. Of course, this may not be an optimal strategy in a competitive market because it leads to quite high retail pricing levels. However, this is something that will become evident in the business plan. The example operation is also one which uses aggressive market expansion, illustrating a growth profile which is found in many ISP businesses today.

The first step is to identify the business objective. For our sample ISP enterprise, we use an approach of a competitive market entrant, able to withstand a period of early operating loss in order to consolidate the enterprise with a significant market share.

The next step is to estimate the size of the market across the period of the plan. This sample business plan uses two market sectors: a dial service based around a target residential market and a business service market based on outsourcing of Internet access services. The operation is based within two major cities. The market penetration levels are admittedly quite low in this example, indicating a market that will require some marketing stimulus to develop into significant proportions. Figure 13.10 indicates the anticipated market size for dial-up customers within the target area, the level of uptake of ISP services, and the anticipated market share achievable by the ISP in question.

From this initial step in forming the ISP business plan, we must look at cost structures. The first analysis is to translate the market projections of client numbers into ISP resource requirements. Modem ports for the dial-access segment will be provisioned using a 4:1 access ratio, positioning the enterprise at a relatively high level of modem pool management quality. The business clients are also distributed across a range of access speeds. The ISP's access service profile is indicated in Figure 13.11.

The analysis of an international circuit is indicated in Figure 13.12. The assumption is being made that the maximum sustainable line occupancy factor is 68 percent, and the break-even point is a line occupancy of 60 percent.

	Year 1	Year 2	Year 3	Year 4	Year 5
Residential Market					
Market Size	400,000	416,000	432,640	449,946	467,943
Total Uptake Rate	1%	5%	20%	35%	42%
ISP Market Share	20%	25%	35%	40%	40%
Projected Client Numbers	800	5,200	30,285	62,992	78,614
Business Market					
Market Size	10,000	10,400	10,816	11,249	11,699
Total Uptake Rate	3%	10%	20%	25%	28%
ISP Market Share	20%	25%	35%	40%	40%
Projected Client Numbers	60	260	757	1,125	1,310

Figure 13.10 Example market share projections.

		Year 1	Year 2	Year 3	Year 4	Year 5
Dial Access						
	dial modems	210	1,320	7,590	15,750	19,680
Network Access						
	64K	40	145	522	750	860
	128K	15	80	150	250	300
	256K	5	30	70	100	120
	512K	0	5	15	25	30

Figure 13.11   Access port projections.

International Circuit cost calculation

Capacity of the circuit	Kbps		2,048
Cost of the circuit - total lease cost	monthly	$	120,000
Megabytes	monthly		685,670
Target line loading factor			**60%**
Taget carriage volume	monthly		411,402
Breakeven cost using unidirectional tariffing	per Mbyte	$	**0.29**

Domestic Circuit cost calculation

Capacity of the circuit	Kbps		2,048
Cost of the circuit - total lease cost	monthly	$	8,000
Megabytes	monthly		685,670
Target line loading factor			**60%**
Taget carriage volume			411,402
Breakeven cost using unidirectional tariffing	per Mbyte	$	**0.02**

Traffic Balance

International	35%	$	0.20
Trunk	22%	$	0.00
Local	13%	$	-
Total Delivered cost per Mb		$	**0.21**

Figure 13.12   Unit cost of carriage.

	Year 1	Year 2	Year 3	Year 4	Year 5
Provisioning Forecasts					
Modem Ports	210	1,320	7,590	15,750	19,680
Router ports	60	260	757	1,125	1,310
Capacity Forecasts					
International Capacity	2	10	43	82	100
Domestic Capacity	2	8	35	68	84

Figure 13.13   Provisioning and capacity forecasts.

The circuit's total unidirectional carriage capacity can be calculated from the circuit's bandwidth and the target line occupancy used to derive the target unit cost for this form of circuit. A similar analysis is undertaken for a domestic trunk circuit. These two unit costs now can be used to calculate the marginal cost of carriage, using a number of simple assumptions about the domestic topology of the network and assumptions regarding the balance of traffic flows. This model assumes no significant levels of Web caching, so that a large proportion of the traffic flow is inflow from offshore origins. The resulting calculation of the unit cost of data is also indicated in Figure 13.12.

With the inclusion of the assumption of data volumes associated with each form of service, the traffic flow assumptions also allow for the generation of network capacity forecasts, as well as forecasts of modem access pool sizes to service the market. These forecasts are indicated in Figure 13.13.

This is sufficient to create a complete cost description of the example enterprise, as indicated in Figure 13.14.

	$ Year 1	$ Year 2	$ Year 3	$ Year 4	$ Year 5
ISP Business Costs					
Equipment	111,000	686,000	3,870,712	7,987,486	9,971,024
Line Lease	1,572,864	7,766,016	32,636,928	62,226,432	76,283,904
Staff	250,000	350,000	450,000	500,000	600,000
Marketing	0	150,000	250,000	250,000	300,000
Overheads	120,000	200,000	250,000	300,000	300,000
TOTAL	**2,053,864**	**9,152,016**	**37,457,640**	**71,263,918**	**87,454,928**

Figure 13.14   ISP business costs.

As described in Step 3, the plan must include a revenue model and the associated adoption of a pricing system. The model chosen here is a flat fee plus overflow charges for dial clients and a volume-based pricing structure for permanently connected clients, using received traffic as the pricing element. The pricing structure and the resulting financial outcome of the business plan are indicated in Figure 13.15.

Of course, as an example plan, assumptions are being made here that would ordinarily require some detail in their justification. The model also would require some risk analysis, based on linkage of price levels to anticipated market share, to determine the points of flexibility for the total model, as well as analysis of competitive factors to the overall integrity of the business plan.

The example has also assumed that the operation will work in the market using a rollout of retail services. This is of course a very limited view of the set of potential business activities, and an ISP would normally use more than a single approach to the market to reduce risks and maximize potential outcomes. Acquisition is a useful mechanism to rapidly achieve a critical level of market share, and branching out into related services of, say, web hosting, and virtual private network support, are also commonly adopted strategies.

Tariff Schedule

Dial Access	$100.00	per month, flat fee
Network Access at 64Kbps	$1,800.00	per month, flat fee
Other	$0.26	variable volume charged

		$ Year 1	$ Year 2	$ Year 3	$ Year 4	$ Year 5
ISP Revenue						
	Dial Access	960,000	6,240,000	36,341,760	75,590,861	94,337,394
	Network Access					
	64 K	72,000	261,000	939,816	1,349,755.2	1,548,434.857
	128 K	90,192.96	481,029.12	901,929.6	1,503,216	1,803,859.2
	256 K	60,128.64	360,771.84	841,800.96	1,202,572.8	1,443,087.36
	512 K	0	120,257.28	360,771.84	601,286.4	721,543.68
	TOTAL	1,182,322	7,463,058	39,386,078	80,247,691	99,854,319
Expenses		2,053,864	9,152,016	37,457,640	71,263,918	87,454,928
Profit / Loss		-871,542	-1,688,958	1,928,438	8,983,773	12,399,391

Figure 13.15   ISP business income projection.

chapter fourteen

Interacting with Other ISPs

The Internet is not, and never has been, a single network. The Internet is a collection of interconnected component networks that share a common addressing structure, a common view of routing, and a common view of a naming system. This interconnection environment spans more than 60,000 component networks, and this number continues to grow and grow.

Underneath the veneer of a competitive ISP retail environment is a somewhat different environment, in which every Internet service provider network must interoperate with neighboring Internet networks in order to produce an outcome of efficient and comprehensive connectivity and end-to-end service—the essential attribute of the total client offering. No ISP can operate in complete isolation from others while participating in offering Internet servers, and therefore, every ISP must not only coexist with other ISPs but also must operate in cooperation with other ISPs.

Within this chapter, we explore this environment of interaction, examining the issues from a business perspective. The three areas covered here are the structure of ISP interaction within the Internet in terms of roles, the physical structures of ISP interaction, and the financial issues of ISP interaction.

ISP Roles: Retailing, Reselling, and Wholesaling

At some stage in the evolution of the ISP business, each ISP must confront the resale of their services. The initial business model of many ISPs is one based on a retail model of a direct relationship between the user and the ISP. This relationship is relatively sustainable within a dial-up host network access service. However, after the ISP expands to encompass clients who use a permanent connection to the ISP and who peer their network to that of the ISP, then sustaining a retail-only operation becomes difficult for the ISP. A natural outcome of the Internet model is that the control of the service environment rests with the client of the service rather than with the service provider. Therefore, a network client of an ISP access service has the ability to resell the access service to third-party clients. In this environment, reselling and wholesaling are very natural developments within the ISP activity sector, with or without the explicit concurrence of the provider ISP. The original ISP may see this reselling as an additional channel to the market for its own Internet carriage services. The ISP could take a positive stance by actively encouraging resellers into the market as a means of overall market stimulus, while tapping into the marketing, sales, and support resources of these reselling entities to continue to drive the underlying Internet carriage service portfolio.

Given that a retail operation can become a provider to resellers at the effective discretion of the reselling retail client, is a wholesale transit ISP restricted from undertaking retail operations? No such restriction exists from a technical perspective.

Internet carriage service is a commodity service, which does not allow for a significant level of intrinsic product discrimination. The relative low level of value added by a wholesale operation implies a low rate of financial return for that operation. This low financial return forces a wholesale provider into the retail sector as a means of improving the financial performance of the service operation. Many retail ISPs first move into greater levels of provisioning capacity to support an increased scope of retail operations. The low barriers to entry to the wholesale market allow for another means of increasing the scope of the operation. To lift business cash-flow levels, the business enters into wholesale agreements that effectively resell the carriage components of the operation without the bundling of other services normally associated with the retail operation. This process allows the ISP to gain higher volumes of carriage capacity, that in turn allow the ISP to gain access to lower unit costs of transmission from carriage providers.

As a reseller, a network operates both as a client and as a provider. This role ambiguity is by no means uncommon on the Internet. Few, if any, reasonable technical-based characterizations draw a clear and unambiguous distinction between a client and service provider when access services to networks are considered. A campus network may be a client of one or more service providers, while the network is also a service provider to campus users. Indeed most networks in a similar situation take on the dual role of client and provider, and the ability to resell an access service can extend to almost arbitrary depths of the reselling hierarchy. From this technical perspective, very few natural divisions of the market support a stable segmentation into exclusively wholesale and exclusively retail market sectors. The overall structure of roles is indicated in Figure 14.1.

The resultant business environment is one characterized by a reasonable degree of fluidity, in which no clear delineation of relative roles or markets exists. The ISP market environment is, therefore, one of competitive market forces in which each ISP has to create a market following using a market positioning strongly based on the service price and some aspects of service quality.

However, no ISP can operate in isolation. Each client has the expectation of universal and comprehensive reachability, such that any client of any other Internet ISP can reach the client, and the client can reach a client of any other ISP. The client of an ISP is not undertaking a service contract that limits connectivity only to other clients of the same ISP. Because no provider can claim ubiquity of access, every provider relies on every other provider to complete

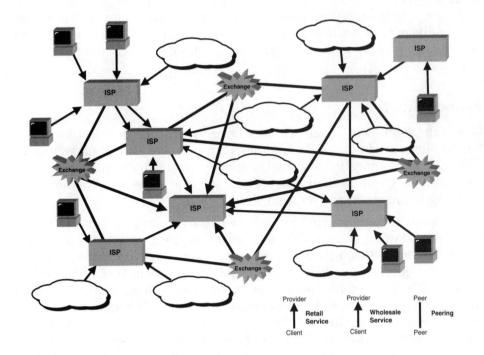

Figure 14.1   ISP roles and relationships.

the user-provided picture of comprehensive connectivity. Because of this dependent relationship, an individual provider's effort to provide substantially superior quality of carriage may have little overall impact on the totality of client-delivered service quality. Quality of service becomes something that can be impacted negatively by poor local engineering but cannot be improved beyond the quality provided by the network's peers, and their peers in turn. Internet wholesale carriage services, therefore, are a commodity service, in which scant opportunity exists for service-based differentiation. The wholesale activity becomes a price-based service with low levels of added value.

The implication in terms of ISP positioning is that the retail operation (rather than the wholesale activity) is the major area where the ISP can provide discriminating service quality. Within the retail operation, the ISP can offer a wide variety of services with a set of associated service levels, and base a market positioning on factors other than commodity carriage pricing.

Accordingly, the environment of interconnection between ISPs does not break down into a well-ordered model of a set of wholesale carriage providers and associated retail service providers. The environment currently is one with a wide diversity of retail-oriented providers, where each provider may operate both as a retail service operator, and a wholesale carriage provider to other retailers.

Peer or Client?

One of the significant issues that arises here is whether an objective determination can be made of whether an ISP is a peer to, or a client of, another ISP. This is a critical question, as, if a completely objective determination cannot be made, the question then becomes one of who is responsible for making such a determination, and on what basis.

This question is an inevitable outcome of the reselling environment, where the reseller starts to make multiple upstream service contracts, with a growing number of downstream clients of the reselling service. At this point, the profile of the original reseller is little distinguished from that of the original provider. The original reseller sees no unique value being offered by the original upstream provider and may conclude that it is in fact adding value to the original upstream provider by offering the upstream provider volume carriage and close access to the reseller's client base. From the perspective of the original reseller, the roles have changed, and the reseller now perceives itself as a peer ISP to the original upstream ISP provider.

This role reversal is perhaps most significant when the generic interconnection environment is one of zero sum financial settlement, in which the successful assertion by one party of a change to peer interconnection status, from a previous relationship of a client, to the second party results in the dropping of client service revenue without any net change in the cost base of the operation. The party making the successful assertion of peer interconnection sees the opposite, with an immediate drop in the cost of the ISP operation with no net revenue change.

The traditional public regulatory resolution of such matters has been through an administrative process of *licensed* service providers, who become peer entities through a process of administrative fiat. In this model, an ISP becomes a licensed service provider through the payment of license fees to the communications regulatory body. The license then allows the enterprise access to interconnection arrangements. A client is an entity that operates without a carrier license, and a peer is one that has been granted such an instrument. However, such heavily regulated environments are quite artificial in their delineation of the entities that operate in this market, and this process acts as a depressant to large-scale private investment. The regulatory environment is changing worldwide to shift the burden of communications infrastructure investment from the public sector, or a uniquely positioned small segment of the private sector, to an environment that encourages private investment. The Internet industry is at the leading edge of this trend, and the ISP domain typically operates within a deregulated valued-added communications service provider regulatory environment. Individual licenses are replaced with generic class licenses or similar deregulated structures, in which formal applications or payments of license fees to operate in this domain are unnecessary. Therefore, no authoritative external entity makes the decision as to whether the relationship between two ISPs is that of a provider and client or that of peers.

If no public regulatory body wants to make such a determination, is there a comparable industry body? The early attempts of the Commercial Internet eXchange (CIX) arrangements were based on a description of the infrastructure of each party, in which acknowledgments of peer capability were based on the operation of a national transit infrastructure of a minimum specified capability. This specification of peering within the CIX subsequently was modified so that CIX peer status for an ISP was based on payment of the CIX Association membership fee. This CIX model was not one that intrinsically admitted bilateral peer relationships. The relationship was a multilateral one, in which each ISP executed a single agreement with the CIX Association and then effectively had the ability to peer with all other association member networks. The consequence of this multilateral arrangement is that the peering settlements can be regarded as an instance of zero sum financial settlement peering.

Other models use a functional peer specification. If the ISP attaches to a nominated physical exchange structure, then the ISP is in a position to open bilateral negotiations with any other ISP also directly attached to the structure. This model is inherently more flexible, as the bilateral exchange structure enables each represented ISP to make its own determination of whether to agree to a peer relationship or not with any other ISP. This model also enables each bilateral peer arrangement to be executed individually, admitting a wider diversity of financial settlement arrangements.

The bottom line is that a true peer relationship is based on the supposition that either party can terminate the interconnection relationship and that the other party does not consider such an action a competitively hostile act. If one party has a high reliance on the interconnection arrangement and the other does not, then the most stable business outcome is that this reliance is expressed in terms of a service contract with the other party, and a provider/ client relationship is established. If a balance of mutual requirement exists between both parties and if the ability to address these requirements in other ways is open to both parties, then a stable basis for a peer relationship exists. Such a statement has no intrinsic metrics that allow the requirements to be quantified. Peering in such an environment is best expressed as the balance of perceptions, in which each party perceives an acceptable approximation of equal benefit in the interconnection relationship in their own terms.

This conclusion leads to the various tiers of accepted peering that are evident in the Internet today. Local ISPs see a rationale to view local competing ISPs as peers, and they still admit the need to purchase trunk transit services from one or more upstream ISPs under terms of a client contract with the trunk provider ISP. Trunk ISPs see an acceptable rationale in peering with ISPs with a similar role profile in trunk transit but perceive an inequality of relationship with local ISPs. Of course, this balance of perceptions becomes clouded when a trunk ISP also participates in local markets as a peer retail player. We examine this in further detail when looking at the financial aspects of peering models later in this chapter.

Physical Interaction: Exchanges and NAPs

One of the physical properties of electromagnetic propagation is that the power required to transmit an electromagnetic pulse over a distance varies in accordance with this distance. The shorter the distance between the transmitter and the receiver, the lower the power budget required; *closer is cheaper*.

This statement holds true not only for power budgets but also for data protocol efficiency. Minimizing the delay between the sender and receiver allows the protocol to operate faster and operate more efficiently; *closer is faster,* and *closer is more efficient.*

These observations imply that distinct and measurable advantages are gained by localizing data traffic, that is by ensuring that the physical path traversed by the packets passed between the sender and the receiver is as short as possible. These advantages are realizable in terms of performance, efficiency, and cost. How then are such considerations factored into the structure of the Internet?

The Exchange Model

A strictly hierarchical model of Internet structure is one in which a small number of global ISP transit operators is at the "top"; a second tier is of national ISP operators; and a third tier consists of local ISPs. At each tier the ISPs are clients of the tier above, as shown in Figure 14.2. If this hierarchical model were strictly adhered to, traffic between two local ISPs would be forced to transit a national ISP, and traffic between two national ISPs would transit a global ISP, even if both national ISPs operated within the same country. In the worst case, traffic between two local ISPs would need to transit a national ISP,

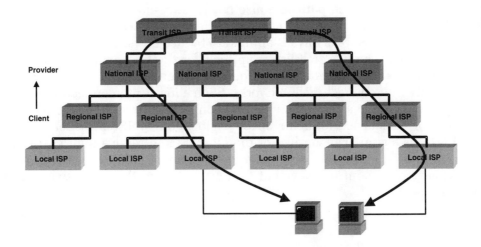

Figure 14.2　A purely hierarchical structure for the Internet.

and then a global ISP from one hierarchy, then a second global ISP, and a second national ISP from an adjacent hierarchy in order to reach the other local ISP. If the two global providers interconnect at a remote location, the transit path of the traffic between these two local ISPs could be very long indeed.

---

*O*n the campus where I worked in the late 1980s, data traffic between the campus and one of its technology vendors had to be passed from Australia to the east coast of the United States and back again, just to cross the street to the vendor's office in Australia. That this process worked at all was a constant source of wonder. That the ISP managed to deliver messages in seconds was a source of amazement at the time. At the same time the majority of traffic between Internet service networks in Europe included two Atlantic transits. Such stories of well-traveled packets that transit large amounts of the global communications infrastructure to arrive within a few meters of where the traffic originated are still, unfortunately, all too common in the Internet today. Ultimately, the cost of such inefficient traffic engineering is expressed in the retail price of Internet-based goods and services.

Such extended paths are inefficient, and the extended transit delay yields poor performance. Such paths are also costly, and such costs are ultimately part of the cost component of the price of Internet access. In a competitive market, strong pressure always is applied to reduce costs. Within a hierarchical environment, strong pressure is applied for the two national providers, who operate within the same market domain, to modify this strict hierarchy and directly interconnect their networks. Such a local interconnection allows the two networks to service their mutual connectivity requirements without payment of transit costs to their respective global transit ISP providers. At the local level is a similar incentive for the local ISPs to reduce their cost base, and a local interconnection with other local ISPs would allow local traffic to be exchanged without the payment of transit costs to the respective transit providers.

Although constructing a general interconnection regime based on point-to-point bilateral connections is possible, this approach does not exhibit good scaling properties. Between N providers, who want to interconnect, the outcome of such a model of single interconnecting circuits is $N^2/2$ circuits and $N^2/2$ routing interconnections, as indicated in Figure 14.3. Given that intercon-

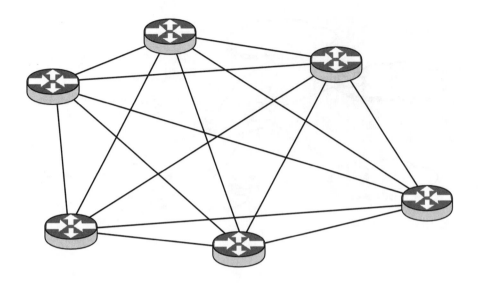

Figure 14.3   Fully meshed peering.

nections exhibit the greatest leverage within geographical local situations, simplifying this picture within the structure of a local exchange is possible. In this scenario each provider draws a single circuit to the local exchange and then executes interconnections at this exchange. Between *N* providers who want to interconnect, the same functionality of complete interconnection can be constructed using only *N* point-to-point circuits.

The Exchange Router

One model of an exchange is to build the exchange itself as a router, as indicated in Figure 14.4. Each provider's circuit terminates on the exchange router, and each provider's routing system peers with the routing process on the exchange router. This structure also simplifies the routing configuration, so that full interconnection of *N* providers is effected with *N* routing peer sessions. However, the exchange router model does become an active component of the interconnect peering policy environment. In effect, each provider must execute a multilateral interconnection peering with all of the other connected providers. Selectively interconnecting with a subset of the providers present at such a router-based exchange is not easily achieved. In addition, this type of exchange must execute its own routing policy. When two or more providers are advertising a route to the same destination, the exchange router must execute a policy decision as to which provider's route is loaded in the router's

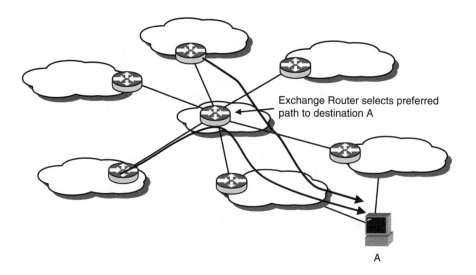

Exchange Router selects preferred
path to destination A

A

Figure 14.4   An exchange router.

forwarding table, making a policy choice of transit provider on behalf of all other exchange-connected providers. Because the exchange is now an active policy element in the interconnection environment, the exchange is no longer completely neutral to all participants. This imposition on the providers may be seen as unacceptable, in that some of their ability to devise and execute an external transit policy is usurped by the exchange operator's policies.

Typically, providers have a higher expectation of flexibility of policy determination from exchange structures than this base level of functionality provided by an exchange router. Providers want the flexibility to execute interconnections on a bilateral basis at the exchange, and to make policy decisions as to which provider to prefer when the same destination is advertised by multiple providers. They require the exchange to be neutral with respect to such individual policy decisions.

The Exchange LAN

The modification to the inter-provider exchange structure is to use a LAN as the exchange element. In this model a participating provider draws a circuit to the exchange and locates a dedicated router on the exchange LAN. This structure is indicated in Figure 14.5. Each provider executes a bilateral peering agreement with another provider by initiating a router peering session

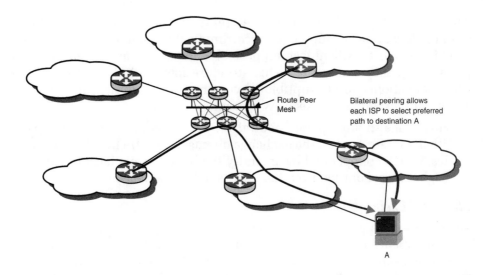

Route Peer
Mesh

Bilateral peering allows
each ISP to select preferred
path to destination A

A

Figure 14.5   An exchange LAN.

with the other party's router. When the same network destination is advertised by multiple peers, the provider can execute a policy-based preference as
to which peer's route will be loaded in the local forwarding table. Such a
structure preserves the cost efficiency of using N circuits to effect interconnection at the N provider exchange, while admitting the policy flexibility of
$N^2/2$ potential routing peer sessions.

Early inter-provider exchanges, such as the U.S. interagency interconnection points FIX-East and FIX-West (FIX stands for Federal Internet eXchange),
were based on an Ethernet LAN as the common interconnection element. This
physical structure was simple, and not all that robust under the pressures of
growth, as the LAN became congested easily. Subsequent refinements to the
model have included the use of Ethernet switches as a higher capacity LAN,
and the use of FDDI rings, switched FDDI hubs, fast Ethernet hubs, and
switched fast Ethernet hubs.

Exchanges are very high traffic concentration points. The desire to manage
ever higher traffic volumes has lead to the anticipation of gigabit Ethernet
switches as the next evolutionary technology step within exchanges. The
model of the exchange location accommodates a model of diversity of access
media, in which the provider's router undertakes the media translation
between the access link protocol and the common exchange protocol.

The local traffic exchange hub does represent a critical point of failure within the local Internet topology. Accordingly, the exchange should be engineered in the most resilient fashion possible, using standards associated with a premium quality data center. This structure may include multiple power utility connections, uninterruptible power supplies, multiple trunk fiber connections, and excellent site security measures.

The exchange should operate neutrally with respect to every participating ISP, with the interests of all the exchange clients in mind. Therefore, exchange facilities, which are operated by an entity that is not also a local or trunk ISP, enjoy higher levels of trust from the clients of the exchange.

Distributed Exchanges

Distributed exchange models also have been deployed in various locations. This deployment can be as simple as a metropolitan FDDI extension, in which the exchange comes to the provider's location rather than the reverse, as indicated in Figure 14.6. Other models that use an ATM-based switching fabric also have been deployed. Distributed exchange models attempt to address the cost of operating a single colocation environment with a high degree of resilience and security, but do so at a cost of enforcing the use of a uniform access technology.

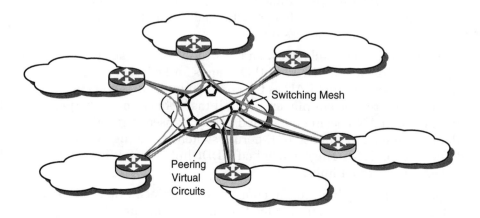

Figure 14.6   A distributed exchange.

However, the major challenge of such distributed models is that of switching speed. Switching requires some element of contention resolution, in which two ingress data elements that are addressed to a common egress path require the switch to detect the resource contention and then resolve it by serializing the egress. Switching, therefore, requires signaling, in which the switching element must inform the ingress element of switch contention. To increase the speed of the switch, the latency of this signaling must be reduced. The dictates of increased switching speed have the corollary of requiring the switch to exist within the confines of a single location.

Besides speed, we must consider the cost shift. In a distributed exchange model, the exchange operator operates the set of access circuits that form the distributed exchange. This process increases costs to providers, while it prevents the providers from using a specific access technology that matches their business requirements of cost and supportable traffic volume. Not surprisingly, to date the most prevalent form of exchange remains the third-party hosted colocation model. This model admits a high degree of diversity in access technologies, while still providing the substrate of an interconnection environment that can operate at high speed and therefore manage high traffic volumes.

Other Exchange-Located Services

The colocation environment is often broadened to include other functions, in addition to a pure routing and traffic exchange role. For a high-volume content provider, the exchange location offers minimal transit distance to a large user population distributed across multiple local service providers, as well as allowing the content provider to exercise a choice in selecting a nonlocal transit provider.

The exchange operator can also add value to the exchange environment by providing additional functions and services, as well as terminating providers' routers and large-volume content services. The exchange location within the overall network topology is an ideal location for hosting multicast services, because the location is quite optimal in terms of multicast carriage efficiency. Similarly, Usenet trunk feed systems can exploit the local hub created by the exchange. The overall architecture of a colocation environment that permits value-added services, which can productively use the unique environment created at an exchange, is indicated in Figure 14.7.

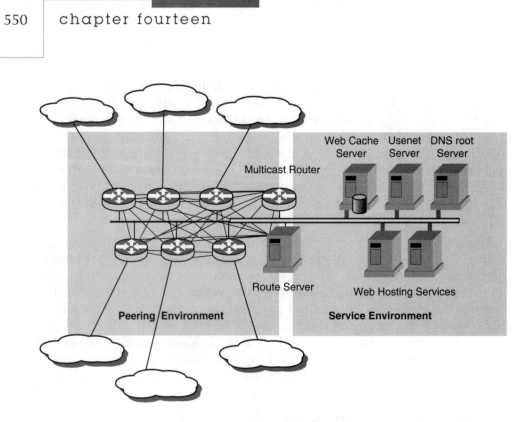

Figure 14.7 Exchange-located service platforms.

Network Access Points

The role of the exchange was broadened with the introduction of the Network Access Point (NAP) in the NSF-proposed post-NSFNET architecture of 1995.

The NAP was seen to undertake two roles: the role of an exchange provider between regional ISPs who want to execute bilateral peering arrangements and the role of a transit purchase venue, in which regional ISPs could execute purchase agreements with one or more of a set of trunk carriage ISPs also connected at the NAP. The *access point* concept was intended to describe access to the trunk transit service. The original four NAPs were established within the framework of a NSF solicitation. These four were located in San Francisco, operated by Pacific Bell; Chicago, operated by Ameritech; New Jersey, operated by Spring; and Washington, DC, operated by Metropolitan Fiber Systems. Similar hybrid local exchange and transit purchase facilities have been set up in other North American cities as well as within cities in Europe and the Asia Pacific area.

This mixed role of both local exchange and transit operations leads to considerable operational complexity, in terms of the transit providers being able to execute a clear business agreement. What is the bandwidth of the purchased service in terms of requirements for trunk transit, versus the access requirements for exchange traffic? If a local ISP purchases a transit service at one of the NAPs, does that imply that the trunk provider is then obligated to present all the ISP's routes at remote NAP? How can a trunk provider distinguish between traffic presented to it on behalf of a remote client versus traffic presented to it by a local service client?

We also should consider the issue that the quality of the purchased transit service is colored by the quality of the service provided by the NAP operator. Although the quality of the transit provider's network may remain constant, and the quality of the local ISP's network and ISP's NAP access circuit may be acceptable, the quality of the transit service may be negatively impacted by the quality of the NAP transit.

One common solution is to use the NAP colocation facility to execute transit purchase agreements and use so-called backdoor connections for the transit service provision role. This usage restricts the NAP exchange network to a theoretically simpler local exchange role. Such a configuration is illustrated in Figure 14.8.

Exchange Business Models

For the ISP industry, a number of attributes are considered highly desirable for an exchange facility. The exchange should be as follows:

- Operated by a neutral party who is not an ISP (to ensure fairness and neutrality in the operation of the exchange)
- Constructed in a robust and secure fashion
- Located in areas of high density of Internet market space
- Able to scale in size
- Operate in a fiscally sound and stable business fashion

A continuing concern exists about the performance of exchanges and the consequent issue of quality of services that traverse the exchange. Many of these concerns stem from an exchange business model that may not be adequately robust under pressures of growth from participating ISPs.

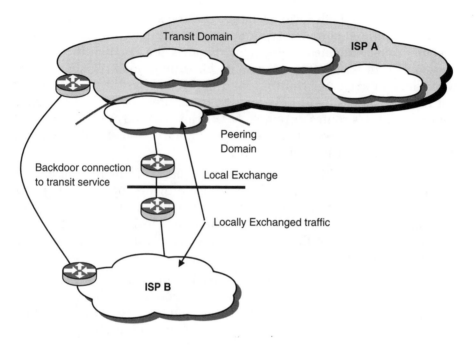

Figure 14.8 Peering and transit purchase.

The exchange business models typically are based on a flat-fee structure. The most basic model uses a fee structure based on the number of rack units used by the ISP to colocate equipment at the exchange. When an exchange participant increases the amount of traffic presented over an access interface, under a flat-fee structure, this increased level of traffic is not accompanied by any increase in exchange fees. However, the greater traffic volumes do imply that the exchange itself is faced with a greater traffic load. This greater load places pressure on the exchange operator to deploy further equipment to augment the switching capacity, without any corresponding increase in revenue levels to the operator.

For an exchange operator to base tariffs on the access bandwidths is not altogether feasible, given that such access facilities are leased by the participating ISPs and the access bandwidth may not be known to the exchange operator. Nor is using a traffic-based funding model possible, since an exchange operator should refrain from monitoring individual ISP traffic across the exchange, given the unique position of the exchange operator. Accordingly, the exchange operator has to devise a fiscally prudent tariff structure at the outset that enables the exchange operator to accommodate large-scale traffic growth, while maintaining the highest possible traffic throughput metrics.

Alternatively there are business models in which the exchange is structured as a cooperative entity between a number of ISPs. In these models the exchange is a nonprofit common asset of the cooperative body. This model is widely used, but also one that is prone to the economic condition of the *Tragedy of the Commons*. It is in everyone's interest to maximize his or her exploitation of the exchange, while no single member wants to underwrite the financial responsibility for ensuring that the quality of the exchange is maintained.

Fourteenth-century Britain was organized as a loosely aligned collection of villages, each with a common pasture for villagers to graze horses, cattle, and sheep. Each household attempted to gain wealth by putting as many animals on the commons as it could afford. As the village grew in size, more and more animals were placed on the commons, and the overgrazing ruined the pasture. No stock could be supported on the commons thereafter. As a consequence of population growth, greed, and the tragedy of the commons, village after village collapsed.

The conclusion that can be drawn is that the exchange is an important component of Internet infrastructure, and the quality of the exchange is of paramount importance if it is to be of any relevance to ISPs. Using an independent exchange operator whose income is derived from the utility of the exchange is one way of ensuring that the exchange is managed proficiently and that the service quality is maintained for the ISP clients of the exchange.

A Structure for Connectivity

Enhancing the Internet infrastructure is quantified by the following objectives:

- ◆ Extension of reachability
- ◆ Enhancement of policy matching by ISPs
- ◆ Localization of connectivity
- ◆ Backup arrangements for reliability of operation

- Increasing capacity of connectivity
- Enhanced operational stability
- The creation of a rational structure of the connection environment to allow scalable structuring of the address and routing space in order to accommodate orderly growth

We have reached a critical point within the evolution of the Internet. The natural reaction of the various network service entities in response to the increasing number of ISPs will be to increase the complexity of the interconnection structure to preserve various direct connectivity requirements. Today, we are in the uncomfortable position of an increasingly complex inter-provider connectivity environment which is stressing the capability of available technologies and equipment. The inability to reach stable cost distribution models in a transit arrangement creates an environment in which each ISP attempts to optimize its position by undertaking as many direct 1:1 connections with peer ISPs as it possibly can. Some of these connections are managed via the exchange structure. Many more are implemented as direct links between the two entities. Given the relative crudity of the inter-AS routing policy tools that we use today, this structure must be a source of some considerable concern. The result of a combination of an increasingly complex mesh of inter-AS connections, together with very poor tools to manage the routing space, is an increase in the overall instability of the Internet environment. In terms of meeting critical immediate objectives, however, such dire general predictions do not act as an effective deterrent to these actions.

The result is a situation in which the inter-AS space is the critical component of the Internet. This space can be viewed correctly as the demilitarized zone within the politics of today's ISP-based Internet. In the absence of any coherent policy, or even a commonly accepted set of practices, the lack of administration of this space is a source of paramount concern.

Interaction Financials: Peering and Settlements

Any large multiprovider distributed service sector has to address the issue of cost distribution at some stage in its evolution. Cost distribution is the means by which various providers can participate in the delivery of a service to a customer who purchases a service from a single provider, and each provider can be compensated for their costs in an equitable structure of inter-provider settlement.

When an airline ticket is purchased from one air service provider, various other providers and service enterprises may play a role in the delivery of the service. The customer does not separately pay the service fee of each airport baggage handler, caterer, or other form of service provider. The customer's original fare, paid to the original service provider, is distributed by the service provider to other providers who incurred cost in providing components of the total service. These costs are incurred through sets of service contracts, and are the subject of various forms of inter-provider financial settlements, all of which are invisible to the customer.

The Internet is in a very similar situation. Some 60,000 constituent networks must interconnect in one fashion or another to provide comprehensive end-to-end service to each client. In supporting a data transaction between two clients, the two parties often are not clients of the same network. Indeed, the two client service networks often do not directly interconnect, and one or more additional networks must act in a transit provider role to service the transaction. Within the Internet environment, how do all the service parties to a transaction, who incur cost in supporting the transaction, receive compensation for their cost? What is the cost distribution model of the Internet?

Here, we examine the basis for Internet inter-provider cost distribution models and then look at the business models currently used in the inter-provider Internet environment. This area commonly is termed *financial settlement*, a term the Internet has borrowed from the telephony industry.

The Currency of Interconnection

What exactly is being exchanged between two ISPs who want to interconnect? In the sense of the meaning of currency as *the circulating medium*, the question is: What precisely is being circulated at the exchange and within the realm of interconnection? The answer to the question is: *routing entries*. When two parties exchange routing entries, the outcome is that traffic flows in response to the flow of routing entries. The route advertisement and traffic flows move in opposite directions, as indicated in Figure 14.9, and a bilateral routing-mediated flow occurs only when routes are passed in both directions.

Within the routing environment of an ISP there are a number of different classes of routes, with the classification based predominately on the way in which the route has been acquired by the ISP:

- ◆ **Client routes** are passed into the ISP's routing domain by virtue of a service contract with the client. The routes may be statically configured at the edge of the ISP's network, learned by a BGP session with the client, or part of an ISP pool of addresses that are dynamically assigned to the client as part of the dial-up session.

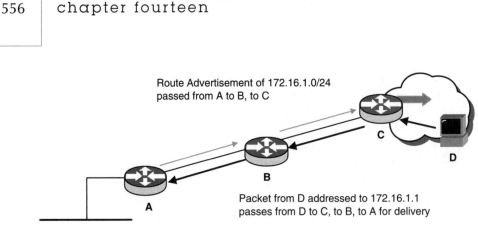

Route Advertisement of 172.16.1.0/24
passed from A to B, to C

C

D

B

Packet from D addressed to 172.16.1.1
passes from D to C, to B, to A for delivery

A

172.16.1.0/24

Figure 14.9   Routing and traffic flows.

- ◆ **Internal ISP routes** fall into a number of additional categories. Some routes correspond to client services operated by the ISP, solely for access to the clients of the ISP, such as Web caches, POP mail servers, and game servers. Some routes correspond to ISP-operated client services that require Internet-wide access, such as DNS forwarders and SMTP relay hosts. Lastly are internal services with no visibility outside the ISP network, such as SNMP network management platforms.

- ◆ **Upstream routes** are learned from upstream ISPs as part of a transit service contract the ISP has executed with the upstream provider.

- ◆ **Peer routes** are learned from exchanges or private interconnections, corresponding to routers exported from the interconnected ISP.

How then should the ISP export routes so that the inbound traffic flow matches the outbound flows implied by this route structure? The route export policy is generally structured along the following lines:

Clients.   All available routes in the preceding four categories, with the exception of internal ISP service functions, should be passed to clients, either in the form of a default route or as explicit route entries passed via a BGP session.

Upstream providers.   All client routes and all internal ISP routes corresponding to Internet-wide services should be passed to upstream providers. Some clients may want further restrictions placed on their routes being advertised in such a fashion. The ability for a client to specify such caveats on the routing structure, and the mechanism used by the ISP to allow this to happen, should be clearly indicated in the service contract.

Peer ISPs. All client routes and all ISP routes corresponding to Internet-wide service should be passed to peer ISPs. Again the client may want to place a restriction on such an advertisement of their routes as a qualification to the ISP's own route export policy.

This structure is shown in Figure 14.10.

The implicit outcome of this structure is that the ISP does not act in a transit role to peer ISPs and does not permit peer-to-peer transit nor peer-to-upstream transit. Peer ISPs have visibility only to clients of the ISP. From the service visibility perspective, client-only services are not visible to peer ISPs or upstream ISPs. Therefore, value-added client services are implicitly visible only to clients and only when they access the service through a client channel.

Settlement Options

Financial settlements have been a continual topic of discussion within the domain of Internet interconnection. To look at the Internet settlement environment, let's first look at the use of inter-provider financial settlements

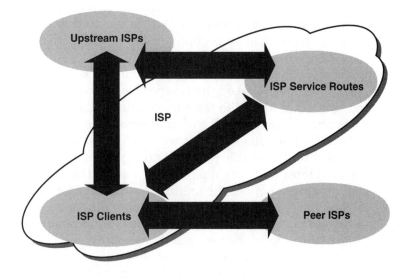

Figure 14.10   External routing interaction.

within the international telephony service industry. Then, we will look at the application of these generic principles to the Internet environment.

Within the traditional telephony model, inter-provider peering takes place within one of three general models:

- **Bilateral settlements.** The first, and highly prevalent, international peering model is that of *bilateral settlements*. A *call* is the unit of settlement accounting. A call is originated by a local client, and the local client's service provider charges the client for the entire end-to-end call. The call may pass through, or transit, a number of providers, and then terminate within the network of the remote client's local provider. The settlement model is a cost distribution mechanism intended to allow each provider to be compensated for costs incurred in the carriage of the call across each provider's network. The cost distribution mechanism of settlements is handled bilaterally. In the most general case of this settlement model the originating provider pays the next hop provider to cover the costs of termination of the call. The next hop provider then either terminates the call within the local network, or undertakes a settlement with the next hop provider to terminate the call. The general telephony trunk model does not admit many multi-party transit arrangements. The majority of telephony settlements are associated with trunk calls that involve only two providers: the originating and terminating providers. Within this technology model, the bilateral settlement becomes easier, as the model simplifies to the case where the terminating provider charges the originating provider a per-call cost within an accounting rate that has been bilaterally agreed between the two parties. As both parties can charge each other using the same accounting currency, the ultimate financial settlement is based on the net outcome of the two sets of call transactions with the two call termination accounting rates applied to these calls. (There is no requirement for the call termination rates for the two parties to be set at the same level.) Each provider invoices the originating end user for the entire call, and the financial settlements provide the accounting balance intended to ensure equity of cost distribution in supporting the costs of the calls made between the two providers. Where there is equity of call accounting rates between the two providers the bilateral inter-provider financial settlements are used in accordance with originating call imbalance, in which the provider hosting the greater number of originating calls pays the other party according to a bilaterally negotiated rate as the mechanism of cost distribution between the two providers.

The accounting settlement call rate is measured in units of call minutes, and the actual rate used is negotiated bilaterally between the two parties. The Federal Communications Commission of the United States (FCC) asserts that U.S. telephone operators paid out some $5.6 billion in settlement rates in 1996, and the FCC is voicing the view that accounting rates have now shifted into areas of non-cost-based settings, rather than working as a simple cost distribution mechanism.

This accounting settlement issue is one of the drivers behind the increasing interest in Voice over IP solutions, because typically no accounting rate settlement component exists in such solutions, and the call termination charges are cost-based, without bilateral price setting. In those cases where accounting rates have come to dominate the provider's call costs, Voice over IP is perceived as an effective lever to bypass the accounting rate structure and introduce a new price point for call termination in the market concerned.

◆ **Sender Keep All.** The second general model is that of *Sender Keep All* (SKA) in which each service provider invoices their originating client's user for the end-to-end services, but no financial settlement is made across the bilateral peering structure. Within the bilateral settlement model, SKA can be regarded as a boundary case of bilateral settlements, where both parties simply deem the outcome of the call accounting process to be absolutely equal, and consequently no financial settlement is payable by either party as an outcome of the interconnection.

◆ **Transit fees.** The third model is that of *transit fees*, in which the one party invoices the other party for services provided. For example, this arrangement is commonly used as the basis of the long-distance provider/local access provider interconnection arrangements. Again, this can be viewed as a boundary case of a general bilateral settlement model, where in this case the parties agree to apply call accounting in only one direction, rather than bilaterally.

The telephony settlement model is by no means stable, and currently significant pressure is being placed on the international accounting arrangements to move away from bilaterally negotiated call accounting rates to a more general adoption of an SKA model. Simultaneously, communications deregulation within many national environments is changing the transit fee model, as local providers extend their network into the long-distance area and commence peering arrangements with similar entities. Criticism also has been directed at the bilaterally negotiated settlement rates, because of the observation that in many cases the accounting rates are not cost-based rates but are based on a desire to create a revenue stream from accounting settlements.

Internet Settlements

A number of critical differences exist between the telephony models of interconnection and the Internet environment, which have confounded all attempts to cleanly map telephony interconnection models into the Internet environment.

Internet interconnection accounting is a packet-based accounting issue, because there is no call in the Internet. Therefore, the most visible difference between the two environments is the replacement of the call with the packet as the currency unit of interconnection. Although we can argue that a TCP session has much in common with a call, this concept is not readily identified within the packet forwarding fabric, and accordingly it is not readily apparent to the network who initiated the TCP session. Unlike a telephony call, no concept of state initiation exists to pass a call request through a network and lock down a network transit path in response to a call response. The network undergoes no state change in response to a TCP session, and therefore, no method is readily available to identify that a call has been initiated, and by which party.

Packets may be dropped. When a packet is passed across an interconnection from one provider to another, no firm guarantee is given by the second provider that the packet will definitely be delivered to the destination. The second provider (or subsequent providers in the transit path) may drop the packet for quite legitimate reasons, and will remain within the protocol specification in so doing. Indeed, the TCP protocol uses packet drop as a rate-control signal. For the efficient operation of the TCP protocol, some level of packet drop is a useful and anticipated event. However, if a packet is used as the accounting unit in a general cost distribution environment, should the provider who receives and subsequently drops the packet be able to claim an accounting credit within the interconnection? The logical response is that such accounting credits should apply only to successfully delivered packets, but such an accounting structure is highly challenging to implement accurately within the Internet environment.

Packet header contents are within the explicit control of the end user, not the provider.   Users can exercise some significant level of control of the path a packet takes to transit the Internet if source routing is honored, so that the relative packet flows between two providers can be arbitrarily manipulated by any client, if so desired.

Packet forwarding is not a verified operation.   A provider may choose to forward a packet to a second provider without reference to the particular routes the second provider is advertising to the first party. A packet also may be forwarded to the second provider with a source address that is not being advertised to the second provider. Given that the generic Internet architecture strives for robustness under extreme conditions, attempts to forward a packet to its addressed destination are undertaken irrespective of how the packet may have arrived at this location in the first place, and irrespective of how a packet with reverse header IP addresses will transit the network.

Routing information is not uniformly available.   Complete information is not available to the Internet regarding the status and reachability of every possible Internet address. Only as a packet is forwarded closer to the addressed destination does more complete information regarding the status of the destination address become apparent to the provider. Accordingly a packet may have incurred some cost of delivery before its ultimate undeliverability becomes evident. An intermediate transit provider can never be completely assured that a packet is deliverable.

These points indicate that a packet-based accounting system for interconnection is the only available rational basis for an inter-provider settlement mechanism. Such a model is prone to significant levels of vulnerability. Arbitrary numbers of packets can be passed across an interconnection in either direction under the explicit control of an end user or a provider, and even without the existence of a valid end-to-end traffic flow. This foundation is not the most stable for a large-scale and high-value monetary settlement structure.

Settlement Models for the Internet

Where a wholesale or retail service agreement is in place, one ISP is in effect a customer of the other ISP. In this relationship, the customer ISP (downstream ISP) is purchasing transit and connectivity services from the supplier

ISP (upstream ISP). The downstream ISP resells this service to its clients. The upstream ISP must announce the downstream ISP's routes to all other customers and other egress points of the ISP's networks to honor the service contract to the downstream ISP customer.

However, given two ISPs who interconnect, the decision as to which party should assume the upstream provider role and which party should assume the downstream customer role is not always immediately obvious to either party or even to an outside observer. Greater geographic coverage may be the discriminator here that allows the customer/provider determination. However, this factor is not the only possible one within the scope of the discussion. One ISP may host significant content and may observe that access to this content adds value to the other party's network, which may be used as an offset against a more conventional customer relationship. In a similar vein, an ISP with a very large client population within a limited geographic locality may see this large client base as an offset against a more uniform customer relationship with the other provider. In many ways, the outcome of these discussions can be likened to two animals meeting in the jungle at night. Each animal sees only the eyes of the other, and from this limited input, the two animals must determine which animal should attempt to eat the other!

An objective determination of which ISP should be the provider and which should be the client is not always possible. In many contexts, the question is inappropriate, given that for some traffic classes the respective roles of provider and client may swap over. The question often is rephrased along the lines of, "Can two providers interconnect without the implicit requirement to cast one as the provider and the other as the client?" Exploration of some concepts of how the question could possibly be answered is illustrative of the problem space here.

PACKET COST ACCOUNTING

One potential accounting model is based on the observation that a packet incurs cost as it is passed through the network. For a small interval of time, the packet occupies the entire transmission capacity of each circuit over which it passes. Similarly, for a brief interval of time, the packet is exclusively occupying the switching fabric of the router. The more routers the packet passes through, and the greater the number and distance of transmission hops the packet traverses, the greater the incurred cost in carrying the packet.

A potential settlement model could be constructed from this observation. The strawman model is that whenever a packet is passed across a network boundary, the packet is effectively sold to the next provider. The sale price increases as the packet transits through the network, accumulating value in direct proportion to the distance the packet traverses within the network. Each boundary packet sale price reflects the previous sale price, plus the value added in transiting the ISP's infrastructure. Ultimately, the packet is sold to the destination client. This model is indicated in Figure 14.11.

As with all strawman models, this one has a number of critical weaknesses, but let's look at the strengths first. An ISP gains revenue from a packet only when delivered on egress from the network, rather than in network ingress. Accordingly, a strong economic incentive exists to accept packets that will not be dropped in transit within the ISP, given that the transmission of the packet only generates revenue to the ISP on successful delivery of the packet to the next hop ISP or to the destination client. This factor places strong pressure on the ISP to maintain quality in the network, because dropped packets imply foregone revenue on local transmission. Because the packet was already purchased from the previous provider in the path, packet loss also implies financial loss. Strong pressure also is exerted to price the local transit function at a commodity price level, rather than attempt to undertake opportunistic pricing. If the chosen transit price is too great, the downstream provider has the opportunity to extend the network to reach further upstream in the path,

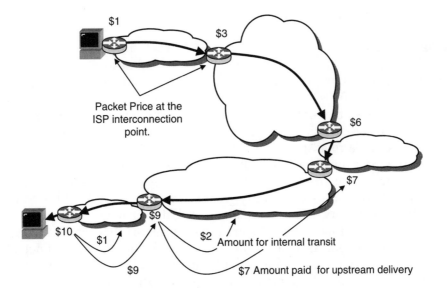

Figure 14.11 Financial inter-provider settlement via packet cost accounting.

bypassing the ISP and purchasing the traffic directly from the upstream source. Accordingly, this model of per-packet pricing, using a settlement model of egress packet accounting, and locally applied value increments to a cumulative per-packet price, based on incremental per hop transmission costs, does allow for some level of reasonable stability and cost distribution in the inter-provider settlement environment.

However, weaknesses of this potential model cannot be ignored. First, some level of packet drop is inevitable irrespective of traffic load. Generally, the more remote the sender from the destination, the less able the sender is to ascertain that the destination address is a valid IP address, and the destination host is available. To minimize the liability from such potential packet loss, the ISP should maintain a relatively complete routing table and only accept packets in which a specific route is maintained for the network. More critical is the issue that the mechanism is open to abuse. Packets, which are generated by the upstream ISP, can be transmitted across the interface, which in turn results in revenue being generated for the ISP. Of course, per-packet accounting within the core of the network is a significant refinement of existing technology. Within a strict implementation of this model, packets require the concept of an attached value that ISPs augment on an ingress-to-egress basis, which could be simplified to a hop-by-hop value increment. Implementations feasibly can use a level of averaging to simplify this by using a tariff for domestic transit and a second for international transit.

TCP SESSION ACCOUNTING

These traffic-based metrics do exhibit some weaknesses because of their inability to resist abuse and likelihood of exacting an inter-provider payment even when the traffic is not delivered to an ultimate destination. Of more concern is that this settlement regime has a strong implication in the retail pricing domain, where the method of payment on delivery is then one of the more robust ways that a retail provider can ensure that there is an effective match between the inter-provider payments and the retail revenue. Does an alternative settlement structure that can address these weaknesses exist? One approach is to perform significantly greater levels of analysis of the traffic as it transits a boundary between a client and the provider or between two providers and to adopt financial settlement measures that match the type of traffic being observed. As an example, the network boundary could detect the initial TCP SYN handshake, and all subsequent packets within the TCP session could be accounted against the session initiator, while UDP traffic could be accounted against the UDP source.

Although such settlement schemes are perhaps limited more by imagination in the abstract, however, very real technical considerations must be borne to bear on this speculation. For a client-facing access router to detect a TCP flow and correctly identify the TCP session initiator requires the router to correctly identify the initial SYN handshake, the opening packet, and then all packets within this TCP flow against this accounting element. This identification may be completely impossible within the network at an inter-provider boundary. The outcome of the routing configuration may be an asymmetric traffic path, so that a single inter-provider boundary may see only traffic passing in a single direction.

However, the greatest problem with this, or any other traffic accounting settlement model, is the diversity of retail pricing structures that exist within the Internet today. Some ISPs use pricing based on received volume, some on sent volume, some on a mix of sent and received volume, and some use pricing based on the access capacity irrespective of volume. This discussion leads to the critical question when considering financial settlements: Considering that the end client is paying the local ISP for comprehensive Internet connectivity, when a client's packet is passed from one ISP to another at an interconnection point, where is the revenue for the packet? Is the revenue model one where the packet sender pays or where the packet receiver pays? The packet egress model described here assumes a uniform retail model in which the receiver pays for Internet packets. The TCP session model assumes the session initiator pays for the entire traffic flow. This uniformity of retail pricing is simply not mirrored within the retail environment of the Internet today.

Although this session-based settlement model does attempt to promote a quality environment with fair carriage pricing, it cannot address the fundamental issue of financial settlements.

CRITERIA FOR SETTLEMENTS

For a financial settlement structure to be viable and stable, the settlement structure must be a uniform abstraction of a relatively uniform retail tariff structure. This conclusion is critically important to the entire Internet financial settlement debate.

The financial structure of interconnection must be an abstraction of the retail models used by the two ISPs. If the uniform retail model is used, the party originating the packet pays the first ISP a tariff to deliver the packet to its destination within the second ISP; then the first ISP is in a position to fund the second ISP to complete the delivery through an interconnection mechanism. If, on the other hand, the uniform retail model is used in which the receiver of the packet funds its carriage from the sender, then the second ISP funds the upstream ISP. If no uniform retail model is used, when a packet is passed from one provider to the other, no understanding exists about which party receives the revenue for the carriage of the packet, and which party settles with the other party for the cost incurred in transmission of the packet.

The answer to these issues within the Internet environment has been to commonly adopt just two models of interaction. These models sit at the extreme ends of the business spectrum, where one is a customer/provider relationship, and the other is a peering relationship without any form of financial settlement, or SKA. These approximately correspond to the second and third models described previously from traditional models of interconnection within the communications industry. However, an increasing trend has moved towards models of financial settlement in a bilaterally negotiated basis within the Internet, using non-cost-based financial accounting rates within the settlement structure. Observing the ISP industry repeat the same well-trodden path, complete with its byways into various unproductive areas and sometimes mistakes, of the international telephony world is somewhat interesting, to say the least. Experiential learning is often observed to be a rare commodity in this area of Internet activity.

No Settlement and No Interconnection

Examining the option of complete autonomy of operation, without any form of interaction with other local or regional ISPs, is instructive within this examination of settlement options.

One scenario for a group of ISPs is that a mutually acceptable peering relationship cannot be negotiated, and all ISPs operate disconnected network domains with dedicated upstream connections and no interconnection. The outcome of such a situation is that third-party connectivity would take place, with transit traffic flowing between the local ISPs being exchanged within the domain of a mutually connected third-party ISP (or via transit across a set of third-party ISPs). For example, for an Asian country, this situation would result in traffic between two local entities, both located within the same country, being passed across the Pacific, routed across a number of network domains within the United States, and then passed back across the Pacific. Not only is this inefficient in terms of resource utilization, this structure also adds a significant cost to the operation of the ISPs, a cost that ultimately is passed to the consumer in higher prices for Internet traffic.

Note that this situation is not entirely novel; the Internet has seen such arrangements appear in the past, and such situations are still apparent in today's Internet. Such arrangements have arisen, in general, as the outcome of an inability to negotiate a stable local peering structure.

However, such positions of no interconnection have proved to be relatively short-lived due to the high cost of operating such international transit environments, the instability of the significantly lengthened interconnection paths, and the unwillingness of foreign third-party ISPs to act (often unwittingly) as agents for domestic interconnection in the longer term. As a result of these factors such off-shore connectivity structures generally have been augmented with domestic peering structures.

The general operating environment of the Internet is that effective isolation is not in the best interests of the ISP, nor is isolation in the interests of other ISPs, nor in the best interests of the consumers of the ISPs' services. In the interests of a common desire to undertake rational and cost-effective use of communications' resources, each national (or regional) collection of ISPs act to ensure local interconnectivity between such ISPs. A priority is to reach acceptable ISP peering arrangements.

SKA Settlement

SKA peering arrangements are those in which traffic is exchanged between two or more ISPs without mutual charge (an interconnection arrangement with no financial settlement). Within a national structure, typically the marginal cost of international traffic transfer to and from the rest of the Internet is significantly higher than domestic traffic transfer. In such cases, any SKA peering is likely to relate to only domestic traffic, and international transit would either be provided by a separate agreement or provided independently by each party.

This SKA peering model is most stable where the parties involved perceive equal benefit from the interconnection. This interconnection model generally is used in the context of interconnection or with providers with approximate equal dimension, as in peering regional providers with other regional providers, national providers with other national providers, and so on. Oddly enough, the parties themselves do not have to agree on what that value or dimension may be in absolute terms. Each party makes an independent assessment of the value of the interconnection, in terms of the perceived size and value of the ISP and the value of the other ISP. If both parties reach the conclusion that in their terms a net balance of value is achieved, then the interconnection is on a stable basis. If one party believes that it is larger than the other and SKA interconnection would result in leverage of its investment by the smaller party, then an SKA interconnection is unstable.

Even with the mutual perception of equality of dimension and value, SKA peering is unlikely to remain stable unless both networks provide infrastructure functions independently or share the operational load of provision of infrastructure functions. These functions include USENET news flows, NTP reference signals, DNS forwarders and caching services, information caches, multicast services, and similar infrastructure services.

The essential criteria for a stable SKA peering structure is perceived equality in the peering relationship. This can be achieved in a number of ways, including the use of entry threshold pricing into the peering environment or the use of peering criteria (such as the specification of ISP network infrastructure or network level of service and coverage areas as eligibility for peering).

A typical feature of the SKA peering environment is to define an SKA peering in terms of traffic peering at the client level only. This definition forces each peering ISP to be self sufficient in the provision of transit services and ISP infrastructure services (such as the requirement to provide services including DNS, NTP, USENET, and so on) that would not be provided across a peering point. This process may not result in the most efficient or effective Internet infrastructure, but it does create a level of approximate parity and reduces the risks of leverage within the interconnection. In this model, each ISP presents at each interconnection or exchange only those routes associated with the ISP's customers and accepts only traffic from peering ISPs at the interconnection or exchange directed to such customers. The ISP does not accept transit traffic destined to other remote exchange locations, nor to upstream ISPs, nor traffic directed to the ISP's infrastructure services. Equally, the ISP does not accept traffic, which is destined to peering ISPs, from upstream transit providers. The business model here is that each client of an ISP is contracting the ISP to present their routes to all other customers of the ISP, to the upstream providers of the ISP, and to all exchange points where the ISP has a presence. The particular tariff model chosen by the ISP in servicing the customers is not material to this interconnection model. Traffic passed to a peer ISP at the exchange becomes the responsibility of the peer ISP to pass to their customers at their cost.

Another means of generating equity within an SKA peering is to peer only within the terms of a defined locality. In this model, an ISP would present routes to an SKA peer in which the routes corresponded to customers located at a particular access POP, or a regional cluster of access POPs. The SKA peer's ability to leverage advantage from the greater level of investment (assuming that the other party is the smaller party) is now no longer a factor, because the smaller ISP sees only those parts of the larger ISP that sit within a well-defined local or regional zone. This form of peering is indicated in Figure 14.12.

The probable outcome of widespread use of SKA interconnections is a generalized ISP domain along the lines of Figure 14.13. Here, the topology is segregated into two domains—consisting of a set of transit ISPs, whose predominate investment direction is in terms of high-capacity carriage infrastructure and high-capacity switching systems, and a collection of local ISPs, whose predominate investment direction is in service infrastructure supporting a string retail focus. Local ISPs participate at exchanges and announce local routes at the exchange on an SKA basis of interconnection with peer ISPs. Such ISPs are strongly motivated to prefer to use all routes presented at the exchange within such peering sessions, as the ISP is not charged any transit cost for the traffic under an SKA settlement structure. The exchange does not provide comprehensive connectivity to the ISP, and this connectivity

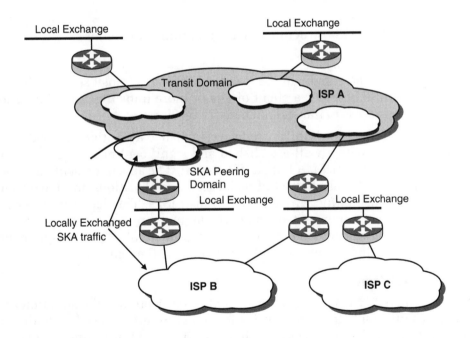

Figure 14.12 SKA peering using local cells.

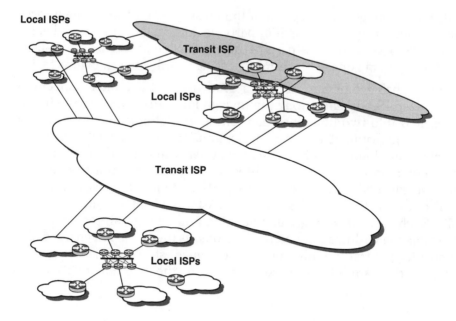

Figure 14.13   ISP structure of local and transit operations.

needs to be complemented with a separate purchase of transit services. In this role, the local ISP becomes a client of one or more transit ISPs explicitly for the purpose of access to transit connectivity services.

In this model, the transit ISP must have established a position of broad ranging connectivity, with a well-established and significant market share of the wholesale transit business. A transit ISP also must be able to present customer routes at a carefully selected set of major exchange locations and have some ability to exchange traffic with all other transit ISPs. This latter requirement has typically been implemented using private interconnection structures, and the associated settlements often are negotiated bilaterally. These settlements possibly may include some element of financial settlement.

Financial Settlement

The alternative to SKA and provider/client role selection is the adoption of a financial settlement structure. The settlement structure is based on both parties effectively selling services to each other across the interconnection point, with the financial settlement undertaking the task of balancing the relative sales amounts.

The simplest form of undertaking this settlement is to measure the volume of traffic being passed in each direction across the interconnection and to use a single accounting rate for all traffic. At the end of each accounting period, the two ISPs would financially settle based on the agreed accounting rate applied to the net traffic flow.

Which way the money should flow in relationship to traffic flow is not immediately obvious. One model assumes that the originating provider should be funding the terminating provider to deliver the traffic, and therefore, money should flow in the same direction as traffic. The reverse model assumes that the overall majority of traffic, to the level of 80–85 percent of all ISP-carried traffic, is traffic generated by an action of the receiver, such as Web page retrieval or the downloading of software. Therefore, the network cost should be imposed on the discretionary user, so that the terminating provider should fund the originating provider. This latter model has some degree of supportive evidence, because a larger provider will, generally, provide more traffic to a smaller attached provider than it receives from that provider. Observation of traffic statistics would bear this out, indicating that traffic-received volumes are a preferable means of determining the relative interconnection benefit to two providers.

The accounting rate can be negotiated to be any amount. There is a caveat on this ability to set an arbitrary accounting rate, as is certainly the case in the telephony industry settlement domain where an accounting rate is not cost-based, business instability issues arise. For greater stability the agreed settlement traffic unit accounting rate would have to match the average marginal cost of transit traffic in both ISP networks for the settlement to be attractive to both parties.

Refinements to this approach can be introduced, although they are accompanied by significant expenditure on traffic monitoring and accounting systems. The refinements are intended to address the somewhat arbitrary determination of financial settlement based on the receiver or the sender. One way is to undertake flow-based accounting, in which the cost accounting for the volume of all packets associated with a TCP flow is directed to the initiator of the TCP session. Here, the cost accounting for all packets of a UDP flow is directed to the UDP receiver. The session-based accounting is significantly more complex than simple volume accounting, and such operational complexity would be reflected in the cost of undertaking such a form of accounting. However, asymmetric paths are a common feature of the inter-AS environment, so that it may not always be possible to see both sides of a TCP conversation and perform an accurate determination of the session initiator.

Another refinement is to use a different rate for each provider, where the base rate is adjusted by some agreed size factor to ensure that the larger provider is not unduly financially exposed by the arrangement. The adjustment factor can be the number of POPs, range of the network, volume carried on the network, number of routes advertised to the peer, or any other metric related to the ISP's investment and market share profile. Alternatively, a relative adjustment factor can simply be a number without any basis in a network metric, to which both parties agree.

Of course, traffic flows on the Internet are not as rigidly structured as those within the telephony environment, and within this Internet interconnection environment, readily determining which party's client generated a bi-directional traffic flow across the peering structure is not easily achieved. This is why the coarse metric of traffic volumes in each direction is often chosen as the basis of the financial settlement. Such a metric of relative traffic volume balance is not very robust either, and the metric is one that is infinitely adjustable and potentially infinitely abused. The capability to adjust the relative traffic balance comes from the direct relationship between the routes advertised and the volume of traffic received. To reduce the amount of traffic received, the ISP reduces the number of routes advertised to the corresponding peer. Increasing the number of routes, and at the same time increasing the number of specific routes, increases the amount of received traffic. Where there is a rich mesh of connectivity, there is a strong financial incentive for each party to adjust the routing parameters to match the lowest financial expenditure by using restricted route advertisements with the greatest levels of revenue by using a local preference for received routes (with the highest preference for client-advertised routes and the next level of preference for financially settled peer advertised routes). Such settings of the routing system may not necessarily correspond to the optimal traffic path in network engineering terms, nor will these settings necessarily result in a highly stable routing and traffic configuration.

Of far greater concern is the ability to abuse the interconnection arrangements. One party can generate and then direct large volumes of traffic to the other party. Although overt abuse of the arrangements is often easy to detect, greed is a wonderful stimulant to ingenuity, and more subtle forms of abuse of this interconnection are always possible. To address this, both parties would typically indicate in an interconnection agreement their undertaking not to indulge in such forms of deliberate abuse of the interconnection. Notwithstanding such undertakings by the two providers, third parties can still abuse the interconnection in various ways. Loose source routing can generate traffic flows which pass across the interconnection in either direction.

The ability to remotely trigger traffic flows through source address spoofing is possible even where loose source routing is disabled. This window of financial vulnerability is far wider than many ISPs are comfortable with, because it opens the provider to a significant liability over which it has a limited ability to detect and control. Consequently, financial settlement structures based on traffic flow metrics are not a commonly deployed mechanism, as they introduce unacceptable financial risks to the ISP into the interconnection environment.

The Settlement Debate

The issue of Internet settlements, and associated financial models of settlement, has occupied the attention of a large number of ISPs, traditional communications carriers, public regulators, and other interested bodies for many years. Despite these concentrated levels of attention and analysis, the Internet interconnection environment remains one where there are no soundly based models of financial settlement in widespread use today.

It is useful to look further into this matter, and pose the question: "Why has the Internet managed to pose such a seemingly intractable challenge to the ISP industry?"

The prime reason is likely to be found within the commonly adopted retail model of ISP services. The tariff for an ISP retail service does not implicitly cover the provision of an Internet transmission service from the client to all other Internet-connected hosts. In other words, the Internet service, as retailed to the client, is not a comprehensive end-to-end service.

In a simple model of the operation of the Internet, each ISP owns and operates some local network infrastructure, and may choose to purchase services from one or more upstream service providers. The service domain offered to the clients of this network specifically encompasses an Internet sub-domain limited to the periphery of the ISP network together with the periphery of the contracted upstream provider's service domain. (This is a recursive domain definition, in that the upstream provider in turn may have purchased services from an upstream provider at the next tier, and so on.) Once the client's outbound traffic leaves this service domain, the ISP ceases to directly, or indirectly, fund the carriage of the client's traffic, and the funding burden passes over to a funding chain linked to the receiver's retail service. For example, when traffic is passed from an ISP client to a client of another provider, the ISP funds the traffic as it transits through the ISP and indirectly funds the cost of carriage through any upstream provider's network. When the traffic leaves the provider's network, to be passed to either a different client, another ISP, or to a peer provider, the sender's ISP ceases to fund the further carriage of the traffic. In other words, these scenarios illustrate the common theme that the retail base of the Internet is not an end-to-end tariff base. The sender of the traffic does not fund the first hop ISP for the total costs of carriage through the Internet to the traffic's destination, nor does the ultimate receiver pay the last hop ISP for these costs. The ISP retail pricing structure reflects an implicit division of cost between the two parties, and there is no structural requirement for inter-provider financial balancing between the originating ISP and the terminating ISP.

An initial reaction to this partial service model would be to wonder why the Internet works at all, given that no single party funds the carriage of traffic on the complete path from sender to receiver. Surely this would imply that once the traffic had passed beyond the sending ISP's service funded domain the traffic should be discarded as unfunded traffic. The reason why this is not the case is that the receiver implicitly assumes funding responsibility for the traffic at this handover point, and the second part of the complete carriage path is funded by the receiver. In an abstract sense the entire set of connectivity paths within the Internet can be viewed as a collection of bilaterally funded paths, where the sender funds the initial path component and the receiver funds the second terminating path component. This underscores the original observation that the generally adopted retail model of Internet services is not one of end-to-end service delivery, but instead one of partial path service, with no residual retail price component covering any form of complete path service. This is not an encouraging situation for those clients who want to purchase an end-to-end quality differentiated service from their ISP.

Financial settlement models typically are derived from a different set of initial premises than those described here. The typical starting point is that the retail offering is a comprehensive end-to-end service, and that the originating service provider utilizes the services of other providers to complete the delivery of all components of the retailed service. The originating service provider then makes some form of financial settlement with those providers who have undertaken some form of an operational role in providing these service elements. This cost-distributed business structure allows both small and large providers to operate with some degree of financial stability, which in turn allows a competitive open service market to thrive. Through the operation of open competition the consumer gains the ultimate price and service benefit of cost-efficient retail services.

The characteristics of the Internet environment tend to create a different business environment than a balanced cost distribution structure. Here there is a clear delineation between a customer-provider relationship and a peer relationship, with no middle ground of a financially settled inter-ISP bilateral relationship. An ISP customer is one who assumes the role of a customer of one or a number of upstream providers, with an associated flow of funding from the customer to the upstream provider, whereas an ISP upstream service provider views the downstream provider as a customer. An ISP peer relationship is two ISPs executing a peering arrangement, where traffic is exchanged between the two providers without any financial settlement, and such peering interactions are only stable while both providers perceive some degree of parity in the arrangement, such as where the two providers present to the peering point Internet domains of approximate equality in market coverage and market share. An ISP may have multiple simultaneous relationships, being a customer in some cases, an upstream provider in others, and a peer in others. In general the relationships are unique within an ISP pairing, and efforts to support a paired relationship that encompasses elements of both peering and customer-provider pose significant technical and business challenges.

The most natural business outcome of any business environment is for each provider to attempt to optimize their business position. This optimization is not simply a case of a competitive impetus to achieve cost efficiency in the service operation, as the realization of cost efficiencies within the service provider's network does not result in any substantial change in the provider's financial position with respect to upstream costs or peering positioning. The provider's path towards business optimization includes a strong component of increasing the size and scope of the service provider operation, so that the benefits of providing funded upstream services to customer providers can be maximized, and non-financially settled peering occurs with other larger providers.

The conclusion drawn is that the most natural business outcome of the Internet settlement environment is one of aggregation of providers, a factor quite evident in the present Internet provider environment.

Futures

A number of aspects of the ISPs' interconnection environment may have ramifications in terms of the future profile of the ISP industry worldwide.

Currently, the growth of the Internet market is acting as the major impetus to the ISP market. When this level of growth tapers off, the widespread expectation is that some level of rationalization will occur, with the number and diversity of ISPs tapering off as a part of this rationalization. The rationale behind this expectation is that in a more static market, larger players can use both investment pressure and various economies of scale to ensure that their operation is highly cost efficient. This efficiency can be reflected in their retail pricing structure, with immediate consequences in acquiring additional retail market share. Also, larger investors can afford to take longer term positions on the market, sustaining an initial period of operating loss to realize desired longer term market share positions.

However, another factor is at play in the longer term future of the industry. This factor is the basic issue of cost distribution within a multi-provider environment. Without a robust and well founded mechanism that allows for the incremental costs associated with the carriage of traffic to be apportioned to each provider within the transit path, a fundamental barrier exists to the stability of a well-populated diverse ISP marketplace servicing vertical market sectors. The business outcomes from this lack of effective cost distribution structures are inevitably that smaller industry players are unable to establish a stable revenue stream from the transit costs associated with interconnection.

Cost distribution is an essential attribute of a diverse provider environment. In the absence of viable and stable cost distribution structures, cost distribution will not happen within the service provider industry. In such an environment it is a challenge to sustain a diverse provider industry, and the business domain outcome is highly likely to be a consolidation into a very small number of ISP transit operators providing service on a global scale. All other providers will align to become customers of one or more of these global ISP transit operators. This very small number of global transit providers (or tier 1 providers, to use a popular term for such enterprises) probably will never coalesce into just one, but a set of global alliances may be an outcome along these lines. While this is the realm of speculation, it is reasonable to suggest a likely outcome of small number of tier 1 ISPs. To be more specific, there may well be between two and six such major global transit providers, with each transit operator undertaking private peering using SKA settlement with its transit peers. All other ISPs will align as direct or indirect customers of such tier 1 ISPs, and may peer locally within their tier of operation. Some industry observers would argue that this industry evolution is already largely in place, and all that remains now is the widespread recognition that this aggregation phase is now underway within the ISP world.

Within the local ISP environment there is more scope for a multiplicity of players in an SKA-based interconnection environment, and this environment can be sustained relatively easily. Consolidation, if occurring in this sector, will be a result of economies of scale rather than an outcome of the economics of interconnection.

Strong pressure to change the technology base to accommodate more sophisticated settlement structures is unlikely to emerge. The fundamental observation is that any financial settlement structure is robust only where a retail model exists that is relatively uniform in both its nature and deployment, and encompasses the provision of services on an end-to-end basis. Where a broad diversity of partial service retail mechanisms exists within a multi-provider environment, the stability of any form of inter-provider financial settlement structure will always be dubious at best.

With the ISP industry, the overall business model alternatives tend to cluster to either a diverse competitive industry with inter-provider settlements, or an environment with no inter-provider settlements, with the creation of strong pressures for provider aggregation. The industry has already made a decision between these alternative business models, as provider aggregation is well and truly evident in today's Internet. Public acceptance of this global business model, particularly within the various national regulatory sectors, is yet to emerge.

chapter fifteen

Public Policy and the Internet

The Internet has presented a number of fundamental challenges to the process of evolution of public policy in the communications sector. The traditional view of the communications market and the associated regulatory structure saw a regulated public telephone operator, as well as radio, television, and print operators, all operating within varying degrees of regulatory control from country to country.

The regulatory control placed on the telephone operator in particular was designed to achieve a number of social objectives, principally relating to ubiquity of access, affordability of the service, and reliability and robustness of the service platform. Such objectives fit well within the context of the Internet, because they are worthy social objectives of any truly useful public communications system. Although the policy objectives may have remained constant, the landscape has changed. No longer is there a single monopoly service provider, often working as a public agency with direct accountability to government. The Internet is being constructed on a wave of policy deregulation, with a significant level of private investment. In this chapter, we look at this landscape in further detail and then look at the likely directions of public policy with respect to the Internet and its evolution.

The Deregulated Communications Market

The traditional regulatory structure of the communications market was seriously questioned in the 1970s. At that time, the model of a public utility monopoly operation of critical public infrastructure elements was complemented by a visible shift into monopoly trading models. As digital technology entered the telephony world, the operating cost efficiencies achieved through the adoption of this technology shift were not always passed directly to the consumer in the form of lower retail tariffs. Telephone operators were perceived to be using the advantages of this technology shift to move to a pricing model that charged the consumer on the value of the voice service, rather than the marginal cost of the provision of a switched voice circuit. This digital technology also had the effect of reducing the entry price for sector-based communications service providers. This reduced barrier to entry, coupled with expectations of continued buoyant financial returns, generated strong pressure on the regulator to open the telecommunications market to private investment. The typical public policy response to this situation was to advocate competitive business practices as a means of reintroducing cost-based pricing models into the communications market. Of course, this was not a uniform call for competition across the world. In some countries, the exploitation of the incumbent operator's monopoly position had allowed the international call accounting rates to be inflated so far above cost that they had become a highly valued source of foreign currency. In these countries, the public telephone monopoly had become a critical component of the national economy.

The call for the introduction of competition into the telephone operations area was phrased as a call for deregulation of the communications market. The stream of argument within this call for competition was that the excessively regulated telephone service had created an environment in which the consumer price was being inflated artificially through exploitation of the regulatory environment. Consequently, the telephone system was no longer an effective enabler for domestic commerce, but was, at best, a source of indirect public taxation, and, at worst, an overhead of massive inefficiency and waste. The call for deregulation indicated that the primary outcome of a competitive market was the removal of inefficient and wasteful operational practices, and the longer term outcome was the expectation of a cost-efficient market operation where the realization of efficiencies of operation was passed to the consumer through lower prices. As it related to the telephone industry, deregulation implied a shift in the public investment profile of the national telephone network, advocating its replacement by a structure of private investment and private operators, operating competitively.

Many countries have responded to this call for deregulation positively, although the initial measures of deregulation have often been incremental steps with some caution evident in such steps. The national monopoly telecommunications service provider has been one of the major public sector elements of many national economies, and in those cases, a shift of this economic activity into the private sector does have quite profound longer term economic implications. Accordingly, the regulatory changes to effect this move typically have been incremental in nature, rather than an overnight shift to a fully deregulated environment, commencing often with deregulation of the value-added service market as a precursor to complete deregulation.

Into this public policy environment, focused predominately on the deregulation of the telephone industry, entered the digital communications market and the explosive growth of the Internet service market in particular. The expectations of deregulation centered around a small number of large investors making significant investments into infrastructure and service operations. The outcomes have been quite different to the policy-makers' expectations. Deregulation and the Internet have worked together to see a large number of smaller investors, exploiting the low entry price of the Internet service industry to enter the market with minimal, if any, infrastructure investment. In addition, the Internet industry now offers the promise of competition in the core voice service market, exploiting the economies and operational profile of the Internet service model to provide a significantly cheaper voice product in the long distance and international call markets. Consequently, this model of deregulation of the communications industry, where it has been adopted as a national policy, has had very far reaching implications, as it has spread far beyond a simple shift of the regulatory framework surrounding the operation of the telephone network into the broader area of communications services, and the Internet in particular.

Where deregulation of the provider market is in force, the barriers between various sectors in the market are being broken down. The nature of the industry is changing, with the natural boundaries between various sectors of the communications industry being blurred by the digital medium. Television operators now complement their traditional programming and content dissemination with Web content. They can use digital streaming audio and video content to recreate some of the attributes of the original television medium, allowing the reuse of some of their product. The print media have created electronic papers to reach an online readership, and online electronic games have created a new industry within the entertainment market. This quite fluid environment is one in which ISPs find themselves operating today. However, the environment will continue to evolve, and the aspects of this evolution probably will be more prevalent in the area of regulation and policy than in technology, as far as the Internet is concerned. The Internet has accelerated the pace of deregulation of the industry to an extent never thought possible, and it is now offering the potential to rewrite the economics of service provision, not only of data-based services, but also the economics of voice services. The outcomes of this process are quite unclear at this stage, and although the appellation of *policy on the fly* may be somewhat extreme, evidence certainly exists of learning through experience across both the industry and within public policy sectors.

The Internet Policy Environment

Who *governs* the Internet? Where does the *authority* lie to set and enforce policy? The answers are far more complex than the simple nature of these questions would infer. The Internet policy environment is far ranging and highly dynamic in nature, presenting significant challenges to policy makers. Internet policy issues cover an extremely broad area of activity, ranging though operational service quality levels, name and address distribution structures, privacy issues, connectivity requirements, content regulation, taxation, and commerce, to name but a few. Obviously, not all of these areas are amenable to strict regulation, even if it were contemplated. The stakes, however, are very high in this area of policy-making:

- First, billions of dollars of telephony revenues will be diverted into the Internet market. Some $3.5 billion is expected to be diverted by 2001.

- Second, existing universal service obligation structures, that, worldwide, also account for billions of dollars within the telephone markets also will be diverted to an Internet infrastructure, which to date has concentrated service only in the wealthiest and most populous areas of the world.

- Third, in the same way that efficient transport infrastructures were a key component of national wealth creation in the industrial age, an efficient communications system will be a critical component of national wealth creation in the global information market. The leverage in this latter category can be estimated to lie somewhere in the trillions of dollars.

Strong pressure exists within policy making to preserve the status quo of the communication industry, and equally strong pressure is being exerted by the different operational paradigm of the Internet to reduce the relevance of such historically based policy frameworks.

In looking at this topic, it's useful to phrase a few policy objectives for the Internet and then examine how they can be achieved. A generally accepted set would include the following set of outcomes:

- Develop the Internet as a part of mainstream public communications
- Build on a structure of private investment into the Internet service industry
- Ensure that the Internet continues to be cost efficient to use
- Ensure that the Internet continues to be useful
- Ensure that the Internet is ubiquitous

Internet-Effective Policies

Policies must be effective within the context of the Internet itself. For this to happen, a necessary precondition is that any such policies reflect an adequate understanding of the current nature and environment of the Internet and to voice a coherent objective in terms of a future vision of the Internet and its role in supporting broader social objectives. Sadly, such positions of understanding and coherent vision are not visibly abundant within the Internet today, and ample evidence remains of policy positions, which are more concerned with attempting to revisit previous policy issues rather than adopting a forward-looking stance within a policy framework. In an environment that is evolving as rapidly as the Internet, it is inappropriate to create policies for the past. The policy framework must adopt a forward-looking stance.

The Changing Internet

To understand the changing requirements for policy determination, we must observe the changing characterization of the Internet. To adopt a forward-looking stance effectively necessitates a more dynamically positioned policy framework that reflects the current and likely future positioning of the Internet as it continues to grow. The Internet environment is not one that remains static on a yearly, or perhaps even on a monthly basis. The changes within the Internet are not only within a dimension of more participants, but also within a dimension of an evolving and expanding activity environment. The policy challenges are effectively based on the likely outcomes of further rapid growth in this environment and the areas of opportunity that are presented within such a process.

However, to understand such changing policy requirements, we must observe the changing characterization of the Internet up to the present and draw out a likely future scenario based on a projection of these pressures and forces.

In the late 1980s, the Internet had reached beyond a research experiment and was a utility network, servicing a community of interest. Its predominate characteristic at the time was that of an academic and research community activity. Within the language of the regulatory framework of the day, the Internet was a common-interest service network, with a well-defined membership and activity scope. The characteristics of the governance of the network through the 1980s was that the Internet was through a collection of service providers, consumers, developers, and researchers, all operating within a largely homogeneous environment. The outcome of this collective process appeared to bear all the appropriate hallmarks of a *collaborative community* characterization, including aspects of common policies, derived through a process of *consensus seeking*. The common forward policy agenda was strongly concerned with technological refinement, also derived in a collaborative manner. The common nature of the various participatory partners and their shared objective effectively ensured that a consensus seeking a collaborative policy determination process would indeed terminate quickly, with readily acceptable outcomes.

A major area of common motivation of this community was an interest in the underlying technology of the Internet. Areas of strong commonality were to be found within this area of collaborative technological development, which strengthened both the cooperative nature of the Internet community and the cohesion of the network itself. This allowed the Internet to develop as a *single environment of uniform connectivity* rather than as fragmented islands of connectivity.

The outcomes of this collaborative community can be characterized within the following parameters:

♦ No formal regulation of the Internet as an externally imposed constraint

♦ An associated position of self-moderation of the Internet by the Internet community itself

♦ A high level of policy adaptability within the constraints of collaborative community expectation

Such a self-moderated, highly adaptable policy environment precisely matched the requirement of the process of technology evolution, in which the Internet assumed the roles of both a research project and a production service platform simultaneously. The collaborative nature of the community and the relatively small size of the community allowed rapid evolution of the environment in both technology and policy terms. In general, such highly adaptable environments are a typical feature of small cohesive communities undertaking developmental efforts. They typically possess the inherent capability to adjust the parameters of self-moderation to suit the requirements of the day and possess suitably flexible control structures to allow policy adaptability at a similar scale.

Although such a collaborative process can operate in an extraordinarily effective manner within a small homogeneous community, and indeed such a process is probably an optimal choice for such communities, such a process does not maintain robustness under growth. The effectiveness of this process is a catalyst for the growth of the community. This growth is readily apparent within the Internet, due in no small part to the particular characteristics of openness and effectiveness of the underlying technology. The collaborative unregulated environment has made increased levels of participation easier, rather than acting as an inhibitor for many. This growth in community population has, in turn, necessitated some significant changes in the community's collaborative consensus-seeking process.

This growth manifests itself in very visible ways, such as the increasing population of the Internet domain in both computer and human population counts and the amount and diversity of information and communication domains that together form the total Internet service domain. However, another metric is also a factor in terms of a policy-based perspective—the increasing level of investment into Internet-based services and programs. This investment level is also increasing, when measured in both monetary terms and in terms of programs and services that are now critically reliant on functionally capable access to a coherent worldwide Internet environment. This investment becomes a major factor in assessing whether the Internet can be seen as a migratory phase on the path to some as yet ill-defined global information and communications infrastructure, or whether the Internet itself is the platform upon which the existing investment levels act as a strong attractor for further investment.

The outcomes of this intense growth factor are visible within the original collaborative academic and research sector, in which the flexibility of the refinement of the underlying technology base becomes limited by the increasing size and investment levels made by this sector. The Internet technical community often has proudly claimed that the SNMP network management protocol was developed and deployed within a period of nine months on the

Internet. This same feat probably could not be performed today. Although defining new technologies as backward-compatible extensions to the existing technology base is possible, the issues of transition to incompatible technologies hinge centrally around the incremental costs, which would be borne by each user entity, and the issue that such costs would not be readily met if the existing technology matched the service expectations of such clients.

As with technology innovation, so with policy evolution. Policy flexibility suffers similar constraints under such growth, where major policy shifts within one section of the community imply a forced change in policy across the remainder of the network. The costs of such forced changes may be prohibitive. As an example of forced policy matching, one can see that if a critical mass within the ISP industry sector moved to, say, financial settlement models, then the remainder of the sector will be effectively forced to adopt similar measures in order to ensure parity of approximate peering across the network. The result of the process is that common interest within the relatively homogeneous worldwide academic and research community has allowed common policy formation to occur. Each component player now becomes reliant on the outcomes of such common policies as the means of ensuring continuity and functionality of the total common communications environment. The overall environment shifts from active to passive as each player, rather than being reliant on direct and frequent involvement in collaborative processes as the means of self-regulation, shifts to simply adopting the outcome of such processes, without any direct involvement in their operation.

Where policy becomes a more static factor, rather than a commonly agreed *modus operandi*, each ISP player within the environment must devote some time and attention to generating stable commonly agreed policies to ensure functional operational interaction of each component network. Without such stability of policy, the collaborative nature of the community quickly breaks down, to be replaced by an aggressive short-term, self-interest optimization pattern.

This transition of the environment appears to have largely taken place. As well as a process of visible change within the nature of the initial collaborative community, as a reflection of the growth of the Internet within this domain, the other major feature of recent times has been the outgrowth of the Internet. This outgrowth is one in which the Internet is encompassing additional service domains in the government, corporate, public service, educational, and industrial areas. This area of growth becomes self-sustaining when a certain level of initial uptake is obtained. A strong client base allows a service operation to operate within acceptable parameters of scale and efficiency, and the presence of providers and relevant services acts as a strong attractor for more clients, as long as there are perceived areas of leverage and benefit in so doing.

The observation made within this context, however, is that the motivation of both the client base and the service providers within these areas is not directly motivated by the original collaborative community's objectives and agenda. These new user domains typically regard the Internet in the same way as any other customer service product, and tend to interpret the environment of the Internet as being one with levels of stability of service. The inferred expectation of stability of the underlying technologies is, at some level of difference with the inherently more dynamic models, assumed by the academic and research collaborative community.

The Current Policy Environment

The current policy environment is best described as one of unresolved tension over the very nature of the Internet and its regulatory model between four policy sectors:

◆ The collaborative community
◆ The deregulated competitive market
◆ The established communications industry
◆ The regulator in the guise of public resource management

This environment is indicated in Figure 15.1.

The Collaborative Community

The collaborative community still has a strong base of influence of policy within the Internet, although its level of influence over the technology of the service and the resulting Internet service environment is waning. Its major contribution remains in the aspect of a statement of ethos of collaboration and active involvement, eschewing a role as a passive consumer in an Internet-mediated, one-way content delivery network.

PUBLIC FUNDING VERSUS COMMERCIALIZATION

The characterization of the collaborative community has been explored in the previous section looking at the evolution of the Internet environment and can be summarized as one based largely on the area of the technological base of

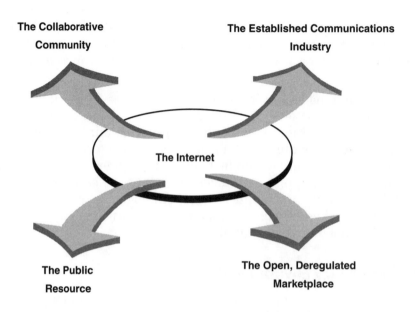

Figure 15.1 The current policy environment of the Internet.

the Internet, with a strong focus on the aspects of academic and research activities into both the Internet as a dynamic technology platform and in the use of the Internet for other academic and research pursuits.

In characterizing the Internet as a research platform, the position within publicly funded academic and research domains is evident in the provision of services through public-funding programs. The NSFnet program of the early 1990s in the United States, and the current U.S. Internet II project, are instances of this public policy. The inevitable side effect is that such programs do not readily admit a component user base exploiting the services on a commercial basis. Public policy generally dictates that such publicly funded research and development programs are intended to effectively develop and harden technology artifacts up to the point of viability of commercial exploitation. When commercial exploitation is considered viable, further public funding of the resource is not a realistic role for public money, on the basis of market skew by public policy being considered harmful and inefficient. The manner by which such broad policy agendas are expressed within the Internet are through *Appropriate Use Policies* in which use of a publicly funded component of the Internet is restricted on a policy basis to certain types of users. Within a homogenous collaborative user community of publicly funded academic and research folk, this presents few issues of contention—

within a broader environment of users and user domains such efforts of user sector delineation based on administrative policies presents all players with significant problems in implementation.

MOTIVATION FOR COMMON SOLUTIONS THROUGH COOPERATION

The community characterization of the policy environment of the Internet within this sector is the careful construction of consensus within the community and the strong level of motivation for common-solution seeking by the academic and research sector members. The reasons for such common consensus approaches are based on the understanding of the role of the Internet as a common technology base. Consensus, if achieved, allows all players, both now and in the future, equal access to the technology elements, and it effectively constructs an open technology environment that can be exploited on equal terms by all players, if they so choose.

The Deregulated Market Commodity

The deregulated competitive market is now the dominating factor in the Internet. It is strongly dominant in terms of metrics of usage, such as traffic volumes and metrics of influence, such as investment levels. The ISP industry and the clients of their service offerings view the Internet as an open, and unregulated, marketplace in which goods and services are freely traded based on perceptions of need and demand. Here, the communications environment is seen as an opportunity for exploitation by market forces in the same way that other media, such as the radio spectrum, are employed by the market.

THE DEREGULATED COMMUNICATIONS ENVIRONMENT

The Internet operates as a service layered above basic transmission elements and within many countries it operates under the terms and conditions of a value-added reseller, rather than being an intrinsic activity of a duly authorized common communications carrier. Within many countries, this area of value-added resellers is an area that is in the process of complete deregulation. The motivation for deregulation being to encourage private investment within the national communications industry, to effectively induce levels of competitive activity, which allow an open competitive market to operate. The overall intent is to stimulate levels of investment in national infrastructure and to provide consumers with a range of services, which are geared to efficient and effective service operation.

Within such a perspective, the Internet operates as any other value-added service, in which service definition, pricing, policy of operation, and all other aspects of the service are defined through the operation of market forces within a competitive market. Within such a marketplace, artificial denial of service through appropriate use policies play no discernible role, and differential tariffing of services fulfills no role other than market penetration and competitive market acquisition.

IMPLICIT DECISION MAKING THROUGH MARKET FORCES

The interesting observation to make is whether such a market-oriented view of the Internet allows integration of basic technology change into the sector's characterization of the Internet, as is the case within the collaborative community. Although the deployment of new services based on technology evolution could be seen as a competitive advantage within a market, if such changes also effectively isolate existing market sectors, then it is not clear whether they would be openly embraced by the marketplace. The major observation of the open market is that policies are derived through the interplay of market pressures and client expectation, and service and infrastructure roles are derived not through common collaborative agreement, but through attempts to generate both price, and more critically, service differentiation within the marketplace.

The Established Communications Industry

The established communications industry had envisioned a data environment more on terms similar to telephony, in which the characteristics of the data service were an intrinsic attribute of the network rather than the host. This model admitted many more elements of control into the network provider domain, viewing host computer platforms as simple data-processing stations. This vision was espoused within the X.25 protocols, Frame Relay, and ATM Virtual Circuit services, which are feature-rich network services.

The requirements of the Internet are far more basic in nature. The requirement to support the Internet is for simple bit carriage services, without any service overlay. For the established communications industry, this is not a market that admits a high degree of added value elements. For some time, the established communications industry resisted this Internet approach to supporting networking services, offering an OSI-based network service architecture as an alternative approach to the industry. This has largely receded in importance, and the current approach from this sector is to quickly come to terms with the market, recovering from a somewhat slow response to the arrival of the Internet as a significant market force.

MOTIVATIONS FOR THE COMMUNICATIONS INDUSTRY

The communications industry has been accused of operating in a fashion not unlike a cartel. While the investment levels were significant, and the rates of financial return very low, it was necessary to take a long-term investment position within the market and then protect this investment from short-term risks. The position of national providers as operators with limited competitive interests and much in common, implied that significant benefits were possible in working within a common framework to protect their long-terms investments and develop their respective markets. All this is changing under the pressure of an altered technology base, in which the barriers to entry are coming down and alternative services threaten the revenue streams from the voice market. The widespread deregulation of the environment now implies that no national boundary exists to competition, so that this common approach to policy determination is now rapidly dwindling in this sector.

In a policy sense, the initial motivation of this sector is to ensure that this activity does not erode their current market position or net worth, and the secondary motivation is now to develop this market in a way that enhances the value of their total enterprise.

This sector has not been occupying the forefront of the policy debate. Their current approach appears to be a preference to use their considerable financial capabilities to purchase a strategic position within the Internet market sector at this stage, while coming to grips with the considerable changes occurring across all facets of their business. However, this is a major sector of any national economy. The established communications service providers are one of the major employment groups in the service sector and one of the major areas of strong revenue performance. Massive change in the environment may be a source of threat to this sector, and the sector will use its resources to resist such changes. Accordingly, although the collaborative community and the deregulated market may see continued change and evolution as a positive attribute of the environment, the established communications sector may be more interested in establishing a somewhat slower pace of change in this area.

The Public Resource

A fourth area of policy tension is that of public regulation pressures. Here, there may be many roles for regulation to ensure that the stated social objectives are being achieved within the competitive marketplace.

MOTIVES FOR PUBLIC REGULATION

The first pressure is that of ensuring fair trading. Fair trading within a competitive marketplace is a balance between a market trend to aggregation of supply channels and the need to ensure that genuine open competition exists to allow market forces to exert pressures on providers to operate in an efficient fashion. The oversight of such regulators can take many forms. The specific objectives include ensuring that incumbent market dominance by any one player is not abused, that consumers are tariffed at a fair price for the service, that new entrants are not artificially excluded from participation in the market, and that the provider environment is fair and open to all players.

The second point of regulation is concerned with longer term social objectives. Such objectives recognize that the Internet is a nationally important resource, and one that would appear to be significant to the public interest over the forthcoming years. Accordingly, public resource management measures would be imposed to ensure the efficient and effective exploitation of the resource in the common national interest. Here, the precise nature of the deployed technology is irrelevant to the public resource perspective, as distinct to the central, and indeed vital, role played by technology evolution within the collaborative community. Within the public resource domain and from the perspective of public regulatory measures, the issue is the current and likely future areas of uptake of the service and whether there is a significant proportion of the national population, or a nationally significant set of sectors, who could benefit from the service. If unacceptable risks are perceived through lack of regulation and lack of public management measures, then it is natural to expect that national public communications regulatory bodies will voice the need to apply public management policies onto the Internet.

The third such area of motivation for national public resource management regimes is concerned with taking appropriate measures to avoid outcomes that are regarded as negative from a national perspective. Such negative outcomes include the assumption of an unregulated monopoly position over a strategically critical or widely used resource or the deliberate disenfranchisement of areas of the population through the deliberate actions of service providers operating outside of any national policy framework, or, at times, issues relating to the control of a nationally strategic resource by nonnational interests. We are accustomed to active public resource management in many areas: water, electricity, air quality, and closer to the communications industry, the print media, the use of the radio spectrum, and the telephone service. The issue here is whether the Internet has achieved sufficient penetration of the national population to be considered as being subjected to *universal service obligations* in any nation to date and whether the Internet has as yet achieved sufficient national strategic importance to effectively ensure the need for a public resource management role in order to achieve the objectives as stated. Within the policy area of universal service obligation lie the issues of *universal equity of access* to the service, *uniform service coherency, quality of the service* as supplied to all subscribers, and the *structure of the service environment.* These considerations are intended to ensure that the infrastructure and services can be positioned as a national asset and are uppermost within the public resource characterization of the Internet. The role of the regulator in this guise can be summarized as that of a national public resource manager, with the objective of ensuring the maximal positive outcome of a public commodity or service for the benefit of the nation and the benefit of the national population.

In this case, the public management question that can be posed is not whether more visible and stricter public management regulatory measures will ever be applied to the Internet, but simply when this will happen.

Internet Policy Issues

The characterization of the Internet today is therefore seen as being within an unresolved area of tension between these four major policy domains. To illustrate this from the perspective of the Internet, a number of critically important issues within the Internet can be analyzed in terms of the tension between these three areas. The analysis presented here is intended to highlight the policy issues that are germane to each subject, rather than a more detailed description of the topic itself.

Domain Name Management

As an exercise in collective policy formulation across the Internet, this topic has certainly seen the greatest level of community attention through 1997 and 1998. It bears the dubious distinction of being the first area to trigger explicit involvement of the U.S. administration into an active role in Internet policy determination, as distinct from adopting a more passive policy stance in encouraging industry self-regulation.

The operation of domain name management is indeed a very good example of this tension between these areas of policy formulation. The collaborative community had exercised administrative control over the domain space for some time, and although the policies were effective to a point, the imposition of service fees by the incumbent registry operator, as a response to scaling issues, brought the entire area under public pressure. Strong pressure from the incumbent registry was brought to bear to maintain its monopoly trading position, and strong pressure came from others to introduce competitive market practices into the domain as a means of creating a market-driven service price for domain names. The collaborative community's response was to attempt to devise a model that admitted both the elements of competitive practices in the service activity, while using a collaborative model of the registry itself to ensure that the collective interests of each registrar was served equally. The stance taken by the U.S. administration was that the inability of the industry to reach consensus between these approaches was perhaps a greater problem than those presented by either outcome. The involvement of the public administration was, as a primary motivation, to reach an outcome rather than continue within an impasse over authority models. Even this measure is one in which authority to undertake a decision is questionable, and, in international matters, such as those raised by the domain name issues, consensus, if achievable, is far better than the attempt to impose through assumption of authority.

The intent of the collaborative community is to consider the domain name space as one with far-reaching implications, and the ability to undo any decision regarding new domains is highly questionable. The often voiced view of many of the ISPs is that such issues are of little concern, and their desire is to secure a domain name for a paying client as quickly and as painlessly as possible. The view voiced by a smaller minority of ISPs is to question whatever the current framework of name administration may be, and regard the space as one that should be open to commercial exploitation without regard to any longer term implications. The public regulatory position currently in vogue is to create a self-regulatory framework within the industry and to indicate that such a framework allows the resource to be administered without further public expense.

Address Space Management

Address space management had for many years been largely operated in an *ad hoc* fashion, in which any entity requesting network address space was allocated space without charge and without question. The address registries allocated address blocks to entities on a freely available, first-come, first-served allocation basis, within the scope of a number of administrative grounds, which attempt to direct the allocation process to result in rational use of the space and to achieve a result of a level of equity of availability.

The address space management policies have a number of attributes in common with other public space resources, and there are parallels in an economic analysis of this resource that include:

The finite nature of the resource.   This attribute is a consequence of the underlying technology, which has defined addressed entities in terms of a 32-bit address value. The total pool is composed of 2^{32} distinct values. Given the rapid expansion of the Internet in the past decade, the finite nature of the address space can now be accurately called *visibly finite*.

The address space has considerable market value.   This valuation is a consequence of the availability and extensive deployment of the under-lying Internet technology that allows uniquely addressed entities the capability to conduct direct end-to-end transactions with peer entities via the Internet. The parameters of this valuation also are influenced by considerations of efficiency of use of the allocated space, availability of end system-based Internet technologies, the availability of Internet-based service providers, and the resulting Internet market size.

Address space management is a necessary activity.   Management processes are required to ensure unique allocation and fair access to the resource, as well as the activity of continuing maintenance of allocation record databases.

Issues relating to perceived future scarcity of addresses and the risk of domination of the Internet space through domination of the address space have led the Internet community to agree on a number of additional constraining measures within the activity of address allocation, increasing the administrative overheads within this activity. The free market approach and the public resource-management perspective would coincide in this area to see the address space as being fundamentally no different from, say, the radio spectrum, in which access to the common resource is managed through normal resource management measures to ensure fair and equitable access to the underlying resource and fair and efficient pricing of such access.

In the absence of the capability to price the management of the Internet address space at administrative cost levels, let alone setting the price of address leasing to reflect the finite nature of the resource and the market value of the resource, as a component of overall common address management practices, the most likely scenario is a continuation of the current address allocation policies until exhaustion of the unallocated address pool occurs. A sad reflection of the conflict of short-term objectives and longer term considerations is that the evident short-term motivations of ready and equitable access to the IPv4 address (which were the motivational factors in determining the current Internet address allocation policies) run the consequent risk of monopoly-based restrictive trade and barrier-based pricing as a longer term outcome of unallocated address space exhaustion.

Although free address allocation and the adoption of policies that include pricing components both ultimately produce strong pressure for increased address space utilization efficiency, the removal of the neutral presence of the unallocated address pool does induce considerable risk of open market failure within the Internet itself if free address allocation policies continue until pool exhaustion has occurred.

Further strengthening of the current address allocation policies, in an effort to induce higher address utilization efficiencies across the remaining address space, is not a viable address management strategy refinement, insofar as the trading market then will commence before unallocated pool exhaustion, trading in large address blocks, which are precluded from such strengthened address allocation policies. The most negative aspect of this is that these processes will erode levels of confidence in the self-regulatory capability of the Internet community, so that significant doubts will be expressed by the larger community, the Internet process is one that is appropriate for effective formulation of common administrative policy of one of the core common assets of the Internet. These outcomes can all be interpreted as policy failure outcomes.

The seriousness of these outcomes must be assessed in the terms of the anticipated timeframe of such policy failure. Current expectations of unallocated address pool lifetime of 6–12 years does allow the Internet community some time to revisit their methods of administrative process definition, but this observation is tempered by the IPv6 process and by increasing levels of pressure on the address space in terms of growth in address demand through growth of deployment of the Internet itself.

An appropriate conclusion is to acknowledge the impediments of existing processes to admit any significant process or policy change that would produce a more efficient and effective address space-management regime. However, it is this policy failure to efficiently utilize the IPv4 address space through inadequate address pool management policies, rather than the exhaustion of the pool *per se*, which is perhaps the driving force to design, and to deploy an evolutionary technology to IPv4 that possesses a significantly larger address space as a major attribute.

Any outside observer of the IPv6 refinement process will look to see whether there is any evidence of experiential learning in address management policies. If there is to be a successor technology for IPv4, it would be reasonable to anticipate that associated address pool management mechanisms show a greater degree of understanding of public resource space management capability in the light of this experience. If no such evidence is forthcoming, then no clear mechanism exists to instill sufficient levels of consumer and industry confidence in these technologies in such a way that would admit large-scale public deployment, irrespective of the technical attributes of the successor technology. Such potential mechanisms may include pricing components irrespective of the actual size of the address resource, because the number's uniqueness is a resource with inherent market value irrespective of whether scarcity pricing premiums are relevant in such an address space.

A continuation of current address space management policies runs a very strong risk of restrictive and monopoly-based trading in address space, with consequence of the same trading practices being expressed within the deployed Internet itself.

Routing Table Management

The routing table growth is a similar area of common pressure on a shared resource. Each time an entity wants to express a unique routing policy for an address block, the address block is advertised into the common routing table with unique attributes, adding entries into the common routing table. In addition, each time the route is withdrawn and each time it is reestablished, all routers carrying a complete set of routing tables must make adjustments to their table, computing a new forwarding table that includes the current status of the routing entry.

The response to this could be characterized as a collaborative policy response, in which three measures have been adopted to attempt to impose a more rational use of the routing table resource. First, the use of strong peer pressure exerted on ISPs to adopt a CIDR-based route advertisement structure, minimizing the number of route entries being generated by the ISP into the Internet-wide routing tables. Second, the widespread adoption of address fragment route filters, intended to ensure that the routing space does not fragment into unique routing policy being expressed for very small address fragments. Finally, the adoption of route-damping filters placed onto route peering sessions is intended to filter out route table entries that generate a large number of route withdrawals and reestablishment events over a short-time interval. The characterization of this as a collaborative community response of common pressure on elements of the network to invest in CIDR techniques, together with the rapid development of routing tools, is the Internet community response to a significant problem within the routing space.

Without this collaborative policy creation function, the deregulated market and public resource management policy response to such an issue normally would be somewhat different, again tending to a mechanism that imposes a price on a scarce public resource as a mechanism to ensure rational exploitation across competing interests. In the routing space, this does present some issues in the levels of indirection between cause and effect, and the consequent pricing flow may not accurately capture the dynamics of the routing infrastructure. The conclusion is that although pricing is an often used mechanism of policy determination, and in a deregulated market pricing is a very common means of enacting policy outcomes, pricing is not a panacea, and collaborative mechanisms may present superior outcomes to particular issues.

Administrative Infrastructure Operation

The collaborative community typically works under the assumption that within a homogeneous community personal and common interests coincide, to the extent that common administrative tasks are often undertaken on a basis of funding in which services are provided freely to the end-user community. The deregulated market approach would tend to advocate a position of pricing such functions in order to ensure that sufficient funding is derived from the operation so that the function can be undertaken free of inherent bias or undue influence. Such a view of the operation also tends to avoid the adoption of voluntary effort within critical administrative functions, and a natural tendency exists to call for institutionalization of the operation in order to provide it with a level of robustness and certainty in its outcomes. It is a commonly held position of current public policy environments to offer industry self-regulation as the appropriate mechanism for governance of such functions while withholding reserve powers to regulate if such self-regulation fails to meet critical public policy objectives.

The preceding three issues—name administration, address administration, and route administration—fall within this area of administrative infrastructure. In addition, in the broader sense of the Internet as a protocol suite, is the task of protocol number assignment and the specification of standards for the protocol itself. This function has been undertaken under the auspices of the Internet Assigned Numbers Authority (IANA) for many years, operated through a funding contract with U.S. federal agencies and through agreements executed with the Internet Architecture Board and through this with the Internet standards effort of the Internet Engineering Task Force. It is likely that this view of industry self-regulation will become the dominant policy direction in this area of administrative function, and the institutionalization of the IANA function within the overall structure of a self-regulatory body will be the outcome here.

Connectivity Management

Connectivity management is a similar area of policy consideration. Within the telephony world, we are accustomed to an environment in which the user functionality is that any telephone number is accessible from any other. The current Internet model is a more constrained model of connectivity in which connectivity is bartered within a process of ISPs' various connection policies and their competitive market position.

This poses a number of questions regarding policy formulation in this domain. Is it reasonable to phrase an objective of the public process that comprehensive connectivity is a strict requirement of every ISP operating with the domain of the public policy? If so, how can such a condition be audited and enforced? Will a deregulated marketplace necessarily result in the common attribute of comprehensive connectivity? Can a collaborative approach create such an outcome in the ISP marketplace?

Here, the differences between a regulated approach to the service environment and a deregulated approach is at its most visible. Within a regulated approach, the regulator has the ability to impose a number of conditions on the operators, including a requirement to implement interconnection, and even going as far as setting an interconnection tariff that is a mandatory requirement for licensing of a service operator. Such constraints from the regulator are not unknown in other service industries, such as banking, for example, in which it is common to see such regulatory conditions imposed on the granting of authorities to operate a banking service. Indeed, such constraints are quite consistent with the general objectives of public policy within service sectors, in which the objectives of a rational, efficient, reliable, and ubiquitous total service environment can best be served by extensive functional interconnections between service operators.

However, the fit of such a broad policy objective to its implementation within a deregulated competitive market is not a comfortable one. Individual operators may perceive connectivity as a competitive advantage, and may view their interconnection structures as business assets that they would be reluctant to expose to their competitors unless there are commercial agreements in place. If these commercial agreements cannot be reached, then, in a fully deregulated market, there is no underlying forcing function for connectivity arrangements to be enacted. This exposes one of the major risks in a completely deregulated market in terms of outcomes; that market size becomes a determinant in the competitive positioning of an enterprise, and the outcome of such a characteristic is typically the aggregation of the marketplace into a small number of large enterprises.

It remains a significant public policy challenge to create an environment that enforces a functional level of interconnection, while not discouraging significant private investment into the sector. Indeed, it may well be the major policy issue of the next few years, as the ISP market is already coalescing into a smaller number of enterprises, who do perceive connectivity agreements as business assets, so that increasing barriers to entry into the market already are becoming evident.

The Internet within the Marketplace

The assumption being made within these areas is that the Internet will not be operated as a single entity either nationally, or globally, now or in the foreseeable future. Issues of ISP interaction and competition will continue to rise in importance within the activity of policy determination as the number and diversity of service providers continues to rise worldwide.

The underlying direction noted here is that the Internet, as a marketplace for carriage provision, has a likely future as a price-driven commodity market in packet switching and packet transmission. The fundamental shift that has occurred with the Internet as a communications environment is that service definition now occurs as a function of the end computer systems, and the communications system imposes no service constraints, nor adds any further service value above this end-to-end service definition.

This position is one which can anticipate some resistance from the market perspective. Basic transmission data units, or packets, are not necessarily purchased by the user in different inherent service qualities. This would tend to direct the competitive Internet market to be a price-driven market, in which each player attempts to operate profitably within parameters of the marginal cost of production of the carriage service. This marketplace is one that results in low rates of return on financial investment, and within such a marketplace, each provider attempts to introduce competitive bias and higher value services by introducing additional differentiators. The consequent market push is evident to attempt to differentiate on service profiles, which brings into question the transparent end-to-end service and uniform technology model of the Internet. Perhaps, one of the best examples of this is the deployment of *transparent* Web caches, in which all packets directed to a remote system's port 80 are intercepted by the network and redirected to a local cache. Although such a system could offer superior performance to many users, it also disturbs any form of end-to-end security mechanisms that rely on a clear channel between the requester and the server.

Policy Directions

A number of pressures indicate that the original aspects of the collaborative community will not continue to exert the same level of policy determination as it has achieved historically. The community of usage is becoming more heterogeneous, and the technical development community also is exhibiting increasing diversity under growth. There is also the issue of areas of finite capacity within the address and routing components of the Internet and the issue of competitive pressure for access to such resources in which scales of demand growth differ from various user and provider sectors.

All such considerations indicate that the process of collaborative determination of consensus policies as a management technique of the Internet is being faced with increasing fragmentary pressure as the Internet continues to grow.

Agile or Inflexible?

However, the collaborative community does possess sufficient agility and flexibility to identify such pressures and respond productively, both in terms of responses at a technical level to pressures on the underlying technology base and to pressures at a policy level to current management practices and style. Indeed, very few management mechanisms exhibit such inherent flexibility and attuned responsiveness to the evolution of common requirements. This attribute of the collaborative community remains its central asset in validly asserting a continuing role within the Internet.

The major positive factor of deregulated market self-regulation is that ability of the market to react to new information markets and new information services very quickly, and an open market can act as a powerful catalyst for national development at a very rapid pace.

Institutionalized operations tend to exhibit greater levels of inflexibility in terms of policy responses to rapidly evolving situations and tend to operate to preserve a status quo rather than to constantly impose pressure to adapt and change the mode of operation of servicing the marketplace. The risk of such institutions is that their output becomes decreasingly relevant to the realities of the evolving market, and unless there is some forcing pressure to implement flexibility within the institutions, they quickly become irrelevant. This is already evident within the institutional structures, which service the common policy instruments of the telephone world, in which their ability to encompass the policy issues of the Internet environment in a timely fashion has been visibly lacking to date.

Regulation of Service Providers

A number of areas exist in which public management practices may be applied to the Internet. Within a number of national domains are emerging conditions for the role of communications' Value Added Reseller, which would apply specifically to ISPs. Under the constraint of a licensing system of operation, which presumably would entail a license fee as a startup cost and allow administrative policy to determine the size and number of Internet Service Providers operating within the country, the opportunity exists to enumerate a number of desired conditions onto the Internet operation. Such conditions may include policies concerning the carriage of offensive material, scope of market access, the service definition, and potentially service limitation and even the domain of inter-provider interactions.

The fact that regulation of the national ISP industry is an option for public policy does not necessarily make it a viable or productive course of action, and the real substance of the underlying motivations for enacting such regulation is a clear understanding of the social objectives, which are intended through such regulation. Highly regulated markets are often an inhibitory factor for private investment, in which the barriers to market entry now must factor in local regulatory constraints as well as other market and business environmental factors.

Regulation can be designed to have particular business outcomes, such as the active encouragement of small businesses within the service market, or the encouragement of the creation of national service operators over offshore operations entering the domestic market. Such an outcome could be generated by the adoption of public policies relating to interconnection of service providers, through differential taxation structures relating to financial investment in this sector, or in the adoption of competitive regulations that encourage diversity of service operators. The questions posed by such measures are whether it is more critical in terms of the development of Internet infrastructure and market stimulation to have many service providers offering many channels into the retail market space, or whether the costs of sustaining such a diverse service environment creates a cost-inefficient market that suffers in terms of international competitiveness through higher service costs for hosting Internet business operations.

Regulations can be phrased with a different social objective in mind. Regulation of the service provider industry can be undertaken with the objective of providing basic consumer protection measures rather than attempting to shape the industry itself. It could encompass efficient and inexpensive channels for consumers to raise disputes with their service provider, using industry funding to create a dispute resolution venue in which third-party adjudication has binding outcomes on the service provider.

Is There a Demand for Public Resource Management?

Such public management structures are invariably initiated within an environment of worthy motives, and indeed, roles potentially need to be undertaken here that the unregulated market would find difficult to fulfill within appropriate parameters of fairness, equity, impartiality, and adequate quality of the service sector. Within such areas of policy determination, the collaborative community can voice the need for such policies, but in terms of funding requirements for such common administrative elements, it invariably falls to public management to create the framework to support such roles.

However, such public management roles do severely test the quality of public administration, particularly where the entity being administered is relatively novel and requires a degree of care and sensitivity in terms of management programs and their desired effect. Public administration generally operates without such fine levels of graduation in the application of policy, and the quality of the administrative role, particularly where there is a requirement for a highly user-attuned service and detailed technical knowledge, must be stated as a challenging milestone for any area of public administration.

All that can be realistically anticipated from the area of public administration is a static administrative model of the ISP sector, with a management approach that is either a model which assumes that administrative responsibility equates to overall control, or a model which equates to self-regulation by deregulated market interests, with a government position of reserve powers rather than active involvement.

Accordingly, it is unlikely that the public management role will be one that is initiated by reason of popular demand. The only realistic scenario, which would see an active role for public administration, is one in which the communications industry regulators successfully advocate the need for an active stance or in which the incumbent monopoly telecommunications service provider invokes public resource management as a response to business leakage to the unregulated value-added reseller business. In both cases, the role of public management would be as a defensive move, rather than as a move to further enable and encourage expansion of access to the common service, and it is unlikely that public resource management roles would be commonly adopted within many nations as a consequence.

Likely Directions

As each of these policy domains interact across the Internet, the question posed by this examination of policy structure remains: What is the likely near-term policy future of the Internet? Obviously, the best I can offer here are personal views rather than fact, and the reader should be aware that predicting the future is always easy—the hard bit is getting it right!

Increasing skew between market-driven expansion and historical community objectives. The collaborative community's influence over the policy framework of the Internet will continue to wane. Already the skew between the ethos of an Internet as a community resource heavily populated with voluntary effort, and the Internet as a medium for mass-marketed commerce and entertainment is readily visible. However, it is both inevitable and correct that the policy initiative of the service network shifts to those who make the investment in operating the service network.

Technical stability requires collaboration. Underlying the competitive service environment is a single communications architecture that is the technology of the Internet. Allowing clients of a provider to conduct transactions with the clients of any other provider, hiding the underlying intricacies of network engineering such as routing policy, transit agreements, and the like requires the adoption of common functional technology standards and the operation of stable interconnection structures. Such an environment does not readily admit the imposition of external authority models, and instead, relies strongly on peer inter-action within a collaborative environment to determine what is accept-able to all as a functioning solution.

Public policy will focus on industry self-regulatory models.   It is unlikely that an active public regulatory position will be as significant within this perspective. The issues already outlined relating to the likely responsiveness of public resource management within this area and the pace at which opportunities are identified and subsequently exploited is such that an active and interventionist public regulation regime probably will not be a significant factor within the Internet pol-icy environment. Minimal levels of regulation, probably regarding trading practices, consumer protection, and investment regulation, are the major anticipated tangible public outcomes for some time yet, and the dominant policy characterization for the near-term future will be the interplay between the established collaborative community and their focus on technical standards and a self-regulatory position for the emerging open market for Internet-based services.

Barriers to entry increase.   Although the number of ISPs servicing mar-ket demand has been rising sharply in the mid-1990s, it is a natural tendency of the incumbent service providers to set the policy structure so that the entry standards are comparable to the position of the already established operators. The overall summary of the situation is that for new Internet providers, the learning curve that new providers must master in order to establish the service and the initial investment required to meet self-determined industry service standards continues along a increasingly steep incline. This can be translated into the observation that the barriers for the Internet are getting higher rather than lower.

Outcomes.   In a policy sense, this effectively indicates that, where fea-sible, a public policy position that encourages investment into the national communications service sector for servicing the Internet ser-vice market would appear to be a reasonable public policy stance, and an associated policy direction that brings a number of providers into the basic transmission services of cable and data switching area would allow this service-based market to be constructed above a relatively efficient transportation and carriage market.

However, this picture is by no means uniform, and many countries are entering the Internet service domain within a framework of a fragmentary pic-ture of commercial service requirements, voiced most visibly by multinational corporate entities. Within this environment, the public regulatory position is generally structured more tightly around the national telephone service operator as a monopoly provider. Due consideration of the desire to continue to operate such a strategic service within a national entity, rather than as an offshore operation of a foreign corporate entity, and economic considerations of this approach effectively preclude an openly positioned domestic communications environment. Within this more restrictive public regulatory environment, the formative ISP is faced with both a highly constrained area of local operation and a more complex Internet environment into which the domestic service has to interconnect. The consequent observation is that for these national environments, which tend to coincide with developing national economies, the task of establishing a healthy ISP industry is more daunting from a regulatory perspective.

Summary

A gulf certainly exists between the typical method of constructing a public policy framework for the communications industry and the exigencies of the Internet.

- The Internet ethos of collaboration as the mechanism for policy formulation has failed to meet the demands of an environment of widespread deployment across many market sectors. Collaboration simply does not scale.
- Industry self-regulation is perhaps more of an expression of faith in the outcomes of the competitive market, as being an efficient distributor of a public resource of service, than it is a well-understood mechanism to achieve the desired objectives in all situations. Industry self-regulation is a faith, not a science.
- The established communications industry players perceive a substantial threat to their existing mode of business within the guise of the Internet. The established communications industry wants to resist change.
- The traditional methods of policy formulation in the public sector are attuned to gradual and well-researched changes to a relatively static policy framework, and a very strong tendency exists to preserve the status quo within the process. Public policy is often too little, too late.

The Internet is a rapidly moving target, and policy determination is akin to management of chaos. Chaos theory predicts that complex systems will self-organize, although it cannot predict what that organization may be!

Solutions will always emerge to meet demands, in the same way as nature abhors a vacuum. In a rapidly evolving and somewhat chaotic market, the opportunities will be available for the nimble, although the larger and more ponderous operators will follow behind with the weight of organization and institutionalization to convert ideas and concepts into robust ubiquitous services. This is perhaps the best that can be expected from the Internet.

chapter sixteen

Futures for the ISP Industry

In this book, we've explained the current technology, business, and policy landscape of the ISP industry. In this chapter, we explore the potential directions for this industry, looking at potential technology, business, and policy futures.

The one constant factor of the pace of the Internet has been its ability to confound most soothsayers, and it is with some trepidation that we indulge in some predictions for the ISP industry. Such predictions do not come with any guarantees of authenticity or authority. Rather, it is a positive aspect of the Internet that the technology can continue to surprise these efforts of divination. However, business investment thrives on some level of certainty of outcome, and in this closing chapter, we attempt to provide what certainty we can within this environment.

Technology Futures

In this section, we briefly look at the futures for the ISP industry from the perspective of the technology base. We cover the areas of evolution of carriage and access and then discuss the futures of the Internet protocol itself.

Carriage Futures

The explosive growth of the Internet and the ISP industry was never planned. No allocation was planned and reserved for Internet use from the world's stocks of carriage capacity. The carriage capacity currently consumed by the Internet has been largely provided from reserve stocks, from the margins of oversupply of the existing voice carriage network. By the late 1990s, the existing trans-Pacific and trans-Atlantic submarine cable systems had been effectively consumed, and the carefully planned roll-out of submarine cable capacity had been all but obliterated in a buying frenzy. The question to be posed is: What happens when this practice extends further and exhausts all existing carriage stocks?

The answer may not necessarily be to build more voice carriage infrastructure and in so doing create additional reserves of carriage capacity for Internet use. Given the large differential between the growth levels of voice-based services and Internet-based services, no appreciable large-scale demand exists for additional voice carriage infrastructure. Instead, we appear to be moving into a phase of construction of carriage infrastructure, which is explicitly designed to meet data carriage requirements.

This poses some significant design challenges for the carriage provider. One direction is for the carriage system to explicitly segment the network, permitting the overlay of a variety of service provider networks. Such a design would tend towards an ATM-based infrastructure, offering end-to-end virtual circuits as a means of allowing each service provider direct access to the end client. Of course, such a model assumes that the Internet access market will continue to be operated along competitive lines and that the costs associated with including an additional layer of switching are a necessary expenditure. However, within a fully deregulated carriage industry, such a supposition that the carriage provider will explicitly design a network that permits competitive access, may not be a valid assumption. A different approach is to dispense with circuit switching altogether in the carriage network and use IP packet switching as an end-to-end solution. This approach would lead towards pushing routers into the role of the customer access device rather than use of circuit-based or time-multiplexed devices, and then using a single IP routing plane within the carriage network. The simplicity of this carriage infrastructure is certainly compelling, in that it yields both high capacity and low cost, but this approach does assume a business model that is substantially different from that of the present.

At this stage, we appear to be still grappling with two sides of the Internet carriage environment. On the access side, an overwhelming majority of clients are still using modems as a data overlay on an analogue voice system. Advances in modem design have managed to bring the speed up to 56Kbps under ideal conditions, but the conditions are typically not that ideal, and the analogue encoding delays and complexities of the dial scripts do not make for an efficient or robust Internet access environment. This will change. The more promising avenue of development for access lies in the reuse of the PSTN copper access loop, using some form of DSL technique. This direction offers the prospect of lifting access speeds into the area of megabits per second, and, depending on the access model chosen, creating an Internet *socket* in which the ease of the corporate service network *plug'n'play* environment can be replicated for the residential and small business market.

Of course, this is not the only contender for the next generation of high-speed access systems. The DSL service does have distance limitations, and some significant investment is called for on the part of the consumer and the access provider to deploy the DSL termination equipment on either end of the access loop. Of some interest in this scenario is whether the adopted technologies for access continue to support the split between the carriage access provider and the Internet access provider. Will a DSL customer, if DSL is the adopted access technology, be able to shift the Internet access service between various ISPs, while remaining on a single access provider's infrastructure? Alternatively, will the distinction between carriage access and Internet access be removed as carriage itself becomes more interwoven with the Internet? The greatest area of commercial opportunity presented by the Internet is competitive positioning within the global information industry. Will the artifice of enforcing competitive access to the client loop create a more efficient national communications infrastructure, or will it become a burdensome overhead and an impediment to a truly competitive national position in the global marketplace?

The other side of the carriage issue is how to engineer for greater and greater levels of IP volume within the bearer networks. The current large-scale trunk ISPs now use circuits of 155Mbps and 622Mbps, with some well-founded expectation of deployment of 2.4Gbps IP trunk systems before the end of the 1990s. This is no longer a margin of the voice bearer network, but is a trunk network in its own right. The issues of trunk carriage of IP over ATM network substrates have largely receded, and the current issues appear to concentrate on the use of SONET as a framing protocol for high-speed IP trunks. An alternative is to place the packet on the fiber without a SONET framing protocol, and some developmental effort that exploits the use of IP over Wave Division Multiplexing (WDM) on fiber circuits is now showing promising results for the large IP carriers. Hence, the issues for high-speed, high-volume trunks for the Internet are no longer how to fit Internet traffic within a circuit-switched network that has a number of other applications. The current carriage issues appear to center on whether a dedicated IP over SONET infrastructure offers sufficient resiliency and ease of operational management to justify the investment in SONET switching equipment or whether a more lightweight approach, using IP as a channel within a WDM, offers acceptable resiliency at some lower level of carriage cost.

Accordingly, and here the prediction is prefaced by the time of making the prediction, in the late 1990s, the carriage futures appear to be concentrating on IP over DSL as a ubiquitous high-speed access technology, and IP over SONET or WDM as a trunk carriage technology. However, the level of uncertainties continue to dominate this area, and these predictions are more of a preface to a debate, rather than a firm prediction of outcomes.

Internet Futures

The next area of technology future lies in the Internet itself. This area continues to experience significant levels of innovation and development, and some of these will impact on the ISP operation. A number of these areas of development are discussed here. This is not intended to be an inclusive discussion of all areas of Internet technology futures, and the selection here is a very short, arbitrary list. However, the discussion of these topics is more general, and the chosen topics are used to focus on the discussion points. The discussion of the technology options is intended to illustrate the important generic aspects that are shaping the future of the Internet itself, highlighting the interplay between technology capabilities and business imperatives.

IP Version 6

Despite the large effort that has been undertaken throughout the 1990s to develop IPv6 as a successor technology platform to the current IPv4 environment, current indications are that IPv4 will provide a stable network platform for some time yet.

The major pressure point was that of the IPv4 address space. The 32-bit space was being used with an efficiency of far less than 1 percent, so that the 32-bit address space would be exhausted once the Internet had encompassed more than 200 million hosts. Widespread use of dynamic address assignment, techniques, and address translation gateways have increased the address utilization factors by more than an order of magnitude, and the immediacy of exhaustion of the address space is now not considered a major factor in the future of IPv4. An open question remains as to how far into the future that address space exhaustion has been postponed. Any prediction will need to factor in the likely emergence of a massive Internet utility appliance consumer market and take into account the demonstrated ability to incorporate new technologies into IPv4, which can alleviate some elements of address exhaustion.

IPv6 did introduce some new concepts of service support into the protocol domain, which has acted as a catalyst for further evolution of IPv4 to accommodate these concepts. To date, many additional service functions have been engineered into the Internet without the need to alter the underlying IPv4 base, and it would be imprudent to discount this factor when assessing the future of IP itself. Will the Internet community be willing to pay the cost of a massive upgrade of the millions of end hosts to support IPv6? The cost is considerable, and the benefits from a local perspective are scant at best. No immediate scenario of doom and disaster looms for the current deployment of IPv4. With this in mind, the question asked by the customer is, "What is the nature of the benefit in undertaking the transition to IPv6?" The answers from the technical Internet community are not well phrased, and the conclusion being reached by many customers is that the cost is considerable, and the benefits from a local perspective are not apparent. From the ISP community is the equally pragmatic answer that if customers do not want it, then there is no point in providing the service. The conclusion to be drawn is that there is no current demand for ISPs to support IPv6, and there is no sign of this changing in the short term.

Even with IP as a consistent base, this does not imply that other changes will not occur. Indeed, in the technology domain of IP some change is preferred.

Quality of Service

Expect some technology change here. The current model of uniform best-effort service quality simply does not reflect the realities of a highly diverse market. Clients want to be able to determine a preferred level of differentiated service for a network transaction and then have the network obey this preference.

Of course, as we discussed in Chapter 8, "Quality of Service," when examining quality-of-service issues, stating the problem is easier than phrasing how the solution may appear. The issues involved in engineering a differentiated service environment on the Internet extend far beyond defining the semantics of bits in the IP header. Is the engineering of quality of service involved with the imposition of state into the network? Does the approach taken by RSVP, in which a virtual circuit with various service parameters is dynamically imposed onto a set of routers, offer a solution path that will scale to the size of the Internet? Alternatively, can stateless per-hop behaviors offer outcomes that can provide the service guarantees, which are an intrinsic component of the demand for quality of service? There is no clear outcome within this technology debate as yet.

The challenge also lies in creating the inter-provider agreements that will permit meaningful end-to-end differentiated service environments. These challenges are not technical but are concentrated around the issues of financial settlement between service providers. When a packet with an elevated service request is passed to an ISP for delivery, the ISP will, quite reasonably, look for some agent to compensate it for the disproportionate amount of resources devoted to honoring the differentiated service requirements.

At this stage, determining what this will look like is not easy, but given the extent of the market demand for this particular service, it is likely that some form of solution will be deployed.

Virtual Private Networks

This is another area of significant activity at present. As with quality of service, there is a strong customer demand for the capability to overlay private networks on top of the Internet itself, with some diversity of approaches as to how to meet this demand. The demand, stated briefly, is to overlay a private security domain, with potentially a defined level of service, associated with a set of access locations and a set of individual clients.

Various solutions have been proposed in this area, which can be characterized as falling within one of two approaches. First, the approach of configuring the network so that it is aware of the segmentation and the network enforces the segmentation via the maintenance of secure virtual circuits, which defines the private network. This approach is an evolution of the private leased circuit as the base technology of private networks, and in the Internet domain, such configurations can be constructed from a number of base tools, including tunnels, controlled route leakage, router filters, payload encryption, and label switching. Here, a state is imposed on the network, which is that of the connectivity and security requirements of the private network. Second, the approach of viewing the requirement for privacy and quality of communication as an end-to-end issue. Here, the end systems use payload encryption and tunnels to dynamically join a private network domain, and the underlying networks are effectively unaware of the end-to-end segmentation that has occurred. In such environments, the virtual private network can span a number of providers and accommodate a mix of network and individual access environments.

Both approaches also need to address service quality issues, and it would appear natural to assume that a state-based virtual private network structure would tend towards the adoption of quality of service techniques that also are stateful in nature, while end-to-end stateless private network domains would more naturally tend towards stateless per-hop quality mechanisms.

It is unclear if any consensus will emerge from these activities in the medium term. The effort to place functionality into the network does increase the value of the service to the VPN customer. This direction to lift the value proposition of the network service from a base level carriage commodity product into a customer solution to meet a business objective does fit well with the strategic objective of many ISPs today. However, the diverse provider environment does imply that a network state-based VPN may lock the customer into a single provider to an unacceptable degree, and the end-to-end VPN approaches do offer the customer considerable flexibility in constructing private communications domains without locking the service into a single provider.

As a consequence, the likely outcomes in the medium term are similar to that of quality of service solutions: Various solutions will be deployed to meet the large scale of demand, but at this stage, no evidence of any uniformity of approach is arising from the technology domain.

Routing

The increasing complexity of the interconnection environment between ISPs is not well matched to the available tools to manage this interaction. The flow of traffic through the Internet between networks is an outcome of an imprecise match between the various routing policies of every provider. When one provider undertakes a local policy change to the local routing configuration, such changes have the potential to generate a significant impact on traffic flows in remote areas of the network. Creating a stable equilibrium within the routing environment calls for constant manual adjustment of local routing configurations to match remote changes in the routing system. Such continual manual adjustment of a distributed system does not appear to be consistent with a theme of stability, and this challenge is one faced by the Internet routing system.

As the number of providers increases, and as the inter-provider interconnection mesh becomes richer, an increasing number of potential paths occur between any two provider networks. The transitivity of routing contributes to this, because each routing advertisement is further qualified by each transit network, so that the routing space has the potential to increase in size at a rate limited only by the factorial product of the number of providers. In a space populated by some 30,000 providers across the world, this is an impossibly large number. Managing routing systems is as much a task of masking out poor local routing decisions as it is a task of promulgating sound local routing decisions.

The pressure to increase the routing space also is based on path attributes. Some paths through the network may possess various technical and policy attributes, which are of significance to the provider's path selection. Some policies are readily expressed within current routing protocols, and others are more challenging. For example, a provider may want to express the policy, "Provider A prefers to select paths that traverse an Internet exchange where provider A is connected," or, a more challenging policy, "Provider A prefers to use a sequence of transit connections that honor a consistent quality of service selection within the IP packet header." The richer the policy language to describe policy preferences, the greater the complexity of the resulting routing policies. It is unclear how this leads to increased stability of the routing system.

In addition to a policy matching requirement, an emerging requirement exists to express within the routing system the desire to use the interconnection mesh to load balance traffic flows across multiple paths. In a telephone network, there is a well-defined concept of *overflow paths*, in which alternate paths are selected when the primary path is fully occupied. Mapping this functionality to the Internet routing environment falls most obviously within the domain of quality of service routing, where the static and dynamic attributes of the path selected for a traffic flow match a set of defined criteria. Quality-of-service routing remains an area of active investigation within the IETF, and although some progress has been made with interior routing protocols, it remains unclear how this can be mapped seamlessly into the exterior routing environment.

Whether imposing these additional requirements on the routing system is a positive move is not obvious. The risk is that such changes will put at risk the essential attributes of the routing system—that of stability and predictability of the behavior. The simple exercise of scaling the current BGP-based routing environment to accommodate further growth in the number of ISPs and the number of interconnections will prove to be a major challenge to the Internet routing environment. Augmenting the functionality of this environment with a richer set of path selection parameters may push this routing environment into areas of instability. In the desire to augment functionality, the basic attribute of stable connectivity cannot be taken for granted.

ISP Business and Policy Futures

The first half of the 1990s was characterized by the emergence of providers to service the demand for Internet access. The emerging vibrant market space was populated by a large number of commercial startup ventures, many of which were garage operations, as well as some more liberally funded ventures. The notable missing element was the large-scale presence of the more established communication service providers. These large players viewed the Internet market as an opportunity to sell higher volumes of carriage and access services, rather than viewing this as a market that they wanted to participate in directly.

The middle of the 1990s has seen the startups continue, although the incidence of low-cost garage startups is decreasing. The entry cost to the service market is increasing as the market itself matures, requiring larger initial investments in service infrastructure as a precondition to gaining a foothold in the market. However, the more prevalent feature in this period has been the wave of aggregation and acquisitions that have occurred across the entire ISP industry. This appears to be a feature in common with the venture startup technology industry, in which the principal objective of many business ventures is to be acquired.

Why has the ISP industry changed in this way? What are the drivers behind the change, and what are the likely directions of the nature of the industry and its participants?

Acquisitions and Mergers

One of the critical factors driving acquisitions is what is referred to in a joking manner as the *clue factor*; in an expanding world with a constant level of *clue*, the result is ever decreasing *clue density*. Acquisitions attempt to concentrate clue. One of the critical factors in the ISP industry is that of the level of availability of individuals with the skill set to support the ISP's technical, operational, and business imperatives. The industry is certainly expanding far faster than the expansion of a skilled labor force to drive the industry. In addition, the skill set is becoming more demanding, with increasing complexity in the operational environment as ISP networks expand into a more complex mesh of ISP interconnection, as client service requirements become more sophisticated, and as the operation itself scales in size. Acquisitions allow an enterprise to acquire expertise and staff skill sets as well as other business assets. As it is sometimes phrased, *clue* is a highly valued business asset in the ISP industry.

Associated with skill sets and capability within the human assets of an ISP are the assets of intellectual property or technology capability. This business is rapidly evolving, and the manner in which technologies are deployed and the innovations in the approach to technology solutions within the ISP are often unique solutions. Such uses of technologies are part of the business assets of the ISP, and such assets form a significant component of the value of the ISP and are part of the acquisition drivers.

Acquisition may actually be the business objective of the ISP. The business plan of the enterprise may encompass the objective of developing a new market space, servicing it to the point where longer term outcomes of the viability and associated financial picture of the enterprise has achieved a reasonable degree of certainty. At this point, the ISP may execute the phase of the business plan that actively seeks a purchaser to acquire the enterprise and the business assets that have been developed.

Many startup small business enterprises do fail. In the broader small business enterprise area, some three quarters of small businesses fail in their first year of operation. In the Internet market, and the ISP market in particular, the picture has been more forgiving, in that the highly robust growth of demand has tended to support a lower threshold of business and marketing acumen than is the case elsewhere. However, the high growth rates do stress the capability of the business to raise capital in order to deploy services in advance of market uptake. In this position of business capital stress, the ISP does become the target for acquisition, based on an under-valuation of its staff, technology, capital assets, and market assets, due to these weaknesses in its business position.

These reasons indicate that the ISP does possess an asset base, based on the ISP's chosen market sector, market share, and state of development of that market, as well as the skills and capabilities of staff, technology innovation, and intellectual property assets as well as capital equipment. These then are the assets of the seller, but for an acquisition to proceed, there must be a buyer. What are the motivations for a buyer in the ISP marketplace?

Larger enterprises often are more conservative in their investment and activity profiles, reflecting the longer time it takes to make strategic decisions, which often is the hallmark of larger enterprises. This conservatism is also a reflection of the desire to protect shareholder value by working within markets that have a suitably low business risk. Being a late entrant to the market-place, acquisition of an existing operation makes sound business sense. Acquisition offers the enterprise an immediate position in the retail market, with skills, capabilities, and a market share. Acquisition represents an alternative form of expenditure to marketing costs to gain market share, and the acquisition also is an expenditure that achieves a known outcome in terms of resulting market share and size of the operation.

The ISP enterprise also can realize economies of scale of operation through acquisition. These economies of scale can be realized in carriage costs, in the costs of maintaining routing and switching systems, in service operations, and in customer service processes. An acquisition would not necessarily integrate the identity of the two enterprises into a resulting single market presence. The identity of the operations may be preserved as a reflection of the market value of the trading name and as a means of operating a number of channels into the retail market.

A further basic driver in this area of acquisition and aggregation lies within the financial models of interconnection. The Internet possesses no inherent capability to undertake rational cost distribution in a multiprovider environment. No current stable method exists to distribute part of the revenue collected to a network transaction and apportion this to various transit providers according to their incurred cost. In the absence of cost-distribution mechanisms, cost distribution will not take place. In the absence of cost distribution, interconnection is forced into one of two models: firstly, that of an equal peer using mutual sender keep all settlement, and secondly, that of a customer and a provider. Here lies a further objective with acquisition: a larger ISP has an increased capability to assert a provider role to other ISPs.

Taking these factors into account, the conclusion is that aggregation is a natural tendency for the ISP industry, and, in the absence of a balancing factor, aggregation will exert a strong downward pressure on the number of ISPs operating in the marketplace. What is keeping the numbers up at present is the continuing entry of new ISPs, drawn by niche market opportunities. These opportunities are opened up by the sustained vigorous levels of retail demand, coupled with the relatively low barriers to entry into the service provider role. This offers the new entrant short-term growth opportunities and the longer term prospect of a profitable sale or, alternatively, a public float within an investor climate that currently has very high expectations of the value of Internet-based business enterprises. The dynamics of interaction within this industry are indicated in Figure 16.1.

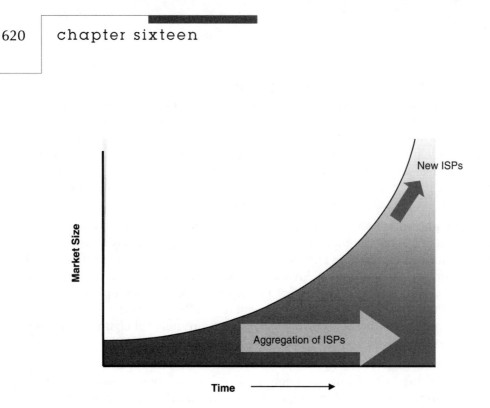

Figure 16.1   ISP market dynamics.

The Entry of the Telco

The large players entering the market are now the established communications industry enterprises (or *telco* as the telephone operator is commonly called), who are seeing competition in terms of other enterprises from their sector, as well as the largest of the established ISPs. Their motivations for entering the market are a combination of risk coverage and exploitation of opportunity.

The risk is that a significant proportion of the existing consumer expenditure on communications services is diverted into expenditure on Internet-based services. Much of this expenditure is in capital cost components of platform and software, leaving only the carriage component as expenditure with the established communications enterprises. In a deregulated competitive environment, carriage is a competitive commodity. In such a market, if left to operate without intervention, the commodity price will stabilize to a level close to the cost of production (either just above or just below the cost of production, depending on the balance between short and longer term outlooks). Such a commodity market does not admit high retail margins, and the risk is one of substantially reduced income with associated reduced operating margins.

The opportunity is one presented by additional retail demand for communications services, based on a broader Internet service environment. Augmenting the traditional services of voice and fax are new opportunities presented by electronic messaging, content publications, electronic commerce, collaboration support, games, and entertainment services. For the established communications enterprises, the Internet offers the opportunity to retail the under-lying carriage services into new service activities. If successful, the activity allows the enterprise to address the risks and produce an advantaged outcome through embracing Internet services into their service portfolio.

This entry into the Internet service industry by large players with significant established market presence and investment capability, who already have significant portfolios of carriage assets, will have a profound impact on the emerging ISP industry profile. The current visible attributes of this shift are strong pressures to aggregate established ISP entities into larger service operations in order to be in a position to compete with this new market entrant.

Where Are We Headed?

As the retail marketplace matures there will be increasing sophistication of the demand for services, coupled with an increasing expectation of service quality. Such expectations will be met by greater levels of investment in service infrastructure by the ISP. This, in turn, raises the cost of market entry for an ISP, demanding greater levels of initial service infrastructure investment. This will be most evident when the explosive growth in the retail market starts to taper off, and when such a state is reached, the entry of new ISPs will also start to taper off.

Will the market continue to aggregate, or are there competing pressures to fragment? One of the most effective fragmentary pressures is through franchising, offering small enterprises the leverage in marketing and expertise of larger enterprises through the franchise operation. Exercises in franchising ISPs have not been a major influence on the ISP industry to date. Although franchising offers some opportunity to share technology skills and technology innovation between multiple ISPs, franchising does not offer many other advantages of economies in scale of operation. The structures that operational processes control to achieve operational excellence, which is a typical aspect of the value proposition of a franchise, do not readily find application within an ISP business profile. The other pressure to fragment is when business agility, rather than investment pressure, and scale of operation are a key determinant in business success. Although this was the case in the first half of the 1990s, and although this remains the case in the leading edge of exploiting new market opportunities, for the bulk of the ISP industry, the trend is now one of aggregation.

A valid conclusion appears to be the expectation of further aggregation to be a continuing feature of the ISP industry, particularly in servicing the requirements of the established retail market. Inside such large market spaces, aggregation of ISP operations continue to offer the opportunities to reduce operational unit costs and simultaneously increase service quality.

In the absence of any form of regulatory constraints, such an activity has a small number of ultimately stable outcomes: Aggregation continues until a de facto monopoly provider emerges with comprehensive market share or until the number of industry participants will be sufficiently small to mutually equilibrate or stabilize within some bounds of market share in which case an effective cartel may ensue. Both outcomes have happened in other industries and service sectors in the past, where the wholesale diamond industry is an example of the formation of a monopoly trading block, and the wholesale oil industry has seen the formation of cartels in the past. In both cases of outcomes, the environment offers the remaining participants the opportunity to lift retail prices above commodity levels.

Such outcomes are not normally the socially desired outcomes of a service industry. If this is the tendency of a fully deregulated market, then it is a reasonable expectation to see a resurgence of regulatory control. The intent of such regulation is to ensure the continued operation of a competitively serviced marketplace, and the regulatory intent would be to ensure the continued viability of the competitive ISP. From a technology perspective, the Internet does not readily support cost distribution models, and the fundamental requirement of a competitive environment is for interconnection and cost distribution between competitive providers. Anticipating that the regulator will impose competition in the Internet access market seems reasonable, but at a price. The price will be higher retail costs for Internet access, and, in a globally competitive market for information and commerce, such a move will not foster national information-based industries at a level that will engender a globally competitive national information industry.

The Future of the ISP

In an engineering environment constructed for the Internet, that includes both access and trunk carriage services, the adopted design does tie in the access medium provider to the ISP. HFC systems, for example, do not readily admit equal access offerings given the nature of the access medium.

Generally, a design that admits competitive access to the client requires a circuit structure within the network. This allows packets to be framed and delivered to the remote service provider destination without the assistance of IP routing. However, circuits require the imposition of state into the network, and the requirement for operational input to set up and maintain such state. This is not without its attendant cost, and such engineering costs, to permit competitive access to the client, are ultimately passed to the client within retail tariffs. Single provider networks are often cheaper to engineer, because the packet can be encapsulated into the carriage media framing format without the engineering and management costs of maintaining a differentiating circuit state.

However, it is more likely that the carriage technology will follow rather than drive the market and that this aspect of engineering will likely resolve into circuit models, which are imposed upon access media to allow the broadest possible set of uses for access investment. It is folly to assume an enduring aspect of technology. The future of the ISP will be shaped by the market and business imperatives, more than by considerations of technology.

The primary observation is that the Internet has achieved critical mass, and widespread deployment of Internet technologies into the public communications environment is now inevitable. This shift in the communications environment has offered an extraordinarily fertile set of opportunities for the ISP industry. The capability to position Internet services above established data carriage services, the low-entry costs to participate, the high growth in levels of demand, and the functional flexibility of the Internet all combine to create a vibrant new industry.

Such functional changes to the base communications model do present a unique set of challenges and opportunities. The established communications industry players have to address the challenge of new market opportunities, coupled with some level of erosion of current markets. The set of acquisitions, mergers, and realignments within this sector are illustrative of the scope of these challenges to the enterprises.

To the regulator, the Internet poses some very interesting challenges. The wave of deregulation within the communications industry is prefaced by the proposition that a competitive market is the most efficient distributor of a public good. Set in juxtaposition to this is the difficulty of servicing the Internet within a heavily dispersed provider environment in which the fundamental economic models of interprovider cost distribution are missing. The natural outcome in a commodity-based provider market is aggregation of service providers, in order to achieve economies of scale. Will a regulatory-imposed competitive market structure act as a longer term deterrent to large-scale investment in Internet infrastructure? Will such regulatory measures act in a way contrary to the policy expectation, and will the regulator be ultimately responsible for higher retail prices for Internet access and carriage? Obviously, the answers will be forthcoming in the fullness of time. However, the immediate outcome is a regulatory environment that encourages the entry of yet further ISPs, and in the current regime the ISP does enjoy the special favor of the regulator.

The potential outcomes of the carriage and access components of the ISP industry appear to point towards very significant levels of aggregation. Although this may be alleviated to some extent by regulatory activity, the strong downward pressure on Internet access and carriage pricing ultimately will only be met by large-scale provider operations, exploiting all possible economies of scale, rather than as an outcome of any regulatory activity. Where is the future of the ISP within this environment?

The ISP provider space is occupied by many highly agile, technically proficient, small business enterprises. This space is unlikely to break down completely, as technical innovation continues to be one of the driving factors behind the Internet's continued growth. More likely, we will see the emphasis of the ISP service portfolio shift to new areas of demand, which exploit these attributes of technical capability and business agility. Many ISPs are already shifting focus to the small- and medium-size enterprise market, offering business solutions based on exploitation of the Internet's capabilities, rather than working in a commodity access market. Here, the ISP is shifting into a higher valued relationship with its clients, offering the client enterprise technology-based business solutions.

The areas of new ISP activity are almost boundless. These areas encompass commerce solutions that map a provider into a global market, supporting the concept of a competitive global small business. New ISP activity also encompasses solutions that use virtual private domains to support both a mobile workforce and the use of semi-private network domains, which support business retail networks and extend into support for various communities of interest.

The opportunities for ISPs are now shifting away from the overlay of IP packets on communications plumbing. Instead of basic access and carriage, the business opportunities for ISPs are now focusing on continued use of the ISP's expertise and agility to create innovative and high-value business solutions. In this form, the ISP sector will continue to exert a role of leadership in determining the future of the Internet.

A Final Word

Any business enterprise has associated business risks. The ISP business is no exception here. Some ISPs will fail, and others will grow beyond their wildest expectations. One of the key ingredients to business success is understanding the environment in which the ISP operates, allowing the business to correctly identify opportunities as they arise.

In its modest way, this book has attempted to address this understanding of the environment of ISP operation, looking at the technology, business, and policy landscape of the Internet. If this book assists an ISP to achieve business success, then I, as the author, will be content.

glossary

AAL *ATM Adaptation Layer*. A connection of protocols that takes data traffic and frames it into a sequence of 48-byte payloads for transmission over an ATM (Asynchronous Transfer Mode) network. Currently, four AAL types are defined that support various service categories. *AAL1* supports constant bit-rate connection-oriented traffic. *AAL2* supports time-dependant variable bit-rate traffic. *AAL3/4* supports connectionless and connection-oriented variable bit-rate traffic. *AAL5* supports connection-oriented variable bit-rate traffic.

ABR *Available Bit Rate*. One of the service categories defined by the ATM Forum. ABR supports variable bit-rate traffic with flow control. The ABR service category supports a minimum guaranteed transmission rate and peak data rates.

ACF/VTAM *Advanced Communications Facility/Virtual Telecommunications Access Method*. In traditional legacy SNA networks, ACF/ VTAM on the IBM mainframe is responsible for session establishment and activation of network resources.

ACK *Acknowledgment*. A message that indicates the reception of a transmitted packet.

ANSI *American National Standards Institute*. One of the American technology standards organizations.

API *Application Programming Interface*. A defined interface between an application and a software service module or operating system component. Conventionally, an API is defined as a subroutine library with a common definition set that extends across multiple computer platforms and operating systems.

APPN *Advanced Peer-to-Peer Networking*. APPN represents IBM's second-generation SNA networking architecture, which accommodates peer-to-peer communications, directory services, and dynamic data routing between SNA subdomains.

ARP *Address Resolution Protocol*. The discovery protocol used by host computer systems to establish the correct mapping of Internet layer addresses, also known as IP addresses, to Media Access Control (MAC) layer addresses.

ARPA *Advanced Research and Projects Agency*. A U.S. federal research funding agency credited with initially deploying the network now known as the Internet. The agency was referred to as DARPA (Defense Advanced Research and Projects Agency) in the past, indicating its administrative position as an agency of the U.S. Department of Defense.

AS *Autonomous System*. The term used to describe a collection of networks administered by a common network-management organization. The most common use of this term is in interdomain routing, where an Autonomous System is used to describe a self-connected set of networks that share a common external policy with respect to connectivity, or in other words, networks that generally are operated within the same administrative domain.

ASIC   *Application Specific Integrated Circuit.* An integrated circuit that is an implementation of a specific software application or algorithm within a silicon engine.

ATM   *Asynchronous Transfer Mode.* A data-framing and transmission architecture that features fixed-length data cells of 53 bytes, consisting of a fixed format of a 5-byte cell header and a 48-byte cell payload. The small cell size is intended to support high-speed switching of multiple traffic types. The architecture is asynchronous, so there is no requirement for clock control of the switching and transmission.

B-Channel   *Bearer Channel.* Traditionally refers to a single, full-duplex physical ISDN (Integrated Services Digital Network) interface that operates at 64 Kbps.

BECN   *Backward Explicit Congestion Notification.* A notification signal passed to the originator of traffic indicating that the path to the destination exceeds a threshold load level. This signal is defined explicitly in the Frame Relay frame header.

BGP   *Border Gateway Protocol.* An Internet routing protocol used to pass routing information between different administrative routing domains or ASs (Autonomous Systems). The BGP routing protocol does not pass explicit topology information. Instead, it passes a summary of reachability between ASs. BGP is most commonly deployed as an inter-AS routing protocol.

border router   Generally describes routers on the edge of an AS (Autonomous System). Uses BGP to exchange routing information with another administrative routing domain. However, this term also can describe any router that sits on the edge of a routing subarea, such as an OSPF (Open Shortest Path First) area border router. *See also edge device.*

BRI   *Basic Rate Interface.* A user interface to an ISDN (Integrated Services Digital Network) that consists of two 64-Kbps data channels (B-Channels) and one 16-Kbps signaling channel (D-channel) sharing a common physical access circuit.

bridging   The process of forwarding traffic based on address information contained at the data-link framing layer. Bridging allows a device to flood, forward, or filter frames based on the MAC (Media Access Control) address. Contrast with *routing.*

CBQ   *Class Based Queuing.* A queuing methodology by which traffic is classified into separate classes and queued according to its assigned class in an effort to provide differential forwarding behavior for certain types of network traffic.

CBR   *Constant Bit Rate.* An ATM service category that corresponds to a constant bandwidth allocation for a traffic flow. The CLP (Cell Loss Priority) bit is set to 0 in all cells to ensure that they are not discard eligible in the event of switch congestion. The service supports circuit emulation as well as continuous bitstream traffic sources (such as uncompressed voice or video signals).

CDV   *Cell Delay Variation.* An ATM QoS (Quality of Service) parameter that measures the variation in transit time of a cell over a Virtual Connection (VC). For service classes that are jitter sensitive, this is a critical service parameter.

CHAP   *Challenge Handshake Authentication Protocol.* An authentication mechanism for PPP (Point-to-Point Protocol) connections that encrypts the user password.

CIDR   *Classless Inter Domain Routing.* An Internet routing paradigm that passes both the network prefix and a mask of significant bits in the prefix within the routing exchange. This supercedes the earlier paradigm of *classful* routing, where the mask of significant bits is inferred by the value of the prefix (where Class A network prefixes infer a mask of 8 bits, Class B network prefixes infer a mask of 16 bits, and Class C network prefixes infer a mask of 24 bits). CIDR commonly is used to denote an Internet environment in which no implicit assumption exists of the Class A, B, and C network addresses. BGP (Border Gateway Protocol) version 4 is used as the de facto method of providing CIDR support in the Internet today.

CIR   *Committed Information Rate.* A Frame Relay term describing a minimum access rate at which the service provider commits to provide the customer for any given Permanent Virtual Circuit (PVC).

CLP   *Cell Loss Priority.* A single-bit field in the ATM cell header to indicate the discard priority. A CLP value of 1 indicates that an ATM switch can discard this cell in a congestion condition.

CLR   *Cell Loss Ratio.* An ATM QoS metric defined as the ratio of lost cells to the number of transmitted cells.

CoS   *Class of Service* or *Classes of Services.* A categorical method of classifying traffic into separate classes to provide differentiated service to each class within the network.

CPE   *Customer Premise Equipment.* The equipment deployed on the customer's site when the customer subscribes (or simply connects) to a carrier's service.

CPU   *Central Processing Unit.* The arithmetic, logic, and control unit of a computer that executes instructions.

CSU/DSU   *Channel Service Unit/Data Service Unit.* A Customer Premise Equipment (CPE) device that provides the telephony interface for circuit data services, including the physical framing, clocking, and channelization of the circuit.

CTD   *Cell Transfer Delay.* An ATM QoS metric that measures the transit time for a cell to traverse a Virtual Connection (VC). The time is measured from source UNI (User-to-User Interface) to destination UNI.

D-Channel   *Data Channel.* A full-duplex control and signaling channel on an ISDN BRI (Basic Rate Interface) or PRI (Primary Rate Interface). The D-Channel is 16 Kbps on an ISDN BRI and 64 Kbps on a PRI.

DCE   *Data Communications Equipment.* A device on the network side of a User-to-Network Interface (UNI). Typically, this is the Customer Premise Equipment (CPE), such as a modem or Channel Service Unit/Data Service Unit (CSU/DSU).

DE   *Discard Eligible.* A bit field defined within the Frame Relay header indicating that a frame can be discarded within the Frame Relay switch when the local queuing load exceeds a configured threshold.

DHCP   *Dynamic Host Configuration Protocol.* A protocol that is beginning to be used quite pervasively on end-system computers to automatically obtain an IP (Internet Protocol) host address, subnet mask, and local gateway information. A DHCP server dynamically supplies this information in response to end-system broadcast requests.

Dijkstra algorithm   Also commonly referred as SPF (Shortest Path First). The Dijkstra algorithm is a single-source, shortest-path algorithm that computes all shortest paths from a single point of reference based on a collection of link metrics. This algorithm is used to compute path preferences in both OSPF (Open Shortest Path First) and IS-IS (Intermediate System to Intermediate System). *See also SPF.*

DLC *Data Link Control.* Refers to IBM data-link layer support, which supports various types of media, including mainframe channels, SDLC (Synchronous Data Link Control), X.25, and token ring.

DLCI *Data Link Connection Identifier.* A numerical identifier given to the local end of a Frame Relay Virtual Circuit (VC). The local nature of the DLCI is that it spans only the distance between the first-hop Frame-Relay switch and the router, whereas a VC spans the entire distance of an end-to-end connection between two routers that use the Frame Relay network for link-layer connectivity.

DLSw *Data Link Switching.* Provides a standards-based method for forwarding SNA (Systems Network Architecture) traffic over TCP/IP (Transmission Control Protocol/ Internet Protocol) networks using encapsulation. DLSw provides enhancements to traditional RSRB (Remote Source-Route Bridging) encapsulation by eliminating hop-count limitations, removes unnecessary broadcasts and acknowledgments, and provides flow-control.

DS0 *Digital Signal Level 0.* A circuit-framing specification for transmitting digital signals over a single channel at 64 Kbps on a T1 facility.

DS1 *Digital Signal Level 1.* A circuit-framing specification for transmitting digital signals at 1.544 Mbps on a T1 facility in the United States, or at 2.108 Mbps on an E1 facility elsewhere.

DS3 *Digital Signal Level 3.* A circuit-framing specification for transmitting digital signals at 44.736 Mbps on a T3 facility.

DSBM *Designated Subnet Bandwidth Manager.* A device on a managed subnetwork that acts as the Subnet Bandwidth Manager (SBM) for subnetwork to which it is attached. This is done through a complicated election process specified in the SBM protocol specification. The SBM protocol is a proposal in the IETF (Internet Engineering Task Force) for handling resource reservations on shared and switched IEEE (The Institute of Electrical and Electronics Engineers) 802-style local area media. *See also SBM.*

DTE *Data Terminal Equipment.* A device on the user side of a User-to-Network Interface (UNI). Typically, this is a computer or a router.

E1 A WAN (Wide-Area Network) transmission circuit that carries data at a rate of 2.048 Mbps. Predominantly used outside the United States.

E3 A WAN transmission circuit that carries data at a rate of 34.368 Mbps. Predominantly used outside the United States.

edge device Any device on the edge or periphery of an administrative boundary. Traditionally used to describe an ATM-attached host or router that interfaces with an ATM network switch. *See also border router.*

end-system Any device that terminates an end-to-end communications relationship. Traditionally used to describe a host computer. However, may also include intermediate network nodes in situations where a particular end-to-end communications substrate relationship terminates on an intermediate device (e.g., a router and an ATM VC).

EPD *Early Packet Discard.* A congestion-avoidance mechanism generally found in ATM networks. EPD uses a method to preemptively drop entire AAL5 (ATM Adaptation Layer 5) frames instead of individual cells in an effort to anticipate congestion situations and make the most economic use of explicit signaling within the ATM network.

Ethernet A LAN (Local Area Network) specification invented by the Xerox Corporation and then jointly developed by Xerox, Intel, and Digital Equipment Corporation. Ethernet uses CSMA/CD (Carrier Sense Multiple Access/Collision Detection) and operates on various media types. It is similar to the IEEE 802.3 series of protocols.

FAQ *Frequently Asked Questions.* Compiled lists of the most frequent questions and their answers on a particular topic. An FAQ generally can be found in various formats, such as HTML (Hyper Text Markup Lanuage) Web pages, as well as traditional printed material.

FDDI *Fiber Distributed Data Interface.* A LAN standard defined in ANSI (American National Standards Institute) Standard X3T9.5 that operates at 100 Mbps, uses a token-passing technology, and uses fiber-optic cabling for physical connectivity. FDDI has a base transmission distance of up to 2 kilometers and uses a dual-ring architecture for redundancy.

FECN *Forward Explicit Congestion Notification.* A notification signal passed to the receiver of traffic indicating that the path to the originator exceeds a threshold load level. This signal is defined explicitly within the Frame Relay frame header.

FEP *Front-End Processor.* Typically, FEP describes the function of an IBM 3745, which provides a networking interface to the SNA (Systems Network Architecture) network for downstream nodes that have no knowledge of network data forwarding paths. The IBM 3745 FEP functions as an intermediary networking arbiter.

FIFO *first in, first out.* FIFO queuing is a strict method of transmitting packets that are presented to a device for subsequent transmission. Packets are transmitted in the order in which they are received.

FIN *FINish flag.* Used in the TCP header to signal the end of TCP data.

FRAD *Frame Relay Access Device* or *Frame Relay Assembler/ Disassembler.* A device that operates natively at the Frame Relay data-link layer and is less robust than multi-protocol routers (and in fact, usually does not provide network-layer routing). A FRAD simply frames and transmits traffic over a Frame Relay network, and a FRAD on the opposite side of a Frame Relay network unframes the traffic and places it on the local media.

FTP *File Transfer Protocol.* A bulk, TCP-based, transaction-oriented file transfer protocol used in TCP/IP networks, especially the Internet.

Gbps *Gigabits per second.* The data world avoided using the term *billion*, which invariably is interpreted as one thousand million or one million million, in favor of the term *giga* as one thousand million. Of course, some confusion between the telecommunications and data-storage worlds still exist as to whether a *giga* is really the value 10^9 or 2^{30}.

GCRA *Generic Cell Rate Algorithm.* A specification for implementing cell-rate conformance for ATM VBR (Variable Bit Rate) Virtual Connections (VC). The GCRA is an algorithm that uses traffic parameters to characterize traffic that is conformant to administratively defined admission criteria. The GCRA implementation commonly is referred to as a *leaky bucket.*

HDLC *High-Level Data Link Control.* A bit-oriented, synchronous data-link layer transport protocol developed by the ISO (International Standards Organization). HDLC provides an encapsulation mechanism for transporting data on synchronous serial links using framing characters and checksums. HDLC was derived from SDLC (Synchronous Data Link Control).

HSSI *High Speed Serial Interface.* The networking standard for high-speed serial connections for wide-area networks (WANs), accommodating link speeds up to 52 Mbps.

HTML *Hyper Text Markup Language.* A simple hypertext document-formatting language used to format content that is presented in Web pages on the World Wide Web (WWW), which is read using one of the many popular Web browsers.

HTTP *Hyper Text Transfer Protocol.* A TCP-based application-layer protocol used for communicating between Web servers and Web clients, also known as Web browsers.

IAB *Internet Architecture Board.* A collection of individuals concerned with the ongoing architecture of the Internet. IAB members are appointed by the trustees of the Internet Society (ISOC). The IAB also appoints members to several other organizations, such as the IESG (Internet Engineering Steering Group).

iBGP *Internal BGP* or *Interior BGP.* A method to carry exterior routing information within the backbone of a single administrative routing domain, obviating the need to redistribute exterior routing into interior routing. iBGP is a unique implementation of BGP (Border Gateway Protocol) rather than a separate protocol unto itself.

ICMP *Internet Control Message Protocol.* A network-layer protocol that provides feedback on errors and other information specifically pertinent to IP packet handling.

I-D *Internet Draft.* A draft proposal in the IETF submitted as a collaborative effort by members of a particular working group or by individual contributors. I-Ds may or may not be subsequently published as IETF Requests for Comments (RFCs).

IEEE *The Institute of Electrical and Electronics Engineers.* A professional organization that develops communications and network standards—traditionally, link-layer LAN signaling standards.

IESG *Internet Engineering Steering Group.* IESG members are ap- pointed by the Internet Architecture Board (IAB) and manage the operation of the IETF.

IETF *Internet Engineering Task Force.* An engineering and protocol standards body that develops and specifies protocols and Internet standards, generally in the network layer and above. These include routing, transport, application, and occasionally, session-layer protocols. The IETF works under the auspices of the Internet Society (ISOC).

Integrated Services In a broad sense, this term encompasses the transport of audio, video, real-time, and classical data traffic within a single network infrastructure. In a more narrow focus, it also refers to the Integrated Services architecture (the focus of the Integrated Services working group in the IETF), which consists of five key components: QoS requirements, resource-sharing requirements, allowances for packet dropping, provisions for usage feedback, and a resource-reservation model (RSVP).

Internet The global Internet. Commonly used as a reference for the loosely administered collection of interconnected networks around the globe that share a common addressing structure for the interchange of traffic.

intranet Generally used as a reference for the interior of a private network, either not connected to the global Internet or partitioned so that access to some network resources is limited to users within the administrative boundaries of the domain.

I/O *Input/Output.* The process of receiving and transmitting data, as opposed to the actual processing of the data.

IP   *Internet Protocol.* The network-layer protocol in the TCP/IP stack used in the Internet. IP is a connectionless protocol that provides extensibility for host and subnetwork addressing, routing, security, fragmentation and reassembly, and as far as QoS is concerned, a method to differentiate packets with information carried in the IP packet header.

IP precedence   A bit value that can be indicated in the IP packet header and used to designate the relative priority with which a particular packet should be handled.

IPng   *IP Next Generation.* A vernacular reference to the follow-on technology for IP version 4, otherwise known as IP version 6 (IPv6).

IPv4   *Internet Protocol version 4.* The version of the Internet protocol that is widely used today. This version number is encoded in the first 4 bits of the IP packet header and is used to verify that the sender, receiver, and routers all agree on the precise format of the packet and the semantics of the formatted fields.

IPv6   *Internet Protocol version 6.* The version number of the IETF standardized next-generation Internet protocol (IPng) proposed as a successor to IPv4.

IPX   *Internet Packet eXchange.* The predominant protocol used in NetWare networks. IPX was derived from XNS (Xerox Networking Services), a similar protocol developed by the Xerox Corporation.

IRTF   *Internet Research Task Force.* Composed of a number of focused and long-term research groups, working on topics related to Internet protocols, applications, architecture, and technology. The chair of the IRTF is appointed by the Internet Architecture Board (IAB). The IRTF is described more fully in RFC2014.

ISDN   *Integrated Services Digital Network.* An early adopted protocol model currently offered by many telephone companies for digital end-to-end connectivity for voice, video, and data.

IS-IS   *Intermediate System to Intermediate System.* A link-state routing protocol for connectionless OSI (Open Systems Interconnection) networks, similar to OSPF (Open Shortest Path First). The protocol specification for IS-IS is documented in ISO 10589.

ISO   *International Standards Organization.* The complete name for this body is the *International Organization for Standardization and International Electrotechnical Committee.* The members of this body are the national standards bodies, such as ANSI (American National Standards Institute) in the United States and BSI (the British Standards Institution) in the United Kingdom. The documents produced by this body are termed *International Standards.*

ISOC   *Internet Society.* An international user society of Internet users and professionals that share a common interest in the development of the Internet.

ISP   *Internet Service Provider.* A service provider that provides external transit for a client network or individual user, providing connectivity and associated services to access the Internet.

ISSLL   *Integrated Services over Specific Link Layers.* An IETF working group that defines specifications and techniques needed to implement Internet Integrated Services capabilities within specific subnetwork technologies, such as ATM or IEEE 802.3z Gigabit Ethernet.

jitter   The distortion of a signal as it is propagated through the network, where the signal varies from its original reference timing. In packet-switched networks, jitter is a distortion of the interpacket arrival times compared to the interpacket times of the original signal transmission. Also known as *delay variance*.

Kbps *Kilobits per second.* A measure of data-transfer speed. Some confusion exists as to whether this refers to a rate of 10^3 bits per second or 2^{10} bits per second. The telecommunications industry typically uses this term to refer to a rate of 10^3 bits per second.

L2TP *Layer 2 Tunneling Protocol.* A proposed mechanism whereby discrete virtual tunnels can be created for each dial-up client in the network, each of which may terminate at different points upstream from the access server. This allows individual dial-up clients to do interesting things, such as to use discrete addressing schemes and have their traffic forwarded, via the tunneling mechanisms, along completely different traffic paths. At the time of this writing, the L2TP protocol specification is still being developed with the IETF.

LAN *Local Area Network.* A local communications environment, typically constructed using privately operated wiring and communications facilities. The strict interpretation of this term is a broadcast media in which any connected host system can contact any other connected system without the need for explicit assistance of a routing protocol.

LANE *LAN Emulation.* A technique and ATM forum specification that defines how to provide LAN-based communications across an ATM subnetwork. LANE specifies the communications facilities that allow ATM to be interoperable with traditional LAN-based protocols, so that among other things, address resolution and broadcast services will function properly.

LAT *Local-Area Transport.* An older virtual terminal network protocol developed by Digital Equipment Corporation. LAT has been notorious for its inability to be routed in a network, as well as its insensitivity to induced latency.

Layer 1 Commonly used to describe the physical layer in the OSI (Open Systems Interconnection) reference model. Examples include the copper wiring or fiber-optic cabling that interconnects electronic devices.

Layer 2 Commonly used to describe the data-link layer in the OSI reference model. Examples include Ethernet and ATM (Asynchronous Transfer Mode).

Layer 3 Commonly used to describe the network layer in the OSI reference model. Examples include IP (Internet Protocol) and IPX (Internet Packet eXchange).

leaky bucket Generally, a traffic-shaping mechanism in which the input side of the shaping mechanism is an arbitrary size, and the output side of the mechanism is of a smaller, fixed size. This implementation has a smoothing effect on bursty traffic, because traffic is "leaked" into the network at a fixed rate. Contrast with *token bucket*.

LEC *Local Exchange Carrier.* Usually considered the local telephone company or any local telephony entity that provides telecommunications facilities within a local tariffing area. *See also RBOC.*

LIJ *Leaf Initiated Join.* A feature introduced in the ATM Forum Traffic Management 4.0 Specification in which any remote node in an ATM network can connect arbitrarily to a point-to-multipoint Virtual Connection (VC) without explicitly signaling the VC originator.

LIS *Logical IP Subnetwork.* An IP subnetwork in which all devices have a direct communication path to other devices sharing the same LIS, such as on a shared LAN or point-to-point circuit. In an NBMA (Non Broadcast Multi Access) ATM network where all devices are attached to the network via VCs, the LIS is a method by which attached devices can communicate at the IP layer so that the IP protocol believes all devices are connected directly to a local network media, although they are not.

LLC   *Link Layer Control.* The higher of the two sublayers of the data-link layer defined by the IEEE. The LLC sublayer handles flow control, error correction, framing, and MAC-sublayer addressing. *See also MAC.*

LSA   *Link State Advertisement.* A packet-forwarding link-state routing process to neighboring nodes that includes information concerning the local node, the link state of attached interfaces, or the topology of the network. LSAs are generated by link-state routing protocols such as OSPF (Open Shortest Path First) and IS-IS (Intermediate System to Intermediate System).

MAC   *Media Access Control.* The lower of the two sublayers of the data-link layer defined by the IEEE. The MAC sublayer handles access to shared media—for example, Ethernet and token ring, and whether methods such as media contention or token passing are used. *See also LLC.*

MARS   *Multicast Address Resolution Server.* A mechanism for supporting multicast in ATM (Asynchronous Transfer Mode) networks. The MARS serves a collection of nodes by proving a point-to-multipoint overlay for multicast traffic.

maxCTD   *Maximum Cell Transfer Delay.* An ATM QoS metric that measures the transit time for a cell to traverse a VC (Virtual Connection). The time is measured from the source UNI (User-to-Network Interface) to the destination UNI.

Mbps   *Megabits per second.* A unit of data transfer. The communications industry typically refers to a *mega* as the value 10^6, whereas the data-storage industry uses the same term to refer to the value 2^{20}.

MBS   *Maximum Burst Size.* An ATM QoS metric describing the number of cells that may be transmitted at the peak rate while remaining within the Generic Cell Rate Algorithm (GCRA) threshold of the service contract.

MCR   *Minimum Cell Rate.* An ATM service parameter related to the ATM Available Bit Rate (ABR) service. The allowed cell rate can vary between the Minimum Cell Rate (MCR) and the Peak Cell Rate (MCR) to remain in conformance with the service.

MIB   *Management Information Base.* A database of network-management information used by the network-management protocol SNMP (Simple Network Management Protocol). Network-managed objects implement relevant MIBs to allow remote-management operations. *See also SNMP.*

MPLS   *Multi Protocol Label Switching.* An emerging technology in which forwarding decisions are based on fixed-length labels inserted between the data-link and network layer headers to increase forwarding performance and path-selection flexibility.

MPOA   *Multi Protocol Over ATM.* An ATM Forum standard specifying how multiple network-layer protocols can operate over an ATM substrate.

MSS   *Maximum Segment Size.* A TCP option in the initial TCP SYN (Synchronize Sequence Numbers) three-way handshake that specifies the maximum size of a TCP data packet that the remote end can send to the receiver. The resultant TCP data-packet size is normally 40 bytes larger than the MSS: 20 bytes of IP header and 20 bytes of TCP header.

MTU *Maximum Transmission Unit.* The maximum size of a data frame that can be carried across a data-link layer. Every host and router interface has an associated MTU related to the physical media to which the interface is connected, and an end-to-end network path has an associated MTU that is the minimum of the individual-hop MTUs within the path.

NANOG *North American Network Operators Group.* A group of Internet operators who share a mailing list. A subset of this group meets regularly in North America. The conversation on the mailing list ranges from the pertinent to the inane. The overall characterization of the group manages to remain as the conspicuous absence of suits and ties.

NAS *Network Access Server.* A modernized and "kinder, gentler" form of its precursor, the terminal server. In other words, a device used to terminate dial-up access to a network. Predominantly used for analog or digital dial-up PPP (Point-to-Point Protocol) access services.

NBMA *Non Broadcast Multi Access.* Describes a multiaccess network that does not support broadcasting or on which broadcasting is not feasible.

NetWare A Novell, Inc. network operating system still largely popular in the corporate enterprise. The use of NetWare is experiencing somewhat of a decline because of the popularity and critical success of TCP/IP. IPX (Internet Packet eXchange) is the principal protocol used in NetWare networks.

NGI *Next Generation Internet.* An obligatory inclusion in every current network research proposal. Also used as a reference for a U.S. government sponsored advanced Internet research initiative, called the Next Generation Internet Initiative, which is somewhat controversial.

NHOP *Next Hop,* as referenced as an object within the Integrated Services Architecture protocol specifications.

NHRP *Next Hop Resolution Protocol.* A protocol used by systems in an NBMA (Non Broadcast Multi Access) network to dynamically discover the MAC address of other connected systems.

NLRI *Network Layer Reachability Information.* Information carried within BGP updates that includes network-layer information about the routing-table entries and associated previous hops, annotated as prefixes (IP addresses).

NMS *Network Management System.* The distant dream of many a network operations manager: a computer system that understands the network so well that it can warn the operator of impending disaster (humor implied).

NNI *Network-to-Network Interface.* An ATM Forum standard that defines the interface between two ATM switches operated by the same public or private network operator. The term also is used within Frame Relay to define the interface between two Frame Relay switches in a common public or private network.

NNTP *Network News Transfer Protocol.* An application protocol used to support the transfer of network news (Usenet) within the Internet. The protocol is used for bulk news transfer and remote access from clients to a central server. NNTP uses TCP to support reliable transfer. This protocol is a point-to-point transfer protocol. Efforts to move to a reliable multicast structure for Usenet news are still an active area of protocol refinement and research.

NOC   *Network Operations Center.* The people you try to ring when your network is down. Traditionally staffed 24 hours a day, 7 days a week, the NOC primarily logs network-problem reports and attempts to redirect responsibility for a particular network problem to the appropriate responsible party for resolution. The NOC is analogous to a Help Desk.

nrt-VBR   *Non-Real-Time Variable Bit Rate.* One of two variable-bit rate ATM service categories in which timing information is not crucial. Generally used for delay-tolerant applications with bursty characteristics.

NSF   *National Science Foundation.* A U.S. government agency that funds U.S. scientific research programs. This agency funded the operation of the academic and research NSFnet (a successor of the ARPAnet and a predecessor to the current commodity Internet) network from 1986 until 1995.

OSI   *Open Systems Interconnection.* A network architecture developed under the auspices of ISO (International Standards Organization) throughout the 1980s as a standards-based technology suite to allow multivendor interoperability. Now primarily of historical interest.

OSPF   *Open Shortest Path First.* An interior gateway routing protocol that uses a link-state protocol coupled with a Shortest Path First (SPF) path-selection algorithm. The OSPF protocol is widely deployed as an interior routing protocol within administratively discrete routing domains.

PAP   *PPP Authentication Protocol.* A protocol that allows peers connected by a PPP link to authenticate each other using the simple exchange of a username and password.

PCR   *Peak Cell Rate.* An ATM service parameter. PCR is the maximum value of the transmission rate of traffic on an Available Bit Rate (ABR) service category Virtual Connection (VC).

PHOP   *Previous Hop*, as referenced as an object within the Integrated Services architecture protocol specifications.

PNNI   *Private Network-to-Network Interface.* The ATM Forum specification for distribution of topology information among switches in an ATM network to allow the computation of end-to-end paths. The specification is based on similar link-state routing protocols. Otherwise known as the *ATM routing protocol.*

PPP   *Point-to-Point Protocol.* A data-link framing protocol used to frame data packets on point-to-point links. PPP is a variant of the HDLC (High-Level Data Link Control) data-link framing protocol. The PPP specification also includes remote-end identification and authentication (PAP and CHAP), a link-control protocol (to establish, configure, and test the integrity of data transmitted on the link), and a family of network-control protocols specific to different network-layer protocols.

PRA   *Primary Rate Access.* Commonly used as an off-hand reference for ISDN PRI network access.

PRI   *Primary Rate Interface.* An ISDN user-interface specification. In North America, a PRI is a single 64-Kbps D-Channel used for signaling and 23 64-Kbps B-Channels used for voice or data (using a T1 access bearer). Elsewhere, the specification is two 64-Kbps D-Channels and 30 64-Kbps B-Channels (using an E1 access bearer).

PSTN   *Public Switched Telephone Network.* A generic term referring to the public telephone network architecture.

PTSP *PNNI Topology State Packet*. A link-state advertisement distributed between adjacent ATM switches that contain node and topology information. Analogous to an OSPF Link State Advertisement (LSA).

PVC *Permanent Virtual Connection* or *Permanent Virtual Circuit*. An end-to-end Virtual Circuit (VC) that is established permanently.

QoS *Quality of Service*. Read this book and find out. Better yet, buy your own copy and then read it.

QoSR *Quality of Service Routing*. A dynamic routing protocol that has expanded its path-selection criteria to consider issues such as available bandwidth, link and end-to-end path utilization, node-resource consumption, delay and latency, and induced jitter.

RAPI *RSVP Application Programming Interface*. An RSVP-specific API that enables applications to interface explicitly with the RSVP (Resource ReSerVation Setup Protocol) resource-reservation process.

RBOC *Regional Bell Operating Company*. Specific to the United States. Basically, the terms *LEC* (Local Exchange Carrier) and *RBOC* are interchangeable. RBOCs were formed in 1984 with the breakup of AT&T. RBOCs handle local telephone service, while AT&T and other long-distance companies, such as MCI and Sprint, handle long-distance and international calling. The seven original RBOCs after the AT&T breakup were Bell Atlantic, Southwestern Bell (recently changed to SBC, which acquired Pacific Bell on April 1, 1996), NYNEX (recently merged with Bell Atlantic), Pacific Bell (bought by SBC), Bell South, Ameritech, and U.S. WEST. Independent telephone companies also exist, such as GTE, that cover particular areas of the United States. The current landscape in the United States is still evolving. The Telecommunications Deregulation Act of 1996 now allows both RBOCs and long-distance companies to sell local, long-distance, and international services.

RED *Random Early Detection*. A congestion-avoidance algorithm developed by Van Jacobson and Sally Floyd at the Lawrence Berkeley National Laboratories in the early 1990s. In a nutshell, when queue depth begins to fill on a router to a predetermined threshold, RED begins to randomly select packets from traffic flows that are discarded in an effort to implicitly signal the TCP senders to throttle back their transmission rate. The success of RED is dependent on the basic TCP behavior, where packet loss is an implicit feedback signal to the originator of a flow to slow down its transmission rate. The ultimate success of RED is that congestion collapse is avoided.

RFC *Request For Comments*. RFCs are documents produced by the IETF for the purpose of documenting IETF protocols, operational procedures, and similarly related technologies.

RIP *Routing Information Protocol*. RIP is a classful, distance-vector, hop-count-based, interior-routing protocol. RIP has been moved to a "historical" status within the IETF and is widely considered to have outlived its usefulness.

routing The process of calculating network topology and path information based on the network-layer information contained in packets. Contrast with *bridging*.

RSRB *Remote Source-Route Bridging*. A method for encapsulating SNA traffic into TCP for reliable transport, and the capability to be routed over a wide-area network (WAN).

RSVP *Resource ReSerVation Setup Protocol.* An IP-based protocol used for communicating application Quality of Service (QoS) requirements to intermediate transit nodes in a network. RSVP uses a *soft-state* mechanism to maintain path and reservation state in each node in the reservation path.

RTT *Round Trip Time.* The time required for data traffic to travel from its origin to its destination and back again.

rt-VBR *Real-Time Variable Bit Rate.* One of the two variable-bit rate ATM service categories in which timing information is indeed critical. Generally used for delay-intolerant applications with bursty transmission characteristics.

SAP *Service Advertisement Protocol.* A broadcast-based, Novell NetWare protocol used to advertise the availability of individual application services in a NetWare network.

SBM *Subnet Bandwidth Manager.* A proposal in the IETF for handling resource reservations on shared and switched IEEE 802-style local-area media. *See also DSBM.*

SCR *Sustained Cell Rate.* An ATM traffic parameter that specifies the average rate at which ATM cells may be transmitted over a given Virtual Connection (VC).

SDH *Synchronous Digital Hierarchy.* The European standard that defines a set of transmission and framing standards for transmitting optical signals over fiber-optic cabling. Similar to the SONET standards developed by Bellcore.

SDLC *Synchronous Data-Link Control.* A serial, bit-oriented, full-duplex, SNA data-link layer communications protocol. Precursor to several similar protocols, including HDLC (High-Level Data Link Control).

SECBR *Severely Errored Cell Block Rate.* An ATM error parameter used to measure the ratio of badly formatted cell blocks (or AAL frames) to blocks that have been received error-free.

SLA *Service Level Agreement.* Generally, a service contract between a network service provider and a subscriber guaranteeing a particular service's quality characteristics. SLAs vary from one provider to another and usually are concerned with network availability and data-delivery reliability. Violations of an SLA by a service provider may result in a prorated service rate for the next billing period for the subscriber as a compensation for the service provider not meeting the terms of the SLA, for example.

SMTP *Simple Mail Transfer Protocol.* The Internet standard protocol for transferring electronic mail.

SNA *Systems Network Architecture.* General reference for the large, complex network systems architecture developed by IBM in the 1970s.

SNMP *Simple Network Management Protocol.* A UDP (User Datagram Protocol)-based network-management protocol used predominantly in TCP/IP networks. SNMP can be used to monitor, poll, and control network devices. SNMP traditionally is used to manage device configurations, gather statistics, and monitor performance thresholds.

SONET *Synchronous Optical Network.* A high-speed synchronous network specification for transmitting optical signals over fiber-optic cable. Developed by Bellcore. SONET is the North American functional equivalent of the European SDH (Synchronous Digital Hierarchy) optical standards. SONET transmission speeds range from 155 Mbps to 2.5 Gbps.

SPF *Shortest Path First.* Also commonly referred as the *Dijkstra algorithm.* SPF is a single-source, shortest-path algorithm that computes all shortest paths from a single point of reference based on a collection of link metrics. This algorithm is used to compute path preferences in both OSPF and IS-IS. See also *Dijkstra algorithm.*

SRB *Source-Route Bridging.* A method of bridging developed by IBM and used in token ring networks, where the entire route to the destination is determined prior to the transmission of the data. Contrast with *transparent bridging.*

SVC *Switched Virtual Connection* or *Switched Virtual Circuit.* A Virtual Circuit (VC) dynamically established in response to UNI (User-to-Network Interface) signaling and torn down in the same fashion.

SYN *SYNchronize sequence numbers flag.* Contained in the TCP header. A bit field in the TCP header used to negotiate TCP session establishment.

T1 A wide-area network (WAN) transmission circuit that carries DS1-formatted data at a rate of 1.544 Mbps. Predominantly used within the United States.

T3 A WAN transmission circuit that carries DS3-formatted data at a rate of 44.736 Mbps. Predominantly used within the United States.

TCP *Transmission Control Protocol.* TCP is a reliable, connection- and byte-oriented transport layer protocol within the TCP/IP protocol suite. TCP packetizes data into segments, provides for packet sequencing, and provides end-to-end flow control. TCP is used by many of the popular application-layer protocols, such as HTTP, Telnet, and FTP.

TDM *Time Division Multiplexing.* A multiplexing method popular in telephony networks. TDM works by combining several signal sources onto a single circuit, allowing each source to transmit during a specific timing interval.

Telnet A TCP-based terminal-emulation protocol used in TCP/IP networks predominantly for connecting to and logging into remote systems.

TLV *Type, Length, Value.* A standard IETF format for protocol packet formats, where individual fields are allocated to indicate the *type* and *length* of a particular packet, as determined by a specific *value* expressed in each field.

token bucket Generally, a traffic-shaping mechanism by which the capability to transmit packets from any given flow is controlled by the presence of tokens. For packets belonging to a specific flow to be transmitted, for example, a token must be available in the bucket. Otherwise, the packet is queued or dropped. This particular implementation controls the transmit rate and accommodates bursty traffic. Contrast with *leaky bucket.*

TOS *Type of Service.* A bit field in the IP packet header designed to contain values indicating how each packet should be handled in the network. This particular field has never been used much, though.

transparent bridging A method of bridging used in Ethernet and IEEE 802.3 networks by which frames are forwarded along one hop at a time, based on forwarding information at each hop. Transparent bridging gets its name from the fact that the bridges themselves are transparent to the end-systems. Contrast with *SRB* (Source-Route Bridging).

TTL *Time To Live.* A field in an IP packet header that indicates how long the packet is valid. The TTL value is decremented at each hop, and when the TTL equals 0, the packet no longer is considered valid, because it has exceeded its maximum hop count.

UBR   *Unspecified Bit Rate.* An ATM service category used for best-effort traffic. The UBR service category provides no QoS controls, and all cells are marked with the Cell Loss Priority (CLP) bit set. This indicates that all cells may be dropped in the case of network congestion.

UDP   *User Datagram Protocol.* A connectionless transport-layer protocol in the TCP/IP protocol suite. UDP is a simplistic protocol that does not provide for congestion management, packet loss notification feedback, or error correction; UDP assumes these will be handled by a higher-layer protocol.

UNI   *User-to-Network Interface.* Commonly used to refer to the ATM Forum specification for ATM signaling between a user-based device, such as a router or similar end-system, and the ATM switch.

UPC   *Usage Parameter Control.* A reference to the traffic policing done on ATM traffic at the ingress ATM switch. UPC is performed at the ATM UNI level and in conjunction with the GCRA (Generic Cell Rate Algorithm) implementation.

VBR   *Variable Bit Rate.* An ATM service characterization for traffic that is bursty by nature or is variable in the average, peak, and minimum rates in which data is transmitted. There are two service categories for VBR traffic: Real-Time and Non-Real-Time VBR. *See also rt-VBR and nrt-VBR.*

VC   *Virtual Connection or Virtual Circuit.* An end-to-end connection between two devices that spans a Layer 2 switching fabric (for example, ATM or Frame Relay). A VC may be permanent (PVC) or temporary (SVC) and is wholly dependent on the implementation and architecture of the network. Contrast with *VP.*

VCI   *Virtual Connection Identifier or Virtual Circuit Identifier.* A numeric identifier used to identify the local end of an ATM VC. The local nature of the VCI is that it spans only the distance between the first-hop ATM switch and the end-system (for example, router), whereas a VC spans the entire distance of an end-to-end connection between two routers that use the ATM network for link-layer connectivity.

VLAN   *Virtual Local Area Network or Virtual LAN.* A networking architecture that allows end-systems on topological disconnected subnetworks to appear to be connected on the same LAN. Predominantly used in reference to ATM networking. Similar in functionality to *bridging.*

VP   *Virtual Path.* A connectivity path between two end-systems across an ATM switching fabric. Similar to a VC. However, a VP can carry several VCs within it. Contrast with *VC.*

VPDN   *Virtual Private Dial Network.* A VPN tailored specifically for dial-up access. A more recent example of this is L2TP (Layer 2 Tunneling Protocol), where tunnels are created dynamically when subscribers dial into the network, and the subscriber's initial Layer 3 connectivity is terminated on an arbitrary tunnel end-point device that is predetermined by the network administrator.

VPI   *Virtual Path Identifier.* A numeric identifier used to identify the local end of an ATM VP. The local nature of the VPI is that it spans only the distance between the first-hop ATM switch and the end-system (for example, router), whereas a VP itself spans the entire distance of an end-to-end connection between two routers that use the ATM network for link-layer connectivity.

VPN *Virtual Private Network.* A network that can exist discretely on a physical infrastructure consisting of multiple VPNs, similar to the "ships in the night" paradigm. There are many ways to accomplish this, but the basic concept is that many individual, discrete networks may exist on the same infrastructure without knowledge of one another's existence.

WAN *Wide Area Network.* A network environment where the elements of the network are located at significant distances from each other, and the communications facilities typically use carrier facilities rather than private wiring. Typically, the assistance of a routing protocol is required to support communications between two distant host systems on a WAN.

WDM *Wave Division Multiplexing.* A mechanism to allow multiple signals to be encoded into multiple wavelengths, so that the light signals can be transmitted on a single strand of fiber-optic cable.

WFQ *Weighted Fair Queuing.* A combination of two distinct concepts —fair queuing and preferential weighting. WFQ allows multiple queues to be defined for arbitrary traffic flows, so that no one flow can starve other, lesser flows of network resources. The weighting component in WFQ is that the administrator can create the queue size and also delegate what traffic is identified for a particular-sized queue.

WRED *Weighted Random Early Detection* or *Weighted RED.* A variant of the standard RED mechanism for routers, in which the threshold for packet discard varies according to the IP precedence level of the packet. The weighting is such that RED is activated at higher queue-threshold levels for higher-precedence packets.

WWW *World Wide Web.* A global collection of Web servers interconnected by the Internet that use the HTTP (Hyper Text Transfer Protocol).

X *X Windows Protocol.* A protocol developed in the 1980s to provide a common graphical user interface that is independent of the host computer architecture and includes a specification of a remote access mechanism to allow distributed access to remote applications from a single workstation. The protocol specification covers the screen, keyboard, and mouse of the workstation.

bibliography

[Aiken 1997] *Architecture of the Multi-Modal Organizational Research and Production Heterogeneous Network (MORPHnet)*, R. Aiken, R. Carlson, I. Foster, T. Kuhfuss, R. Stevens, L. Winkler, January 1997.

[ATMF 1997] *Multi-Protocol Over ATM Specification v1.0*, ATM Forum, af-mpoa-0087.000, July 1997.

[Baran 1964] *On Distributed Communications*, P. Baran et al., Vols. 1–11, RAND Corporation Research Documents, 1964.

[Bellman 1952] *Dynamic Programming*, R. E. Bellman, Princeton, N.J.: Princeton University Press, 1957.

[Callon 1997] *A Framework for Multiprotocol Label Switching*, Internet Draft, draft-ietf-mpls-framework-02.txt, R. Callon, P. Doolan, N. Feldman, A. Fredette, G. Swallow, A. Viswanathan, November 1997.

[Callon 1998] *Multiprotocol Label Switching Architecture*, Internet Draft, draft-ietf-mpls-arch-01.txt, R. Callon, A. Viswanathan, E. Rosen, April 1998.

[Cerf-Kahn 1974] *A protocol for packet network interconnection*, V.G. Cerf, R.F. Kahn, IEEE Transactions on Communications, Col. COM-22, No. 5, 1974.

[Clark 1988] *The Design Philosophy of the DARPA Internet Protocols*, D. D. Clark, Proc SIGCOMM 88, ACM CCR Vol. 18, Number 4, August 1988, pp. 106–114 (reprinted in ACM CCR Vol. 25, Number 1, January 1995, pp. 102–111).

[Demera 1989] *Design and Analysis of a Fair Queuing Algorithm*, A. Demera, S. Keshav, S. Shenker, ACM SIGCOMM'89, Austin, September 1989.

[Dierks 1997] *The TLS Protocol—Version 1.0*, Internet Draft, draft-ietf-tls-protocol-05.txt, T. Dierks, C. Allen, November 1997. For more information on the IETF TLS working group, see www.ietf.org/html.charters/tls-charter.html.

[Dijkstra 1959] *A Note on Two Problems in Connection with Graphs*, E. W. Dijkstra, Nimerische Mathematic, Vol. 1, pp. 269–271, 1969.

[Feng 1997] *Understanding TCP Dynamics in an Integrated Services Internet*, W. Feng, D. Kandlur, D. Saha, K. Shin, NOSSDAV '97, May 1997.

[Fites 1989] *The Computer Virus Crisis*, Fites, Johnson, Kratz, Van Nostrand Reinhold, 2nd Edition, 1992.

[Floyd 1993] *Random Early Detection Gateways for Congestion Avoidance*, S. Floyd, V. Jacobson, IEEE/ACM Transactions on Networking, v.1, n.4, August 1993.

[Ford Fulkerson 1962] *Flows in Networks*, I. R. Ford, Jr., D. R. Fulkerson, Princeton, N.J.: Princeton University Press, 1962.

[Garcia-Kuna-Aceves 1989] *A Unified Approach to Loop-Free Routing Using Distance Vector or Link States*, J. J. Garcia-Luna-Aceves, ACM Sigcomm '89 Symposium, September 1989.

[Hamzeh 1996] *Point-to-Point Tunneling Protocol—PPTP*, K. Hamzeh, G. Singh Pall, W. Verthein, J. Taarud, W. A. Little, June 1996. See also: *www.microsoft.com/backoffice/communications/morepptp.htm* and *infodeli.3com.com/infodeli/tools/remote/general/pptp/pptp.htm*.

[Heinanen 1998] *VPN Support with MPLS*, Internet Draft, draft-heinanen-mpls-vpn-01.txt, J. Heinanen, E. Rosen, March 1998.

[IEEE 1993] *MAC Bridges*, ISO/IEC 10038, ANSI/IEEE Std. 802.1D, 1993.

[IEEE 1997] *Supplement to MAC Bridges: Traffic Class Expediting and Dynamic Multicast Filtering*, IEEE P802.1p/D6, May 1997.

[Jacobson 1988] *Congestion Avoidance and Control*, V. Jacobson, Computer Communication Review, vol. 18, no. 4, pp. 314–329, August 1988.

[Jagannath 1997] *End-to-End Traffic Issues in IP/ATM Internetworks*, Internet Draft, draft-jagan-e2e-traf-mgmt-00.txt, S. Jagannath, S. Yin, August 1997.

[Jordan 1985] *Reference Data for Engineers: Radio, Electronics, Computer, and Communications*, E. Jordan, ed., Indianapolis, IN.: Howard Sams & Co., 1985.

[Katz 1998] *NBMA Next Hop Resolution Protocol (NHRP)*, Internet Draft, draft-ietf-rolc-nhrp-13.txt, J. Luciani, D. Katz, D. Piscitello, B. Cole, January 1998.

[Keshav 1997] *An Engineering Approach to Computer Networking*, S. Keshav, Addison-Wesley, 1997.

[Kleinrock 1961] *Information Flow in Large Communication Nets*, L. Kleinrock, RLE Quarterly Progress Report, July 1961.

[Kleinrock 1964] *Communication Nets: Stochastic Message Flow and Delay*, L. Kleinrock, New York: McGraw-Hill, 1964.

[Kleinrock 1975] *Queuing Systems, Volume 2: Computer Applications*, L. Kleinrock, New York: John Wiley & Sons, 1975.

[Lin 1997] *Dynamics of Random Early Detection*, D. Lin, R. Morris (Harvard University), presented at ACM SIGCOMM 1997.

[Lottor 1998] *Internet Domain Survey*, M. Lottor, 1998. *www.nw.com/zone/WWW/top.html*.

[Mills 1988] *The Fuzzball*, D. Mills, Proceedings of the ACM SIGCOMM '88 Workshop, pp. 115–122, ACM SIGCOMM, New York, 1988.

[Nichols 1998] *Differentiated Services Operational Model and Definitions*, Internet Draft, draft-nichols-dsopdef-00.txt, K, Nichols, S. Blake (editors), February 1998.

[Perkins 1998] *Mobile IP Design Principles and Practices*, C. Perkins, Addison-Wesley, 1998.

[Raymond 1993] *The New Hacker's Dictionary, Third Edition*, Compiled by Eric S. Raymond, published by MIT Press, 1993. The Jargon File online: *www. ccil.org/jargon/*.

[RFC 1058] *Routing Information Protocol*, C. L. Hedrick, June 1988.

[RFC 1105] *Border Gateway Protocol (BGP)*, K. Lougheed, Y. Rekhter, June 1989.

[RFC 1163] *Border Gateway Protocol (BGP)*, K. Lougheed, Y. Rekhter, June 1990.

[RFC 1191] *Path MTU Discovery, J. Mogul*, S. Deering, November 1990.

[RFC 1267] *Border Gateway Protocol 3 (BGP-3)*, K. Lougheed, Y. Rekhter, October 1991.

[RFC 1483] *Multiprotocol Encapsulation over ATM Adaptation Layer 5*, J. Heinanen, July 1993.

[RFC 1528] *Principles of Operation for the TPC.INT Subdomain: Remote Printing—Technical Procedures*, C. Malamud & M. Rose, October 1993.

[RFC 1587] *The OSPF NSSA Option*, R. Coltun, V. Fuller, March 1994.

[RFC 1633] *Integrated Services in the Internet Architecture: An Overview*, R. Braden, D. Clark, S. Shenker, June 1994.

[RFC 1701] *Generic Routing Encapsulation*, S. Hanks, T. Li, D. Farinacci, P. Traina, October 1994.

[RFC 1771] *A Border Gateway Protocol 4 (BGP-4)*, Y. Rekhter, T. Li, March 1995.

[RFC 1774] *BGP-4 Protocol Analysis*, P. Traina, ed., March 1995.

[RFC 1793] *Extending OSPF to Support Demand Circuits*, J. Moy, April 1995.

[RFC 1812] *Requirements for IP Version 4 Routers*, F. Baker, June 1995.

[RFC 1861] *Simple Network Paging Protocol - Version 3 - Two-Way Enhanced*. A. Gwinn. October 1995.

[RFC 1958] *Architectural Principles of the Internet*, B. Carpenter, ed., IAB, June 1996.

[RFC 1997] *BGP Communities Attribute*, R. Chandra, P. Traina, T, Li, August 1996.

[RFC 2002] *Mobile-IPv4 Configuration Option for PPP IPCP*, J. Solomon, S. Glass, February 1998.

[RFC 2014] *IRTF Research Group Guidelines and Procedures*, A. Weinrib, J. Postel, October 1996.

[RFC 2065] *Domain Name System Security Extensions*, D. Eastlake, C. Kaufman, January 1997. For further information regarding DNSSec, see: *www.ietf.org/html.charters/dnssec-charter.html.*

[RFC 2138] *Remote Authentication Dial In User Service (RADIUS)*, C. Rigney, A. Rubens, W. Simpson, S. Willens, April 1997.

[RFC 2205] *Resource ReSerVation Protocol (RSVP) - Version 1 Functional Specification*, R. Braden, L. Zhang, S. Berson, S. Herzog, S. Jamin, September 1997.

[RFC 2208] *Resource ReSerVation Protocol (RSVP) Version 1 Applicability Statement, Some Guidelines on Deployment*, A. Mankin, F. Baker, R. Braden, S. Bradner, M. O'Dell, A. Romanow, A. Weinrib, L. Zhang, September 1997.

[RFC 2211] *Specification of the Controlled-Load Network Element Service*, J. Wroclawski, September 1997.

[RFC 2212] *Specification of Guaranteed Quality of Service*, S. Shenker, C. Partridge, R. Guerin, September 1997.

[RFC 2267] *Network Ingress Filtering: Defeating Denial of Service Attacks which employ IP Source Address Spoofing*, P. Ferguson, D. Senie, January 1998.

[RFC 2300] *Internet Official Protocol Standards*, J. Postel, ed., May 1998.

[RFC 791] *Internet Program, DARPA Internet Program, Protocol Specification*, J. Postel, ed., September 1991.

[RFC1281] *Guidelines for the Secure Operation of the Internet*, R. Pethia, S. Crocker, B. Fraser, November 1991.

[RFC1700] *Assigned Numbers*, J. Reynolds, J. Postel, October 1994.

[RFC1702] *Generic Routing Encapsulation over IPv4 networks*, S. Hanks, T. Li, D. Farinacci, P. Traina, October 1994.

[RFC1705] *Distance Vector Multicast Routing Protocol*, D. Waitzman, C. Partridge, S. Deering, November 1988. For historical purposes, see also *ftp://ftp.isi.edu/mbone/faq.txt.*

[RFC1998] *An Application of the BGP Community Attribute in Multi-home Routing*, E. Chen, T. Bates, August 1996.

[RFC2039] *Recommendations on Queue Management and Congestion Avoidance in the Internet*, B. Braden, D. Clark, J. Crowcroft, B. Davie, S. Deering, D. Estrin, S. Floyd, V. Jacobson, G. Minshall, C. Partridge, L. Peterson, K. Ramakrishnan, S. Shenker, J. Wroclawski, L. Zhang. April 1998.

[RFC2131] *Dynamic Host Configuration Protocol*, R. Droms, March 1997.

[RFC2196] *Site Security Handbook*, B. Fraser, ed., September 1997.

[RIPE 181] *Representation of IP Routing Policies in a Routing Registry (ripe-81++)*, T. Bates, E. Gerich, L. Joncheray, J. Jouanigot, D. Karrenberg, M. Terpstra, J. Yu, October 1994. www.ripe.net/docs/ripe-181.html.

[Roberts 1966] *Toward a Cooperative Network of Time-Shared Computers*, L. Roberts, T. Merrill, Fall AFIPS Conference., October 1966.

[Roberts 1967] *Multiple Computer Networks and Intercomputer Communication*, L. Roberts, ACM Gatlinburg Conf., October 1967.

[Saltzer 1984] *End-To-End Arguments in System Design*, J. H. Saltzer, D. P. Reed, D. D. Clark, ACM TOCS, Vol. 2, Number 4, November 1984, pp. 277–288.

[Seaman 1997] *Integrated Service Mappings on IEEE 802 Networks*, Internet Draft, draft-ietf-issll-is802-svc-mapping-01.txt, M. Seaman, A. Smith, E. Crawley, November 1997.

[Valencia 1997] *Layer Two Forwarding (Protocol) 'L2F'*, Internet Draft, draft-valencia -l2f-00.txt, A. Valencia, M. Littlewood, T. Kolar, October 1997.

[Valencia 1998] *Layer Two Tunneling Protocol 'L2TP'*, Internet Draft, draft-ietf-pppext-l2tp-11.txt, A. Valencia et al, May 1998.

[Yavatkar 1998] *SBM (Subnet Bandwidth Manager): A Proposal for Admission Control over IEEE 802-style networks*, Internet Draft, draft-ietf-issll-is802-bm-06.txt, R. Yavatkar, F. Baker, D. Hoffman, Y. Bernet, M. Speer, March 1998.

[Zhang 1990] *Oscillating Behavior of Network Traffic: A Case Study Simulation*, L. Zhang, D. Clark, Internetwork: Research and Experience, Volume 1, Number 2, New York: John Wiley & Sons, 1990, pp. 101–112.

Index